INTERPLAY

DORIS

张潆

Fourth Canadian Edition

INTERPLAY

The Process of Interpersonal Communication

DORIS zhang

Ronald B. Adler
Lawrence B. Rosenfeld
Russell F. Proctor II
Constance Winder

OXFORD
UNIVERSITY PRESS

OXFORD
UNIVERSITY PRESS

Oxford University Press is a department of the University of Oxford.
It furthers the University's objective of excellence in research, scholarship,
and education by publishing worldwide. Oxford is a registered trade mark of
Oxford University Press in the UK and in certain other countries.

Published in Canada by
Oxford University Press
8 Sampson Mews, Suite 204,
Don Mills, Ontario M3C 0H5 Canada

www.oupcanada.com

First Edition published in 2006
Second Edition published in 2009
Third Edition published in 2012

Original edition published by Oxford University Press, Inc.,
198 Madison Avenue, New York, N.Y. 10016-4314, USA.

Library and Archives Canada Cataloguing in Publication
Adler, Ronald B. (Ronald Brian), 1946–, author
Interplay : the process of interpersonal communication / Ronald
B. Adler, Lawrence B. Rosenfeld, Russell F. Proctor II, and Constance
Winder. -- Fourth Canadian edition.
Revision: Interplay, 3rd Canadian edition. Don Mills, Ont. : Oxford
University Press, 2012.
Includes bibliographical references and index.
ISBN 978-0-19-900962-6 (paperback)
1. Interpersonal communication--Textbooks.   I. Rosenfeld, Lawrence
B., author   II. Winder, Constance, 1961–, author   III. Proctor, Russell F.,
author   IV. Title.
BF637.C45A35 2016   302.2   C2015-906395-7

Cover image: sumkinn/Shutterstock.com

Brief Contents

Contents

PART TWO | Creating and Responding to Messages

Chapter 5 Listening   150

PART FOUR | Contexts of Interpersonal Communication

Chapter 11 Communicating with Family   358

Chapter 12 Work, Group, and Team Communication   380

FROM THE PUBLISHER

This fourth edition of *Interplay* builds on the successful approach used in the previous Canadian editions that have served instructors and students well. It gives first-time students a useful, compelling, and accurate introduction to the academic study of interpersonal communication. The reader comes away with a new appreciation of how scholarship about communication in interpersonal relationships can make a difference in everyday life. To that end, this fourth edition presents new and expanded coverage, while still retaining the trusted qualities and features of the previous editions.

Key Features

- An accessible writing style based on the belief that even complicated ideas can be presented in a straightforward way.
- A commitment to showing how scholarship offers insights about the process of interpersonal communication.
- The use of thought-provoking photos and cartoons that illustrate points in the text in a way that is more interesting and compelling than text alone.

Increased Application of Theory to Everyday Life

- To help students better understand the application of theory for everyday life, this edition features expanded content on technology, work, and culture throughout. Some new sections include:

Technology

- Chapter 2 – managing personal disclosure with technology
- Chapter 8 – social media and romantic relationships

Work

- Chapter 9 – emotion labour for human service providers
- Chapter 12 – networking and interviewing

Culture

- Chapter 1 – Canadian versus US interpersonal communication
- Chapter 11 – First Nations concepts of families

Engaging Pedagogy

This edition of *Interplay* builds on the pedagogical approach that has successfully helped students appreciate how scholarship leads to a better understanding of communication in the "real world."

- *"Take Two" boxes* recap core concepts and terms to ensure students understand their meaning and draw linkages between them.

TAKE TWO

- **Abstractions:** convenient ways of generalizing similarities between several objects, people, ideas, or events.
- **Advantages:** provide an easy shorthand; help avoid confrontations and embarrassment.
- **Disadvantages:** can lead to stereotyping; can confuse others.
- **Euphemisms:** innocuous terms substituted for blunt ones (e.g., *thrifty* instead of *cheap*).
- **Relative language:** words that gain meaning by comparison (e.g., *fast*, *short*).
- **Static evaluation:** the usually mistaken assumption that people or things are totally consistent and unchanging (descriptions that contain the word *is*— e.g., "She *is* rude").

- *"Check It!" questions* give students a great tool for study and review.

 **CHECK IT!**

Describe the Gibb categories of defensive and supportive behaviours and how they can contribute to creating a more defence-arousing or a less defence-arousing response.

- *"Focus on Technology" boxes* draw attention to current research on interpersonal communication and new technology while showing how core material relates to topics such as text-message syntax, cellphones and forced eavesdropping, and the influence of culture on computer-mediated business negotiation.

266 **PART THREE** Dimensions of Interpersonal Relationships

Focus on TECHNOLOGY

SOCIAL MEDIA AND INTIMACY

Computer-mediated communication provides opportunities to meet and interact with people whose interests and experiences are similar to our own. Chat rooms, blogs, social networking sites, and online dating services allow us access to people we may otherwise never have a chance to meet. This is one of the main advantages of online dating sites—they provide access to a much larger pool of potential romantic partners than our personal social networks could ever provide (Finkel et al., 2012). Online social gaming provides us with opportunities to interact with both old and new friends, some of whom we interact with in person and some of whom we engage with exclusively online (Domahidi et al., 2014). Social media platforms allow us to connect with others socially and professionally, while text messaging allows us constant contact with our loved ones. There is no doubt that CMC is often personal and helps us establish and maintain our intimate relationships. However, it is somewhat ironic that CMC *feels* so intimate. When we are online we are often alone, in the privacy of our homes sending messages intended for a chosen few. But there is no guarantee that our chosen recipients are our only audience. Recall from Chapter 2 that privacy settings can be breached (never mind what you agreed to when you checked that box in the "terms and conditions") and there are a variety of organizations that have a vested interest in knowing more about us (Madrigal, 2012).

In addition, there are times when members of our own social networks can hurt us, either intentionally or accidently, by sharing information we wanted to keep private. In a clever experiment, researchers at the University of Haifa found that contrary to popular thought it is not the anonymity or invisibility afforded by the Internet that predicts how unkind people are to each other, but the lack of eye contact (Lapidot-Lefler and Barak, 2012). In their experiment 71 pairs of college students were instructed to debate an issue, and agree on a solution, while using instant messaging. Each partner was seated in a different room, using a computer to communicate. Partners debated in one of three conditions. One group of partners was asked to share personal, identifying details before debating. A second group could see the profiles of their partners, and a third group was instructed to maintain eye contact via close up cameras attached to their monitors. Participants in the first two conditions (in which eye contact was unavailable) were twice as likely to send hostile messages to their partners as compared to the pairs who were required to maintain eye contact. The researchers speculated that lack of eye contact reduces empathy and allows greater aggressiveness. All of the factors that contribute to peoples' lack of inhibition on the Internet have yet to be identified, but there is increasing evidence that people online behave in ways that they are less likely to behave in person. Recall from Chapter 2 that people often disclose more personal information about themselves online compared to when they are face-to-face with others (Christofides et al., 2012) and that sharing information about ourselves triggers reward pathways in our brains (Tamir and Mitchell, 2012). Being aware of the inhibition that is associated with CMC, combined with the knowledge that the privacy we experience online is not the reality of the Internet, helps us monitor our communication to ensure that the messages we send via CMC are those we would be comfortable sending in face-to-face interactions.

contrast, members of more individualistic cultures—such as those of Canada, the United States, and Australia—make less distinction between personal and casual relationships. They are more familiar with strangers and reveal more personal information, making them excellent "cocktail party conversationalists." Social psychologist Kurt Lewin (1936) captured the difference nicely when he noted that Americans were easy to meet, but difficult to get to know, while Germans were difficult to meet, but easy to know well.

Differences like these mean that the level of self-disclosure that is appropriate in one culture may seem completely inappropriate in another one. If you were raised in Canada or the United States, you may view people from other cultures as reserved and perhaps standoffish. The

REFLECTION

WIN–WIN SOLUTION REDUCES FRICTION

After four months of living together, my two neat roommates were fed up with cleaning up after me and the other messy member of our little household, and the two of us were tired of hearing the neat freaks complain about our habits.

Last week, we had a meeting (again) about the dishes and glasses. But this time, we didn't argue about who was right or wrong. Instead, we looked for a win–win solution. And once we started looking, we found it. Each of us gets his own dishes, glasses, and silverware—two of each item per person. We are responsible for cleaning only our own things. Now, if you look in our kitchen cabinets, you find only eight glasses, eight plates, and so on. There isn't enough stuff to make a mess, and each of us has to wash his own things if he wants to eat. Everybody is happy. Some people might think our solution is silly, but it has certainly worked well for us—and that's all that matters.

- *"Reflection" sidebars* offer first-person accounts of how principles covered in the text apply to real life.

- *"Self-Assessment" quizzes* allow readers to analyze their current communication behaviour and its consequences.

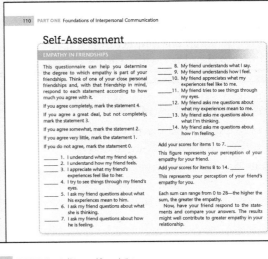

- *"Building Work Skills" exercises* help students apply knowledge they have gained about interpersonal communication to situations they are likely to encounter in the workplace.

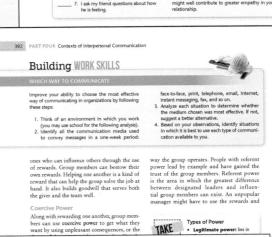

- *"Focus on Research" profiles* highlight scholarship that students will find interesting and useful on topics ranging from workplace bullying to how social status and self-identification are influenced by material possessions.

Contemporary Design

We have created a design that reflects the vibrancy and excitement of interpersonal communication today without sacrificing content or authoritativeness.

Aids to Student Learning

Textbooks today must speak to the needs and interests of today's students, providing them with an accessible introduction to a body of knowledge. To accomplish this, numerous features to promote student learning are incorporated throughout the book.

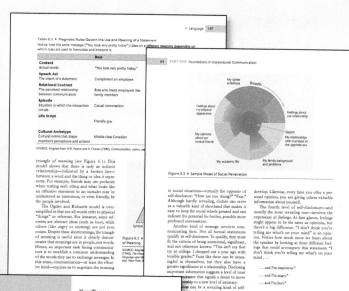

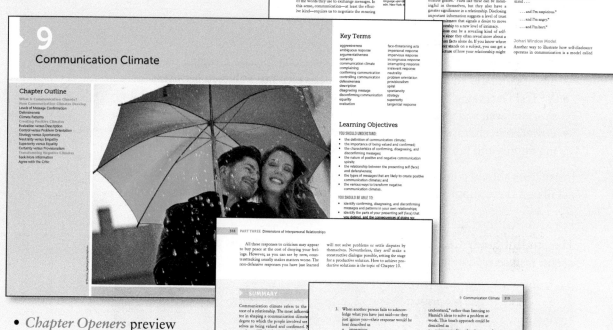

- *Chapter Openers* preview the contents of each chapter with key terms and learning objectives that provide a concise overview of the key concepts to be covered.

- *Chapter Summaries* ensure a thorough understanding of key concepts and aid in reviewing for tests and exams.

End-of-Chapter Learning Tools

- *Multiple-Choice Quizzes* provide students with a quick assessment tool to ensure comprehension of material discussed in the chapter.
- *Student Activities* reinforce concepts and ideas through practical, interactive exercises.
- *Discussion Questions* draw out key issues while encouraging readers to form their own conclusions about interpersonal communication
- *Journal Ideas* encourage students to think in depth about concepts and strategies discussed in the chapter and how they relate to their personal goals.

Online Supplements

Interplay: The Process of Interpersonal Communication (4th edition) is supported by an outstanding array of ancillary materials for both students and instructors, all available on the companion website: www.oupcanada.com/Interplay4e

For the Instructor

- An "Instructor's Manual" includes comprehensive outlines of the text's various parts and chapters, additional questions for encouraging class discussion, and suggestions on how to use videos to enhance lectures.
- A "Test Generator" offers a comprehensive set of multiple-choice, true-or-false, short-answer, and essay questions, with suggested answers, for every chapter.
- PowerPoint slides, summarizing key points from each chapter and incorporating figures and tables from the textbook are available to adopters of the text.

Instructors should contact their Oxford University Press sales representative for details on these supplements and for login and password information.

For the Student

The Student Study Guide offers self-testing study questions, annotated links to useful resources, and much more.

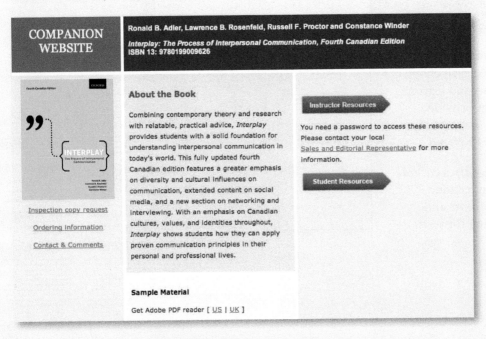

COMPANION WEBSITE

Ronald B. Adler, Lawrence B. Rosenfeld, Russell F. Proctor and Constance Winder

Interplay: The Process of Interpersonal Communication, Fourth Canadian Edition
ISBN 13: 9780199009626

Inspection copy request

Ordering information

Contact & Comments

About the Book

Combining contemporary theory and research with relatable, practical advice, *Interplay* provides students with a solid foundation for understanding interpersonal communication in today's world. This fully updated fourth Canadian edition features a greater emphasis on diversity and cultural influences on communication, extended content on social media, and a new section on networking and interviewing. With an emphasis on Canadian cultures, values, and identities throughout, *Interplay* shows students how they can apply proven communication principles in their personal and professional lives.

Sample Material

Get Adobe PDF reader [US | UK]

Instructor Resources

You need a password to access these resources. Please contact your local Sales and Editorial Representative for more information.

Student Resources

PREFACE

The fourth Canadian edition of this book was developed and shaped by many important people. First, I am indebted to my reviewers, who offered sage advice, and pointed me in the right direction.

Kathy Jarrell, Mount Royal University
Coleen Brown, Douglas College
Laura Doan, Thompson Rivers University
Barbara Rice, Conestoga College

I would also like to thank my colleagues and students at George Brown College for their ongoing support, generosity, and insight.

I am grateful to the brilliant team at Oxford University Press in Toronto, who have guided me through four editions of this book. In particular, I'd like to thank acquisitions editors Carolyn Starr and Stephen Kotowych, who initiated this new edition, and assistant managing editor, Eric Sinkins, who deftly handled the seemingly infinite details from start to finish. Developmental editor Meg Patterson provided many intelligent and thoughtful suggestions, while Shelly Stevenson made the new edition clearer, more accurate, and easier to read, and was, like the entire Oxford team, a pleasure to work with. On the production side, I'd like to thank Michelle Welsh and the talented designer Laurie McGregor.

Finally, the fourth edition of this book was once again generously supported by my family. Zoe Waelchli provided some of the beautiful photos that enrich this edition. Thanks, Zoe! Gerlando, Owen, and Oliver, spending time with you is the very best thing. Thank you for the encouragement, laughter, and love in such abundance.

Connie Winder
George Brown College, Toronto

PART ONE
Foundations of Interpersonal Communication

1

Interpersonal Process

Chapter Outline

© Geber86/iStockphoto

Key Terms

asynchronous 异步的；不同时的
channel 电视台；频道
co-culture 共同培养
cognitive complexity 认知复杂性
communication competence 交际能力
computer-mediated 计算机介导
    communication (CMC)
content message
culture
dyad 双；一对
environment
ethnocentrism 民族优越感
in-groups 小圈子
intercultural communication 跨文化交流
interpersonal 人际的
    communication
media richness 媒介丰富度

noise (external, 外部的
    physiological, 生理的
    psychological) 心理的
out-groups
permanence 持久
prejudice 偏见
qualitative interpersonal 定性的人
    communication 际关系
quantitative interpersonal
    communication 定量的人际关系
relational messages
self-monitoring 自我监控
stereotyping 刻板印象
synchronous 同步的
transactional 交易型的
    communication

Learning Objectives

YOU SHOULD UNDERSTAND:

- the needs that effective communication can satisfy;
- five insights from the communication model;
- five key principles of communication;
- four misconceptions about communication;
- quantitative and qualitative definitions of interpersonal communication; and
- the characteristics of competent communication.

YOU SHOULD BE ABLE TO:

- identify examples of the physical, identity, social, and practical needs you attempt to satisfy by communicating;
- demonstrate how the communication model applies to your interpersonal communication;
- describe the degrees to which your communication is qualitatively impersonal and interpersonal, and describe the consequences of this combination; and
- identify situations in which you communicate competently and those in which your competence is less than satisfactory.

Everyone communicates. Students and professors, parents and children, employers and employees, friends, strangers, and enemies—all communicate. We have been communicating with others from the moment of our birth and will keep on doing so until we die.

Why study an activity you've been doing your entire life? There are many reasons (Morreale and Pearson, 2008), but let's consider three. First, studying **interpersonal communication** will give you a new look at a familiar topic. For instance, in a few pages, you will find that some people can go years—even a lifetime—without communicating in a truly interpersonal manner. In this sense, exploring human communication is rather like studying anatomy or botany—everyday objects and processes take on new meaning.

A second reason for studying the subject has to do with the staggering amount of time we spend communicating. For example, college students spend approximately 13 hours a day engaged in some type of interpersonal communication (Emanuel et al., 2008). An informal, Internet-based survey of business professionals revealed that they spend an average of more than 4 hours a day communicating via email, telephone, Facebook, and Twitter, not to mention the time spent meeting with colleagues and clients face-to-face (Moore, 2010). North Americans spend increasing amounts of time each year social networking online (Nielsenwire, 2010), and Canadians are the world leaders in Internet use (Canadian Internet Registration Authority, 2013).

There is a third, more compelling reason for studying interpersonal communication. To put it bluntly, all of us could learn to communicate more effectively. Our friendships, jobs, and studies suffer because we fail to interact with others as effectively as is necessary. A survey by the Canadian Council of Chief Executives (2014) revealed that "people skills," or relationship-building skills and communication skills, were the top two attributes that employers were looking for in new hires. In a US survey, "lack of effective communication" was given as the cause of relational breakups—including divorce—more often than anything else, including money, relatives or in-laws, sexual problems, previous relationships, or children (National Communication Association, 1999). In addition, workplace communication errors account for interpersonal conflict, loss of productivity, and unnecessary waste, and in fields such as aviation (Tiewtrakul and Fletcher, 2010) and health care, even loss of life (Carter et al., 2009; Vilensky and MacDonald, 2011). If you pause now and make a mental list of communication problems you have encountered, you'll see that, no matter how successful your relationships are at home, with friends, at school, or at work, there is plenty of room for improvement in your everyday life. The information that follows will help you improve the way you communicate with some of the people who matter most to you.

Interpersonal communication occurs when people treat one another as unique individuals, regardless of the context or the number of people involved. Why should we study something that happens every day?

© iStockPhoto/Leonardo Patrizi.

Why We Communicate

Research demonstrating the importance of communication has been around longer than you might think. Frederick II, emperor of the Holy Roman Empire from 1220 to 1250, was called *stupor mundi*—"wonder of the world"—by his admiring subjects. Along with his administrative and military talents, Frederick was a leading scientist of his time. A medieval historian described one of his dramatic, and inhumane, experiments:

> He bade foster mothers and nurses to suckle the children, to bathe and wash them, but in no way to prattle with them, for he wanted to learn whether they would speak the Hebrew language, which was the oldest, or Greek, or Latin, or Arabic, or perhaps the language of their parents, of whom they had been born. But he laboured in vain because all the children died. For they could not live without the petting and joyful faces and loving words of their foster mothers. (Ross and McLaughlin, 1949, p. 366)

Fortunately, contemporary researchers have found less drastic ways to illustrate the importance of communication. In one study of isolation, five subjects were paid to remain alone in a locked room. One lasted for eight days. Three held out for two days, one commenting, "Never again." Another of the subjects lasted a mere two hours (Schachter, 1959, pp. 9–10).

The need for contact and companionship is just as strong outside the laboratory, as people who have led solitary lives by choice or necessity have discovered. W. Carl Jackson (1978), an adventurer who sailed across the Atlantic Ocean alone in 51 days, summarized the feelings common to most loners:

> I found the loneliness of the second month almost excruciating. I always thought of myself as self-sufficient, but I found life without people had no meaning. I had a definite need for somebody to talk to, someone real, alive, and breathing.

You might argue that solitude would be a welcome relief from the irritations and unrelenting demands of everyday life. It's true that all of us need solitude, often more than we get. On the other hand, each of us has a point beyond which we do not *want* to be alone. Beyond this point, solitude changes from a pleasurable to a painful condition. In other words, we all need people. We all need to communicate.

Physical Needs

Communication is so important that its presence or absence affects physical health. Recent studies confirm that people who process a negative experience by talking about it report improved life satisfaction, as well as enhanced mental and physical health, compared to those who only think about it (Lyubomirsky et al., 2006; Sousa, 2002). A study conducted with police officers found that being able to talk easily to colleagues and supervisors about work-related trauma was connected to better physical and mental health (Stephens and Long, 2000).

In extreme cases, communication can even become a matter of life or death. It is not surprising that one of the worst punishments that inmates in Western prisons are subjected to is solitary confinement. Known to North American convicts as "the hole," segregation units have been described by both psychologists and inmates as far more damaging and harder to bear than physical punishment. The isolation from both the physical world (so that one does not know if it is day or night, or what the weather is like) and the complete lack of meaningful communication with other people combine to create a situation in which most inmates would prefer to die (Jackson, 2002).

Satisfying communication isn't a necessity just for prisoners. Evidence gathered by medical researchers (e.g., Amieva et al., 2010; Hall and Havens, 2002; Maté, 2003; Orth-Gomér and Leineweber, 2005) and social scientists (e.g., Duck, 1998; Zheng and Hart, 2004) shows that satisfying relationships can literally be a matter of life and death. For example:

- People who lack strong relationships run two to three times the risk of early death, regardless of whether they smoke, drink alcoholic beverages, or exercise regularly.
- People who reported satisfying interpersonal relationships had a reduced risk of dementia and Alzheimer's disease.
- Divorced, separated, and widowed people are 5 to 10 times more likely to need psychiatric hospitalization than their married counterparts.
- Perceived loneliness is one of the strongest predictors of poor health among the elderly.
- Pregnant women under stress and without supportive relationships have three times as many complications as pregnant women who suffer from the same stress, but have strong social support.
- Social isolation is a major risk factor contributing to heart disease, comparable to physiological factors such as an inadequate diet, cigarette smoking, obesity, and lack of physical activity.
- Socially isolated people are four times as susceptible to the common cold as those who have active social networks.

Research like this demonstrates the importance of satisfying personal relationships, and it explains the conclusion of social scientists that communication is essential (Baumeister and Leary, 1995; Statistics Canada, 2006b). Not everyone needs the same amount of contact, and the quality of communication is almost certainly as important as the quantity. Nonetheless, the point remains: personal communication is essential for our well-being. To paraphrase an old song, "people who need people" aren't "the luckiest people in the world"—they're the *only* people!

Identity Needs

Communication does more than enable us to survive. It is the way—indeed, the *major* way—we learn who we are (Fogel et al., 2002; Khanna, 2004, 2010). As you'll read in Chapter

2, our sense of identity comes from the way we interact with other people. Are we smart or stupid, attractive or ugly, skilful or inept? The answers to these questions don't come from looking in the mirror. We decide who we are on the basis of how others react to us.

Deprived of communication with others, we would have no sense of identity. This is illustrated by the famous Wild Boy of Aveyron, who spent his early childhood without any apparent human contact. The boy was discovered in January 1800 when he was digging for vegetables in a French village garden. He showed no behaviour one would expect in a social human. He could not speak, but uttered only weird cries. More significant than this absence of social skills was his lack of any identity as a human being. As author Roger Shattuck (1980, p. 37) put it, "The boy had no human sense of being in the world. He had no sense of himself as a person related to other persons." Only through the influence of a loving "mother" did the boy begin to behave—and, we can imagine, think of himself—as a human.

Modern stories support the essential role that communication plays in shaping identity. In 1970, the authorities discovered a twelve-year-old girl (whom they called Genie) who had spent virtually all her life in an otherwise empty, darkened bedroom with almost no human contact. The child could not speak and had no sense of herself as a person until she was removed from her family and "nourished" by a team of caregivers (Rymer, 1993).

Like Genie and the Wild Boy of Aveyron, each of us enters the world with little or no sense of identity. We gain an idea of who we are from the way others define us. As we explain in Chapter 2, the messages children receive in their early years are the strongest identity shapers, but the influence of others continues throughout our lives.

Social Needs

Some social scientists have argued that besides helping define who we are, communication is the principal way relationships are created

(Duck and Pittman, 1994; Hubbard, 2001). For example, Julie Yingling (1994) asserts that children "talk friendships into existence." Canadian teenagers value friendships the most, ahead of a comfortable life, recognition, and excitement (Bibby, 2001), and they spend a great deal of time developing and maintaining these relationships through communication. As we explain in Chapter 8, sometimes we deal with social needs directly by discussing our relationships with others. But more often, communication satisfies a variety of social needs without our ever addressing them overtly. Communication helps us to help and be helped by others, to feel included and worthwhile, to have fun and relax with others, and to exert influence and control in social situations (Rubin et al., 1988). Because relationships with others are so vital, some theorists have gone so far as to argue that communication is the primary goal of human existence. Anthropologist Walter Goldschmidt (1990) calls the drive for meeting social needs "the human career." Positive social interaction and support appear to be the strongest determinants of quality of life (Leung and Lee, 2005).

Beyond our immediate circle of contacts, we can satisfy social needs by communicating with a larger community. There appears to be an increasing trend in North American society for people to live more socially isolated lives than their parents and grandparents did (Putnam, 2000). Since the 1950s, we eat together less often, belong to fewer social clubs, and enjoy fewer visits from friends (Putnam, 2000). Large-scale social changes such as industrialization, capitalism, and the proliferation of cheap and efficient transportation have changed the communities in which we live. Many of us live farther away from our families, friends, and places of work than our ancestors did. In addition, more recent advances in technology have allowed us to do our banking, shop for groceries, visit the library, and be entertained and go to work without leaving our homes. While there are numerous advantages to being able to connect to the world remotely, there is increasing evidence that active, meaningful involvement with other people is essential to our happiness and well-being (Burke at al., 2010; Sagioglou and Greitemeyer, 2014; Turkle, 2011).

Practical Needs

We shouldn't overlook the everyday, important functions of communication. It is the tool that lets us tell the hairstylist to take just a little off the sides, direct the doctor to where it hurts, and inform the plumber that the broken pipe needs attention *now*!

Beyond these obvious needs, a wealth of research demonstrates that communication is an essential part of effectiveness in a variety of daily situations. The abilities to speak and listen effectively have been called the most important factors in helping graduating university and college students to gain employment and advance in their careers—more important than technical competence, work experience, and academic background (Canadian Council of Chief Executives, 2014; Hart Research Associates, 2013; Northeastern University, 2013). Employment and Social Development Canada (2014) includes communication skills and the ability to work effectively with others as essential for success at work. Employers increasingly value in their workers transferable employability skills such as effective communication, problem solving, teamwork skills, respect for others, and active listening (Learning Partnership, 2004; Munroe and Watt, 2014.).

Communication is just as important outside of work. Over two decades of research findings suggest that, married couples who communicate effectively are more likely to enjoy greater marital satisfaction than couples who lack effective communication skills (Kirchler, 1988; Litzinger and Gordon, 2005; Rehman and Holtzworth-Munroe, 2007; Ridley et al., 2001). Similarly, same-sex couples' satisfaction with their long-term relationships is strongly influenced by their communication and problem-solving skills (Peplau and Fingerhut, 2007; Quam et al., 2010). On the scholastic front, the grade point averages of US college students were related positively to their communication competence (Rubin and Graham, 1988), and school adjustment, dropout rates, and overall school achievement and academic competence were found to be highly related to students' having strong, supportive relationships (Rosenfeld and Richman, 1999; Rosenfeld et al., 1998; Whitten and Weaver, 2010).

Psychologist Abraham Maslow (1968) suggests that human needs fall into five categories, each of which must be satisfied before we concern ourselves with the next one. As you read on, think about the ways in which communication is often necessary to satisfy each need. The most basic needs are *physical*: sufficient air, water, food, and rest, and the ability to reproduce as a species. The second category of Maslow's needs involves *safety*: protection from threats to our well-being. Beyond physical and safety concerns are the *social* needs we have already mentioned. After those necessities are met, Maslow suggests that each of us has the need for *self-esteem*: the desire to believe that we are worthwhile, valuable people. The final category of needs involves *self-actualization*: the desire to develop our potential to the maximum, to become the best people we can be.

 **CHECK IT!**

> Why do we communicate? Describe the four types of needs communication helps us to meet.

The Communication Process

So far, we have talked about communication as if its meaning was perfectly clear. In fact, scholars have debated the definition of communication for years with no simple conclusions (Littlejohn and Foss, 2008). One thing is clear: human communication is a complex process with many components. In this section, we will discuss some features and principles of communication.

A Model of Communication

As the old saying goes, "a picture is worth a thousand words." That's what scientists had in mind when they began creating models of the communication process in the 1950s.

Over time, communication models have become increasingly sophisticated in an attempt to represent all the factors that affect human interaction. No model can completely represent the process of communication, any more than a map can capture everything about the neighbourhood where you live. Still, the model in Figure 1.1 provides a starting point for explaining the insights and principles discussed below.

Insights from the Communication Model

Figure 1.1 illustrates a number of important characteristics of communication. As you read on, note how the following insights help explain the richness of this process.

Sending and Receiving Are Usually Simultaneous

In the following scenarios, ask yourself who is sending a message and who is receiving one.

- A teacher is explaining a difficult concept to a student after class.
- A parent is lecturing a teenager about the family's curfew rules.
- A salesperson is giving a customer information about a product.

The natural impulse is to identify the teacher, parent, and salesperson as senders, while the student, teenager, and customer are receivers. Now imagine a confused look on the student's face; the teenager interrupting defensively; the customer blankly staring into the distance. It's easy to see that these verbal and non-verbal responses are messages being "sent," even while the other person is talking.

Because it's often impossible to distinguish sending from receiving, our communication model replaces these roles with a more accurate word: *communicator*. This term reflects the fact people can simultaneously be senders and receivers who exchange multiple messages.

Meanings Exist in and among People

Messages, whether they are verbal or nonverbal, don't have meanings in themselves; rather, meanings reside in the people who express and interpret them. Imagine that a friend says "I'm sorry" after showing up two hours late for a pre-arranged meeting. There are several possible "meanings" that this expression might have: a genuine apology, an insincere attempt to defuse your anger, or even a sarcastic jibe. It's easy to imagine that your friend might mean one thing and you might have a different interpretation of it. The possibility of multiple interpretations means that it is often necessary to negotiate a shared meaning in order for satisfying communication to occur.

Environments Affect Communication

Problems often arise because communicators occupy different environments (sometimes called *contexts*)—that is, fields of experience that help them make sense of other people's behaviour. In communication terminology, **environment** refers not only to a physical location, but also to the personal experiences and cultural backgrounds that the participants bring to a conversation. Environments aren't always obvious. For example, several studies have revealed that playing cooperative video games, or even playing violent video games cooperatively (in a team), increases pro-social thoughts and helping behaviours (Gentile, et. al. 2009; Granic, Lobel, and Engels, 2014; Greitemeyer and Osswald, 2010; Velez et al., 2014).

Notice how the model in Figure 1.1 shows that the environments of *A* and *B* overlap. This intersecting area represents the background that the communicators have in common. If this overlap didn't exist, communication would be difficult, if not impossible.

Whereas similar environments facilitate satisfying communication, different backgrounds can make effective communication more challenging. Consider just some of the factors that might contribute to different environments and to difficulties:

- *A* might belong to one cultural group and *B* to another.
- *A* might be rich and *B* poor.
- *A* might be rushed and *B* have nowhere to go.

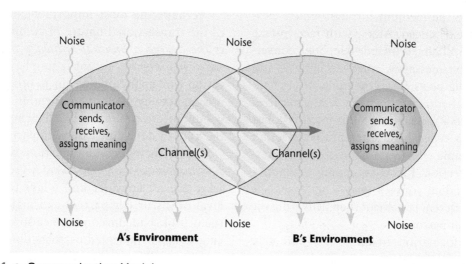

Figure 1.1 ● Communication Model

- *A* might have lived a long, eventful life, and *B* might be young and inexperienced.
- *A* might be passionately concerned with the subject and *B* indifferent to it.

Noise Affects Communication

Another factor that makes communication difficult is what scientists call **noise**: anything that interferes with the transmission and reception of a message. Three types of noise can disrupt communication. *External noise* includes those factors outside the receiver that make it difficult to hear or listen, as well as many other kinds of distractions. For instance, someone sitting next to you and speaking loudly on their cellphone, or a siren going by may prevent you from hearing a speaker's remarks. *Physiological noise* involves biological factors in the receiver that interfere with accurate reception, such as hearing loss, illness, and so on. *Psychological noise* refers to cognitive factors that make communication less effective. For instance, a woman who hears the word *gal* or *lady* may become so irritated that she has trouble listening objectively to the rest of a speaker's message. Likewise, an insecure employee may interpret a minor suggestion the boss makes as ridicule or criticism.

Channels Make a Difference

Communication scholars use the term **channel** to describe the medium through which messages are exchanged. Along with face-to-face interaction, channels include telephone conversations, text messages, email exchanges, and social media posts. The communication channel being used can affect the way a receiver responds to a message (O'Sullivan, 2000). For example, a typed love letter probably won't have the same effect as a handwritten expression of affection. Likewise, ending a relationship by sending your ex-lover a text message makes a different statement than delivering the bad news in person.

The information in Table 1.1 can help you answer some important questions about channel selection. Is it better to say "I'm sorry" in person or over the phone? Which channel is the best for expressing your anger? Should you approach the boss directly or put it in writing when asking for a raise? Will asking a merchant for a refund by email work better than a personal request? Generally, trust is built through face-to-face interactions (Rockmann and Northcraft, 2008) and people prefer to share highly emotional messages (e.g., romantic break up, resigning from a job) via media-rich, synchronous channels such as face-to-face encounters or telephone conversations (Choi and Toma, 2014), but all channels have their advantages and disadvantages for both the sender and the receiver.

Communication Principles

In addition to the insights offered by the communication model, there are other principles that guide our understanding of communication.

Communication Is Transactional

One shortcoming of communication models is that they don't adequately capture a sense of the give-and-take in interpersonal relationships. In fact, communication is **transactional communication**—that is, a dynamic process created by the participants through their interaction with one another.

Perhaps the most important consequence of the transactional nature of communication is *the degree of mutual influence that occurs when we interact*. To put it simply, communication isn't something we do *to* others; rather, it is an activity we do *with* them. In this sense, communication is rather like dancing—at least the kind of dancing we do with partners.

Like dancing, communication *depends on the involvement of a partner*. A great dancer who doesn't consider and adapt to the skill level of his or her partner can make both of them look bad. In communication and dancing, even two talented partners don't guarantee success. When two skilled dancers perform

Table 1.1 ● Factors to Consider When Choosing a Communication Channel

	Time Required for Feedback	Amount of Information Conveyed	Sender's Control over How Message Is Composed	Control over Receiver's Attention	Effectiveness for Detailed Messages
Face-to-Face	Immediate	High	Moderate	Highest	Low
Telephone	Immediate	Moderate	Moderate	Moderate (less than in face-to-face setting)	Low
Voice Mail	Delayed	Moderate	Higher	Low	Low
Email	Varies	Low	High	Low	High
Instant Messaging	Varies	Low	High	Varies	Low
Text Messaging and Twitter	Can be immediate.	Low	High	Low	High (brief messages)
Hard Copy (e.g., handwritten or typed message)	Delayed	Low (words, numbers, and images, but limited non-verbal cues)	Highest	Low	High

SOURCE: Adapted from R.B. Adler and J. Elmhorst (2008), *Communicating at work: Principles and practices for business and the professions*, 9th edn. New York: McGraw-Hill.

without coordinating their movements, the results feel bad to the dancers and look foolish to an audience.

Finally, relational communication—like dancing—is a *unique creation* that arises out of the way in which the partners interact. The way you dance probably varies from one partner to another because of the co-operative, transactional nature of dancing. Likewise, the way you communicate almost certainly varies with different partners. Psychologist Kenneth Gergen (1991) captures the transactional nature of communication well when he points out how our success depends on interaction with others: "One cannot be 'attractive' without others who are attracted, a 'leader' without others willing to follow, or a 'loving person' without others to affirm with appreciation" (p. 158). The transactional nature of relationships requires that we communicate *with* other people, not *to* them.

REFLECTION

CHOOSING THE CHANNEL

I am an average person in just about every way, except that I have a speech impediment. I have good days and bad days with my speech. On the bad days, I get the idea that strangers think I'm slow and incompetent, even though people who know me don't think I'm either.

Texting and email have become a very satisfying way for me to communicate, especially with people I don't know very well. With text messages and email, people can form opinions about me without thinking just about how I sound. I've found that my impediment isn't a problem once people know me, but at first, I think it is a real barrier; text and email remove that barrier completely.

CHECK IT!

When developing a model for interpersonal communication, what insights regarding the nature of interpersonal communication must we consider, and why?

Communication Can Be Intentional or Unintentional

Some communication is clearly deliberate: you probably plan your words carefully before asking the boss for a raise or offering constructive criticism. Some scholars (e.g., Motley, 1990) argue that only intentional messages like these qualify as communication. However, others (e.g., Baxter and Montgomery, 1996; Buck and VanLear, 2002) suggest that even unintentional behaviour is communicative. Suppose, for instance, that a friend overhears you muttering complaints to yourself. Even though you didn't intend her to hear your remarks, they certainly did carry a message. In addition to these slips of the tongue, we unintentionally send many non-verbal messages. You may not be aware of your sour expression, impatient shifting, or sigh of boredom, but others notice them nonetheless.

REFLECTION

MY WIFE'S EYEBROWS

My wife doesn't know it, but whenever she thinks something I'm saying is foolish, she arches her eyebrows in a special way (just before she tells me something I said was "ridiculous"). So now, when I see her eyebrows take this funny shape, I stop and ask her what's wrong. She immediately tells me, "I didn't say anything." Then I tell her what she's doing with her eyebrows, and she tells me, "You're crazy; I told you I didn't say anything." She doesn't seem to understand that she's sending messages while she's also listening, and that her eyebrow message is loud and clear!

Even the seeming absence of a behaviour has communicative value. Recall the times when you sent an email or left a voice mail message and received no reply. You probably assigned some meaning to the lack of a reply. Was the other person angry? Indifferent? Too busy to reply? Whether or not your hunch was correct, the point remains that all behaviour has communicative value. "Nothing" never happens.

In this book, we will look at the communicative value of both intentional and unintentional behaviour. We take the position that whatever you do—whether you speak or remain silent, confront or avoid a person, show emotion or keep a poker face—you provide information to others about your thoughts and feelings. In this sense, we are like transmitters that can't be shut off.

Communication Has a Content and a Relational Dimension

Virtually all **messages** have a **content** component, which involves the information being explicitly discussed (i.e., "Please pass the salt," "Not now, I'm tired," "You forgot to buy milk") and a relational component (Dillard et al., 1999; Watzlawick et al., 1967), which expresses how you feel about the other person (i.e., whether you like or dislike him or her, feel in control or subordinate, feel comfortable or anxious, and so on). For instance, consider how many different **relational messages** you could communicate by simply saying "thanks a lot" in different ways.

Sometimes, the content of a message is all that matters. For example, you may not care how the directory assistance operator feels about you, as long as you get the phone number you're looking for. In a qualitative sense, however, the relational dimension of a message is often more important than the content under discussion. This explains why disputes over apparently trivial subjects become so important. In such cases, we're not really arguing over whose turn it is to take out the garbage or whether we should play tennis or swim. Instead, we're disputing the nature of the relationship. Who is in control? How important are we to each other? In Chapter 8, we will explore several key relational issues in detail.

Communication Is Irreversible

We sometimes wish that we could back up in time, erasing words or acts and replacing them with better alternatives. Unfortunately, such reversal is impossible. Sometimes, further explanation can clear up the confusion or an apology can mollify another person's hurt feelings, but other times, no amount of explanation can erase the impression you have created. It is no more possible to "unreceive" a message than to "unsqueeze" a tube of toothpaste. Words said and deeds done are irretrievable. Nowhere is this more evident than with social media. Once you have sent or posted that comment or those pictures they can live on forever in cyberspace, well beyond your control.

© TatyanaGl/iStockphoto.

Communication is irreversible, and sometimes it affects more than just the person with whom you're communicating. Think back to a time when you wished to take back something you communicated to another person. How did it affect your relationship with that person? How did it affect other relationships in your life?

Communication Is Unrepeatable

Because communication is an ongoing process, an event cannot be repeated. The friendly smile that worked so well when you met a stranger last week may not succeed with the person you encounter tomorrow. It may feel stale and artificial to you the second time around, or it may be wrong for the new person or occasion. Even with the same person, it is impossible to recreate an event. Why? Because both you and the other person have changed. You have both lived longer. The behaviour isn't original. Your feelings about each other may have changed. You need not constantly invent new ways to act around familiar people, but you should realize that the "same" words and behaviour are different each time they are spoken or performed.

Communication Misconceptions

Now that we have described what communication is, we need to identify some things that it is not. Avoiding these common misconceptions (adapted from McCroskey and Richmond, 1996) can save you a great deal of trouble in your personal life.

Not All Communication Seeks Understanding

Most people operate on the implicit, but flawed, assumption that the goal of all communication is to maximize understanding between communicators. While some understanding is

TAKE TWO

Dimensions of Every Message

- **Content:** refers to the information explicitly being discussed.
- **Relational:** refers to how the communicators feel about each other.

REFLECTION

HURTFUL WORDS CAN'T BE RETRACTED

I was adopted at the age of five. My adoptive parents were verbally abusive. On a few occasions, they said things to me in anger that I will never forget and which changed our relationship forever. "Nobody wanted you—you should be thankful that we took you in" was one of their major hurtful messages. Even though they would apologize later, no amount of explanations ease the pain those words have caused me.

necessary for us to coordinate our interaction, there are some types of communication in which understanding as we usually conceive it is not the primary goal. Consider, for example, the following situations:

- *The social rituals we enact every day*: "How's it going?" you ask. "Great," the other person replies. The primary goal in exchanges like these is mutual acknowledgment: there is obviously no serious attempt to exchange information.
- *Many attempts to influence others*: A quick analysis of most television commercials shows that they are aimed at persuading viewers to buy products, not helping viewers understand the content of the ad. In the same way, many of our attempts to persuade others to act as we want don't involve a desire to get the other person to understand what we want—just to comply with our wishes.
- *Deliberate ambiguity and deception:* When you decline an unwanted invitation by saying, "I can't make it," you probably want to create the impression that the decision is really beyond your control. (If your goal were to be perfectly clear, you might say, "I don't want to get together. In fact, I'd rather do almost anything than accept your invitation.") In fact, we often equivocate precisely because we want to hide our true

thoughts and feelings (this is explained in detail in Chapter 9).

More Communication Is Not Always Better

While failure to communicate effectively can certainly cause problems (Richmond, 1995), *too much* talking can also be a mistake. Sometimes, excessive communication is simply unproductive, as when two people "talk a problem to death," going over the same ground again and again without making progress. There are other times when talking too much actually aggravates a problem. We've all had the experience of "talking ourselves into a hole"—making a bad situation worse by pursuing it too far. As McCroskey and Wheeless (1976, p. 5) put it, "More and more negative communication merely leads to more and more negative results." In one study, college roommates revealed that thinking and talking about conflicts can actually increase relational problems (Cloven and Roloff, 1991).

There are even times when *no* interaction is the best course. When two people are angry and hurt, they may say things they don't mean and will later regret. In such cases, it is probably best to spend time cooling off, thinking about what to say and how to say it. In Chapter 4, we will help you decide when and how to share feelings.

✓ CHECK IT!

What are the five principles that guide our understanding of interpersonal communication? Describe them and explain their significance.

TAKE TWO

Not all communication seeks understanding. Some examples include:
- everyday social rituals;
- persuasion and coercion; and
- deliberate ambiguity and deception.

Communication Will Not Solve All Problems

Sometimes, even the best-planned, best-timed communication won't solve a problem. For example, imagine that you ask an instructor to explain why you received a poor grade on a project you believe deserved top marks. The instructor clearly outlines the reasons why you received the low grade and sticks to that position after listening thoughtfully to your protests. Has communication solved the problem? Hardly.

Sometimes, clear communication is even the cause of problems. Suppose, for example, that a friend asks you for an honest opinion of an expensive outfit she just bought. Your clear and sincere answer, "I think it makes you look fat," might do more harm than good. Deciding when and how to self-disclose isn't always easy. See Chapter 2 for suggestions.

Effective Communication Is Not a Natural Ability

Most people assume that communication is an aptitude that is developed without the need for training—rather like breathing. Although nearly everyone does manage to function passably without much formal communication training, most people operate at a level of effectiveness far below their potential. In fact, communication skills are similar to athletic ability. Even the least gifted among us can improve with training and practice.

Interpersonal Communication Defined

Now that you have a better understanding of the overall process of human communication, it's time to look at what makes some types of communication uniquely interpersonal.

Quantitative and Qualitative Definitions

Interpersonal communication has been defined in two ways (Redmond, 1995). Most definitions describe a **quantitative interpersonal communication** as any interaction between two people. Social scientists call two people who are interacting a **dyad**, and they often use the adjective *dyadic* to describe this type of communication. So, in a quantitative sense, the terms *dyadic communication* and **interpersonal communication** can be used interchangeably. If we use a quantitative definition, a sales clerk helping a customer or a police officer ticketing a speeding driver would be examples of interpersonal acts, whereas a teacher leading a class or an actor performing before an audience would not.

Dyadic communication *is* different from the kind of interaction that occurs in larger groups (Wilmot, 1995). In a group, participants can form coalitions to get support for their positions. In a dyad, though, the partners must work matters out with each other. This difference explains why, if a task calls for competition, children prefer to play in three- or four-person groups, and if it calls for co-operation, they prefer to be in dyads (Benenson et al., 2000).

Despite the unique qualities of dyads, you might object to the quantitative definition of interpersonal communication. For example, consider a routine transaction between a sales clerk and customer, or the rushed exchange when you ask a stranger on the street for directions. Communication of this sort hardly seems the same as when you talk to a friend about a personal problem or share with family members your experiences of a year in school.

The impersonal nature of some two-person exchanges—the kind when you think, "I might as well have been talking to a machine"—has led some scholars (e.g., Miller and Steinberg, 1975; Stewart and Logan, 1998) to argue that quality, not quantity, is what distinguishes interpersonal communication. **Qualitative interpersonal communication** occurs when people treat one another as unique individuals, regardless of the context in which the interaction occurs or the number of people involved. When quality of interaction is the criterion, the opposite of interpersonal

"You invented a time machine to come back and hit Reply instead of Reply All?"

Tom Toro *The New Yorker Collection/The Cartoon Bank.*

communication is *impersonal* interaction, not group, public, or mass communication.

Several features distinguish qualitatively interpersonal communication from less personal exchanges. The first is *uniqueness.* Whereas impersonal exchanges are governed by the kind of social rules we learn from parents, teachers, and etiquette books, the way we communicate in a truly personal relationship is unlike our behaviour with anyone else. In one relationship, you might exchange good-natured insults, while in another, you are careful never to offend your compatriot. Likewise, you might handle conflicts with one friend or family member by expressing an opinion as soon as a disagreement arises, whereas the unwritten rule in another relationship is to withhold expressions of disagreement until resentments build up and then to clear the air periodically. Communication scholar Julia Wood (2009) coined the term *relational culture,* in which people in close relationships create their own unique ways of interacting.

A second characteristic of qualitatively interpersonal communication is *irreplaceability.* Because interpersonal relationships are unique, they cannot be replaced. This explains why we usually feel so sad when a close friendship or love affair cools down. We know that no matter how many other relationships we have in our lives, none of them will ever be quite like the one that just ended.

Interdependence is a third characteristic of qualitatively interpersonal relationships. Here, the fate of the partners is connected. You might be able to brush off the anger, affection, excitement, or depression of someone you're not involved with interpersonally, but in an interpersonal relationship, the other's life affects you. Sometimes, interdependence is a pleasure, and at other times, it is a burden. In either case, interdependence is a fact of life in qualitatively interpersonal relationships.

A fourth yardstick of interpersonal communication is *disclosure of personal information.* In impersonal relationships, we don't reveal much about ourselves, but in many interpersonal ones, communicators feel more comfortable sharing their thoughts and feelings. This does not mean that all interpersonal relationships are warm and caring, or that all self-disclosure is positive. It's possible to reveal negative, personal information: "I'm really mad at you . . ."

In impersonal communication, we seek payoffs that have little to do with the people involved. You listen to professors in class or talk to potential buyers of your used car in order to reach goals that have little to do with developing personal relationships. By contrast, you spend time in qualitatively interpersonal relationships with friends, lovers, and others because of the fifth characteristic of such communication, *intrinsic rewards.* It often doesn't

REFLECTION

IRREPLACEABLE LOSS

My dad died when I was 29 years old. Ever since I was a child, I had always thought I would never reach 30. Fortunately, I did and have made it well past, but something changed forever when I was 29. I lost a relationship that could never be replaced. After my dad died, I felt suddenly "grown up" or as if I didn't have a "safety net" any more. Nothing had really changed in my life to account for this feeling of being on my own except the absence of my dad and our unique ways of interacting. No one else called me by the nickname he did. It was gone. Our ways of talking, our jokes, our shared memories seemed to be evaporating. I couldn't hold on to them all by myself. I remembered sitting beside my dad at his mom's funeral. I was 10 years old. I felt sad, but a bit relieved that she had died because she had been sick with Alzheimer's disease for some time. It was the first funeral I had been to, and I was nervous, so I watched my dad carefully to see what to do. At one point in the service, he turned to me and with a wink said, "Well, I'm an orphan now." (His father had deserted the family when he was a child.) I burst out laughing. Thinking back now, I wonder if there was a little tinge of truth in his joke. I wonder if he felt the same way I did when he died—all grown up and alone without that relationship to catch him if he fell.

TAKE TWO

Defining Interpersonal Communication: Quantity versus Quality

- **Quantitative interpersonal communication:** definitions focus on *the number of people* involved.
- **Qualitative interpersonal communication:** definitions focus on *the nature of the interaction* between the people involved in terms of its uniqueness, irreplaceability, amount of disclosure, and intrinsic rewards, as well as the interdependence of the people involved.

The rarity of qualitatively interpersonal communication is not necessarily unfortunate. Most of us do not have the time or energy to create personal relationships with everyone we encounter. In fact, the scarcity of interpersonal communication contributes to its value. Like precious and one-of-a-kind works of art, qualitatively interpersonal relationships are special because they are rare.

Personal and Impersonal Communication: A Matter of Balance

Now that the differences between qualitatively interpersonal and impersonal communication are clear, we need to ask some important questions. Is personal communication better than the impersonal variety? Is more personal communication the goal?

Most relationships are neither personal nor impersonal. Rather, they fall somewhere between these two extremes. Consider your own communication and you will find that there is often a personal element in even the most impersonal situations. You might appreciate the unique sense of humour of a supermarket cashier or spend a few moments sharing private thoughts with the person cutting your hair. And even the most tyrannical,

matter what you talk about, as developing the relationship is what's important.

Because interpersonal communication is characterized by the qualities of uniqueness, irreplaceability, interdependence, disclosure, and intrinsic rewards, it forms only a small fraction of our interaction. Most of our communication is relatively impersonal. We chat pleasantly with shopkeepers or fellow passengers on the bus or plane, discuss the weather or current events with most classmates and neighbours, and deal with co-workers and teachers in a polite way; but considering the number of people with whom we communicate, interpersonal relationships are by far the minority.

demanding, by-the-book boss might show an occasional flash of humanity.

Just as there's a personal element in many impersonal settings, there is also an impersonal side to our relationships with the people we care about most. There are occasions when we don't want to be personal: when we're distracted, tired, busy, or just not interested. In fact, interpersonal communication is somewhat like rich food—it's fine in moderation, but too much can make you uncomfortable. The blend of personal and interpersonal communication can shift in various stages of a relationship. The communication between young lovers who talk only about their feelings may change as their relationship develops. Several years later, their communication has become more routine and ritualized, the percentage of time they spend on personal, relational issues drops, and the conversation about less intimate topics increases. In Chapter 8, we discuss how communication changes as relationships pass through various stages; and in Chapter 2, we describe various theories of self-disclosure. As you read this information, you will see even more clearly that, while interpersonal communication can make life worth living, it isn't possible or desirable all the time.

Self-Assessment

HOW INTERPERSONAL ARE YOUR RELATIONSHIPS?

Select three important relationships to assess. These might include your relationships with people at work or school, with friends, or with your family. For each relationship, answer the following questions:

1. To what extent is the relationship characterized by uniqueness? How much is this relationship one of a kind?

   Low level of uniqueness 1 2 3 4 5 6 7 High level of uniqueness

2. To what extent is the relationship irreplaceable?

   Very easy to replace 1 2 3 4 5 6 7 Very hard to replace

3. To what extent are you and your relationship partner interdependent; that is, to what extent do your actions affect the other?

   Little interdependence 1 2 3 4 5 6 7 High interdependence

4. To what extent is communication in the relationship marked by high disclosure of personal information?

   Little disclosure 1 2 3 4 5 6 7 High disclosure

5. To what extent does the relationship create its own intrinsic rewards?

   Little Intrinsic Value 1 2 3 4 5 6 7 High Intrinsic Value

Referring to your answers, decide how qualitatively interpersonal (or how impersonal) each relationship is. (If you have more fives, sixes, and sevens in your answers, then your relationship is more interpersonal. If you have more ones, twos, and threes, then the relationship is more impersonal.) How satisfied are you with your findings? What can you do to improve your satisfaction with these relationships?

Interpersonal Communication and Technology

Until about a generation ago, face-to-face communication seemed essential to starting and maintaining most, if not all, personal relationships. Other channels did exist: the telephone (in an era of expensive long-distance rates and less-than-perfect technology) may have worked during temporary absences, and postal correspondence may have bridged the gap until the people involved could reconnect in person. Nonetheless, interpersonal communication seemed to require physical proximity.

Technological changes have given us new options for communicating personally. Computers now fit in the palms of our hands and wireless technology allows us access to the Internet from almost everywhere. **Computer-mediated communication** (CMC) provides us with other ways to interact both socially and at work. For work related communication, email remains the most popular form of CMC, but text messaging, instant messaging, social networking, picture and video sharing, blogging, and other social media provide friends, family, colleagues, acquaintances, and even strangers with a variety of ways to communicate (Zickuhr, 2010). Some critics argue that the almost hypnotic attraction of the Internet and social media discourages people from spending "face time" with others. A small body of research supports this position. Some research has found that heavy Internet users spend less time talking in person and on the phone with friends and family members (Bower, 1998; Nie, 2001), habits that can lead to high levels of emotional loneliness (Moody, 2001). Problematic Internet use, which is Internet use that interferes with the ability to accomplish daily routines, is associated with social anxiety, loneliness, and depression, but sorting out whether the Internet is the cause or symptom of such problems is difficult (Tokunaga, 2014). For some individuals Internet use can and does interfere with the quality of their face-to-face personal relationships. Email, texting, Twitter, Facebook and online video games are ways to stay in touch and interact with others, but, as Sherry Turkle (2011) points out, they are no substitute for real conversation and physical human connection. You can't give someone a hug, wipe away tears, or really share all the sensations of a delicious meal using CMC.

On the other hand, there is considerable research that suggests that the Internet can actually enhance interpersonal communication. Social networking and use of the Internet can create opportunities for meaningful social exchanges among people. People who use social networking sites tend to have close social ties "on the ground" and social networking sites provide opportunities for people to meet and interact with a more diverse group of people than they might meet otherwise (Wellman and Rainie, 2012). In their analyses of the effects of the Internet on social life and civic participation, Ben Veenhof, Barry Wellman, and their colleagues (2008) analyzed data from several surveys conducted between 2003 and 2007 that included almost 150,000 Canadians. Not surprisingly, given Canadians' high Internet use and fondness for email, the majority of adults surveyed used the Internet daily, and email appeared to support existing social contacts and not to replace telephone and face-to-face communication. People who visited and called each other frequently also emailed each other frequently. Similar, large scale studies in the United States have also found that mobile phone use and certain social media activities (e.g., sharing photos) are associated with larger and more diverse social networks (Hampton et.al., 2011). Clearly, face-to-face communication is essential for our health and well-being, but CMC can also play a vital role in establishing and maintaining our interpersonal relationships.

Characteristics of Computer-Mediated Communication

Like face-to-face communication, mediated communication contains the same elements described in the communication model introduced earlier in this chapter (communicators, environments, messages, channels, and noise). It also satisfies the same communication needs (physical, identity, social, and practical), while having some unique features, such as media richness, synchronicity, and permanence.

Media Richness

Media richness or information richness is a concept developed by social scientists (Daft and Lengel, 1984) to describe the amount and type of information that can be conveyed through a communication channel. While all communication channels present challenges, text-based messages are inherently leaner than verbal messages delivered on the phone or in person. They lack non-verbal cues that help communicators better understand each other's intentions and emotions, and thus are more easily misunderstood. For some people the absence of non-verbal cues such as voice tone, facial expressions, etc. makes text-based

A lot of people argue that the Internet has a negative effect on communication, while others argue that now we can communicate better than we ever have before. What do you think?

communication more comfortable. For shy individuals in particular, CMC can actually enhance the quality of their friendships and reduce their anxiety about participating in discussions (Hammick and Lee, 2014). Social networking sites such as Facebook appear to help shy people get to know people better, enabling them to achieve greater intimacy and closer friendships (Baker and Oswald, 2010). However, pared down, text-based communication creates more opportunities for misunderstanding. Without non-verbal cues such as facial expressions, gestures, and voice tone it is easy to misinterpret messages, particularly those that might be interpreted as conveying humour, irony, or sarcasm. When sending a message it is essential to try to be as unambiguous as possible; and when receiving text messages it is important to remember that we tend to interpret positive text-based messages as more neutral than intended and neutral messages as more negative than intended (Byron, 2008).

Synchronicity

Synchronous communication occurs in real time. Examples of synchronous CMC would be cellphone conversations and video conferencing (e.g., Skype, FaceTime, etc.). However, most mediated communication is **asynchronous**, which means there is a time gap between when the message was sent and when it is received. Email, voice mail, text messages, and social networking posts are asynchronous. Asynchronous messages are different from synchronous messages because you have more time to respond to them as well as the option to not respond at all. But as we learned earlier this chapter, not responding is still communicating—all behaviour has communicative value. The *asynchronous* nature of many types of mediated communication provides a way to share information that otherwise might be impossible. For example, recent immigrants to Canada are more likely to use the Internet (email, text messaging, and Skype) every day to communicate with relatives and friends abroad (Statistics Canada, 2008). CMC provides not only increased opportunities for communication locally, but also the ability to maintain relationships over long distances.

Permanence

A third difference between face-to-face and mediated communication is **permanence**, or how long the message endures. Unlike our face-to-face conversations, the messages, photos, and videos we post or send to each other, via CMC, can be saved indefinitely and shared with individuals for whom they were never intended. This can be a tremendous advantage. For example, when your doctor or specialist electronically records your conversation about a health condition you are able to access it anytime in the future; or when you have forgotten where to meet your friend you can look up the address she texted to you earlier. But there are obvious disadvantages too.

For instance, people are more comfortable disclosing personal information online or via text-based messaging (Marriott and Buchanan, 2014; Reid and Reid, 2007). While this can be a good thing, it can also contribute to people posting pictures or sending messages that they might later regret. For instance, a study conducted by Internet Watch Foundation found that 88 per cent of the sexually explicit photos and videos of young people they found on public websites were self-generated (e.g., selfies, sexting messages sent privately). These images had never been intended for public viewing (Smith, 2012), but were still accessible and distributed by unintended viewers. Even with privacy settings and other safeguards, the reality is we have little control over the information we share online, it can potentially be accessed by anyone, and it can never truly be deleted from the Internet. We will look at some of the challenges of CMC when we discuss personal disclosure in Chapter 2 as well as when we examine communication climates and conflict in later chapters. In the meantime, however, it is wise to treat CMC communication in the same way you treat messages you send in person. Think twice before communicating something you might later regret.

Interpersonal Communication and Cultural Diversity

Almost a half century ago, communication guru Marshall McLuhan (1964) coined the metaphor of the world as a "global village" where members of all nations are connected by communication technology. Just as with members of a traditional village, McLuhan suggested, the affairs and fate of the occupants of Planet Earth are connected—for better or worse. This analysis has proved to be increasingly true in the years since McLuhan introduced it. The growth in communication technology, including international telephone service, the Internet, and global television coverage brings the world into our homes. Although relatively cheap transportation has reduced the barrier of distance, making travel easier for more people than ever before, Canadians don't need to go far to be exposed to the global village.

Demographic changes have been transforming Canada into a microcosm of the global village. Canada has the second-highest proportion of foreign-born citizens and the highest immigration rate in the world (Adams, 2007b; Statistics Canada, 2011b). In 2011, 6.7 million, or 20.6 per cent of the total population of Canadians were born outside the country. The Canadian concept of multiculturalism, where people value, celebrate, and preserve their cultural heritage rather than becoming assimilated into the dominant culture, helps to create this microcosm of global diversity. More than any other country, Canada values the contributions of immigrants (Adams, 2007a; Reitz, 2011).

REFLECTION

POSITIVE POWER OF TEXTING

I was about 17 when my parents split up and my dad took a job overseas. I found that through texting I was able to maintain and even deepen my relationship with him. I could contact him when I wanted to, not according to a "schedule of visits." I didn't like the fact that he didn't live with us anymore, but I felt like I could still joke with him and we could share important things going on in our lives, along with all the stupid, everyday stuff that makes us both laugh, cringe, cry or growl with irritation. When we see each other it makes things so much easier because we know what's up.

 **CHECK IT!**

What is the general consensus regarding the effects of technology on interpersonal communication?

Economic integration also creates ties that bind nations and people. National economies are increasingly connected with and affected by developments around the world. According to Industry Canada, no other major economy is as trade-oriented as Canada. The country depends on international trade to grow and prosper; because Canada's economy is very small, domestic-based companies increasingly enter global markets in order to remain viable and competitive (Poloz, 2005).

Given all this information, it makes sense to examine how interpersonal communication operates between members of different cultures. Throughout this book, we will see that when people from different backgrounds interact, they face a set of challenges that are often different from when members of the same culture communicate.

Culture

Defining **culture** is not an easy task. One survey of scholarly literature revealed 500 definitions, phrasings, and uses of the concept (Kroeber and Kluckhohn, 1952). For our purposes, Larry Samovar and his colleagues (2012) offer a clear and comprehensive definition of *culture* as "the language, values, beliefs, traditions, and customs people share and learn."

This definition shows that culture is, to a great extent, a matter of *perception* and *definition*. When you identify yourself as a member of a culture, you must not only share certain characteristics, but you must also recognize yourself, and others like you, as possessing these features; and see others who don't possess them as members of different categories. For example, eye colour doesn't seem like a significant factor in distinguishing "us" from "them," whereas skin colour is more important—at least in some cases. It's not hard to imagine a society where the opposite is true. Social scientists use the term **in-groups** for groups with which we identify and **out-groups** for those that we view as different (Tajfel and Turner, 1992).

Intercultural Communication

Having defined culture, we can go on to define **intercultural communication** as the process by which members of two or more cultures exchange messages in a manner that is influenced by their different cultural perceptions and symbol systems (Samovar et al., 2012). Note that intercultural communication (at least as we'll use the term here) doesn't always occur when people from different cultures interact. The cultural backgrounds, perceptions, and symbol systems of the participants must have a significant influence on the exchange before we can say that culture has made a difference. Consider a few examples where culture does and doesn't play a role:

- A group of preschool children is playing in a park. These three-year-olds don't realize that their parents may have come from different countries or even that they don't all speak the same language. At this point, we could not say that intercultural communication is taking place. Only when different norms become apparent—about diet, sharing, or parental discipline, for example—do the children begin to think of one another as different.
- Members of a school basketball team from a variety of cultural backgrounds—some East Asian, some South Asian, some Caribbean, and some European—are intent on winning the league championship. During a game, cultural distinctions aren't important. There's plenty of communication, but it is not fundamentally intercultural. Away from their games, the players are friendly when they meet, but they rarely socialize. If they did, they might notice some fundamental differences in the way members of each cultural group communicate.
- A husband and wife were raised in homes with different religious traditions. Most of the time, their religious heritage makes little difference and the partners view themselves as a unified couple. Every so often, however—perhaps during holidays or when

meeting members of each other's family—the different backgrounds are highlighted. At those times, we can imagine the partners feeling quite different from each other—thinking of themselves as members of separate cultures.

This group could be participating in intercultural communication or in co-cultural communication. Can they participate in both?

These examples show that in order to view ourselves as members of a culture, there has to be some distinction between "us" and "them," between in- and out-group. We may not always be able to say precisely what the differences are. We may have only a feeling that something is different. There are occasions when cultural influences are powerful, but so subtle that they go unrecognized.

Many social scientists use the term **co-culture** to describe a subgroup that is part of an encompassing culture. For example, in North American culture it is easy to recognize categories such as age (teen, senior citizens), ethnicity (Asian, European), race, gender, sexual orientation, physical disabilities, and religion. Some scholars (e.g., Mulac et al., 2001; Tannen, 1990, 1994; Wood, 2009) and writers in the popular press (e.g., Gray, 1992) have even characterized men and women as belonging to different co-cultures because their communication styles are so different.

Interpersonal and Intercultural Communication

At this point, you may be wondering whether there is any communication that *is not* intercultural, or at least co-cultural. Indeed, there are many cases when communication isn't influenced by intercultural considerations. Even in an increasingly diverse world, there are still plenty of relationships in which people share a basically common background. The

Irish marchers in a St Patrick's Day parade; the group of men from a small town who play poker every other Friday night; and the members of a university sorority or fraternity are likely to share fundamentally similar personal histories and, therefore, have similar norms, customs, and values. Even when people with different cultural backgrounds communicate, shared values and experiences are often far more important than the cultural backgrounds they bring to the relationship (Merkin, Taras and Steel, 2014; Singer, 1998). David may be a Jewish man whose ancestors came from Eastern Europe, while Lisa is a third-generation Japanese-Canadian woman whose parents are practising Christians, but they have created a life together that is usually more important than their differences, and that enables them to deal comfortably with those differences when they do arise.

Rather than classifying some exchanges as intercultural and others as free from cultural influences, we may more accurately talk about *degrees* of cultural significance (Lustig and Koester, 1999). Encounters can fit along a spectrum of interculturalness. At the most intercultural end are situations where differences between the backgrounds and beliefs of communicators are high. A traveller visiting a new country for the first time with little knowledge of local society would be an obvious example. At the least intercultural end of the spectrum fall exchanges where cultural differences matter little. A student from Montreal who attends a small university in the Maritimes may find life somewhat different, but the adjustment would be far less difficult than that for the international traveller. In between these extremes falls a whole range of encounters in which culture plays varying roles.

What is the relationship between intercultural communication and interpersonal relationships? William Gudykunst and Young Kim (2003) summarize an approach that helps answer this question. They suggest that interpersonal and intercultural factors combine to form a two-by-two matrix in which the importance of interpersonal communication forms one dimension and intercultural significance forms the other (see Figure 1.2). This model shows that some interpersonal transactions (for example, a conversation between two siblings who have been raised in the same household) have virtually no intercultural

elements. Other encounters (such as a traveller from Senegal trying to get directions from an Iranian-Canadian taxi driver in Vancouver) are almost exclusively intercultural, without the personal dimensions that we discuss throughout this book.

Still other exchanges—the most interesting ones for our purposes—contain elements of both intercultural and interpersonal communication. This range of encounters is broad in the global village: business people from different backgrounds try to wrap up a deal; Canadian-born and immigrant children learn to get along in school; health-care educators seek effective ways to serve patients from around the world; neighbours from different racial or ethnic backgrounds look for ways to make their streets safer and cleaner; middle-class teachers seek common ground with students from low-income neighbourhoods—the list seems almost endless. In situations like these, communicators are trying to establish some degree of relationship and understanding. When they do find ways of connecting that account for, and even transcend, cultural differences, communicators

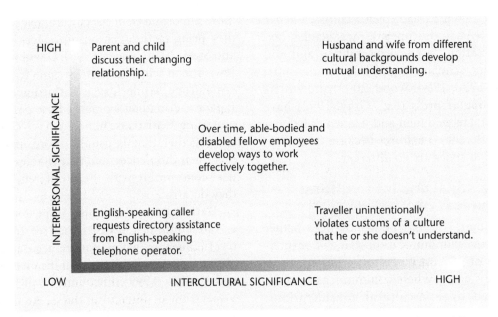

Figure 1.2 ● Possible Interactions among Interpersonal and Intercultural Dimensions of Person-to-Person Communication

have created what Fred Casmir (1991) calls a "third culture," a unique relationship shared by two or more people.

Comparison of Canadian and US Culture

Since the population of the United States is roughly 10 times that of Canada and 5 times that of the United Kingdom (United States Census Bureau, 2014; World Gazetteer, 2005), it follows logically that a very large proportion of the research on interpersonal communication in Western culture has been conducted with US citizens. Canadians have a much smaller database of homegrown studies to inform them about their interpersonal communication practices. So, to what extent can we apply US findings to the Canadian context? In order to answer this question, we need to examine the similarities and differences between the two cultures, particularly in areas that are relevant to interpersonal communication.

Differences in word choice, phrasing, grammatical structure, and pronunciation that occur in various North American dialects (see Chapter 6 for examples of language differences) can undoubtedly make it hard to understand the speech of people from some parts of Canada and the United States—even though they are all speaking English. But these speech differences do not necessarily change speakers' judgments about the appropriateness or effectiveness of various types of interpersonal communication. In contrast, there are some documented differences between Canadian and American values that may well influence our perceptions of appropriate and effective interpersonal communication.

How are Canadian values similar to US values, and how are they different? There has been considerable discussion, debate, and research comparing the values and behaviour of Canadians and Americans (Adams, 2003; Boucher, 2004; Jedwab, 2004b; Krauss, 2003). The consensus appears to be that, although the two cultures are very similar when placed in the context of the many cultures in the world (Hofstede, 1980, 2001), there are some differences that are important to many Canadians. For instance, Michael Adams, co-founder of the social research organization Environics, has reported on three large social-values surveys conducted in Canada and the United States in 1992, 1996, and 2000. He and his Environics colleagues used those surveys in combination with over 14,000 individual interviews and previously compiled Canadian survey findings (dating back to 1983), to conduct a comparative analysis of Canadian and American culture and to track shifts in social values (Adams, 2003). In the surveys, participants were questioned about more than 100 social values. Values were defined as "ideas that motivate people to behave the way they do, good, bad or neither" (Adams, 2003, p. 12).

Canadians and Americans described different values, attitudes, and beliefs in many different areas. Some of the most significant in terms of their impact on interpersonal communication are attitudes toward violence, tolerance of diversity, and the relative status of men and women.

Concepts in Intercultural Communication

- **Culture:** the language, values, beliefs, traditions, and customs people share and learn.
- **In-groups:** groups of people with whom we identify.
- **Out-groups:** groups of people whom we view as different.
- **Co-culture:** a subgroup that is part of an encompassing culture.
- **Intercultural communication:** the process by which members of two or more cultures exchange messages in a manner that is influenced by their different cultural perceptions and symbol systems.

Liam Francis Walsh *The New Yorker Collection/The Cartoon Bank.*

"What part of Canada that I know nothing about are you from?"

Attitudes toward Violence

Michael Adams (2003) argues that Canadians are markedly differentiated from Americans by their attitudes toward violence. Generally, fewer Canadians perceive that they are surrounded by violence than do their US counterparts. Canadians are less likely to perceive violence as a normal part of everyday life or as a way of solving problems. When compared with Americans, far fewer Canadians endorsed the view that it was acceptable to use a little violence to relieve tension or frustration (Adams, 2003). Similarly, almost twice as many Americans as Canadians thought it was acceptable to use violence to get what you want (23 per cent compared to 13 per cent). Predictions that Canadians would be more likely to endorse the use of violence and be more deferential to authority in the wake of the 11 September 2001 (9/11) attacks proved untrue. Investigations immediately following 9/11 revealed that Canadians were not ready to curtail their Charter of Rights and Freedoms without justification based on reality, not on fear (Baker, 2002). Similar predictions that the

events of 9/11 would contribute to less tolerance for diversity and multiculturalism in Canada also proved unfounded.

Tolerance of Diversity

Canadians consistently express more positive attitudes toward immigration (Adams 2007b, 2010; Pew Research Centre, 2003; Soroka and Robertson, 2010) when compared to the United States and many Western countries. Public opinion surveys conducted over the past decade suggest that the majority of Canadians endorse the idea that immigrants have a good influence on their country. The majority of Americans surveyed did not appear to share that belief (Soroka and Robertson, 2010). The Canadians surveyed were also less willing than Americans to endorse overtly racist statements such as, "Non-whites should not be allowed to immigrate to this country." (Adams, 2003; Environics Institute, 2012). Even if respondents in both countries were not being completely truthful in order to appear more socially acceptable, Canadians appear to believe that in Canadian culture, intolerance of immigrants is not socially acceptable. It is important to note that these data have the potential to be misleading, because they might be interpreted to imply that Canadians are neither ethnocentric, nor racist and prejudiced toward immigrants and minorities. There is abundant evidence that Canadians can be ethnocentric, racist, and prejudiced (Canadian Council on Social Development, 2000; Henry and Tator, 2003; Jedwab, 2004a; Teelucksingh and Galabuzi, 2005). Regardless, the point is that Canadians are different from Americans to the extent in which we believe these things are not acceptable in Canada.

In addition to being open-minded toward cultural diversity, Canadians are more accepting of diversity in people's sexuality than Americans. Data from World Values Surveys indicate that Canadians are more open-minded toward lesbians and gay men than are Americans (Anderson and Fetner, 2008). Similarly, American university students showed more negative attitudes toward lesbians and gay men than did Canadian university students (Morrison et al., 2009). Canadian attitudes both influence and are influenced by Canadian laws that guarantee equal rights to all people regardless of their sexual orientation, including the right for same-sex couples to be legally married. Lesbian, gay, bisexual, transgendered, and queer (LGBTQ) people do not have these same legal protections in all states in the US. Again, greater acceptance of sexual diversity in Canada does not mean LGBTQ people do not experience prejudice and discrimination, but it does appear that Canadians are aware that these negative attitudes and prejudiced behaviours are wrong.

Relative Status of Men and Women

Similarly, discrimination against women exists in Canada (Morris et al., 1999), but Canadians are less willing than their US counterparts to endorse a view of patriarchal authority (the father must be master in his own home) or a view that men are naturally superior to women. According to the Environics 2000 survey data, 18 per cent of Canadians and 49 per cent of Americans said the father of a household must be the boss (Adams, 2003). Michael Adams (2003, 2005) argues that Canadians' more egalitarian views regarding the status of women and their unwillingness to endorse traditional family models of patriarchal authority have contributed to making us take a more relaxed view of what constitutes a family. More Canadians support the view that common-law partners and same-sex couples are "proper" families). Americans appear to be less accepting of these kinds of variations in family structure (Adams, 2003; Galloway and Moore, 2005; Mitchell, 2014).

At the same time that we see differences, we are also aware that in a global context, the values that are the basis for Canadian society are perceived as more similar to those of US society than to those of many other cultures (Grabb and Curtis, 2010). A study commissioned by the Association for Canadian Studies reported that 55 per cent of Canadians believe that Canadian society has values that are similar to those of the United States (Jedwab, 2004b). Furthermore, when we look at the cultural dimensions such as individualism versus collectivism, uncertainty avoidance, and "power distance" (social hierarchy), Canada and the United States have very similar rankings. Geert Hofstede (1980, 2001) used extensive statistical data to examine cultural values in 53 different countries around the world. One value dimension he measured indicated the extent to which people's personal goals take priority over their allegiance to the group, "that is, individualism as opposed to collectivism." The United States ranks first in promoting individualism; followed by Australia (ranked second); Britain (ranked third); and Canada and the Netherlands (tied for fourth place). Similarly, Canada and the United States rank 42nd and 43rd respectively in regard to the degree to which each country can be classified as one that does not like uncertainty—the higher the ranking, the greater the tolerance for uncertainty in that country. Finally, power distance, which is a concept similar to that of social hierarchy, is also very similar in the United States and Canada (ranked respectively 38th and 39th out of 53 countries)—the higher the ranking, the more egalitarian the culture. We discuss these cultural dimensions in more detail in Chapter 2.

Given the similarities between the two cultures, at least in a global context, it seems fair to assume US interpersonal communication research findings have at least some applicability to Canadians. At the same time, it is important to be sensitive to the fact that there are real and significant differences between the two cultures and to keep a critical eye open to the

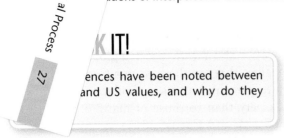

K IT!

ences have been noted between
and US values, and why do they

possibility that these cultural differences might influence our interpretations of US research.

Communication Competence

"What does it take to communicate better?" is probably the most crucial question to ask as you read this book. Answering it has been one of the leading challenges for communication scholars. While all the answers aren't in yet, research has discovered a great deal of important and useful information about communication competence.

Communication Competence Defined and Described

Defining **communication competence** isn't as easy as it might seem. Although scholars continue to argue over a precise definition, most agree that competent communication is both *effective* and *appropriate* (Spitzberg, 2000). To understand these two dimensions, consider how you might handle everyday communication challenges, such as declining an unwanted social invitation or communicating about a friend's annoying behaviour. In cases like these, *effective* communication would get the results you want. *Appropriate* communication would do so in a way that, in most cases, enhances the relationship in which it occurs (Wiemann et al., 1997). You can appreciate the importance of both appropriateness and effectiveness by imagining approaches that would satisfy one of these criteria, but not the other. Effectiveness without appropriateness might satisfy your goals, but leave others unhappy. Conversely, appropriateness without effectiveness might leave others content, but you frustrated.

With the goal of balancing effectiveness and appropriateness, in the following paragraphs we outline several important characteristics of communication competence.

Motivation and Open-Mindedness Are Key

In order to become a more competent communicator, you must have some desire to improve your communication skills with a variety of people. You need to be open to new ways of thinking and behaving. Without an open-minded attitude, a communicator will have trouble interacting competently with people from different backgrounds. To understand open-mindedness, it is helpful to consider three traits that are incompatible with it. **Ethnocentrism** is the belief that one's own culture is superior to others. An ethnocentric person thinks—either privately or openly—that anyone who does not belong to his or her in-group is somehow strange, wrong, or even inferior.

Ethnocentrism leads to an attitude of **prejudice**—an unfairly biased and intolerant attitude toward others who belong to an out-group. (Note that the root term in *prejudice* is "prejudge.") An important element of prejudice is **stereotyping**—exaggerated generalizations about a group. Stereotypical prejudices include the obvious exaggerations that all women are emotional, all men are sex-crazed and insensitive goons, all older people are out of touch with the modern world, and all gay men are flamboyant. Stereotyping can even be a risk when it comes

Obstacles to Open-Mindedness
- **Ethnocentrism:** the belief that one's own culture is superior to others.
- **Prejudice:** an unfairly biased and intolerant attitude toward others who belong to an out-group.
- **Stereotyping:** exaggerated generalizations about a group.

to one's knowledge of the cultural characteristics within one's own milieu, which we explore in Chapter 2. Despite general similarities within a culture, not every individual group member shares the same values and beliefs. It's encouraging to know that open-minded communicators can overcome pre-existing stereotypes and learn to appreciate people from different backgrounds as individuals.

There Is No Single Ideal or Effective Way to Communicate

Your own experience shows that a variety of communication styles can be effective. Some very successful communicators are serious, while others use humour; some are gregarious, while others are quieter; and some are more straightforward, while others hint diplomatically. Just as there are many kinds of beautiful music or art, there are many kinds of competent communication. Furthermore, a type of communication that is competent in one setting might be a colossal blunder in another. The joking insults you routinely trade with one friend might offend a sensitive family member, and last Saturday night's romantic approach would probably be out of place at work on Wednesday morning. This means that there can be no surefire list of rules or tips that will guarantee your success as a communicator.

Flexibility is especially important when members of different cultures meet. Some communication skills seem to be universal (Ruben, 1989)—for example, every culture has rules that require speakers to behave appropriately. But the definition of what kind of communication is appropriate in a given situation varies considerably from one culture to another (Chen and Starosta, 1996; Ulrey, 2001). On an obvious level, customs like belching after a meal or appearing nude in public, which might be appropriate in some parts of the world, would be considered outrageous in others. But there are more subtle differences in competent communication. For example, qualities like self-disclosure and speaking in a straightforward manner—much valued in North America—are likely to be considered overly aggressive and insensitive in many Asian cultures, where subtlety and indirectness are considered important (Kim et al., 1998; Merkin et al., 2014).

Culture has a significant influence on how we experience our personal relationships. In a comparison of perceptions of interpersonal closeness, Turkish students reported feeling closer to others and ideally wanted greater closeness in their interpersonal relationships than did Canadian students (Uskul et al., 2004). Similarly, Li (2002) found that Chinese students felt closer to their family members and friends than did Canadian students.

These and other research studies—for example, a study by Johnson and colleagues (2001) of what people from different cultures perceive as competent communication behaviour in initial interactions—suggest how a knowledge of other people's cultural backgrounds might help you become a more competent intercultural communicator. If, for example, you understand that a potential friend's background is likely to regard displays of respect as especially important, you could adjust your communication accordingly.

Even within a single society, members of various co-cultures may have different notions of appropriate behaviour. One study revealed that ideas of how good friends should communicate varied among people with different cultural backgrounds (Collier, 1996). As groups, people from Hispanic backgrounds valued relational support most highly, while people from African backgrounds prized respect and acceptance. Those with an Asian heritage emphasized a caring, positive exchange of ideas, and people with a European heritage prized friends who recognized their needs as individuals. Findings like these mean that there can be no list of rules or tips that will guarantee your success as a communicator. They also suggest that competent communicators are able to adapt their style to suit the individual and cultural preferences of others (Chen, 1997).

Focus on RESEARCH

CALL-CENTRE CUSTOMER SERVICE: NEITHER INTERPERSONAL NOR IMPERSONAL, JUST BIZARRE

The values and beliefs of a culture are often invisible to members of the group. One way that social scientists have revealed these beliefs is to breach the social rules and observe people's reactions. For instance, a person in a supermarket takes items out of another person's cart and puts them in her own—when confronted she says that she thought that was her cart (which makes no sense). Or, a person playing tic-tac-toe erases his opponent's move, places the mark in another spot, and then makes his move. When we are confronted by such behaviours we are surprised and often indignant, because they violate social rules we all know and take for granted. Deborah Cameron (2008) argues that telephone conversations with customer service representatives of large companies often parallel these bizarre rule violations, because large companies often pre-script and manage what their employees can actually say to customers. As a result, employees cannot respond to our questions and requests with the information they understand we want; instead, they must follow the company script. Cameron calls this "top-down" talk, because managers and executives at the top in companies establish very tight rules about what employees at the bottom can and can't say. She reviewed call-centre conversations between customer service representatives of an insurance company and their clients, and found they violated many of the social

rules for conversation and as a result often frustrated and angered customers, even though the company's employees were always polite. For example, when a customer asked for something, the insurance company representative, rather than saying he or she could not oblige, proposed another option. The customer could figure out that the request was being denied, but might easily perceive the insurance company as being evasive. For many of us, speaking with these employees feels a lot like speaking with a machine—recall the voice at the grocery store self-checkout that keeps repeating the same request no matter what we do: "Place the item in the bagging area," or the virtual agents, part of interactive voice-response systems many companies use to deal with customer calls, that intone "Just say 'billing.'" Speaking with machines often frustrates and annoys us, because a human voice should be attached to a human brain that operates according to unspoken but well-known cultural rules of conversation.

Critical thinking: *Can you think of times when your cultural rules about communication have been made clearer because someone has broken one of them? On the flip side, have you ever been in a situation where you became aware of a communication norm because you inadvertently violated it? Why do you think these norms are often "invisible"?*

Competence Is Situational

Because competent behaviour varies so much from one situation and person to another, it's a mistake to think that communication competence is a trait that a person either possesses or lacks (Spitzberg, 1991). It's more accurate to talk about *degrees* or *areas* of competence.

You and the people you know are probably quite competent in some areas and less so in others. For example, you might deal quite skilfully with peers, but at the same time feel clumsy interacting with people much older or younger, wealthier or poorer, or more or less "attractive" than you. In fact, your

competence may vary from situation to situation. This means it's an overgeneralization to say, in a moment of distress, "I'm a terrible communicator!" It's more accurate to say, "I didn't handle this situation very well, but I'm better in others."

Competence Requires Mindfulness

Knowledge of how to communicate with people from different backgrounds is often "culture-specific," to use Samovar and his colleagues' terminology (2012). The rules and customs that work with one group might be quite different from those that succeed with another. The ability to "shift gears" and adapt one's style to the norms of another culture or co-culture is an essential ingredient of communication competence (Kim et al., 1996).

How can a communicator acquire the culture-specific information that leads to competence? One important element is what Stella Ting-Toomey (1999) and others call *mindfulness*—awareness of one's own behaviour and that of others. Communicators who lack this quality blunder mindlessly through intercultural encounters, oblivious of how their own behaviour may confuse or offend others, and how behaviour that they consider bizarre may simply be different from their norm.

Charles Berger (1979) suggests three strategies for moving toward a more mindful, competent style of intercultural communication. *Passive observation* involves noticing what members of a different culture do and using these insights to communicate in ways that are most effective. *Active strategies* include reading, watching films, asking experts and members of the other culture how to behave, and taking academic courses related to intercultural communication and diversity (Carrell, 1997). The third strategy, *self-disclosure*, involves volunteering personal information to people from the other culture with whom you want to communicate. One type of self-disclosure is to confess your cultural ignorance: "This is very new to me. What's the right thing to do in this situation?" This approach is the riskiest of the three we describe here, since some cultures may not value candour and self-disclosure as much as others. Nevertheless, most people are pleased when strangers attempt to learn the practices of their culture, and they are usually more than willing to offer information and assistance.

Competence Can Be Learned

To some degree, biology is destiny when it comes to communication style (Beatty and McCroskey, 1997). Studies of identical and fraternal twins suggest that some traits, including sociability, a short temper, and the ability to relax seem to be partially a function of our genetic makeup. In addition, a recent study by Beatty and colleagues (2001) found that social composure and wit are highly heritable. (The same study showed that articulation ability and appropriate disclosure are not.)

Fortunately, biology isn't the only factor that shapes how we communicate. Communication competence is, to a great degree, a set of skills that anyone can learn (Fortney et al., 2001). For instance, people with high communication apprehension often benefit from communication-skills training (Ayres and Hopf, 1993). Sometimes, even a modest amount of training can produce dramatic results. For example, after only 30 minutes of instruction, one group of observers became significantly more effective in detecting deception in interviews (deTurck and Miller, 1990). Even without systematic training, it is possible to develop communication skills through the processes of observation and trial and error. We learn from our own successes and failures, as well as from observing other models—both positive and negative. One study revealed that education does lead to improved communication skills: for college students, communication competence increases over the course of their undergraduate studies (Rubin et al., 1990).

Characteristics of Competent Communication

Despite the fact that competent communication varies from one situation to another, scholars have identified several common denominators that characterize effective communication in most contexts.

A Large Repertoire of Skills

As we have already seen, good communicators do not use the same approach in every situation. They know that it's best sometimes to be blunt and, at other times, to be tactful—that there is a time to speak up and a time to be quiet. They understand that some situations require seriousness and others call for playfulness.

The chances of behaving competently increase with the number of options you have about *how* to communicate. For example, if you want to start a conversation with a stranger, your chances of success increase as you have more options available (Kelly and Watson, 1986). All it might take to get the conversational ball rolling is a self-introduction. In other cases, seeking assistance might work well: "I've just moved here. What kind of neighbourhood is the east end?" A third strategy is to ask a question about some situational feature: "I've never heard this band before. Do you know anything about them?" You could also offer a sincere compliment and follow it up with a question: "Great shoes! Where did you get them?" Just as a golfer has a wide range of clubs to use for various situations, a competent communicator has a large array of behaviours from which to choose.

Adaptability

Having a large repertoire of possible behaviours is one ingredient of competent communication, but you have to be able to choose the *right* one for a particular situation (Brashers and Jackson, 1999; Hample and Dallinger, 2000; Stamp, 1999). To repeat, an approach that works well

Competent communication requires choosing the right form of communication for the situation. What are some ways these two people can competently communicate to one another given the situation?

in one situation might be disastrous somewhere else. Effective communication means choosing the right response for the situation.

Ability to Perform Skilfully

Once you have chosen the best way to communicate, you have to do it effectively. In communication, as in other activities, practice is the key to skilful performance. Much of the information in this book will introduce you to new tools for communicating, and the "Skill Builder" activities at the end of each chapter will help you practise them.

Involvement, Empathy, and Perspective Taking

Not surprisingly, effective communication takes place when the people care about one another and the topic at hand (Cegala et al., 1982). Rod Hart suggests that this involvement has several dimensions (adapted here from Knapp and Vangelisti, 2009). It includes commitment to the other person and the relationship, concern about the message being discussed, and a desire to make the relationship clearly useful. Even in relationships that are less central to our lives, people have the best chance of developing an effective message when they understand the other person's perspective (Ifert and Roloff, 1997). And since that person may not be good at expressing his or her thoughts and feelings clearly, empathy—the ability to imagine how an issue might look from someone else's perspective—suggests why listening is such an important communication skill. Not only does empathy help you understand others, it also provides information for developing strategies about how best to influence people. Empathy is such an important element of communicative competence that researcher Mark Redmond (1989, p. 594) flatly states, "By definition, a person cannot produce a message that is empathic that is not also communicatively competent."

Cognitive Complexity

The ability to construct a variety of different frameworks for viewing an issue is termed

cognitive complexity. Imagine that a long-time friend seems to be angry with you. One possible explanation is that she is offended by something you've done. Another possibility is that something has happened in another part of her life that is upsetting. Or perhaps nothing at all is wrong and you're just being overly sensitive. Researchers have found that a large number of constructs for interpreting the behaviour of others leads to greater "conversational sensitivity," thereby increasing the chances of acting in ways that will produce satisfying results (Burleson and Caplan, 1998; Kline and Chatani, 2001).

Self-Monitoring

Psychologists use the term **self-monitoring** to describe the process of paying close attention to one's own behaviour and using these observations to shape the way one behaves.

Self-monitors are able to move a part of their consciousness outside of themselves to observe their behaviour from a detached viewpoint. In doing so, they're able to think such thoughts as these:

"I'm making a fool of myself."

"I'd better speak up now."

"This approach is working well. I'll keep it up."

It's no surprise that self-monitoring generally increases one's effectiveness as a communicator (Kolb, 1998; Sypher and Sypher,

CHECK IT!

What are the characteristics of a competent communicator?

Building WORK SKILLS

TAKING THE OTHER PERSON'S PERSPECTIVE WHEN SENDING MESSAGES

Have you ever received a telephone or email message that left you wondering what the sender wanted you to do or why they wanted you to know what they had to say? A message may have been missing the most important information (e.g., the person's name or phone number). Or a message may have had so much detailed, irrelevant information that you couldn't wade through it all. These kinds of messages are particularly frustrating at work. We have probably all received them and sent them. Often, we leave these messages before we have really thought through our requests of others—before we have taken their perspective.

For this skill-building exercise, you need a partner from the class. First, think about a need to communicate with someone at your workplace or at school: a request to make or information to share. If you can't think of a real example, you and your partner can use one of the examples below:

• A colleague has asked you to switch shifts because she has an appointment. You are willing

to do so, but must get the permission of your supervisor. Leave a message for your supervisor.
• You have come down with some sort of illness and will have to miss class. You have a test and an assignment due. Leave a message for your teacher.

Jot down your message. Now, read your message from the point of view of the person you are leaving it for. Is it complete? Is it well-organized? Will the recipient understand the context? Are there irrelevant details that could be omitted? Have you told him or her what you want or why he or she needs to know? Once you are satisfied with your message, you can do one of the following: leave it on the voice mail of your partner from class; email it to your partner; or just read it, uninterrupted, to your partner.

Ask your partner to imagine he or she is the person you intended to send the message to. Ask your counterpart to give you some feedback about the quality of your message, particularly your ability to take the recipient's perspective.

1983). The ability to ask yourself the question, "How am I doing?" and to change your behaviour if the answer isn't positive, is a tremendous asset for communicators. People with poor self-monitoring skills often blunder through life, sometimes succeeding and sometimes failing, without the detachment to understand why.

How does your behaviour as an interpersonal communicator measure up against the standards of competence described in this chapter? Like most people, you will probably find some areas of your life that are very satisfying and others that you would like to change. As you read on in this book, realize that the information we provide in each chapter offers advice that can help your communication become more productive and rewarding.

Although the qualities described here do play an important role in communicative competence, they can be ineffective when carried to excess (Spitzberg, 1994). For example, too much self-monitoring can make a person so self-conscious that the concern for appearance ("How do I sound?" "How am I doing?") overshadows the need to be faithful to one's true beliefs. Likewise, an excess of empathy and cognitive complexity can lead you to see all sides of an issue so well that you become incapable of acting. In other words, both a deficiency and an excess can lead to incompetent communication.

SUMMARY

Communication is important for a variety of reasons. Besides satisfying practical needs, meaningful communication contributes to physical health, plays a major role in defining our identity, and forms the basis for our social relationships.

Communication is a complex process that can be represented in a communication model. The model we present in this chapter depicts how communicators usually send and receive messages simultaneously. The meaning of these messages resides in the people who exchange them, not in the messages themselves. Environment and noise affect communication, as do the channels we choose for sending our messages.

A variety of principles help explain how communication operates. Communication is transactional—that is, it's a dynamic process that people create through interaction. Messages can be intentional or unintentional, and they almost always have both a content and a relational dimension. Once expressed, messages cannot be withdrawn. Also, communication is unrepeatable.

Interpersonal communication can be defined quantitatively (by the number of people involved) or qualitatively (by the nature of interaction between them). In a qualitative sense, interpersonal relationships are unique, irreplaceable, interdependent, intrinsically rewarding, and usually characterized by self-disclosure. Qualitatively interpersonal communication is relatively infrequent, even in many close relationships. While some research suggests that computer-mediated communication (CMC) is more impersonal than face-to-face communication, other research shows that it can enhance interpersonal relationships.

Increasing multiculturalism in Canada and closer, globalized economic connections between Canada and other nations compel us to look at interpersonal communication in the context of cultural diversity. Intercultural communication is the process by which people belonging to two or more cultures share messages in a manner that is influenced by their different cultural perceptions and symbol systems.

When we review interpersonal communication research, it is important to keep in mind that the majority of studies have been conducted in the United States and, although Canadians and their US counterparts are very similar in many respects, they do differ in terms of some significant social values. These include attitudes toward violence, ethnic and cultural diversity, and the relative status of men and women.

To understand the communication process, it is important that we recognize and avoid several common misconceptions. Despite the value of self-expression, more communication is not always better than less. In fact, there are times when more communication can make problems worse. Even at its best, communication is not a panacea that will solve every problem. Effective communication is not a natural ability. While some people have greater aptitude at communicating, everyone can learn to interact with others more effectively.

Communication competence is the ability to be both effective and appropriate—that is, to get desired results from others in a manner that maintains the relationship on terms that are acceptable to everyone. There is no single ideal way to communicate. Flexibility and adaptability are characteristics of competent communicators, as is the skillset that includes being able to be involved, have empathy, and have perspective. Also important to being a competent communicator are the abilities to utilize cognitive-complexity skills and self-monitor. The good news is that communication competence can be learned.

MULTIPLE-CHOICE QUESTIONS

1. Social isolation is a major contributor to heart disease. This finding provides support for the idea that communication fills which type of human need?
   a. physical
   b. identity
   c. social
   d. practical
2. An example of physiological noise is
   a. worrying about an upcoming test.
   b. a loud siren.
   c. hearing loss.
   d. a crowded, smelly room.
3. Your friend says she is sorry after she has spilled coffee on your new top. You think she is insincere, but another friend thinks her apology is genuine. This difference of opinion best illustrates which insight from the communication model presented in this chapter?
   a. Sending and receiving are usually simultaneous.

   b. Meanings exist in and among people.
   c. Noise affects communication.
   d. Channels make a difference.
4. The idea that communication is transactional refers to
   a. the dynamic process created by communicators interacting with each other.
   b. the mutual influence that happens when people interact.
   c. the unique creation that arises out of the interaction between people.
   d. all of the above.
5. The part of every message that expresses how the person feels about their communication partner is called the
   a. intentional dimension.
   b. transactional dimension.
   c. relational dimension.
   d. content dimension.
6. Which of the following statements is true about communication?

a. All communication seeks understanding.
b. Communication is a natural ability that cannot be developed.
c. Communication will solve all problems.
d. Communication is unrepeatable.

7. Disclosure, uniqueness, irreplaceability, interdependence, and intrinsic rewards are all features that distinguish
   a. impersonal communication from interpersonal communication.
   b. dyadic communication from small group communication.
   c. intentional communication from unintentional communication.
   d. all of the above.

8. The consensus among researchers is that computer-mediated communication is inferior to face-to-face communication and negatively affects interpersonal relationships.
   a. true
   b. false

9. Intercultural communication doesn't always occur when people from two different cultures interact.
   a. true
   b. false

10. By definition a person cannot produce a message that is empathic that is not also communicatively competent.
    a. true
    b. false

Answers: 1. a; 2. c; 3. b; 4. d; 5. c; 6. d; 7. a; 8. b; 9. a; 10. a

ACTIVITIES

1. Invitation to Insight

How much time do you spend communicating? Conduct an informal study to answer this question by keeping a two-day log of your activities. Using your findings, answer the following questions:
a. What percentage of your waking time is spent speaking with and listening to others?
b. Using the explanation on pages 15–17 of this chapter, describe what percentage of your entire communication is qualitatively interpersonal.
c. How satisfied are you with your findings? How would you like to change your everyday communication?

2. Critical Thinking Probe

As you have read in this chapter, communication is transactional—it is something we do *with* others and not *to* them. How does face-to-face communication differ from computer-mediated communication, such as email? Are they equally transactional?

3. Invitation to Insight

How competent are you as a communicator? You can begin to answer this question by interviewing people who know you well, such as family members, friends, or co-workers. Conduct interviews with different people to determine if you are more competent in some relationships than in others.
a. Describe the characteristics of competent communicators outlined on pages 31–34 of this chapter. Be sure your interviewee understands each of them.
b. Ask your interviewee to rate you on each of the observable qualities. (It won't be possible for others to evaluate internal characteristics, such as cognitive complexity and self-monitoring.) Be sure this evaluation considers your communication in a variety of situations, because it's likely you aren't uniformly competent—or incompetent—in all of them.
c. If your rating is not high in one or more areas, discuss with your partner how you could raise it.

d. Consider whether another person might rate you differently. Why might this happen?

4. Skill Builder

Knowing how you want to communicate isn't the same as being able to do it competently. The technique of behaviour rehearsal provides a way to improve a particular communication skill before you use it in real life. Behaviour rehearsal consists of four steps:

a. Define your goal. Begin by deciding how you want to behave.

b. Break the goal into the kinds of behaviour it involves. Most goals are made up of several verbal and non-verbal parts. You may be able to define these parts by thinking about them yourself, by observing others, by reading about them, or by asking others for advice.

c. Practise each behaviour before using it in real life. You can practise a new behaviour by rehearsing it alone and then with others before you put it into action. Another approach is to picture yourself behaving in new ways. This mental image can increase your effectiveness.

d. Try out the behaviour in real life. You can improve your chances of success in two ways. First, work on only one subskill at a time, and start with easy situations. Don't expect yourself suddenly to behave flawlessly in the most challenging situations. Second, begin by practising your new skills in situations where you have a chance of success.

DISCUSSION QUESTIONS

1. Why do humans communicate? Which reasons are most relevant to you?

2. Why study interpersonal communication? How might you benefit?

3. Think of someone who you believe is an effective interpersonal communicator. Give examples of the characteristics of competent communication that this person demonstrates.

4. Give an example of each of the four communication misconceptions described in Chapter 1. How have these misconceptions affected you?

5. Is it important to consider interpersonal communication in the context of cultural diversity? Why or why not?

JOURNAL IDEAS

At the end of each chapter you will find a couple of ideas to help you keep a reflective journal. There is considerable evidence (Armarego, 2007; Bolton, 2005; Brown, 2009; Sinclair and Woodward, 1997) that journal writing helps students integrate theory into practice. In order to become better at performing particular skills (communication skills, perhaps) people need to reflect on, analyze, and critically evaluate their current practice. We hope these questions stimulate the beginnings of such self-reflection.

1. Review the misconceptions people have about communication and describe an example of each that you have experienced or directly observed.

2. How does technology affect your interpersonal communication in positive and negative ways?

2

Communication and the Self

Chapter Outline

© Todor Tsvetkov/iStockphoto

Key Terms

benevolent lie
breadth
cognitive conservatism
collectivistic culture
depth
distorted feedback
equivocal language
face
facework
identity management
individualistic culture
Johari Window
lie
myth of perfection
negative mood

obsolete information
perceived self
presenting self
reference groups
reflected appraisal
self-concept
self-control
self-disclosure
self-esteem
self-fulfilling prophecy
significant other
social comparison
social expectations
social penetration model

Learning Objectives

YOU SHOULD UNDERSTAND:

- the characteristics and development of the self-concept;
- the influence of language, cultural values, and self-fulfilling prophecies in shaping the self-concept;
- how it is possible to change one's self-concept;
- the nature and extent of identity management;
- the characteristics of and reasons for self-disclosure; and
- the risks of, benefits of, and alternatives to self-disclosure.

YOU SHOULD BE ABLE TO IDENTIFY:

- the influence of other people, language, culture, and self-fulfilling prophecies on the development of your self-concept;
- different cultural values that could result in different communication patterns;
- your influence on the self-concept of others;
- the elements of yourself that you may inaccurately perceive as desirable or undesirable;
- the differences between your perceived self and various presenting selves, and the identity management strategies you use;
- use the social penetration and Johari Window models to examine self-disclosure in one of your relationships;
- identify the potential risks and benefits of disclosing in a selected situation; and
- for a given situation, compose responses that reflect varying degrees of candour and equivocation.

Who are you? Before reading on, take a few minutes to try a simple experiment. First, make a list of the 10 words or phrases that describe the most important features of who you are. Some of the items on your list may involve social roles: student, employee, son/daughter, parent, and so on. Or you could define yourself by physical characteristics: fat, skinny, tall, short, beautiful, or ugly. You may focus on your intellectual characteristics: smart, stupid, curious, or inquisitive. Perhaps you can best define yourself in terms of moods, feelings, or attitudes: optimistic, critical, or energetic. Or you could consider your social characteristics: outgoing, shy, or defensive. You may see yourself in terms of belief systems: pacifist, Buddhist, vegetarian, Christian, or liberal. Finally, you could focus on particular skills (or lack of them): swimmer, artist, carpenter, or klutz. In any case, choose 10 words or phrases that best describe you, and write them down.

Next, choose the 1 item from your list that is the most fundamental to who you are, and copy it onto another sheet of paper. Then pick the second-most fundamental item and record it as number two on your new list. Continue ranking the 10 items until you have reorganized them all.

Now comes the most interesting part of the experience. Create a mental image of yourself. Try to paint a picture that captures not only your physical characteristics, but also the attitudes, aptitudes, feelings, and beliefs included on your list. Take plenty of time to create this image.

Now, imagine how you would be a different person if the lowest-ranked item on your list were not part of your personality or physical makeup. How would its absence affect the way you act? The way you feel? The way others behave toward you? Was it easy to give up that item? Do you like yourself more or less without it? Take a few minutes with your eyes closed to answer these questions.

Without taking back the item you've just given up, continue your fantasy by removing item number nine. What difference does its absence make for you?

Continue the process by jettisoning one item at a time until you have given them all up. Notice what happens at each step of the process. After you have gone through your entire list, reclaim the items one by one until you are back to where you started.

How do you feel after trying this exercise? Most people find the experience a powerful one. They say that it clarifies how each of the items selected is fundamental to their identity. Many people say that they gain a clear picture of the parts of themselves they value and the parts they are unhappy with.

Communication and the Self-Concept

The way you regard yourself in the exercise you just completed offers clues about your **self-concept**, that is, the relatively stable set of perceptions you hold of yourself. One way to understand the self-concept is to imagine a special mirror that not only reflects physical features, but also allows you to view other aspects of yourself—emotional states, talents, likes, dislikes, values, roles, and so on. The reflection in that mirror would be your self-concept.

Any description of your self-concept that you constructed in this exercise is only a partial one. To make it complete, you would have to keep adding items until your list ran into hundreds of words. Of course, not every dimension of your self-concept list is equally important. For example, the most significant part of one person's self-concept might consist of social roles, whereas for another, it might be physical appearance, health, friendships, accomplishments, or skills.

Self-esteem is the part of the self-concept that involves evaluations of self-worth. A communicator's self-concept might include being quiet, argumentative, or serious. His or her self-esteem would be determined by how he or she felt about these qualities. Our competence in doing things we value, such as maintaining satisfying relationships, influences how good we feel about ourselves, and, in turn, our feelings of self-esteem influence how we approach the things we do. As Figure 2.1 shows, people who feel good about themselves have positive expectations about how they will communicate (Baldwin and Keelan, 1999). Self-esteem depends on our assessment of how well we do things that matter to us. As we will discuss in the next few pages, other people have a great deal of influence over the things we value and our assessment of our worth.

Self-control is sometimes called self-regulation, and it involves your ability to change your thoughts, emotions, moods, impulses, or performance of some task in order to achieve a personal goal or meet a social or cultural expectation (Baumeister and Alquist, 2009). Self-control has been associated with many positive outcomes, including secure and satisfying relationships. The most impressive evidence regarding the value of self-control comes to us from a study done by Yuichi Shoda, Walter Mischel, and Philip Peake (1990), often referred to as the "marshmallow experiment." Four-year-old children were asked to choose between getting one marshmallow immediately or getting three marshmallows if they were able to wait (delayed gratification), while in the presence of that one marshmallow (temptation). The children who displayed more self-control, able to wait for the larger reward, were, as a group, more successful both socially and academically as adults than the children who were unable to delay gratification. Additional studies have demonstrated that higher levels of self-control are associated with a variety of positive outcomes including interpersonal success (Baumeister et al., 2006; Findley, Carvallo and Bartak, 2014; Finkel and Campbell, 2001; Tangney et al., 2004; Vohs et al., 2005). People with greater self-control are able to respond to problems in interpersonal relationships by talking constructively about the problem rather than by reacting negatively or avoiding the other person (Finkel and Campbell, 2001). Now you may think, "Well, I would have eaten that marshmallow. I couldn't wait." Fortunately, self-control can be developed—you can build self-control, strength, and stamina. Practising self-control in one area (e.g., engaging in an academic study program) can help you develop self-control in other areas (e.g., smoking and drinking less) (Oaten and Cheng, 2006; also see Baumeister et al., 2006 for a review of evidence).

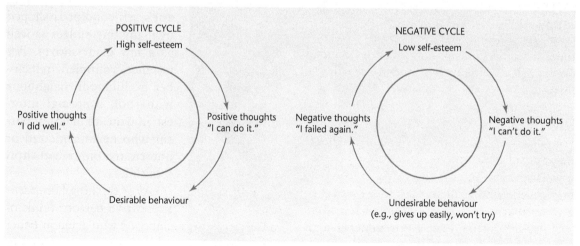

Figure 2.1 ● **The Relationship between Self-Esteem and Communication Behaviour**

SOURCE: Adapted from H.M. Johnson (1998), *How do I love me?* 3rd edn (pp. 3, 5). Salem, WI: Sheffield Publishing Co.

- **Self-concept:** the relatively stable set of perceptions you hold of yourself.
- **Self-esteem:** the part of the self-concept that involves evaluations of self-worth.
- **Self-control:** the ability to change (one's thoughts, behaviours, emotions, etc.) in order to conform to an expectation.

How the Self-Concept Develops

Researchers generally agree that the self-concept does not exist at birth (Rosenblith, 1992). An infant lying in a crib has no notion of self, no notion—even if verbal language were miraculously made available—of how to answer the question "Who am I?" At about six or seven months, the child begins to recognize "self" as distinct from surroundings. If you have ever watched children at this age, you have probably marvelled at how they can stare with great fascination at a foot, a hand, and other parts of their bodies that float into view, almost as if they were strange objects belonging to someone else. Then the connection is made, almost as if the child were realizing, "The hand is me," "The foot is me." These first revelations form the child's earliest concept of self. At this early stage, the self-concept is almost exclusively physical, involving the child's basic realization of existing and of possessing certain body parts over which he or she exerts some control.

As the child develops, this rudimentary sense of identity expands into a much more complete and sophisticated picture that resembles the self-concept of adults. This evolution is almost totally a product of social interaction (Goodvin et al., 2008; Schmidt, 2006). Two complementary theories describe how interaction shapes the way individuals view themselves: **reflected appraisal** and **social comparison** (Harter, 2006; Sedikides and Skowronski, 1995).

Reflected Appraisal

Before reading on, try the following exercise. Either by yourself or aloud with a partner, think of someone you know or once knew who helped enhance your self-concept by acting in a way that made you feel accepted, worthwhile, important, appreciated, or loved. This person needn't have played a crucial role in your life, as long as the role was positive. Often, one's self-concept is shaped by many tiny nudges as well as a few giant shoves. For instance, you might remember a childhood neighbour who took a special interest in you, or a grandparent who never criticized or questioned your youthful foolishness.

After thinking about this supportive person, think of someone who acted in either a big or small way to diminish your self-esteem. For instance, you may have had a coach who criticized you

© Zoe Waelchli.

Self-concept starts developing when we're only a few months old, but continues into adulthood, largely due to social interaction. What interactions have you had in the past year that changed the way you saw yourself?

in front of the team, or a teacher who said or implied that you wouldn't amount to much.

After thinking about these two types of people, you should begin to see that everyone's self-concept is shaped by reflected appraisal—that is, perceptions of the judgments of those around her or him. To the extent that you have received supportive messages, you have learned to appreciate and value yourself. To the extent that you perceive critical signals, you are likely to feel less valuable, lovable, capable, and secure (Felson, 1985; Lemay and Dudley, 2009). Your self-concept can be seen, at least in part, as a product of the messages you've received throughout your life.

Social scientists use the term **significant other** to describe a person whose evaluations are especially influential. Messages from parents, of course, are an early and important influence on the self-concept. Parents with poor, negative, or deviant self-concepts are at greater risk of parenting their children in ways that have negative consequences for children's well-being and self-concept development (Stith et al., 2009). By contrast, supportive parents are more likely to raise children with healthy self-concepts. Along with family, the messages from many other significant others shape our self-concept. A teacher from long ago, a special friend or relative, or even a barely known acquaintance whom you respected can all leave an imprint on how you view yourself (Snapp and Leary, 2001).

Carol Dweck (2006, 2010) advises that when an adult says things to children, such as, "I think you worked hard to solve the problem," they understand that their abilities to work hard and persist produce good results. As a result they are more likely to show tenacity and perseverance when faced with the next challenge, and with this "growth" mindset they understand that they can develop their abilities. On the other hand, if adults say, "You're smart" when children solve problems, children are more likely to develop a "fixed" mindset. They may come to believe that people are born with their abilities (e.g., intelligence)

and no amount of practice, perseverance, or effort is going to change the outcome. People with fixed mindsets are more likely to quit after they have failed and much less likely to take chances and tackle difficult projects, because they believe that they do not possess the ability to be successful—they live up to their fixed expectations and limit their opportunities for learning and growth.

As we grow older, the power of messages from significant others remains (Voss et al., 1999). Some social scientists have coined the term "Michelangelo phenomenon" to describe the way significant others sculpt each other's self-concept (Drigotas, 2002; Drigotas et al., 1999). Romantic partners, co-workers, friends, and many others can speak and act in ways that have a profound effect on the way we view ourselves.

You might argue that not every part of your self-concept is shaped by others, that there are certain objective facts recognizable by self-observation alone. After all, nobody needs to tell you whether you are taller than others, speak with an accent, and have curly hair, and so on. These facts are obvious. Indeed, some features of the self are immediately apparent. But the *significance* we attach to them—that is, the rank we assign them in the hierarchy of our list and the interpretation we give them—depends greatly on the opinions of others. After all, many of your features are readily observable, yet you don't find them important at all because nobody has regarded them as important.

Social Comparison

So far, we have looked at the way messages from other people shape the self-concept. In addition to using these messages, each of us forms our self-image by the process of **social comparison**: evaluating ourselves in terms of how we compare with others (Festinger, 1954; Garcia and Tor, 2007)

We decide whether we are superior or inferior and similar or different by comparing ourselves to what social scientists call reference groups—those people we use to evaluate our own characteristics. You might feel ordinary or inferior in talent, friendships, or attractiveness if you compare yourself with an unsuitable reference group. In a meta-analysis of 115 studies conducted between 1970 and 2005, Brittany Gentile and her colleagues (2009) found that men scored significantly higher than women in their satisfaction with their physical appearance, but only in the studies conducted after 1980. These researchers argue that women's lower self-esteem about their appearance may be due to the increased media focus on appearance, beginning in the 1980s, which has provided a totally unrealistic beauty ideal to use for comparison.

Comparing yourself to attractive Hollywood stars, agile professional athletes, Mensa geniuses, or successful billionaires are perfect examples of relating to unsuitable reference groups. Whether you are as attractive, agile, talented, intelligent, or wealthy doesn't mean you're worth less than such people. Even comparing yourself to a more suitable reference group, such as the social networking profiles of your friends and acquaintances, can create unrealistic expectations (Chou and Edge, 2012; Qiu et al., 2012). Simply because, people on social networking sites tend to focus on the positive aspects of their lives, and without complete information about them it is easy to relate yourself to them negatively. Once you place yourself alongside a truly representative sample, you have a better chance of developing a more accurate understanding of yourself. Nonetheless, many people judge themselves against unreasonable standards and suffer accordingly (Grodin and Lindolf, 1995). You will read more about how to avoid placing perfectionistic demands on yourself in Chapter 4.

CHECK IT!

Describe the processes of reflected appraisal and social comparison in the development of self-concept.

Self-Concept Development in Context

Whose opinions about us matter the most? Which reference groups are available to us for comparison? When we think about how the self-concept develops, we need to consider forces that are larger than our family, friends, and immediate community members. Our identities are shaped by our age and place in history, our sex, our sexual orientation, our physical ability or disability, and our cultural background. These elements create the larger social context in which our self-concepts develop.

Language and Identity

Some aspects of culture, such as language, have obvious implications for shaping the way we think and feel about ourselves. If you live in a culture where everyone speaks the same language, then language will have little noticeable impact on how you view yourself and others. But when some members of a society speak the dominant language and others speak a minority tongue or dialect, or when that second language is not prestigious, the sense of being a member of an out-group is strong. At this point, the speaker of a non-dominant language can either feel obliged to assimilate by speaking the "better" language, or refuse to accommodate him or herself to the majority language and maintain loyalty to the ethnic tongue (Giles, Mulac et al., 1992). In either case, the impact of language on the self-concept is powerful. On one hand, the feeling is most likely, "I'm not as good as speakers of the native language"; and on the other hand, the belief is most likely, "There's something unique and worth preserving in my language."

The issue of language and identity is evident in Canada's diverse multicultural society. It is strongly felt by two groups in particular: First Nations peoples and francophone Canadians. The residential school system for Natives, which was developed in the late nineteenth century and existed until the 1990s, has been implicated in the loss of First Nations languages and culture. These schools separated First Nations children from their families and communities, taught them English or French, and attempted to impart Christian values. First Nations children lost their languages and their traditions. Many Native leaders assert that the loss of indigenous languages has caused Aboriginal peoples to lose their spirit as well.

> The loss of hundreds of languages that have already passed into history is an intellectual catastrophe in every way comparable in magnitude to the ecological catastrophe we face today as the earth's tropical forests are swept by fire. Each language still spoken is fundamental to the personal, social, and—a key term in the discourse of indigenous peoples—spiritual identity of its speakers. They know that without these languages they would be less than they are, and they are engaged in the most urgent struggles to protect their linguistic heritage. (Prodanovic, 2013; Zepeda and Hill, 1991)

Although the federal government has apologized for the atrocities committed by the residential school system, the pain and loss of relationships, culture, and identity remain a notorious legacy. Only about one-sixth of Canada's North American Indian, Métis, or Inuit peoples know an Aboriginal language well enough to carry on a conversation (Statistics Canada, 2011a,). There are several programs aimed at helping Canadian First Nations peoples to preserve their languages (First People's Cultural Foundation) and their Aboriginal identities (CBC News, 2010).

The preservation of the French language in Canada, particularly in Quebec, has created considerable controversy over the years. Perhaps the most hotly debated measure was Bill 101. Under this legislation, which was passed in 1977 by the Quebec National Assembly, the only language permitted on commercial signs was French, and the right to attend an English-language elementary school was severely restricted. Many Quebeckers believed that, in order for francophone culture to survive, the French language needed to be protected in an increasingly English-speaking world. Since 1977, several amendments to the legislation have helped to ease some of the tensions between French and English-speaking Quebeckers. The fight to preserve the French language and culture in Canada continues, and although the majority of English-speaking Canadians appear to believe that French and French culture in Quebec are safe, French-speaking Canadians are less convinced (Jedwab, 2003).

Even within a language system, the labels that members of a co-culture use to define themselves can both reflect and help define their sense of identity. In one study, Sharon Boatswain and Richard Lalonde (2000) surveyed 101 Canadian black university students ranging in age from 18 to 50 years old in order to find out which labels they preferred, as well as what was the personal meanings they assigned

How is a child practising her letters learning not only how to write words, but learning a culture and identity as well?

© iStockPhoto/acilo.

to their preferred labels. Their work was based on a similar US study (Smith, 1992) that found "black" and "African-American" to be the preferred labels. While "black" was the most popular first choice in the Canadian study (35 per cent of respondents), it was not as strongly preferred as in the United States. The Canadian investigation found far more diversity in preferred labels than did the US study. Choosing from 35 different labels, respondents ranked their first, second, and third choices, and 20 different labels were listed as a first preference. The researchers hypothesized that this may be due to Canada's policy of multiculturalism, which encourages Canadians to retain various aspects of their heritage culture. For example, 30 per cent of the respondents in the Canadian study selected as their first choice a label that referred to a Caribbean country or the West Indies. The personal meanings respondents gave usually referred to ethnic identity or place of birth. Finally, US studies have found "African American" to be a clear choice along with "black," but in the Canadian study, there was little preference for the equivalent—"African Canadian"—perhaps because this term refers to a more distant cultural heritage (Boatswain and Lalonde, 2000).

Cultural Values and Norms

In addition to language, there are several cultural values that shape our identities and our perceptions of others. Sometimes, they influence our thoughts, feelings, and perceptions of ourselves and others in ways we may not even be aware of. We will examine several of these cultural differences in Chapter 3 when we look at how culture shapes our views of other people. In addition, we will look at cultural differences in the use of language, silence, and context in Chapter 6. While all these cultural values influence our perceptions of ourselves and others, the most powerful dimension of culture on our identities is the emphasis different cultures place on the importance of the individual versus the importance of the group.

Members of an **individualistic culture** view their primary responsibility as helping themselves, whereas communicators in a **collectivistic culture** feel loyalties and obligations to an in-group: one's extended family or community, or even the organization one works for (Triandis, 1995). Individualistic cultures are also characterized by self-reliance and competition, whereas members of a collectivistic culture are more attentive to and concerned with the opinions of significant others. The individualism–collectivism dimension has been relied on most heavily to examine and explain differences in communication patterns across cultures (Merkin, Taras and Steel, 2014).

Among the world's most individualistic countries are the United States, Canada, Australia, and Britain. Latin American and Asian cultures are generally more collectivistic (Hofstede, 1980, 2001). Table 2.1 summarizes some differences between individualistic and collectivistic cultures.

The differences between individualistic and collectivistic cultures show up in communication patterns. For instance, people from more individualistic cultures tend to be more expressive, straightforward, and direct in their communication; while people from more collectivist cultures are more likely to be more indirect and restrained in their communication and use persuasion, ambiguity, and third-party communication in order to preserve relationship harmony (Merkin et al. 2014). It's important to realize that differences in the use of direct communication do not mean that shyness is a "problem" in some cultures. In fact, just the opposite is true: in these societies, reticence is valued. When the goal is to avoid being "the nail that sticks out," it's logical to feel nervous when you make yourself appear different by calling attention your way. A self-concept that includes "assertive" might make a Westerner feel proud, but in much of Asia, it would more likely be cause for shame. People from collectivist cultures are less likely to promote themselves or report positive self-perceptions when compared to individuals from more

Table 2.1 ● The Self in Individualistic and Collectivistic Cultures

Individualistic Cultures	Collectivistic Cultures
Self is a separate, unique individual; should be independent, self-sufficient.	People belong to extended families or in-groups; "we" or group orientation.
Individual should take care of himself or herself and immediate family.	Person should take care of extended family before self.
Many flexible group memberships; friends based on shared interests and activities.	Emphasis on belonging to a very few permanent in-groups, which have a strong influence over the person.
Reward for individual achievement and initiative; individual decision encouraged; individual credit and blame assigned.	Reward for contribution to group goals and well-being; co-operation with in-group members; group decisions valued; credit and blame shared.
High value on autonomy, change, youth, individual security, and equality.	High value on duty, order, tradition, age, group security, status, and hierarchy.

SOURCES: Adapted by Sandra Sudweeks from H.C. Triandis (1990), "Cross-cultural studies of individualism and collectivism," in J. Berman (ed.), *Nebraska symposium on motivation* (pp. 41–133). Lincoln, NB: University of Nebraska Press; and E.T. Hall (1959), *Beyond culture*. New York: Doubleday.

individualistic cultures (Merkin et al. 2014). Collectivist cultures place a great deal of value on modesty and unlike individualists' desire to stand out or "shine brighter" collectivists would prefer to minimize individual attention as reflected in the Japanese maxim, "the nail that sticks out gets pounded down." It must be noted that while cultural values of individualism and collectivism describe general cultural differences between nations they are not necessarily accurate when describing the values or communication styles of specific individuals within a culture or a nation. There are many other factors that influence individuals' values and their communication styles such as their personality, gender, age, education level, occupational status, political beliefs, and so forth. This conceptualization of cultures differing, in terms of the value placed on the individual versus the group, helps us to understand how groups of people from different cultural backgrounds might differ in terms of their conceptualizations of themselves and their preferred communication styles. However, it doesn't help us know how to communicate effectively with an individual—for that we need to keep an open mind and remember and apply the characteristics of competent communication, as described in Chapter 1.

Characteristics of the Self-Concept

Now that you have a better idea of how your self-concept has developed, we can take a closer look at some of its characteristics.

The Self-Concept Is Subjective

The way we view ourselves may be at odds with other people's perceptions—and often with the observable facts (Simine and Carlson, 2010). For instance, people are notoriously bad judges of their own communication skills. A random sample of men was asked to rank themselves on their ability to get along with others. Defying mathematical laws, every subject put himself in the top half of the population. Sixty per cent rated themselves in the top 10 per cent of the population, and an amazing 25 per cent believed they were in the top 1 per cent. In the same study, 70 per cent of the men ranked the quality of their leadership in the top quarter of the population, whereas only 2 per cent thought they were below average. Sixty per cent said they were in the top quarter in athletic ability, whereas only 6 per cent viewed themselves as

REFLECTION

INDIVIDUALS' AND COLLECTIVISTS' CULTURAL VALUES

As a child growing up in a family with strong ties to the Netherlands, I learned that many of our customs and traditions were different from those of my friends at school. I lived in a very multicultural neighbourhood. My friends' cultural heritages included East Asian, South Asian, Caribbean, and southern European. Growing up, I was taught you had to work for everything. Possessions were earned by hard-working individuals. At the age of 15, I got my first job so I could pay for my share of the groceries. By the time I was 17, and in my final year of high school, I was working full-time to support myself. In my family, when you reach 17 you are considered an adult. As an adult, I was expected to leave the family home and move out on my own. My friends could not believe that my parents would ask me to leave home. They wondered if my parents really loved me. I was hurt that they would think that about my parents. Of course they loved me—they were helping me to be a strong, independent individual. This was a value we held deeply. I see now that our family's values were very much rooted in an individualistic culture. Many of my friends' families' values grew out of more collectivistic traditions. Of course, our parents loved us all—their values influenced how they expressed their love to us.

below average (Myers, 1980). These results are consistent with people's bias to overestimate their abilities and rate themselves more favourably than others in a wide variety of areas (Vazire and Carlson, 2010; Wilson, 2009).

There are several reasons why some people have a self-concept that others would

CHECK IT!

Briefly describe how individualism and collectivism influence the development of the self-concept and interpersonal communication.

regard as unrealistically favourable. First, a self-estimation might be based on **obsolete information**. Perhaps your jokes used to be well-received, or your grades were high, or your work was superior, but now the facts have changed. A self-concept might also be excessively favourable because of **distorted feedback** from others. A boss may claim to be an excellent manager because his assistants pour on false praise in order to keep their jobs. A hot-tempered professor's inflated ego may be based on the deference paid to her ideas by her colleagues in order to avoid nasty arguments.

There are also times when we view ourselves more harshly than the facts warrant. We have all experienced a temporary case of the "uglies," convinced we look much worse than others say that we do. Research confirms what common sense suggests—people are more critical of themselves when they are experiencing a **negative mood** than when they are feeling more positive (Brown and Mankowski, 1993; Cantazaro and Wei, 2010). Although everyone suffers occasional bouts of self-doubt that affect communication, some people suffer from long-term or even permanent states of excessive self-doubt and criticism (Gara et al., 1993). It's easy to understand how this chronic condition can influence the way these people approach and respond to others.

What are the reasons for such excessively negative self-evaluations? As with unrealistically high self-esteem, one source for an overabundance of self-criticism is obsolete information. A string of past failures in school or with social relations can linger to haunt a communicator long after they have occurred. Similarly, we have known slender people who still think of themselves as overweight and high-achieving students who still insist they are underachievers.

An inaccurate self-concept can also be caused by distorted feedback. Growing up in an overly critical family is one of the most common causes of a negative self-image. In other cases, the remarks of cruel friends, inconsiderate teachers, excessively demanding employers, or even memorable strangers can have a lasting effect. As we have seen, the impact of significant others and reference groups in forming your self-concept can be huge, and their effect on your self-esteem can be just as great.

Along with obsolete information, distorted feedback, and negative moods, another cause for low self-esteem is the **myth of perfection** that is common in our society. From the time most of us learn to understand language, we are exposed to models who appear

Thinkstock/Laikwunfai.

How do perfectionism and social expectations relate to low self-esteem?

to be perfect at whatever they do. This myth is clearest when we examine the stories commonly told to children. In these stories, the hero and heroine are wise, brave, talented, and victorious, whereas villains are totally evil and doomed to failure. This kind of model is easy for a child to understand, but it hardly paints a realistic picture of the world. Children learn that in order to gain acceptance they must pretend to "have it all together," even though they know they don't. Given this naive belief that everyone else is perfect and the knowledge that you are not, self-esteem will naturally suffer. We will have a great deal to say about perfection and other irrational ideas both in this chapter and in Chapter 4.

A final reason people often sell themselves short is also connected to **social expectations**. It is strange that the perfectionistic society we belong to rewards those people who downplay the strengths that we demand they possess. We term these people "modest" and find their behaviour agreeable. On the other hand, we consider some of those who honestly appreciate their own strengths to be braggarts or egotists, confusing them with the people who boast about accomplishments they do not possess (Miller et al., 1992). This convention leads most of us to talk freely about our shortcomings while downplaying our accomplishments. It's all right to proclaim that you are miserable if you have failed to do well on a project, but it's boastful to express your pride at a job well done.

Self-esteem may be based on inaccurate thinking, but it still has a strong effect on the way we relate to others. Table 2.2 summarizes some important differences between communicators with positive and negative self-esteem. Differences like these make sense when you realize that people who dislike themselves tend to believe that others won't like them either. Even online studies have found that people with low self-esteem are more likely to disclose negative and pessimistic information and receive unwanted negative responses from other people (Forest and Wood, 2012). People with unjustified positive self-views do not seem to fare any better. Several studies suggest that while these overly confident individuals may make a good first impression they come to be seen more negatively over time (Anderson et al., 2012; Carlson et al., 2011; Kwan et al., 2004). Although the self-concept is subjective, accuracy is possible and desirable. People who perceive themselves accurately enjoy more positive and satisfying interpersonal relationships with others, even when controlling for factors like intelligence,

Table 2.2 ● Characteristics of Communicators with Positive and Negative Self-Esteem

Persons with Positive Self-Esteem	Persons with Negative Self-Esteem
1. Are likely to think well of others.	1. Are likely to disapprove of others.
2. Expect to be accepted by others.	2. Expect to be rejected by others.
3. Evaluate their own performance more favourably.	3. Evaluate their own performance less favourably.
4. Perform well when being watched and are not afraid of the reactions of others.	4. Perform poorly when being watched and are sensitive to possible negative reactions.
5. Work harder for people who demand high standards of performance.	5. Work harder for undemanding, less critical people.
6. Are inclined to feel comfortable with others they view as superior in some way.	6. Feel threatened by people they view as superior in some way.
7. Are able to defend themselves against negative comments of others.	7. Have difficulty defending themselves against others' negative comments; are more easily influenced.

SOURCE: Adapted from D.E. Hamachek (1982), *Encounters with others: Interpersonal relationships and you.* New York: Holt, Rinehart and Winston.

emotional stability, and agreeableness (Tenney, Vazire and Mehl, 2013). So, despite the subjective nature of our understanding, increasing the accuracy of our self-knowledge is a worthwhile goal with interpersonal, not to mention philosophical, benefits.

A Healthy Self-Concept Is Flexible

People change. From moment to moment, we aren't the same. We wake up in the morning in a jovial mood and become irritated by lunchtime. You might be a relaxed conversationalist with people you know, but at a loss for words with strangers. You might be patient when explaining things on the job, but have no tolerance for such explanations at home. The self-concepts of most communicators react to these changes ("I'm patient at work, but I'm not patient at home"), and these changes affect self-esteem ("I'm not as good a person at home as I am in the office").

As we change in these and many other ways, our self-concept must also change in order to stay realistic. An accurate self-portrait today would not be exactly the same as the one we had a year ago, a few months ago, or even yesterday. This does not mean that a person changes radically from day to day. Long-term

changes in self-concept appear to take place in response to major life transitions. These might include leaving high school and going to college or university, starting a job, having children, or retiring (Manzi et al., 2010). The fundamental characteristics of your personality may stay the same for years, perhaps for a lifetime. However, it is likely that you are changing in other important ways—physically, intellectually, emotionally, and spiritually.

The Self-Concept Resists Change

A realistic self-concept should recognize the way we have changed over time, but the tendency to resist revision of our self-perception is strong. Once we fasten onto a self-concept, the tendency is to seek out people who confirm it. Numerous studies (e.g., North and Swann, 2009; Stets and Cast, 2007; Swann et al., 1992) show that both university/college students and married couples with high self-esteem seek out partners who view them favourably, whereas those with low self-esteem are more inclined to seek out people who view them unfavourably. This tendency to look for information that conforms to an existing self-concept has been labelled **cognitive conservatism** (Greenwald, 1995; Kihlstrom and Klein, 1994).

Understandably, we are reluctant to revise a favourable self-concept. If you were a thoughtful, romantic partner early in a relationship, it would be hard to admit that you might have become less considerate and attentive lately. Likewise, if you used to be a serious student, it isn't easy to admit that you have slacked off recently. Curiously, the tendency to cling to an outmoded self-perception holds even when the new image would be more favourable. We can recall scores of attractive, intelligent students who continue to view themselves as the gawky underachievers they were at the beginning of their studies. This sort of cognitive conservatism fosters unnecessary doubt and negative self-perceptions. These students can become their own worst enemies, denying themselves the validation they deserve, and need, to enjoy satisfying relationships.

Once the self-concept is firmly rooted, only a powerful force can change it. At least four requirements must be met for an appraisal to be regarded as important (Bergner and Holmes, 2000; Gergen, 1971). First of all, the person who offers a particular appraisal must be *someone we see as competent to offer it*. Parents satisfy this requirement extremely well because as young children, we perceive that our parents know so much about us—sometimes more than we know about ourselves. Second, *the appraisal must be considered highly personal*. The more the other person seems to know about us and adapts what is being said to fit us, the more likely we are to accept judgments from this person. Third, the appraisal must be *reasonable in light of what we believe about ourselves*. If an appraisal is similar to one we give ourselves, we will believe it; if it is somewhat dissimilar, we will probably still accept it; but if it is completely dissimilar, we will probably reject it. Finally, appraisals that are consistent *and* numerous are more persuasive than those that contradict usual appraisals or those that occur only once. As long as only a *few* students yawn in class, a teacher can safely disregard them as a reflection of his or her teaching ability. In like manner, you could

TAKE TWO **Cognitive conservatism:** the tendency to look for information that conforms to an existing self-concept.

safely disregard the appraisal of the angry date who tells you in no uncertain terms what kind of person behaves as you did. Of course, when you get a second or third similar appraisal in a short time, the evaluation becomes harder to ignore.

The Self-Fulfilling Prophecy and Communication

The self-concept is such a powerful influence on the personality that it not only determines how you see yourself in the present, but also can actually affect your future behaviour and that of others. Such occurrences come about through a phenomenon called the **self-fulfilling prophecy**.

A self-fulfilling prophecy occurs when a person's expectations of an event and her or his subsequent behaviour based on those expectations make the anticipated outcome more likely to happen than it would otherwise be. Self-fulfilling prophecies occur all the time, although you may never have given them that label. For example, think of some experiences you may have had:

- You expected to become nervous and botch a job interview, and later did so.
- A boss explained a new task to you, saying that you would probably find it difficult, and indeed you did.

In each of these cases, there is a good chance that the event took place as it did because you predicted that it would. You needn't have botched the interview, and you might have done better on the job if your boss hadn't spoken up. In other words, what helped make each event happen the way it did was your expectation of things going a certain way.

Types of Self-Fulfilling Prophecies

There are two types of self-fulfilling prophecies. *Self-imposed prophecies* are ones that influence your behaviour. You've probably had the experience of waking up in a cross mood and saying to yourself, "This will be a bad day." Once you come to such a conclusion, you will likely act in ways that make it come true. If you avoid the company of others because you expect they have nothing to offer, your suspicions will have been confirmed—nothing exciting or new is likely to happen. On the other hand, if you approach the same day with the idea that it could be a good one, this expectation may well be met. Smile at people, and they're more likely to smile back. Enter a class determined to learn something, and you probably will. In these cases and other similar ones, your attitude has a great deal to do with how you see yourself and how others see you.

Research has demonstrated the power of self-imposed prophecies. In one study, communicators who believed they were incompetent proved less likely than others to pursue rewarding relationships and more likely to sabotage their existing relationships than people who were less critical of themselves (Kolligan, 1990). On the other hand, students who considered themselves capable achieved more academically (Zimmerman, 1995). In another study, subjects who were sensitive to social rejection tended to expect rejection, see it where it may not have existed, and overreact to their exaggerated observations in ways that jeopardized the quality of their relationships (Downey and Feldman, 1996).

A second category of self-fulfilling prophecy is one that governs someone else's actions (Blank, 1993). The classic example was demonstrated by Robert Rosenthal and Lenore Jacobson in a study they described in their book *Pygmalion in the Classroom* (1968). The experimenters told teachers that 20 per cent of the children in a certain elementary school showed unusual potential for intellectual growth. The names of the 20 per cent were drawn by means of a table of random numbers—much as if they were drawn out of a hat. Eight months later, these unusual or "magical" children showed significantly greater gains in IQ than the remaining children, who had not been singled out for the teachers' attention. The change in the teachers' behaviour toward these allegedly "special" children led to changes in the intellectual performance of the randomly selected children. Among other things, the teachers gave the "smart" students extra time to answer questions and provided more feedback to them. These children did better, not because they were any more intelligent than their classmates, but because their teachers (significant others) communicated the expectation that they could. In other words, it wasn't just what the teachers *believed* that made a difference, it was how these beliefs were conveyed by the teachers' *behaviour*.

Influence of Self-Fulfilling Prophecies

The influence of self-fulfilling prophecies on communication can be strong, acting either to improve or to harm relationships. If you assume that another person is unlikeable, you will probably act in ways that communicate your feelings. In such a case, the other person's behaviour will probably match your expectations, since we usually do not go out of our way to be nice to people who aren't nice to us. If, on the other hand, you treat the other person as likeable, the results will probably be more positive.

The self-fulfilling prophecy is an important force in interpersonal communication, but we don't want to suggest that it explains all behaviour. There are certainly times when the expectation of an event will not bring it about. Your hope of drawing an ace in a card game will not in any way affect the chance of that

 CHECK IT!

In order for an appraisal to change a firmly rooted self-concept, it must meet four requirements. What are they?

card turning up in an already shuffled deck. Nor will your belief that good weather is coming stop the rain from falling. In the same way, believing you'll do well in a job interview when you're clearly not qualified for the position is unrealistic. To connect the self-fulfilling prophecy with the "power of positive thinking" is an oversimplification.

Changing Your Self-Concept

You have probably begun to realize that it is possible to gain a more accurate and satisfying self-concept. In the next sections, we discuss some methods for making such a change.

Have Realistic Expectations

It is important to realize that some of your dissatisfaction might come from expecting too much of yourself. Nobody is able to handle every conflict productively, to be totally relaxed and skilful in conversations, to ask perceptive questions all the time, or to be 100 per cent helpful when others have problems. Expecting yourself to reach such unrealistic goals is to doom yourself to unhappiness at the start.

It is important to judge yourself in relation to your own growth and not to the accomplishments of others. Rather than feeling miserable because you are not as talented as an expert, realize that you probably are a better, wiser, or more skilful person than you used to be, and that this growth is a legitimate source of satisfaction. Perfection is fine as an ideal, but you are being unfair to yourself if you actually expect to reach it.

Have a Realistic Perception of Yourself

One source of low self-esteem is inaccurate self-perception. As you've already read, such unrealistic pictures

Self-fulfilling prophecy: occurs when a person's expectations of an event and her or his subsequent behaviour based on those expectations make the outcome more likely than it would otherwise be. Such prophecies can be self-imposed (influenced by your own behaviour) or governed by the behaviour of others.

sometimes come from being overly harsh toward yourself, from believing that you're worse than the facts suggest. Of course, it would be foolish to deny that you could be a better person than you are, but it is also important to recognize your strengths.

Unrealistically low self-esteem can also come from the inaccurate comments of others. Workers with overly critical supervisors, children with cruel "friends," and students with unhelpful teachers are all prone to suffer from low self-esteem because of excessively negative feedback. If you fall into this category, it's important to put the unrealistic evaluations you receive into perspective and then to seek out supportive people who will acknowledge

"I want to be feared as a tyrant, loved as a father, and revered as a god, but I also want them to think I'm funny."

© Zachary Kanin The New Yorker Collection/The Cartoon Bank.

Building WORK SKILLS

Imagine yourself at work or school. Pretend you have to interact with someone (a customer, colleague, client, supervisor, etc.) who has a reputation for being difficult. If you can't imagine a situation, try one of the scenarios described below.

You are the assistant coach of a soccer team of eight-year-old girls and boys. The mother of a child on your team has left you a voice mail to call her back. The last time you saw her, she accused your colleague, the head coach, of playing other children more frequently and not giving her child enough shifts. She claimed the head coach didn't know how to put together a winning team. In her message, she didn't say what she wanted to talk to you about.

You work at the returns counter of a major department store. There is a man in line whom you saw a colleague assist last week. At that time, he attempted to return a pair of pants that he had bought a month earlier and had worn and washed. He said he didn't like the style and it didn't suit him, and he wanted a full refund. He yelled at your colleague and accused him of being incompetent when he explained that the store's return policy did not allow such returns. You have to serve this man next.

List the ways in which your prior knowledge of this person might negatively affect your perception of her or his communication. How might your expectations influence your communication? What could you do to reduce the effects of the self-fulfilling prophecy in this situation?

your assets as well as point out your shortcomings. Doing so is often a quick and sure boost to your self-esteem.

Have the Will to Change

Often, we say we want to change, but are not willing to do the necessary work. In such cases, the responsibility for not growing rests squarely on your shoulders. At other times, we maintain an unrealistic self-concept by claiming that we *can't* be the person we'd like to be, when, in fact, we are simply not willing to do what is necessary. You can change in many ways, but only if you are willing to make the effort.

Have the Skill to Change

Trying is often not enough. You also have to know how.

First, you can seek advice—from books such as this one and a variety of other printed sources. You can also get advice from instructors, counsellors, and other experts, as well as from friends. Of course, not all the advice you receive will be useful, but if you read widely

and talk to enough people, you will have a good chance of learning the things you want to know.

A second method of learning how to change is to observe models—people who handle themselves in the ways you would like to master. It has often been said that people learn more from models than in any other way; by taking advantage of this principle, you will find that the world is full of teachers who can show you how to communicate more successfully. Become a careful observer. Watch what people you admire do and say, not so that you can copy them, but so that you can adapt their behaviour to your own personal style.

At this point, you may be overwhelmed by the difficulty of changing the way you think about yourself and the way you act. Remember, no one is saying that this process will be easy (although it sometimes is). But, even when change is difficult, it's possible if you are serious. You don't need to be perfect, but you *can* change your self-concept and raise your self-esteem, and, as a result, your communication—*if you choose to.*

Do you think it's dishonest for people to have public selves and private selves?

iStockPhoto/silverkblack.

Presenting the Self: Communication as Identity Management

So far, we have described how communication shapes the way communicators view themselves. Now we turn the tables and focus on the topic of **identity management**—the communication strategies that people use to influence how others view them. In the following pages, you will see that many of our messages are aimed at creating certain impressions.

Public and Private Selves

To understand why identity management exists, we have to discuss the notion of self in more detail. So far, we have referred to the self as if each of us had only one identity. In truth, however, each of us possesses several selves, some private and others public. These selves are often quite different.

The **perceived self** is the person you believe you are in moments of honest self-examination. The perceived self may not be accurate in every respect. For example, you may think you are much more (or less) empathetic than an objective test would suggest. Accurate or not, the perceived self is powerful because you believe it reflects who you are. The perceived self is called "private" because you are unlikely to reveal all of it to another person. You can verify the private nature of the perceived self by thinking of elements of your self-perception that you would not disclose. For example, you might be reluctant to share some feelings about your appearance ("I think I'm rather unattractive"), your goals ("The most important thing to me is becoming rich"), or your motives ("I care more about myself than about others").

In contrast to the perceived self, the **presenting self** is a public image—the way we want to appear to others. In most cases, the presenting self we seek to create is a socially approved image: diligent student, loving partner, conscientious worker, loyal friend, and so on. Sociologist Erving Goffman (1959, 1971) used the word **face** to describe this socially approved identity, and he coined the term **facework** to describe the verbal and non-verbal ways in which we act to maintain our own presenting image and the images of others. (See Chapter 9 for more on presenting self and face.) He argued that each of us can be viewed both as a kind of playwright who creates roles that we want others to believe and as the performer who acts out those roles. Goffman suggested that each of us maintains face by putting on a *front* when we are around others whom we want to impress. In contrast, behaviour in the *back region*—when we are alone—may be quite different. You can recognize the difference between public and backstage behaviour

- **Perceived self:** the person you believe yourself to be in moments of honest self-examination; physical traits, personality characteristics, attitudes, aptitudes, and all other parts of the image you want to present to the world
- **Presenting self:** a public image, the way you want to appear to others.
- **Face:** your socially approved identity; different selves we present to different people.
- **Facework:** the verbal and non-verbal ways in which you act to maintain your own presenting image and the images of others.

by remembering a time when you observed a driver, alone in his or her car, behaving in ways that would never be acceptable in public. All of us engage in backstage ways of acting that we would never exhibit in front of others. Just think about how you behave in front of the bathroom mirror when the door is locked, and you will appreciate the difference between public and private behaviour. If you knew someone was watching, would you behave differently?

Characteristics of Identity Management

Now that you have a sense of what identity management is, we can look at some characteristics of this process.

We Strive to Construct Multiple Identities

It is an oversimplification to suggest we use identity-management strategies to create just one identity. In the course of even a single day, most people play a variety of roles: "respectful student," "joking friend," "friendly neighbour," and "helpful co-worker," to suggest just a few. We even play a variety of roles around

the same person. As you grew up, you almost certainly changed characters as you interacted with your parents. In one situation, you acted as the responsible adult ("You can trust me with the car") and at another time, you were the helpless child ("I can't find my socks!"). At certain times—perhaps on birthdays or holidays—you were a dedicated family member, and at other times, you may have played the role of rebel. Likewise, in romantic relationships, we switch among many ways of behaving, depending on the context: friend, lover, business partner, scolding critic, apologetic child, and so on.

The ability to construct multiple identities is one element of communication competence. For example, the style of speaking or even the language itself can reflect a choice about how to construct one's identity. Many bilingual Haitians living in Montreal understand this principle and often choose whether to use English or French depending on the kind of identity they are seeking in a given conversation (Baker, 2001).

Identity Management Is Collaborative

As we perform like actors trying to create a front, our "audience" is made up of other actors who are trying to create their own characters. Identity-related communication is a kind of process theatre in which we improvise scenes where our character reacts with others. For example, perhaps you try to present yourself as easygoing and funny by joking about something that has gone wrong, but your partner does seen the humour or the appropriateness of a relaxed approach. Your partner's response may well elicit another version of yourself.

Virtually all conversations provide an arena in which communicators construct their identities in response to the behaviour of others. As we saw in Chapter 1, communication is not made up of discrete events that can be separated from one another. Instead, what happens at one moment is influenced by what each communicator brings to the interaction and by

Focus on TECHNOLOGY

Use of online communication for identity experiments designed to explore self-concept is relatively common in adolescents (Valkenburg et al., 2005). Mechthild Maczewski (2002, 2007) of the University of Victoria studied youth identity exploration through the Internet. Maczewski suggests that the anonymity, connectivity, and interactivity of cyberspace provide youth with unique opportunities to explore multiple identities. Because physical and local identities can be hidden in online spaces, youth could conceptualize multiple identities and interact with diverse groups of people—as well as engage in roles they might not be provided with in their "on-ground" lives. The youth who participated in Maczewski's study described the Internet as a space of their own where they were able to connect with people they felt they could really talk to and engage in similar interests with. They reported that their online relationships reduced their sense of isolation and expanded their consciousness. One participant,

despite being a teenager, was given a promotion in her online job that allowed her to supervise a chat room; this experience helped her develop confidence, skills, and self-awareness that would have been difficult to attain in her on-ground life.

Similarly, Elizabeth Mazur and Lauri Kozarian (2010) found that adolescents and young adults use blogs to present themselves in flattering and positive terms; the blogs serve primarily as monologues about their daily experiences, social issues, academic and career goals, family, and friends. The researchers' analysis of a randomly selected sample of 124 blogs from a variety of hosting websites revealed that young people use their blogs to explore their identities, play with their presenting selves, and engage with others, perhaps in a venue that is more comfortable than in face-to-face interactions. Clearly, CMC provides people with additional opportunities to communicate with others and better explore and understand themselves.

---

what had happened in their relationship up to that point.

Identity Management Can Be Deliberate or Unconscious

There's no doubt that sometimes we are highly aware of managing the impressions we create. Most job interviews and first dates are clear examples of deliberate identity management. But in other cases, we unconsciously act in ways that are actually small public performances. For example, experimental subjects expressed facial disgust in reaction to eating sandwiches laced with a supersaturated solution of salt water only when there was another person present; when they were alone, they made no faces upon eating the same snack (Brightman et al., 1975). Another study showed that communicators engage in facial mimicry (such as smiling or looking sympathetic in response to another's message) only in face-to-face settings, when their expressions can be seen by the other

REFLECTION

MULTIPLE ME'S

An assignment in my English class showed me how much I change my identity in different relationships. We had to write letters to two different people describing how we were doing in life. I wrote the first one to my grandmother, and the other to my best friend. I was amazed at the difference between the two. I was much more positive and superficial with my grandma. I talked about events—school, work, and what I was doing with other members of our family. When writing to my friend, I talked about my non-family relationships and shared a lot of information that would probably have shocked and confused my grandmother. I also used entirely different writing styles—very formal with my grandmother, lots of slang with my friend.

This assignment helped me realize that I show different sides of myself to different people. It's not that I lie to anybody, it's just that I have different identities in different relationships.

person. When they are speaking over the phone and their reactions cannot be seen, they do not make the same expressions (Chovil, 1991). Facial mimicry is also influenced by social factors such as whether the other person belongs to the same group (e.g., another basketball player) or is familiar to the person (Bourgeois and Hess, 2007). Studies like these suggest that much of our behaviour is aimed at sending messages to others—in other words, is identity management.

You can see by now that much identity management is unconscious. The experimental subjects described by Brightman and colleagues didn't consciously think, "Somebody is watching me eat this salty sandwich so I'll make a face" or "Since I'm in a face-to-face conversation, I'll show I'm sympathetic by mimicking the facial expressions of my conversational partner." Decisions like these are often made instantaneously and outside of our conscious awareness.

Despite the claims of some theorists, it seems an exaggeration to suggest that *all* behaviour is aimed at making impressions. Young children are certainly not strategic communicators. A baby spontaneously laughs when she is pleased and cries when she is sad or uncomfortable, without any notion of creating an impression on others. Likewise, there are almost certainly

times when we as adults act spontaneously. But when a significant other questions the presenting self that we offer up, the likelihood of our acting to "improve" it increases.

People Differ in Their Degree of Identity Management

Some people are much more aware of their identity-management behaviour than others (Kopp, 1988; Snyder, 1979). There are advantages to being able to effectively self-monitor and adjust our communication. People who pay attention to themselves are generally able to handle social situations smoothly, often putting others at ease. They are also good "people readers" who can adjust their behaviour to get the desired reaction from others (Flynn et al. 2006).

Along with these advantages, there can be drawbacks to being an extremely high self-monitor (Leone and Hall, 2003; Leone and Hawkins, 2006; Oyamot et al., 2010). Such people's analytical nature may prevent them from experiencing events completely, since part of their attention will always be taken up with viewing the situation from a detached position. High self-monitors' ability to act makes it difficult to tell how they are really feeling. For example, high self-monitors have been observed to manipulate their Facebook profiles in order to appear more extraverted, happy, and popular when compared to lower self-monitors (Hall and Pennington, 2013). In fact, because high self-monitors change roles often, they may have a hard time *themselves* knowing how they really feel. By contrast, low self-monitors express what they are thinking and feeling without paying much attention to the impression they create. While they may be more in touch with their

© skodonnell/iStockphoto

What are some advantages and disadvantages of managing your identity?

feelings, their reactions may not help them to achieve their desired outcomes in some interpersonal situations.

By now, it should be clear that neither extremely high nor low self-monitoring is the ideal. There are some situations when paying attention to yourself and adapting your behaviour can be useful, and other times when reacting without considering the effect on others is a better approach. This need for a range of behaviour demonstrates once again the notion of communicative competence, as outlined in Chapter 1—flexibility is the key to successful relationships.

Why Manage Impressions?

Why bother trying to shape the opinions of others? Sometimes, we create and maintain a front to follow social rules. As children, we learn to act politely, even when we are bored. In fact, part of growing up consists of acquiring a set of manners for various occasions, such as meeting strangers, attending school, and going to church. Young children who haven't learned all the do's and don'ts of polite society often embarrass their parents with their behaviour ("Mommy, why is that man so fat?"), but by the time they enter school, behaviour that may previously have been excusable or even amusing just isn't acceptable. Good manners are often intended to make other people more comfortable. For example, able-bodied people often hide their discomfort upon encountering someone who is disabled by acting nonchalantly or stressing the similarities between themselves and the disabled person (Coleman and DePaulo, 1991).

Social rules govern our behaviour in a variety of settings. For example, it would be impossible to keep a job without meeting certain expectations. Salespeople are supposed to treat customers with courtesy. Employees need to appear reasonably respectful when talking to the boss. Some forms of clothing would be considered outrageous at work. By agreeing to take on a job, you are signing an unwritten contract that dictates you will present a certain

 **CHECK IT!**

> Describe four reasons why people manage impressions of themselves.

face at work, whether or not that face reflects the way you might be feeling at a particular moment.

Even when social roles do not dictate the proper way to behave, we often manage the impression we create for personal reasons or to achieve relational goals. You might, for example, dress up for a visit to traffic court in the hope that your front (responsible citizen) will persuade the judge to treat you sympathetically. You might act in a more friendly and lively way than you feel when you meet someone new so that you will appear likeable. In situations like these, you aren't being deceptive as much as "putting your best foot forward."

All these examples show that it is difficult—perhaps even impossible—*not* to create impressions. After all, you have to send some sort of message. If you don't appear friendly when you meet a stranger, you have to appear aloof, indifferent, hostile, or so on. If you don't act in a businesslike way, you have to act in a different way: casually or jokingly, for example. Often, the question isn't whether or not to present a face to others, but which face to present.

How Do We Manage Impressions?

How do we create a public face? In our technological age, which provides many options for communicating, the answer depends in part on the communication channel chosen.

Face-to-Face Identity Management

In face-to-face interaction, communicators can manage their front in three ways: with their manner, their appearance, and the setting. *Manner* consists of a communicator's words and non-verbal actions. Your manner plays a major role in shaping how others view you. In Chapters 6 and 7, we describe in detail how words and non-verbal behaviour create impressions. Since you *have* to speak and act, the question is not whether or not your manner sends a message, but rather whether or not these messages will be intentional.

Along with manner, a second dimension of identity management is *appearance*—the personal items people use to shape an image. Sometimes, appearance is part of creating a professional image. A physician's white lab coat and a police officer's uniform set the wearer apart as someone special. A tailored suit and a rumpled outfit create very different impressions in the business world. Off the job, clothing is just as important. We choose clothing that sends a message about ourselves: "I'm stylish," "I'm sexy," "I'm athletic," and a host of other possible messages.

A final way to manage impressions is through the choice of *setting*—physical items we use to influence how others view us. In the car culture of modern Western society, the automobile is a large part of identity management. This explains why many people lust after cars that are far more expensive and powerful than they really need. A sporty convertible or fancy imported sedan doesn't just get a driver from one place to another; it also makes a statement about the kind of person he or she is. The physical setting we choose and the way we arrange it is another important way to manage impressions. What colours do you choose for the place you live? What artwork is on your walls? What music do you play? If possible, we choose a setting that we enjoy, but in many cases, we create an environment that will present the desired front to others. If you doubt this fact, just remember the last time you straightened up the house before important guests arrived.

Identity Management in Mediated Communication

Most of the preceding examples involve face-to-face interaction, but identity management is just as pervasive and important in other types of communication.

"Sean and I like each other better on-line."

© Liza Donnelly *The New Yorker* Collection/The Cartoon Bank.

At first glance, the technology of computer-mediated communication (CMC) seems to limit the potential for identity management. Texting and email, for example, appear to lack the "richness" of other channels. They don't convey the tone of your voice or your posture, gestures, or facial expression. Recently, though, communication scholars have begun to recognize that what is missing in CMC can actually be an *advantage* for communicators who want to manage the impressions they make.

When sending electronic messages, people can choose their level of clarity or ambiguity, seriousness or humour, logic or emotion. Unlike face-to-face communication, electronic correspondence allows a sender to say difficult things without forcing the receiver to respond immediately, and it permits the receiver to ignore a message rather than give an unpleasant response. Options like these show that CMC can serve as a tool for identity management at least as well as face-to-face communication can (Walther, 1996; Walther et al., 2010).

Like email and texting, personal profiles on social networking sites, blogs, and personal websites allow their creators to manage their identities. Some observers have pointed out that the creation of online profiles involves much more than what appears on the computer screen, and that people are also managing their public identities (Chandler, 1998; Madden and Smith, 2010; Mazur and Kozarian, 2010). The words, images, and sounds that people choose make a statement about who they are—or at least how they want to be regarded by others.

People who construct personal profiles, websites, blogs, and so on create identity both by what they *include* and what they *exclude* from their home page. Consider how featuring or withholding the following kinds of information affects how people might regard your online profile: age, photo, educational or career accomplishments, sexual orientation, job title, interests, personal philosophy and religious beliefs, and organization affiliations. You can easily think of a host of other kinds of material that could be included or excluded, and the effect that each would have on how others regard you. Despite the potential for self-enhancement and deception, research suggests that online social networking profiles (e.g., Facebook, LinkedIn, etc.) tend to fairly accurately convey the personality profile and identity of the profile owners (Wilson et al., 2012).

Identity Management and Honesty

At first, identity management might sound like an academic label for manipulation or phoniness. And there certainly are situations where impression management is dishonest. A manipulative date who pretends to be affectionate or thoughtful in order to gain sexual favours is clearly unethical and deceitful. So is a job applicant who lies about her or his academic record to get hired or a salesperson who pretends to be dedicated to customer service when the real goal is to make a quick buck.

But not all cases of identity management are so clearly wrong. In a job interview, is it

legitimate to appear more confident and reasonable than you really feel? Likewise, in a boring conversation are you justified in being more attentive than you feel like being, out of courtesy to the other person? And there are times you would be foolish to provide complete and truthful information online. Managing your online identity helps to protect your privacy and security. Situations like these suggest that managing impressions doesn't necessarily make you a liar. In fact, it is almost impossible to imagine how we could communicate effectively without making decisions about which front to present in one situation or another. Each of us has a repertoire of faces—a cast of characters—and part of being a competent communicator is to choose the best role for a situation. It is an oversimplification to say that there is only one honest way to behave in each circumstance and that every other response would be insincere and dishonest. Instead, identity management involves deciding which face—which part of yourself—to reveal. Which face to show to others is an important decision, but, in any case, you are sharing a real part of yourself.

Disclosing the Self

What we share about ourselves and what we keep hidden is part of our identity management. You might argue that aside from secrets, it is impossible *not* to make yourself known to others. After all, every time you open your mouth to speak, you're revealing your tastes, interests, desires, opinions, beliefs, or some other bit of information about yourself. Even when the subject is not a personal one, your choice of what to talk about tells the listener something about who you are. In Chapter 7, we will discuss the fact that each of us communicates non-verbally even when we're not speaking.

If every verbal and non-verbal behaviour in which you engage is self-revealing, how can self-disclosure be distinguished from any other act of communication? According to

CHECK IT!

What are the advantages and disadvantages of mediated communication when partaking in identity management?

psychologist Paul Cozby (1973), the subject of self-disclosing communication is the *self*, and information about the self is *purposefully communicated verbally to another person*. Although this definition is a start, it ignores the fact that some messages intentionally directed toward others are not especially revealing. For example, telling an acquaintance, "I don't like clams" is quite different from announcing, "I don't like you." Let us take a look at several factors that further distinguish self-disclosure from other types of communication.

Honesty

It almost goes without saying that true self-disclosure has to be honest. It's not revealing to say, "I've never felt this way about anyone before" to every Saturday-night date, or to preface every lie with the statement "Let me be honest . . ."

As long as you are honest and accurate to the best of your knowledge, communication can qualify as an act of self-disclosure. On the other hand, painting an incomplete picture of yourself (telling only part of what is true) is not genuine disclosure. We will talk more about the relationship between honesty and disclosure later in this chapter.

Depth

A self-disclosing statement is generally regarded as being personal—containing relatively "deep" rather than "surface" information. Of course, what is personal and intimate for one person may not be for another. You may feel comfortable admitting your spotty academic record, short temper, or fear of spiders to anyone who asks, whereas others would be embarrassed to do so. Even basic demographic information, such as age, can be extremely personal for some people.

Availability of Information

Self-disclosing messages must contain information that the other person is not likely to know at the time or to be able to obtain from another source without a great deal of effort.

If as little as 2 per cent of our communication qualifies as self-disclosure, how do we get to know one another?

© kerriekerr/iStockphoto.

For example, describing your conviction for a drunk-driving accident might feel like an act of serious disclosure because the information concerns you, is offered intentionally, is honest and accurate, and is considered personal. However, if the other person could obtain that information elsewhere without much trouble—from a glance at the morning newspaper or from various gossips, for example—your communication would not disclose very much.

Context of Sharing

Sometimes, the self-disclosing nature of a statement comes from the setting in which it is uttered. For instance, relatively innocuous information about family life seems more personal when a student shares it with the class (Myers, 1998), or when an athlete tells it to her coach (Officer and Rosenfeld, 1985). This sort of sharing creates a more personal atmosphere because it changes the relationship from a purely "business" level to a more personal one.

We can summarize our definitional tour by saying that **self-disclosure** (1) has the self as subject, (2) is intentional, (3) is directed at another person, (4) is honest, (5) is revealing, (6) contains information generally unavailable from other sources, and (7) gains much of its intimate nature from the context and culture in which it is expressed.

Although many acts of communication may be self-revealing, this definition makes it clear that few of our statements may be classified as self-disclosure. Most conversations—even among friends and romantic partners—focus on everyday mundane topics and disclose little or no personal information (Alberts et al., 2005; Dindia et al., 1997; Duck and Miell, 1986).

Models of Self-Disclosure

Although our definition of self-disclosure is helpful, it doesn't include the important fact that not all self-disclosure is equally revealing—that some disclosing messages tell more about us than others do. The social penetration model captures the breadth and depth of disclosure, while the Johari Window model (see page 64) describes the aspects of yourself that you are aware of and those that you reveal to others.

Social Penetration Model

Social psychologists Irwin Altman and Dalmas Taylor (1973; Taylor and Altman, 1987) describe two ways in which communication can be more or less disclosing. Their **social penetration model** is pictured in Figure 2.2. The first dimension of self-disclosure in this model involves the **breadth** of information volunteered—the range of subjects being discussed. For example, the breadth of disclosure in your relationship with a fellow worker will expand as you begin revealing information about your life away from the job, as well as on-the-job details. The second dimension

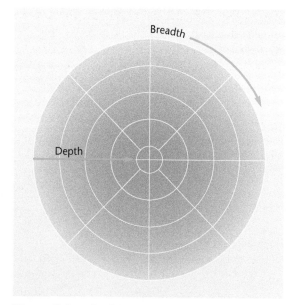

Figure 2.2 ● Social Penetration Model

of disclosure is the **depth** of the information being volunteered—the shift from relatively unrevealing messages to more personal ones.

Depending on the breadth and depth of information shared, a relationship can be defined as casual or intimate. In a casual relationship, the breadth may be great, but not the depth. A more intimate relationship is likely to have much depth in at least one area. The most intimate relationships are those in which disclosure is great in both breadth and depth. Altman and Taylor see the development of a relationship as a progression from the periphery of their model to its centre, a process that usually takes place gradually. Each of your personal relationships probably has a different combination of breadth of subjects and depth of revelation. Figure 2.3 pictures a student's self-disclosure in one relationship.

One way to classify the depth of disclosure is to look at the types of information that can be revealed. *Clichés* are ritualized, stock responses

CHECK **IT!**

Describe all the qualities of self-disclosure.

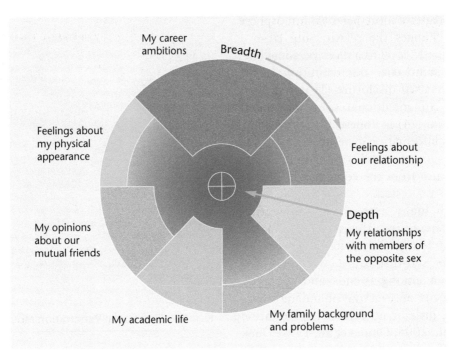

Figure 2.3 ● Sample Model of Social Penetration

to social situations—virtually the opposite of self-disclosure: "How are you doing?" "Fine." Although hardly revealing, clichés can serve as a valuable kind of shorthand that makes it easy to keep the social wheels greased and can indicate the potential for further, possibly more profound conversation.

Another kind of message involves communicating *facts*. Not all factual statements qualify as self-disclosure. To qualify, they must fit the criteria of being intentional, significant, and not otherwise known: "This isn't my first try at college. I dropped out a year ago with terrible grades." Facts like these can be meaningful in themselves, but they also have a greater significance in a relationship. Disclosing important information suggests a level of trust and commitment that signals a desire to move the relationship to a new level of intimacy.

Opinions can be a revealing kind of self-disclosure since they often reveal more about a person than facts alone do. If you know where the speaker stands on a subject, you can get a clearer picture of how your relationship might

develop. Likewise, every time you offer a personal opinion, you are giving others valuable information about yourself.

The fourth level of self-disclosure—and usually the most revealing one—involves the expression of *feelings*. At first glance, feelings might appear to be the same as opinions, but there's a big difference. "I don't think you're telling me what's on your mind" is an opinion. Notice how much more we learn about the speaker by looking at three different feelings that could accompany this statement: "I don't think you're telling me what's on your mind . . .

. . . and I'm suspicious."

. . . and I'm angry."

. . . and I'm hurt."

Johari Window Model

Another way to illustrate how self-disclosure operates in communication is a model called the **Johari Window**, developed by Joseph Luft and Harry Ingham (Janas, 2001; Luft, 1969).

Imagine a frame that contains every-thing there is to know about you: your likes and dislikes, your goals, your secrets, your needs—everything. This frame could be div-ided into information you know about your-self and things you don't know. It could also be split into things others know about you and things they don't know. Figure 2.4 illustrates these divisions.

Part 1 represents the information that both you and the other person already have. This part is your *open area*. Part 2 represents the *blind area*: information of which you are unaware, but that the other person knows. You learn about information in the blind area primarily through feedback from others. Part 3 of the Johari Window represents your *hid-den area*: information that you know, but are not willing to reveal to others. Items in this hidden area become public primarily through self-disclosure. Part 4 of the Johari Window represents information that is *unknown* to both you and to others. At first, the unknown area seems impossible to verify. After all, if neither you nor others know what it contains, how can you be sure it exists at all? We can

- **Social penetration model:** two ways, measured by breadth and depth, that communication can be more or less disclosing.
- **Breadth:** the range of sub-jects discussed.
- **Depth:** the personal nature of information (significant and private self-disclosures, clichés, facts, opinions, and feelings).

deduce its existence because we are constantly discovering new things about ourselves. For example, it is not unusual to discover that you have an unrecognized talent, strength, or weakness. A newly discovered item moves from the unknown area into the open area when you share your insight, or into the hid-den area when you keep it secret.

The relative size of each area in our per-sonal Johari Window changes from time to time according to our moods, the subject we are discussing, and our relationship with the other person. Despite these changes, a single Johari Window could represent most people's overall style of disclosure.

Benefits and Risks of Self-Disclosure

By now, it should be clear that neither all-out disclosure nor complete privacy is desirable. In the following pages we will outline both the risks and benefits of opening yourself to others.

Benefits of Self-Disclosure

Although the amount of self-disclosure varies from one person and relationship to another, all of us share important information about ourselves at one time or another. What leads us to open up? Derlega and Grzelak (1979), Kelly (1999), and Agne et al. (2000) present a variety of reasons for disclosing in any par-ticular situation. We can build upon their work by showing how these reasons have at least potential benefits.

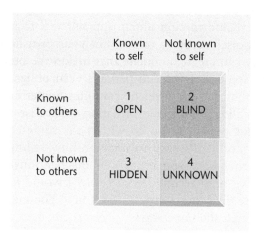

Figure 2.4 ● Johari Window

SOURCE: Figures 2.4 and 2.5 are from *Group process: An introduction to group dynamics.* Copyright © 1963, 1970 by Joseph Luft. Used with the permission of Mayfield Publishing Company.

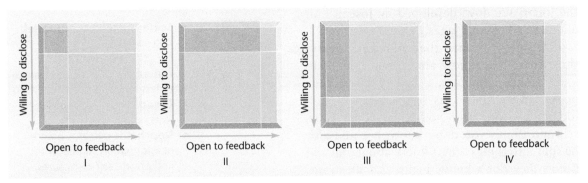

Figure 2.5 ● How Limited Disclosure Blocks Communication

Catharsis Sometimes, you might disclose information in an effort to "get it off your chest." Catharsis can indeed relieve the burden of pent-up emotions, but when it is the *only* goal of disclosure, the results of opening up may not be good. Later in this chapter, you will read guidelines for self-disclosure that improve your chance of achieving catharsis in a way that helps, instead of harming, relationships.

Self-Clarification It is often possible to clarify your beliefs, opinions, thoughts, attitudes, and feelings by talking about them with another person. This gaining of insight by "talking the problem out" occurs in many psychotherapies, but it also goes on in other relationships, ranging all the way from close friendships to conversations with bartenders or hairdressers. When the purpose of disclosing is to gain new insights, people who self-disclose tend to feel more positive about their secrets and come to terms with them (Kelly et al., 2001).

Self-Validation If you disclose information with the hope of seeking the listener's agreement ("I think you did the right thing"), you are seeking validation of your behaviour—confirmation

of a belief you hold about yourself. On a deeper level, this sort of self-validating disclosure seeks confirmation of important parts of your self-concept. Self-validation through self-disclosure is an important part of the "coming out" process through which gay and lesbian people recognize their sexual orientation and choose to integrate this knowledge into their personal, familial, and social lives (Han, 2001; Savin-Williams, 2001).

Reciprocity A well-documented conclusion from research is that one person's act of self-disclosure makes it more likely that the other person will reveal personal information (Derlega et al., 1994; Dindia, 2000b, 2002). There is no guarantee that revealing personal information about yourself will trigger self-disclosures by others, but your own honesty can create a climate that makes the other person feel safer, and perhaps even obligated to match your level of candour. Sometimes, revealing personal information will cause the other person to do so within the same conversation. It's easy to imagine how telling a partner how you feel about the relationship ("I've been feeling bored lately") would generate the same degree of candour ("You know, I've felt the same way!"). Reciprocity does not always occur at the same time. Telling a friend today about your job-related problems might help her feel comfortable telling you about her family history later, when the time is right for this sort of disclosure.

 CHECK **IT!**

Describe the four quadrants of the Johari Window and the relationship of each to receptivity to feedback.

Self-Assessment

ANALYZING YOUR SELF-DISCLOSURE CHOICES

Part 1: Why you disclose

Use the following scale to indicate your reasons for self-disclosing. These reasons are likely to vary for each relationship you analyze, so you may choose to repeat this self-assessment more than once. Keep one relationship in mind as you complete the self-assessment.

1 = This is definitely not a reason I self-disclose.
2 = This is probably not a reason I self-disclose.
3 = I am unsure whether this is a reason I self-disclose.
4 = This is probably a reason I self-disclose.
5 = This is definitely a reason I self-disclose.

_____ 1. I disclose as a means to get something off my chest—to vent my feelings.

_____ 2. I disclose as a way to clarify my beliefs, feelings, opinions, thoughts, and so on—to use the other person as a "sounding board."

_____ 3. I disclose to get the other person to agree with me about how I see the situation.

_____ 4. I disclose as a way to encourage the other person to talk to me.

_____ 5. I disclose certain pieces of information so as to create a particular impression of myself.

_____ 6. I disclose to keep the other person current with what is happening to me, so that our relationship "doesn't fall behind."

_____ 7. I disclose to achieve some particular goal—for example, to increase my control over the other person, the situation, or our relationship.

_____ 8. I disclose so I can get advice, support, or assistance from this person.

_____ 9. I disclose because I "owe it" to this person, or feel obligated, because this person has the right to know.

_____ 10. I disclose to the other person because we care for each other, trust one another, and support one another.

Part 2: Reasons for not disclosing

Use the scale below to identify your reasons for not disclosing personal information. As before, you may choose to repeat this self-assessment for each of your important relationships, but keep one relationship in mind for each evaluation.

1 = This is definitely not a reason I avoid self-disclosing.
2 = This is probably not a reason I avoid self-disclosing.
3 = I am unsure whether this is a reason I avoid self-disclosing.
4 = This is probably a reason I avoid self-disclosing.
5 = This is definitely a reason I avoid self-disclosing.

_____ 1. I can't find the opportunity to self-disclose.

_____ 2. I don't want to upset or hurt the person—perhaps put the person's life in an uproar.

_____ 3. I can't think of a way to self-disclose.

_____ 4. The information I disclose might be used against me in some way.

_____ 5. I might be treated differently after I self-disclose.

_____ 6. I might be treated as if I were "crazy" after I self-disclose.

_____ 7. I don't think I'll get support if I self-disclose.

_____ 8. I might not be understood.

_____ 9. My self-disclosure might hurt our relationship.

_____ 10. What I self-disclose might be told to people I would prefer not know.

_____ 11. I don't self-disclose because our relationship isn't close enough.

_____ 12. What I self-disclose might be told to people whom I would prefer to tell myself.

_____ 13. I don't know how to put what I want to say into words.

What are your most important or usual reasons for disclosing? What are your most important or usual reasons for not disclosing? What does this information reveal to you about how you use self-disclosure in your relationships, and the kinds of relationships you have?

Impression Formation   Sometimes, we reveal personal information to make ourselves more attractive, and research shows that this strategy seems to work. One study revealed that both men's and women's attractiveness was associated with the amount of self-disclosure in conversations (Stiles et al., 1996). Consider a couple on their first date. It's not hard to imagine how one or both partners might share personal information to appear more sincere, interesting, sensitive, or curious about the other person. The same principle applies in other situations. A salesperson might say, "I'll be honest with you . . ." primarily to show that she is on your side, and a new acquaintance might talk about the details of his past in order to seem more friendly and likeable. Whether or not you try to create a good impression depends on whether you expect to have future dealings with this person (Tidwell, 1998).

Maintenance and Enhancement of Relationships   Research demonstrates that we like people who disclose personal information to us. In fact, the relationship between self-disclosure and liking works in several directions. We like people who disclose personal information to us, we reveal more about ourselves to people we like, and we tend to like others more after we have disclosed to them (Dindia, 2000b).

Beyond fostering liking, disclosure (if it is appropriate, of course) can keep relationships healthy and satisfying both online and in person (Bane et al., 2010; Lippert and Prager, 2001; Vittengl and Holt, 2000). Appropriate self-disclosure is associated with greater martial satisfaction across numerous cultures (Cordova, Gee, and Warren, 2005; Kito, 2005; Quek and Fitzpatrick 2013).Not surprisingly, partners who reveal personal information to each other often avoid the sorts of misunderstandings that lead to unhappiness and build greater trust and intimacy.

Moral Obligation   Sometimes, we disclose personal information out of a sense of moral obligation. People who are HIV positive, for example, are often faced with the choice of whether or not they should tell their partners. Hirsch Allen and his colleagues in British Columbia (2014) found that 73 per cent of HIV-positive men and women in their study disclosed their HIV-positive status to their sexual partners. This rate of disclosure is slightly higher than studies done in countries where there is less criminalization of nondisclosure. However, additional research has revealed that it is people's belief that they have a moral duty to tell their partners that consistently predicts disclosure rates among people who are HIV positive. Laws criminalizing nondisclosure in a particular jurisdiction have been much less influential (O'Byrne, 2012).

Social Influence   People sometimes reveal personal information to help others. This practice is common in self-help groups such as Alcoholics Anonymous (Hegelson and Gottlieb, 2000) and a variety of support groups, including those offered online. Group members are able to support each other in overcoming many types of adversity by sharing their struggles and building a supportive community (Barak et al., 2008). Two high-profile examples, of people disclosing personal information in order to help others, include actress Angelina Jolie and American football player Michael Sam. In Jolie's case, she revealed that she had undergone a preventive double mastectomy as well as a preventative partial hysterectomy. She talked openly about her decision to have this surgery in order to raise public awareness about the rare, but potentially fatal, gene mutation that causes a small proportion of breast and ovarian cancer cases. With Sam, he disclosed, prior to the NFL draft, that he was gay. Sam was the first openly gay player to be drafted into the NFL. His acceptance speech for the ESPN/ESPY Arthur Ashe Courage Award reflected his motivation to reveal personal and potentially career-limiting information in order to help others. Below are a couple of excerpts from his speech, as quoted in the *Globe and Mail* (Doura, 2014).

> My responsibility at this moment in history is to stand up for everybody out there who wants nothing more than to be themselves openly . . . To anyone out there, especially young people, who are feeling like they don't fit in and will never be accepted, please know this: Great things can happen if you have the courage to be yourself.

Self-Defence Sometimes, you may choose to disclose something before someone else discloses it for you. A review of the social influence literature by Williams and Dolnik (2001) suggests that disclosing negative or damaging information about oneself is frequently used as an adaptive social influence strategy.

Benefits of Self-Disclosure

- **Catharsis:** revealing thoughts, feelings, and emotions to release emotional burden.
- **Self-clarification:** talking about beliefs, thoughts, opinions, and attitudes to gain insight.
- **Reciprocity:** disclosing information to increase the likelihood that the other person will do the same.
- **Impression formation:** revealing personal information in order to make ourselves more attractive.
- **Maintenance and enhancement of relationships:** foster liking and maintain healthy relationships through disclosure.
- **Social influence:** disclosing information to exert control over others.
- **Self-defence:** disclosing something before someone else does.

The Risks of Self-Disclosure

While the benefits of disclosing are certainly important, opening up can also involve risks that make the decision to disclose a difficult and sometimes painful one (Christofides et al., 2012; Niederhoffer and Pennebaker, 2002). The risks (and fears) of self-disclosure fall into six common categories (Derlega et al., 2000; Rosenfeld, 1979, 2000), including: rejection, causing a negative impression, deceased relational satisfaction, loss of influence, loss of control, and hurting the other person. We will take a closer look at these in the following pages.

Rejection John Powell (1969) summed up the risks of disclosing in answering the question that forms the title of his book *Why Am I Afraid to Tell You Who I Am?* "I am afraid to tell you who I am, because, if I tell you who I am, you may not like who I am, and that's all I have." The fear of disapproval is powerful. Sometimes, it is exaggerated and illogical, but there are real dangers in revealing personal information:

> A: I'm starting to think of you as more than a friend. To tell the truth, I think I love you.
> B: I think we should stop seeing one another.

Negative Impression Even if disclosure does not lead to total rejection, it can create a negative impression.

> A: You know, I've never had a relationship with a woman that lasted more than a month.
> B: Really? I wonder what that says about you.

Decrease in Relational Satisfaction Besides affecting other people's opinions of you, disclosure can lead to a decrease in the satisfaction that comes from a relationship. Consider a scenario like this, where the incompatible wants and needs of both people become clear through disclosure:

> A: Let's get together with Youssef and Sahar on Saturday night.

B: To tell you the truth, I'm tired of seeing Youssef and Sahar. I don't have much fun with them, and I think Youssef is kind of a jerk.

A: But they're my best friends!

Loss of Influence   Another risk of disclosure is a possible loss of influence in the relationship. Once you confess a secret weakness, your control over how the other person views you can be diminished.

A: I'm sorry I was so sarcastic. Sometimes, I build myself up by putting you down.

B: Is that it? I'll never let you get away with that again!

Loss of Control   Revealing something personal about yourself means losing control of the information. What might happen if the person tells someone else what you disclosed—people you prefer not to know, or whom you would like to tell yourself?

A: I never really liked Nor. I agreed to go out because it meant a good meal in a nice restaurant.

B: Really? Nor would certainly like to know that!

Hurt the Other Person   Even if revealing hidden information leaves you feeling better, it might hurt others—cause them to be upset, for example. It's probably easy to imagine yourself in a situation like this:

A: Well, since you asked, I have felt less attracted to you lately. I know you can't help it when your skin breaks out, but it is kind of a turnoff.

B: I know! I don't see how you can stand me at all!

Alternatives to Self-Disclosure

Though self-disclosure plays an important role in interpersonal relationships, it's not the only

type of communication available. To understand why complete honesty is not always easy or ideal, consider some familiar situations:

You don't find your co-worker's jokes funny and you resent her lack of effort at work. She says, "What's up with you? Don't you like working with me anymore?"

Your friend, who is headed out the door for an important job interview, says, "I know I'll never get this job! I'm really not qualified, and besides, I look terrible." You agree with your friend's assessment.

You have just been given a large, extremely ugly lamp as a gift by a relative who visits your home often. How would you answer the question, "Where will you put it?"

Although honesty is desirable in principle, it often has risky, unpleasant consequences.

Risks of Self-Disclosure

- **Rejection:** disclosure may cause disapproval.
- **Negative impression:** even if disclosure doesn't cause outright rejection, it can make you look bad.
- **Decrease in relational satisfaction:** relationships can suffer from disclosure.
- **Loss of influence:** disclosure may reveal your weakness, and you may have less influence over others.
- **Loss of control:** people can tell others what you have disclosed and thus control information that you want to manage.
- **Hurt the other person:** disclosure might cause the other person to be upset.
- **Increased awareness:** self-discovery through disclosure can be difficult or painful.

Focus on TECHNOLOGY

ALWAYS ON: "BUTLER LIES" HELP US MANAGE OUR AVAILABILITY

Cellphones have created a world in which we can always be connected, whether we want to be or not. So, how do we manage our "availability"? In the past, people struggled to establish a time and place to connect, but now, with constant connectivity, people increasingly seek strategies to avoid communication, particularly when communicating would be disruptive, socially awkward, or when we need to focus our attention on something else. Jeff Hancock and his colleagues at Cornell University's Social Media Lab (Hancock et al., 2009; Reynolds et al., 2013) coined the term *butler lies* to describe small lies that help us manage our availability, in much the same way as a butler might manage the access to his employer. Here are a few examples:

"I'm on my way" (when you haven't left).

"Can't meet later. Busy" (when you are not busy).

"Sorry, just got your message" (when you got it a while ago).

They make use of ambiguities which arise from the fact that both communicators are not in the same place. People report using butler lies to avoid hurting other people's feelings or to save face. In their analysis of 2341 text messages sent by 82 American university student dyads, these researchers found that:

- butler lies occurred more frequently in everyday texting than other types of lies;
- receiver's expected more butler lies than other types of lies;
- despite their expectations, receivers were less likely to perceive butler lies as deceptive compared to other types of lies; and
- on average senders reported feeling worse about their deceptive messages than receivers (Reynolds et al., 2013).

They conclude that deception is commonly used to help us manage the pressure of being expected to always be available. Recent systems, that provide senders with notifications that messages have been read and automatic location-sharing features, threaten our ability to use butler lies. Based on their research findings they argue that this may not be a good thing because to some extent people expect to be lied to some of the time and while these investigators do not advocate lying to hurt others, they do acknowledge that we need some socially sensitive mechanisms to avoid communication overload, particularly if social norms continue to demand constant availability.

It's tempting to sidestep situations where self-disclosure would be difficult, but examples like the ones you just read show that avoidance is not always possible. Research and personal experience show that communicators—even those with the best intentions—are not always completely honest when they find themselves in situations when honesty would be uncomfortable (Ennis et al., 2008; O'Hair and Cody, 1993). Five common alternatives to self-disclosure are remaining silent or being secretive, lying, equivocating, hinting, and avoiding. We will take a closer look at the first four of these alternatives in the following pages. Avoiding is discussed in Chapter 10.

Silence and Secrecy

When confronted directly by your spouse about your lack of affection, for example, you don't really have the luxury of the "No comment" verbal response (or the non-verbal "speak to the hand" gesture) favoured by many politicians, lawyers, and movie stars. There are situations, however, when you can keep information to yourself. Keeping silent is one way to avoid disclosing information you would rather keep private, particularly in situations when you are not asked directly about it. In their exploration of the dark and light sides of avoidance and secrets, Tamara Afifi, John Caughlin, and Waid Afifi (2007) discuss what characterizes secrecy. They suggest that secrets involve intentionally concealing private information that the individual considers too risky to reveal. Not all silence is secretive; however, when you choose silence over disclosure you have made a choice to conceal information, at least in that particular situation. As we have discussed throughout this text, talk–silence patterns vary by culture, and many Canadians find prolonged silences uncomfortable, but this is not the case in many Asian and Canadian First Nations cultures. Within any culture, some people are more inclined to keep their emotions and thoughts to themselves (Vrij et al., 2003). Determining whether or not information is private (others have no claim to it) or whether it is a secret (we are keeping it from people who have a right to know) involves considering the ethics of evasion, which we will discuss a little later in this chapter.

Lying

A **lie** is a deliberate attempt to hide or misrepresent the truth.

Lying to gain unfair advantage over an unknowing victim seems clearly wrong, but another kind of untruth—the "benevolent lie"—is not so easy to condemn as completely unethical. A **benevolent lie** is defined (at least by the person who tells it) as not being malicious—and perhaps it is even helpful to the person it is told to. Though most people favour honesty in close relationships, they do admit that there are cases when benevolent lying is not only necessary, but also the right thing to do. The most obvious reason for benevolent lying is to protect the other person's feelings. You can almost certainly recall times when you have been less than truthful in order to avoid hurting someone you care for.

Whether or not they are innocent, benevolent lies are certainly common. Some researchers have found considerable evidence that deception is part of everyday life. Burgoon and Buller (2008) estimate that almost a third of everyday conversations include some kind of deception (e.g., exaggeration, evasiveness, and outright lies). What reasons do people give for being deceitful? When subjects in DePaulo and colleagues' study (1996) were asked to give a lie-by-lie account of their motives for concealing or distorting the truth, five major reasons emerged, including: preventing embarrassment of oneself and others; avoiding tension and conflict; helping to guide social interaction to gain power; and further developing or terminating relationships. The most common reason reported was preventing embarrassment.

Most people think benevolent lies are told for the benefit of the recipient. For example, the majority of subjects in the DePaulo et al. study (1996) claimed such lying was "the right thing to do." Other research paints a less flattering picture of who benefits most from lying. One study found that two out of every three lies are told for "selfish reasons" (Hample, 1980). Other research by Paula Lippard

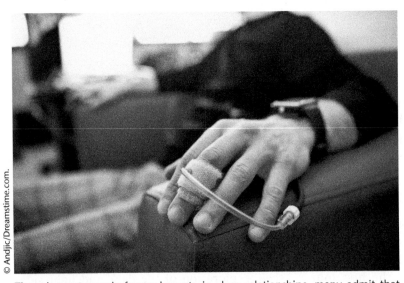

© Andjic/Dreamstime.com.

Though most people favour honesty in close relationships, many admit that there are times when benevolent lying is the right thing to do. When do you think benevolent lying is the right thing to do? When is it harmful?

(1988) suggests that this figure is too low. Of 322 lies recorded, 75.8 per cent were for the benefit of the liar. Fewer than 22 per cent were for the benefit of the person hearing the lie, and a mere 2.5 per cent were intended to aid a third person. Table 2.3 presents some common reasons given for lying.

Lies can elicit different responses. An occasional benevolent lie in an otherwise honest relationship does not pose much threat. Major deception though—especially when it is part of a pattern of deceit—is likely to provoke a relational crisis (McCornack and Levine, 1990).

Lying about major parts of your relationship can lead to the end of that relationship. So, if preserving a relationship is important to you, then honesty—at least about important matters—really does appear to be the best policy.

Equivocation

Lying is not the only alternative to self-disclosure. When faced with the choice between lying and telling an unpleasant truth, communicators can—and often do—equivocate.

 **CHECK IT!**

What reasons do people give for lying and what are the effects of lies?

Equivocal language has two or more equally plausible meanings.

Sometimes, we send equivocal messages without meaning to, resulting in confusion. "I'll meet you at the apartment." could refer to more than one place. But other times we are deliberately vague. When a friend asks what you think of an awful outfit, you could say, "It's really unusual—one of a kind!" Likewise, if you are too angry to accept a friend's apology, but don't want to appear petty, you might say, "Don't mention it."

The value of equivocation becomes clear when you consider the alternatives. Consider the dilemma of what to say when you have been given an unwanted present—an ugly painting, for example—and the giver asks what you think of it. How can you respond?

Table 2.3 ● Some Reasons for Lying

Reason	Example
To save face for self.	"Oh, I never got that shower invitation!"
To save face for others.	"Don't worry about forgetting my get-together. It really was no big deal."
To acquire resources.	"Oh, please let me add this class. If I don't get in, I'll never graduate on time!"
To protect resources.	"I'd like to lend you the money, but I'm short myself."
To initiate and continue interaction.	"Excuse me, I'm lost. Do you live around here?"
To avoid conflict.	"It's not a big deal. We can do it your way. Really."
To avoid interaction.	"That sounds like fun, but I'm busy Saturday night."
To be able to leave.	"Oh, look what time it is! I've got to run!"
To present a competent image.	"Sure I understand. No problem."
To increase social desirability.	"Yes, I've done a fair amount of skiing."
To exaggerate.	"You think this is cold? Let me tell you about how cold it was on that trip . . ."

SOURCE: Adapted from categories originally presented in C. Camden, M.T. Motley, and A. Wilson (1984), "White lies in interpersonal communication: A taxonomy and preliminary investigation of social motivations," *Western journal of speech communication, 48,* 315.

Focus on RESEARCH

WHAT IS A LIE, AND WHEN IS IT A GOOD THING?
CROSS-CULTURAL COMPARISONS

In a fascinating study, investigators from Canada and the People's Republic of China explored adults' concepts about lying and the truth (Fu et al., 2001, 2010). Their purpose was to further examine the findings of a previous study (Lee et al., 1997), in which Chinese and Canadian children had been told stories about characters who did pro-social or anti-social deeds. The children were then questioned by their teachers about what the characters had done. The Chinese children evaluated the characters who lied about their pro-social deeds more favourably than the characters who told the truth about their pro-social deeds. In contrast, the Canadian children evaluated the characters who told the truth about their pro-social deeds more favourably than the characters who lied. Lee and his colleagues (1997) suggested the Chinese children were influenced by the emphasis in their culture on modesty and self-effacement. These children believed that lying for reasons of modesty was a good thing and that telling the truth about good deeds was morally undesirable. The older the Chinese children were, the more likely they were to evaluate lying to hide one's good deeds as positive and telling the truth about one's good deed as undesirable.

Fu and colleagues (2001; Xu et al., 2009) wondered whether these same differences, in evaluating the morality of lying, between Asian and Western children would hold up for Asian and Western adults. They conducted a very similar experiment with Canadian and Chinese adults. Like the Chinese children, the Chinese adults evaluated the character of the person who lied about doing a pro-social act more favourably than the character of the person who told the truth. However, unlike the children, the Chinese adults considered the untruthful statements made to conceal the person's own good deeds not to be lies. Almost all the Canadian adults considered these untruthful statements to be lies, as did almost all the Canadian and Chinese children in the previous study.

This series of studies was the first to find evidence that concepts of lying may not be universal and may be determined by social-cultural conventions. In this instance, the untruthful statement may not be considered a lie because it serves a highly valued virtue in Chinese collectivistic culture—modesty. Modesty is important for maintaining group cohesiveness and harmony. The conclusions that came from these studies clearly support the notion that conceptualizations and evaluations of lying are not universal and continue to develop well into adulthood.

Critical thinking: *What other communication strategies discussed in this chapter might be evaluated differently depending on an individual's individualist-collectivist values? How would they be different?*

On the one hand, you need to choose between telling the truth and lying. At the same time, you have a choice of whether to make your response clear or vague. Figure 2.6 displays these choices.

After considering the alternatives, we clearly see that the first option—an equivocal, true response—is far preferable to the other choices in several respects. Mainly, because it spares the receiver embarrassment. Rather than flatly saying no to an unappealing invitation, it may be kinder to say, "I have other plans"—even if those plans are to stay home and watch television.

A study by Sandra Metts and her colleagues (1992) shows how equivocation can save face in difficult situations. Several hundred college students were asked how they would turn down unwanted sexual overtures from a person whose feelings were important to them: a close friend, a prospective date, or a dating partner. The majority of students chose a diplomatic reaction ("I just don't think I'm ready for this right now") as being more face-saving and comfortable than a direct statement like "I just don't feel sexually attracted to you." The diplomatic reaction seemed sufficiently clear to get the message across, but

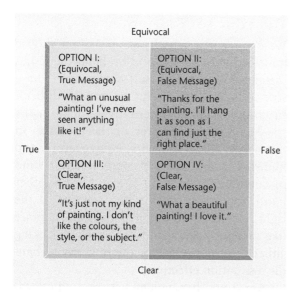

Figure 2.6 ● Dimensions of Truthfulness and Equivocation

not so blunt as to embarrass or humiliate the other person.

As Bavelas and colleagues (1990, p. 171) put it, "Equivocation is neither a false message nor a clear truth, but rather an alternative used precisely when both of these are to be avoided."

In addition to preventing dishonesty, saving face, and minimizing stress, equivocation can be quite effective at making a point. Renee Edwards and Richard Bello (2001) explored how receivers interpreted equivocal statements, such as being told by a friend that his or her speech was "interesting" instead of being told, "You messed up." Besides regarding the equivocal statements as more polite, they had no trouble discerning the intended meaning—that the speech was poor.

Given these advantages, it is not surprising that most people will usually choose to equivocate rather than tell a lie. In a series of experiments, subjects chose between telling a face-saving lie, the truth, and equivocating (Bavelas et al., 1990). Only 6 per cent chose the lie, and between 3 and 4 per cent chose the hurtful truth. By contrast, more than 90 per cent chose the equivocal response. People may say they prefer telling the truth to equivocating, but given the choice, they prefer to finesse the truth (Robinson et al., 1998).

Hinting

Hints are more direct than equivocal statements. Whereas an equivocal message is not necessarily aimed at changing another's behaviour, a hint seeks to get the desired response from the other person. As Michael Motley (1992) suggests, some hints are designed to save the receiver from embarrassment. For example:

Direct Statement	Face-Saving Hint
You're too overweight to be ordering dessert.	These desserts are terribly overpriced.
I'm too busy to continue with this conversation. I wish you would let me go.	I know you're busy; I'd better let you go.

Other hints are less concerned with protecting the receiver than with saving the sender from embarrassment, such as:

Direct Statement	Face-Saving Hint
Please don't smoke here; it bothers me.	I'm pretty sure that smoking isn't permitted here.
I'd like to invite you out for lunch, but I don't want to risk a "no" answer to my invitation.	Gee, it's almost lunch time. Have you ever eaten at that new Italian restaurant around the corner?

The success of a hint depends on the other person's ability to pick up the unexpressed message. Your subtle remarks may go right over the head of an insensitive receiver or one who chooses not to respond to them. If this happens, you still have the choice to be more direct. If the costs of a straightforward message seem too high, you can withdraw without risk.

Alternatives to Self-Disclosure

- **Silence or secrecy:** saying nothing.
- **Lying:** deliberately attempting to hide or misrepresent the truth.
- **Equivocation:** giving a response that has two or more equally plausible meanings.
- **Hinting:** making a face-saving remark designed to get a desired response.

The Ethics of Evasion

We can clearly see why people often choose hints, equivocations, and/or benevolent lies instead of complete self-disclosure. These strategies are easier ways to manage difficult situations than the alternatives for both the speaker and the receiver of the message. In this sense, successful liars, equivocators, and hinters can be said to possess a certain kind of communicative competence. On the other hand, there *are* times when honesty is the right approach, even if it is painful. At times like these, evaders could be viewed as lacking either the competence or the integrity to handle a situation effectively.

Are hints, benevolent lies, and equivocations ethical alternatives to self-disclosure? Some of the examples in these pages suggest the answer is a qualified yes. Many social scientists and philosophers agree. For example, researchers David Buller and Judee Burgoon (1994) argue that the morality of a speaker's motives for lying, not the deceptive act itself, ought to be judged. Another approach is to consider whether the effects of a lie will be worth the deception. Ethicist Sissela Bok (1978) says deception may be justified if it does good things, prevents harm, and/or protects a larger truth. Perhaps the right questions to ask, then, are whether an indirect message is truly in the interests of the receiver, and whether this sort of evasion is the only effective way to behave. Bok suggests another way to check the justifiability of a lie: imagine how others would respond if they knew what you were really thinking or feeling. Would they accept your reasons for not telling the truth?

Guidelines for Self-Disclosure

Self-disclosure is a special kind of sharing that is not desirable in every situation. Let us look at some guidelines that can help you recognize

Building WORK SKILLS

DISCLOSURE AT WORK

Imagine a situation at work where you have made a mistake. Imagine that part of the reason for your error is related to something personal (for example, a conflict in a relationship, a disability you have, or a bias you have). In order for the problem to be corrected, you need to tell either your co-worker, or your boss or supervisor. Whom would you tell? What would you say? How much information would you reveal? Describe the risks and benefits of the choices you made. Share your approach and list of the risks and benefits with a classmate. Does he or she agree with your analysis? Why or why not?

how to express yourself in a way that's rewarding for you and for the others involved.

Is the Other Person Important to You?

There are several ways in which someone might be important. Perhaps you have an ongoing relationship deep enough that sharing significant parts of yourself justifies keeping your present level of togetherness intact. Or perhaps the other person is someone you know, but not intimately. Now you see a chance to grow closer, and disclosure may be the path toward developing that personal relationship.

Is the Risk of Disclosing Reasonable?

Most people intuitively calculate the potential benefits of disclosing against the risks of doing so (Fisher, 1986; Vangelisti et al., 2001). This approach makes sense. Even if the probable benefits are great, opening yourself up to almost certain rejection may be asking for trouble. For instance, it might be foolhardy to share your important feelings with someone who is likely to betray your confidences or ridicule them. On the other hand, knowing that your partner will respect the information makes the prospect of speaking out more reasonable.

Revealing personal thoughts and feelings can be especially risky on the job (Eisenberg, 1990; Eisenberg and Witten, 1987). The politics of the workplace sometimes require communicators to keep their feelings to themselves in order to accomplish both personal and organizational goals. You may find the opinions of a boss or customer personally offensive, but decide to bite your tongue rather than risk your job or lose goodwill for the company.

REFLECTION

EQUIVOCATION PROVIDES COMFORT

My mother made her share of mistakes in raising my sisters and me. Now, her health is failing and I am aware that every conversation we have may be our last one.

My mom is understandably scared of death and in need of comfort. Last week, I told her, "You have taught me a lot about being a mother." I didn't tell her that many of the lessons I learned from her taught me what not to do when I have daughters of my own.

My vagueness wasn't a lie, but it wasn't the entire truth either. I'm comfortable with my equivocation here. This is no time for complete, brutal honesty.

Is the Self-Disclosure Appropriate?

It is important, and quite interesting, to recognize that revealing your emotions and thoughts to others activates the same reward centres in

© iStockPhoto/Susan Chiang.

Self-disclosure has its risks and rewards. When has disclosing something about yourself helped a relationship you've had? When has it hurt a relationship?

the brain that are activated by food and sex (Tamir and Mitchell, 2012). However, while self-disclosure is intrinsically rewarding, it is not always the best course of action. Generally, it is not wise to reveal highly personal secrets in public forums such as in classrooms or on social media sites. One of the problems with online communication is that the experience of being online (often in a private place such as your home) is not the same reality as is found on the Internet, where privacy settings can and are breached, and monitoring by companies and third parties is routine. As the saying goes, "If you are not paying for something, you are not the customer; you're the product being sold." On the other hand, sharing personal information in private settings is part of relationship development and can promote trust and intimacy (Greene et al. 2006).

But even during a phase of high disclosure, sharing *everything* about yourself isn't necessarily constructive. Self-disclosure is not an all-or-nothing proposition. It's possible to reveal information in some situations and keep it to yourself in others. In any case, disclosure should be relevant and appropriate to the situation at hand.

Is the Disclosure Reciprocated?

There is nothing quite as disconcerting as talking your heart out to someone, only to discover that the other person has yet to say anything to you that is even half as revealing. You think to yourself, "What am I doing?" Unequal self-disclosure creates an unbalanced relationship, one with potential problems.

The reciprocal nature of effective disclosure doesn't mean that you are obliged to match every one of another person's revelations. In order to maintain mutual investment in a relationship, disclosure needs to be balanced over time.

Will the Effect Be Constructive?

Self-disclosure can be a vicious tool if it is not used carefully. Every person has a psychological boundary to subjects that are extremely sensitive to them. Intruding in that area is a sure way to disable another person, and usually at a great cost to the relationship. It's important to consider the effects of your candour before opening up to others. Comments such as "I've always thought you were pretty unintelligent," or "Last year, I made love to your best friend," may sometimes resolve old business and thus be constructive, but they can also be devastating—to the listener, to the relationship, and to your self-esteem.

✓ CHECK IT!

Describe the six factors you need to consider before disclosing information about yourself to others.

SUMMARY

The self-concept is a relatively stable set of views that people hold about themselves. It begins to develop soon after birth, being shaped by the appraisals of significant others and by social comparisons with reference groups. The self-concept develops in the context of the larger social–cultural environment. Language affects the development of our self-concept, as do a number of cultural values. The most fundamental of these values is a culture's individualistic–collectivistic orientation. The self-concept is subjective and can be substantially different from the way a person is perceived by others. Although the self may evolve, the self-concept resists change.

A self-fulfilling prophecy occurs when a person's expectations of an event influence the outcome. A prophecy can consist of predictions (positive or negative) by others, or it may be self-imposed. It is possible to change one's self-concept in ways that lead to more effective communication. Identity management consists of an individual's strategic communication designed to influence other people's perceptions. Identity management aims at presenting one or more faces to others, which may be different from the spontaneous behaviour that takes place in private. Some communicators are high self-monitors who are very conscious of their own behaviour, while others are less aware of how their words and actions affect others.

Communicating through mediated channels can enhance a person's ability to manage impressions. Since each person has a variety of faces that she or he can reveal, choosing which one to present is a central concern of competent communicators.

Self-disclosure consists of honest, revealing messages about the self that are intentionally directed toward others. Disclosed communication contains information that is generally unavailable from other sources. The percentage of messages that are truly self-disclosing is relatively low.

Two models for examining self-disclosure in relationships are the social penetration model and the Johari Window. The social penetration model describes two dimensions of self-disclosure: breadth and depth. The Johari Window uses four window panes to illustrate how much information a person reveals to others, hides, is blind to, and is unaware of.

Communicators choose to disclose or not to disclose personal information for a variety of reasons. Four alternatives to revealing self-disclosures are silence, lies, equivocations, and hints. When deciding whether or not to disclose, communicators should consider a variety of factors, such as the importance of the other person to them; the risk involved; and the appropriateness, relevance, and constructiveness of the disclosure.

MULTIPLE-CHOICE QUESTIONS

1. What is a relatively stable set of perceptions you hold about yourself called?
   a. significant other
   b. self-esteem
   c. self-concept
   d. self-control
2. What are the two theories that explain how social interaction shapes the self-concept?

   a. reflected appraisal and social comparison
   b. reflected appraisal and self-control
   c. reference groups and significant others
   d. power distance and uncertainty avoidance
3. A cultural group whose members value group consensus and cohesion and

feel strong obligations to fellow group members could described as

a. collectivistic.
b. resistant.
c. avoidant.
d. individualistic.

4. Which of the following statements about the self-concept is true?
   a. The self-concept changes easily.
   b. The self-concept is subjective.
   c. The self-concept is unaffected by social expectations.
   d. The self-concept is based entirely on obsolete information.

5. Rose is nervous about her job interview and has convinced herself that she will not do well. Her nervousness causes her to be tongue-tied during the interview and she does not impress the employer. Rose's expectations and subsequent behaviour demonstrate the power of
   a. reference groups.
   b. the myth of perfection.
   c. distorted feedback.
   d. self-fulfilling prophecies.

6. The person you believe yourself to be at moments of private self-examination is called the perceived self.
   a. true

b. false

7. Which of the following statements about identity management is true?
   a. We strive to construct a single, coherent identity.
   b. Identity management is done privately.
   c. People differ in the degree of identity management.
   d. Identity management is always deliberate.

8. Computer-mediated communication has very limited potential for identity management.
   a. true
   b. false

9. When we manage our identities through face-to-face interactions with other people we can
   a. change our manner (words and non-verbal actions).
   b. change our appearance.
   c. change the setting.
   d. all of the above.

10. It is an oversimplification to say there is only one honest way to behave in each circumstance.
    a. true
    b. false

Answers: 1. c; 2. a; 3. a; 4. b; 5. d; 6. a; 7. c; 8. b; 9. d; 10. a

ACTIVITIES

1. Invitation to Insight

What reference groups do you use to define your self-concept? You can recognize your social comparison groups by answering the following questions:

a. Select one area in which you compare yourself to others. In what area is the comparison made? (For example, is the comparison based on wealth, intelligence, social skill?)
b. In the selected area, ask yourself, "Which people am I better or worse than?"
c. In the selected area, ask yourself, "Which people am I the same as or different from?"

What is the effect of using these groups as a basis for judging yourself? How might you view yourself differently if you used other reference groups as a basis for comparison?

2. Invitation to Insight

Describe two incidents in which self-fulfilling prophecies you imposed on yourself affected your communication. Explain how each of these predictions shaped your behaviour, and describe how you might have behaved differently if you had made a different prediction.

3. Critical Thinking Probe

What social forces affect the development of self-concept in childhood and beyond? To what degree do these forces contribute to healthy or unhealthy self-concepts? Use three specific messages to illustrate your answers. Then, discuss how individuals can reduce the effect of unhealthy forces in their everyday lives.

4. Skill Builder

Describe one communication-related part of your self-concept you would like to change. Use the guidelines on pages 51–53 to describe how you could make that change. Also keep in mind:

a. Decide whether your expectations for change are realistic. Don't expect to become a new person; it should be enough to become a better one.

b. Recognize your strengths as well as your shortcomings. You may not be as bad as you think you are!

c. Decide whether you are willing to make the necessary effort to change. Good intentions are an important start, but hard work is also necessary.

d. Develop a specific plan to change the way you behave. You may want to consult books and experts as well as to observe models to gain a clear idea of your new goals and how to achieve them.

5. Skill Builder

a. Make a list of some personal information you have not shared with a family member. Then, make a second list of information you haven't disclosed to a friend.

b. For each item on your lists, consider the worst consequences if you were to reveal this information and the best possible consequences from disclosing this information

c. Evaluate the most likely outcome if you were to disclose, and then conduct a risk–benefit analysis to decide whether or not to keep the information private or share it.

6. Ethical Challenge

You can gain a clearer sense of the ethical implications of impression management by following these directions:

a. Make a list of the different presenting selves you try to communicate at school or work, to family members, to friends, and to various types of strangers—in either face-to-face communication or by computer-mediated communication.

b. Which of these selves are honest, and which are deceptive?

c. Are any deceptive impressions you try to create justified? What would be the consequences of being completely candid in the situations you have described?

Referring to your answers to these questions, develop a set of guidelines to distinguish ethical and unethical impression management.

7. Ethical Challenge

For each of the following evasive approaches, recall a recent situation in which you used that approach: silence, benevolent lying, equivocating, and hinting. Write an anonymous description of each situation on a separate sheet of paper. Submit the cases to a panel of "judges" (most likely fellow students), who will use the criteria of justifiable motives and desirable effects to evaluate the morality of this deception. Invite the "judges" to consider how they would feel if they knew that someone used these evasive approaches with them.

8. Role Play

With a partner, imagine yourselves in each of the following situations. Choose your respective parts in each scenario, and then choose the most effective way you could act. Role-play your choices.

a. You offer to teach a friend a new skill, such as playing the guitar, using a computer program, or sharpening up a tennis backhand. Your friend is making slow progress, and you find yourself growing impatient.

b. At a party, you meet someone you find very attractive, and you are pretty sure that the feeling is mutual. You feel an obligation to spend most of your time with the person you came with, but the opportunity here is very appealing.

c. At work, you face a belligerent customer. You don't believe that anyone has the right to treat you this way.

d. A friend or family member makes a joke about your appearance that hurts your feelings. You aren't sure whether or not to make an issue of the remark or to pretend that it doesn't bother you.

DISCUSSION QUESTIONS

1. What is the difference between self-concept and self-esteem? How does each affect interpersonal communication?

2. Are language and culture important in the development of one's self-concept? Why or why not?

3. Given the characteristics of self-concept, how amenable is it to change? Support your position by referring both to the characteristics of the self-concept and to the guidelines for changing the self-concept.

4. Where do you draw the line between identity management as competent communication and dishonest manipulation? Support your position by referring to arguments presented in this chapter.

5. What are the risks and benefits of lying?

6. How are lying, silence, hinting, and equivocation different? Are they morally different?

JOURNAL IDEAS

1. Create a list of words or a collage of pictures (or a bit of both) that represents aspects of your self-concept that you present to others (presenting self). Create a second word list or collage that represents your private self. How did you learn about these aspects of yourself? Consider the processes of reflected appraisal and social comparison in your analysis—who are your significant others and reference groups? How accurate is this representation? What are possible reasons for an inaccurate assessment?

2. Recall a couple of times when you disclosed personal information with very different outcomes (one positive situation and one negative situation). Review the guidelines for self-disclosure (found on page 76) to analyze each situation and the different outcomes.

3

Perceiving Others

Chapter Outline

Key Terms

achievement culture
androgynous
attribution
confirmation bias
empathy
fundamental attribution
   error
gender
halo effect
interpretation
narratives

negotiation
nurturing culture
organization
perception checking
power distance
psychological sex type
punctuation
selection
self-serving bias
standpoint theory
uncertainty avoidance

Learning Objectives

YOU SHOULD UNDERSTAND:

- how the processes of selection, organization, interpretation, and negotiation affect a communicator's perception of others;
- how physiological, psychological, social, and cultural factors lead communicators to perceive one another and other phenomena differently;
- the common tendencies in perception that can sometimes lead to misperceptions; and
- the value of empathy in interpersonal communication and relationships.

YOU SHOULD BE ABLE TO:

- describe the factors that shape your perceptions of important people and events, and explain how these and other factors could lead another person to perceive the same people and events differently;
- describe an interpersonal issue from the other person's point of view, showing how and why the other person experiences the issue differently; and
- use perception checking to clarify your understanding of another person's point of view.

"Look at it my way."

"Put yourself in my shoes."

"YOU DON'T UNDERSTAND ME!"

Statements like these reflect one of the most common communication challenges. We can talk to (or at) one another until we're hoarse and exhausted, yet we still do not really understand one another. In fact, research has found that typical dyads can interpret and explain only 25 to 50 per cent of each other's behaviour accurately (Spitzberg, 1994), and that spouses consistently overestimate the degree to which they agree with their partners (Sillars et al., 1992). Some communication scholars (e.g., Eisenberg and Goodall, 2001) have suggested that complete understanding could lead to more disagreement and dissatisfaction, not smoother relationships. Nonetheless, failing to share each other's view of the world can leave us feeling isolated and frustrated, despairing that our words don't seem able to convey the depth and complexity of what we think and feel.

Just like the boxes in Figure 3.1, virtually every interpersonal situation can be seen from many points of view. Take a minute to study that figure. How many ways can you discover to view this image? If you see only one or two, keep looking. (You can see at least four ways of viewing the image by looking at Figure 3.2.) If it is hard to make quick and accurate sense of simple drawings, imagine the challenge involved in trying to understand the perspectives of other human beings, who are far more complex and multi-dimensional.

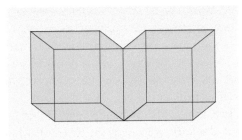

Figure 3.1 ● Two Cubes Touching

In this chapter, we provide tools for communicating in the face of perceptual differences. We begin by examining some of the many reasons why the world appears so different to each of us. After examining the perceptual factors that make understanding so difficult, we will look at tools for bridging the perceptual gap.

The Perception Process

How do we make sense of the world? How do our perceptions affect our communication with others? Recall from the communication model presented in Chapter 1, meanings exist in and among people. Each of us actively constructs our own reality. So, how do we do this? We will begin to answer these questions by taking a look at the steps by which we attach meanings to our experiences: selection, organization, interpretation, and negotiation.

Selection

Since we are exposed to more input than we can possibly manage, the first step in perception is the **selection** of which data we will attend to. There are several factors that cause us to notice some messages and ignore others.

Stimuli that are *intense* often attract our attention. Something that is louder, larger, or brighter stands out. This explains why—other things being equal—we are more likely to remember extremely tall or short people, and why someone who laughs or talks loudly at a party attracts more attention (although not always favourable) than quieter guests do.

Repetitious stimuli, repetitious stimuli, repetitious stimuli, repetitious stimuli, repetitious stimuli, repetitious stimuli also attract attention.* Just as a quiet, but steadily dripping tap can come to dominate our awareness, people to whom we are often exposed will become noticeable.

---

*The graphic demonstrations of factors influencing perception in this and the following paragraphs are borrowed from D. Coon (2001), *Psychology: Gateways to mind and behaviour*, 9th edn. Belmont, CA: Wadsworth.

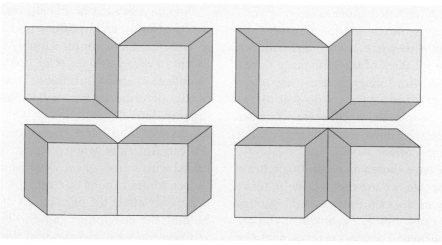

Figure 3.2 ● Four Ways of Viewing Two Cubes Touching

Attention is also frequently related to contrast or change in stimulation. Put differently, unchanging people or things become less noticeable. This principle offers an explanation (or possibly an excuse?) for why we take consistently wonderful people for granted if we see them often. Many times it's only when they go away—or stop being so wonderful—that we appreciate them.

Motives also determine how we perceive people. For example, someone on the lookout for a romantic adventure will be especially aware of attractive potential partners, whereas the same person in an emergency might be oblivious to anyone, but the police or medical personnel.

Our *emotional state*, as well, shapes what we select. Paula Neidenthal and her colleagues (2001) discovered that our mood affects our ability to detect other people's emotional states. They discovered that people in a happy mood were quick to notice when happy-appearing characters in a film appeared sadder, whereas unhappy subjects were quicker at noticing when sad characters appeared happier.

Organization

After selecting information from the environment, we must arrange it in some meaningful way in order to make sense of the world. We call this stage **organization**. The raw sense data we perceive can be organized in more than one way. (See Figure 3.2 for a visual example of this principle.) We do this by using *perceptual schema*, which are cognitive frameworks that allow us to give order to the information we have selected (Macrae and Bodenhausen, 2001).

Organizing Perceptions of People

We use four types of schema to classify other people (Andersen, 1991; Freeman and Ambady, 2011). As you read about each one, think about how you use it to organize your perceptions. *Physical constructs* classify people according to their appearance and the way they sound: fat or thin, accent or no accent, young or old, and so on. *Role constructs* use social position, such as student, lawyer, and spouse. *Interaction constructs* focus on social behaviour: friendly, helpful, aloof, and sarcastic, for example. The final organizing scheme uses *psychological constructs*: generous, nervous, insecure, and so on.

The kinds of constructs we use strongly affect the way we relate to others. Katherine Kinzler and her colleagues (2009) found that when shown only photographs of unfamiliar children, five-year-olds chose same-race children as friends, but when the photographs were paired with voice recordings, children chose native speakers of their language rather than children with foreign accents, regardless of their race. What constructs do you use to classify the people you encounter? Consider how your relationships might change if you used different schema.

Once we have chosen an organizing scheme to classify people, we use that scheme to make generalizations about members of the groups who fit our categories. For example, if you are especially aware of a person's sex, you might be alert to the differences between the way men and women behave or the way they are treated. If religion plays an important part in your life, you might think of members of your faith differently than you do of others. If ethnicity is important for you, you probably notice the differences between members of various ethnic groups. There's nothing wrong with making generalizations—in fact, it would be impossible to get through life without them—but they need to be made accurately. When generalizations lose touch with reality, they lead to stereotyping. Stereotypes may be based on a kernel of truth, but they go beyond the facts at hand and make claims that usually have no valid basis.

Two characteristics distinguish stereotypes from reasonable generalizations. The first involves *categorizing others on the basis of easily recognized, but not necessarily important characteristics.* For example, perhaps the first thing you notice about a person is the colour of her skin—but that may not be nearly as significant as the person's intelligence or achievements. The second feature that characterizes stereotypes is *ascribing a set of characteristics to most or all members of a group.* For example, you might unfairly assume that all older people are doddering or that all men are insensitive to women's concerns. When we apply these generalizations to an individual, our attitude would be described as prejudiced (recall from Chapter 1 that the root term in *prejudice* is "pre-judge").

Stereotypes exist in all cultures around the world (Cuddy et al., 2009) and can plague intercultural communication (Allen, 1995; Buttny, 1997; Kashima et al., 2013). Surveys of college students' attitudes show that many blacks describe whites as "demanding" and "manipulative," while many whites describe blacks as "loud" and "ostentatious." Many African American women report having been raised with stereotypical views of whites (e.g., "most whites cannot be trusted"). Stereotypes don't only affect the perceptions of the person holding the belief, they can also influence the self-perceptions of the target of the stereotype. For instance, a Canadian lawyer recalled being the only black person at a social function and feeling torn about having some watermelon. "I should have no issue with walking up to that table and having a big piece of watermelon, but I found myself questioning that, well, what will it look like, how will it be perceived and that's a dilemma that Black people face a lot of the time" (Gosine, 2008, p. 320).

By adulthood, we tend to engage in stereotyping frequently, effortlessly, and often unconsciously (Zenmore et al., 2000). Once we create and hold stereotypes, we seek out information that supports our inaccurate beliefs (Kashima et al., 2013). Interpersonal communication has been found to play a role in stereotype maintenance. For example, researchers have found that when people are relaying stories to each other they tend to communicate information that is consistent with our stereotypes and leave out information that is inconsistent with our stereotypes (e.g., gossip, news, reports of their own experiences, and even children's stories) (Lyons and Kashima, 2003, 2006).

One way to avoid the kinds of communication problems that come from excessive stereotyping

 CHECK IT!

What are stereotypes and how are they different from other generalizations we make about people?

is to "de-categorize" others, giving yourself a chance to treat people as individuals instead of assuming that they possess the same characteristics as every other member of the group to which you assign them.

Organizing Perceptions of Events

Perceptual differences do not involve only the general categories we use to classify other people. We can also organize specific communication transactions in different ways, and these differing

How can we work to "de-categorize" our views of others?

organizational schemes can have a powerful effect on our relationships. Communication theorists have used the term **punctuation** to describe the determination of causes and effects in a series of interactions (Watzlawick et al., 1967). You can begin to understand how punctuation operates by visualizing a running quarrel between a husband and wife. The husband accuses the wife of being a nag, while she complains that he is withdrawing from her. Notice that the order in which each partner punctuates this cycle affects how the dispute looks. The husband begins by blaming the wife: "I withdraw because you nag." The wife organizes the situation differently, starting with the husband: "I nag because you withdraw." Once the cycle gets rolling, it is impossible to say which accusation is accurate, as Figure 3.3 shows. The answer depends on how the sequence is punctuated.

Anyone who has seen two children argue about "who started it" can understand that squabbling over causes and effects is not likely to solve a conflict. In fact, the kind of finger-pointing that goes along with assigning blame will probably make matters worse. Rather than arguing about whose punctuation of an event is correct, it's far more productive to recognize that a dispute can look different

to each party and then move on to the more important question: "What can we do to make things better?"

Interpretation

Once we have selected and organized our perceptions, we interpret them in a way that

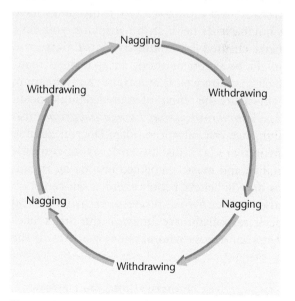

Figure 3.3 ● Communication Sequence

The way a communication sequence is punctuated affects its perceived meaning. Which comes first, the nagging or the withdrawing?

makes some sort of sense. **Interpretation** is part of almost every interpersonal act. Is the person who smiles at you across a crowded room interested in romance or simply being polite? Is a friend's kidding a sign of affection or irritation? Should you take an invitation to "drop by any time" literally or not?

There are several things that cause us to interpret a person's behaviour in one way or another. The first is our *degree of involvement* with the person. For example, research suggests that we tend to view people with whom we have—or seek to have—a relationship more favourably than those whom we observe from a detached perspective (Manusov, 1993; Neuliep and Grohskopf, 2000).

Relational satisfaction is a second factor that influences our interpretation. The behaviour that seems desirable when you are happy with a partner might seem completely different when the relationship isn't satisfying. For example, couples in unsatisfying relationships are more likely than satisfied partners to blame one another when things go wrong (Bradbury and Fincham, 1990; Manusov, 1993).

A third factor that influences interpretations is *past experience*. What meanings have similar events held? If, for instance, you have been cheated by landlords in the past, you might be skeptical about an apartment manager's assurances that careful housekeeping will ensure the refund of your cleaning deposit.

Assumptions about human behaviour also influence our interpretations. Do you assume people are lazy, dislike work, avoid responsibility, and must be coerced into doing things, or do you believe people exercise self-direction and self-control, possess creativity, and seek responsibility? Imagine the differences between a boss who assumes workers fit the first description and one who assumes they fit the second (McGregor, 1960; Neuliep, 1996).

Expectations make up another factor that shapes our interpretations. For example, insecure people with low self-esteem who expect their friends to view them as vulnerable and insecure perceive their friends' honest and genuine behaviour as less authentic (perpetuating their insecurities) than do confident people without such expectations (Lemay and Dudley, 2009). *Knowledge of others* also affects the way we interpret their actions. For instance, if you know a friend has just been jilted by a lover or fired from a job, you'll interpret his aloofness differently than if you were unaware of what happened. If you know an instructor is rude to all students, you will be unlikely to take her remarks personally.

Although we have talked about selection, organization, and interpretation separately, the three phases of perception can occur in different sequences. For example, a parent's or babysitter's past interpretations (such as "Jason is a troublemaker") can influence future selections (his behaviour becomes especially noticeable)

REFLECTION

PROBLEMATIC PUNCTUATION

When I was living with my parents, my father was always asking where I was going or where I had been. I interpreted his questions as too nosy, and I usually responded with hostility or silence. This made him even more concerned about what I was doing.

Now, I recognize that each of us was punctuating this situation differently. He saw me as being the problem: "I ask you what you are doing because you never tell me." I saw him as the cause of the problem: "I never tell you what I'm doing because you are always pestering me." Who started the cycle? Either way, we both lost. I have come to realize how hanging onto our different ways of punctuating the situation kept us from understanding one another.

TAKE TWO

Punctuation: the determination of causes and effects in a series of interactions.

and the organization of events (when there's a fight, the assumption is that Jason started it). Like all communication, perception is an ongoing process in which it is hard to pin down the beginnings and endings.

Negotiation

In Chapter 1 you read that meaning is created both *in* and *among* people. So far, our discussion has focused on the inner components of perception—selection, organization, and interpretation—that take place in each individual's mind. Now, we need to examine the part of our sense-making that occurs *among* people. The process by which communicators influence one another's perceptions through communication is known as **negotiation.**

One way to explain negotiation is to view interpersonal communication as the exchange of stories. Scholars call the stories we use to describe our personal worlds **narratives** (McLean and Fournier, 2008; Shaw, 1997). Just as the cubes in Figure 3.1 (on page 86) can be viewed in several ways, almost every interpersonal situation can be described by more than one narrative. These narratives often differ. Some political liberals refer to conservatives as heartless, whereas conservatives call their liberal critics unrealistic. Children may say their parents are too controlling, while the parents talk about their children as irresponsible and naive. People who value cleanliness and order may label their housemates as dirty and sloppy, while those housemates would likely describe a concern for tidiness as obsessive. When our narratives clash with those of others, we can either hang onto our own point of view, and refuse to consider anyone else's (usually not productive), or try to negotiate a narrative that creates at least some common ground.

CHECK IT!

Describe the factors that influence the way we interpret human behaviour.

The best chance for smooth communication is to have shared narratives. For example, romantic partners who celebrate their successful struggles against relational obstacles are happier than those who do not have this shared appreciation (Flora and Segrin, 2000). Likewise, couples who agree about the important turning points in their relationships are more satisfied than those who have different views of what incidents were most important (Baxter and Pittman, 2001).

Shared narratives do not have to be accurate to be powerful (Martz et al., 1998; Murray et al., 1996). Couples who report being happily married after 50 or more years seem to collude in a relational narrative that does not always jibe with the facts. They agree that they rarely have conflicts, although objective analysis reveals that they have had their share of disagreements. Without overtly agreeing to do so, they choose to blame outside forces or unusual circumstances for their problems, instead of blaming each other. They offer the most charitable interpretations of each other's behaviour, believing that their spouse acts with good intentions even when things don't go well. They seem willing to forgive, or even forget transgressions. Examining this research, Judy Pearson asks:

> Should we conclude that happy couples have a poor grip on reality? Perhaps they do, but is the reality of one's marriage better known by outside onlookers than by the players themselves? The conclusion is evident. One key to a long happy marriage is to tell yourself and others that you have one and then to behave as though you do! (Pearson, 2000, p. 186)

Influences on Perception

How we select, organize, interpret, and negotiate data about others is influenced by a variety of factors. Some of our perceptual judgments are affected by physiology, others by cultural and social factors, and still others by psychological factors (Hochberg, 1998).

Physiological Influences

Sometimes, our different perspectives come from our physical environment and the ways that our bodies differ from others.

The Senses

The differences in how each of us sees, hears, tastes, touches, and smells stimuli can affect interpersonal relationships (Clark, 2000). Consider the following everyday situations:

"Turn down the TV! It's going to make me go deaf."

"It's not too loud. If I turn it down, it'll be impossible to hear it."

"It's freezing in here."

"Are you kidding? We'll suffocate if you turn up the heat!"

"Why don't you pass that truck? The highway's clear for half a mile."

"I can't see that far, and I'm not going to get us killed."

These disputes aren't just over matters of opinion. Our reception of sensory data is different. Differences in vision and hearing are the easiest to recognize, but other gaps also exist. There is evidence that identical foods taste different to different people (Bartoshuk, 1980; 2000). Odours that please some people repel others (Montcrieff, 1966). Likewise, temperature variations that are uncomfortable to some of us are inconsequential to others. Remembering these differences won't eliminate them, but it will remind us that other people's preferences aren't crazy, just different.

Age

Older people view the world differently than younger ones because of a greater scope and number of experiences. Developmental differences also shape perceptions. Developmental psychologists (Lourenco and Machado, 1996; Piaget, 1952) describe a series of stages that children pass through on their way to

The Four Steps in Perception

1. **Selection:** the process of determining which information we will pay attention to; influenced by stimuli intensity, repetition, contrast, or change as well as our motives and emotional state.
2. **Organization:** the process by which we arrange information in a meaningful way using perceptual schema (physical, role, interaction, and psychological constructs).
3. **Interpretation:** the process of making sense of perceptions within our own minds.
4. **Negotiation:** the process by which communicators influence one another's perceptions.

adulthood. Younger children are incapable of performing mental feats that are natural to the rest of us. Until they approach the age of seven, for example, they have difficulty taking another person's point of view. This fact helps explain why youngsters often seem egocentric, selfish, and uncooperative. A parent's exasperated, "Can't you see I'm too tired to play?" just won't make sense to a four-year-old full of energy, who imagines that everyone else feels the same as she does.

Health and Fatigue

Think of the last time you came down with a cold, flu, or some other ailment. Do you remember how different you felt? You probably had much less energy than usual. It's likely that you felt less sociable and that your thinking was slower than usual. Such changes have a strong impact on how you relate to others. It's good to realize that someone else may be behaving differently because of illness. In the same way, it is important to let others know when you feel ill so they can give you the understanding you need. Just as illness can affect your relationships, so can excessive fatigue. When you have been working long hours or studying late for an exam, the world can seem quite different than when you are well rested. Lack of sleep negatively affects our moods and our ability to concentrate, and increases our anxiety (Babson et al., 2010). People who are sleep deprived have a reduced frustration tolerance, increased negative mood and perception and greater difficulty processing emotions and using them to make sound judgments (Killgore, 2010). This helps to explain why problems often seem less insurmountable after a good sleep.

Our biological states can strongly affect how we perceive the world. Can you think of a time when your perception was affected by pain or fatigue?

Hunger

Our digestive system often rules our behaviour. Hungry people pay greater attention to food despite their conscious efforts to ignore food-related information and attend to the task at hand (Piech et al., 2010). In addition, being hungry seems to affect our capacity for decision making. Researchers in Israel found that judges' decision making appeared to be influenced by the length of time since they had last eaten (Danzinger et al., 2013). Hunger also appears to be related to a propensity for increased anger and aggression. Brad Bushman and his colleagues (2014) found that when married couples' blood sugar was lower (increased hunger) they were more inclined to behave aggressively toward each other in a laboratory setting (e.g., inflict a loud noise upon each other).

Biological Cycles

Are you a "morning person" or a "night person"? Most of us can answer this question easily, and there's a good physiological reason why. Each of us has a daily cycle in which all sorts of changes constantly occur, including variations in body temperature, sexual drive, alertness, tolerance to stress, and mood (Touitou, 1998; Tsaousis, 2010). We often aren't conscious of these changes, but they can affect the way we relate toward each other. For example, Jeffrey Larson and his associates (1991) discovered that couples with mismatched waking and sleeping patterns (e.g., an evening person and a morning person) reported significantly more conflict, less sexual intimacy, and less time spent conversing on important topics than couples with similar sleeping patterns.

Behavioural Neurological Challenges

There are a wide range of conditions and disorders that affect the brain and nervous system and can cause considerable variation in human perception. These include challenges such as attention deficit disorder and autism spectrum disorder, as well as mental health challenges (e.g., bipolar, schizophrenia) and degenerative conditions (e.g., dementia, Alzheimer's disease). The common element among these challenges is that they involve differences in brain and nervous system functioning. For example,

© CREATISTA/iStockphoto

many people with autism spectrum disorder experience difficulty understanding the actions of others and they often struggle with social relationships. Recent discoveries suggest that these difficulties may be related to differences in mirror neuron system functioning (Greimel et al., 2010; Iacoboni and Dapretto, 2006). Mirror neurons help us understand the actions of others. Not just the "what" of other peoples' behaviour, but the "why" of their actions as well (Pfeifer et al, 2008; Rizzolatti and Craighero, 2004). Understanding other people's intentions and emotions is a key component of interpersonal interaction and a prerequisite for empathy. It may be that people with autism perceive social interactions differently because of differences in their neurology. Similarly, there is evidence to suggest people with Alzheimer's disease experience a variety of brain changes including reduced activation of the mirror neuron system (Lee et al., 2013). As we learn more about the mechanisms and functioning of the human brain involved in social interactions we will get better at understanding individual differences in perception and behaviour.

Psychological Influences

Along with physiology, our psychological state also influences the way we perceive others.

Mood

Our emotional state strongly influences how we view people and events, and, therefore, how we communicate. Sadness, for instance, impairs our ability to accurately interpret social cues (Ambady and Gray, 2002). When we are sad, we are more likely to overanalyze and misinterpret social signals given off by others. An experiment using hypnotism dramatically demonstrated how our varying moods influence our perceptions of events (Lebula and Lucas, 1945). Each subject was shown the same series of six pictures, each time having been put in a different mood. The descriptions of the pictures differed radically depending on the emotional state of the subject. The following examples are from one subject in various emotional states while describing a picture of children digging in a swampy area:

> *Happy mood*: "It looks like fun, reminds me of summer. That's what life is for, working out in the open, really living—digging in the dirt, planting, watching things grow."

> *Anxious mood*: "They're going to get hurt or cut. There should be someone older there who knows what to do in case of an accident. I wonder how deep the water is."

> *Critical mood*: "Pretty horrible land. There ought to be something more useful for kids of that age to do instead of digging in that stuff. It's filthy and dirty and good for nothing."

Such evidence shows that our judgments often say more about our own attitudes than about the other people involved.

Although there's a strong relationship between mood and happiness, it is not clear which comes first—the perceptual outlook or the amount of relational satisfaction. There is some evidence that perception leads to satisfaction rather than the other way around (Fletcher et al., 1987). In other words, the attitude or expectation we bring to a situation shapes our level of happiness or unhappiness. Once started, this process can create a spiral. If you are happy about your relationship, you will be more likely to interpret your partner's behaviour in a charitable way. This, in turn, can lead to greater happiness. Of course, the same process can work in the opposite direction. One remedy for serious distortions—and unnecessary conflicts—is to monitor your own moods. If you are aware of being especially critical or sensitive, you can avoid overreacting to others.

Self-Concept

A second factor that influences perception is the self-concept (Hinde et al., 2001). For example, the recipient's self-concept has

One remedy for serious distortions—and unnecessary conflicts—is to monitor your own moods. What are some things you can do to change your mood in the moment?

proved to be the greatest factor in determining whether people who are being teased interpret the teaser's motives as being friendly or hostile, and whether they respond comfortably or defensively (Alberts et al., 1996). As discussed in Chapter 2, the way we think and feel about ourselves strongly influences how we interpret others' behaviour.

Social Influences

Within any culture, one's personal point of view plays a strong role in shaping perceptions.

Social scientists have developed **standpoint theory** to describe how a person's position in the world shapes his view of society in general and of specific individuals (Harding, 1991; Orbe, 1998). Standpoint theory is most often applied to the difference between the perspectives of privileged social groups and of people who have less power, as well as to the different perspectives of women and men (Dougherty, 2001). Unless one has been disadvantaged, it can be difficult to imagine how different the world might look to someone who has been treated badly because of race, ethnicity, gender, biological sex, sexual orientation, or socio-economic class. After some reflection, though, it is easy to understand how being marginalized can make the world seem like a very different place.

Sex and Gender Roles

Physiological differences aren't the only factors that shape the differing perceptions of men and women. Personal experiences and social expectations are also influential. For example, one study found that women and men judge the same behaviour quite differently. Some types of behaviour that men find innocuous have been judged by women as harassing (Dougherty, 2001). Not surprisingly, much of the difference comes from experience. That is, women who report having been harassed are more likely to find harassment in subsequent interactions (Singer et al., 1998).

Early theorizing by Sandra Bem (1974) suggested that stereotypical masculine and feminine ways of behaving are not opposite poles of a single continuum, but instead are two separate sets of behaviour. With this view, a person—regardless of the person's biological sex—can act in a masculine manner or a feminine manner, or exhibit both types of characteristics. The masculine–feminine dichotomy, then, is replaced with four **psychological sex types**—masculine, feminine, **androgynous** (combining masculine and feminine traits), and undifferentiated (neither masculine nor feminine). The word **gender** is a shorthand term for psychological sex type. Combining the four psychological sex types with the traditional biological sex types produces four categories for men (masculine males, feminine males, androgynous males, and undifferentiated males) and four categories for women

Focus on RESEARCH

DO YOU SEE WHAT I SEE?

Chris Davis, 28 years old, was apprehended last night on charges of domestic abuse. Two police officers arrived at the location of the dispute at 7:05 p.m. At that time they found Robin Brown, 28 years old, Chris's partner, on the living-room couch bleeding with a black eye. Robin reported that Chris had become angry about a telephone call and had begun shouting obscenities and then grabbed, punched, and kicked Robin to the floor before leaving the house.

After reading this report, ask yourself:

- If you had witnessed this interaction between Chris and Robin would you report it to the police?
- Do you think Chris should be convicted of assault?
- As crimes go, how violent was the incident?
- Should Robin leave Chris for good?
- Do you think Chris has acted this way in the past?

Did you assume that Chris was a man and Robin a woman? If you didn't, would your answers be different? What if you found out that Chris and Robin were both men or both women, or if you knew that Robin was a man and Chris was a woman? Nicole Cormier and Michael Woodworth (2008) found that Canadian university students did perceive incidents of intimate partner violence differently when the experimenters varied the genders of the perpetrator

and victim. Cormier and Woodworth presented four identical crime reports to 108 first-year psychology students at a western Canadian university and 62 Canadian police officers. The investigators varied the gender of the perpetrator and victim and discovered that the students perceived the same-sex scenarios (perpetrator and victim—both male or both female) and the less common opposite-sex scenario (i.e., female perpetrator and male victim) to be less abusive than the more common opposite-sex scenario (i.e., female victim and male perpetrator). Students were more likely to report the male perpetrator and female victim scenario to the police and were more likely to believe that the heterosexual male perpetrator should be convicted of assault compared to the other three perpetrators. The students in this study were also more adamant that the heterosexual female victim should leave the relationship compared to the homosexual victims and the heterosexual male victim. Police officers were also influenced by the gender of victim and perpetrator, but significantly less so than the students, and while the police officers were not completely free of bias in their perceptions, they were more inclined to take all forms of abuse more seriously than the students. These researchers point out that gender stereotypes, previous experience, and occupational roles all have a powerful influence on our perceptions.

Critical thinking: *Can you think of other instances where sexual orientation might influence people's perceptions differently, depending on occupational roles?*

(masculine females, feminine females, androgynous females, and undifferentiated females). Although there are women and men who fit into each category, in general, people see themselves as either sex-typed (masculine male or feminine female) or androgynous (Korabik and McCreary, 2000).

A person categorized in one of these eight combined psychological–biological sex types perceives interpersonal relationships differently from someone in another category. For

example, masculine males probably see their interpersonal relationships as opportunities for competitive interaction, as opportunities to win something. Feminine females probably see their interpersonal relationships as opportunities to be nurturing, to express their feelings and emotions. Androgynous males and females, on the other hand, probably differ little in their perceptions of their interpersonal relationships.

Androgynous individuals tend to see their relationships as opportunities to behave in a

variety of ways, depending on the nature of the relationships themselves, the context in which a particular relationship takes place, and the myriad other variables affecting what might constitute appropriate behaviour. These variables are usually ignored by the sex-typed masculine males and feminine females, who have a smaller repertoire of behaviour.

Occupational Roles

The kind of work we do also governs our view of the world. Imagine five people taking a walk through a park. One, a botanist, is fascinated by the variety of trees and plants. Another, a zoologist, is on the lookout for interesting animals. The third, a meteorologist, keeps an eye on the sky, noticing changes in the weather. The fourth, a psychologist, is totally unaware of nature, concentrating instead on the interactions among the people in the park. The fifth, a pickpocket, quickly takes advantage of the others' absorption to collect their wallets. There are two lessons in this little story. The first, of course, is to watch your wallet carefully. The second is that our occupational roles often govern our perceptions.

Perhaps the most dramatic illustration of how occupational roles shape perception occurred in the early 1970s. Stanford University psychologist Philip Zimbardo (1971; Haney and Zimbardo, 2009) recruited a group of well-educated, middle-class young men. He randomly chose 11 to serve as "guards" in a mock prison set up in the basement of Stanford's psychology building. He issued uniforms, handcuffs, whistles, and billy clubs to the guards. The remaining ten subjects became "prisoners" and were put in rooms with metal bars, bucket toilets, and cots.

"I don't see liking trucks as a boy thing. I see it as a liking-trucks thing."

Liza Donnelly/*The New Yorker* Collection/The Cartoon Bank.

Zimbardo let the guards establish their own rules for the experiment. The rules were tough: no talking during meals, rest periods, or after lights out. They took head counts at 2:30 a.m. Troublemakers received short rations.

Faced with these conditions, the prisoners began to resist. Some barricaded their doors with beds. Others went on hunger strikes. Several ripped off their identifying number tags. The guards reacted to the rebellion by clamping down hard on protesters. Some became sadistic, physically and verbally abusing the prisoners. The experiment was scheduled to go on for two weeks, but after six days Zimbardo realized that what had started as a simulation had become too real, and stopped it. It seems that *what* we are is determined largely by society's designation of *who* we are.

Cultural Influences

Cultural selection, organization, interpretation, and negotiation exert a powerful influence on the way we view communication by other people. In this section we will explore cultural differences regarding the value of talk and silence, approaches to logic and thinking, views of social obligations, distribution of power, and the extent to which people avoid uncertainty and value achievement and nurturance. These are just some of the ways in which cultures differ, and these differences influence our perceptions of ourselves and other people.

Talk and Silence

Western cultures tend to view talk as desirable and use it for social purposes as well as to perform tasks. Silence has a negative value in these cultures. It is likely to be interpreted as lack of interest, unwillingness to communicate, hostility, anxiety, shyness, or a sign of interpersonal incompatibility. Westerners are uncomfortable with silence, which they find embarrassing and awkward.

On the other hand, Asian cultures tend to perceive talk quite differently. For thousands of years, Asian cultures have discouraged the expression of thoughts and feelings. Silence is valued, as Taoist sayings indicate: "In much talk there is great weariness" or "One who speaks does not know; one who knows does not speak." Unlike Westerners, who are uncomfortable with silence, many people in Asian cultures believe that remaining quiet is the proper state when there is nothing to be said. In fact, a talkative person is often considered a show-off or a fake.

It is easy to see how these different views of speech and silence can lead to communication problems when people from various cultures meet. Both the "talkative" Westerner and the "silent" Asian are behaving in ways they believe are proper, yet each views the other with disapproval and mistrust. Only when they recognize the different standards of behaviour can they adapt to one another, or at least understand and respect their differences.

Social Obligations

People from collectivistic and individualistic cultures perceive interpersonal behaviour and obligations differently. For example, Au et al. (2001) gave hotel-school students in China and Canada a description of how a service provider

REFLECTION

CULTURAL DIFFERENCES IN HUMOUR

I was born and raised in Russia. One thing I find very different here [Canada] is the way people use humour. When I first arrived in this country, I noticed that my host family joked and teased me a lot. I was often offended and hurt. The problem was that neither my host family nor I understood the differences in meaning people attach to the same way of behaving. In Russia, people do not tease to express affection. In Canada, though, joking is often a way to show friendship. Once I realized this cultural difference, I became better at socializing.

handled a complaint from a customer whose coat was stained with tea. Results showed that the students from China (collectivists) were more likely than the students from Canada—(individualists) to see the service provider as the person at fault. In addition, Janoff-Bulman and Leggatt (2002), looking at motivational differences in the perception of social obligations by Hispanic (collectivistic) undergraduates and Anglo-Saxon (individualistic) undergraduates, found that although individuals from both cultures reported a strong sense of obligation toward close friends and family members, Hispanics felt a stronger motivation than Anglos to help more distant family and friends.

Thinking and Logic

The way members of a culture are taught to think and reason shapes the way they interpret other people's messages (Gudykunst and Kim, 2003). One important force that affects thinking is a culture's system of logic. Members of individualistic cultures, such as Canadians and Americans, prize rationality and linear, logical thinking. They value the ability to be impartial—to analyze a situation from a detached perspective. They rely on facts, figures, and experts to make decisions. Members of individualistic societies tend to see the world in terms of dichotomies, such as good–bad,

Focus on TECHNOLOGY

PERCEPTIONS OF CELLPHONE ETIQUETTE

Is it rude to interrupt a conversation while dining in a restaurant by answering your cellphone or replying to a text? Does it depend on what type of restaurant you are in, or who you are dining with? Is it okay to discuss personal information on a cellphone in a public place? How long do you expect to wait for a reply to your text message? People's perceptions of appropriate cellphone etiquette vary considerably. Cellphone natives (those who have grown up with cellphones) are generally more tolerant of their use, while older people, who are not cellphone natives, are often less willing to abide their ubiquitous use (Forgays et al., 2014; Ling, 2004; Ling et al., 2011).

Scott Campbell and Tracy Russo (2003) suggest that our opinions about cellphone etiquette are shaped by the way our family and friends behave with cellphones. They found that people's perceptions of when and how to use their cellphones were very similar to those of the people in their personal social networks (i.e., friends, family, and co-workers). Similarly, Jeffery Hall and his colleagues (2014) found that young Americans (under 25 years old) thought adhering to their own *personal*—and shared—norms for cellphone use was more important in predicting relationship quality than adhering to *societal* norms for appropriate cellphone use. The more similar the friends' personal cellphone rules were, the more they liked each other. The participants in Hall's study reported having higher standards for cellphone use in public situations such as restaurants, bars, and cars—that is, talking, texting, and using social media when in the presence of someone else was seen as less appropriate than when in private situations. However, participants' perceptions of their friends'

adherence to these public norms was not predictive of their commitment to, or liking of, their friends. Hall and his colleagues suggest that in private people are only accountable to each other, and therefore friends' personal, shared rules about cellphone use matter most. In public situations, societal norms matter more because there is more visibility and scrutiny by others. However, friends' observance or disregard for societal cellphone norms doesn't appear to affect relationship satisfaction.

In a study involving both cellphone natives and non-natives (subjects ranged in age 18 to 68 years old), Deborah Kirby Forgays and her colleagues (2014) found that across all age groups texting was perceived as more acceptable than phone calls in a wide variety of situations, except driving. Younger participants in this study, however, embraced texting as the best channel for many more types of messages (including ending a relationship) when compared to older participants (non-natives). As we will explore in Chapter 12, norms for civilized cellphone use at work are considerably more restrictive (Washington et al., 2014).

While this lack of consensus may seem like a new problem that is unique to our times, the rules governing how and when to use new technologies have always evolved along with the technology. Believe it or not, people felt awkward answering their landline phones—in their homes!—when they were first adopted. The etiquette and comfort with the use of technology is always evolving, but being considerate of others (especially those who may not share your personal cellphone norms) will reduce your chances of being inadvertently offensive with your phone.

right–wrong, happy–sad, and so on. In contrast, members of collectivistic cultures are more likely to be intuitive. They prefer to get a feel for the big picture and are less impressed by precision, classification, or detachment. Collectivistic cultures are also less prone to see the world in either–or terms. They accept the fact that people, things, or ideas can be both right and wrong, good and bad at the same time. Such categorizing doesn't mean that

members of individualistic cultures are never intuitive or that collectivistic ones are never rational. The differences in ways of thinking are a matter of degree. Nonetheless, it's easy to imagine how an individualist raised in mainstream Canadian culture and someone from an extremely collectivistic Asian or First Nations culture could find their interactions perplexing. For instance, consider what might happen when a conflict arises between two romantic partners, friends, or co-workers. "Why don't we look at this rationally," the individualist might say. "Let's figure out exactly what happened. Once we decide whose fault the problem is, we can fix it." By contrast, the partner with a more collectivistic way of thinking might say, "Let's not get caught up in a lot of details or an argument about who is right or wrong. If we can get a feel for the problem, we can make things more harmonious." Although both partners might be speaking the same language, their modes of thinking about their relationship would be dramatically different.

Distribution of Power

The Canadian Charter of Rights and Freedoms states that "every individual is equal before the law and under the law and has the right to equal protection and equal benefit of the law without discrimination." For members of democratic societies, this principle of equality is so fundamental that we accept it without question. However, not all cultures share this belief. Some operate on the assumption that certain groups of people (an aristocracy or an economic class, for example) and some institutions (such as a church or the government) have the right to control the lives of individuals. Geert Hofstede (1980, 2001) coined the term **power distance** to describe the degree to which members of a society accept an unequal distribution of power.

Cultures with low power distance believe in minimizing the difference between various social classes. Rich and poor, educated and uneducated groups may still exist, but there is a pervasive belief that one person is as good as another regardless of a person's station in life. Low-power-distance cultures also support the notion that challenging authority is acceptable—even desirable. Citizens are not necessarily punished for raising questions about the status quo. According to Hofstede's research, Canadian and US societies have relatively low power distance, though not the lowest in the world. Austria, Denmark, Israel, and New Zealand proved to be the most egalitarian

countries. At the other end of the spectrum are countries with a high degree of power distance: Philippines, Mexico, Venezuela, India, and Singapore.

The degree of power distance in a culture is reflected in key relationships (Lustig and Koester, 1999). Children who are raised in cultures with high power distance are expected to obey their parents and other authority figures to a degree that would astonish most children raised in Canada or the United States. Power automatically comes with age in many countries. For example, the Korean language has separate terms for *older brother*, *oldest brother*, *younger sister*, *youngest sister*, and so on. Parents in cultures with low power distance do not expect the same unquestioning obedience and are not surprised when children ask why when requested or told to do something.

Differences between high- and low-power-distance cultures also show up in school (Richardson and Smith, 2007; Yook and Albert, 1998) and at work (Farh et al., 2007). In societies that accept high power distance, students and employees are expected to obey their teachers and employers without question. Students are discouraged from asking questions, which might seem like an attack on the teacher's authority or knowledge. Similarly, employees have much less say about how they do their work. In fact, workers from these cultures are likely to feel uncomfortable when given the freedom to make their own decisions or when a more egalitarian boss asks for their opinion, because they prefer to view their bosses as benevolent decision makers. In contrast, in countries where low power distance is the norm, students are more likely to be rewarded for showing initiative and for questioning their teachers, and employees expect more of a say in decisions and may feel unappreciated when they are not consulted.

Uncertainty Avoidance

The desire to resolve uncertainty seems to be a trait shared by people around the world (Berger, 1988). While uncertainty may be universal, cultures have different ways of coping with an unpredictable future. Hofstede (1980, 2001) uses the term **uncertainty avoidance** for the degree to which members of a culture feel threatened by ambiguous situations and how much they try to avoid them.

A culture's degree of uncertainty avoidance is reflected in the way its members communicate. In countries where people avoid uncertainty, such as Portugal, Belgium, Greece, and Japan, deviant people and ideas are considered dangerous and intolerance is high (Samovar et al., 2012). People in these cultures are especially concerned with security, so they have a strong need for clearly defined rules and regulations. It's easy to imagine how most relationships in cultures with a high uncertainty avoidance—family, work, friendships, and romance—are likely to fit a predictable pattern. By contrast, people in a culture that is less threatened by the new and unexpected are more likely to tolerate—or even welcome— people who don't fit the norm. Residents of countries such as Singapore, Britain, Denmark, Sweden, Hong Kong, the United States, and Canada are relatively unthreatened by change. Following established rules and patterns isn't necessarily expected, and different behaviour may even be welcomed.

Achievement and Nurturing

The term **achievement culture** describes societies that place a high value on material success and a focus on the task at hand, while **nurturing culture** is a descriptive term for societies that regard the support of relationships as an especially important goal. Achievement or "hard" cultures, which emphasize materialism, include Japan, Switzerland, and Germany. Nurturing or "soft" cultures include Spain, France, and the Scandinavian countries (i.e., Norway, Sweden, and Denmark). Canada is considered a moderately achievement-oriented culture. The portrait of an effective communicator varies from one type of culture to another. Research shows that people from achievement-oriented cultures tend to behave more competitively, express more assertiveness, and show less concern for others. In contrast, people from more nurturing cultures are more inclined to behave in ways that promote harmony and use a more sensitive and indirect communication style (Merkin et al., 2014).

As you think about the cultural values described here, realize that cultural misunderstandings do not occur just between people from different countries. In Canada's increasingly multicultural society, people from different cultural backgrounds are likely to encounter one another "at home," in the communities they share. Many Canadians have both a "Canadian" culture to which they belong and one or more cultures that make up their ethnic heritage. For some people, there is considerable harmony in the values and norms that exist in their co-cultures; for others, there is considerable discord. What we all share is the fact that our cultural values shape our perceptions.

 **CHECK IT!**

Describe the four general areas of influence on our perceptions and provide examples within each area.

Common Tendencies in Perception

It is obvious that many factors distort the way we interpret the world. Social scientists use the term **attribution** to describe the process of attaching meaning to behaviour. We attribute meaning both to our own actions and to the actions of others, but we often use different yardsticks. Research has uncovered several perceptual tendencies that may lead to inaccurate attributions (Hamachek, 1992).

We Judge Ourselves More Charitably than We Do Others

In an attempt to convince ourselves and others that the positive face we show to the world is true, we tend to judge ourselves in the most generous terms possible (Balcetis, 2009; Farah and Atoum, 2002). On the one hand, when others suffer, we often blame the problem on their personal qualities and we underestimate the impact of the situation. Social scientists have labelled this tendency the **fundamental attribution error** (Ross, 1977, 2001). For instance, recipients of a work-related email containing spelling and grammatical errors are more likely to assume the sender is unintelligent (personal quality) than to assume that English is not the sender's first language (contextual factor) (Vignovic et al., 2010). On the other hand, when we experience failure, like making spelling mistakes of our own in an email message, we quickly find explanations outside ourselves, such as being in a hurry. When we have done something well, however, we are quick to take personal credit rather than attribute the success to the situation (Ross and Nisbett, 1991). This tendency to protect our self-esteem by blaming the situation for our failures and taking personal credit for our successes is called the **self-serving bias**. Consider a couple of examples:

- When *they* botch a job, we think they weren't listening well or trying hard enough; when *we* make the mistake, the problem was unclear directions or not enough time.
- When *she* lashes out angrily, we say she's being moody or too sensitive; when *we* blow off steam, it is because of the pressure we've been under.

Not surprisingly, these biased perceptions are especially common in troubled relationships. In one study of couples in conflict (Schütz, 1999), people were more likely to blame their partners for the problem than to accept responsibility for their role in the problem. The researchers point out that these results came from couples dealing with ordinary relational challenges. They observe that the fundamental attribution error and

self-serving bias are likely to be even stronger in troubled relationships. In contrast, people who make more complex attributions about other people's behaviour (that is, those who take into account many different causes for behaviour) are more accurate in their social judgments and less prejudiced and punitive in their conclusions about other people (Tam et al., 2008). In addition, people who take into account many different reasons for other people's behaviour are viewed by their peers as thoughtful, empathic, socially skilled, and wise (Fast et al., 2008). Research also shows that when people are aware of both the positive and negative characteristics of another person, they tend to be more influenced by the undesirable traits (Baumeister et al., 2001; Kellermann, 1989; Sparks and Baumeister, 2008). This attitude sometimes makes sense. If the negative quality clearly outweighs any positive ones, you would be foolish to ignore it. For example, a surgeon with shaky hands and a teacher who hates children would be unsuitable for their jobs, regardless of their other virtues. But much of the time, it's a bad idea to pay excessive attention to negative qualities and overlook good ones.

We Are Influenced by Our Expectations

Suppose you took a class and were told in advance by several friends that the instructor is terrific, and that she is very funny. Would this affect the way you perceive the teacher? Probably so. There is a good chance that you would view the instructor positively and laugh at her jokes—perhaps more than you would have if you hadn't been told about her in advance. In this situation, as in others, our expectations influence our perceptions.

However, expectations do not always lead to more positive appraisals. There are times when we raise our expectations so high that we are disappointed with the events that occur. If you are told that someone you are about to meet is extremely attractive, you may create a picture in your mind of a professional model, only to be disappointed when the person doesn't live up to your unrealistic expectations. What if you had been told that the person isn't very good-looking? In that case, you might have been pleasantly surprised by the person's appearance, and perhaps you would rate the person's attractiveness more positively. The point is that our expectations influence the way we see others, both positively and negatively.

It is important to be aware of the influence of our expectations when we are making decisions about others. Many professions require that proposals be evaluated through "blind review"—that is, the person submitting the proposal is not allowed to offer identifying information that might influence the evaluator's appraisal. In the same way, you can probably think of times when it would be wise to avoid advance information about another person so that you will perceive the person as neutrally as possible.

We Are Influenced by the Obvious

Being influenced by what is most obvious is understandable. As you read earlier, we select stimuli from our environment that are noticeable—that is, intense, repetitious, unusual, or otherwise attention-grabbing. The problem is that the most obvious factor is not necessarily the only cause—or the most significant one—of an event. For example:

- When two children (or adults, for that matter) fight, it may be a mistake to blame the one who lashes out first. Perhaps the other one was at least equally responsible, by teasing or refusing to co-operate.
- You might complain about an acquaintance whose malicious gossiping or arguing has become a bother, forgetting that by putting up with that kind of behaviour you have been at least partially responsible.
- You might blame an unhappy work situation on the boss, overlooking other factors beyond her control, such as a change in the economy, the policy of higher management, or demands of customers or other workers.

These examples show that it is important to take time to gather all the facts before arriving at a conclusion.

We Cling to First Impressions

Labelling people according to our first impressions is a part of the perception process that is difficult to avoid. Such labels are a way of making quick interpretations: "She seems cheerful," "He seems sincere," "They sound awfully conceited."

If impressions are accurate, they can be useful in helping us decide how to respond best to people in the future. However, problems arise when the labels we attach are inaccurate, for once we form an opinion of someone, we tend to hang onto it and make any conflicting information fit that opinion.

Social scientists have found that first impressions are often based on physical appearance and tend to be inaccurate (Olivola and Todorov, 2010). When our first impressions of others are positive, they are described as having a **halo effect**. For instance, people who are physically attractive are judged to be interpersonally skilled (Dion et al., 1972; Lemay et al., 2010). The power of the halo effect has been demonstrated by research on how employers rate job applicants (Dougherty et al., 1994). Interviewers usually form strong impressions of candidates in the first few minutes after meeting them. Once these impressions are formed, they often ask questions that confirm their image of the applicant. For example, when an interviewer forms a positive impression, she might ask leading questions aimed at supporting her positive views ("What lessons did you learn from that setback?"), interpret answers in a positive light ("Ah, taking time away from school to travel was a good idea!"), encourage the applicant ("Good point!"), and sell the company's virtues ("I think you would like working here").

Likewise, applicants who create a negative first impression are operating under a cloud that may be impossible to dispel. Our tendency to seek out, remember, and organize information that supports our impressions and beliefs is referred to as **confirmation bias** (Nickerson, 1998). We all have a tendency to confirm what we already believe to be true. A distinguishing feature of the scientific method is to seek to falsify our hypotheses, in order to overcome this pervasive human tendency to pursue information that supports our predictions, but even scientists are vulnerable to this feature of human perception. For instance, a careful review of the research literature by economist Julie Nelson (2013) revealed that the perception of women being more financially risk adverse than men has far less empirical support than previously claimed. Nelson suggests that because this stereotype about women has been

We all form first impressions when meeting new people. How can we avoid letting those first impressions inform all of our understanding and interactions with others?

so widely held in the community of economists it has led them to inadvertently draw misleading conclusions from their research data. Given the almost unavoidable tendency to form first impressions, the best approach is to keep an open mind, look for information that might challenge your initial beliefs and be willing to change your opinion if events prove you mistaken.

We Assume Others Are Similar to Us

We commonly imagine that others have the same attitudes and motives that we do (Human and Biesanz, 2011). The frequently mistaken assumption that other people's views are similar to our own applies in a wide range of situations. For example:

- You've heard a slightly raunchy joke that you found funny. You assume that it won't offend a friend. It does.
- You've been bothered by an instructor's tendency to get off the subject during lectures. If you were a professor, you would want to know if you were creating problems for your students, so you decide that your instructor will probably be grateful for some constructive criticism. Unfortunately, you are wrong.
- You lost your temper with a friend a week ago and said some things you regret. In fact, if someone said those things to you, you would consider the relationship finished. Imagining that your friend feels the same way, you avoid making contact. In fact, your friend feels that he was partly responsible and has avoided you because he thinks you are the one who wants to end things.

These examples show that others don't always think or feel the way we do and that assuming similarities can lead to problems. Sometimes, you can find out the other person's real position by asking directly; other times, by checking with someone else; and still other times, by making an educated guess after you

- **Fundamental attribution error:** the tendency to blame other people's problems on their personal qualities and underestimate the impact of the situation.
- **Self-serving bias:** the tendency to protect our self-esteem by blaming the situation for our failures and taking personal credit for our successes.
- **Halo effect:** the power of a first impression to influence subsequent perceptions.
- **Confirmation bias:** the tendency to seek out, remember and organize information that supports our impressions and beliefs.

 **CHECK IT!**

Summarize the five common tendencies in our perceptions of other people.

Perception Checking

With the likelihood for perceptual errors so great, it is easy to see how a communicator can leap to the wrong conclusion and make false assumptions. Consider the defence-arousing potential of incorrect accusations like these:

"Why are you mad at me?" (Who said I was?)

"What's the matter with you?" (Who said anything was the matter?)

"Come on now. Tell the truth." (Who said I was lying?)

Even if your interpretations are correct, these kinds of mind-reading statements are likely to generate defensiveness. The skill of **perception checking** is a better way to share your interpretations. A complete perception check has three parts:

1. a description of the behaviour you noticed;
2. two or more possible interpretations of the behaviour; and
3. a request for clarification about how to interpret the behaviour.

Perception checks for the preceding three examples would look like this:

"When you left quickly and slammed the door [*behaviour*], I wasn't sure whether you were mad at me [*first interpretation*] or just in a hurry [*second interpretation*]. How did you feel? [*request for clarification*]"

"You haven't laughed much in the last couple of days [*behaviour*]. It makes me wonder whether something's bothering you [*first interpretation*] or whether you are just being quiet [*second interpretation*]. What's up? [*request for clarification*]"

have thought the matter out. All these alternatives are better than simply assuming that everyone would react the way you do.

We don't always fall into the kind of perceptual tendencies described in this section. Sometimes, for instance, people *are* responsible for their misfortunes, or our problems *are not* our fault. Likewise, the most obvious interpretation of a situation may be the correct one. Nonetheless, a large amount of research has shown again and again that our perceptions of others are often distorted in the ways we have described. The moral, then, is clear: do not assume that your negative appraisal of a person is accurate or unbiased.

Perceiving Others More Accurately

After reading this far, you can appreciate how flawed our perceptions of one another can be. It's easy to understand how these distorted perceptions can interfere with our communication. What we need, then, are tools to improve the accuracy of our attributions. In the following section, we will introduce two such tools.

"You said you really liked the job I did [*behaviour*], but there was something about your voice that made me think you may not like it [*first interpretation*]. Maybe it is just my imagination, though [*second interpretation*]. How do you really feel? [*request for clarification*]"

Perception checking is a tool to help us understand others instead of assuming that our first interpretation is correct. Because its goal is mutual understanding, perception checking is a co-operative approach to communication. Besides leading to more accurate perceptions, it signals an attitude of respect and concern for the other person, saying, in effect, "I know I'm not qualified to judge you without some help."

The straightforward approach of perception checking has the best chance of working in what we identify in Chapter 6 as *low-context cultures*—ones in which members use language as clearly and logically as possible. The dominant cultures of North America and Western Europe fit into this category, and members of these groups are most likely to appreciate the kind of straightforward approach that perception checking embodies. On the other hand, members of *high-context cultures* (more common in traditional First Nations Canadian communities, Latin America and Asia) value social harmony over clarity. High-context communicators are more likely to regard candid approaches like perception checking as potentially embarrassing, preferring instead less direct ways of understanding one another. Thus, a "let's get this straight" perception check might work well with a Canadian manager of British or European descent who was raised to value clarity, but it could be a serious mistake with an First Nations Canadian boss who has spent most of his life in a high-context culture (see Chapter 6).

Building Empathy

Perception checking can help us decode messages more accurately, but it doesn't give us enough information that we can claim to fully understand another person. For example, a professor who uses perception checking might learn that a student's reluctance to ask questions is due to confusion and not lack of interest. This information would be helpful, but imagine how much more effective the professor would be if she could get a sense of how it feels to be confused, and could consider how the material that is so familiar to her appears to the student who is seeing it for the first time. Likewise, parents whose perception checks reveal that their teenager's outlandish behaviour grows from a desire to be accepted by others may not understand (or perhaps remember) what it feels like to crave that acceptance.

Empathy Defined

What we need, then, to understand others more completely is **empathy**—the ability to recreate another person's perspective and to experience the world from

© hotblack/iStockphoto.

Perception checking is a tool to help us understand others instead of assuming that our first interpretation is correct. Have you done any perception checking recently?

Building WORK SKILLS

PERCEPTION CHECKING

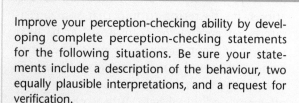

Improve your perception-checking ability by developing complete perception-checking statements for the following situations. Be sure your statements include a description of the behaviour, two equally plausible interpretations, and a request for verification.

You made what you thought was an excellent suggestion to your boss. He said, "I'll get back to you about that right away." It's been three weeks, and you haven't received a response yet.

You disagreed with a co-worker's suggestions during a meeting. When the meeting was over, you asked if anyone wanted to go for lunch and everyone agreed, with the exception of that same co-worker. The next day when you pass him in the hall, he nods, but doesn't say hello or smile as he usually does.

---

her point of view. It is impossible to achieve total empathy, but with enough effort and skill, we can come closer to this goal (Buckman and Baile, 2005; Buckman et al., 2011; Long et al., 1999).

As the term will be used here, empathy has three dimensions (Stiff et al., 1988). The first dimension involves *perspective taking*—the ability to take on the viewpoint of another person. This understanding requires a suspension of judgment, so that for the moment you set aside your own opinions and take on those of the other person. Besides cognitive understanding, empathy also has an affective dimension—what social scientists term *emotional contagion*. In everyday language, emotional contagion means that we experience the same feelings that others have. We know their fear, joy, sadness, and so on. A third dimension of empathy is a genuine *concern* for the welfare of the other person. Not only do we think and feel as others do, but we have a sincere interest in their well-being. Full empathy requires both intellectual understanding of the other person's position and an affective understanding of her feelings (Kerem et al., 2001).

Empathy involves *experiencing* the other's perception—in effect, temporarily becoming that person. This kind of understanding is different from *sympathy* which involves having compassion for another person's circumstances, but from your own point of view. As

this definition implies, when you feel sympathetic, you stand beside the other person. You feel compassion, but you do not share the other person's emotions. Despite your concern, sympathy involves less identification than does empathy. When you sympathize, the confusion, joy, or pain belongs to another. When you empathize, the experience becomes your own, at least for the moment. Empathy does not, however, require agreement with another person. You can empathize with others without endorsing their behaviour.

The ability to empathize seems to exist in a rudimentary form in even the youngest children (Goleman, 1995). Virtually from birth, infants become visibly upset when they hear another baby crying, frequently crying themselves and showing facial expressions of distress (Geangu et al., 2010). Toddlers prefer animated characters whom they have observed to be helpful over those who have hindered someone else, and even when adults show no emotion after they have been hurt or their property has been damaged, very young children show appropriate concerned looks and pro-social helping responses (Vaish et al., 2009). While empathy has been found to have a genetic component, environmental factors influence its development in the early years (Knafo et al., 2008). Empathy is supported and developed by parenting practices which include modelling empathy, encouraging appropriate emotional expressiveness, and explaining the effects of one's actions on others (Strayer and Roberts, 2004). In adults, York University psychologist Raymond Mar and his colleagues have found that those who read fiction have greater abilities to take another person's perspective and to be empathetic than those who read nonfiction or who don't read at all (Mar and Oatley, 2008; Mar et al., 2009). These researchers suggest that reading fictional stories takes us to new places where we experience the social worlds of the story's characters, where we use the same thinking skills and empathic abilities that we would use in our own real-life social situations. Reading fiction gives us opportunities to practise using these skills, which leads to greater accuracy in understanding others in real life.

The Value of Empathy

As we saw in Chapter 1, the ability to empathize is so important that it is an essential ingredient of communicative competence. Empathy can have benefits for both the person who is doing the empathizing and the person who is being understood (Redmond, 1986; Rumble et al., 2009).

The recipient of empathy incurs several benefits. The first is increased *self-esteem*. Others usually respond to your point of view with judgments such as "That's right" or "No, it's not that way at all." An empathic response is different. It suggests the listener is willing to accept you as you are, without any evaluations. It's flattering to find that someone is interested enough in your position to hear you out without passing judgment. The act of being understood can also be very *comforting*, whether or not the other person's reflections offer any additional help. When others empathize, a common thought is "I'm not alone." Finally, the target of empathy learns to *trust* the empathizer in a way that probably would not be otherwise possible.

There is considerable evidence of the value of empathy for both medical patients and health-care professionals. Dr Robert Buckman, was, among many things, an oncologist at Toronto's Princess Margaret Hospital and professor at the University of Toronto. He and his colleagues (2011) found that when doctors take the time to really listen and understand patients' emotional responses, they actually save time, decrease the likelihood of malpractice lawsuits, and avoid burnout. In addition, patients are happier, more satisfied with their care, and more motivated to take their medications—all factors associated with better health outcomes. Unfortunately, investigators have also found that more often than not doctors miss opportunities to be empathic (Morse et al., 2008). Empathy, like any other skill, can be learned (Buckman et al., 2011). In health care, showing empathy and tuning in to the integral well-being of the patient are essential hallmarks of good care (Vanlaere et al., 2010). Perhaps Hippocrates described the health-care provider's role best: "To cure sometimes, to treat often, to comfort always." The requirements for responding empathetically will be

William Steig/The New Yorker Collection/The Cartoon Bank.

"How would you feel if the mouse did that to you?"

Building WORK SKILLS

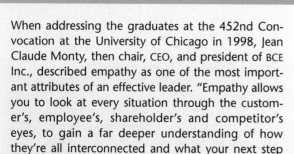

When addressing the graduates at the 452nd Convocation at the University of Chicago in 1998, Jean Claude Monty, then chair, CEO, and president of BCE Inc., described empathy as one of the most important attributes of an effective leader. "Empathy allows you to look at every situation through the customer's, employee's, shareholder's and competitor's eyes, to gain a far deeper understanding of how they're all interconnected and what your next step should be" (Monty, 1998).

Often, the hardest time to empathize with someone is when we are involved in an argument or conflict with that person. Think about a disagreement you had recently with someone at work or school. Take a moment to jot down your perspective on the issue. Now, try honestly and accurately to imagine the other person's thoughts and feelings about the same issue. Describe the two sides of the argument to a friend or classmate. Does your friend or classmate think you have genuinely tried to perceive the issue from the other person's point of view? Has your position on the issue changed at all? Why or why not?

described after we consider the relationship between empathy and ethics.

Empathy and Ethics

The golden rule of treating others as we want to be treated points to the clear relationship between the ability to empathize and the ethical principles that enable society to function in a manner that we consider civilized. In fact, research has found a link between empathy and ethical altruism (Hoffman, 1991; Midlarsky et al., 2005). Bystanders who feel empathy for victims are more likely to intervene and offer help than those who are indifferent. On a larger scale, studies in Canada, the United States, and Germany have revealed a relationship between feelings of empathy and the willingness of people to follow the moral principle that resources should be allocated according to people's needs. Empathetic people have "an interest in understanding life rather than taking sides" (Adams, 2003).

Requirements for Empathy

Empathy may be valuable, but it is not always easy to achieve. In fact, research shows that it's hardest to empathize with people who are radically different from us in age, sex, socio-economic status, intelligence, and so forth (Cronkhite, 1976; Samovar et al., 2012). In order to make such perceptual leaps, you need to develop several skills and attitudes.

Open-Mindedness   Perhaps the most important characteristic of an empathic person is the ability and disposition to be open-minded—to set aside for the moment your own beliefs, attitudes, and values and to consider those of the other person. Open-mindedness is especially difficult when the other person's position is radically different from your own. The temptation is to think (and sometimes say), "That's crazy!" "How can you believe that?" or "I'd do it this way . . ."

Being open-minded is often difficult because people confuse *understanding* another's position with *accepting* it. These are quite different matters. To understand why a friend

- **Empathy:** recreating another person's perspective and experiencing the world from his point of view ("feeling inside").
- **Sympathy:** feeling compassion for someone, but not experiencing that person's point of view or emotions ("feeling with").

Self-Assessment

EMPATHY IN FRIENDSHIPS

This questionnaire can help you determine the degree to which empathy is part of your friendships. Think of one of your close personal friendships and, with that friendship in mind, respond to each statement according to how much you agree with it.

If you agree completely, mark the statement 4.

If you agree a great deal, but not completely, mark the statement 3.

If you agree somewhat, mark the statement 2.

If you agree very little, mark the statement 1.

If you do not agree, mark the statement 0.

_____ 1. I understand what my friend says.
_____ 2. I understand how my friend feels.
_____ 3. I appreciate what my friend's experiences feel like to her.
_____ 4. I try to see things through my friend's eyes.
_____ 5. I ask my friend questions about what his experiences mean to him.
_____ 6. I ask my friend questions about what she is thinking.
_____ 7. I ask my friend questions about how he is feeling.

_____ 8. My friend understands what I say.
_____ 9. My friend understands how I feel.
_____10. My friend appreciates what my experiences feel like to me.
_____11. My friend tries to see things through my eyes.
_____12. My friend asks me questions about what my experiences mean to me.
_____13. My friend asks me questions about what I'm thinking.
_____14. My friend asks me questions about how I'm feeling.

Add your scores for items 1 to 7. _____

This figure represents your perception of your empathy for your friend.

Add your scores for items 8 to 14. _____

This represents your perception of your friend's empathy for you.

Each sum can range from 0 to 28—the higher the sum, the greater the empathy.

Now, have your friend respond to the statements and compare your answers. The results might well contribute to greater empathy in your relationship.

disagrees with you, for example, does not mean you have to give up your position and accept hers.

Imagination   Being open-minded is often not enough to make you empathetic. You also need enough imagination to be able to picture another person's background and thoughts. A happily married or single person needs imagination to empathize with the problems of a friend considering divorce. A young person needs it to empathize with a parent facing retirement. A teacher needs it to understand the problems of students, just as students can't be empathic without trying to imagine how their instructor feels.

Commitment   Because empathizing is often difficult, a third necessary quality is a sincere desire to understand another person. Listening to unfamiliar, often confusing information takes time and is not always pleasant. If you aim to be empathic, be willing to accept the challenge. Empathy requires considerable energy and effort and you need to make sure that your own

 CHECK IT!

What are the three requirements for empathy, and why do people often have difficulty with the first requirement?

needs for comfort and compassion are met in order to be prepared for the challenge.

By now, you can see the tremendous difficulties we encounter when we want to understand one another. Physiological distortion, psychological interference, and social and cultural conditioning all insulate us from our fellow human beings. But the news is not all bad, for with a combination of determination and skill, we can do a better job of spanning the gap that separates us and, as a result, enjoy more satisfying interpersonal relationships.

 CHECK IT!

Name and describe two tools that can improve the accuracy of our attributions.

SUMMARY

Many communication challenges arise because of differing perceptions. The process of interpersonal perception is a complex one, and a variety of factors influence each person's view of reality.

Interpersonal perception involves four phases: selection, organization, interpretation, and negotiation. A number of influences can affect how we perceive others' behaviour. Physiological factors include our senses, age, health, fatigue, hunger, and biological cycles. Psychological factors such as mood and self-concept also have a strong influence on how we regard others. In addition, social influences, such as sex and gender roles and occupational roles, play an important part in the way we view those with whom we interact. Finally, cultural influences shape how we recognize and make sense of others' words and actions. Our cultural values influence our perceptions of talk and silence, thinking and logic, social obligations, distribution of power, avoidance of uncertainty, and the value of achievement and nurturance.

Our perceptions are often affected by common perceptual tendencies. We are more likely to blame others than ourselves for misfortunes, and we are more influenced by negative information than positive information. We are influenced by our expectations, and we are also influenced by obvious stimuli, even if they are not the most important factors. We cling to first impressions, even if they are mistaken, and we assume others are similar to us.

One way to verify the accuracy of our interpretations is through perception checking. Instead of jumping to conclusions, communicators who check their perceptions describe the behaviour they noticed, offer two or more equally plausible interpretations, and ask for clarification from their partner.

Empathy is the ability to experience the world from another person's perspective. There are three dimensions to empathy: perspective taking, emotional involvement, and concern for the other person. Empathy has benefits for both the empathizer and the recipient. The requirements for developing greater empathy include open-mindedness, imagination, and commitment.

MULTIPLE-CHOICE QUESTIONS

1. Perception of other people is organized using
   a. perceptual schema.
   b. selection constructs.
   c. negotiation constructs.
   d. all of the above.
2. Determining the cause and effects of a series of social interactions is referred to as
   a. stereotyping.
   b. punctuation.
   c. grammar.
   d. narratives.
3. Culture influences people's perceptions of
   a. silence.
   b. logic.
   c. power.
   d. all of the above.
4. Exaggerated beliefs about all members of a group that are based on an easily recognizable, but unimportant characteristic are called stereotypes.
   a. true
   b. false
5. Sara is in a bad mood and is very skeptical about the salespersons' explanation of a supposedly better cellphone plan. Sara's mood is an example of
   a. a physiological influence on perception.
   b. a social influence on perception.
   c. a psychological influence on perception.
   d. a narrative influence on perception.
6. Explaining other people's failures by blaming their personal characteristics rather than situational factors is referred to as
   a. the self-serving bias.
   b. uncertainty avoidance.
   c. standpoint theory.
   d. the fundamental attribution error.
7. A common tendency in perception is to
   a. judge others more charitably than ourselves.
   b. be influenced by our expectations.
   c. favour positive impressions.
   d. all of the above.
8. The power of a first impression to influence subsequent perceptions is called the halo effect.
   a. true
   b. false
9. The requirements for empathy include
   a. selection, organization, and negotiation.
   b. relational satisfaction, realistic expectations, and knowledge.
   c. open-mindedness, imagination, and commitment.
   d. attributions, androgyny, and amplification.
10. When health-care professionals practise empathy with their patients it ends up taking more time and they are at increased risk of burnout.
    a. true
    b. false

Answers: 1. a; 2. b; 3. d; 4. a; 5. c; 6. d; 7. b; 8. a; 9. c; 10. b

ACTIVITIES

1. Critical Thinking Probe

Complete the following sentences:

a. Women _____.

b. Men _____.

c. Francophones _____.

d. Anglophones _____.

e. Muslims _____.

f. Older people _____.

Now, ask yourself the degree to which each of your responses was a stereotype and/or a generalization. Is it possible to make generalizations about the groups listed above? How could your answers to these questions change the way you perceive and respond to people in these groups?

2. Invitation to Insight

You can get a better appreciation of the importance of punctuation by using the format pictured in Figure 3.3 (on page 89) to diagram the following situations:

a. A father and daughter are growing more and more distant. The daughter withdraws because she interprets her father's coolness as rejection. The father views his daughter's aloofness as a rebuff and withdraws further.

b. The relationship between two friends is becoming strained. One makes jokes to lighten up the tension, and the other becomes more tense.

c. A couple is on the verge of breaking up. One partner frequently asks the other to show more affection; the other withdraws physical contact.

Explain how each of these situations could be punctuated differently by the two participants. Next, use the same procedure to explain how an event from your experience could be punctuated in at least two different ways. Describe the consequences of failing to recognize the plausibility of each of these punctuation schemes.

3. Invitation to Insight

Choose one of the following situations, and describe how it could be perceived differently by each person. Be sure to include the steps of selection, organization, and interpretation. What might their narratives sound like as they negotiate their perceptions? List any relevant physiological, psychological, social,

and cultural influences, and also suggest how the communicators' self-concepts may have affected their perceptions.

a. A customer complains to a salesperson about poor service in a busy store.

b. A parent and teenager argue about the proper time for the teen to return home after a Saturday-night date.

c. A quiet student feels pressured when called upon by an instructor to speak up in class.

d. A woman and a man argue about whether to increase the balance in the workplace by making special efforts to hire employees from under-represented groups.

4. Invitation to Insight

On pages 101–105 of this chapter, we outlined several common perceptual tendencies. Describe instances in which you committed each of them, and explain the consequences of each one. Which of these perceptual tendencies are you most prone to make, and what may be the results of making it? How can you avoid these tendencies in the future?

5. Skill Builder

You can develop your empathy skills by putting yourself in the shoes of someone with whom you have an interpersonal relationship. With that person's help, describe *in the first person* how the other person views an issue that is important to him. In other words, try as much as possible to become that person and see things from his perspective. Your partner will be the best judge of your ability to make this perceptual jump, so use his comments to modify your account. After doing the exercise, describe how your attempt changed the way you might relate to the other person.

6. Role Play

With a partner, choose one of the situations described below or recall a situation in which someone displayed ambiguous non-verbal behaviour, and construct a perception-checking statement. Be sure to include a description of the behaviour, two plausible, but different interpretations of the behaviour, and a request for clarification. Now, have your partner act out the ambiguous behaviour and role-play your perception-checking statement with your partner. Reverse roles.

Situation One
Your sister arrives home from school, loudly drops her books, and walks by you without a greeting. You hear her bedroom door slam shut.

Situation Two
You call a close friend to talk about your exciting plans for the weekend and he is quiet, answering your questions, but not elaborating on the plans, asking questions, or offering his opinion. His mood seems very subdued and a bit distant.

Situation Three
You arrive at work and your boss gives you a list of things to be done. She is not as talkative as usual and she quickly walks away after giving you instructions.

DISCUSSION QUESTIONS

1. Imagine yourself at a family meal or celebration. How might the participants' perceptions of this event differ? Consider all the influences on perception described in this chapter to gain insight into the ways in which various family members might perceive the situation differently.

2. Consider the cultural influences on perception described in this chapter. How might the common perceptual tendency to assume that others are like us create problems in Canada's multicultural society?

3. In what types of situations can our common tendencies in perception work to our advantage, and where would these same tendencies work to our disadvantage?

4. Some communication researchers argue that empathy is perhaps the most important element of communication competence. Would you agree or disagree? Why?

JOURNAL IDEAS

1. Consider the influences on perception discussed in this chapter and describe examples of how they have influenced your perceptions and have possibly influenced other people's perceptions of you.

2. Think of someone you strongly disagree with about a particular issue. Try to describe how they think and feel about the issue as accurately as possible. Remember, understanding their position does not mean that you accept or agree with it.

4

Emotions

Chapter Outline

© Ekaterina Minaeva/iStockphoto

Key Terms

cognitive reappraisal
debilitative emotions
emotions
emotional contagion
emotional intelligence
emotionally counterfeit
facilitative emotions
fallacy of approval
fallacy of catastrophic
    expectations

fallacy of causation
fallacy of helplessness
fallacy of overgeneralization
fallacy of perfection
fallacy of *should*
rational–emotive approach
rumination
self-talk

Learning Objectives

YOU SHOULD UNDERSTAND:

- the three components of emotion;
- the factors that influence the expression of emotion in contemporary society;
- the influence of culture, biological sex, and gender on emotional expressiveness and sensitivity;
- the relationships among activating events, thoughts, emotions, and communication behaviour;
- seven fallacies leading to unnecessarily debilitative emotions that can interfere with effective communication; and
- the steps in the rational–emotive approach for coping with debilitative emotions.

YOU SHOULD BE ABLE TO:

- observe the physical and cognitive manifestations of some of the emotions you experience;
- label your own emotions accurately;
- identify the degree to which you express your emotions and the consequences of this level of expression;
- follow the guidelines in this chapter in deciding when and how to express your emotions in an important relationship;
- realize which of your emotions are facilitative and which are debilitative;
- identify the fallacious beliefs that have caused you to experience debilitative emotions in a specific situation; and
- in a specific situation, apply the rational–emotive approach to managing your debilitative emotions.

Imagine how different life would be if you lost your ability to experience emotions. An emotionless world would be free of boredom, frustration, fear, and loneliness. But the cost of such a pain-free existence would be the loss of emotions like joy, pride, and love. Few of us would be willing to make that sort of trade-off. Being aware of and experiencing emotions is fundamental to the quality of our lives. People who have suffered damage to the areas of the brain that allow them to process emotional information have serious difficulty making decisions in daily life, despite the fact that their regular cognitive abilities are still functioning normally (Bechara, 2004; Eslinger and Tranel, 2005). Making decisions and navigating our lives require the combination of cognitive processes and emotional responses. Emotions help humans solve the basic problems of social living (Keltner and Haidt, 2001; Pfister and Bohm, 2008).

The role of emotions in human affairs is apparent to social scientists and lay people alike. The concept of emotional intelligence has become part of our everyday understanding about how effectively people get along with others. **Emotional intelligence** involves the ability to recognize emotions in ourselves and others, to manage our emotions and to use emotions to enhance our self-motivation, our empathy and our relationships with others. People who are high in emotional intelligence pay attention to and manage their emotions in adaptive ways that benefit themselves and others (Mayer et al., 2004, 2008). People with high emotional intelligence appear to be more socially competent, have better-quality interpersonal relationships, and are judged as more sensitive than people lower in

emotional intelligence (Brackett et al., 2005; Mayer et al., 2008). Because emotions are such an important part of human communication, we will take a close look at them in the following pages. We will explore what feelings are, discuss the ways they are handled in contemporary society, and see how recognizing and expressing them can improve relationships. We'll also look at some guidelines that should give you a clearer idea of when and how to express your emotions constructively. In the final section, we'll explore a method for coping with troublesome, debilitating feelings that inhibit rather than help your communication.

What Are Emotions?

Suppose an extraterrestrial visitor asked you to explain emotions. How would you answer? You might start by saying that emotions are things that we feel. But this doesn't say much, for, in turn, you would probably describe feelings as synonymous with emotions. There isn't consistent agreement among researchers on exactly what an emotion is (Izard, 2010; 2011). Psychologist Caroll Izard distinguishes between first-order emotions, which

"You just take all those feelings of rejection, and pour them into something you can sell on Etsy."

Focus on RESEARCH

COLD AND LONELY? THE PHYSICAL PERCEPTION OF OSTRACISM

In English, loneliness is often described as cold, as in "I am cold and lonely without you," and when we are left out or rejected by others we might say they gave us the "cold shoulder." Other languages have similar metaphors and idioms. Chen-Bo Zhong and Geoffrey Leonardelli (2008) of the University of Toronto did a study to see if we actually feel colder when we are left out. They randomly assigned 65 undergraduate students to one of two conditions. The first group of participants were asked to recall a time when they were socially isolated or excluded. The second group were asked to recall a time when they were included. Then both groups were asked to estimate the temperature of the room they were in (under the cover story that university maintenance staff needed this information). Participants who recalled being rejected estimated the room to be colder than did those who recalled a time when they were included. Zhong and Leonardelli did a second experiment that had

52 undergraduate students play a virtual ball game in which the computer was programmed to exclude some participants. Afterward, participants were asked to fill out a supposedly unrelated marketing questionnaire in which they had to rate the desirability of different food products which included warm drinks (e.g., coffee or soup) and cold drinks (e.g., icy Coke). They found that participants who had been excluded desired a warm drink more than did those who had been included. These findings support the idea that our social experiences do affect our physical experiences, and that satisfying interactions with others influence not only our physical well-being, but also our perceptions of our physical reality.

Critical thinking: *What other interpersonal situations are associated with physical characteristics through metaphors or idioms? What reasons might explain the connection?*

are simpler and operate in infancy and early childhood, and emotion schemas. Emotion schemas are what we typically experiences as adults. They require more sophisticated cognitive skills (e.g., beyond interpreting a sensation of pain or pleasure) and involve an interaction between feeling and thinking. Much of the debate regarding what emotions are seems to revolve around the role of cognition in emotions. For our purposes (understanding the role of emotions in interpersonal communication) we will define **emotions** as a feeling state that includes physiological changes, a cognitive interpretations, and an outward expression. While finding an agreed upon definition of emotion is challenging, there is considerable consensus that emotions play an important role in motivating and focusing human behaviour and in social interactions. In the context of interpersonal communication it is useful to examine three components of our definition in order to better understand the role of emotion

in our social interactions (Planalp, 1999; Scherer, 2000).

Physiological Changes

When a person has strong emotions, many bodily changes take place. For example, the physical components of fear include an increased heartbeat, a rise in blood pressure, an increase in adrenalin secretions, a high blood-sugar level, a slowing of digestion, and a dilation of the pupils (Schauer and Elbert, 2010). Some of these changes are recognizable to the person having them. Such physiological messages can offer a significant clue to your emotions once you become aware of them. A churning stomach or tense jaw can also be a signal that something is wrong.

Cognitive Interpretations

Although there may be cases in which there is a direct connection between physical behaviour and emotional states, in most situations, the mind plays an important role in determining how we feel. As we noted, some physiological components of fear are a racing heart, perspiration, tense muscles, and raised blood pressure. Interestingly enough, these symptoms are similar to the physical changes that accompany excitement, joy, and other emotions. In other words, if we were to measure the physical condition of someone having a strong emotion, we would have a hard time knowing whether that person was trembling with fear or with excitement. The recognition that the bodily components of most emotions are similar led some psychologists to conclude that the experience of fright, joy, or anger comes primarily from the labels—and the accompanying cognitive interpretations—we give to our physical symptoms (Valins, 1966). In his book *Shyness: What It Is, What to Do about It*, psychologist Philip Zimbardo (1977, p. 53) offers a good example of this principle:

> I notice I'm perspiring while lecturing. From that I infer I am nervous. If it occurs often, I might even label myself a "nervous person." Once I have the label, the next question I must answer is, "Why am I nervous?" Then I start to search for an appropriate explanation. I might notice some students leaving the room, or being inattentive. I am nervous because I'm not giving a good lecture. That makes me nervous. How do I know it's not good? Because I'm boring my audience. I am nervous because I am a boring lecturer and I want to be a good lecturer. I feel inadequate. Maybe I should open a delicatessen instead. Just then a student says, "It's hot in here, I'm perspiring and it makes it tough to concentrate on your lecture." Instantly, I'm no longer "nervous" or "boring."

Zimbardo discusses the consequences of making inaccurate or exaggerated attributions such as these. In a survey of more than 5000 people, over 80 per cent described themselves as having been shy at some time in their lives, and more than 40 per cent considered themselves to be shy at present. Most significantly,

those who labelled themselves "not shy" behaved in virtually the same way as their shy counterparts. They would blush, perspire, and feel their hearts pounding in certain social situations. The biggest difference between the two groups seemed to be the label with which they described themselves. This is a significant difference. Someone who notices the symptoms we've described and thinks, "I'm such a shy person!" will most likely feel more uncomfortable and communicate less well than another person with the same symptoms who thinks, "Well, I'm a bit shaky (or excited) here, but that is to be expected."

We'll take a closer look at ways to reduce unpleasant emotions through cognitive processes later in this chapter.

Outward Expression

Feelings are often apparent by observable changes. Some of these changes involve a person's appearance: blushing, sweating, and so on. Other changes involve behaviour: a distinctive facial expression, a particular posture, certain gestures, different vocal tone and rate, and so on.

Although it's reasonably easy to tell when someone is feeling a strong emotion, it's more difficult to be certain exactly what that emotion might be. A slumped posture and a sigh may be a sign of sadness or fatigue. Likewise, trembling hands may indicate excitement or fear. As we shall see in Chapter 7, non-verbal behaviour is usually ambiguous, and it's dangerous to assume that it can be "read" with much accuracy.

Although we usually think of non-verbal behaviour as the reaction to an emotional state, there may be times when the reverse is true—when non-verbal behaviour actually causes emotions. When volunteers were coached to smile, they reported feeling better, and when they altered their expressions to look unhappy, they felt worse (Kleinke et al., 1998). Previous research by Paul Ekman and his colleagues (1983) produced similar results, with subjects feeling afraid, angry, disgusted,

Focus on RESEARCH

EMOTIONS SHAPE PERCEPTIONS

Is love blind? Stephen Most and his colleagues (2010) at the University of Delaware are pretty sure that *jealousy* is. In their study, heterosexual couples, sitting beside each other, but with a curtain between them, viewed a series of pictures on computer monitors. First the women looked at a rapidly presented series of landscape pictures and tried to pick out the target image, which wasn't upright, and to indicate which way it was rotated (right or left). Within this series of pictures was a distracter picture (an emotional or erotic picture). At the same time, the men were asked to rate the attractiveness of a series of landscape pictures. In the next step, the women were told that they would complete the same task again, but this time their partners would be rating the attractiveness of pictures of single women, some of whom attended the same university. The women reported their feelings of uneasiness about their partners completing this task. Only data for women who felt more uneasy about their partners rating pictures of women than rating landscapes were used in the analysis.

Women were significantly better at accurately seeing the rotated target pictures when their partners were rating landscapes compared to when their partners were rating women. The more uneasy the women felt about their partner rating other women, the more often they missed the target picture. The investigators suggest that the women's uneasy feelings of jealousy impaired their ability to accurately see the pictures—evidence that in some situations jealousy is blinding.

Critical thinking: *Do you think these investigators would have found similar results if they had switched the tasks and had the men complete the task that required seeing the rotated pictures?*

---

amused, sad, surprised, and contemptuous when they created facial expressions that mimicked those feelings. As behavioural scientists like to say, it can be easier to act yourself into new ways of feeling than to feel yourself into new ways of acting.

Non-verbal behaviour is a powerful way of communicating emotion. In fact, non-verbal actions are better at conveying attitudes than they are at expressing ideas. But sometimes, words are necessary to express feelings. Is your friend's uncharacteristically short temper a sign of anger at you, or does it mean something less personal? Is a lover's unenthusiastic response a sign of boredom with you or the result of a long workday? Is a new acquaintance mistaking your friendliness for a come-on? There are times—especially in our low-context culture—when you cannot rely on perceptiveness to make sure a message is communicated and understood accurately.

The ability to communicate clearly about feelings has been characterized as part of *emotional intelligence*, which we discussed earlier in this chapter. Awareness of the intensity of emotions and the vocabulary to describe them accurately is important. Reluctance or an inability to express emotions is associated with depression and unhappiness (Barr et al., 2008). Although we understand many words that describe emotions in varying intensity, we tend to rely on a few basic emotional labels (happy, sad, mad, etc.), and increase or decrease their intensity with words like "really," "kind of," and so on. Rather than using these modifiers—"I was really, really happy" and "I was kind of angry"—to increase or decrease the intensity of our descriptions, we can enhance others' understanding of our experiences by choosing more accurate descriptors such as ecstatic or annoyed.

Research by John Gottman and his associates (1997) has shown that the way parents talk to their children about emotions has a strong influence on the children's development. They show how the "coaching approach" gives children skills for communicating their feelings in later life which in turn leads to much more

Describe the three components of emotions and provide examples of each.

satisfying relationships. The researchers identified two distinct parenting styles: "emotion coaching" and "emotion dismissing." Parents who encourage their children to reflect on and talk constructively about emotions have children who report greater self-confidence, increased well-being, and more positive relationships compared to children whose parents are dismissive of their emotions (Young, 2009). Later in this chapter, you will find some guidelines for communicating effectively about emotions.

Influences on Emotional Expression

Each of us is born with the disposition to reveal our emotions, at least non-verbally. But over time, a wide range of differences develops in emotional expression. In the next few pages, we will look at some influences that shape how people communicate their feelings.

Personality

Science has established an increasingly clear relationship between personality and the way people experience and communicate emotions (Gross et al., 1998). For example, extroverted people—those with a tendency to be cheerful and optimistic, and to enjoy social contact—report more positive emotions in everyday life than more introverted individuals (Costa and McCrae, 1980; McCrae and Costa, 2008). Conversely, people with neurotic personalities—those with a tendency to worry, be anxious, and feel apprehensive—report more negative emotions than less neurotic individuals. In addition, individuals with neurotic tendencies are less accurate when identifying negative emotions in others (Edgar et al., 2012; Matsumoto et al., 2000).

Although personality can be a strong force, it does not have to govern your emotions or communication satisfaction. Think of shyness, which can be considered the opposite of extroversion. Introverted people can devise comfortable and effective strategies for reaching out. For example, the absence of auditory and visual cues in text-based communication has been found to help shy people feel less apprehension about communicating with new people (Hammik and Lee, 2014). The Internet provides a way for shy people to initiate communication and gain confidence that will support them in their face-to-face interactions.

Culture

Over 100 years of research confirms the fact that certain basic emotions are experienced by people around the world (Gudykunst and Kim, 2003), no matter where a person is born and regardless of his background. The ability to feel happiness, anger, and fear, as well as the similar ways people express these emotions seems to be universal, at least in regard to their facial expressions and vocal qualities. A smile or scowl, for example, is understood everywhere, and people from different cultures can recognize anger, fear, and happiness in other people's voice quality even when they do not understand the language spoken (Bryant and Barrett, 2008).

Of course, this does not mean that the same events generate the same emotion in all cultures. The notion of eating cod tongues might bring a smile of delight to some residents of Newfoundland, though it would cause many other Canadians to grimace in disgust. More to the point, research has shown that fear of strangers and risky situations is more common among people living in North America and Europe than those living in Japan, whereas Japanese tend to be more apprehensive about relational communication than North Americans and Europeans (Ting-Toomey, 1991).

There are also differences in the degree to which people in various cultures display their feelings (Cole et al., 2002; Safdar et al., 2009).

There are a lot of influences that shape how we communicate our feelings. How do you see the influences discussed in this chapter shaping the way you communicate?

members of highly individualistic cultures like Canada and the United States feel comfortable revealing their feelings to people they are close to (Gallois, 1993; Matsumoto, 1991; Park et al., 2013). Individualists and collectivists also handle emotional expression with members of out-groups differently. Whereas collectivists are quite frank about expressing negative emotions toward outsiders, individualists are more likely to hide emotions such as dislike (Triandis, 1994). It's easy to see how differences in display rules can lead to communication problems. For example, individualistic North Americans might view collectivistic Asians as less than candid, whereas a person raised in Asia could easily regard North Americans as being overly demonstrative.

For instance, in a cross-cultural investigation of display rules for seven basic emotions (happiness, sadness, anger, fear, disgust, contempt, and surprise) researchers found that Canadian university students believed showing positive emotions (e.g., happiness, surprise) and powerfully negative emotions (e.g., anger, disgust) was appropriate more often than Japanese students. Japanese students had more varied rules for displaying emotions, depending on whom they were interacting with, compared to the Canadian students (Safdar et al., 2009). These differences in ideas about appropriate displays of emotions are consistent with general norms for emotional expression among collectivistic and individualistic cultures (Matsumoto et al., 2008). Clearly, expressing strong negative emotions such as anger and disgust could easily threaten interpersonal harmony.

In fact, one of the most significant factors influencing emotional expression is the position of a culture on the individualism–collectivism spectrum. Members of collectivistic cultures (such as Japan and India) prize harmony among members of their in-group and discourage the expression of any negative emotions that might upset relationships among people who belong to it. By contrast,

Cultural background influences the way we interpret others' emotions as well as the way we express our own. Recognition of emotion is generally more accurate when the person expressing the emotion and the person judging the emotional display belong to the same cultural group (Dailey et al., 2010; Elfenbein and Ambady, 2002a). It makes sense that it would be easier to judge another person's emotional expressions accurately if you were familiar with the subtle differences in expressive style that are part of their culture. In a comparison of university students from Africa (Gabon) and North America (Quebec), Hillary Elfenbein and her colleagues (2007) found that members of these two groups of students had their own culturally unique differences in facial expressions of some emotions. Knowledge of these unique variations in emotional expression gave members of the same culture a distinct advantage for accurately reading emotions within their cultural group. The investigators compared these uniquely distinct variations in emotional expression to dialects—variations in a standard language.

In addition to knowledge of unique variations in facial expressions, members of different cultures pay closer attention to different facial cues when interpreting emotional expressions. People in individualistic cultures, such as Canada and the United States, pay closer attention to a person's mouth. Conversely, people in collectivist cultures, such as China, South Korea, and Japan, are more likely to look more carefully at a person's eyes. These cultures even differ in their use of emoticons, with people from individualistic cultures usually using symbols that direct attention to the mouth [:) or :–( ] while people from collectivist cultures are more likely to vary the direction of the eyes [^_^ or ; _ ;] (Park, Barash et al., 2013; Yuki et al., 2007).

There is evidence that in cultures where interdependence is valued, people are more skilled at reading the emotions of others. For example, Jeffrey Sanchez-Burks and his colleagues (2003) found that Koreans were better able to infer feelings and attitudes of employers than Americans were. An emphasis on relationships within a culture encourages concern about other people's feelings. Just as people from the same culture seem to be significantly better at recognizing each other's emotions, dating and married couples are significantly better at recognizing each other's emotional cues than strangers are (Elfenbein and Ambady, 2002b). Similarly, people are more likely to express emotions with those they know well in both face-to-face and computer-mediated communication (Derks et al., 2008).

Biological Sex and Gender

Even within our culture, biological sex and gender roles often shape the ways in which men and women experience and express their emotions (Wester et al., 2002).For instance, women have been observed to differ from men in their subjective ratings of facial emotional expressions. Women appear more sensitive to extreme expressions of emotion (both positive and negative) than men. Women also seem to have a better memory for the facial expressions they observe in daily life and a better memory for emotional events (Sawada et al., 2014; Seidlitz and Diener, 1998).

Research on emotional expression also suggests that there is some truth in the cultural stereotype of the inexpressive male and the more demonstrative female. In many cultures males are socialized not to express emotions such as sadness, but their expression of anger is deemed acceptable. In contrast, women's expressions of sadness fits with the female stereotype for emotional expression, but their expressions of anger do not. Megan McCarty and her colleagues (2014) found that when men and women experience counter stereotypic emotions in public places (e.g., men feeling sad and women feeling angry) it interfered with performance on a cognitive task. This was true even if they did not express their emotions publicly. These researchers suggest that experiencing emotions in which we have been socialized not to express, is taxing. Similarly, when women buck social conventions and express counter stereotypic emotions such as contempt, they report feeling more unhappy

© Georgethefourth/iStockphoto.

Women appear to be better at detecting and interpreting emotional expressions. Do you think this is an advantage or disadvantage for women?

Focus on RESEARCH

SAVOURING HAPPINESS

Most people seem to want to understand their emotions and behaviours. Research regarding self-reflection on negative emotions has produced some contradictory findings. On the one hand, understanding our emotional responses to negative experiences can help us to adapt, as well as cope with and solve problems. On the other hand, repeatedly focusing on negative emotions (sometimes called rumination) can make bad feelings last much longer than necessary and make us more vulnerable to depression (Cox et al., 2010). We will examine the negative effects of rumination later in this chapter, when we consider common irrational beliefs and how they perpetuate debilitative emotions. But what about reflecting on positive emotions? Can reflecting on positive emotions make us happier and increase our life satisfaction?

Jordi Quoidbach from the University of Liege, Belgium; Elizabeth Berry from the University of British Columbia; and their colleagues (2010) compared eight strategies that can help people either savour or dampen their positive emotions. The four savouring strategies involved increasing positive experiences by expressing positive emotions with non-verbal behaviours:

- *Behavioural display:* smiling.
- *Being present:* deliberately paying attention to the pleasant experience.
- *Capitalizing:* celebrating positive events by communicating about them with others.
- *Positive mental time:* remembering or anticipating positive events.

The four dampening strategies were:

- *Suppression:* hiding positive emotions.
- *Distraction:* not paying attention to positive events.
- *Fault finding:* paying attention to negative elements in otherwise positive situations.

- *Negative mental time travel:* remembering positive events as a consequence of situational factors ("I got an A because the test was easy") and anticipating negative future consequences ("My luck will run out soon").

These investigators gave 282 people (university students and employees) detailed descriptions of situations that would elicit contentment, joy, awe, excitement, pride, and gratitude along with the eight possible reactions based on the savouring and dampening strategies described above. They also measured the participants' emotional well-being, life satisfaction, and overall happiness using standardized questionnaires. They found that people's emotional well-being was associated with remembering or anticipating positive events (positive mental time travel) and paying attention to the pleasant experience (being present). Not surprisingly, life satisfaction was lower for those who found fault and engaged in negative mental time travel, and higher for participants who capitalized on the positive events by sharing their experiences with others. The more savouring strategies the participants used, the greater their self-reported happiness. Essentially the more you can be present in the moment, share your positive experiences with others, show your positive emotions, and reflect on previous happy times or anticipate good things to come, the happier you will be. These investigators suggest that people need to develop the ability to engage in all these savouring strategies if they want to cultivate lasting happiness in their lives.

Critical thinking: *These investigators found that using a* single *savouring strategy was not related to increased happiness. Whereas, participants who use a* variety *of strategies reported greater happiness. How does this fit with other things you have learned about effective communication and well-being?*

than men do (Crowley and Knowles, 2014). In addition, when men express anger in a professional context they are generally given higher status by their peers, but when women do the same they lose status (Brescoll and Uhlmann, 2008). When women display anger at work they are often described as angry people ("*She's* out of control") whereas male expression of anger in the workplace is attributed to the situation at hand ("*The situation* was frustrating"). Recall the fundamental attribution error and stereotypes described in Chapter 3. Clearly we are susceptible to stereotypes about emotional expression and the simplistic causal attributions that perpetuate them.

On the whole, women are more likely than men to express a wide range of feelings verbally and non-verbally (Kunkel and Burleson, 1999; Naito et al., 2005). The same differences between male and female emotional expressiveness appear to apply in text messages too. Women are more likely to be more emotionally expressive and more likely to use emoticons when sending messages.

Social Conventions

Canadians have a reputation for being polite, deferential, and law-abiding people (Adams, 2003). Mainstream North American culture generally discourages the direct expression of most emotions. Count the number of genuine emotional expressions you hear over a two- or three-day period and you will discover that such expressions are rare. People are generally comfortable making statements of fact and often delight in expressing their opinions, but they rarely disclose how they feel.

Not surprisingly, the emotions that people do share directly are usually positive. Communicators are reluctant to send messages that embarrass or threaten the face of others (Shimanoff, 1988). For instance, contemporary society discourages expressions of anger. When compared to past centuries, many societies today strive to suppress this "unpleasant" emotion and its expression in almost every situation, including child-rearing, the workplace, and personal relationships (Pinker, 2011; Stearns and Stearns, 1986). One study of married couples (Shimanoff, 1985) revealed that the partners shared complimentary feelings ("I love you") or face-saving ones ("I'm sorry I yelled at you"). They also willingly disclosed both positive and negative feelings about absent third parties ("I like Fred," "I'm uncomfortable around Gloria"). On the other hand, they rarely verbalized face-threatening feelings ("I'm disappointed in you") or hostility ("I'm mad at you").

In computer-mediated communication, as well, people are more likely to express positive emotions. Emoticons are used in CMC primarily to express emotions that strengthen the verbal part of the message and express humour (Derks et al., 2008). It is interesting that people favour the use of emoticons to convey positive emotions, as some research suggests that people receiving emails at work (where the use of emoticons is usually discouraged) are more likely to misinterpret the emoticons as being more emotionally negative or neutral than intended (Kock, 2005; Kruger et al., 2005).

Social Roles

Expression of emotions is also limited by the requirements of many social roles. Salespeople are taught always to smile at customers, no matter how obnoxiously they are behaving. Teachers are portrayed as paragons of rationality, supposedly representing their field of expertise and instructing their students with total impartiality. Students are often rewarded for asking "acceptable" questions and otherwise being submissive creatures (Trenholm and Rose, 1980). Emergency personnel, health-care providers, and people who work in a wide variety of human services are often required to manage their own emotions as well as the emotions of others when they are on the job (Scott and Myers, 2005; Williams, 2013).

The result of all these restrictions is that many of us lose the ability to feel deeply. Just as a muscle withers away when it is unused, our capacity to recognize and act on certain emotions decreases without practice. It's hard to cry after spending most of one's life fulfilling the role society expects of a man, even when the tears are inside. After years of denying anger, the ability to recognize that feeling takes real effort. For someone who has never acknowledged love for one's friends, accepting that emotion can be quite difficult.

REFLECTION

EMAIL AS A SAFE CHANNEL FOR EMOTIONAL EXPRESSION

I've never been very close to my sister, but last year we started sending emails to each other. At first, we "e-chatted" about once a week; now, it's almost daily. What's interesting is that my sister does not show her emotions very much in person, but in her emails, she "bares her soul" to me.

Last week, we got together in person for the first time in months. I thought we would pick right up at the same level of emotional exchange that had become the norm in our online discussions. Wrong! In face-to-face conversation, it still seemed hard for her to express her feelings. It was kind of hard for me, too.

Funny thing is, she sent me an emotional email after she got home, telling me how much she enjoyed our get-together. It was warm and touching. It was also something she would never say to me in person.

Fear of Self-Disclosure

In a society that discourages the expression of feelings, emotional self-disclosure can seem risky to people. For a parent, boss, or teacher whose life has been built on the image of confidence and certainty, it may be frightening to say, "I'm sorry. I was wrong."

Moreover, someone who musters up the courage to share feelings such as these still risks unpleasant consequences. Others might misunderstand. An expression of affection might be construed as a romantic invitation, and a confession of uncertainty might appear to be a sign of weakness. Another risk is that emotional honesty might make others feel uncomfortable. Finally, there's always a chance that emotional honesty could be used against you, either out of cruelty or thoughtlessness. In Chapter 2, we discussed alternatives to complete disclosure and suggested circumstances when it can be both wise and ethical to keep your feelings to yourself.

Emotional Contagion

Along with cultural rules, social roles, and self-induced fears, our emotions are also affected by the feelings of those around us through **emotional contagion**, the process by which emotions are transferred from one person to another. As Daniel Goleman (1995, p. 115) observed, "We catch feelings from one another as though they were some kind of social virus." Husbands and wives influence each other's emotions, both positive and negative (Segrin and Flora, 2005) as do co-workers—sometimes "catching" burnout from each other (Robbins and Judge, 2010). Service providers can catch the angry emotions of complaining customers (Dallimore et al., 2007) sometimes making it difficult to provide "service with a smile."

Although people differ in the extent to which they are susceptible to emotional contagion (Doherty, 1997; Ilies et al., 2007; Papousek et al., 2008), most of us recognize the degree to which emotions are "infectious." You can probably remember times when being around a calm person made you feel more at peace, or when your previously sunny mood was spoiled by contact with someone bad-tempered. Researchers have demonstrated that this process can happen quickly, and with little or no verbal communication. In one study (Sullins, 1991), two volunteers completed a survey that described their moods. They spent two unsupervised minutes together, ostensibly waiting for the researcher to return to the room. At the end of that time, they completed another emotional survey. Time after time, the brief exposure resulted in the less expressive partner's moods coming to resemble those of

 **CHECK IT!**

Describe seven influences on emotional expression that shape how people communicate their feelings.

© MorelSO/iStockphoto.

Emotions can be contagious, so it's important that we express them well. Can you think of a time you "caught" an emotion from someone else?

the more expressive one. If an expressive communicator can shape another person's feelings with so little effort in such a short time, it's easy to understand how emotions can be even more infectious with prolonged contact.

Guidelines for Expressing Emotions

A wide range of research supports the value of expressing emotions appropriately. While research shows that people who know how to share their feelings are typically healthier than those who do not, both types of people can suffer physiologically if their emotions are not expressed *constructively*. For example, inexpressive people—those who value rationality and self-control, try to keep their feelings and impulses under wraps, and deny distress—are more likely to suffer from ailments such as cancer, asthma, and heart disease (Burton and King, 2008; DeAngelis, 1992; Mayne, 1999). As well, people who are overly expressive—those who freely demonstrate their emotions through words and facial expressions—are more likely to suffer from high blood pressure. Some research shows that their blood pressure jumps an average of 20 points, and in

some people as much as 100 points (Mayne, 1999; Siegman and Snow, 1997). To reiterate, the key to health, then, is to learn how to express emotions effectively and constructively.

Beyond the physiological benefits, another advantage of expressing emotions effectively is the chance of improving relationships (Garfield, 2010; Kennedy-Moore and Watson, 1999). As we explain in Chapter 8, self-disclosure is one path (though not the only one) to intimacy. Even on the job, many managers and organizational researchers are contradicting generations of tradition by suggesting that expressing emotions constructively can lead to career success and also help workers feel better (Nelton, 1996; O'Neill, 2009).

Despite its benefits, expressing emotions effectively is not a simple matter (Fussell, 2002). It's obvious that showing every feeling of boredom, fear, anger, or frustration would get you into trouble. Even the indiscriminate sharing of positive feelings—love, affection, and so on—is not always wise. On the other hand, withholding emotions can be personally frustrating and can keep relationships from growing and prospering.

The following suggestions can help you decide when and how to express your emotions. Combined with the guidelines for self-disclosure in Chapter 2, they can improve the effectiveness of your emotional expression.

Recognize Your Feelings

Answering the question, "How do you feel?" is not as easy for some people as others (Peper, 2000). Communication researchers Melanie Booth-Butterfield and Steven Booth-Butterfield (1998) have found that some people (whom they term "affectively oriented") are much more aware of their own emotional states and use information about those feelings when they make important decisions. By contrast, people with a low affective orientation are usually unaware of their emotions and tend to consider feelings to be useless and unimportant. The researchers summarize studies showing a relationship between awareness of feelings and a wide range of valuable traits, including having positive relationships between parents and children, being able to comfort others, being sensitive to non-verbal cues, and even being able to skilfully use humour to communicate. In other words, being aware of your feelings is an important ingredient in effective communication.

Sometimes recognizing your emotions can be difficult. Journaling can help, as can talking to someone close to you. What are some other ways you come to recognize your emotions?

As we saw earlier in this chapter, there are a number of ways in which feelings become recognizable. Physiological changes can be a clear sign of your emotional state. Monitoring your non-verbal behaviour is another excellent way to keep in touch with your feelings. You can also recognize your emotions by observing your thoughts, as well as the verbal messages you send to others. It's not far from the verbal statement, "I hate this!" to the realization that you are angry (or bored, nervous, or embarrassed).

Choose the Best Language

Most people suffer from impoverished emotional vocabularies. Ask them how they are feeling, and the response will almost always include the same terms: *good* or *bad*, *terrible* or *great*, and so on. Take a moment now and see how many feelings you can write down. After you have done your best, look at the "Self-Assessment" activity on page 131 and see which ones you have missed from this obviously incomplete list.

Many communicators think they are expressing feelings when, in fact, their statements are **emotionally counterfeit**. For example, it sounds emotionally revealing to say, "I feel like going to a show" or "I feel we've been seeing too much of each other." But, in fact, neither of these statements has any emotional content. In the first sentence, the word *feel* really stands in for an intention: "I *want* to go to a show." In the second sentence, the "feeling" is really a thought: "I *think* we've been seeing too much of each other." You can recognize the absence of emotion in each case by adding a genuine word of feeling to it— for instance, "I'm *bored* and I want to go to a show" or "I think we've been seeing too much of each other and I feel *confined*."

Relying on a small vocabulary of feelings is as limiting as using only a few terms to describe colours. To say that the ocean in all its moods, the sky as it varies from day to day, and the colour of your true love's eyes are all "blue" tells only a fraction of the story. Likewise, it's overly broad to use a term like *good* or *great* to describe how you feel in situations as different as earning a high grade, finishing a marathon, and hearing the words "I love you" from a special person.

There are several ways to express a feeling verbally:

- Through *single words*: "I'm angry" (or "excited," "depressed," "curious," and so on).
- By describing *what's happening to you metaphorically*: "My stomach is tied in knots," "I'm on top of the world."
- By describing *what you'd like to do*: "I want to run away," "I'd like to give you a hug," "I feel like giving up."

One way to clarify emotional expression is to avoid overqualifying or downplaying your emotions—"I'm a *little* unhappy," "I'm *pretty* excited," or "I'm *sort of* confused." Of course, not all emotions are strong ones. We do feel degrees of sadness and joy, for example, but some communicators have a tendency to discount almost every feeling. Do you?

Finally, you can improve emotional expression by making it clear that your feeling is centred on a specific set of circumstances, rather than the whole relationship. Instead of saying, "I resent you," say, "I get resentful when you do not keep your promises." Rather than, "I'm bored with you," say, "I get bored when you talk about money."

Share Multiple Feelings

Many times, the feeling you express is not the only one you are experiencing. For example, you might often express your anger, but overlook the confusion, disappointment, frustration, sadness, or embarrassment that preceded it. To understand the importance of expressing multiple emotions, consider the following examples. For each one, ask yourself two questions: How would I feel? What feelings might I express?

Emotionally counterfeit: statements that appear to describe feelings, but lack emotional content.

- An out-of-town friend has promised to arrive at your house at six o'clock. When your guest hasn't arrived by nine, you are convinced there has been a terrible accident. Just as you pick up the phone to call the police and local hospitals, your friend strolls in with an offhand remark about getting a late start.
- You and your companion have a fight just before leaving for a party. Deep inside, you know you were mostly to blame, even though you are not willing to admit it. When you arrive at the party, your companion leaves you and flirts with several other attractive guests.

In situations like these, you would probably feel several emotions. Consider the case of the late friend. Your first reaction to his arrival would probably be relief: "Thank goodness, he's safe!" But you would also probably feel anger: "Why didn't he phone to tell me he'd be late?" The second example would probably leave you with an even greater number of emotions: guilt at contributing to the fight, hurt and perhaps embarrassment at your friend's flirtations, and anger at this sort of vengefulness.

Despite the commonness of experiencing several emotions at the same time, we often communicate only one feeling—usually, the most negative one. In both of the preceding examples, you might show only your anger, leaving the other person with little idea of the full range of your feelings. Consider the different reaction you would get by describing *all* your emotions in these situations as well as others (see the "Reflection" box on page 133 for example.)

Recognize the Difference between Feeling and Acting

Just because you feel a certain way does not mean you must always act on it. In fact, there is compelling evidence that people who act out angry feelings—even by hitting a punching bag—actually feel worse than those who

Self-Assessment

Check off the emotions that you experience often. Then put a plus sign next to those that you express effectively, and a minus sign next to the ones that you communicate in less-than-satisfactory ways. (If one or more of your most-used or expressed emotions is not on this short list of all the possibilities, add it to the list.)

____ affectionate	____ afraid	____ agitated	____ irritable	____ isolated	____ jealous
____ alienated	____ amazed	____ ambivalent	____ joyful	____ lazy	____ lively
____ angry	____ annoyed	____ anxious	____ lonely	____ lovable	____ loving
____ apathetic	____ ashamed	____ bashful	____ love struck	____ mad	____ mean
____ beaten	____ bewildered	____ bored	____ melancholy	____ miserable	____ misunderstood
____ bothered	____ brave	____ calm	____ mixed up	____ mortified	____ needy
____ cantankerous	____ carefree	____ caring	____ neglected	____ nervous	____ optimistic
____ cheerful	____ cocky	____ cold	____ overwhelmed	____ paranoid	____ passionate
____ comfortable	____ compassionate	____ concerned	____ peaceful	____ pessimistic	____ phony
____ confident	____ confused	____ content	____ playful	____ pleased	____ possessive
____ crazy	____ creative	____ cruel	____ preoccupied	____ prejudiced	____ pressured
____ curious	____ defeated	____ defensive	____ protective	____ puzzled	____ quiet
____ delighted	____ depressed	____ desperate	____ refreshed	____ regretful	____ relieved
____ detached	____ devastated	____ disappointed	____ rejected	____ remorseful	____ repulsed
____ disgusted	____ disturbed	____ eager	____ repulsive	____ resentful	____ restless
____ ecstatic	____ edgy	____ elated	____ restrained	____ ridiculous	____ romantic
____ embarrassed	____ empty	____ enthusiastic	____ sad	____ sadistic	____ secure
____ envious	____ evil	____ excited	____ seductive	____ self-pitying	____ self-reliant
____ exhausted	____ exhilarated	____ fearful	____ sentimental	____ sexy	____ shaky
____ fed up	____ fidgety	____ fixated	____ shocked	____ shy	____ silly
____ flattered	____ flirtatious	____ foolish	____ sincere	____ sinful	____ smug
____ forlorn	____ friendly	____ frightened	____ sorry	____ strong	____ stubborn
____ frustrated	____ furious	____ generous	____ stupid	____ subdued	____ superior
____ gentle	____ glad	____ glum	____ suicidal	____ supported	____ surprised
____ grateful	____ guilty	____ gutless	____ suspicious	____ sympathetic	____ tender
____ happy	____ harassed	____ hateful	____ tense	____ terrified	____ tired
____ helpless	____ high	____ hopeful	____ touchy	____ trapped	____ triumphant
____ hopeless	____ horrible	____ hostile	____ two-faced	____ ugly	____ uneasy
____ humiliated	____ hurried	____ hurt	____ unsure	____ useless	____ vindictive
____ hyper	____ hysterical	____ impatient	____ violent	____ vulnerable	____ warm
____ impressed	____ incompetent	____ inhibited	____ weak	____ weary	____ weepy
____ indecisive	____ inferior	____ insecure	____ wonderful	____ worried	____ wacky
____ insincere	____ interested	____ intimidated	____ youthful	____ zany	____ zonked

What lessons do your responses show? In what ways are you satisfied with your emotional expression? In what areas would you like to improve it? Keep your findings in mind as you continue reading this chapter.

experience anger without lashing out (Bushman et al., 1999; Parlamis, et. al, 2010). In addition, venting anger has many negative personal and interpersonal outcomes (Gibson and Callister, 2010; Parlamis, 2012).

Recognizing the difference between feeling and acting can liberate you from the fear that getting in touch with certain emotions will commit you to some disastrous course of action. If, for instance, you think, "I'm so nervous about the interview that I want to cancel it and pretend I'm sick," it becomes possible to explore why you feel so anxious and then work to remedy the problem. Pretending that nothing is the matter, on the other hand, will do nothing to diminish your anxiety, which can then block your chances for success.

Accept Responsibility for Your Feelings

As you will soon read, people do not *make us* like or dislike them, and believing that they do denies accepting accountability and the responsibility each of us has for our own emotions. It's important to make sure that your emotional expressions do not blame others for the way you feel. The "I" language described in Chapter 6 makes it clear that you own your feelings. For example, instead of saying, "You're making me angry," it is more accurate to say, "I'm feeling angry." Instead of uttering, "You hurt my feelings," a more responsible statement is, "I feel hurt when you do that."

Choose the Best Time and Place to Express Your Feelings

Often, the first flush of a strong feeling is not the best time to speak out. If you are awakened by the racket caused by a noisy neighbour and you storm over to complain, you may say things you will later regret. In such a case, it's probably wiser to wait until you have thought out carefully how you might express your feelings in a way that would be most likely to be heard.

Even after you have waited for the first flush of feeling to subside, it's still important to choose the time that is best suited to

CHECK IT!

What are the six guidelines to keep in mind when expressing emotions?

the message. If you are rushed or tired or disturbed by some other matter, that is probably a good reason for postponing the expression of your feeling. Often, it can take a great amount of time and effort to attend to your emotions, and fatigue or distraction will make it difficult to follow through on the matter you have started. Similarly, you ought to be sure that the recipient of your message is ready to hear you out before you begin.

The private articulation of emotion through expressive writing has been associated with a variety of benefits for health and well-being (Crowley, 2014; Knowles et al., 2011; Krpan et al., 2013; Romero, 2008). It is unclear exactly why writing about emotional experiences is associated with positive outcomes. It may be that the process of writing provides individuals with insight into themselves and their experiences and by creating meaning and gaining personal insight they decrease their stress (Pennebaker and Chung, 2007). In any case, private, written expression of emotions is an option when you want to express, but not share your emotions.

There are also cases where you may choose to never express your feelings. Even if you are dying to tell an instructor that her lectures leave you bored to a stupor, you might decide it's best to answer her question "How's class going?" with an innocuous "Okay." And even though you may be irritated by the arrogance of a police officer who stops you for speeding, the smartest approach might be to keep your feelings to yourself.

Managing Difficult Emotions

Perceiving others more accurately is not the only challenge that communicators face. At times, we view *ourselves* in a distorted way. These distorted self-perceptions can generate a wide range of feelings—insecurity, anger, and guilt, to name a few—that interfere with effective communication. To begin understanding how this process works, read on.

Facilitative and Debilitative Emotions

We need to make a distinction between **facilitative emotions**, which contribute to effective functioning, and **debilitative emotions**, which hinder or prevent effective performance. A classic example of a debilitative emotion is *communication apprehension*—feelings of anxiety that plague some people at the prospect of communicating in an unfamiliar or difficult situation such as giving a speech, meeting strangers, or being interviewed for a job.

Not surprisingly, debilitative emotions like communication apprehension can lead to a variety of problems in personal, business, educational, and even medical situations (McCroskey, 2009). The difference between facilitative and debilitative emotions is often not one of quality as much as degree. For instance, a certain amount of anger or irritation can be constructive, since it often stimulates a person to improve the unsatisfying conditions. Rage, on the other hand, usually makes matters worse. The same is true of fear. A little bit of nervousness before a job interview may inspire you just enough to improve your performance (athletes or actors who are too relaxed usually do not do well), but a job candidate who is visibly nervous is not likely to impress potential employers (Ayres and Crosby, 1995). One big difference, then, between facilitative and debilitative emotions is their *intensity*.

A second characteristic of debilitative feelings is their *extended duration*. Feeling depressed for a while after the breakup of a relationship or the loss of a job is natural. Spending the rest of one's life grieving over the loss accomplishes nothing. In the same way, staying angry at someone for a wrong inflicted long ago can be just as punishing to the grudge holder as to the wrongdoer. **Rumination** involves recurrent thoughts not demanded by the immediate environment (Sullivan et al., 2005). Prolonged brooding over past events has been associated with increased risk of depression, interpersonal conflict hostility, and aggression (Bushman, 2002; Bushman et al., 2005; Ray et al., 2008; Spasojevic and Alloy, 2002). Rehashing negative events over and over in your mind just prolongs the duration of negative emotions and makes them

REFLECTION

CHOOSING THE EMOTION TO EXPRESS FIRST

Not long ago, our seventeen-year-old daughter spent the entire night out—without telling us about her plans to stay at a friend's. By 2:00 a.m., we were in a panic. We frantically called the police and the local hospitals, but she couldn't be found anywhere. My wife and I spent the entire sleepless night praying that she was all right and imagining all the awful things that might have happened to her.

When our daughter's car came up the driveway at 7:30 a.m., I was never so relieved in my life! But as soon as she walked in the door and I realized she was okay, I really let her have it. "What were you thinking? How irresponsible can you be?" You can imagine how I sounded, and how defensively she reacted.

After a couple of minutes, I could see our "conversation" headed in the wrong direction, and that it was at least partly my fault. I had shared only my anger, and not the feelings of relief, concern, and love that were even more important. "Let's start over," I suggested. Then, I explained to her how worried we had been all night long, and what a relief it was for us to know that she was safe. What a difference! Our daughter still knew how angry we were, but she also understood that the anger came from love and concern. This experience taught me how important it is to share multiple feelings. Hearing the positive ones makes negative feelings a lot easier to accept.

more debilitating. While it is sometimes hard to stop ruminating, as we will soon see, it is possible.

Finally, debilitative emotions are frequently based on irrational thinking that we might be unaware of. In order to minimize these emotions, we first need to examine the relationship between thinking and feeling and then explore some of the irrational beliefs people commonly hold.

Experts argue that it is not events that cause people to feel bad, but the beliefs people hold about these events. Think about the last time you were upset. What role did your beliefs play in your emotional response?

Thoughts as a Cause of Feelings

The goal, then, is to find a method for getting rid of debilitative feelings while remaining sensitive to the more facilitative emotions. Fortunately, such a method—termed a **rational–emotive approach**—does exist (Ellis, 2001). This method is based on the idea that the key to changing feelings is to change unproductive thinking. Let's see how it works.

For most people, emotions seem to have a life of their own. They wish they could feel calm when approaching strangers, yet their voices quiver. They try to appear confident when asking for a raise, but their eyes twitch nervously. Many people would say that the strangers or the boss *makes* them feel nervous, just as they would say that a bee sting causes them to feel pain:

Activating Event	Consequence
bee sting	physical pain
meeting strangers	nervous feelings

When looking at emotions in this way, people may believe they have little control over how they feel. However, the causal relationship between activating events and emotional discomfort (or pleasure) is not as great as it seems. Cognitive psychologists and therapists argue that it is not events, such as meeting strangers or being jilted by a lover, that cause people to feel bad, but rather the *beliefs they hold* about these events.

American psychologist Albert Ellis (best known for his development of cognitive–behavioural therapies), tells a story that clarifies this point. Imagine yourself walking by a friend's house and seeing your friend come to a window and call you a string of vile names. Under the circumstances, it's likely that you would feel hurt and angry. Now, imagine that instead of walking by the house, you were passing a psychiatric hospital when the same friend, who was obviously a patient there, shouted the same offensive names at you. In this case, your reaction would probably be quite different—most likely, you'd feel sadness and pity.

In this story, the activating event—being called names—was the same in both cases, and yet the emotional consequences were very different. The reason for different feelings has to do with the pattern of thinking in each case. In the first instance, you would most likely think that your friend was angry with you and that you must have done something terrible to deserve such a response. In the second case, you would probably assume that your friend had experienced some psychological difficulty, so you would probably feel sympathetic. This example illustrates that people's interpretations of events determine their feelings:

Activating Event	Thought or Belief	Consequences
being called names	"I don't deserve to be treated like this."	hurt, anger
being called names	"My friend must be sick."	pity, sympathy

The same principle applies in more common situations. For example, the words "I love you" can be interpreted in a variety of ways. They could be taken at face value as a genuine expression of deep affection. They might also be interpreted in a variety of other ways: for example, as an attempt at manipulation, a sincere, but mistaken declaration uttered in a moment of passion, or an attempt to make the recipient feel better. It's easy to imagine how different interpretations of a statement like "I love you" can lead to different emotional reactions:

Event	Thought	Feeling
hearing "I love you"	"This is a genuine statement"	genuine delight (perhaps)
hearing "I love you"	"She's just saying this to manipulate me."	anger

The key, then, to understanding and changing feelings lies in the pattern of thought, which manifests itself through **self-talk** (Vocate, 1994)—the non-vocal, internal monologue that is our process of thinking. To understand how self-talk works, pay attention to the part of you that, like a little voice, whispers in your ear. Take a moment now and listen to what the voice is saying.

Did you hear the voice? It was quite possibly saying, "What little voice? I don't hear

any voices!" This little voice talks to you almost constantly:

"Better pick up a loaf of bread on the way home."

"I wonder when he's going to stop talking."

"It certainly is cold today!"

At work or at play, while reading the paper or brushing our teeth, we all tend to think. This thinking voice rarely stops. It may fall silent for a while when you are running, riding a bike, or meditating, but most of the time, it rattles on.

Irrational Thinking and Debilitative Emotions

This process of self-talk is essential to understanding the debilitative feelings that interfere with effective communication. Many debilitative feelings come from accepting a number of irrational thoughts—we'll call them *fallacies* here—that lead to illogical conclusions and, in turn, to debilitating feelings. We are not usually aware of these thoughts, and that makes them especially powerful (Bargh, 1988).

The Fallacy of Perfection

People who accept the **fallacy of perfection** believe that a worthwhile communicator

- **Facilitative emotions:** contribute to effective functioning.
- **Debilitative emotions:** hinder and prevent effective performance; they are usually more intense and longer lasting than facilitative emotions and are frequently based on irrational thinking.
- **Rational–emotive approach:** a cognitively-based therapeutic approach that involves getting rid of debilitative emotions by changing one's thinking.

Self-Assessment

SELF-TALK AND RESILIENCE

There is considerable evidence that the little voice in your head is a major contributor to your ability to adapt to the challenges that life presents (Reivich and Shatte, 2002; Seligman, 1991). Research into resilience (the ability to persevere and adapt when things go awry) and optimism (looking to the future as an opportunity for achievement and happiness) suggests that flexible, accurate thinking skills are what separate people who cope well with stress from those who do not. Flexible, accurate thinking contributes to better overall physical and mental health because it mediates the negative effects of stress. Several longitudinal studies conducted at Harvard University found that flexible, accurate thinking styles in young adults predicted better physical and mental health, a more active social life, more stable long-term relationships, and greater overall life satisfaction at age 80 (Vaillant, 2002; Werner and Smith, 2001). Clearly, a resilient coping style has tremendous benefits, but how do we develop our own?

We develop our "thinking habits" or the "scripts" for that little voice in our heads throughout our lives, often by observing significant people in our lives (such as parents, teachers, and friends). We can learn more productive ways of thinking about and dealing with adversity at any age. One thing we can do is examine our explanatory style—our habitual ways of explaining why things happen to us. Explanatory style can be viewed in terms of three dimensions: *personalization*, *permanence*, and *pervasiveness* (Seligman, 1991). Each dimension needs to be viewed as a continuum:

When something goes wrong . . .

Who is to blame? (personalization)	Me	Not me
How long will it last? (permanence)	Always	Not always
How much of my life does it affect? (pervasiveness)	Everything	Not everything

There is no "right" end to the continuum. The truth is usually somewhere in the middle, and a flexible, accurate thinker is able to see this. Often, however, when things go wrong, we reflexively assess these three dimensions and fall into habitual thinking traps. Some of us routinely blame ourselves and give way to despair, convinced that the difficulties confronting us will last forever and ruin our lives. Some of us are quick to blame others before giving the situation much thought, and we angrily conclude that other people have permanently ruined everything. Think about a problem you have had recently. What is your typical explanatory style, your "explanation reflex"? Now, look at the situation more carefully. Rarely is a problem created as a result of just one person's actions, and how much of your life it affects and for how long may just depend on your point of view. Slow down and challenge your beliefs. Why not make that little voice in your head into an optimistic friend or "life coach" rather than a harsh critic?

should be able to handle any situation with complete confidence and skill. Although such a standard of perfection can serve as a goal and a source of inspiration (rather like making a hole-in-one for a golfer), it's totally unrealistic to expect that you can reach or maintain this level of behaviour. The truth is, people simply are not perfect. Perhaps the myth of the perfect communicator comes from people believing too strongly in novels, television, or films. In these media, perfect characters are often depicted: the perfect mate or child, the imperturbable and gregarious host, the amazingly competent professional. Although these fabrications are certainly appealing, real people will inevitably come up short compared to them.

People who believe that it's desirable and possible to be a perfect communicator come to think that they will not be appreciated if they are imperfect. Admitting mistakes, saying "I don't know," or sharing feelings of uncertainty or discomfort thus seem to be social defects.

Given the desire to be valued and appreciated, these people are tempted at least to try to *appear* perfect. They assemble a variety of social masks, hoping that if they can fool others into thinking that they are perfect, perhaps they'll find acceptance. The costs of such deception are high. If others ever detect that this veneer of confidence is false, the person hiding behind it is considered a phony. Even if the facade goes undetected, the performance consumes a great deal of psychological energy and diminishes the rewards of approval.

Not only can the myth of perfection keep others from liking you, but it also acts as a force to diminish self-esteem. How can you like yourself when you do not measure up to your own standards?

You become more liberated each time you comfortably accept the idea that you are not perfect. For example, like everyone else, you sometimes have a hard time expressing yourself. Like everyone else, you make mistakes from time to time, and there is no reason to hide it. You are honestly doing the best you can to realize your potential, to become the best person you can be.

The Fallacy of Approval

Another mistaken belief is based on the idea that it is vital—not just desirable—to obtain everyone's approval. Communicators who subscribe to the **fallacy of approval** go to extreme lengths to seek acceptance from others, even to the extent of sacrificing their own principles and happiness. Adherence to this irrational myth can lead to some ludicrous situations, such as feeling nervous because people you really do not like seem to disapprove of you, or feeling apologetic when you are not at fault.

The myth of approval is irrational. It implies that some people are more respectable and more likeable because they go out of their way to please others. Often, this implication simply is not true. How respectable are people who have compromised important values simply to gain acceptance? Are people highly regarded when they repeatedly deny their own needs as a means of buying approval? Genuine affection and respect are hardly due such characters. In addition, striving for universal acceptance is irrational because it is simply not possible.

Don't misunderstand: abandoning the fallacy of approval does not mean living a life of selfishness. It's still important to consider the needs of others. It's also pleasant—perhaps even necessary—to strive for the respect of certain people. The point is that the price is too high if you must abandon your own needs and principles in order to gain this acceptance.

The Fallacy of *Should*

One huge source of unhappiness is the inability to distinguish between what *is* and what *should be*, or the **fallacy of *should***. For instance, imagine a person who is full of complaints about the world:

> "There should be no rain on weekends."

> "People should live forever."

> "Money should grow on trees."

> "We should all be able to fly."

Beliefs such as these are obviously foolish. However pleasant such wishing may be, insisting that the unchangeable should be altered won't affect reality one bit.

In each of these cases, the person would *prefer* that people behaved differently. Wishing that things were better is perfectly legitimate, and trying to change them is, of course, a good idea; but it is unreasonable to insist that the world operate just as one wants it to. Parents wish that their children were always considerate and neat. Teachers wish that their students were fascinated with the subjects discussed in class and willing to study diligently. As the old saying goes, those wishes and a quarter (now considerably more) will get you a cup of coffee.

An obsession with what *should* be yields three bad consequences: First, it leads to

Focus on TECHNOLOGY

SOCIAL INCLUSION, THE INTERNET, WEBCAMS, AND TEXT MESSAGES

Why do we seek approval from others and why does it hurt so much when they reject us? Kipling Williams has conducted a great deal of research on social exclusion and ostracism, and he and his colleagues have found that not only is it painful when other adults choose not to play a cyberball game with us, it is also painful just to watch others be rejected from the online game (Wesselmann et al., 2009). Incredibly, it is even painful when we are rejected by groups of people we despise (Gonsalkorale and Williams, 2007). In an extensive review of the literature regarding social and physical pain, Geoff MacDonald and Mark Leary (2005) suggest that the need to belong to a group is central to our survival as a species, and that some of the same brain mechanisms that signal physical pain (e.g., stubbing your toe) are also activated by social pain (e.g., not being invited to a party). In fact, taking a pain reliever such as acetaminophen dulls the social pain of rejection and exclusion just as it does physical pain (DeWall et al., 2011). It is interesting that we seldom ruminate about episodes of physical pain that we have experienced, but we frequently relive social pain over and over again in our minds, often reconstructing the argument or incident and replacing what we said with what we wish we had said. People who take conflict personally are more inclined to brood about it and make the pain last (Wallenfelsz and Hample, 2010). Some researchers suggest that the pain of social exclusion may be at the heart of what hinders shy and anxious people from engaging in social interactions. People with shy temperaments may learn to avoid social interaction because of the painful feelings they have experienced during social interactions in the past (Panksepp, 2011).

For many people who are shy or socially anxious, venturing forth into the social world and risking social rejection can be truly challenging. Researchers have been interested in the social opportunities provided by the Internet and text messaging (Baker and Oswald, 2010; Buote et al., 2009; Campbell et al., 2006; Ledbetter et al., 2011; Ramirez and Broneck, 2009; Reid and Reid, 2007, 2010; Selfhout et al., 2009; Valkenburg and Peter, 2007). They have found that the Internet provides benefits to people who have experienced social difficulties (Baker and Oswald, 2010; Ledbetter et al., 2011; Modayil et al., 2003; Selfhout et al., 2009; Valkenburg and Peter, 2007). It allows them to connect with people who share the same interests and provides opportunities to rehearse behaviour and communication skills that may help them in face-to-face social interactions. In a study of people using cellphones to either text or talk, Donna Reid and Fraser Reid (2007, 2010) found that, in comparison with talkers, texters were more socially anxious and more likely to disclose information about themselves through text rather than in face-to-face or phone conversations. Reid and Reid conclude that there is something special about texting that allows some people to translate their social anxiety into productive relationships.

While shy and socially anxious people may not necessarily use computer-mediated communication channels more than their more socially confident peers do, they may experience greater benefits from the social opportunities these channels provide. Sarah Stevens and Tracy Morris (2007) found in their sample that although the university students with dating anxiety were not more likely to develop online relationships than their less-anxious peers, they were more likely to use webcams to make and maintain their relationships. Stevens and Morris speculated that perhaps the blushing and trembling that socially anxious people experience when dating are less noticeable in webcam interactions compared to face-to-face encounters. Similarly, Levi Baker and Debra Oswald (2010) found that shy people reported greater associations between Facebook use and friendship quality. Facebook and other social networking sites may not be the first choice of some shy individuals, perhaps because these sites are less private, and individuals have less control over what is posted about themselves compared to more traditional forms of CMC, such as email or text messaging. For instance, Andrew Ledbetter and his colleagues (2011) found that shy and socially anxious university students were less likely than their more confident peers to share personal information and connect with others using Facebook. Regardless of the preferred format, it would appear that technology gives people a wider range of choices about how to initiate and maintain relationships with others and avoid the pain of exclusion.

unnecessary unhappiness. People who are constantly dreaming about the ideal are seldom satisfied with what they have. For instance, partners in a marriage who focus on the ways in which their spouse could be more considerate, sexy, or intelligent have a hard time appreciating the qualities of character that drew them together in the first place.

Second, the obsession keeps you from changing unsatisfying conditions. One employee, for example, constantly complains about problems on the job: there should be better training, the pay ought to be higher, the facilities should be upgraded, and so on. This person could be using the same energy to improve such conditions. Of course, not all problems have solutions, but when they do, complaining is rarely very productive. As one college manager puts it, "Rather than complain about the cards you are dealt, play the hand well."

Finally, this obsession tends to cause defensiveness in others. Imagine living around someone who insisted that people be more punctual, work harder, or refrain from using certain language. This kind of carping is obviously irritating. It's much easier to be around people who comment without preaching.

The Fallacy of Overgeneralization

The **fallacy of overgeneralization** occurs when a person bases a belief on a *limited amount of evidence*. Consider the following statements:

> "I'm so stupid! I can't understand how to do my income tax."

> "Some friend I am! I forgot my best friend's birthday."

In these cases, people have focused on a single shortcoming as if it represented everything. Sometimes people forget that despite their difficulties, they have solved tough problems, and that although they can be forgetful, they are often caring and thoughtful.

A second, related category of overgeneralization occurs when we *exaggerate shortcomings*:

> "You *never* listen to me."

> "You're *always* late."

> "I can't think of *anything*."

Upon closer examination, such absolute statements are almost always false and they usually lead to discouragement or anger. It's better to replace overgeneralizations with more accurate messages:

> "You often don't listen to me."

> "You've been late three times this week."

> "I haven't had any ideas I like today."

The Fallacy of Causation

People who live their lives in accordance with the **fallacy of causation** believe they should do nothing that can hurt, or in any way inconvenience others because it will cause undesirable feelings. For example, you might visit friends or family out of a sense of obligation rather than a genuine desire to see them, because you believe their feelings will be hurt if you don't visit them. Have you ever avoided objecting to behaviour that you found troublesome because you didn't want to cause anger? You may, on occasion, have pretended to be attentive—even though you were late for an appointment and in a rush—because you didn't want a person to feel embarrassed for "holding you up." Then there were the times when you substituted praise for more honest, negative responses in order to avoid hurting someone.

A reluctance to speak out in such situations often results from assuming that one person can cause another's emotions—that others, for example, are responsible for your feeling disappointed, confused, or irritated, or that you are responsible for others feeling hurt, angry, or upset. Actually, this assumption is sometimes incorrect. We may *act* in provocative ways, for which we are responsible, but each person is also responsible for the way they *react*.

To understand why each person is responsible for their own feelings, consider how strange it sounds to suggest that people *make* you fall in love with them. Such a statement simply doesn't make sense. It would be more correct to say that people first act in one way or another; then you may or may not fall in love as a result of these actions.

In the same way, it's not accurate to say that people *make* you angry, upset, or even happy. Behaviour that upsets or pleases one person might not bring any reaction from another. If you doubt this fact, think about people you know who respond differently to the same

behaviour that you find so bothersome. (You may scream "Idiot!" when you are driving and someone switches lanes in front of you without signalling, while the person driving the car behind you may not even notice, or may notice, but not care.) The contrast between their reactions and yours shows that responses are determined more by our own temperament and thinking than by the actions of others.

The Fallacy of Helplessness

The **fallacy of helplessness** suggests that forces beyond our control determine our satisfaction in life. People with this outlook continually see themselves as victims:

> "There's no way a woman can get ahead in this society. It's a man's world, and the best thing I can do is to accept it."

> "I was born with a shy personality. I'd like to be more outgoing, but there's nothing I can do about that."

> "I can't tell my boss that she is putting too many demands on me. If I did, I might lose my job."

The error in such statements becomes apparent once a person realizes that few paths are completely closed. In fact, most "can't" statements may be more correctly restated in one of two ways:

1. You say that you *won't* act in a certain way—that you choose not to do so. For instance, you may choose not to stand up for your rights or to follow unwanted requests, but it is usually inaccurate to claim that some outside force keeps you from doing so.
2. You say that you *don't know how* to do something. For instance, not knowing how to complain in a way that reduces defensiveness, or not knowing how to conduct a conversation.

Many difficulties a person claims can't be solved do have solutions. The task is to

REFLECTION

THINKING ABOUT AN ANNOYING FRIEND

My friend Maria talks about her personal life at length, but when I talk about myself for more than a couple of minutes, she has few comments and quickly turns the conversation back to her favourite topic: herself.

Until lately, Maria's egocentric focus was beginning to hurt my feelings. When Maria talks about herself, I think that what I have to say isn't interesting or that she doesn't care about me as a friend. I feel neglected, as if our relationship is one-sided.

Lately, I've started to think about other reasons Maria talks so much. For example, she's told me that I am a great listener and that I help her by lending an ear. Also, I've realized that Maria seldom gets to talk about herself (she spends all day talking to customers on the phone and is engaged to a very talkative guy).

So now I have started to take Maria's self-centred approach less personally. I still wish she would listen to me more, but I don't think that her egocentrism is making me resentful. It's my choice whether to accept her as she is, speak up about what I want, or see less of her.

discover those solutions and to work diligently at applying them.

When viewed in this light, many "can't" statements are really rationalizations to justify an unwillingness to change. Research supports the dangers of helpless thinking (Marangoni and Ickes, 1989). Lonely people tend to attribute their poor interpersonal relationships to uncontrollable causes. "It's beyond my control," they think. For example, lonely people are more negative than non-lonely ones about ever finding a mate. Also, they expect their relational partners to reject them. Notice the self-fulfilling prophecy in this attitude: believing that your relational prospects are dim can lead you to act in ways that make you an unattractive prospect. Once you persuade yourself that there's no hope, it's easy to give up trying. On the other hand, acknowledging that there is a way to change—even though it may be difficult—puts the responsibility for the predicament on your shoulders. Knowing that you can move closer to your goals makes it difficult to complain about the present. You *can* become a better communicator.

The Fallacy of Catastrophic Expectations

Some fearful people operate on the assumption that if something bad can happen, it probably will. This is the **fallacy of catastrophic expectations**—a position similar to Murphy's Law. These statements are typical of such an attitude:

"If I invite them to the party, they probably won't want to come."

"If I speak up in order to try to resolve a conflict, things will probably get worse."

Which of these fallacies do you struggle with the most? What are some things you can do to overcome irrational thoughts?

© iStockPhoto/Shelly Perry.

"If I apply for the job I want, I probably won't be hired."

"If I tell them how I really feel, they'll probably just laugh at me."

Once you start imagining terrible consequences, a self-fulfilling prophecy can begin to build. One study revealed that people who believed that their romantic partners would not change for the better were likely to behave in ways that contributed to the breakup of the relationship (Metts and Cupach, 1990).

Minimizing Debilitative Emotions

How can you overcome irrational thinking? Social scientists have developed a simple yet effective approach (Ellis, 2001; Ellis and Ellis, 2011). When practised conscientiously, it can help you cut down on the self-defeating thinking that leads to many debilitative emotions.

 CHECK IT!

List the seven fallacies or irrational types of thinking that can create debilitative emotions. Provide an example of each fallacy.

Monitor Your Emotional Reactions

The first step is to recognize when you are having debilitative emotions. (Of course, it's also nice to be aware of pleasant feelings when they occur!) As we suggested earlier, one way to notice feelings is through physical stimuli: butterflies in the stomach, racing heart, blushing, and so on. Although such reactions might be symptoms of food poisoning, more often they reflect a strong emotion. You can also recognize certain ways of behaving that suggest your feelings—stamping instead of walking normally, being unusually quiet, and speaking in a sarcastic tone of voice are some examples.

It may seem strange to suggest that it's necessary to look for emotions—they ought to be immediately apparent. However, the fact is that we often suffer from debilitative feelings for some time without noticing them. For example, at the end of a trying day you have probably caught yourself frowning and realized that you have been wearing that face for some time without knowing it.

Remember the two key characteristics of debilitating emotions, intensity (they are *too* intense) and duration (they last *too* long), and use them to guide your assessment.

Note the Activating Event

Once you realize how you are feeling, the next step is to figure out what activating event triggered your response. Sometimes, it is obvious. If your sweetheart keeps calling you by the name of a former lover, you are likely to become upset. In other cases, however, the activating event is not so apparent.

Sometimes, there is no single activating event, but instead a series of small incidents that finally trigger a debilitative feeling. This sort of thing happens when someone teases you over and over about the same thing, or when you suffer a series of small disappointments.

The best way to begin tracking activating events is to notice the circumstances in which you have debilitative feelings. Perhaps they happen when you are around *specific people.*

For example, you may feel tense or angry every time you encounter a person you have struggled with in the past (Gayle and Preiss, 1999). Until those issues are dealt with, feelings about past events can trigger debilitative emotions, even in apparently innocuous situations.

In other cases, you might discover that being around certain *types of individuals* triggers debilitative emotions. For instance, you might become nervous around people who seem more intelligent or self-confident than you are. In other cases, certain *settings* can stimulate unpleasant emotions: parties, work, or school.

Sometimes, the *topic of conversation* is what sets you off, whether it is politics, religion, sex, or some other sensitive subject. There is evidence to suggest that the *channel* or information source can play a role too. Recall from Chapter 3 that there are considerable variations in people's perceptions of appropriate cellphone etiquette and civility. Social media, with its exclusive and nonexclusive message features, and friending and defriending, can also contribute to feelings of jealousy, envy, sadness, and social isolation (Cohen et al., 2014; Kross et al., 2013; Sagioglou, Greitemeyer, 2014). Recognizing your activating events is an important step in minimizing debilitative emotions.

Record Your Self-Talk

This is the point at which you analyze the thoughts that are the link between the activating event and your feelings. If you are serious about getting rid of debilitative emotions, it's important to actually write down your self-talk when you are learning to use this method. Putting your thoughts on paper will help you see whether or not they make any sense.

Monitoring your self-talk might be difficult at first. This is a new skill, and any new activity seems awkward. If you persevere, however, you will be able to identify the thoughts that lead to your debilitative feelings. Once you get into the habit of recognizing this internal monologue, you will be able to identify your thoughts quickly and easily.

Dispute Your Irrational Beliefs

The key to success in the rational–emotive approach is to dispute your irrational beliefs. Rethinking or reinterpreting the meaning of a situation in ways that change the emotional impact is referred to as **cognitive reappraisal** (Ochsner and Gross, 2008). There is considerable evidence that reappraisal helps both in the short and long term in reducing negative, debilitating emotions (Deny and Ochsner, 2014; Ray et al., 2010). For instance, imagine you and your friend Puja are able to get discounted tickets to an upcoming concert through your mutual friend Mohamed. You arrive at the concert location just before it is scheduled to start only to find that Mohamed has forgotten the tickets at home. You and Puja agree to wait while Mohamed rushes home to get the tickets. As you wait you can faintly hear one of your favourite songs being played and you think about what a bonehead Mohamed is and how you can't believe you got all the way to the concert only to miss the best part. You think about your irritation and frustration and your brooding makes you angrier by the minute. Puja on the other hand is initially frustrated, but quickly reminds herself about the great discount Mohamed got on the tickets and what a generous person he is. Puja thinks about how she really couldn't have afforded the full price of the tickets and looks forward to having fun at a concert she would have otherwise missed. Research conducted by Rebecca Ray and her colleagues (2008) found that people who think like Puja, reappraising the situation, recover from negative experiences faster than people who ruminate about events. They stop feeling angry and stop thinking about the situation much more quickly when they reappraise the event rather than ruminate on it, and that's better for their interpersonal relationships and their health. Use the discussion of irrational fallacies on pages 135–141 to find out which of your internal statements are based on mistaken thinking.

You can do this most effectively by following three steps. First, decide whether each belief you have recorded is rational or irrational. Next, explain why the belief does or does not make sense. Finally, if the belief is irrational, write down an alternative way of thinking that is more sensible and that can leave you feeling better when you are faced with the same activating event in the future.

After reading about this method for dealing with unpleasant emotions, some readers may have objections such as:

"This rational–emotive approach sounds like nothing more than trying to talk yourself out of feeling bad." This accusation is totally correct. After all, since we talk ourselves into feeling bad, what's wrong with talking ourselves *out* of bad feelings, especially when they are based on irrational thoughts? Rationalizing may be an excuse and a self-deception, but there's nothing wrong with being rational.

"The kind of disputing we just read sounds phony and unnatural. I don't talk to myself in sentences and paragraphs." There's no need to dispute your irrational beliefs in any special literary style. You can be as colloquial as you want. The important thing is to clearly understand what thoughts led you into your debilitative feeling so you can clearly dispute them. When the technique is new to you, it's a good idea to write or talk out your thoughts in order to make them clear. After you have had some practice, you will be able to do these steps in a quicker, less formal way.

"This approach is too cold and impersonal. It seems to aim at turning people into cold-blooded, calculating, emotionless machines." This is simply not true. A rational thinker can still dream, hope, and love. There's nothing necessarily irrational about feelings like those. Rational people usually indulge in a bit of irrational thinking once in a while. But they usually know what they are doing. Like healthy eaters who occasionally

Building WORK SKILLS

Debilitative emotions at work or school can prevent you from making decisions and solving problems. Choose an important situation you faced at work or school in which you experienced debilitative emotions that interfered with your ability to communicate effectively. Use the four steps on pages 141–144 to challenge the rationality of your beliefs. How has the rational–emotive approach affected your communication in this situation?

treat themselves to a snack of junk food, rational thinkers occasionally indulge in irrational thoughts, knowing that they'll return to their healthy lifestyle soon with no real damage done.

"This technique promises too much. There's no chance I could rid myself of all unpleasant feelings, however nice that might be." We can answer this by assuring you that rational–emotive thinking probably will not solve all your emotional problems. What it can do is reduce their number, intensity, and duration. This method is not the answer to all your problems, but it can make a significant difference—which is not a bad accomplishment.

SUMMARY

Emotions have several dimensions. They are signalled by internal physiological changes, manifested by verbal and non-verbal reactions, and defined in most cases by cognitive interpretations. There are several reasons why people do not verbalize many of the emotions they feel. Certain personality types respond to emotions more negatively than others. Some cultures encourage, while others discourage, the expression of emotions. Personality, biological sex, and gender all influence how people experience and express their emotions. Social rules discourage the expression of some feelings, particularly negative ones. Many social roles do not allow expression of certain feelings. Some people express emotions so rarely that they lose the ability to recognize when they are feeling them. Fear of the consequences of disclosing some emotions leads people to withhold expression of them, and emotions can be transferred from one person to another through a process called emotional contagion.

Since total expression of feelings is not acceptable in adults, several guidelines help define when and how to share emotions. Self-awareness, clear language, and expression of multiple feelings are important. Willingness to accept responsibility for one's feelings instead of blaming them on others leads to better reactions. Choosing the proper time and place to share feelings is also important.

While some emotions are facilitative, debilitative feelings inhibit effective functioning. Many of these debilitative emotions are caused by various types of irrational thinking. It is often possible to communicate more confidently and effectively by recognizing troublesome emotions, identifying the activating event and self-talk that triggered them, and replacing any irrational thoughts with a more logical analysis of the situation.

MULTIPLE-CHOICE QUESTIONS

1. Paying attention to and regulating emotions in ways that help you adapt to your environment is called
   a. cognitive interpretation.
   b. rumination.
   c. emotional intelligence.
   d. facilitative emotion.

2. Owen notices that just before he steps on the ice for the playoff hockey game, his heart is beating faster and his hands feel a little shaky. He interprets these signals as evidence that he is nervous. This is an example of the
   a. verbal expression component of emotion.
   b. non-verbal expression component of emotion.
   c. rumination component of emotion.
   d. cognitive interpretation component of emotion.

3. Sadaf is laughing when Jim enters the room. Jim feels happier and starts smiling himself even though he doesn't know what Sadaf is laughing about. This phenomenon is called
   a. emotional contagion.
   b. counterfeit emotions.
   c. rumination.
   d. the rational–emotive approach.

4. In order to express your emotions constructively you need to
   a. avoid using precise language.
   b. avoid sharing multiple feelings.
   c. avoid blaming others for your feelings.
   d. all of the above.

5. Intense emotions that last too long and hinder your effective performance are called
   a. facilitative emotions.
   b. the myth of perfection.
   c. distorted feedback.
   d. debilitative emotions.

6. Any worthwhile communicator should be able to handle any communication situation with confidence and skill. This statement is an example of the fallacy of
   a. perfection.
   b. overgeneralization.
   c. causation.
   d. helplessness.

7. A belief based on a limited amount of evidence such as "I am so stupid! I can't understand how to do my income tax" is an example of which fallacy?
   a. causation
   b. should
   c. overgeneralization
   d. perfection

8. When you have recurrent thoughts not demanded by the situation, this mental process is called rumination.
   a. true
   b. false

9. Taking acetaminophen has been found to reduce the pain of social rejection in much the same way that it relieves physical pain.
   a. true
   b. false

10. The internal monologue of your thoughts is called the rational–emotive approach.
    a. true
    b. false

Answers: 1. c; 2. d; 3. a; 4. c; 5. d; 6. a; 7. c; 8. a; 9. a; 10. b

ACTIVITIES

1. Invitation to Insight

The "Self-Assessment" exercise on page 136 explored your "favourite" emotions without focusing on any particular personal relationship. What happens when you have a specific relationship in mind? Using the list of emotions in the "Self-Assessment" box, do the following exercise:

a. Think of an important personal relationship.

b. Identify the few emotions that are the most important for *you* in the relationship.

c. Name the few emotions that you think are the most important for the *other person* in the relationship.

d. Describe how you express each emotion you chose as most important for you. Think of the frequency with which you express each feeling, the circumstances in which you express it, and the ways you express it.

e. Describe how the other person expresses each emotion you identified as most important for her. Think of the frequency with which the other person expresses each feeling, the circumstances in which it is expressed, and how she expresses it.

f. What have you learned about yourself, the other person, and your relationship by conducting this analysis?

If possible, invite the other person to do the same analysis and compare your results.

2. Skill Builder

Choose an important emotion you experience in one of your relationships. This relationship needn't be highly personal. You might, for example, focus on an employer, an instructor, or a neighbour. Use the guidelines on pages 128–132 to determine whether, and how, you might express this emotion.

3. Ethical Challenge

According to the rational–emotive approach, we cause our own feelings by interpreting an event in one way or another. If this is true, it is a fallacy to claim we "make" others feel happy or sad. Do you accept this position? To what degree are you responsible for communicating in ways that "cause" others to feel happy or sad? Use a specific incident from your life to illustrate your answer.

4. Role Play

Choose a partner. Together, develop a specific scenario in which you have sent an email that your partner has interpreted much more negatively than you intended. Discuss your options to clarify this situation and then role-play your solution to the problem. Now, switch roles.

DISCUSSION QUESTIONS

1. What are emotions? What do they contribute to the human experience of life?

2. Seven influences on emotional expression are described in this chapter. Explain how each has influenced your ability and motivation to communicate your feelings.

3. Six guidelines for expressing emotions are described in this chapter. Do you think these guidelines are complete? Are there any guidelines you would add? Remove? Why?

4. American psychologist Albert Ellis has argued that thoughts cause emotions. Would you agree or disagree? Why?

5. Several common, but flawed beliefs, or fallacies, are described in this chapter. Which ones are you most susceptible to? Why do you think that is?

6. Discuss the value of self-talk in managing difficult emotions. How is the recent emergence of "life coaches" related to this concept?

emergence of "life coaches" related to this concept?

JOURNAL IDEAS

1. Explore the fallacy of helplessness by describing two important difficulties you have in communicating with (a) family members, (b) people at school or at work, (c) strangers, and (d) friends. Use the following format for each difficulty:

   I can't _____,

   because _____.

   Now, read the list, but with a slight difference. For each *can't*, substitute the word *won't*. Note which ones are actually "won't" statements. Read the list again, but this time substitute "I do not know how to" for your original *can't*. Rewrite any sentences that are truly "do not know how," statements, then decide what you could do to learn the skill that you currently lack.

   On the basis of your experience, decide whether you subscribe to the fallacy of helplessness and what you could do to eliminate this sort of debilitative thinking from your life.

2. The "Focus on Research" box, on page 125, included four savouring strategies that can help to increase happiness and well-being. The way to expand happiness through these strategies is to pay closer attention to times when we are feeling contentment, joy, awe, excitement, pride, and gratitude. Keep track of times when you have experienced these emotions and describe these experiences in some detail. Pay attention to your mood—do you feel happier when you pay attention to positive emotions? Why or why not?

PART TWO
Creating and Responding to Messages

© pixdeluxe/iStockphoto

5

Listening

© Kanmu/iStockphoto

Key Terms

advising response
ambushing
analyzing response
attending
closed questions
counterfeit questions
defensive listening
empathizing response
evaluating response
filling in the gaps
hearing
insulated listening
listening

open questions
paraphrasing
pseudo-listening
questioning response
remembering
responding
selective listening
silent listening
sincere questions
stage hogging
supporting response
understanding

Learning Objectives

YOU SHOULD UNDERSTAND:

- the importance of listening;
- the reasons for listening to others;
- the error of common myths that suggest that listening is easy;
- the habits of people who listen ineffectively;
- the components of the listening process;
- the differences among the listening responses introduced in this chapter; and
- the advantages and disadvantages of various listening styles.

YOU SHOULD BE ABLE TO:

- identify specific instances when you listen (a) to understand and retain information, (b) to build and maintain relationships, (c) to help others, and (d) to evaluate;
- describe the circumstances in which you listen ineffectively and the poor listening habits you use in these circumstances;
- identify the response styles you commonly use when listening to others; and
- demonstrate a combination of listening styles you could use to respond effectively to another person.

The grizzled army sergeant faced a roomful of new US Signal Corps cadets, about to begin their training as radio operators. "The equipment is a snap to operate," he explained. "All you have to do to send a message is to push this button on the microphone, and your voice goes out to anyone who's tuned in. Go ahead . . . give it a try."

Each recruit picked up a microphone and began speaking. The sound of thirty amplified voices all transmitting at the same time created a loud, painful squeal. "Okay, soldiers," the sergeant announced. "You just learned the first principle of radio communication. Any fool can send a message. The only way communication works is if you are willing and able to receive one too."

The sergeant's lesson is a good one for every communicator. Speaking is important, but without listening, a message might as well never be sent. Attentive listening is fundamental to effective interpersonal communication and perhaps the most difficult skill to develop. In this chapter, you will learn about the many factors that make good listening difficult, and you'll also find reasons for tackling those challenges. You'll see what really happens when listening takes place. Finally, you will read about a variety of listening responses that you can use to increase your own understanding, improve your relationships, and help others.

The Nature of Listening

When people think about improving their communication skills, they usually think of developing their ability to send messages. We have all heard simplistic prescriptions for better listening (e.g., "just shut up and listen"), but this advice doesn't begin to capture all the challenges inherent in attentive and effective listening. Listening effectively requires a number of skills, not the least of which is really paying attention in the midst of our constantly connected, digitally distracting world. Listening well is hard to do and the value of listening skills is often overlooked, but, as we will see,

investing our time in improving those skills has innumerable benefits. *Information gathering functions*

The Importance of Listening

How important is listening? If we use frequency as a measure, it ranks at the top of the list (Janusik and Wolvin, 2009). Among college students, listening makes up over 50 per cent of their communication activities (Emanuel et al., 2008), followed, at a distant second, by speaking (less than 20 per cent of their communication time). Students spend equal amounts of time engaged in interpersonal listening and listening to media. As Figure 5.1 illustrates, reading and writing combined don't consume as much time as listening. In the workplace, listening is an activity that executives engage in a lot. W.F. Keefe (1971) and L.K. Steil (1996) report that executives spend approximately 70 per cent of their communication time listening.

Besides being the most frequent form of communication, listening may be a more highly valued skill than speaking. Andrew Wolvin, Carolyn Coakley, and Carolyn Gwynn (1999; Wolvin and Coakley, 1991) summarize

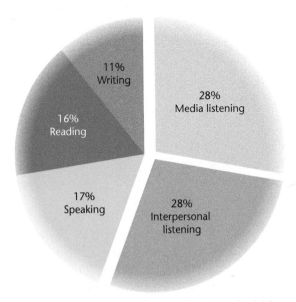

Figure 5.1 ● **Types of Communication Activities**

SOURCE: R. Emanuel et al., 2008. "How college students spend their time communicating," *International Journal of Listening, 22*, 13–28.

handwritten margin notes at top:
listening errors significantly influence productivity
Improvement in listening skills · Positively correlated with increase in relational standing.

Unfortunately, there is no connection between how well most communicators think they listen and how competent they really are in their ability to understand others. Are there times when you're a better listener than others?

numerous studies that find listening to be the most important communication skill for entry-level workers, subordinates, supervisors, and managers on several fronts: job and career success, productivity, upward mobility, communication training, and organizational effectiveness. When several hundred human-resource executives were asked to identify skills of the ideal manager, the ability to listen effectively ranked at the top of the list (Winsor et al., 1997). In problem-solving groups, effective listeners are judged as having the most leadership skills (Johnson and Bechler, 1998). When asked what skills were most important on the job, senior executives, students, and employers identified listening as the primary requirement, more often than any other skill, including technical competence, computer knowledge, creativity, and administrative talent (Gabric and McFadden, 2001; Marchant, 1999).

handwritten margin note: who/how/when we listen

The business world is not the only place where listening is vital. When a group of adults was asked to rank various communication skills according to their importance, listening topped their family and social lists, alongside their career lists (Wolvin, 1984). In fact, it has been found that among people in committed relationships,

listening to personal information in everyday conversations was considered an important ingredient of satisfaction (Prager and Buhrmester, 1998).

Unfortunately, there is no connection between how well most communicators think they listen and how competent in understanding others they really are (Carrell and Willmington, 1996). While virtually everyone acknowledges the importance of listening, regrettably, people rarely view themselves as needing to improve their own skills in receiving and understanding. A study by Judi Brownell (1990) illustrates this point vividly. A group of managers in her study was asked to rate their listening skills. Astonishingly, not one of the managers described himself or herself as a "poor" or "very poor" listener. Indeed, 94 per cent rated themselves as "good" or "very good." The favourable self-ratings contrasted sharply with the perceptions of the managers' subordinates, many of whom said their bosses' listening skills were weak. As you will soon read, a certain amount of poor listening is inevitable. The good news is that listening skills can definitely be improved through instruction and training (Lane et al., 2000; McGee and Cegala, 1998; Spinks and Wells, 1991).

Listening Defined

handwritten margin note: listening > Hearing. learned communication skill

So, what exactly is listening? **Listening** is the process of receiving, interpreting, and responding to spoken and non-verbal messages. Listening involves more than just hearing. **Hearing** is the process by which sound waves strike the eardrum and cause vibrations that are transmitted to the brain. Listening takes place when the brain reconstructs these electrochemical impulses into a representation of the original

handwritten margin note: thoughtful process

sound and then gives them meaning (Fernald, 2001). Barring illness, injury, or earplugs, hearing cannot be stopped. Your ears will pick up sound waves and transmit them to your brain whether you want them to or not.

Listening, however, is not so automatic. Many times, we hear, but do not listen. Sometimes, we deliberately do not listen. Instead of paying attention to words or other sounds, we avoid them. Often, we block out irritating sounds, such as a neighbour's lawn mower or the roar of nearby traffic. We also stop listening when we find a subject unimportant or uninteresting. Boring stories, television commercials, and nagging complaints are common examples of messages we avoid. Other times, we think we are listening, but in fact, we are simply receiving sounds and our minds are elsewhere. Listening requires not just hearing, but the effort of paying attention, understanding, remembering, and responding, as we will discuss later in this chapter.

Reasons for Listening

A first step in becoming a better listener is to realize that there are several different reasons to listen and each requires a different set of attitudes and skills.

To Understand and Remember

The most obvious reason for listening is to *understand and remember information*. People who are adept at this are more likely to become successful, both personally and professionally (Floyd, 1985). In virtually every job, it is important to understand the instructions, advice, needs, reactions, and concerns of the people you work with. Unquestionably, understanding others requires listening to them. From lawyers, judges, and accountants to nurses, physicians, and health professionals, and almost every job in between, listening skills have been identified as central to effectiveness (Ala-Kortesmaa and Isotalus, 2014; Browning and Waite, 2010; Stone et al., 2013).

To Evaluate

A second type of listening involves *evaluating the quality of messages*. In their book, *Teaching as a Subversive Activity*, Neil Postman and Charles Weingartner (1969) discuss this function of listening in a unique way, referring to it as "crap detecting." They define a crap detector as someone who not only functions in a society but also observes it, noting its obsessions, fears, strengths, and weaknesses. Critical listeners are able to hear a speaker's words and understand the ideas without necessarily accepting them or agreeing with them. The ability to listen analytically and critically differs radically from empathic and supportive listening, but it is equally important.

To Build and Maintain Relationships

A third reason for listening, which is especially relevant for interpersonal communication, is to *build and maintain relationships*. Research shows that effective listening "builds better relationships, and poor listening weakens relationships, or prevents relationships from developing at all" (Kaufmann, 1993, p. 4). In one survey, marital counsellors identified "failing to take the other's perspective when listening" as one of the most frequent communication problems for client couples (Vangelisti, 1994; Long et al., 1999).

To Help Others

A fourth type of listening involves *helping others*, another important interpersonal skill. Listening is an essential tool that professionals use to help their clients. Doctors, lawyers, teachers, managers, supervisors, clergy, and therapists must listen carefully so they can offer sound assistance. Professionals are not the only people we call on for help; we also seek the counsel of friends and family. When others listen to us with understanding and concern, we can gain different and useful perspectives for solving problems.

The Challenge of Listening

Despite its importance, most people misunderstand what is required for proper listening. Many believe, quite simply, that if they've *heard* another person's message, they've *listened*. What these people fail to realize is that good listening is not simple; in fact, it's a challenge. The challenge can be met, but only by those who do not buy into popular misconceptions about listening. Let's look at several of these misconceptions.

Listening Is Not Easy

A common myth is that listening is like breathing—a natural activity that people do without conscious effort. The fact is, there are numerous obstacles that must be overcome for

people to listen effectively, and doing so sometimes involves time, concentration, and work. Researchers have identified several barriers to listening (Golen, 1990; Hulbert, 1989). A look at some of them will show why good listening is so difficult.

Information Overload

The sheer amount of speech most of us encounter every day makes it impossible to listen carefully to everything we hear. We often spend five or more hours a day listening to people talk. If you add these hours to the amount of time we devote to text messages, Internet media, radio, and television, you can see that it is virtually impossible for us to keep our attention totally focused for so long. Therefore, we periodically let our attention wander.

Personal Concerns

A second reason we don't always listen carefully is that we are often wrapped up in personal concerns that we perceive as being more immediately important to us than the messages others are sending. It's hard to pay attention to someone else when we are anticipating an upcoming test or thinking about the wonderful time we had last night with our friends. When we still feel that we have to "listen" politely to others, listening becomes a charade.

Rapid Thought

Listening carefully is also difficult because our minds are so active. Although we are capable of understanding speech at rates up to 600 words a minute (Versfeld and Dreschler, 2002), the average person speaks much more slowly—between 100 and 140 words a minute. Therefore, we have a lot of "spare time" to spend with our minds while someone is talking. The temptation is to use this time in ways that are not related to the speaker's ideas, such as thinking about personal interests, daydreaming, planning a rebuttal, and so on. The trick is to use this spare time to understand the speaker's ideas better, rather than to let your attention wander.

 CHECK IT!

> Define the term *listening*. Describe four reasons for listening and provide an example of each.

Noise

Finally, our physical and mental worlds often present distractions that make it hard for us to pay attention to others. The sounds of other conversations, traffic, and music, as well as the kinds of psychological noise that we discussed in Chapter 1, all interfere with our ability to hear well. For example, research has supported the common-sense suspicion that background noise from a television set reduces the ability of a communicator to understand messages (Armstrong et al., 1991). Similarly, the background noise in a typical elementary school classroom has been shown to interfere with listening and require children to exert greater effort (Howard et al., 2010). Fatigue or other forms of discomfort can also distract us. For instance, consider how the efficiency of your listening decreases when you are seated in a crowded, hot, stuffy room full of moving people and other noises. In such circumstances, even the best intentions are not enough to ensure cogent understanding.

Before going any further, we want to make it clear that intensive listening is not always desirable. Given the number of messages we're exposed to, it is impractical to expect yourself to listen well 100 per cent of the time. Our main concern is that you have the ability to be an accurate receiver when it really does matter.

All Listeners Do Not Receive the Same Message

When two or more people are listening to a speaker, we tend to assume that they are each hearing and understanding the same message. In fact, that is not the case. Recall our discussion of perception in Chapter 3, where we pointed out the many factors that cause each of us to perceive an event in a different manner. Physiological factors, social roles, cultural background, and personal interests and needs all shape and distort the raw data we hear into very different messages. Because every person interprets data in a unique way, we have to accept the fact that we can never completely understand another person. It is no wonder

CHECK IT!

Describe four barriers to listening.

that dyads typically achieve only 25 to 50 per cent accuracy in interpreting or representing each other's behaviour (Spitzberg, 1994). Our listening is always coloured and limited by our unique view of the world.

Types of Non-listening

Most people have experienced the frustration of being misunderstood. Similarly, most of us have one or more bad habits that keep us from understanding the messages of others. As you read about the following types of non-listening behaviours, see which ones describe you.

Pseudo-listening is an imitation of the real thing. "Good" pseudo-listeners give the appearance of being attentive: they look you in the eye, nod and smile at the right times, and even answer you occasionally, but their minds are elsewhere. Pseudo-listeners use a polite facade to mask their inattention.

Stage hogging involves people who are interested only in expressing their own ideas and don't care about what other people have to say. These offenders allow you to speak from time to time, but only so they can catch their breath and use your remarks as a basis for their own chatter. Research on "conversational narcissism" (Vangelisti et al., 1990) shows that self-centred stage hogs ask questions, but not other-oriented, information-seeking ones. Rather, these conversational domineers ask counterfeit questions to demonstrate their superiority and hold the floor (we'll talk more about *counterfeit* versus *sincere* questions later in this chapter).

People who use **selective listening** respond only to the parts of a speaker's remarks that interest them, rejecting everything else. Unless you bring up one of these pet subjects, you might as well be talking to a tree.

People with a tendency of **filling in the gaps** like to think that what they remember makes a whole story. These people manufacture

REFLECTION

FAKE LISTENING

I went parachuting for the first time last month. Before our first jump, we spent four hours in "ground school." I listened very carefully, especially during the part where they told us what to do if our chute didn't open after jumping from the plane. This was life-and-death material, and I didn't want to miss anything.

That's not the way I listen at school most of the time. I sit through most classroom lectures and it all seems like gibberish to me. I act as if I'm listening—nod at what I hope are the right times, smile when people laugh, and even scratch my head as if I'm thinking—so the teacher will assume I am listening. But I don't remember a thing afterward. I used to think it was all the teacher's fault, but I guess part of it has to do with whether or not I bother to turn up my "listening volume."

information so that when they retell what they listened to, they can give the impression they "got it all." The message left is actually a distorted (not merely incomplete) version of the real message.

The habit of **insulated listening** is almost the opposite of selective listening. Instead of looking for something, these listeners avoid it. Whenever a topic arises that they would rather not deal with, insulated listeners simply fail to hear or acknowledge it.

People who engage in **defensive listening** take innocent comments as personal attacks. It's fair to assume that many defensive listeners are suffering from shaky self-images, and they avoid facing this problem by projecting their own insecurities onto others.

A person who uses **ambushing** methods will listen carefully to you, but only because the person is collecting information that she will use to attack what you have to say. Needless to say, using this kind of strategy will justifiably initiate defensiveness from the other person.

Components of Listening

By now, you can begin to see that there is more to listening than sitting quietly while another person speaks. In truth, *listening*—at least listening effectively—consists of five separate elements: hearing, attending, understanding, remembering, and responding.

Hearing

As we have already discussed, hearing is the physiological aspect of listening. It is the non-selective process of sound waves impinging on the ear. Hearing is the most fundamental part of listening. It can be diminished by physiological disorders, background noise, and auditory fatigue, a temporary loss of hearing caused by continuous exposure to the same tone or loudness. People who spend an evening at a rock concert or a fireworks display may experience auditory fatigue and, if they are exposed often enough, permanent hearing loss.

We miss out on things when we don't listen. Do you think it's possible to be a good listener all of the time?

About one-quarter of Canadians report some form of hearing loss (The Canadian Hearing Society, 2007).

Attending

While hearing is a physiological process, **attending** is a psychological one and is part of the process of selection that we described in Chapter 3. It is hard to pay attention to every message, especially when we receive so many, often more than one at once. Many times our face-to-face conversations are interrupted by phone calls, text messages, Internet-related distractions, and things going on around us. Even when we want to pay attention, we can be distracted. Really listening to a message requires a significant amount of effort and brain power, and there is plenty of evidence that trying to have a conversation while doing something else (e.g., driving or even walking!) results in poorer performance on both tasks (Drews et al., 2008; Horrey and Wickens, 2006; Hyman et al., 2010).

We would go crazy if we attended to every sound we hear, so we filter out some messages and focus on others. Needs, wants, desires, and interests determine what is attended to. Not surprisingly, research shows that we attend most carefully to messages when there is a benefit in doing so (Burleson, 2007). If you are planning to see a movie, you will listen to a friend's description of it more carefully than you otherwise would. And when you want to get better acquainted with someone, you'll pay careful attention to almost anything they say, in hopes of improving the relationship. We are motivated to listen to others when we care about what they are saying.

In addition to paying attention to verbal communication, listening involves attending to the non-verbal messages people send us as well. Notice that the Chinese characters which make up the verb meaning "to listen" in Figure 5.2 include not just ears, but eyes, too. Some people fail to notice non-verbal signals, but for others, attending to non-verbal communication poses unique challenges. People

with a *non-verbal learning disorder* often miss or misinterpret social cues like facial expressions, gestures, and tones of voice (Poirier and Gaucher, 2009; Rourke, 1998). Children with this disorder often violate social conventions and can become socially isolated if they don't receive proper adult support and intervention. Understanding others requires attention to both verbal and non-verbal messages. John Carton and his colleagues (1999) found that adults' ability to attend to and accurately interpret people's facial expressions and voice tone was positively related to the well-being of their relationships with others.

Surprisingly, attending doesn't just help the listener; it also benefits the message sender. Participants in one study learned to play a new video game and then described the game to listeners who varied in their degrees of agreeableness and attentiveness to the speaker. Later, the researchers tested the speakers' long-term recall of the video game and the conversation

- **Pseudo-listening:** an imitation of real listening.
- **Stage hogging:** the practice of only expressing one's own ideas during conversation.
- **Selective listening:** the act of listening only to the parts of a speaker's remarks that interest them.
- **Filling in the gaps:** the practice of making up information to give the impression that one was listening and can recall the whole story.
- **Insulated listening:** the tendency to avoid or fail to hear or acknowledge certain topics.
- **Defensive listening:** the habit of interpreting innocent comments as personal attacks.
- **Ambushing:** the tendency to listen carefully, but only gather information that can be used to attack the speaker.

Focus on RESEARCH

LISTENERS INFLUENCE OUR PERCEPTIONS OF OUR COMMUNICATION ABILITIES

As we discussed earlier, people are known to overestimate their abilities in many areas, including their communication effectiveness (Fay et al., 2008). Nicolas Fay and his colleagues (2010) wondered why this happens. They were not convinced that we do this because we know what we intend to communicate, and so we assume others know too. In addition, unlike other researchers, they were not persuaded by the "cognitive load" argument—that because speaking requires a lot of brain power we are unable to monitor the reactions of others to ensure they understand what we are saying. They wanted to investigate the possibility of an interpersonal explanation—that the listener influences the speaker's assessment of her communication effectiveness. Their research participants read a series of twelve statements with ambiguous meanings, such as "Allan painted the picture in the kitchen." This statement could mean that he painted the picture that is hanging in the kitchen, or that he painted the picture while he was in the kitchen. Participants were told which of the two meanings they needed to convey—by using non-verbal, non-linguistic cues (see Chapter 7), such as emphasizing certain words in their speech. Half the participants read the statements to a listener whom they could see, but who was not allowed to speak. These listeners indicated to the researchers which of the two meanings they understood. The other half of the participants read statements apparently alone, without being able to see a listener. The researchers listened to all the statements. People who read the statements without seeing a listener rated their communication effectiveness more accurately than did the speakers who had a listener present. Those who could see their listener overestimated the effectiveness of their communication; they thought the listener understood the intended meaning of their statements more often than the listener actually did. The investigators speculate that perhaps the non-verbal feedback from listeners caused the speakers to believe they had effectively communicated the intended meaning. Whatever the reason, their investigation illustrates the transactional nature of communication —it really is an interpersonal endeavour.

Critical thinking: *Can you think of reasons why overestimating our communication effectiveness might be adaptive? Situations where it is detrimental?*

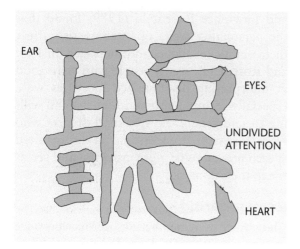

EAR

EYES

UNDIVIDED ATTENTION

HEART

Figure 5.2 ● The Chinese characters that make up the verb meaning "to listen" tell us something significant about this skill.

Calligraphy by Angie Au.

they had about it. Those who had recounted the segments to listeners who were agreeable and attentive remembered more details of the game and the conversation they had had about it (Pasupathi and Hoyt, 2010). Listeners had a similarly positive effect on people's recall of movie details (Pasupathi et al., 1998). The "Focus on Research" box in this section shows how listeners make us feel more competent as speakers.

Understanding

Paying attention—even close attention—to a message does not guarantee that you will understand what is being said. **Understanding** is composed of several elements. First, of course, you must be aware of the syntactic and grammatical rules of the language. But,

Focus on TECHNOLOGY

CELLPHONES AND FORCED EAVESDROPPING

When asked if cellphones disturb people, the majority of Europeans and North Americans will say yes, at least some of the time (Haddon, 2006, 2000; Ling, 2004). There are lots of stories of cellphones ringing at inopportune times (e.g., when the owner is in a public bathroom) and in inappropriate places (e.g., funerals). Another problem that Westerners find disturbing is the "forced eavesdropping" predicament; the generally unwanted situation where the cellphone user carries on a loud conversation in a public space. There are times when it feels almost impossible to ignore the person beside us talking about trivial matters or, worse yet, disclosing personal information that we would rather not know. Why is it so difficult to ignore cellphone conversations? It seems much easier to filter out the face-to-face conversations of people in our close proximity.

Perhaps some features of cellphone conversations grab our attention. First, many people speak more loudly when they are talking on a cellphone than when they are speaking with someone sitting near them (Monk et al., 2004a). This increase in volume certainly makes it easier to listen and harder to ignore. Second, we hear only one side of the cellphone conversation. Unlike face-to-face conversations that occur nearby, the cellphone conversation may attract our attention because of what is missing; its gaps in information may spark our curiosity and engage us in imagining the other side of the conversation. Andrew Monk and his colleagues (2004b) at the University of York tested this hypothesis in the United Kingdom by having actors in train cars carry on two types of one-sided conversations—either on a cellphone, or with another person, who is inaudible, present in the train car. Passengers on the train rated the both types of the one-sided conversations as more noticeable and intrusive than other conversations where both people were present and audible.

Age and culture affect our perceptions of forced eavesdropping too. Younger people are less bothered by having their conversations overheard in public places (Tillema et al., 2009). As well, in cultures where human interaction and connectivity are more highly valued than privacy and personal space, people are far more tolerant of high-volume, one-sided conversations in public places (Plant, 2001, 2003). Clearly, there are numerous factors that influence both our intentional and unintentional listening.

beyond this basic ability, understanding a message depends on several other factors. One is your knowledge about the source of the message. That will help you decide, for example, whether a friend's insulting remark is a joke or a serious attack. The context of a message also helps you understand what is being said. A yawning response to your comments would probably have a different meaning at midnight than at noon.

Finally, understanding often depends on the listener's mental abilities. Generally speaking, the ability to make sense of messages is closely related to the listener's intelligence (Bostrom and Waldhart, 1980). As early as 1948, Ralph Nichols related successful understanding to factors that included verbal ability, intelligence, and motivation. Timothy Plax and Lawrence Rosenfeld (1979) found that the personality traits of listeners also affect their ability to understand messages. In Plax and Rosenfeld's study, people who were good at interpreting disorganized messages were especially secure, sensitive to others, and willing to understand the speaker. Listeners who were successful at understanding disorganized speech proved to be more insightful and versatile in their thinking.

Remembering

The ability of **remembering** information once we've understood it depends on several factors: the number of times the information is heard or repeated, how much information there is to store in the brain, and whether the information may be "rehearsed" or not.

Early research on listening revealed that people remember only about half of what they hear immediately after hearing it (Barker, 1971). They forget half of what is said even if they work hard at listening. The situation would probably not be too bad if the half that people immediately remember was retained, but it is not. Within two months, half of the half is forgotten, bringing what we remember down to about 25 per cent of the original message. In fact, people start forgetting immediately (within eight hours, the 50 per cent remembered drops to roughly 35 per cent). Given the amount of information we are exposed to every day—from teachers, friends, radio, television, and other sources—the *residual message* (what we remember) is a small fraction of what we have heard.

This high rate of forgetfulness is not as depressing as it might seem. While most people recall very few details of their conversations, they do retain an overall impression about the speaker, especially in important relationships (Fisher and Adams, 1994). The more intensity, intimacy, trust, and commitment in the relationship, the more we pay attention to what others are saying. Thus, high recall is one characteristic of healthy interpersonal relationships.

Responding

All the steps we have discussed so far—hearing, attending, understanding, and remembering—are internal activities. A final part of the listening process involves **responding** to a message—giving observable feedback to the speaker (Bostrom, 1996; Cooper et al., 1997). One study of 195 critical incidents in banking and medical settings showed that a major difference between effective and ineffective listening was the

kind of feedback offered (Lewis and Reinsch, 1988). Good listeners showed that they were attentive by displaying non-verbal behaviours, such as keeping eye contact and reacting with appropriate facial expressions. Their verbal behaviour—for example, answering questions and exchanging ideas—also demonstrated their adequate attention. It's easy to imagine how other responses would signal less-effective listening. A slumped posture, bored expression, and barely stifled yawn send clear messages that you are not tuned in to the speaker. Sometimes your listening response may quite unintentionally communicate that something is amiss in the conversation. For example, people who stutter when they speak report that a common negative response they get is "The Look" (Starkweather, 2002). At least one major feature of "The Look" includes a lack of direct eye contact. People who are listening to stuttering speech avert their gaze more frequently than when listening to more fluent speech. When listening to people who stutter, we are more inclined to look at their noses rather than their eyes (Bowers et al., 2010). This gaze aversion often comes to be associated with negative emotions for the

Listening is not a passive activity—at the same time we receive messages, we also send them. What messages do you think this man and woman are sending one another?

stutterer even though that was probably not the intent of the listener.

As discussed in Chapter 1, adding responsiveness to our listening model demonstrates the fact that communication is transactional. Listening is not just a passive activity. As listeners, we are active participants in a communication transaction. At the same time that we receive messages, we also send them.

Types of Listening Responses

Of the five components of listening described above, responding is the one that lets us know if others are truly tuned in to what we are saying. Think for a moment of someone you consider a good listener. Why did you choose that person? It's probably because of the way she behaves while you are speaking: looking you in the eye and nodding when you are talking, staying attentive while you are telling an important story, reacting with an exclamation when you say something startling, expressing empathy and support when you are suffering, and offering another perspective or advice when you ask for it (Bippus, 2001). As Figure 5.3 illustrates, listening responses like these range from reflective feedback that invites the speaker to talk without fear of being judged, to more directive responses that evaluate the speaker's messages. We'll spend the rest of the chapter looking at each of these response styles in detail.

Silent Listening

There are times when the best response is to say nothing. This is certainly true when you

don't want to encourage a speaker to keep talking. For instance, there are times when a boss or instructor drones on and on when you need to leave for an appointment, or when a friend retells the story of a love affair gone bad for what seems like the tenth time. In situations like these, a verbal response would only encourage the speaker to continue—precisely the opposite of the reaction you would be seeking. The best response in these cases may be **silent listening**—staying attentive and nonverbally responsive without saying anything.

Silent listening is not just an avoidance strategy. It also can be the right approach when you are open to the other person's ideas, but your interjections wouldn't be appropriate. If you are part of a large audience hearing a lecture, it would probably be disruptive to ask questions and offer comments. On a more personal level, when a friend tells you a joke, butting in to ask for clarification ("There was a priest, a rabbi, and *who*?") would probably spoil your friend's rhythm.

There are even times when silent listening can help others solve their problems. Sonia Johnson (1987) describes a powerful activity she calls "hearing into being." The process is simple. In brainstorming sessions, each participant has half an hour of uninterrupted floor time. "When we are free to talk without threat of interruption, evaluation, and the pressure of time," notes Johnson, "we move quickly past known territory out into the frontiers of

CHECK **IT!**

Describe the five components of listening.

Silent Listening	Questioning	Paraphrasing	Empathizing	Supporting	Analyzing	Evaluating	Advising

MORE REFLECTIVE
LESS DIRECTIVE

LESS REFLECTIVE
MORE DIRECTIVE

Figure 5.3 ● Types of Listening Responses

Focus on RESEARCH

LISTENING TO CANADIAN FIRST NATIONS PATIENTS

Health-care providers in Canada often work in cross-cultural situations, but frequently have little or no preparation for dealing with the differing values and communication styles that these situations bring. Len Kelly and Judith Belle Brown (2002) were interested in gathering information to help doctors and other health-care professionals who serve First Nations communities. They conducted semi-structured one-hour interviews with 10 non-Native physicians working in these communities. The length of time each participant had worked in these communities ranged from 3 to 30 years, with an average of 14.4 years. The researchers found that the doctors had had to change their understanding of illness as something existing in an individual to something existing in a community, and that they had to think in new ways about the elements of communication and the communication strategies they used. For the doctors, the first indicator of distinct and varied First Nations cultural values was apparent in many Native peoples' different communication styles. The doctors reported that they had had to adapt to a different pace in their discussions with patients—speaking less, listening more, and becoming more comfortable with silence and lack of eye contact. Perhaps the most unfamiliar element of communication for non-Native physicians was the use of silence. One elder explained the importance of silent listening like this: "We are born with two ears, two eyes, and one mouth and should use them accordingly. We should use the mouth half as much as the ears and eyes" (Kelly and Brown, 2002, p. 1647). The doctors said they had received enormous benefits from the cross-cultural experience including changes in their understanding. One of them recalled:

The sense of humility that comes with understanding your limitations, I could illustrate with a quick story: I saw a very elderly Native lady; her daughters brought her in, she was sort of a matriarch and they called me that night and asked would I come to the house and see her and I did. Normal pulse, normal blood pressure, chest clear, everything seemed fine and I had no idea why they called me out at night, but I was pretty annoyed that they had done that . . . when one of the daughters said to me, "Would you like a cup of tea?" and I said, "Sure, that would be great," and that sort of diffused my little reprimand.

I went to the kitchen and sat down to have my cup of tea and while I was having the tea, the daughters went back into the bedroom, and then one of them walked out and said, "Well, she's gone very peacefully now," and I said, "What?" and ran into the bedroom. She was lying there as dead as a doornail and they said, "Thank you very much for coming when mother died. You know we knew she was going to go and we really appreciate just you having been here."

I thought to myself, "Well, first of all am I ever glad that I didn't say what I had intended to say about the unnecessary visit and secondly, how the hell did they know she was dying? I honestly did not have a clue. That injected in me a great sense of humility, like whoa, they know a lot that I don't know, about their mother, but also just about death and dying—and anyway, I've held onto that sense of humility and that's pretty much where I remain." (Kelly and Brown, 2002)

Critical thinking: *Can you think of other cultural differences that might affect listening responses?*

our thought" (p. 132). Johnson, who uses the technique in feminist seminars, reports that some women burst into tears when they first experience "hearing into being" because they are not used to being listened to so seriously and completely. Ask yourself when the last time was that you talked, uninterrupted, to an attentive partner for more than a few minutes?

How would you like the chance to develop your ideas without pausing for another's comments? Silent listening is a response style that many of us could profit from using—and receiving—more often.

Members of high-context and low-context cultures differ in their use of silence. Generally, in high-context cultures (i.e., many Asian

Calvin and Hobbes

by Bill Watterson

and Canadian First Nations cultures), silence is valued as a way to communicate respect and thoughtful consideration of others. People feel content with silence because it communicates mutual understanding (Braithwaite, 1990). However, in low-context cultures such as Canada and the United States, silence is often uncomfortable and people who don't talk are frequently evaluated negatively by others. Silence somehow suggests there is a problem because people are expected to verbalize what they think.

Questioning

Regarded as "the most popular piece of language" (Goodman and Esterly, 1990), a **questioning response** occurs when the listener asks the speaker for additional information. There are several reasons to ask sincere, non-directive questions:

- *To clarify meanings.* By now, you know that people who share words do not always share meanings. Good listeners don't assume they know what their partners mean; they ask for clarification with questions such as: "What did you mean when you said he had been 'unfair' to you?" "You said she's 'religious'—how do you define that term?" "You said you were going 'fast'—could you be more specific?"

Of course, be sure to use an appropriate tone of voice when asking such questions, or else they might sound like an inquisition.

- *To learn about other people's thoughts, feelings, and wants.* A caring listener may want to inquire about more than just "the facts." Opinions, emotions, needs, and even hopes are buried inside many messages; with sensitivity, a sincere question can draw these out. "What do you think about the new plan?" "How did you feel when you heard the news?" and "Were you hoping for something different?" are examples of such probes. When inquiring about personal information, it is usually best to ask **open questions** that allow a variety of extended responses rather than **closed questions** that allow only a limited range of answers. For instance, "How did you feel?" is an open question that allows a variety of responses, while "Did you feel angry?" is a closed question that requires only a yes or no answer (and may direct respondents toward feelings they weren't experiencing).

- *To encourage elaboration.* People are sometimes hesitant to talk about themselves, or perhaps they aren't sure if others are interested. Remarks such as, "Tell me more about that," "Try me again—I'm not sure

I understand," and "Keep going—I'm following you" convey concern and involvement. Notice that none of these examples ends with a question mark. We can encourage elaboration simply by acknowledging that we are listening.

- *To encourage discovery.* People in the helping professions—clergy, counsellors, therapists, and so on—often ask questions to prompt their clients into discovering solutions for their problems. "Playing counsellor" can be a dangerous game, but there are times when you can use questions to encourage others to explore their thoughts and feelings. "So, what do you see as your options?" may prompt an employee to come up with creative problem-solving alternatives. "What would be your ideal solution?" might help a friend get in touch with various wants and needs. Most importantly, encouraging discovery rather than dispensing advice indicates you have faith in others' ability to think for themselves. This may be the most important message that you can communicate as an effective listener.

- *To gather more facts and details.* Just because your conversational partner tells you something, it doesn't mean you understand the whole story. As long as your questions are not intrusive (you will need to monitor the other person's non-verbal behaviour to determine this), people often appreciate listeners who want to learn more. Questions such as, "What did you do then?" and "What did she say after that?" can help a listener understand the big picture.

Not all questions are genuine requests for information. Whereas **sincere questions** are aimed at understanding others, **counterfeit questions** are really disguised attempts to send a message, not receive one. As such, they really fit better at the "more directive" end of the listening response continuum shown in Figure 5.3 on page 162. It's also likely that they'll lead to a defensive communication climate, as we discuss in Chapter 9.

Counterfeit questions come in several varieties:

- *Questions that trap the speaker.* When your friend says, "You didn't like that movie, did you?" you are being backed into a corner. It's clear that your friend disapproves, so the question leaves you with a choice to make. You can disagree and defend your position, or you can devalue your reaction by lying or equivocating—"I guess it wasn't terrific." Consider how much easier it would be to answer the sincere question, "What did you think of the movie?"

  Adding a tag question such as "didn't you?" or "isn't that right?" to the end of a question can be a tip-off that the asker is looking for agreement, not information. Although some listeners use these tag endings to confirm and facilitate understanding (Coates, 1986), tags can be coercive: "You said you'd call at five o'clock, but you forgot, didn't you?" Similarly, questions that begin with "Don't you" (such as, "Don't you think he would make a good boss?") direct others toward a desired response. As a simple solution, changing "Don't you?" to "Do you?" makes the question less leading.

  Leading questions not only signal what the desired answer is, but also affect memory, especially in children. David Bjorklund and his colleagues (2000) showed children and adults a video of a theft and then several days later, interviewed them using both leading and free-recall questions. The adults were unaffected by the type of question asked, but the children who were asked leading questions had a less accurate memory of the video than those who were asked free-recall questions.

- *Questions that make statements.* "Are you *finally* off the phone?" is more a statement than a question—a fact unlikely to be lost on the targeted person. Emphasizing certain words can also turn a question into a statement: "You lent money to *Tony*?" We also use questions to offer advice. The person who asks, "Are you going to stand up to him and give him what he deserves?" has clearly stated an opinion about what should be done.

- *Questions that carry hidden agendas*. "Are you busy Friday night?" is a dangerous question to answer. If you say "no," thinking the person has something pleasant in mind, you won't like hearing, "Good, because I need some help moving my piano." Obviously, such questions are not designed to enhance understanding; they are setups for the proposal that follows. Other examples include, "Will you do me a favour?" and "If I tell you what happened, will you promise not to get mad?" Because they are strategic rather than spontaneous, these questions are likely to provoke defensiveness (Gibb, 1961). Wise communicators answer questions that mask hidden agendas cautiously with responses such as "It depends" or "Let me hear what you have in mind before I answer."

- *Questions that seek "correct" answers*. Most of us have been victims of question askers who want to hear a particular answer. "Which shoes do you think I should wear?" can be a sincere question—unless the asker has a predetermined preference. When this happens, the asker is not interested in listening to contrary opinions, and "incorrect" responses get shot down. Some of these questions may venture into delicate territory. "Honey, do you think I'm overweight?" is usually a request for a "correct" answer—and the listener must have a fair amount of discretion and good judgment to determine a suitable response.

- *Questions based on unverified assumptions*. "Why aren't you listening to me?" assumes the other person is not paying attention. "What's the matter?" assumes that something is wrong. As we explained in Chapter 3, perception checking is a much better way of confirming one's assumptions. You'll recall that a perception check offers a description and interpretations, followed by a sincere request for clarification: "When you kept looking over at the TV, I thought you weren't listening to me, but maybe I was wrong. Were you paying attention?"

No question is inherently sincere or counterfeit. As we will explain further in Chapter 6, the meaning and intent of any statement is shaped by its context. Moreover, a slight change in tone of voice or facial expression can turn a sincere question into a counterfeit one, and vice versa. Nonetheless, the types of questions described above are usually closer to statements than requests for information.

It's also worth noting that counterfeit questions are not always bad; in fact, they can be powerful tools for making a point. Lawyers use them to get confessions in the courtroom, and journalists ask them to uncover concealed information. Our point is that they usually get in the way of effective listening and relationship building—after all, most people don't like feeling trapped or "grilled" in a conversation.

Paraphrasing

Paraphrasing is feedback that restates, in your own words, the message you thought the speaker sent. You may wonder, "Why would I want to restate what is already been said?" Consider this simple exchange:

> "Let's make plans to get together next weekend."

> "So you want to chat next week to make plans for Saturday?"

> "No, what I meant is that we should check our calendars now to see if we're free to go to the game on Sunday."

By paraphrasing, the listener learned that the speaker wanted to make plans now, not later—and that "weekend" meant Sunday, not Saturday. Note that the listener rephrased rather than repeated the message. In effective paraphrasing you restate what you think the speaker has said in your own words as a way of checking the meaning you've assigned to the message. It's important that you paraphrase, not "parrot-phrase." If you simply repeat the speaker's comments verbatim, you will sound foolish or hard of hearing—and just as important you still might misunderstand what is been said.

Types of Paraphrasing Statements

Restating another person's message in a way that sounds natural can sometimes be a difficult skill to master. Here are three approaches to get you started:

1. Change the speaker's wording.

    Speaker: "Bilingual education is just another failed idea of francophones."

    Paraphrase: "Let me see if I've got this right. You're mad because you think bilingual education sounds good, but it doesn't work?"

2. Offer an example of what you think the speaker is talking about. When the speaker makes an abstract statement, you may suggest a specific example, or two, to see if your understanding is accurate.

    Speaker: "Lee is such a jerk. I can't believe the way he acted last night."

    Paraphrase: "You think those jokes were pretty offensive, huh?"

3. Describe the underlying theme of the speaker's remarks. When you want to summarize the theme that seems to have run through another person's conversation, a complete or partial perception check is useful:

    Paraphrase: "You keep reminding me to be careful. Sounds like you're worried that something might happen to me. Am I right?"

There are several reasons why paraphrasing aids in listening. First, as the preceding examples illustrate, paraphrasing allows you to find out if the message received is the message the sender intended. Second, paraphrasing often draws out further information from the speaker, much like questioning (in fact, a good paraphrase often ends with a question such as "Is that what you meant?"). Third, paraphrasing is an ideal way to take the heat out of intense discussions. When conversations become heated, it is often because the people involved believe they aren't being heard. Paraphrasing has been shown to increase the speaker's positive emotions toward the listener (Weger et al., 2010). Rather than escalate the conflict, try paraphrasing what the other person says: "Okay, let me be sure I understand you. It sounds as if you are concerned about . . . " Paraphrasing usually stops a defensive spiral because it assures the other person of your involvement and concern. When you take the time to restate and clarify a speaker's message, your commitment to listening is hard to deny.

There are two levels at which you can paraphrase messages: the first involves feedback of factual information; the second involves describing what you believe the underlying message to be.

Paraphrasing Factual Information

Summarizing facts, data, and details is important during personal or professional conversations. "We've agreed that we'll take another few days to think about our choices and make a decision on Tuesday—right?" might be an effective way to conclude a business lunch. A questioning tone should be used; a listener wants to be sure that meaning has been shared. Even personal topics are sometimes best handled on a factual level: "So, your main problem is that our friends take up all the parking spaces in front of your place. Is that it?" While this "neutral" response may be difficult when you are under attack, it helps to clarify facts before you offer your reaction. It is also a good

Building WORK SKILLS

Practise your ability to paraphrase in order to understand others by following these steps:

1. Choose a partner, and designate one of yourselves as person A and the other as person B. Find a subject on which you and your partner seem to disagree—a personal dispute, a philosophical or moral issue, or perhaps a matter of personal taste.
2. Person A begins by making a statement on the subject. Person B's job is to paraphrase the idea. In this step, B should feedback only what he heard A say, without adding any judgment or interpretation. B's job here is simply to understand A—not to agree or disagree with A.
3. Person A responds by telling B whether or not the response was accurate and by making any necessary additions or corrections to clarify the message.
4. Person B then paraphrases the revised statement. This process should continue until A is sure that B understands her.
5. Now, B and A reverse roles and repeat the procedure in the first four steps. Continue the conversation until both partners are satisfied that they have explained themselves fully and have been understood by the other person.

After the discussion has ended, consider how this process differed from typical conversations on controversial topics. Was there greater understanding here? Do the partners feel better about one another? Finally, ask yourself how your life might change if you used more paraphrasing in everyday conversations.

idea to paraphrase instructions, directions, and decisions before acting on what you *think* has been said.

Paraphrasing Personal Information

While restating factual information is relatively easy, it takes a sensitive ear to listen for the other person's thoughts, feelings, and wants. The "underlying message" is often the more important message, and effective listeners try to reflect what they hear at this level. An attentive conversationalist listens for thoughts, feelings, and wants, and is thus able to address the cognitive (rational), affective (emotional), and behavioural (desired action) domains of the human experience. Read the following statement as if a married, female friend is talking to you, and listen for all three components in her message:

> Jean-Pierre has hardly been home all week—he's been so busy with work. He rushes in just long enough to eat dinner, then he buries himself at his desk until bedtime. Then he tells me today that he's going fishing Saturday with his buddies. I guess men are just like that—job first, play second, family third.

What is the speaker thinking, feeling, and wanting? Paraphrasing can help you find out: "Sounds as if you're unhappy (feeling) because you think Jean-Pierre's ignoring you (thought) and you want him to spend more time at home (want)." Recognize that your paraphrase may not be accurate; the speaker might reply, "No, I really don't want him to spend more time at home—I just want him to pay attention to me when he's here." Recognize also that you could identify an entirely different think–feel–want set: "So, you're frustrated (feeling) because you'd like Jean-Pierre to change (want), but you think it's hopeless because men have different priorities (thought)." The fact that these examples offer such different interpretations of the same message demonstrates the value of paraphrasing.

Your paraphrases don't have to be as long as the examples in the preceding paragraph. In many cases, you'll want to reflect only one or two of the think–feel–want components. The

✓ CHECK IT!

Describe the three approaches to paraphrasing another person's message and explain how paraphrasing aids listening.

REFLECTION

LETTING OTHERS GIVE THEMSELVES ADVICE

Last week, my roommate and her boyfriend were arguing. It seemed to me that she was making a much bigger deal of the situation than she should have, but I knew it would be a mistake to tell her my opinion. Besides, I could have been wrong.

So, instead of telling her what I thought (as I usually would have done), I decided to paraphrase back what she was saying. All of a sudden, she stopped talking and smiled and said, "Gosh, I am being really dumb. This isn't even worth wasting my time on." I was amazed! This was exactly what I had been thinking, but she got there on her own.

This approach worked especially well with my roommate because she is the kind of person who gets defensive if you come out and tell her your opinion. I think I'll use paraphrasing more often—it certainly seems better than giving advice that people do not want to hear.

listeners put the attitude of empathy into verbal and non-verbal responses, they engage in empathizing. Sometimes, these responses can be quite brief: "Uh-huh," "I see," "Wow!" "Ouch!' "Whew!" and "My goodness!" In other cases, empathizing is expressed in statements like these:

"I can see that really hurts."

"I know how important that was to you."

"It's no fun to feel unappreciated."

"I can tell you're really excited about that."

"Wow, that must be rough."

"I think I've felt that way, too."

"Looks like that really made your day."

"This means a lot to you, doesn't it?"

Even statements like these may not fully capture the feeling of effective empathizing, which is not reducible to a technique or skill, but is something that emerges from a relationship (Myers, 2000). Genuine empathizing requires genuine identification with another person.

How often do you empathize with the people you interact with?

key is to give feedback that is appropriate for the situation and to offer it in a way that helps the listening process. Because paraphrasing is an unfamiliar way of responding, it may feel awkward at first. If you start by paraphrasing occasionally and then gradually do it more often, you will begin to see the benefits of this method.

Empathizing

An **empathizing response** is what listeners use when they want to show they *identify* with a speaker. As we discussed in Chapter 3, empathy involves perspective taking, emotional contagion, and genuine concern. When

Empathizing falls near the middle of the listening response continuum shown in Figure 5.3 on page 162. It is different from the more reflective responses at the left end of the spectrum, which attempt to gather information neutrally. It is also different from the more evaluative styles at the right end of the spectrum, which offer more direction than reflection. To understand how empathizing compares to other types of responses, consider these examples:

> "So, your boss isn't happy with your performance and you are thinking about finding a new job." [*paraphrasing*]

> "Ouch—I'll bet it hurt when your boss said you weren't doing a good job." [*empathizing*]

> "Hey, you'll land on your feet—your boss doesn't appreciate what a winner you are." [*supporting*]

Notice that empathizing identifies with the speaker's emotions and perceptions more than paraphrasing does, yet offers less evaluation and agreement than supporting responses. In fact, it is possible to empathize with others while disagreeing with them. For instance, the response "I can tell that this issue is important to you" legitimizes a speaker's feelings without assenting to that person's point of view (note that it could be said to either a friend or a foe at a business meeting). Empathizing is therefore an important skill, not only for interacting with people you agree with, but also for responding to those who see the world differently than you.

Perhaps a better way to explain empathizing is to describe what it *does not* sound like. Many listeners believe they are empathizing when, in fact, they are offering responses that are evaluative and directive. Listeners are probably *not* empathizing when they do the following:

- *Deny others the right to their feelings.* Consider this common response to another person's problem: "Don't worry about it." While the remark may be intended as a reassuring comment, the underlying message is that the speaker wants the person to feel different. The irony is that the suggestion will probably not work—after all, it is unlikely that people can or will stop worrying just because you tell them to. Other examples of denying feelings are "It's nothing to get so upset about" and "That's a silly way to feel"). Research shows that empathizing is more effective than denying the feelings and perspectives of others (Burleson and Samter, 1985, 1994).

- *Minimizing the significance of the situation.* Think about the times someone said to you, "Hey, it's only _____." You can probably fill in the blank a variety of ways: "a game," "words," "a test," "a party." How did you react? You probably thought the person who said it just didn't understand. To someone who has been the victim of verbal abuse, the hurtful message wasn't "just words"; to a child who didn't get an invitation, it wasn't "just a party" (see Burleson, 1984); to a student who has failed an important exam, it wasn't "just a test" (see Burleson and Samter, 1985). When you minimize the importance of someone else's experience, you are not empathizing. Instead, you are interpreting the event from your perspective and then passing judgment—rarely a helpful response.

- *Focus on yourself.* When your response to someone else's troubles is to defend yourself ("Don't blame me; I've done my part"), it is clear you are more concerned with yourself than with the other person. Even well-intentioned comparisons of the speakers' situation to your own experiences (e.g., "I know exactly how you feel, the same thing happened to me . . .") draw attention away from the speaker and are not usually helpful (Burleson, 2008).

- *Raining on the speaker's parade.* Most of the preceding examples deal with difficult situations or messages about pain. However, empathizing involves identifying with the joys of others as well as their sorrows. Many of us can remember coming home with exciting news, only to be told, "A 5 per cent raise? That isn't so great." "An *A*-? Why didn't you get an A?" "Big deal—I got one of those years ago." Taking the wind out of someone's sails is the opposite of empathizing.

Authors Florence Wolff and Nadine Marsnik (1993, p. 100) believe that empathizing requires "fine skill and exquisite tuning to another's moods and feelings." Research suggests that cognitive complexity and flexibility are needed to offer these non-judgmental, other-oriented responses (Applegate, 1990). Fortunately, research also shows that the ability to offer such responses can be learned by both children and adults (Long et al., 1999; Wei and Li, 2001). The "Activities" section at the end of this chapter can offer you valuable practice in developing your skills as an empathic communicator.

Supporting

So far, we have looked at listening responses that put a premium on being reflective and non-evaluative. However, there are times when other people want to hear more than a reflection of how *they* feel—when they would like to know how *you* feel about *them*. A **supporting response** reveals the listener's solidarity with the speaker's situation. There are several types of supportive responses:

Agreement:

"You're right—the landlord is being unfair."

"Yes, that class was tough for me, too."

Offers to help:

"I'm here if you need me."

"Let me try to explain it to him."

Praise:

"I don't care what the boss said. I think you did a great job!"

"You're a terrific person! If she doesn't recognize it, that's her problem."

Reassurance:

"The worst part seems to be over. It will probably get easier from here."

"I know you'll do a great job."

There's no question about the value of receiving support when faced with personal problems. "Comforting ability" and social support have been shown to be among the most important communication skills a friend—or a teacher, or a coach, or a parent—can have (Cunningham and Barbee, 2000; Robbins and Rosenfeld, 2001; Rosenfeld and Richman, 1999; Rosenfeld et al., 1998). The value of personal support is clear when big problems arise, but research shows that smaller, everyday distresses and upsets can actually take a bigger toll on mental health and physical well-being (Ekenrode, 1984). Social support, however, can reduce the psychological distress of people dealing with a wide range of upsets (Schwarzer, 1998). Social support has been linked to improved immune function (Baron et al., 1990), better physical health, and increased lifespan (House et al., 1988). James Pennebaker's research (1995, 1997) suggests that just having someone to talk to about upsetting experiences can make a positive impact on your physical and mental health. Social support is one of the most important resources we have to improve our quality of life.

Men and women differ in the way they act when the opportunity to support others arises. Women are more likely than men to give supportive responses when presented with another person's problem (Hale et al., 1997; Trobst et al., 1994), and are more skilful at composing such messages (Burleson, 1982). By contrast, men tend to respond to other people's

REFLECTION

COMFORTING A CRYING CHILD: "IT'S OKAY" IS NOT OKAY

I have always enjoyed working with young children. Sharing their joy and excitement is such a pleasure and exploring the world with them inspires my curiosity. Another important part of my job as a caring adult in children's lives is providing comfort and support when they are upset. My first reaction when children are hurt and crying has always been to try to reassure them. When I am hugging them I find myself saying, "It's okay. It's all right." And things like that. I realize now that, rather than being reassuring, my words could be seen as actually denying the child's true feelings. Obviously, if you are crying and someone or something has hurt you, it really isn't okay at all in that moment! It hurts. Now, I try to say things like, "I am here. I will try to help you feel better" when I am giving my hugs. I try to acknowledge their feelings and offer to comfort and care for them.

who had recently suffered the death of a loved one said that 80 per cent of the statements made to them were unhelpful (Davidowitz and Myrick, 1984). Nearly half of these unhelpful statements were advice: "You've got to get out more." "Don't question God's will." The next most frequent response was reassurance, such as, "She's out of her pain now." Far more helpful were expressions that acknowledged the mourner's feelings, such as, "I know this is a painful loss for you." One American Red Cross grief counsellor explained to survivors of the 11 September 2001 (9/11) terrorist attacks in the United States, that simply being present can be more helpful than trying to reassure grief-stricken family members who had lost loved ones in the tragedy (Washington Post 2001).

> Don't say anything. Saying "it'll be okay" or "I know how you feel" can backfire. Right now that's not what a victim wants to hear. They want to know people are there and care about them if you need them. Be there, be present, and listen. The clergy refer to it as a ministry of presence. You don't need to do anything, just be there or have them know you're available.

problems by offering advice or by changing the subject (Barbee et al., 1990; Derlega et al., 1994). All these responses can be helpful—it just depends on the perspective of the person seeking the support.

For social support to be effective, it must match the other person's needs (Sarason et al., 1990). This means that even though you might be doing your best to help someone, you might be wasting your effort if what you offer is not what's needed. In one study, hospice workers who received emotional support from their co-workers experienced an increase in stress, whereas those who received technical challenge support experienced a decrease (Richman and Rosenfeld, 1987). The emotional support communicated "you are right to feel overwhelmed," while the technical challenge support communicated "you are smart and motivated to solve the problem" and pushed the workers to find solutions.

Even the most sincere supportive efforts do not always help. In one survey, mourners

Like the other kinds of helping styles, supporting can be beneficial, but only under certain conditions (Halone and Pecchioni, 2001; Goldsmith and Fitch, 1997), such as:

- *Make sure your expression of support is sincere.* Phony agreement or encouragement is probably worse than no support at all, since it adds the insult of your dishonesty to whatever pain the other person is already feeling.
- *Be sure the other person can accept your support.* Sometimes, people are so upset that they aren't ready or able to hear anything positive.
- *Focus on "here and now" rather than "then and there."* While it is sometimes true that "you'll feel better tomorrow," it sometimes is not (you can probably remember times when you felt worse the next day). More

important focusing on the future avoids supporting in the present. Even if the prediction that "10 years from now, you will not even remember her name" proves correct, it gives little comfort to someone experiencing heartbreak today

Analyzing

In an **analyzing response**, the listener offers an interpretation of a speaker's message ("I think what's really bothering you is . . . ," "She's doing it because . . . ,' or "Maybe the problem started when he . . . "). Interpretations are often effective in helping people who have problems consider alternative meanings of a situation, that is, meanings that they would have never thought of without your assistance. Sometimes, an analysis helps clarify a confusing problem and provide an objective understanding of the situation. Research suggests that analytic listeners are able to listen to people who are emotionally upset without experiencing similar emotions, and this can be an advantage in solving problems (Weaver and Kirtley, 1995).

In other cases, an analysis can create more problems than it solves. There are two possible reasons: First, your interpretation may not be correct, in which case the person with the problem may become even more confused by accepting it. Second, even if your analysis is accurate, sharing it with the other person may not be useful. There is a chance that it will arouse defensiveness—offering an analysis could imply being superior and in a position to evaluate. Besides, the person with the problem may not be able to understand your view of the problem without working it out personally.

How can you know when it's helpful to offer an analysis? There are several guidelines to follow:

- *Offer your interpretation in a tentative way rather than as absolute fact.* There's a big difference between saying, "Maybe the reason is . . ." and insisting, "This is the truth."

- *Your analysis ought to have a reasonable chance of being correct.* An inaccurate interpretation—especially one that sounds plausible—can leave a person more confused than before.

- *Make sure that the other person will be receptive to your analysis.* Even if you are completely accurate, your thoughts will not help if the other person is not ready to consider them. Pay attention to the other person's verbal and non-verbal cues to see how your analysis is being received.

- *Be sure that your motive for offering an analysis is truly to help the other person.* It can be tempting to offer an analysis to show how brilliant you are or even to make the other person feel bad for not having thought of the right answer in the first place. Needless to say, an analysis offered under such conditions is not helpful.

Evaluating

An **evaluating response** appraises the sender's thoughts or behaviour in some way. The evaluation may be favourable ("That's a good idea" or "You are on the right track now") or unfavourable ("An attitude like that won't get you anywhere"). In either case, it implies that the person evaluating is in some way qualified to pass judgment on the speaker's thoughts or actions.

Sometimes, negative evaluations are purely critical. How many times have you heard responses such as, "Well, you asked for it!" or "I told you so!" or "You're just feeling sorry for yourself?" Although such a comment can sometimes serve as a verbal slap that "knocks sense" into the problem holder, it usually makes matters worse by arousing defensiveness in that person. After all, suggesting that someone is foolish or mistaken is an attack on the presenting image that most people would have a hard time ignoring or accepting.

Other times, negative evaluations are less critical. These involve what we usually call constructive criticism, which is intended to help the problem holder improve in the future.

Self-Assessment

Learn more about your helping style by indicating how you would most likely respond to each of the statements below. Don't try to guess the "right" response. Choose the response that is closest to what you would probably say after hearing each statement.

1. "I think I understand the material, but I don't know where I stand in the course. I'm not sure what the instructor expects of me, and she doesn't tell me how I'm doing. I wish I knew where I stood."

   a. "Has your instructor ever given you any indication of what she thinks of your work?"
   b. "If I were you, I'd discuss it with her."
   c. "She's probably just trying to give everyone in the class a lot of freedom to do what they want to do."
   d. "It sounds as if you're worried about your grade. Is that it?"
   e. "Don't take it so seriously. Most of the time in school, you don't know where you stand."
   f. "What do you think you can do to solve this situation? What have you tried?"
   g. "I've had teachers like that, and it's a lousy situation."

2. "The policy in the chemistry department is supposed to be to hire lab assistants from people in the advanced chemistry classes. And now I find that this person from a beginning class is getting hired. I had my eye on that job. I've been working hard for it. I know I could be a terrific assistant if I had a chance."

   a. "I can tell how disappointed you are."
   b. "Why do you think they hired the person from the beginning class?"
   c. "If not getting the job means not having enough money to make it through the semester, I can help out with a loan."
   d. "Getting ahead is very important to you, and it sounds as if you feel cheated that someone else got the job as lab assistant."
   e. "You should take some more chemistry classes to help you advance."

   f. "I told you not to get your hopes up."
   g. "You shouldn't complain—they probably hired the best person to be an assistant."

3. "I'm really tired of this. I'm taking more classes than anyone I know, and then on the same day, three of my teachers tell me that there's another assignment due on top of what's already due. I've got so many people asking me to do things that I just can't keep up, and it bothers me. I like my teachers, and my classes are interesting, but I am getting overwhelmed."

   a. "With so many teachers asking you to do extra assignments, it's difficult for you to accomplish all of it, and the pressure gets you down."
   b. "Are all these requests from your teachers required work?"
   c. "I'm really sorry you feel so overwhelmed."
   d. "You seem to have too much work. Why don't you talk it over with your teachers?"
   e. "Yikes! Sounds like things are pretty hectic for you right now."
   f. "You're probably overworked because you are not organized."
   g. "Who told you to take so many classes?"

4. "My teacher tells the class that he would appreciate getting term projects as soon as possible to help him with grading. So I work like mad to get it completed and on his desk early. What's my reward for helping him out? Nothing! No thanks, no nothing. In fact, I think my project will sit on his desk until all the projects are handed in."

   a. "How often do teachers do this to you?"
   b. "And you believed him because . . . ?"
   c. "You ought to tell him how you feel."
   d. "You feel resentful because you think he's taking advantage of you?"
   e. "I hate it when teachers do that to us!"
   f. "I hear you! Been there, felt that—it's no fun."
   g. "Your reward is having finished the work early."

5. "He used to be one of the guys until he was made the team's coach. Now, it's like he's not my friend anymore. I don't mind being told about my mistakes, but he doesn't have to do it in front of the rest of the team. Whenever I get the chance, he's going to get his!"

a. "Revenge is only one way of handling this."
b. "I'll bet that really upset you—and I can understand why."
c. "To be told about your mistakes in front of the rest of the team is embarrassing, especially by a person you once considered a friend."
d. "If you didn't make so many mistakes, the coach wouldn't have to tell you about them."
e. "Why don't we talk it over with a few other people on the team and then go and talk to him about this situation?"
f. "How often does he criticize you in front of the others?"
g. "Seems like he's on a power trip."

Listed below are the possible response types for each of the five situations. For example, if you indicated answer "a" in situation number 1, note that this is a "questioning response." If you indicated answer "b", note that this is an "advising response." Do this for your five responses.

Questioning response: 1a, 2b, 3b, 4a, 5f
Advising response: 1b, 2e, 3d, 4c, 5e
Analyzing response: 1c, 2g, 3f, 4e, 5g
Paraphrasing response: 1d, 2d, 3a, 4d, 5c
Evaluating response: 1e, 2f, 3g, 4b, 5d
Supportive response: 1f (technical challenge support), 2c (tangible support), 3c (emotional support), 4f (listening support), 5a (emotional challenge support)
Empathizing response: 1g, 2a, 3e, 4e, 5b

Do you have a particular way of responding? What does this tell you about how you listen—that is, the kinds of information you listen for? When is your typical way of responding most and least useful? What do you think is the most useful response in each of the five situations?

Friends give this sort of response about the choice of everything from clothing to jobs to friends. A common setting for constructive criticism is school, where instructors evaluate students' work in order to help them master concepts and skills. Even constructive criticism can arouse defensiveness, because it may threaten the self-concept of the person to whom it is directed. Chapter 9 provides guidelines for offering feedback in ways that minimize defensiveness and protect the self-concept of the recipient.

Advising

When we are approached with someone's problem, the most common reaction is to advise (Notarius and Herrick, 1988). An **advising response** involves providing the speaker with your opinion about what they should do. Advice is most welcome under two conditions: when it has been requested, and when the adviser seems concerned with respecting the face-saving needs of the recipient (Goldsmith, 2000; Goldsmith and MacGeorge, 2000; MacGeorge et al., 2002).

Even when advice is requested and offered in a face-saving manner, there are several reasons why it often is not helpful. First, it may not offer the best suggestion about how to act. In fact, it may even be harmful. There may often be a temptation to tell others how you would behave in their place, but it is important to realize that what's right for one person may not be right for another. Second, a related consequence of advising is that it often allows others to avoid responsibility for their decisions. A partner who follows a suggestion of yours that does not work out can always pin the blame on you. Finally, people often do not want advice. They may not be ready to accept it and instead may simply need to talk out their thoughts and feelings. You should offer advice, then, only under the following conditions:

• *You are sure the other person really wants to hear your suggestions.* The best indicator is a clear request for advice. If the person has already made a decision or taken a course of action your advice may not be wanted. If you are not sure whether the other person is seeking your opinion, it may be best to ask.

- *You are confident that your advice is correct.* Resist the temptation to act like an authority on matters you know little about or to make suggestions when you are not positive that they are the best choice. Realize that while a particular course of action worked for you, it probably will not be correct for everybody.

- *You are able to offer the advice in a sensitive manner.* Recall (from Chapter 1) that every message has a relational and content component. Even if the content of your advice is good if you provide it in a way that belittles or threatens the self-concept of the recipient (e.g., implying that they are not as smart as you) it is unlikely to be helpful or heeded.

Which Style to Use?

By now, it should be clear that there are many ways to respond as a listener. You also can see that each style has advantages and disadvantages. Which style is best? There is no simple answer to this question. Research shows that all response styles have the potential to

© iStockPhoto/Mark Bowden.

When we are approached with someone's problem, the most common reaction is to advise. What conditions should exist before you offer someone advice?

TAKE TWO

Types of Listening Responses

- **Silent listening:** staying attentive and non-verbally responsive, without saying anything.
- **Questioning:** asking the speaker for additional information.
  - *Open questions* allow for a variety of extended responses.
  - *Closed questions* only allow a limited range of answers.
  - *Sincere questions* are aimed at understanding others.
  - *Counterfeit questions* are disguised attempts to send a message, not receive one.
- **Paraphrasing:** restating, in your own words, the message you thought the speaker sent.
- **Empathizing:** showing that you identify with a speaker.
- **Supporting:** revealing your solidarity with the speaker's situation.
- **Analyzing:** offering an interpretation of a speaker's message.
- **Evaluating:** appraising the speaker's thoughts or behaviour in some way.
- **Advising:** providing the speaker with your opinion about what she should do.

help others accept their situation, feel better, and have a sense of control over their problems (Albrecht and Adelman, 1987; Burleson, 1994).

As a general rule, it is probably wise to begin with responses from the left and middle of the listening response continuum: silent listening, questioning, paraphrasing, empathizing, and supporting. Once you have gathered the facts and demonstrated your interest and concern, it's likely that the speaker will be more receptive to (and perhaps even ask

Building WORK SKILLS

Explore the various types of listening responses by completing the following steps:

1. Join with two partners to form a trio. Designate members as persons A, B, and C.
2. Person A begins by sharing an actual, current work- or school-related problem with B. The problem need not be a major life crisis, but it should be a real one. Person B should respond in whatever way that seems most helpful. Person C's job is to categorize each of B's responses as either: silent listening, questioning, paraphrasing, empathizing, supporting, analyzing, evaluating, or advising.
3. After a four- to five-minute discussion, C should summarize B's response styles. Person A then describes which of the styles were most helpful and which were not helpful.
4. Repeat the same process twice, switching roles so that each person has been in all of the positions.
5. Based on your findings, your threesome should draw conclusions about what combination of response styles can be most helpful.

for) your analyzing, evaluating, and advising responses.

You can improve the odds of choosing the best style in each situation by considering three factors. First, *think about the situation*, and match your response to the nature of the problem. People sometimes need your advice. In other cases, your encouragement and support will be most helpful, and in still other cases, your analysis or judgment may be truly useful. And, as you have seen, there are times when your questioning and paraphrasing can help others find their own answer.

Second, besides considering the situation, you also should *think about the other person* when deciding which approach to use. It is important to be sure that the other person is open to receiving *any* kind of help. Furthermore, you need to be confident that you will be regarded as someone whose support is valuable. The same response that would be accepted with gratitude when it comes from one communicator can be regarded as unhelpful when

it is offered by the wrong person (Clark et al., 1998; Sullivan, 1996).

It is also important to match the type of response you offer with the style of the person to whom it is directed (Bippus, 2001). Some people are able to consider advice thoughtfully, while others use suggestions to avoid making their own decisions. Many communicators are extremely defensive and are not capable of receiving analysis or judgments without lashing out. Still others are not equipped to think through problems clearly enough to profit from questioning and paraphrasing. Sophisticated listeners choose a style that fits the person.

Finally, *think about yourself* when deciding how to respond. Most of us reflexively use one or two styles (did you notice this when you completed the "Self-Assessment" on pages 174–175?). You may be best at listening quietly, posing a question, or paraphrasing from time to time. Or perhaps you are especially insightful and can offer a truly useful analysis of the problem. Of course, it's also possible to rely on a response style that is *unhelpful*. You may be overly judgmental or too eager to advise, even when your suggestions are not invited or productive. As you think about how to respond to another's problems, consider your weaknesses as well as your strengths.

 CHECK IT!

What factors should you consider before you choose how to respond as a listener?

SUMMARY

Listening is both more frequent and less emphasized than speaking. Despite its relative invisibility, listening is at least as important as speaking. Research shows that good listening is vital to both personal and professional success. There are a variety of reasons why we listen to others. At the most basic level, we listen to understand and retain information. Perhaps more importantly, we listen to build and maintain our interpersonal relationships. We may listen to help others and also to evaluate their messages.

Most people's understanding of listening suffers from several misconceptions, which communicators need to correct. Listening—at least listening effectively—is quite different from merely hearing a message. Skilful listening is not easy; rather, it is a challenge that requires much effort and talent. Several barriers can hamper effective listening: hearing problems, information overload, rapid thought, and both internal and external noise. Even careful listening does not mean that all listeners will receive the same message. A wide variety of factors discussed in this chapter can result in hugely varying interpretations of even simple statements.

Listening consists of several components: *hearing, paying attention to a message, understanding the statement, remembering the message after the passage of time*, and *responding to the speaker*. Listening responses are important, because they let us know if others are truly tuned in to what we're saying. Listening responses can be placed on a continuum. More reflective and less directive responses include silent listening, questioning, paraphrasing, and empathizing. These put a premium on gathering information and showing interest and concern. Less reflective and more directive responses include supporting, analyzing, evaluating, and advising. These put a premium on offering input and direction. It is possible to use the "more reflective" listening responses to help people arrive at their own decisions without offering advice or evaluation. The most effective listeners use several styles, depending on the situation, the other person, and their own personal skills and motivation.

MULTIPLE-CHOICE QUESTIONS

1. If you combine interpersonal listening and media listening college students spend approximately how much of their communication time listening?
   a. 72%
   b. 56%
   c. 17%
   d. 11%
2. Which of the following reasons for listening are accurate?
   a. We listen to understand and remember.
   b. We listen to evaluate the quality of messages.
   c. We listen to build and maintain relationships.
   d. We listen for all the above reasons.
3. While his boss describes a project he would like him to work on, Simon is thinking about asking a colleague he likes to go out for coffee. Simon's thoughts interfere with his ability to listen to his boss and are an example of
   a. information overload.
   b. stage hogging.
   c. noise.
   d. insulated listening.

4. Listening is the process by which sound waves strike the eardrum and cause vibrations that are transmitted to the brain.
   a. true
   b. false
5. Background noise from a television
   a. always reduces the ability of the communicator to understand messages.
   b. is classified as mental noise.
   c. is classified as information overload.
   d. both a and b are true.
6. Listening is like breathing—a natural activity that people do without conscious effort.
   a. true
   b. false
7. When Seema's mother brings up the topic of school, homework, and grades, Seema totally ignores her mother. Seema's non-listening would be best described as
   a. pseudo-listening.
   b. stage hogging.

   c. insulated listening.
   d. selective listening.
8. Members of high-context cultures generally value silence as a way to communicate respect and thoughtful consideration of others.
   a. true
   b. false
9. Which three listening responses would be described as more reflective and less directive?
   a. paraphrasing, silent listening, and questioning
   b. questioning, analyzing, and evaluating
   c. advising, supporting, and empathizing
   d. paraphrasing, empathizing, and supporting
10. In order to choose the best listening response in any situation, you need to rely on the style you use most often.
    a. true
    b. false

Answers: 1. b; 2. d; 3. c; 4. b; 5. c; 6. b; 7. c; 8. a; 9. a; 10. b

ACTIVITIES

1. Invitation to Insight
You can learn to stop believing in some common myths about listening by remembering specific instances when
a. you heard another person's message, but did not pay attention to it.
b. you attended to a message, but forgot it almost immediately.
c. you attended to and remembered a message, but did not understand it accurately.
d. you understood a message, but did not respond sufficiently to convey your understanding to the sender.

2. Invitation to Insight
Keep a three-day journal of your listening behaviour, noting the time you spend listening in various situations. In addition, analyze your reasons for listening. Which goal(s) were you trying to achieve?
a. To understand and retain information.
b. To build and maintain relationships.
c. To help.
d. To evaluate.

3. Critical Thinking Probe
Communication problems can arise from factors that are not easily observed. Based on your experience, decide which of the following steps in the listening process cause the greatest difficulties:
a. hearing,
b. attending,
c. understanding,

d.   remembering, or

e.   responding.

Discuss your findings with your friends, and develop a list of remedies that can help minimize listening problems in the areas you identified.

4. Skill Builder

Explore the benefits of silent listening by using a "talking stick." Richard Hyde (1993) developed this exercise from the Native American tradition of "council." Gather a group of people in a circle, and designate a particular item as the talking stick. Participants will then pass the stick around the circle. Participants may speak

a.   only when holding the stick,

b.   for as long as they hold the stick, and

c.   without interruption from anyone else in the circle.

When a member is finished speaking, the stick passes to the left and the speaker surrendering the stick must wait until it has made its way around the circle and back to him before speaking again.

After each member of the group has had the chance to speak, discuss how this experience differs from more common approaches to listening. Decide how the desirable parts of this method could be introduced in everyday conversations.

5. Ethical Challenge

What responsibility do communicators have to listen as carefully and thoughtfully as possible to other speakers? Are there ever cases where certain types of non-listening (e.g., pseudo-listening, stage hogging, and defensive listening—see page 156) are justified? How would you feel if you knew that others were not listening to you?

6. Role Play

Choose a partner.

a.   One person will provide a factual description of something they know how to do and the other person doesn't (e.g., cook a particular dish, fix something, perform a function on a particular brand of cellphone, etc.). The other person will listen and use paraphrasing to clarify and ensure he understands. Now, reverse roles.

b.   Next, one person will describe a personal situation (ensure you are comfortable disclosing the information) that involves thoughts and emotions. The other person will listen and paraphrase to ensure she understands. Now, reverse roles.

c.   Discuss the strengths and challenges of paraphrasing in both situations from the perspective of the listener and the speaker.

DISCUSSION QUESTIONS

1.   Discuss the benefits of good listening skills.

2.   Describe instances in your own life when you have used the four reasons for listening.

3.   Why is listening not an easy communication task? Describe the four barriers to listening.

4.   Give an example from your own experience of each of the seven types of non-listening.

5.   Explain how things can go wrong in each of the five components of listening.

6.   Describe paraphrasing and its benefits.

7.   When are advising and evaluating appropriate listening responses? When should they be avoided?

JOURNAL IDEAS

1. Keep track of the time you engage in any of the seven types of non-listening (e.g., pseudo-listening, stage hogging, selective listening, filling in the gaps, insulated listening, defensive listening, and ambushing). Note the day, time of day, topic of conversation, location, and people involved. After collecting examples over the course of a week, look at your examples and identify any patterns. Are there people, times of day, topics, or locations that recur in your entries? Analyze your entries and describe what obstacles to listening you encounter regularly and what, if anything, you might do to listen more effectively.

2. Often people don't want to paraphrase or empathize with people with whom they are arguing, because they mistake understanding another person's point of view for agreeing with it. Think about a recent time when you disagreed with someone and try to paraphrase the content of their message as well as the personal elements. Can you understand their point of view even when not agreeing with it? Can you imagine the emotions they might have experienced while talking to you? Would actually using this paraphrasing strategy during a disagreement with that person be helpful? Why or why not?

6

Language

Chapter Outline

Marina99/Shutterstock

Key Terms

abstraction ladder
ambiguous language
"but" statement
convergence
divergence
emotive language
euphemism
factual statement
high-context culture
"I" language
inferential statement
"it" statement
linguistic relativism

low-context culture
opinion statement
phonological rules
powerless speech
    mannerisms
pragmatic rules
relative language
semantic rules
static evaluation
syntactic rules
"we" language
"you" language

Learning Objectives

YOU SHOULD UNDERSTAND:

- the symbolic nature of language;
- that meanings are in people, not words;
- the types of rules that govern the use of language;
- how language affects worldview;
- the influence of language on identity, credibility and status, affiliation, attraction, interest, power, and attitudes about sexism and racism;
- the factors that influence precision and vagueness in language;
- the language patterns that reveal a speaker's level of responsibility for his or her statements;
- three forms of disruptive language;
- the relationship between culture and verbal styles, and the influence of language on perceptions; and
- the relationship between language use, biological sex, gender roles, and non-sex related factors.

YOU SHOULD BE ABLE TO:

- identify cases in which you have attributed meanings to words instead of people;
- analyze a real or potential misunderstanding in terms of semantic or pragmatic rules;
- describe how the principles presented in the section of this chapter titled "The Influence of Language" operate in your life;
- construct a message at the optimal level of specificity or vagueness for a given situation;
- construct statements that acknowledge your responsibility for the content of messages;
- rephrase disruptive statements in less inflammatory terms;
- explain how culture affects verbal style; and
- identify similarities and differences between male and female language.

"I don't know what you mean by 'glory,'" Alice said.

Humpty Dumpty smiled contemptuously. "Of course you do not—till I tell you. I meant 'there's a nice knock-down argument for you!'"

"But 'glory' does not mean 'a nice knock-down argument,'" Alice objected.

"When I use a word," Humpty Dumpty said, in a rather scornful tone, "it means just what I choose it to mean—neither more nor less."

"The question is," said Alice, "whether you can make words mean so many different things."

"The question is," said Humpty Dumpty, "which is to be master—that's all."

—Lewis Carroll, *Through the Looking Glass*

Like Alice, at one time or another everyone has felt trapped in a linguistic wonderland. Words shift meanings until we don't know what other people or even we ourselves are saying. Although language is an imperfect vehicle with which to convey ideas, it is also a marvellous tool. On an everyday level, it allows us to carry on the normal activities that make civilized life possible. Language is a foundation for our personal relationships, and it is a tool for understanding and expressing who we are. To appreciate the tremendous importance of language, imagine how impossible life would be without it. We could survive without eyesight or hearing, and life would still be possible without a limb. But without the ability to use language, we would hardly be human—at least not in the usual sense of the word.

In this chapter, we will examine the relationship between words and ideas. We will describe some important characteristics of language and show how these characteristics affect our day-to-day communication. We will outline several types of troublesome language and show how to replace them with more effective kinds of speech. Finally, we will look at the power language has both to shape and to express our attitudes toward others.

The Nature of Language

We begin our survey by looking at some features that characterize all languages. These features explain both why language is such a useful tool and why it can be so troublesome.

Language Is Symbolic

Words are arbitrary symbols that have no meaning in themselves. For example, the word *five* is a kind of code that represents the number of fingers on your hand only because we agree that it does. As Bateson and Jackson (1964, p. 271) point out, "There is nothing particularly five-like in the number 'five.'" To a speaker of French, the symbol *cinq* conveys the same meaning; to a computer, the same value is expressed by the electronically coded symbol *00110101*.

Even sign language, as "spoken" by most deaf people, is symbolic in nature and not the pantomime it may seem to be. Because this form of communication is symbolic and not literal, there are hundreds of different sign languages used around the world; they have evolved independently whenever significant numbers of deaf people have come together (Sacks, 1989). These distinct languages include American Sign Language, British Sign Language, French Sign Language, Danish Sign Language, Chinese Sign Language, and Australian Aboriginal and Mayan Sign Languages.

Language Is Governed by Rules

The only reason symbol-laden languages work at all is that people agree on how to use them. The linguistic agreements that make communication possible can be codified in rules. Languages contain several types of rules. **Phonological rules** govern how sounds are combined to form words. For instance, the words *champagne*, *double*, and *occasion* have the same meanings in French and English, but are pronounced differently because the languages have different phonological rules.

Syntactic rules govern the way symbols can be arranged. Notice that the following

Focus on TECHNOLOGY

TEXT MESSAGING AND SYNTAX

Since the 1960s, with the increased access to film and television, there has been considerable speculation about the influence of media on language. This interest has only increased in recent years with the exponential changes in media in our lives (Grace et al., 2014; Tagliamonte, 2014). One specific area of concern is that texting and instant messaging negatively influence people's (particularly teens') ability to use conventional grammar. The assumption is that, when text messaging, people's use of abbreviation (e.g., *tmw* for "tomorrow," *u* for "your"); initialization (e.g., *lol* for "laugh out loud"; *ttyl* for "talk to you later"); and rebus (a word game that combines numbers, letters, and pictures to create words—e.g., *GR8* for "great"); as well as other creative adaptations of conventional language, will erode their ability to use normative (conventional or standard) grammar when it is required (e.g., in essays, assignments, and formal letters).

Intrigued by the phenomenon of texting, University of Toronto linguistics researcher Sali Tagliamonte and her undergraduate research partner Derek Denis (2008) analyzed a month's worth of unmonitored instant-messaging conversations of 72 people aged 15 to 20 years old. They also examined a quantity of speech from the same group of young people. The researchers found that, when compared to their oral speech, the subjects' text messages were far more formal in their use of syntactic rules. The messages were not as formal as an essay would be, but the grammar used was that of formal language. They did mix more formal grammar with other types of language, however, the use of short forms such as *lol* made up only a very small proportion of their messages. Tagliamonte and Denis describe the language of text messaging as a unique new hybrid that creatively combines a variety of language features such as speech, written language, formal and informal grammar, and diction. While teachers informally report that some of the abbreviations and initializations characteristic of text messages are showing up in assignments and essays, Tagliamonte responds by saying that school is for teaching students what kind of language is appropriate in particular contexts (Daubs, 2008). The subjects in their study demonstrated very clearly that their grammatical skills were intact.

"Yes, a winky face is correct... But in ancient times, the semicolon was actually used to separate archaic written devices known as 'complete sentences.'"

Loren Fishman/Cartoonstock.com.

statements contain the same words, but the shift in syntax creates quite different meanings:

"Whisky makes you sick when you're well."

"Whisky, when you're sick, makes you well."

Although most of us are not able to describe the syntactic rules that govern our language, it's easy to recognize their existence by noticing how odd a statement that violates them appears. Sometimes, however, apparently ungrammatical speech is simply following a different set of syntactic rules. For example, English spoken in Newfoundland and Labrador has many non-standard features in its grammar, pronunciation, and vocabulary. If you apply the rules of Standard English syntax to the statement, "Throw Mum down the stairs her keys," you would be confused about who or what is going down the stairs. But in parts of Newfoundland and Labrador, this construction clearly means it's Mum's keys, not Mum, that are being thrown down the stairs. There are several well-established English subsystems in the province, each with its own pronunciations and grammar.

Our use of English is also governed by **semantic rules**. Whereas syntax deals with structure, semantics governs the meaning of statements. Semantic rules are what make it possible for us to agree that *bikes* are for riding and *books* are for reading, and they help us know whom we will encounter when we use rooms marked MEN and WOMEN. Without semantic rules, communication would be impossible, because each of us would use symbols in unique ways, unintelligible to others.

Although semantic rules help us understand the meaning of individual words, they often do not explain how language operates in everyday life. Consider the statement, "Let's get together tomorrow." The semantic meaning of the words in this sentence is clear enough, and yet, the statement could be taken in several ways. It could be a request ("I hope we can get together"), a polite command ("I want to see you"), or an empty cliché ("I don't really mean it"). We learn to distinguish the accurate meanings of such speech through **pragmatic rules** that tell us what uses and interpretations of a message are reasonable in a given situation. When these rules are understood by all players in the language game, smooth communication is possible. For example, one rule specifies that the relationship between communicators plays a large role in determining the meaning of a statement. Our example, "I want to see you," is likely to mean one thing when uttered by your boss and another thing entirely when it comes from your sweetheart. Likewise, the setting in which the statement is made plays a role. Saying "I want to see you" will probably have a different meaning at the office than at a cocktail party. Of course, the non-verbal behaviour that accompanies a statement also helps us interpret its meaning.

The *coordinated management of meaning* (CMM) theory describes some types of pragmatic rules that operate in everyday conversations. It suggests that we use rules at several levels to create our own messages and interpret other people's statements (Cronen and Chetro-Szivos, 2001; Cronen et al., 1988). Table 6.1 uses a CMM framework to illustrate how two people might be confused because they are using different rules at several levels. In situations like this, it's important to make sure that the other person's use of language matches yours before jumping to conclusions about the meaning of his or her statements. The skill of perception checking described in Chapter 3 can be useful at times like this.

Language Is Subjective

If the rules of language were more precise and if everyone followed them, we would suffer from fewer misunderstandings. You have an hour-long argument about *feminism* with a friend, only to discover that you were using the term in different ways and that you really were in basic agreement. You tease a friend in what you mean to be a playful manner, but he takes you seriously and is offended.

These problems occur because people attach different meanings to the same message. Ogden and Richards (1923) illustrated this point graphically in their well-known

- **Phonological rules:** govern how sounds are combined to form words.
- **Syntactic rules:** govern the way symbols can be arranged.
- **Semantic rules:** govern the meaning of statements.
- **Pragmatic rules:** tell us what interpretations of a message are reasonable in a given situation.

Pragmatic

They don't work hard, do they?

~~Yes,~~ L of this question

The answer B based on truth.

Yes, they do means they work hard.

No, they don't means they don't work hard.

However, in China, ~~We usually answered question to~~ ~~too just based on the question~~

People usually answer according to the question.

Yes means they don't work hard.

No means they work hard.

A
B
C
D

B.

Table 6.1 ● Pragmatic Rules Govern the Use and Meaning of a Statement 语用规则

Notice how the same message ("You look very pretty today") takes on a different meaning depending on which rules are used to formulate and interpret it.

	Boss	Employee
Content 内容 Actual words	"You look very pretty today."	
Speech Act 言语行为 The intent of a statement	Compliment an employee	Unknown
Relational Contract 关系契约 The perceived relationship between communicators	Boss who treats employees like family members	Subordinate employee, dependent on boss's approval for advancement
Episode 插曲 Situation in which the interaction occurs	Casual conversation	Possible come-on by boss?
Life Script 生活脚本	Friendly guy	Woman determined to succeed on own merits
Cultural Archetype 文化原型 Cultural norms that shape member's perceptions and actions	Middle-class Canadian	Working-class Canadian

SOURCE: Adapted from W.B. Pearce and V. Cronen (1980), *Communication, action, and meaning*. New York: Praeger.

triangle of meaning (see Figure 6.1). This model shows that there is only an indirect relationship—indicated by a broken line—between a word and the thing or idea it represents. For example, friends may use profanity when texting each other, and what looks like an offensive statement to an outsider may be understood as innocuous, or even friendly, by the people involved.

The Ogden and Richards model is oversimplified in that not all words refer to physical "things" or referents. For instance, some referents are abstract ideas (such as *love*), while others (like *angry* or *exciting*) are not even nouns. Despite these shortcomings, the triangle of meaning is useful since it clearly demonstrates that meanings are in people, not words. Hence, an important task facing communicators is to establish a common understanding of the words they use to exchange messages. In this sense, communication—at least the effective kind—requires us to negotiate the meaning

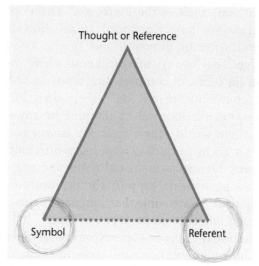

Figure 6.1 ● Ogden and Richards' Triangle of Meaning

SOURCE: Adapted from Charles K. Ogden and I.A. Richards (1946), *The Meaning of meaning: A study of the influence of language upon thought and of the science of symbolism*, 8th edn. New York: Harcourt, Brace and World, 11.

of our language (Duck, 1994). This brings us back to a familiar theme: meaning is both *in* and *among* people.

Language Is Linked to Worldview

Does the language you speak shape the way you see and think about the world? For almost 150 years, theorists have explored issues surrounding the extent to which language influences our thoughts and perceptions of the world. The idea that people who speak different languages organize and view their worlds differently has been supported by a variety of studies. For instance Lera Boroditsky (2009; Boroditsky and Gaby, 2010) describes the Pormpuraawans, a group of Aboriginal people who live in Australia, who don't have spatial terms like *right*, *left*, *back*, and *forward* in their language. Instead they use compass directions to communicate about location (*east*, *west*, *north*, and *south*). So if you asked a Pormpuraawan where she put the keys she wouldn't say, "On the top left shelf of the bookcase" as we might. Instead she would say, "On the northeast shelf of the bookcase." The Pormpuraawans have developed an unbelievably good sense of direction and spatial knowledge. They always need to know where they are (in terms of compass directions) in order to communicate not only their own location, but the location of anything or anyone in their world—they have no language to allow them to think about space differently. These differences in spatial terms and spatial thinking provide support for the notion of **linguistic relativism**—that language exerts a strong influence on perceptions (Allen, 2010). Additional evidence comes from observations of bilingual speakers who seem to think differently when they change languages (Giles and Franklyn-Stokes, 1989). In one study, French-Americans were asked to interpret a series of pictures. When they spoke in French, their descriptions were far more romantic and emotional than when they used English to describe the same kinds of images. Likewise, when students in Hong Kong were asked to

complete a values test, they expressed more traditional Chinese values when they answered in Cantonese than when they spoke in English. In Israel, both Arab and Jewish students saw bigger distinctions between their group and "outsiders" when using their native language than when they spoke in English, which, being a foreign language, was more neutral. Examples like these show the power of language to shape cultural identity—sometimes for better and sometimes for worse.

Some languages contain terms that have no English equivalents (Rheingold, 1988). For example, consider a few words in other languages that have no simple translation in English:

- *unga* (Inuit): dependent love, especially the love of a baby for its mother; wanting to be taken care of; it may also refer to the feeling of spouses or friends when they are apart and miss each other.
- *nemawashi* (Japanese): the process of informally feeling out all the people involved with an issue before making a decision.
- *lagniappe* (French/Creole): an extra gift given in a transaction that wasn't expected by the terms of a contract.
- *lao* (Mandarin): respectful term used for older people, showing their importance in the family and in society.
- *dharma* (Sanskrit): each person's unique, ideal path in life and the knowledge of how to find it.

Once words like these exist and become a part of everyday life, the ideas that they represent are easier to recognize. But even without such terms, each of the concepts above is still

CHECK IT!

Describe four features of language and how each contributes to both the usefulness of language and the potential for misunderstandings.

possible to imagine. Thus, speakers of a language that includes the notion of *lao* would probably treat its older members respectfully, and those who are familiar with *lagniappe* might be more generous. However, these words don't have to be in a language for a communicator to follow these principles. As scholar Harry Hoijer put it, "differences between languages are not so much in what *can* be said, but in what it is *relatively easy* to say" (Steinfatt, 1989, p. 63). While language may shape thoughts and behaviour, it doesn't dominate them absolutely.

The Influence of Language

Besides simply describing the world, language can have a strong effect on our perceptions and how we regard one another. In the following pages, we will examine some of the many ways language can affect our lives.

Naming and Identity

"What's in a name?" Juliet asked rhetorically. If Romeo had been a social scientist, he would have answered, "A great deal." Research has demonstrated that names are more than just a simple means of identification, that, in fact, they shape the way others think of us, the way we view ourselves, and the way we act (Marcus, 1976).

There is research to suggest that names are associated with a variety of life outcomes (Aura and Hess, 2004; Christenfeld and Larsen, 2008). Unusual names and those with unique spellings have been associated with a number of negative outcomes, such as involvement in juvenile delinquency (Kalist and Lee, 2009) and greater difficulty in obtaining job interviews (Bertrand and Mullainathan, 2004).

Linguistic relativism: the idea that language exerts a strong influence on perceptions and thought.

However, mothers' level of education affects naming patterns, and mothers with lower levels of education are more likely to choose unpopular names (as measured by the frequency of their use in the population). These same mothers are more likely to raise their children in disadvantaged home environments and have lower socio-economic status (Kalist and Lee, 2009). While names play a role in shaping our identities and influence the way others see us, there are significantly more substantial factors that affect our chances in life.

Names are one way parents can steep their child in a family's cultural heritage. In Canada, as in many countries around the world, cultural heritage is increasingly complex. Canadian census data (Statistics Canada, 2011c) indicate that the number of mixed-race marriages continues to increase, leading to more mixed-race children. Rosalind Edwards and Chamion Caballero (2008) explored the process of choosing baby names among mixed-race couples in the United Kingdom. Edwards and Caballero found that, in addition to choosing names they liked, the majority of the couples interviewed also wanted names that symbolized the child's heritages. Names our parents choose for us are one of the first ways they transfer cultural and social influences from one generation to the next. Many women in Western society, aware of the power of names to influence identity, view the choice of name to identify themselves with after they marry as an important decision. A woman may choose to take her husband's last name, hyphenate her own name and her husband's, or keep her birth name. Studies done in the Netherlands (Noordewier et al., 2010) and in the United States (Hoffnung, 2006) have found that women who change their names and those who keep their names are different in terms of demographic characteristics and are judged according to stereotypes about what is feminine and what is feminist. In the Netherlands, Marret Noordewier and her colleagues (2010) found that women who take their husband's names were judged to fit the feminine stereotype. Specifically they were judged to be more caring, dependent, and emotional than women who kept their names. In contrast, women who kept their birth names were judged to be closer to the feminist stereotype—more independent, ambitious, intelligent, and competent. In addition, these investigators found that when people reviewed potential applicants for a job, they rated the women who kept their birth names as more likely to be offered a job and estimated higher starting salaries for these women, compared to women who took their husband's last names. In the United States, Michele Hoffnung (2006) found that women who choose to keep their birth names were older on average at the time of marriage and had a higher level of education, higher career commitment, and more feminist attitudes compared to women who chose the traditional practice of taking their husbands' names. Recall, however, that while generalizations are sometimes helpful guides in human perception, they can cause communication problems when they are used as the basis for interacting with individual human beings. Some research suggests that what we can infer about women who either keep or change their

names is not as profound as it might seem. For example, one study (Stafford and Kline, 1996) analyzed 110 well-educated married women, both name-changers and name-keepers. Contrary to what linguistic reformers may have expected, there were no significant differences between the two groups in terms of self-esteem, relationship dependency, autonomy, or feelings about the balance of control in their marriages.

Credibility and Status

The words we use and the way we pronounce them have a strong influence on whether others accept or reject our ideas. A significant amount of research shows that speaking with a foreign accent is associated with a variety of negative stereotypes (Derwing and Munro, 2009b). These include being less competent, less intelligent, less loyal, and less attractive than native English speakers (Gluszek and Dovidio, 2010).

A study of adult Canadians studying English as a second language found that the majority of the non-native English speakers interviewed believed that people would respect them more if they pronounced English well (Derwing, 2003). Although many of the non-native speakers interviewed in his study considered native English speakers to be patient and understanding, and the majority said they did not believe they had been discriminated against because of their accent, they believed that their accents had a negative effect on some of their social interactions with native English-speaking Canadians. Similarly, Kilbride and Ali (2010) found that immigrant women in their study wanted to learn to speak English from native Canadian speakers because they wanted to speak it

© ratluk/iStockphoto

In language, vocabulary and accent come together to shape listener's perspectives. The next time you're watching TV, think about the vocabulary and accent used by the actors to portray their characters. How do these influence your perception and understanding of the characters?

with a Canadian accent. In a workplace-based study, Tracey Derwing and Murray Munro (2009a) found that native Canadian English speakers (mostly engineers) did not show preferences for particular accents, but they did indicate that they would prefer to continue to interact with speakers whose pronunciation was easier to understand. In this study comprehensibility was the most important factor, more important than fluency, grammar, voice quality, and personality in workers' assessments of how successful an individual would be in workplace interactions.

Vocabulary is just as important as accent in shaping perceptions. Scholarly speaking is a good example of this phenomenon. One illustration comes from the Dr Fox research (Naftulin et al., 1973; Peer and Babad, 2014; Ware and Williams, 1980). This research involved Dr Myron L. Fox, who delivered a talk followed by a half-hour discussion on "mathematical game theory as applied to physical education." The original audience included psychiatrists, psychologists, social workers, and educators (Naftulin et al., 1973) and a more recent audience (who saw a film of the original Dr Fox lecture) included both undergraduate and graduate students (Peer and Babad, 2014). Questionnaires, collected after the sessions back in the 1970s and the more recent sessions, revealed that these educated listeners found the lecture thought provoking. Their perceptions of Dr Fox were very positive.

The remarkable thing was that Fox was a complete fraud! He was a professional actor who had been coached by researchers to deliver a lecture of double-talk—a patchwork of information from a *Scientific American* article mixed with jokes, non sequiturs, contradictory statements, and meaningless references to unrelated topics. When wrapped in a linguistic package of high-level professional jargon, and delivered by an engaging, humorous, and well-spoken person the meaningless gobbledygook was judged favourably. In other words, Fox's credibility came more from his style of speaking than from the ideas he expressed.

REFLECTION

WORD CHOICE AND ATTITUDE

I've taken two communication classes this year and they were completely different. I just figured out a big reason why. In one class, my professor used language that made it sound as if communication had nothing to do with us. He would always refer to "people" or "communicators" as if they were from another planet, or at least another species. One day, he announced that his lecture topic would be "How men and women speak when *they* are together." If men and women are *they*, who are *we*?

My other professor talked about how *we* communicate. "Does watching violence on television make us more aggressive?" she would ask. "Do movies teach us how to be husbands or wives or parents?" The two different ways of using language seemed trivial at first, but now I can see that they said a lot about how each professor approached the course.

Affiliation, Attraction, and Interest

Accent and vocabulary are not the only ways in which language reflects the status of relationships. Speech also can be a way of building and demonstrating solidarity with others. An impressive body of research has shown that communicators who want to show affiliation with one another adapt their speech in a variety of ways, including their choice of vocabulary, rate of talking, number and placement of pauses, and level of politeness (Aune and Kikuchi, 1993; Giles, Coupland, and Wiemann, 1992; Giles, Henwood et al., 1992; Giles, Mulac et al., 1992). On an individual level, close friends and lovers often develop a set of special terms that serve as a way of signifying their relationship (Bell and Healey, 1992; Bell et al., 1987). Using the same vocabulary serves to set these people apart from others, reminding themselves and the rest of the world of their relationship. The same process works among members of larger groups, ranging from online communities to street gangs and military units. Communication researchers call the process of adapting one's speech style to that of others with whom the communicator wants to identify **convergence**.

When two or more people feel equally positive about one another, their linguistic convergence will be mutual. But when communicators want or need approval, they often adapt their speech to accommodate the other person's style, trying to say the "right thing" or speak in a way that will help them fit in. We see this process when immigrants who want to gain the reward of material success in a new culture strive to master the host language. Likewise, employees who seek advancement tend to speak more like their superiors, supervisors adopt the speech style of managers, and managers converge toward their bosses.

The principle of speech accommodation works in reverse, too. Communicators who want to set themselves apart from others adopt the strategy of **divergence**, speaking in a way that emphasizes their differences. For example, members of an ethnic group, even though fluent in the dominant language, might use their own dialect as a way of showing solidarity with one another—a sort of "we're proud of our heritage" strategy. Divergence also occurs in other settings. For example, a physician or lawyer who wants to establish credibility with her or his client might speak formally and use professional jargon to create a sense of distance. The implicit message

here is, "I'm different from you (and more knowledgeable)."

Power

Communication researchers have observed a number of language patterns that add to or detract from a speaker's power to influence others. Notice the difference between these two statements:

> "Excuse me, sir. I hate to say this, but I . . . uh . . . I guess I won't be able to turn in the assignment on time. I had a personal emergency and . . . well . . . it was just impossible to finish it by today. I'll have it in your mailbox on Monday, okay?"

> "I won't be able to turn in the assignment on time. I had a personal emergency and it was impossible to finish it by today. I'll have it in your mailbox on Monday."

Whether or not the instructor finds the excuse acceptable, it's clear that the second statement sounds more confident, whereas the tone of the first is apologetic and uncertain. Table 6.2 lists several **powerless speech mannerisms** illustrated in the first statement you just read. A number of studies have shown that speakers whose talk is free of these mannerisms are rated as more competent, dynamic, and attractive than speakers who sound powerless (Ng and Bradac, 1993; Reid and Ng, 1999). The effects of powerful versus powerless speech styles are also apparent in employment interview outcomes: a powerful speech style results in more positive attributions of competence and employability than a powerless one (Parton et al., 2002). Even a single type of powerless speech mannerism appears to make a person appear less authoritative or socially attractive (Hosman, 1989).

However, powerful speech that gets the desired results in mainstream North American and European culture does not succeed everywhere with everyone (Samovar et al., 2012). In Japan, saving face for others is an important

---

TAKE TWO

- **Convergence:** the process of adapting one's speech style to that of others with whom the communicator wants to identify.
- **Divergence:** the process of adapting one's speech in ways that emphasize differences between the speaker and others from whom the speaker wants to distance him or herself.

Table 6.2 ● Examples of Less Powerful Language

Type of Usage	Example
Hedges 模糊朦胧限制语	"I'm kinda disappointed . . ." "I think we should . . ." "I guess I'd like to . . ."
Hesitatitons 犹豫	"Uh, can I have a minute of your time?" "Well, we could try this idea . . ." "I wish you would . . . er . . . try to be on time."
Intensifiers 加强词	"So that's how I feel." "I'm not very hungry."
Polite forms 称谓礼貌式	"Excuse me, sir . . ."
Tag questions 附加问句	"It's about time we got started, isn't it?" "Don't you think we should give it another try?"
Disclaimers 放弃	"I probably shouldn't say this, but . . ."

SOURCE: Adapted from R.B. Adler and J. Elmhorst (2010), *Communicating at work: Principles and practices for business and the professions*, 10th edn. New York: McGraw-Hill, 29.

goal, so communicators there tend to speak in ambiguous terms and use hedge words and qualifiers. In most Japanese sentences, the verb comes at the end of the sentence, so the action part of the statement can be postponed. Traditional Mexican culture, with its strong emphasis on co-operation, also uses hedging to smooth over interpersonal relationships. By not taking a firm stand with their speech mannerisms, Mexicans believe they will not make others feel ill at ease. Canadian First Nations and Koreans are two other cultural groups that prefer "indirect" (e.g., using *perhaps* or *could be*) over "direct" speech.

Even in North American culture, simply counting the number of powerful or powerless statements will not always reveal who has the most control in a relationship. Social rules often mask the real distribution of power. A boss who wants to be pleasant might say to a secretary, "Would you mind retyping this letter?" In truth, both boss and secretary know this is an order and not a request, but the questioning form makes the medicine less bitter. Sociolinguist Deborah Tannen (1994, p. 101) describes how politeness can be a face-saving way of delivering an order:

I hear myself giving instructions to my assistants without actually issuing orders: "Maybe it would be a good idea to . . ." "It would be great if you could . . ." all the while knowing that I expect them to do what I've asked right away. . . . This rarely creates problems, though, because the people who work for me know that there is only one reason I mention tasks—because I want them done. I *like* giving instructions in this way; it appeals to my sense of what it means to be a good person . . . taking others' feelings into account.

As this quotation suggests, high-status speakers—especially higher-status women, according to Tannen—often realize that politeness is an effective way to get their needs met while protecting the face of the less powerful person. Similarly, Denise Lewin Loyd and her colleagues (2010) caution that when people are unaware of your expertise in a particular area, your best approach is to communicate in less powerful ways. However, if your status as an expert is known to the group, then using more powerful language will achieve greater influence and increase your chances of being liked. The importance of achieving

CHECK IT!

Describe six less powerful speech mannerisms and provide an example of each.

both content and relational goals helps explain why a mixture of powerful and polite speech is usually most effective (Geddes, 1992). Of course, if the other person misinterprets politeness for weakness, it may be necessary to shift to a more powerful speaking style. Conversely, in some situations powerful speech can be perceived as insensitive and overbearing and a less powerful approach is what is needed. The key is to be able to adapt your style to your conversational partner (Loyd et al., 2010).

Sexism, Sexual Prejudice, and Racism

Since language and thinking are very much interrelated, the language we use when referring to others can contribute to stereotypic characterizations and prejudice. We will briefly review how language influences our thinking about women and men; lesbian, gay, bisexual, transgendered, and queer (LGBTQ) people; and members of different races.

Sexist language "includes words, phrases, and expressions that unnecessarily differentiate between females and males or exclude, trivialize, or diminish" either sex (Parks and Robertson, 2000, p. 415). This type of speech can affect the self-concepts of women and men, often in subtle ways. Suzanne Romaine (1999) offers several examples of how linguistic terms can stereotype men and women. To say that a woman *mothered* her children focuses on her nurturing behaviour, but to say that a man *fathered* a child talks only about his biological role. We are familiar with terms like *working mother*, but there is no term *working father* because we assume (perhaps inaccurately) that men are the breadwinners in families.

Beyond just stereotyping women, sexist language can stigmatize them. For example, the term *unmarried mother* is common, but we do not talk about *unmarried fathers* because for many people, there is no stigma attached to this status for men. And whereas there are over 200 English words for promiscuous women, there are only 20 for men (Stanley, 1977).

There are at least two ways to eliminate sexist language (Rakow, 1992). The first circumvents the problem altogether by eliminating sex-specific terms or substituting neutral terms. For example, using plural pronouns (i.e., they, theirs, them) in sentence constructions eliminates the necessity to use them simultaneously (i.e., *he and she, his and hers, him and her*, etc.) in writing. When no sex reference is appropriate, you can substitute neutral terms. For example: *mankind* may be replaced with *humankind, humanity, human beings, human race*, and *people*; *man-made* may be replaced with *artificial, manufactured*, and *synthetic*; *manpower* may be replaced with *labour, workers*, and *workforce*; and *manhood* may be replaced with *adulthood*. In the same way, *mailmen* are *letter carriers* and *postal workers*; *firemen* are *firefighters*; *chairmen* are *presiding officers, leaders*, and *chairs*; *foremen* are *supervisors*; *policemen* and *policewomen* are *police officers*; and *stewardesses* and *stewards* are *flight attendants*. Of course, some terms refer to things that could not possibly have a sex; so, for example, a *manhole cover* could be called a *sewer lid*. Research suggests that while gender-neutral language helps to reduce our stereotypical perceptions of previously male dominated occupations (e.g., *entrepreneur* instead of *businessman, news anchor* instead *anchorman*) it doesn't completely eliminate the male bias we have (Lassonde and O'Brien, 2013). Obviously, increased exposure to women in stereotypically male occupations (as well as men in stereotypical female occupations) helps as does using language that explicitly identifies sex.

Clearly marking sex—to heighten awareness of whether the reference is to a female or a male—is the second method for eliminating sexism. For example, rather than substitute *chairperson* for *chairman*, use the terms *chairman* and *chairwoman* to specify whether the person is a man or a woman. (Note also that there is nothing sacred about putting *he* before *she*; in fact, adding *she*, *her*, and *hers* after *he*, *him*, and *his*, without changing the order, continues to imply that males are the more important sex and should come first.)

Eliminating language that discriminates against lesbian, gay, bisexual, transgendered, and queer (LGBTQ) people is an equally important and challenging task. In their study of men's use of anti-gay insults at the University of Calgary, Tyler Brown and Kevin Alderson (2010) found that men used an abundance of homosexual insults to joke with and pressure their peers, and that only about one-quarter of the men surveyed said they would never use the term *fag* or *faggot* to insult another person. The men surveyed also revealed that they rarely if ever believed that the person they were insulting was in fact gay. Brown and Alderson speculate that using these sexually prejudiced insults may help to create a feeling of inclusion among males and may serve as an indicator of greater masculinity to heterosexual women. Regardless of why people use sexually prejudiced insults, they are offensive and contribute to the stigma and stress LGBTQ people experience (Burn et al., 2005).

When confronted with sexually prejudiced language, people often don't feel they know what to do or say. In a study of recently graduated teachers who were faced with sexually prejudiced language in the classroom, researchers found that by their responses, teachers could be categorized into four main groups: avoiders, hesitators, confronters, and interrogators (Zack et al., 2010). The majority of teachers interviewed were hesitators, but a few confident interrogators used the situation to ask questions and explore students' understanding of the words they chose and the larger consequences of their choices. Brian Payne (2010), a high school art teacher, found that students often misused the terms *gay* and *retarded* when discussing art, and he made a point of addressing the hurtful nature of these terms and how using these words to

REFLECTION

GIRLS OR WOMEN?

I'm a member of the women's hockey team at my university—but that's not how most people on campus refer to us. They regularly call us the *girls'* hockey team, even though most of us haven't been "girls" (at least legally) for years. It wouldn't bother me so much except they never refer to the men's hockey team as the *boys'* team. It seems to me like a case of sexist language that refuses to go away.

Sexist language usually defines the world as made up of superior men and inferior women; sexually prejudiced language usually implies that heterosexuality is superior to any other sexual orientation; and racist language reflects a worldview that classifies members of one racial group as superior and others as inferior. How often do you hear these biases in the language of people around you? How often do you use them yourself?

© iStockPhoto/Alina Solovyova-Vincent.

describe things they found gauche, awkward, or uncomfortable made them seem unintelligent. He found that by talking openly about students' choice of words, he not only helped to raise their consciousness, but also improved their vocabularies.

Whereas sexist language usually defines the world as made up of superior men and inferior women, and sexually prejudiced language usually implies that heterosexuality is superior to any other sexual orientation, racist language reflects a worldview that classifies members of one racial group as superior and others as inferior (Asante, 2002). Not all language that might have racist overtones is deliberate. For example, the connotations of many words favour whites over people of colour (Person-Lynn, 1994; Pfeifer, 2009). Words and images associated with *white* are usually positive, whether it's the cowboy hero in white clothing or connotations of *white* as "pure," "clean," "honourable," "innocent," "bright," and "shiny." The words and images associated with "black" are often negative, a concept that reaches from the black hat of the villain cowboy and the black cat that causes bad luck to words and phrases like *black market*, *blackball*, and *blacklist*.

An obvious step toward eliminating racist language is to make sure your communication is free of offensive labels and slurs. Some troublesome language will be easy to identify, while other problematic speech will be more subtle. For instance, you may be unaware of using racial and ethnic modifiers when describing others, such as *black professor* or *Pakistani merchant* (or modifiers identifying sex or sexual orientation, such as *female doctor* or *lesbian poet*). Modifiers like these usually are not necessary, and they can be subtle indicators of prejudiced language. If you would not use the phrases *white professor*, *European merchant*, *male doctor*, or *heterosexual poet*, then modifiers that identify race and sex may be indicators of attitudes and language that need to be changed.

Self-Assessment

SEXIST LANGUAGE*

Respond to each of the following statements by indicating the extent to which you agree with it:

1 = strongly disagree
2 = tend to disagree
3 = undecided
4 = tend to agree
5 = strongly agree

_____ 1. Women who think that being called a chairman is sexist are misinterpreting the word.

_____ 2. When people use the term *man and wife*, the expression is not sexist if the users do not mean it to be.

_____ 3. The elimination of sexist language is an important goal.

_____ 4. Sexist language is related to the sexist treatment of people in society.

_____ 5. When teachers talk about the history of Canada, they should change expressions such as *our forefathers* to expressions that include women.

_____ 6. The English language will never be changed because it is too deeply ingrained in the culture.

Total = _____.

Add your responses to the six statements, making sure to reverse-score (i.e., 5 = 1, 4 = 2, 3 = 3, 2 = 4, and 1 = 5) statements 1, 2, and 6. Scores can range from 6 to 30, and scores that are approximately 24 and higher reflect a negative attitude toward sexist language.

*This "Self-Assessment" box contains 6 of the 21 items on the Inventory of Attitudes toward Sexist/Nonsexist Language-General, developed by Parks and Robertson (2000).

Uses (and Abuses) of Language

By now, it's apparent that language can shape the way we perceive and understand the world. Next, we will look at some specific types of usage and examine both their value and the problems they can cause.

Precision and Vagueness 含米胡不清

Most people assume that the goal of language is to make our ideas clear to one another. Sometimes, however, we want to be less than perfectly clear. In the following pages, we will point out some cases where vagueness serves useful purposes as well as cases where perfect understanding is the goal.

Equivocal ⊂

Ambiguous Language 模棱兩可的

Ambiguous language consists of words and phrases that have more than one commonly accepted definition. Some ambiguous language is amusing, as the following newspaper headlines illustrate:

Police Begin Campaign to Run Down Jaywalkers

Teacher Strikes Idle Kids

20-Year Friendship Ends at the Altar

Many misunderstandings that arise from ambiguity are trivial. We remember eating dinner at a Mexican restaurant and ordering a "tostada with beans." Instead of being served a beef tostada with beans on the side, we were surprised to see the waiter bring us a plate containing a tostada *filled* with beans. As with most such misunderstandings, hindsight showed that the phrase *tostada with beans* has two equally correct meanings.

Other misunderstandings involving ambiguous messages can be more serious. A nurse gave one of her patients a scare when she told him that he "would not be needing" his robe, books, and shaving materials any more. The patient became quiet and moody. When the nurse inquired about the odd behaviour, she discovered that the poor man had interpreted her statement to mean he was going to die soon. In fact, the nurse meant he would be going home shortly.

For another example of ambiguous language, consider the word *love*. People commonly use that term in six very different ways: *eros* (romantic love), *ludus* (game-playing love), *storge* (friendship love), *mania* (possessive, dependent love), *pragma* (logical love), and *agape* (all-giving, selfless love) (Lee, 1973; Hendrick et al., 1998). Imagine the conflicts that would occur between a couple who sincerely pledged their love to one another, each with a different kind of love in mind. We can imagine them asking one another, "If you really love me, why are you acting like this?" without realizing that each of them views the relationship differently.

It's difficult to catch and clarify every instance of ambiguous language. For this reason, the responsibility for interpreting statements accurately rests in large part with the receiver. Feedback of one sort or another—for example, paraphrasing and questioning—can help clear up misunderstandings: "You say you love me, but you want to see other people. In my book, "love" is exclusive. What about you?"

Despite its obvious problems, ambiguous language has its uses. For example, when a hospital system defined the nursing role of "care coordinator" in a strategically ambiguous way, some nurses were excited and

Sask Pork.

REFLECTION

SPILLED MILK AND AMBIGUOUS LANGUAGE

One of my favourite family stories happened when our son, Scott, was about three years old. He wanted to pour his own milk, and my husband, Jerry, was helping him. Little Scott carefully tilted the milk carton to the edge of the glass, and slowly the milk poured from the jug into the glass.

The glass began to fill. Jerry said, "That's good . . . Okay, that's good . . . That's GOOD!" as the milk began to overflow the glass and spill onto the table.

Jerry asked Scott why he didn't stop pouring the milk. It was obvious to me that by saying, "That's good," Jerry meant, "That's enough—you can stop now," but what Scott heard was that he was doing a good job of pouring. You have to be very literal with three-year-olds!

exhilarated by the challenge of crafting a new role (Miller et al., 2000). In Chapter 2, we described how using language that is open to several interpretations can help you avoid the kind of honesty and clarity that can embarrass both the speaker and listener. For example, if a friend proudly shows you a newly completed painting and asks your opinion of it, you might answer equivocally by saying, "Gee, it's really unusual. I've never seen anything like it," instead of giving a less ambiguous, but more hurtful response such as, "This may be the ugliest thing I've ever seen!"

Abstraction

High-level abstractions are convenient ways of generalizing about similarities between several objects, people, ideas, or events. Figure 6.2 shows an **abstraction ladder** that illustrates how to describe the same phenomenon at various levels of abstraction.

We use higher-level abstractions all the time. For instance, rather than saying, "Thanks for washing the dishes," "Thanks for vacuuming the rug," and "Thanks for making the bed," it's easier to say, "Thanks for cleaning up." In such everyday situations, abstractions are a useful kind of verbal shorthand.

Like ambiguity, high-level abstractions also can help communicators find face-saving ways to avoid confrontations and embarrassment by being deliberately unclear (Eisenberg, 1984; Eisenberg and Witten, 1987). If a friend apologizes for arriving late for a date, you can choose to brush off the incident instead of making it an issue by saying, "Don't worry. It wasn't the end of the world"—a true statement, but less specific than saying, "To tell you the truth, I was mad at the time, but I've cooled off now." If your boss asks your opinion of a new idea that you think is weaker than your own approach, but you don't want to disagree, you could respond with a higher-level abstraction by saying, "It might work . . ."

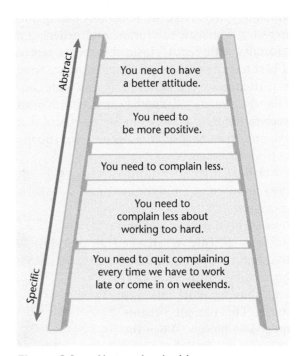

Figure 6.2 ● Abstraction Ladder

A boss gives feedback to an employee about career advancement at various levels of specificity.

Building WORK SKILLS

REDUCING ABSTRACT LANGUAGE

A significant amount of work-related communication consists of stating goals, making requests of others, talking about work-related problems, and complaining! No matter what type of career you have in mind, this will probably be true.

Think about using language at work in one of the following ways. Perhaps you need to make a request of a colleague or someone who reports to you, or you need to give them some negative feedback (criticism) about their work. Write down what you might say and then use Table 6.3, "Abstract and Behavioural Descriptions," to decide whether you have found the right balance between behavioural description and abstract description. How did you do? Could you improve your request or your criticism? How?

Although vagueness does have its uses, highly abstract language can cause several types of problems. The first is stereotyping. Imagine someone who has had one bad experience and, as a result, blames an entire group: "Marriage counsellors are worthless," "Torontonians are all rude," or "Men are no good." Overly abstract expressions like these can cause people to think in generalities, ignoring uniqueness. As we saw in Chapter 2, expecting people to act in a certain way can become a self-fulfilling prophecy. If you expect the worst of people, you have a good chance of getting it.

Besides narrowing your own options, excessively abstract language can also confuse others. Telling the hairstylist "not too short" or "more casual" might produce the look you want, or it might lead to an unpleasant surprise.

Overly abstract language can lead to more serious problems. For instance, accusations of sexual assault can arise because one person claims to have said "no" when the other person insists no such refusal was ever conveyed. In response to this sort of disagreement, specific rules of sexual conduct have become more common in workplaces and educational institutions. An example of such a code of sexual conduct is the one being developed by Colleges Ontario. The Colleges Ontario draft Sexual Assault and Sexual Violence Policy and Protocol (2015) uses low-level abstractions to minimize the chances of anyone claiming confusion about a partner's willingness or consent. Consent is defined as follows:

Consent: The voluntary agreement to engage in the sexual activity in question. It is the act of willingly agreeing to engage in specific sexual behaviour, and requires that a person is able to freely choose between two options: yes and no. This means that there must be an understandable exchange of affirmative words which indicates a willingness to participate in mutually agreed upon sexual activity. It is also imperative that everyone understands the following:

- Silence or non-communication must never be interpreted as consent and a person in a state of diminished judgment cannot consent.
- A person is incapable of giving consent if she/he is asleep, unconscious, or otherwise unable to communicate.
- A person who has been threatened or coerced (i.e., is not agreeing voluntarily) into engaging in the sexual activity is not consenting to it.
- A person who is drugged is unable to consent.
- A person is usually unable to give consent when she/he is under the influence of alcohol and/or drugs.
- A person may be unable to give consent if she/he has a mental disability.
- The fact that consent was given in the past to a sexual or dating relationship does not mean

REFLECTION

SECONDARY SKIN IRRITATION

Before radiation treatment for my stomach cancer, I was told I'd get a prescription for a salve to help heal the burns I would get. After my first treatment, I reminded the doctor about the prescription, saying, "You haven't given me the prescription for the radiation burns." She said, in a powerful act of trying to reduce the horror of what was happening to me with a simple shift in language, "We no longer call them radiation burns—they're now 'secondary skin irritations.'" She can call them anything she wants, but all I know is that the new label didn't make them hurt any less!

that consent is deemed to exist for all future sexual activity.

- A person can withdraw consent at any time during the course of a sexual encounter.
- It is the responsibility of the initiator of sexual activity to obtain clear and affirmative responses at all stages of sexual engagement.

Some critics have ridiculed rules like these as being unrealistically legalistic and inappropriate for romantic relationships. Whatever its weaknesses, the Ontario Colleges' policy illustrates how low-level abstractions can reduce the chances of a serious misunderstanding. Specific language may not be desirable or necessary in many situations, but in an era when misinterpretations can lead to accusations of physical assault, it does seem to have a useful place.

You can make your language—and your thinking —less abstract and more clear by learning to make behavioural descriptions of your problems, goals, appreciations, complaints, and requests. We use the word *behavioural* because such descriptions move down the abstraction ladder to describe the specific, observable objects and actions we're thinking about. Table 6.3 shows how behavioural

descriptions are much more clear and effective than vague, abstract statements.

Euphemism 委婉语

A **euphemism** (from a Greek word meaning "to use words of good omen") is an innocuous 无害的 term substituted for a blunt one. For example, patients with newly diagnosed or poorly controlled diabetes sometimes refer to their condition as "a touch of sugar" or "borderline diabetes" to downplay the seriousness of their condition (Ulrich and Abner, 2010). Euphemisms can soften the impact of information that might be unpleasant. It's easy to imagine how a relational breakup might be easier to handle with the explanation, "I'm not ready for commitment" than with "I want to date other people." However, there are times when a more direct approach may be needed. For instance if health-care professionals were to downplay the seriousness of a medical condition such as diabetes they risk putting people's health in danger. When choosing how to broach difficult subjects, the challenge is to be as kind as possible without sacrificing either your integrity or the clarity of your message.

Relative Language

Relative language gains meaning by comparison. For example, do you attend a large or a small school? This depends on what you compare it to. Compared to the University of Toronto, with about 80,000 students, your university may look small, but compared with a smaller institution, it may seem quite large. Relative words such as *fast* and *slow*, *smart* and *stupid*, *short* and *long* are clearly defined only through comparison.

Using relative terms without explaining them can lead to communication problems. Have you ever answered someone's question about the weather by saying it was warm, only to find out the person thought it was cold? Have you followed a friend's advice and gone to a "cheap" restaurant, only to find that it was twice as expensive as you expected? Did classes you heard were "easy" turn out to be

Table 6.3 ● Abstract and Behavioural Descriptions

	Abstract Description	Who Is Involved	In What Circumstances	Specific Behaviour	Remarks
Problem	I'm no good at meeting strangers.	People I'd like to date.	At parties and in school.	I think, "They'd never want to date me." Also, I don't initiate conversations.	Behavioural description more clearly identifies thoughts and behaviour to change.
Goal	I'd like to be more assertive.	Telephone and door-to-door solicitors.	When I don't want the product or can't afford it.	Instead of apologizing, I want to keep saying, "I'm not interested" until they go away.	Behavioural description clearly outlines how to act; abstract description does not.
Appreciation	"You've been a great boss."	(No clarification necessary)	When I've needed to change my schedule because of school exams or assignments.	"You've rearranged my hours cheerfully."	Give both abstract and behavioural descriptions for best results.
Complaint	"I don't like some of the instructors around here."	Professors A and B.	In class, when students ask questions, the professors think they are stupid.	They either answer in a sarcastic voice (you might demonstrate) or accuse us of not studying hard enough.	If talking to A or B, use only behavioural description. With others, use both abstract and behavioural descriptions.
Request	"Quit bothering me!"	You and your friends X and Y.	When I'm studying for exams.	"Instead of asking me again and again to party with you, I wish you'd accept my reply that I need to study tonight."	Behavioural description will reduce defensiveness and make it clear that you don't always want to be left alone.

hard? The problem in each case resulted from failing to link the relative word to a more measurable term.

One way to avoid the pitfalls of relative language is to use numbers to define relative terms. For instance, physicians have found that by having patients rate their pain on a 10 point scale (with 1 representing no pain and 10 representing the worst possible pain) they can more accurately gage others' pain (Chuang et al., 2014). Numerical ratings are used to make words more measurable in everything from restaurant and movie reviews to student satisfaction.

Static Evaluation 静态评价

"Luis is a nervous guy." "Karen is short-tempered." "You can always count on Wes." A description or evaluation that contains the word *is* can be called a **static evaluation**—the usually mistaken assumption that people or things are totally consistent and unchanging. Instead of labelling Luis as permanently and completely nervous, it would probably be more accurate to outline the situations in which he behaves nervously: "Luis acts nervously until you get to know him." The same goes for Karen, Wes, and the rest of us: we are more changeable than the way static, everyday language describes us.

Edward Sagarian (1976) writes about an unconscious language habit that imposes a static view of others. Why is it, he asks, that we say, "He *has* a cold," but "He *is* a convict" or a genius, a slow learner, or any other kind of behaviour that is also not necessarily permanent? Sagarian argues that such linguistic labelling leads us to typecast others and in some cases forces them to perpetuate behaviour that could be changed.

Alfred Korzybski (1933) suggested the linguistic device of dating to reduce static evaluation. He proposed adding a subscript whenever appropriate to show the transitory nature of a referent. For example, a teacher might write the following as an evaluation of a student: "Susan had difficulty co-operating with her classmates." Although the actual device of subscripting is awkward in writing and impractical in conversation, the idea it represents can still be used. Instead of saying, "I'm shy," a more accurate statement might be, "I haven't approached any new people since I moved here." The first statement implies that your shyness is an unchangeable trait, rather like your height, while the second one suggests that you are capable of changing.

The Language of Responsibility

Besides providing a way to make the content of a message clear or obscure, language reflects the speaker's willingness to take responsibility for her or his beliefs, feelings, and actions. This acceptance or rejection of responsibility says a great deal about the speaker, and it can shape the tone of a relationship. To see how, read on.

"It" Statements

Notice the difference between the sentences of each set:

"It bothers me when you're late."
"I'm worried when you're late."

"It's nice to see you."
"I'm glad to see you."

"It's a boring class."
"I'm bored in the class."

- **Abstractions:** convenient ways of generalizing similarities between several objects, people, ideas, or events.
- **Advantages:** provide an easy shorthand; help avoid confrontations and embarrassment.
- **Disadvantages:** can lead to stereotyping; can confuse others.
- **Euphemisms:** innocuous terms substituted for blunt ones (e.g., *thrifty* instead of *cheap*).
- **Relative language:** words that gain meaning by comparison (e.g., *fast, short*).
- **Static evaluation:** the usually mistaken assumption that people or things are totally consistent and unchanging (descriptions that contain the word *is*—e.g., "She *is* rude").

Though we might describe people as being nervous or attention-seeking just like we describe the colour of their eyes, people are rarely that unchanging. How would your friends describe you? Are you like that all of the time?

© iStockPhoto/ozgurdonmaz.

"You're really a great person, but I think we ought to stop seeing each other."

"You've done good work for us, but we're going to have to let you go."

"This paper has some good ideas, but I'm giving it a 'D' because it's late."

"Buts" *can*, however, be a face-saving strategy worth using at times. When the goal is to be absolutely clear, however, the most responsible approach will deliver the central idea without the distractions that can come with "but" statements.

"I," "You," and "We" Language

We've already seen that "I" language is a way of accepting responsibility for a message. "You" language is quite different. It expresses a judgment of the other person. Positive judgments ("You look great today!") rarely cause problems, but notice how each of the following critical "you" statements implies that the subject of the complaint is doing something wrong:

"You left this place a mess!"

"You didn't keep your promise!"

"You're really crude sometimes!"

Despite its name, "you" language does not have to contain the pronoun *you*, which is often implied rather than stated outright:

"That was a stupid joke!" ("Your jokes are stupid!")

"Don't be so critical!" ("You're too negative!")

"Mind your own business!" ("You're too nosy!")

As the name implies, an **"it" statement** replaces the personal pronoun *I* with the less immediate construction *it*. By contrast, **"I" language** clearly identifies the speaker as the source of a message. Communicators who use "it" statements avoid responsibility for ownership of a message, instead attributing it to some unidentified body. This habit is not just imprecise; more importantly, it's an unconscious way to avoid taking a position. You can begin to appreciate the increased directness of "I" language by trying to use it instead of the less direct and more evasive "it" statements in your own conversations.

"But" Statements

Statements that take the form "X-but-Y" can be quite confusing. A closer look at the **"but" statement** explains why. *But* has the effect of cancelling the thought that precedes it:

Whether the judgment is stated outright or implied, it's easy to see why "you" language can arouse defensiveness. A "you" statement implies that the speaker is qualified to judge the target—not an idea that most listeners are willing to accept, even when the evaluation is correct.

"I" language offers a more accurate and less provocative way to express a complaint (Kubany et al., 1992; Winer and Majors, 1981). "I" language shows that the speaker takes responsibility for the accusation by describing his or her reaction to the other's behaviour without making any judgments about its worth. A complete "I" statement has three parts: it describes (1) the other person's behaviour, (2) your feelings, and (3) the consequences the other's behaviour has for you:

> "I get embarrassed [*feeling*] when you talk about my bad grades in front of our friends [*behaviour*]. I'm afraid they'll think I'm stupid [*consequence*]."

> "When you didn't pick me up on time this morning [*behaviour*], I was late for class and wound up getting chewed out by the professor [*consequences*]. That's why I got so angry [*feeling*]."

> "I haven't been very affectionate [*consequence*] because you've hardly spent any time with me in the past few weeks [*behaviour*]. I'm confused [*feeling*] about how you feel about me."

When the chances of being misunderstood or getting a defensive reaction are high, it's a good idea to include all three elements in your "I" message. In some cases, however, only one or two of them will get the job done:

> "I went to a lot of trouble making this dinner, and now it's cold. Of course I'm annoyed!" (The behaviour is obvious.)

> "I'm worried because you haven't called me up." ("Worried" is both a feeling and a consequence in this statement.)

Despite its obvious advantages, even the best-constructed and masterfully delivered "I"

message will not always receive a non-defensive response. As Thomas Gordon (1970, p. 145) points out, "nobody welcomes hearing that his behaviour is causing someone a problem, no matter how the message is phrased." Furthermore, "I" language in large doses can start to sound egotistical (Proctor, 1989). Research shows that self-absorbed people, also known as "conversational narcissists," can be identified by their constant use of first-person-singular pronouns (Raskin and Shaw, 1988; Vangelisti et al., 1990). For this reason, "I" language works best in moderation.

One way to avoid overuse of "I" language is to consider the pronoun *we*. **"We" language** implies that the issue is the concern and responsibility of both the speaker and receiver of a message. Consider a few examples:

> "We have a problem. We can't seem to talk about money without fighting."

> "We are not doing a very good job of keeping the apartment clean, are we?"

> "We need to talk to your parents about whether we'll visit them for the holidays."

It's easy to see how "we" language can help build a constructive climate. Besides being immediate, it suggests a kind of "we're in this together" orientation (Gorham, 1988). Couples who use "we" language are more satisfied than those who rely more heavily on "I" and "you" pronouns (Honeycutt, 1999; Sillars et al., 1997). On the other hand, using the pronoun *we* can be presumptuous since you are speaking for the other person as well as for yourself. It's easy to imagine someone replying to the statement, "We have a problem . . ." by saying, "Maybe you have a problem, but don't tell me I have!"

As is summarized in Table 6.4, all three pronouns—*I, you,* and *we*—have their advantages and drawbacks. Given this fact, what advice can we give about the most effective pronouns to use in interpersonal communication? A study by Russell Proctor and James Wilcox

Table 6.4 ● Pronoun Uses and Their Effects

Pronoun	Pros	Cons	Recommendations
"I" Language	Takes responsibility for personal thoughts, feelings, and wants. Less defence-provoking than "you" language.	Can be perceived as egotistical, narcissistic, and self-absorbed.	Use descriptive "I" messages in conflicts when the other person does not perceive a problem. Combine "I" with "we" language in conversations.
"We" Language	Signals inclusion, immediacy, cohesiveness, and commitment.	Can speak improperly for others.	Combine with "I" language, particularly in personal conversations. Use in group settings to enhance sense of unity. Avoid when expressing personal thoughts, feelings, and wants.
"You" Language	Signals other-orientation, particularly when the topic is positive.	Can sound evaluative and judgmental, particularly during confrontations.	Use "I" language during confrontations. Use "You" language when praising or including others.

(1993) offers an answer. The researchers found that *I–we* combinations (for example, "I think that we . . ." or "I would like to see us . . . ") were strongly endorsed by college students, particularly for confrontational conversations in romantic relationships. Anita Vangelisti and her associates (1990) made a similar observation: unlike conversational narcissists, non-narcissists combine their "I" references with references to other persons, objects, and events. Since too much of any pronoun sounds wrong, it is generally a good idea to combine pronouns. If your "I" language expresses your position without being overly self-absorbed, your "you" language shows concern for others without judging them, and your "we" language includes others without speaking for them, you will probably come as close as possible to the ideal mix of pronouns.

Disruptive Language 顛覆性語言

Not all linguistic problems come from mis-understandings. Sometimes, people understand one another perfectly and still wind up in conflict. Of course, not all disagreements

can or should be avoided. But eliminating three harmful linguistic habits from your communication repertoire can minimize the kind of clashes that don't need to happen, allowing you to save your energy for the unavoidable and important struggles.

Fact–Inference/Opinion Confusion

A **factual statement** is a claim that can be verified as true or false. By contrast, an **inferential**

- **"I" language:** clearly identifies the speaker as the source of the message.
- **"It" statement:** replaces pronoun *I* with *it* and allows speaker to avoid taking responsibility for ownership of a message.
- **"But" statement:** when *but* is used in a statement, it has the effect of cancelling out the thought that proceeds it.
- **"You" language:** expresses judgment of the other person.

statement is an interpretation of evidence and an **opinion statement** is a belief or judgment that may or may not be based on evidence. A factual statement can be proven, whereas inferential and opinion statements are usually debatable. Consider a few examples of the difference between each:

Fact	Some Possible Inferences	Opinion
It rains more in Vancouver than in Victoria.	Victoria has a more pleasant climate than Vancouver. You have to water your garden much less in Vancouver compared to Victoria.	Victoria is better than Vancouver.
You have not texted or spoken to me in a week.	You are mad at me. You are busy.	You are inconsiderate.

When factual statements, inferences, and opinions are set side-by-side like this, the difference between them is clearer. In everyday conversation, however, we often present our inferences and opinions as if they were facts (e.g., "That was a dumb thing to say!" or "Spending that much money on ____ is a waste!"). By presenting our opinions and deductions as facts we invite unnecessary argument. For example:

A: Why are you mad at me?
B: I'm not mad at you. Why have you been so insecure lately?
A: I'm not insecure. It's just that you've been so critical.
B: What do you mean, "critical?" I haven't been critical.

Instead of trying to read the other person's mind, a far better course is to use the perception checking skills described in Chapter 3.

Identify the observable behaviour (fact) that has caught your attention and describe the interpretation (inference) that you have drawn from it. After describing this train of thought, ask the other person to comment on the accuracy of your interpretation:

"When you didn't return my phone call [*fact*], I got the idea that you were mad at me [*inference*]. Are you? [*question*]"

Emotive Language

Emotive language seems to describe something, but really announces the speaker's attitude toward it (Macagno and Walton, 2010; Richards, 1948). If you approve of a friend's roundabout approach to a difficult subject, you might call her "tactful"; if you don't like it, you might accuse her of "beating around the bush." Whether the approach is good or bad is more a matter of opinion than of fact, although this difference is obscured by emotive language.

You can appreciate that emotive words are really editorial statements when you consider these examples:

If You Approve, Say	If You Disapprove, Say
cautious	cowardly
eccentric	crazy
extrovert	loudmouth
information	propaganda
progressive	radical
thrifty	cheap
traditional	old-fashioned

Research has found that the words healthcare providers use affect patients' responses to illness, medical procedures and their ability cope (Lang et al. 2005; Vranceanu et al., 2011; 2012). For instance, in an investigation into the words typically involved in hand surgery, investigators found that the words *discomfort* or *ache* were perceived more positively than *pain* and the word *tear* was rated more positively than *rupture* (Vranceanu et al., 2012). Since pain intensity and disability are affected by patients' psychological distress these investigators have advised health-care providers to be aware that all words are not equal in terms of their emotional impact. They advise choosing the best words that both accurately describe conditions and procedures and promote effective coping.

Culture and Language

So far, we have described attributes that characterize most languages, with a particular emphasis on English. Although there are some remarkable similarities among the world's many languages (Brown, 1991), they differ in important respects that affect the ways their speakers communicate with one another and with speakers of other tongues. In this section, we outline some of those differences.

Translation

Anyone who has tried to translate ideas from one language to another knows that the potential for misunderstanding is always present. Sometimes, the results of an unfortunate translation can be amusing. For example, Gerber introduced its baby-food products in some French-speaking countries without realizing that *gerber* is a French slang term that means "to vomit."

Even when they choose the right words, there's no guarantee that non-native speakers will use a foreign language correctly. For example, Japanese insurance companies warn their policyholders who are visiting the United States to avoid their cultural tendency to say "excuse me" or "I'm sorry" if they are involved in a traffic accident (Sugimoto, 1991). In Japan, apologizing is a traditional way to express goodwill and maintain social harmony,

✓ CHECK IT!

Describe three harmful linguistic habits that contribute to conflict.

REFLECTION

IDIOMS AND TRANSLATION

I hadn't realized how tricky it can be to learn a new language until I started tutoring some international students who had just arrived on campus from overseas. Most of them have an excellent textbook understanding of English, because they've been studying the language since elementary school. But knowing formal rules and vocabulary hasn't prepared them for the way everyday talk works.

Some of the idioms we take for granted as native English speakers don't make any sense. Yesterday, I counted over twenty of them in just one class lecture: "taking the bull by the horns," "beating around the bush," "shot down," "blowing your top," "up in the air," and so on. Until you can understand idioms like these, you miss a lot. And until you learn to use them, you sound like a textbook instead of a natural speaker.

even if the person offering the apology is not at fault. But in the United States, an apology can be taken as an admission of guilt and result in Japanese tourists being held accountable for accidents for which they may not be responsible.

Difficult as they may be, translation and choosing terminology constitute only two of many communication challenges facing members of different cultures and co-cultures. Now, we need to look at some more subtle challenges that can make decoding messages from members of other cultures a challenging task.

High- versus Low-Context Cultures

Anthropologist Edward Hall (1959) identified two distinct ways that members of various cultures deliver messages. A **low-context culture** uses language primarily to express thoughts, feelings, and ideas as directly and logically as possible. To low-context communicators, the meaning of a statement lies in the words spoken. By contrast, a **high-context culture** relies heavily on subtle, often non-verbal cues

© iStockPhoto/elkor.

To low-context communicators, the meaning of a statement lies in the words spoken. By contrast, a high-context culture relies heavily on subtle, often non-verbal cues to maintain social harmony. Do you ever witness this clash in your interactions with your family or friends? How do you negotiate these differences?

to maintain social harmony (Ambady et al., 1996). Rather than upsetting others by speaking directly, communicators in these societies learn to discover meaning from the context in which a message is delivered: the non-verbal behaviour of the speaker, the history of the relationship, and the general social rules that govern interaction between people. In Table 6.5, we summarize some key differences in how people from low and high-context cultures use language.

Mainstream culture in Canada, the United States, and Northern Europe can be categorized near the low-context end of the scale. Inhabitants of these low-context cultures generally value straight talk and grow impatient with "beating around the bush." By contrast, most Asian and Middle Eastern cultures fit the high-context pattern and favour more indirect and less candid communication.

In many Asian societies, for example, maintaining harmony is important, so communicators avoid speaking clearly if it helps a person to "save face." For this reason, communicators raised in Japanese or Korean cultures are less likely than Canadians to offer a clear "no" to an undesirable request. The design of websites differs too depending on the extent to which a culture depends on language or contextual cues to convey information. In their analysis of 597 global business websites, Jean-Claude Usunier and Nicolas Roulin (2010) found that a low-context communication style worked best for businesses with a global audience, because this style tended to provide more information that was easier to find and read, and these websites allowed users to conduct more transactions when compared to websites that relied more on contextual cues to provide information.

To members of high-context cultures, communicators with a low-context style can appear overly talkative, lacking in subtlety, and redundant. On the other hand, to people from low-context backgrounds, high-context communicators often seem inexpressive or even dishonest. It is easy to see how the clash between directness and indirectness can aggravate problems between, for example, straight-talking, low-context Israelis and their Arab neighbours, whose high-context culture stresses smooth interaction. Israelis might view their Arab counterparts as evasive, while the Arabs might perceive the Israelis as insensitive and blunt.

Verbal Communication Styles

Using language is more than just a matter of choosing a particular group of words to convey an idea. Each language has its own unique character that distinguishes it from others. Matters like the amount of formality or informality, precision or vagueness, and brevity or detail are major ingredients in speaking competently. When a communicator tries to use the

Table 6.5 ● High- and Low-Context Communication

Low Context	High Context
Majority of information carried in explicit verbal messages, with less focus on the situational context.	Important information carried in contextual cues—time, place, relationship, situation; less reliance on explicit verbal messages.
Self-expression valued; communicators state opinions and desires directly and strive to persuade others to accept their own viewpoint.	Relational harmony valued and maintained by indirect expression of options; communicators abstain from saying "no" directly.
Clear, eloquent speech considered praiseworthy; verbal fluency admired.	Communicators talk "around" the point, allowing the others to fill in the missing pieces; ambiguity and use of silence.

verbal style from one culture in a different one, problems are likely to arise.

Gudykunst (2005) describes three important types of cultural differences in verbal style. One is *directness* or *indirectness*. We have already discussed how low-context cultures use language primarily to express thoughts, feelings, and ideas as clearly, directly, and logically as possible, while high-context cultures may speak less directly, using language to maintain social harmony.

Another way in which language styles can vary is in terms of whether they are *elaborate* or *succinct*. For instance, speakers of Arabic commonly use language that is much more rich and expressive than that normally found in English. Strong assertions and exaggerations that would sound ridiculous in English are a common feature of Arabic.

Succinctness is most extreme in cultures where silence is valued. In many First Nations cultures in Canada, for example, the favoured way to handle ambiguous social situations is to remain quiet (Basso, 1970; Hett, 1993). When you contrast this silent style to the talkativeness that is common when people first meet in mainstream Canadian culture, it's easy to imagine how the first encounter between a Cree or Mi'kmaq and an Anglo-Canadian might be uncomfortable for both people.

A third way that languages can differ from one culture to another is in their *formality* or *informality*. The pronouns used in a language may encode politeness and formality. For example, most European languages except English have different pronouns for informal use among friends (e.g., *tu* in French and Italian) and more formal pronouns for addressing superiors and people one does not know well (e.g., *vous* in French, *lei* in Italian). In Japanese, there are even more choices depending on the rank, job, sex, and age of the person being spoken to.

The informal approach that is characteristic of North Americans is quite different from the great concern for propriety in many parts of Asia and Africa. Formality is not so much a matter of using correct grammar as of defining social relationships. For example, there are different degrees of formality for speaking to old friends, non-acquaintances whose background one knows, and complete strangers. One sign of being a learned person in Korea is the ability to use language that recognizes these relational distinctions. When you contrast these sorts of distinctions with the casual friendliness of many North Americans, even when talking to complete strangers, it's easy to see how a Korean might consider North American communicators to be boorish and how a North American might see Koreans as stiff and unfriendly.

Gender and Language

In addition to the differences among languages and cultures, there are other important variables that influence the ways people use language. The most investigated variable is gender. There are varying opinions about the similarities and differences in men and women's use of language, and while gender appears to influence some elements of conversation, there are some other important non-sex variables at play in conversation, such as a person's social philosophy, sexual orientation, occupation, and interpersonal power.

Content

Though there is certainly variation within each sex, on the average, men and women discuss a different range of topics. The first research on conversational topics was conducted over seventy years ago. Despite the changes in male and female roles since then, the results of more recent studies are remarkably similar (Bischoping, 1993; Clark, 1998; Fehr, 1996; Sehulster, 2006). These studies, which analyzed the communication of women and men ranging in age from 17 to 80, examined the topics each discussed with friends of the same sex. Certain subjects were common to both sexes: work, movies, and television proved to be frequent topics for both groups. Both men and women tended to reserve discussions of

sex and sexuality for members of the same sex. Along with the similarities, there were significant differences in the conversations of men and women, especially when talking to friends. Female friends spent much more time discussing relationships, health and reproductive matters, weight, food, and fashion, beauty, and shopping. Men, on the other hand, were more likely to discuss sports, hobbies, and activities. Both men and women were equally likely to discuss family, work, and the opposite sex in same-sex conversations (Sehulster, 2006).

Reasons for Communicating and Amount of Talking

Both men and women, at least in the mainstream cultures of Canada and the United States, use language to build and maintain social relationships. Regardless of the sex of the communicators, the goal of almost all ordinary conversations includes making the conversation enjoyable by being friendly, showing an interest in what the other person says, and talking about topics that interest the other person (Clark, 1998). How men and women accomplish these goals, though, is often different. Although most communicators try to make their interaction enjoyable, men are more likely than women to try to make conversation fun. Their discussions involve a greater amount of joking and good-natured teasing. By contrast, women's conversations focus more often on feelings, relationships, and personal problems (Burleson et al., 1996; Samter et al., 1994).

Female speech often contains statements showing support for the other person, demonstrations of equality, and efforts to keep the conversation going (Clark, 1998). Both women's language (e.g., filling silences,

© iStockPhoto/PeopleImages.

What reasons are there for miscommunication with members of the opposite sex? Have you come across any of these in your own life?

facilitating conversation) and their non-verbal behaviours (e.g., nodding head, smiling) have been interpreted as doing more "conversational work" (Farley et al., 2010; Kollock et al., 1985). Women appear to use speech to connect more with people, particularly if the other person is not well known. Men, on the other hand, are more likely than women to use assertive speech with unfamiliar others (Leaper and Ayers, 2007). In addition, men are more likely to use language to accomplish the job at hand than to nourish relationships, and they tend to pay more attention to language and less attention to non-verbal behaviours when compared to women (Gore, 2009). These differences, however, are more likely to be observed when men and women are communicating with people they do not know well or in research conducted in labs rather than in real-life, interpersonal relationships (Leaper and Ayers, 2007).

In terms of differences in the amount that men and women talk, some researchers have found no differences (Mehl et al., 2007), and others have found that again, it depends on the topic and the conversational partner. Leaper and Ayers' (2007) meta-analysis of sex differences in communication revealed that women talked more than men during socio-emotional activities (e.g., sharing personal information), but that men talked more than women during instrumental tasks (e.g., solving a problem). Overall, across a variety of situations these investigators found that contrary to the stereotype, men actually talked more.

When it comes to electronic communication such as email, however, women tend to write longer responses than men, but, just as in face-to-face conversations, the topic of discussion and communication partner influence the differences in email length (Brajer and Gill, 2010). Victor Brajer and Andrew Gill found that female university students in their study wrote longer emails than men when the topic was parking problems, but not when the topic was choosing their university major. The women also wrote longer responses than the men when

they were communicating with a female professor. Again, these differences were observed in a contrived situation in which men and women were communicating with people they did not know well. The typical length of real-life, text-based messages may well be equivalent for men and women.

Conversational Style

Research suggests that women speak somewhat differently in conversations than men do (Wood, 2009; Turner et al., 1995). For example, Mulac (1998) reports that men are more likely than women to use judgmental adjectives ("Reading can be a drag"), directives ("Think of some more"), and "I" references ("I have a lot to do"). Women are more likely to use intensive adverbs ("He's really interested"), emotional references ("If he really cared about you . . . "), uncertainty verbs ("It seems to me . . . "), and contradictions ("It's cold, but that's okay"). Mulac summarizes style differences by claiming that men's speech is more direct, succinct, personal, and task-oriented. By contrast, female speech is more indirect, elaborate, and focused on relationships. Some theorists have argued that such differences cause women's speech to be less powerful than men's, although research does not always back up this claim (Grob et al., 1997).

Other studies have revealed that men and women behave differently in different conversational settings. For example, in mixed-sex dyads, men talk longer than women, while in same-sex situations, women talk for a longer time. Women speak more tentatively than men when they are in mixed-sex conversations, although their speech is just as confident as men's in same-sex situations. In larger groups, men talk more, whereas in smaller groups, women do more of the talking. In same-sex conversations, there are other differences: women use more questions, justifications, intensive adverbs, personal pronouns, and adverbs. Men use more directives, interruptions, and filler words to begin sentences (Mulac et al., 2001; Mulac et al., 1988).

Focus on RESEARCH

ARE GENDER DIFFERENCES IN COMMUNICATION A MATTER OF WHO'S WATCHING?

Paul Brunet and Louis Schmidt (2010) were interested in finding out whether men and women communicated in sex-stereotyped ways when they were communicating online with people they did not know. These researchers asked undergraduate students at McMaster University in Hamilton, Ontario, to use Yahoo instant messaging to chat with a same-sex stranger for 10 minutes. The participants were told to get to know each other during the 10-minute online conversation. Half of the dyads were randomly assigned to a condition in which they could see each other via webcam, but not hear each other, so that they had to use instant messaging to communicate. Previous research had established that women tend to be more emotionally expressive than men online; in this study women did use significantly more emoticons than men, but only when the webcam was present. This was surprising, since in this condition there was the opportunity for non-verbal expression of emotion (e.g., smiling, frowning). Brunet and Schmidt speculated that women are more likely to conform to stereotypes when they are being observed by others. Perhaps women in the webcam condition felt more pressure to maintain societal norms of friendliness than women who maintained their anonymity in the no-webcam condition.

Critical thinking: *Can you think of other contextual or situational factors that might influence men and women to conform to social expectations in their communication?*

Non-sex Variables

Despite the differences in the way men and women speak, the link between sex and language use is not as clear-cut as it might seem. For example, one analysis of over 1200 research studies found that only 1 per cent of variance in communication behaviour resulted from sex differences (Canary and Hause, 1993). There is no significant difference between male and female speech in areas such as use of profanity; use of qualifiers such as "I guess" or "this is just my opinion," or tag questions; and vocal fluency (Grob et al., 1997; Zahn, 1989). A growing body of research explains some of the apparent contradictions in similarities and differences between female and male speech by pointing out that factors other than the gender of the communicator influence language use. For example, *social philosophy* plays a role. Feminist wives talk more than their husbands do, whereas wives who do not identify themselves as feminists talk less. Orientation toward problem solving also plays a role in conversational style: whether a speaker has a co-operative or competitive orientation has greater influence on interaction than biological sex (Fisher, 1983). *Sexual orientation* may be more powerful than biological sex in determining speech mannerisms. In gay and lesbian relationships, the conversational styles of partners reflect power differences in the relationship (e.g., who is earning more money) more than the biological sex of the communicators (Steen and Schwartz, 1995).

The speaker's *occupation* also influences speaking style. For example, male early childhood educators' speech to their students resembles the language of female teachers more closely than it resembles the language of fathers at home (Gleason and Greif, 1983). At work, task differences exert more powerful effects on whether speakers use sex-inclusive language (such as using *he or she* instead of just *he*) than does biological sex (Rubin et al., 1994). A close study of trial transcripts showed that the speaker's experience on the witness stand and occupation had more to do with language use than did biological sex. The researcher concluded, "So-called women's

REFLECTION

DIFFERENT ROLES, DIFFERENT LANGUAGE

As the first woman in a formerly all-male architectural firm, I feel like something of a guinea pig. Most of the partners and associates have made me feel welcome, but a small group treats me with what seems like a condescending attitude. The structural, mechanical, and electrical engineers we use as consultants are even worse. I don't think they've ever worked with a woman who wasn't a secretary. I've found that with these guys, I've changed the way I speak. I try to use more powerful language with fewer hesitations and hedges. I make more statements and ask fewer questions. In other words, I sound more like a stereotypical man.

I don't know yet whether this approach will make any difference. The point is, I sound like a different person when I'm at work more than in any other setting. It's not really an act: it's more an effort to sound professional. I guess if someone dresses differently when they go to work, there's nothing wrong with sounding different too.

CHECK IT!

Describe the observed differences between male and female speakers in terms of content, reasons for communicating, and conversational style. What non-sex variables have been associated with differences in the ways men and women speak?

language is neither characteristic of all women nor limited only to women" (O'Barr, 1982).

Another factor that trumps sex differences is *power*. For instance, there are few differences between the way men and women use powerful speech (specifically, threats) when they have the same amount of bargaining strength in a negotiation (Scudder and Andrews, 1995), and they are equally likely to change the topic of conversation when they have equal power or status in a task-oriented discussion (Okamoto and Smith-Lovin, 2001). Findings like this suggest that characteristically feminine speech is less a function of gender or sex than of women's historically less-powerful positions in some parts of the social world.

By now, it should be clear that there are differences between the ways men and women speak, but that these differences are determined by a wide variety of factors that may have little or nothing to do with biological sex. As men and women grow to have equal opportunities and more similar social experiences, we can expect that there will be fewer differences in the ways they speak.

SUMMARY

Language is both a marvellous communication tool and the source of many interpersonal problems. Every language is a collection of symbols governed by a variety of rules. Because of its symbolic nature, language is not a precise vehicle: meanings rest in people, not in words themselves. The codes that are used by members of a culture are often the most recognizable factors that shape communication between people from different cultural backgrounds. Verbal codes include language spoken and the worldview created by it, as well as verbal communication style.

Besides conveying meanings about the content of a specific message, language both expresses and shapes the perceptions of its users. Terms used to name people influence the way they are regarded. The terms used to label speakers and the language they use shape other people's evaluations of the speakers' credibility and status. Language also reveals the level of affiliation, attraction, and interest of a speaker toward a subject. In addition, language patterns reflect and shape a speaker's perceived power. Finally, language reflects and influences prejudiced attitudes.

When used carelessly, language can lead to a variety of interpersonal problems. The precision or vagueness of messages can affect a receiver's understanding of them. Both precise messages and vague, evasive messages have their uses in interpersonal relationships, and a competent communicator has the ability to choose the best level of precision for the situation at hand. Language also acknowledges or avoids the speaker's acceptance of responsibility for his or her positions, and competent communicators know how to use "I," "you," and "we" statements to accept the optimal

level of responsibility and relational harmony. Some language habits—confusing facts with opinions or inferences and using emotive terms—can lead to unnecessary disharmony in interpersonal relationships.

Low-context cultures (e.g., North American) rely primarily on language to express thoughts and feelings, while high-context cultures (e.g., Asian) rely heavily on subtle cues to maintain social harmony.

The relationship between the gender of the communicator and language is a complex one. There are many differences in the ways men and women speak. The content of their conversations varies, as do their reasons for communicating and their conversational style. However, not all differences in language use can be accounted for by the speaker's gender. Social philosophy, sexual orientation, occupation, and interpersonal power also influence the use of language, and psychological gender can be more of an influence than biological sex.

MULTIPLE-CHOICE QUESTIONS

1. Phonological rules govern
   a. how symbols can be arranged.
   b. how sounds can be combined to form words.
   c. how words should be interpreted given the situation.
   d. the meanings of words.

2. Ogden and Richards' triangle of meaning suggests
   a. meanings are in and among people.
   b. there is an indirect relationship between a word and the thing or idea it represents.
   c. problems occur because people attach different meanings to the same message.
   d. all of the above.

3. The Pormpuraaw people of Australia don't have words for *right*, *left*, *back*, and *front* in their language; instead they use

compass directions, and as a consequence they think differently about space than people who speak other languages. This is an example of
   a. credibility and status.
   b. pragmatic rules.
   c. coordinated management of meaning.
   d. linguistic relativism.

4. Unusual names and names with unique spellings have been associated with negative outcomes such as involvement in juvenile delinquency.
   a. true
   b. false

5. Canadians learning English as a second language (ESL) report that
   a. their accent has had no effect on their social interactions.
   b. they would prefer to learn English from a fellow ESL learner.

c. people would respect them more if they learn to pronounce English well.

d. all of the above

6. Convergence involves adapting one's speech style to better match the style of others with whom one is communicating.

    a. true

    b. false

7. Hedges, hesitations, intensifiers, polite forms, tag questions, and disclaimers are all examples of

    a. convergent speech.

    b. divergent speech.

    c. powerless speech.

    d. sexist speech.

8. Using unnecessary modifiers when describing others such as in the phrases *black professor* or *Pakistani merchant* can be subtle indicators of racism.

    a. true

    b. false

9. Jane insists that the weather in Victoria is much better than in Vancouver. This is an example of which type of disruptive language?

    a. "but" statement

    b. emotive language

    c. fact–opinion confusion

    d. euphemisms

10. People from high-context cultures, such as many Asian and Middle Eastern cultures, primarily use language to express thoughts, feelings, and ideas directly.

    a. true

    b. false

Answers: 1. b; 2. d; 3. d; 4. a; 5. c; 6. a; 7. c; 8. a; 9. c; 10. b

ACTIVITIES

1. Invitation to Insight

For each of the following scenes, describe one syntactic, one semantic, and one pragmatic rule:

a. Asking an acquaintance out for a first date.

b. Declining an invitation to a party.

c. Responding to a stranger who has just said "excuse me" after bumping into you in a crowd.

2. Invitation to Insight

Recall an incident in which you were misunderstood. Explain how this event illustrates the principle that "meanings are in people, not words."

3. Ethical Challenge

The information about the influence of language, on pages 189–196, shows how the words a communicator chooses can shape the perceptions of others. Create two scenarios for each type of linguistic influence listed below. The first should describe how the type of influence could be used constructively, and the second should describe an unethical application of this knowledge.

a. naming and identity

b. credibility and status

c. attraction and interest

d. power

e. sexism, sexual prejudice, and racism

4. Skill Builder

Translate the following into behavioural language:

• an abstract goal for improving your interpersonal communication (i.e., "Be more assertive" or "Stop being so sarcastic")

• a complaint you have about another person (i.e., he is "selfish," she is "insensitive")

In both cases, describe the person or people involved, the circumstances in which the communication will take place, and the precise behaviour involved. What difference will using the behavioural descriptions likely make in your relationships?

5. Invitation to Insight

Are there ever situations in your life when it is desirable to be less clear and more vague? Use the information on pages 197–202 to answer this question and to decide whether vagueness is the most competent approach to the situation.

6. Skill Builder

You can develop your skill at delivering "I" and "we" messages by following these steps:

a. Visualize situations in your life when you may have sent each of the following messages:
   - "You're not telling me the truth!"
   - "You only think of yourself!"
   - "Don't be so touchy!"
   - "Quit fooling around!"
   - "You don't understand a word I'm saying!"
b. Write alternatives to each statement, using "I" language.
c. Think of three "you" statements you could make to people in your life. Transform each of these statements into "I" and "we" language, and rehearse them with a classmate.

7. Invitation to Insight

What roles do the types of disruptive language described on pages 206–207 play in your life? Recall incidents when you have confused facts and opinions, confused facts and inferences, and used emotive language. Discuss the consequences of each type of language use, and describe how the results might have been different if you had used language more carefully.

8. Invitation to Insight

Some authors believe that differences between male and female communication are quite significant. Other researchers believe the differences are not nearly so dramatic. Which approach seems more accurate to you? Offer experiences from your life to support your point of view.

9. Skill Builder

Rewrite the following sentences to make them gender-neutral.

a. The average student is worried about his grades.
b. Ask the student to hand in his work as soon as he is finished.
c. Writers become so involved in their work that they neglect their wives and children.

10. Role Play

Choose a partner. Think of a real criticism (of someone else) and compose a highly abstract message to convey your complaint (e.g., "You're so selfish"). Briefly describe the situation to your partner (who the other person is and the general situation—avoid providing specific details about the complaint) and have her or him pretend to be the person you are criticizing. Deliver your abstract criticism and have your partner respond. Now, compose a more specific behavioural description of the same complaint and deliver this criticism to your partner and have him or her respond. Discuss the differences between the two messages. What are the advantages of stating your complaints in more specific terms? Now, reverse roles and repeat the exercise.

DISCUSSION QUESTIONS

1. What is the significance of the phrase "meanings are in people, not in words?"
2. Does naming something make it more or less frightening? Recall the outbreak of Severe Acute Respiratory Syndrome (SARS) in the spring of 2003. At first, doctors and public health officials did not have a name for the illness. Later, they described it as SARS—which wasn't really a name, but a description of the illness.

The acronym stuck. Why did the public want to name it? How does language affect our perceptions?

3. We have argued in this chapter that sexist language is a subtle form of bias. Do you agree or disagree? Why?

4. Given the subjective nature of perception, is "we" language ever acceptable? Why or why not?

5. Do you think that news outlets use the confusion between fact and opinion, and fact and inference to their advantage? Do some news reports contain emotive language? Could these distinctions be used to distinguish between news reporting and propaganda? Why or why not?

6. Do you believe that the language a person speaks affects that person's worldview? Why or why not?

7. Given the diversity of verbal styles in different cultures, is it possible not to offend someone when you are communicating cross-culturally? Why or why not?

JOURNAL IDEAS

1. Over the next few days keep track of generalizations you make when speaking to others when offering thanks and criticism. Try to rewrite these comments using more precise language. What might be the benefits and drawbacks of using less abstract language when communicating with others?

2. Think of a couple of times you recently used "you" or "it" language during an argument or conflict. Rewrite your criticisms using "I" language. How might using "I" language change the interaction during a conflict?

7

Non-verbal Communication

Chapter Outline

© Bob Daemmrich / Alamy

Key Terms

barrier behaviours
chronemics
disfluencies
emblems
haptics
illustrators
intimate distance
kinesics
manipulators

non-verbal communication
paralanguage
personal distance
personal space
proxemics
public distance
regulators
social distance
territory

Learning Objectives

YOU SHOULD UNDERSTAND:

- the distinguishing characteristics of non-verbal communication;
- the functions that non-verbal communication can serve;
- the research evidence regarding detecting deception; and
- the various ways in which non-verbal messages are communicated.

YOU SHOULD BE ABLE TO:

- describe your non-verbal behaviour in any situation;
- identify non-verbal behaviour that repeats, substitutes for, complements, accents, regulates, or contradicts a verbal message;
- recognize and adjust the messages you send through your own non-verbal behaviour; and
- share appropriately your interpretation of another's non-verbal behaviour.

People don't always say what they mean . . . but their body gestures and movements tell the truth! Will he ask you out? Is she encouraging you? Know what is really happening by understanding the secret language of body signals. You can . . .

Improve your sex life . . .

Pick up your social life . . .

Better your business life . . .

Read Body Language so that you can penetrate the personal secrets, both of intimates and total strangers . . .

Does her body say that she's a phony?

Does his body say that she's a manipulator?

Does her body say that she's lonely?

Unless you've been trapped in a lead mine or doing fieldwork in the Amazon Basin, "claims" like these are probably familiar to you. Almost every drugstore, supermarket, and airport book rack has its share of "body-language" paperbacks and magazine articles. They promise that, for only a few dollars and with a grade-5 reading ability, you can learn secrets that will change you from a fumbling social failure into a self-assured mind reader who can uncover a person's deepest secrets at a glance.

Claims like these are almost always exaggerations or fabrications. There *is*, of course, a scientific body of knowledge about non-verbal communication, and it *has* provided many fascinating and valuable clues to human behaviour. That's what this chapter is about. But it is unlikely the next few pages will turn you instantly into a rich, sexy, charming communication superstar; however, don't go away. Even without glamorous promises, a quick look at some facts about non-verbal communication shows that it is an important and valuable field to study.

Non-verbal Communication Defined

Since *non* means "not" and *verbal* means "with words," then it seems logical that *non-verbal communication* would involve "communication without words." This definition is an oversimplification, however, because it fails to distinguish between *vocal* communication (by mouth) and *verbal* communication (with words). Some non-verbal messages have a vocal element. For example, the words "I love you" have different meanings depending on the way they are spoken. Furthermore, some non-spoken forms of communication, such as American Sign Language, are linguistic and not really non-verbal in the sense most social scientists use the term. A better definition of **non-verbal communication** is "messages expressed by non-linguistic means."

These non-linguistic messages are important because what we *do* often conveys more meaning than what we *say*. Albert Mehrabian (1972), a psychologist working in the field of non-verbal behaviour, claimed that 93 per cent of the emotional impact of a message comes from a non-verbal source, whereas only 7 per cent is verbal. Anthropologist Ray Birdwhistell (1970) described a 65–35 percentage split between actions and words. Although social scientists have disputed these figures (e.g., Hegstrom, 1979; Lapakko, 1997), it is a fact that non-verbal communication contributes a great deal to shaping perceptions.

You might ask how non-verbal communication can be so powerful. At first glance, it seems as if meanings come from words. To answer this question, think of a time when you watched people speaking a language you didn't understand. Although you didn't understand the words being spoken, there were plenty of clues that gave you an idea of what was going on in the exchange. By watching the speakers' facial expressions, postures, gestures, vocal tones, and other behaviour you probably could make

TAKE TWO

Non-verbal communication: messages expressed by non-linguistic means; they can include vocal communication (e.g., voice tone), but not language (e.g., sign language).

What is the difference between sign language and non-verbal communication?

verbal, linguistic means of communication. We will now take a look at some of the fundamental characteristics of non-verbal communication.

All Behaviour Has Communicative Value

Some theorists have suggested that *all* non-verbal behaviour conveys information. They argue that it is impossible *not* to communicate. You can understand the impossibility of non-communication by considering what you would do if someone told you not to communicate any messages at all. What would you do? Close your eyes? Withdraw into a ball? Leave the room? You can probably see that even those actions communicate messages that mean you are avoiding contact. One study (DePaulo, 1992) took just this approach. When communicators were told not to express non-verbal clues, others viewed them as dull, withdrawn, uneasy, aloof, and deceptive.

The impossibility of not communicating is significant because it means that each of us is a kind of transmitter that cannot be shut off. No matter what we do, we send out messages that say something about ourselves and our relationships with others. If, for instance, someone

assumptions about the way the communicators felt about one another at the moment and got some ideas about the nature of their relationship. Researchers have found that subjects who hear content-free speech—ordinary speech that has been electronically manipulated so that the words are unintelligible—can consistently recognize the emotion being expressed, as well as identify its strength (Knapp and Hall, 2013).

Characteristics of Non-verbal Communication

The many types of non-verbal communication share some characteristics. As Table 7.1 shows, these characteristics are quite different from

Table 7.1 ● Some Differences between Verbal and Non-verbal Communication

Verbal Communication	Non-verbal Communication
mostly voluntary and conscious	often unconscious
usually content-oriented	usually relational
can be clear or vague	inherently ambiguous
primarily shaped by culture	primarily shaped by biology
discontinuous or intermittent	continuous
single channel (words only)	multi-channelled

SOURCE: Adapted from P. Andersen (1999), *Nonverbal communication: forms and functions*, (p. 16). Mountain View, CA: Mayfield.

were observing you now, what non-verbal clues would they get about how you are feeling? Are you sitting forward or reclining back? Is your posture tense or relaxed? Are your eyes wide open, or do they keep closing? What does your facial expression communicate now? Can you make your face expressionless? Don't people with expressionless faces still communicate something to you? Even uncontrollable behaviour can convey a message. You may not intend to show that you are embarrassed, but your blushing can still give you away. Of course, not all behaviour (intentional or not) will be interpreted correctly. Your trembling hands might be taken as a sign of nervousness when you are really just shivering from the cold. But whether or not your behaviour is intentional, and whether or not it is interpreted accurately, all non-verbal behaviour has the potential to create messages.

Although non-verbal behaviour reveals information, we are not always conscious of what we are communicating non-verbally. In one study, less than 25 per cent of the experimental subjects who had been instructed to show increased or decreased liking of a partner

could describe the non-verbal behaviour they used (Byron, 2008; Palmer and Simmons, 1995). Furthermore, the fact that communicators are non-verbally expressive does not mean that others will receive the abundance of unspoken messages that are available.

Non-verbal Communication Is Primarily Relational

Some non-verbal messages serve utilitarian functions. For example, a police officer directs the flow of traffic, or a team of street surveyors uses hand motions to coordinate their work. But non-verbal communication also serves a far more common (and more interesting) series of *social* functions.

The relational component of messages is most often communicated non-verbally. Non-verbal communication allows us to define the kind of relationships we want to have with others (Burgoon and Le Poire, 1999). You can appreciate this fact by thinking about the wide range of ways you could behave when greeting another person. You could wave, shake hands, nod, or smile, clap the other person on the back, give her a hug, kiss him on both cheeks, or avoid all contact. Each one of these actions sends a message about the nature of your relationship with the other person. The relational messages communicated with non-verbal communication include the degree to which people like each other and want involvement with each other, and their status or power relative to each other.

Non-verbal messages perform another valuable social function: they convey emotions that we may be unwilling or unable to express or that we may not even be aware of. In fact, non-verbal communication is much better suited to expressing

© bo1982/iStockphoto.

We are not always conscious of what we are communicating non-verbally, and the fact that communicators are non-verbally expressive does not mean that others will receive the unspoken messages. How can we become more conscious of both the non-verbal messages we're sending and the non-verbal messages of others?

attitudes and feelings than ideas. You can demonstrate this by imagining how you could non-verbally express each of these comments:

1. "I'm tired."
2. "I'm in favour of universal health care."
3. "I'm attracted to another person in the group."
4. "I think prayer should be allowed in schools."
5. "I'm angry at someone in this room."

This experience shows that ideas (such as statements 2 and 4) do not lend themselves to non-verbal expressions nearly as well as attitudes and feelings (statements 1, 3, and 5). This explains why it is possible to understand the attitudes or feelings of others even if you do not understand the subject of their communication.

Text messages, email, and instant messages offer fewer non-verbal cues about the speaker's feelings than do face-to-face encounters or even telephone conversations. Most of us have had the experience of finding out that our email or text message has been misunderstood. The use of emoticons (keyboard characters to simulate facial expressions) and statements about emotion can be used to try to capture non-verbal expressions in text-based messages and reduce the chances for misunderstandings. Research suggests that the use of emoticons to capture emotional expressiveness increases

the involvement and interaction between the people sharing an email or text message (Fabri and Moore, 2005; Walther and D'Addario, 2001). In the "Focus on Technology" box (page 224), we explore the frustrations of misunderstood email and text messages in the workplace. Clearly, the rich mixture of non-verbal and verbal messages that flow in face-to-face exchanges, or even in telephone conversations, cannot be easily replicated in writing, but it is possible to share emotions and compensate for the lack of non-verbal cues in CMC (Walther et al., 2010).

Non-verbal Communication Is Ambiguous

In Chapter 6, we pointed out how some language can be ambiguous. (For example, the statement "Your nose piercing really makes you stand out" could be a compliment or a criticism, and the vague statement, "I'm almost done" could mean you have to wait a few minutes or an hour.) Most non-verbal behaviour has the potential to be even more ambiguous than verbal statements like these. To understand why, consider how you would interpret silence from your companion during an evening together. Think of all the possible meanings of this non-verbal behaviour: affection, anger, preoccupation, boredom, nervousness, thoughtfulness—the possibilities are many.

The ambiguity of non-verbal behaviour was illustrated when a supermarket chain tried

DILBERT © 2002 Scott Adams. Used By permission of Universal UClick. All rights reserved.

Focus on TECHNOLOGY

EMOTIONS, EMAIL, AND TEXT MESSAGES

For Canadians, texting, email, social networking, and instant messaging are the media of choice for communicating at work and for sending personal messages to friends and family (Ipsos Reid, 2012). Increasingly, people use text-based messages to communicate with family and friends, send photos and invitations, and make important announcements such as engagements and births. Email messages, text messages, tweets, and social media posts don't interrupt the flow of activities in the same way telephone conversations and face-to-face meetings do. One of the major drawbacks with written messages, however, is their lack of non-verbal cues that communicate relational messages and emotions. This lack of media richness increases the potential for messages to be misinterpreted.

This is of particular concern at work, where the use of emoticons (graphic representations of facial expressions; e.g., :) and ;-)), initializations (e.g., *lol* means "laugh out loud"), and repeated letters (I am soooo sorry) which help to convey tone and emotion, are usually discouraged by managers and supervisors (Jett, 2005). Emoticons in the workplace are used primarily to indicate or strengthen a positive attitude, identify attempts at humour, act as hedges, and soften directives. Rather than accurately identify the senders' emotions they indicate how the message is supposed to be interpreted by the receiver (Skovholt et al., 2014). The actual expression of the senders' emotion in face-to-face or telephone conversations is only really available to the receiver via non-verbal cues that are absent in email and text messages (Riordan and Kreuz, 2010). This has led some researchers to suggest that email should not or cannot convey emotion. However, investigations have revealed that email often does communicate emotions—sometimes quite unintentionally (Thompsen and Foulger, 1996; Walther and D'Addario, 2001; Walther et al., 2010).

Kristen Byron has explored the factors that contribute to the miscommunication of emotion in email communication in the workplace. In Byron's (2008) theoretical framework, the two most common misinterpretations of emotions in workplace email are (1) receivers are likely to perceive emails intended to convey positive emotions as more neutral, and (2) receivers are more likely to perceive emails as more intensely negative than was intended by the sender. There are a number of factors that influence the likelihood of miscommunication, including the length of the relationship between the sender and the receiver, the gender and relative status of the sender (e.g., colleague or boss), the age and mood (positive or negative) of the receiver, and the established guidelines for the expression of emotion in that workplace. Byron argues that while more research in this area is needed, misperception of emotion in email messages can be reduced by first increasing employees' awareness that emotions can be communicated, both intentionally and unintentionally, in email messages. Second, employees need to recognize that they are fallible as both email senders and receivers. A third step would be to increase the use of cues and the amount of feedback to increase the likelihood of more accurate perceptions. Senders can increase accuracy by actually verbalizing the emotion ("I am so happy you will be able to come to the meeting"), and receivers can ask questions and state their interpretations of messages and invite the sender to respond. These strategies for perception checking (see Chapter 3) are as useful for computer-mediated communication as they are for the face-to-face variety.

---

to emphasize its customer-friendly approach by instructing employees to smile and make eye contact with customers. Several clerks filed grievances when some customers mistook the service-with-a-smile approach as sexual come-ons. As this story suggests, non-verbal cues are much more ambiguous than verbal statements when it comes to expressing willingness to become physically involved (Lim and Roloff, 1999).

Because non-verbal behaviour is so ambiguous, caution is wise when you are responding to non-verbal cues. Rather than jumping to conclusions about the meaning of a sigh, smile, slammed door, or yawn, it is far better to use the kind of perception-checking approach

Focus on RESEARCH

MISINTERPRETING NON-VERBAL BEHAVIOUR: A TRAGEDY FOR CANADIAN FIRST NATION GIRLS

In her review of the treatment of First Nations girls sentenced to Ontario Training Schools from 1933 to 1960, Joan Sangster (2002) describes the devastating effects of misinterpreting non-verbal behaviour because of cultural differences.

Sangster gives heartbreaking accounts of young First Nations girls whose emotional restraint and lack of eye contact were misinterpreted as passivity, secretiveness, and deceitfulness by the reform school staff, who were English-speaking Canadians of European descent.

Many First Nations cultures value silence and listening and do not promote overt emotional expression (either positive or negative). In contrast, the dominant Canadian culture of the 1930s to the 1960s was very much an extension of British culture in which eye contact and direct engagement were highly valued. These young girls showed their respect for and deference to the authority figures by not looking them in the eye and by keeping their feelings to themselves. The staff interpreted the girls' non-verbal behaviour as hostility and sneakiness. One school worker wrote, "She is quiet, deep and cunning. She goes along with training . . . but it is not penetrating. She has no conscience and is not progressing. . . . She appears cooperative, but is deceitful" (Sangster, 2002, p. 38).

In addition, the girls had been raised in First Nations families where the parents teach their children by modelling the right behaviour and refrain from criticizing and punishing. The girls had learned to imitate adults in order to behave appropriately. This imitation was interpreted as a lack of intelligence by the school staff, who described the girls as "dull." The school superintendent described one girl as unable to assimilate her lessons. "She scrapes by

copying," she wrote dismissively (Sangster, 2002, p. 36). Tragically, many girls were transferred to institutions for the mentally retarded, from which it was extremely difficult for them to be released.

There is no question that the training school staff's ethnocentrism and their racist attitudes toward First Nations peoples, which were very much a part of Canadian culture at that time, contributed to the staff's negative interpretations of the girls' behaviour. It is easy to see how an innocent lack of awareness of cultural differences in non-verbal expression can lead to tragic misunderstandings, particularly when one is dealing with children.

Critical thinking: *Can you think of changes that we could make to help to prevent misinterpretations of non-verbal behaviour in a variety of professional settings? Is increasing awareness of cultural influences on communication more essential in some professions? Why or why not?*

described in Chapter 3. "When you yawned, I got the idea I might be boring you. But maybe you are just tired. What's going on?" The ability to consider more than one possible interpretation for non-verbal behaviour illustrates the kind of cognitive complexity that we identified in Chapter 1 as an element of communication competence. Popular advice on the

subject notwithstanding, it is usually not possible to read a person like a book.

Non-verbal Communication Is Influenced by Culture and Gender

Cultures have different non-verbal languages as well as verbal ones. Fiorello LaGuardia, mayor of New York from 1933 to 1945, was fluent in English, Italian, and Yiddish. Researchers who watched films of his campaign speeches with the sound turned off found that they could tell which language he was speaking by the changes in his non-verbal behaviour (Birdwhistell, 1970).

Some kinds of non-verbal behaviour—called **emblems**—are culturally understood substitutes for verbal expressions. Nodding the head up and down is an accepted way of saying "yes" in many cultures. Likewise, a side-to-side head shake is a non-verbal way of saying "no," and a shrug of the shoulders is commonly understood as meaning "I do not know" or "I'm not sure." Remember, however, that some emblems—such as the thumbs-up gesture—vary from one culture to another (it means "good job!" in Canada, the number "1" in Germany, and the number "5" in Japan). Other non-verbal signs can be ambiguous even within a single culture. For example, a wink might mean something entirely different to the person on the receiving end than it does to the person winking (Lindsey and Vigil, 1999; Matsumoto and Hwang, 2013).

Despite differences like these, much non-verbal behaviour is universal. Certain expressions have the same meanings around the world. Smiles and laughter are a universal signal of positive emotions, for example, while the same sour expressions convey displeasure in every culture. Charles Darwin believed that expressions like these are the result of evolution, functioning as survival mechanisms that allowed early humans to convey emotional states before the development of language. The innateness of some facial expressions becomes even clearer when we examine the behaviour of children born deaf and blind (Eibl-Eibesfeldt, 1972). Despite a lack of social learning, these children display a broad range of expression. They smile, laugh, and cry in ways virtually identical to seeing and hearing infants.

While non-verbal expressions like these may be universal, the ways they are used varies widely around the world. In some cultures, the overt expression of feelings like happiness

or anger is discouraged. In other cultures, the same feelings are perfectly acceptable. Thus, a Japanese person might appear much more controlled and placid than an Arab, when in fact their feelings might be identical (Leathers, 1992). Summarizing studies on emotion recognition within and across cultures, Elfenbein and Ambady (2002a, 2002b) found that while emotions were universally recognized at better-than-chance levels, accuracy was higher when emotions were expressed and recognized by members of the same national, ethnic, or regional group, suggesting an in-group advantage. However, not all non-verbal behaviour is equally identifiable. In laboratory settings, subjects are better at identifying positive facial expressions, such as happiness, love, surprise, and interest, than negative ones, like fear, sadness, anger, and disgust (Druckmann et al., 1982). In real life, though, spontaneous non-verbal expressions are so ambiguous that observers are frequently unable to identify accurately what they mean (Elfenbein and Ambady, 2002a, 2002b; Motley, 1993).

Gender also affects non-verbal communication (Hall, 2006; Knapp and Hall, 2013). Generally, women are more expressive than men and better at interpreting non-verbal behaviour (Hall, 2006). Women's greater non-verbal expressiveness includes more eye contact, smiling, facial expressions, touching, head movements and gestures compared to men (Hall, 2006). Women have been found to better at remembering people's appearance and non-verbal cues, and at reading and interesting facial expressions, with the possible exception of male expressions of anger (Knapp and Hall, 2006). Generally, the differences between men and women's non-verbal communication skills are a matter of degree. There are many other factors that also influence people's

CHECK IT!

Describe the four characteristics of non-verbal communication.

abilities to express and interpret non-verbal behaviour. These include age, mental health, self-monitoring ability, personality factors, our moods and the context of the communication (Knapp and Hall, 2006).

Functions of Non-verbal Communication

Although we are dealing with non-verbal communication in this chapter, do not assume that people's words and actions are unrelated. Non-verbal communication interacts with verbal communication to express feelings, and relational messages, to modify a verbal message and to regulate the flow of our interactions with others. Let's take a look at the various relationships between our words and other types of expression.

Regulating 调节

Non-verbal **regulators** help control verbal interaction. The best example of such regulation is the wide array of turn-taking signals in everyday conversation (Drummond and Hopper, 1993; H.M. Rosenfeld, 1987). Research has shown there are three specific non-verbal signals that mean that a speaker has finished talking and is ready to yield to a listener:

1. a change in vocal intonation—a rising or falling in pitch at the end of a clause;
2. a drawl on the last syllable or the stressed syllable in a clause; and
3. a drop in vocal pitch or loudness when speaking a common expression such as "you know."

You can see how these regulators work by observing almost any conversation. Eye contact is another way of regulating verbal communication. Lack of visual contact is one way to signal turn taking or even to exclude an unwanted person from a conversation. Speakers make surprisingly little eye contact during a conversation, but they commonly focus on another person when coming to the end of their turn. Children (and some socially insensitive adults) have not learned all the subtle signals of such turn taking. Through trial and error, children learn how to "read" other people well enough to avoid interrupting.

Repeating 重复

First, non-verbal behaviour may repeat a verbal message. If someone asked you for directions to the nearest drugstore, you could say, "Go north about two blocks" and then repeat your instructions non-verbally by pointing north. This kind of repetition is especially useful when we're describing an idea with a visual element, such as size, shape, or direction. Repeating is so much a part of face-to-face interaction that many people regard it as a necessary part of communication (Kendon, 1994).

Substituting 替换

We can substitute non-verbal messages for verbal ones that we communicate. For instance, the more you know someone, the easier it is to use non-verbal expressions as a kind of shorthand to substitute for words. When you see a familiar friend wearing a certain facial expression, it is not necessary to ask, "What kind of day did you have?" In the same way, experience has probably shown you that certain kinds of looks, gestures, and other clues say, far better than words, "I'm angry at you" or "I feel great." Recall that emblems can replace words to convey a message. Within North American culture emblems such as a head nod, a head shake, and shoulder shrug can substitute for "yes," "no," and "I don't know" respectively.

Complementing and Accenting 重读

Whereas non-verbal emblems convey meaning independently of words, **illustrators** serve the functions of complementing and accenting verbal statements. Illustrators are actions that have no meaning of their own. Snapping your fingers, running your fingers through your hair, or pounding one fist into the other can accompany a positive statement in one instance and

REFLECTION

WISHING TEACHERS WOULD TAKE THE HINT

We students send non-verbal cues to our teachers all the time. When a class session is almost over, we start shifting in our seats, looking at the clock, and putting away our books. Sometimes it gets really loud, especially when we start zipping and unzipping our backpacks. Unfortunately, I know a few teachers who ignore us (and the clock) and just keep talking! I wish we could go back to having bells that signal the end of class. Now that's a regulator teachers can't ignore!

a negative one in others. The meaning of such gestures is specific to their context.

Emblems are used consciously; you roll your eyes and circle your finger around one ear to signal "he's crazy" in Canada or the US (in Argentina, it means you have a phone call). Illustrators are usually unconscious (Ekman et al., 1984). We rarely plan the smiles and frowns, sighs and laughs, and all the other non-verbal behaviours that so richly complement and accent our words.

© iStockPhoto/svetikd.

What non-verbal communication is taking place in this picture? How is that non-verbal communication functioning?

Contradicting 矛盾

Non-verbal behaviour can often *contradict* the spoken word. If you said, "Go north about two blocks," and pointed south, your non-verbal message would be contradicting what you said.

Although sending such incongruous messages might sound foolish at first, there are times when we deliberately do just this. One deliberate use of *mixed messages* (as they're often called) is to send, politely but clearly, a message that might be unacceptable if it were expressed in words. For instance, think of a time when you became bored with a conversation while your companion kept rambling on. At such a time, the most straightforward statement would be, "I'm tired of talking to you and want to go meet someone else." Although it might feel good to be so direct, this kind of honesty is inappropriate in anyone over five years of age. Instead of being blunt in situations like this, a face-saving alternative is to express your lack of interest non-verbally. While nodding politely and murmuring "uh-huh" and "no kidding?" at the appropriate times to indicate your "interest" in what's being said, you can signal a desire to leave by looking around the room, turning slightly away from the speaker, or even making a point of yawning. In most cases, such clues are enough to end the conversation without the awkwardness of expressing outright what you are thinking.

What happens when non-verbal behaviour contradicts the words we speak? In a variety of settings (including job interviews, therapy sessions, and first meetings), adults rely more on non-verbal messages than on words when interpreting the messages of others. Non-verbal cues are especially likely to carry weight when they contradict a speaker's words. In one series of experiments, friendly, neutral, and unfriendly verbal messages were paired with conflicting non-verbal behaviour (Argyle et al., 1971). Raters who judged the verbal and non-verbal messages separately found them equal in strength. But when the two messages were combined, the non-verbal statements carried as much as 12.5 times the weight of the verbal ones. This study shows that when verbal and non-verbal messages contradict each other we tend to believe the non-verbal.

Deception and Non-verbal Communication

Deception is an interesting facet of non-verbal communication, and one that social scientists have studied extensively. As we explained in detail in Chapter 2, people regularly send and receive messages that are not completely

TAKE TWO

The following are five functions of non-verbal communication:
1. Regulating verbal interactions (e.g., changing vocal intonation to signal that one is almost finished talking); regulators comprise a wide array of non-verbal turn-taking signals.
2. Repeating a verbal message (e.g., pointing when giving directions).
3. Substituting for a verbal message (e.g., nodding one's head); emblems are culturally understood substitutes for verbal messages.
4. Complementing or accenting a verbal message (e.g., snapping one's fingers); illustrators have no meaning on their own, but complement a verbal message.
5. Contradicting a verbal message (e.g., sending a mixed message by nodding, but also yawning).

truthful. Not all deception is self-serving or malicious: much of it is aimed at saving the face of the communicators involved. For example, you might tell a "benevolent lie" to avoid hurting the feelings of a friend who asks about a party you attended, but they were not invited to. You might say something like, "It was okay—a bit boring," when, in truth, you really had a great time. In a situation like this, it is easy to see how non-verbal factors can make the face-saving deception either succeed or fail.

Hiding Deceit

Some people are better at hiding deceit than others. Most people become more successful liars as they grow older and become more socially skilled (Feldman et al., 1999; Buller and Burgoon, 1994). High self-monitors are usually better at hiding their deception and detecting deception than their less self-aware peers (Bond and DePaulo, 2008; Burgoon et al., 1994), and raters judge highly expressive liars as more honest than those who are more subdued (Burgoon et al., 1995). People with power are much better at hiding the non-verbal cues that indicate lying than are people with less power (Carney, 2010). People who lie online are less likely to get caught than those who lie in face-to-face interactions (Giordano et al., 2007); however, people are much less likely to choose to lie in an email—probably because email provides a tangible record of their deceit (Hancock, 2007; Hancock, Thom-Santelli, and Ritchie, 2004). People tell the most lies during telephone conversations—perhaps because, unlike in email, there is no permanent record of the untruth and, unlike in face-to-face encounters, there are fewer non-verbal cues to give them away. The least lying occurs in email; lying rates in face-to-face exchanges and text messages are about equal (Hancock, 2007; Hancock, Thom-Santelli, and Ritchie, 2004). Not surprisingly, people whose jobs require them to act differently than they feel, such as actors, lawyers, diplomats, and salespeople, are more successful at deception than the general population (Riggio and Friedman, 1983).

Detecting Deceit

Decades of research have revealed that there are no reliable non-verbal clues that indicate deception (Aamodt and Custer, 2006). Nonetheless, there are some clues that may reveal less than totally honest mistakes in speaking (Andersen, 1999). Liars tend to be tenser and make a more negative impression when compared to truth tellers. They are more likely to experience involuntary shoulder shrugs and speak faster (Carney, 2010). In addition, they are more reserved, often use fewer illustrators, and tell less-compelling tales (DePaulo et al., 2003). For example, deceivers make more speech errors than truth tellers—stammers, stutters, hesitations, false starts, and so on. Vocal pitch often rises when people tell lies, and liars tend to hesitate more in speech (Rockwell et al., 1997; Vrij et al., 2000). Table 7.2 outlines some conditions under which liars are more likely to betray themselves non-verbally.

Table 7.2 ● Circumstances in Which a Deceiver Leaks Non-verbal Clues to Deception

Deception cues are more likely when the deceiver:
• wants to hide emotions being experienced at the moment;
• feels strongly about the information being hidden;
• feels apprehensive or guilty about the deception;
• gets little enjoyment from being deceptive;
• has not had time to rehearse the lie in advance; and/or
• knows there are severe punishments for being caught.

SOURCE: Based on material from P. Ekman (2009), *Telling lies: Clues to deceit in the marketplace, politics and marriage*, 4th edn. New York: W.W. Norton.

Despite clues like these, people's effectiveness in uncovering deceptive messages is generally not much better than chance (Bond and DePaulo, 2006; Vrij, 2000). In general, there are three methods for detecting lies: The first focuses on non-verbal behaviours, such as vocal qualities, facial expressions, posture, and so on. The second involves the use of equipment, such as lie detectors, to monitor physiological responses, and the third involves analyzing the content of what is said (Hancock, Curry et al., 2004). While each method can often distinguish between people telling the truth and those who are lying, no method is consistently reliable. Even when people are warned that one or more subjects may be lying, they cannot consistently identify liars (George et al., 2008). There is debate about whether or not expertise in the detection of deception can be enhanced by specific training (Masip et al., 2009; Porter and Brinke, 2010; Vrij et al., 2010). This type of training has been conducted most often with people working in the law-enforcement system, such as police officers (Hartwig et al., 2006), but even after having been trained, few people can accurately and

Not everyone's nose grows when they're being deceitful. What are some ways we can detect deceit?

consistently detect lies. People vary in their credibility both when they are telling the truth and when they are lying, and it appears that it is the liar's credibility, more than any other factor, that influences the accuracy of our judgments (Bond and DePaulo, 2008).

The bottom line is that non-verbal cues offer important information for detecting deception, but most lies cannot be detected through snap judgments of facial expressions or shifts in posture. Instead, people who suspect a lie tend to collect a variety of clues (including information from third parties as well as physical evidence) over a period of days, weeks, or even longer (Park et al., 2002). Jumping to conclusions based on limited information is not a wise way to react to first communications with a person, and it may lead to relational difficulties. Handle the material we present here about detecting deception with care and good judgment.

Types of Non-verbal Communication

So far, we have talked about the characteristics of non-verbal communication and the ways unspoken messages relate to our use of words. Now, it is time to look at the many types of non-verbal communication.

Face and Eyes

The face and eyes are probably the most noticeable parts of the body, but the non-verbal messages from the face and eyes are not the easiest to read. The face is a tremendously complicated channel of expression to interpret, for several reasons.

First, it is hard to describe the number and kind of expressions commonly produced by the face and eyes. For example, researchers have found that there are at least 8 distinguishable positions of the eyebrows and forehead, eight more of the eyes and lids, and 10 for the lower face (Ekman and Friesen, 1974a, 1975). When you multiply this complexity by the number of emotions we experience, you can see why it would be almost impossible to compile a dictionary of facial expressions and their corresponding emotions.

The eyes themselves can send several kinds of messages. Gazing and glancing are usually signals of the looker's interest. However, the *type* of interest can vary. Sometimes, as we mentioned earlier, looking is a conversational turn-taking signal that says, "I'm finished talking. Now it's your turn." Gazing also is a good indicator of liking (Druckmann et al., 1982). Sometimes, eye contact *reflects* liking that already exists, and at other times, it actually creates or *increases* liking—hence the expression "making eyes." In other situations, eye contact indicates interest, but not attraction or approval, such as when a teacher glares at a rowdy student or a police officer "keeps an eye on" a suspect.

© thefinalmiracle/iStockphoto.

The face and eyes are probably the most noticeable parts of the body, but the non-verbal messages from the face and eyes are not the easiest to read. What are some of the reasons for this?

In addition to influencing verbal responses, research by Stephen Davis and Jamie Kieffer (1998) has found at least one effect of eye contact that influences a particular kind of non-verbal behaviour: tipping in restaurants. Davis and Kieffer discovered that customers, in both small towns and large urban centres, leave bigger tips when their servers (whether male or female) maintain eye contact with them. The authors speculate that good eye contact makes the atmosphere of a restaurant friendlier and allows customers to feel as if they are dining at home.

Patterns of eye contact are very much influenced by culture. In many Asian and Canadian First Nations cultures, and some Caribbean ones, direct eye contact between persons of different status is prohibited. If a person of lower status looks a superior in the eye, it is a sign of disrespect. Imagine how this cultural expectation can cause miscommunication in an elementary school classroom, where the teacher demands eye contact while reprimanding a child ("Look at me when I am talking to you!"), but the child avoids looking the teacher in the eye in order to show respect for the authority figure.

Body Movement

Another way we communicate non-verbally is through the physical movement of our bodies—our posture, gestures, physical orientation to others, and so on. Social scientists use the term **kinesics** to describe the study of how people communicate through bodily movements.

Some social scientists claim that a language of gestures was the first form of human communication, preceding speech by tens of thousands of years (Corballis, 2002). To appreciate the communicative value of kinesics messages, stop reading for a moment and notice how you are sitting. What does your position say non-verbally about how you feel? Are there any other people near you now? What messages do you get from their present posture? By paying attention to the posture of those

around you, as well as to your own, you will find another channel of non-verbal communication that reveals how people feel about themselves and others.

The English language reveals the deep links between posture and communication. English is full of expressions that tie emotional states with body postures:

> "I won't take this lying down!"
>
> "Stand on your own two feet."
>
> "You're all wrapped up in yourself."
>
> "Don't be so uptight!"

Phrases like these show an awareness of posture, even if it is often unconscious. The main reason we miss most posture messages is that they are not very obvious. In daily life, people who feel weighed down by a problem seldom hunch over dramatically. When we're bored, we don't usually lean back or slump enough to embarrass the person with whom we're bored. In interpreting posture, then, the key is to look for small changes that might be shadows of the way people feel.

Gestures are a fundamental element of communication—so fundamental, in fact, that even people who have been blind from birth use them (Iverson, 1999; Iverson and Goldin-Meadow, 1997). Gestures are sometimes intentional—for example, a cheery wave or thumbs-up. In other cases, however, they are unconscious. Occasionally, an unconscious gesture will consist of an unambiguous emblem, such as a shrug that clearly means "I do not know." More often, however, there are several possible interpretations to gestures. A group of ambiguous gestures consists of what we usually call *fidgeting*—movements in which one part of the body grooms, massages, rubs, holds, pinches, picks, or otherwise manipulates another part. Social scientists call these actions **manipulators**. Social rules may discourage us from performing more manipulators in public, but people still do so without noticing.

Research reveals what common sense suggests—that an increased use of manipulators is often a sign of discomfort (Ekman and Friesen, 1974b). But not *all* fidgeting signals uneasiness. People also are likely to use manipulators when relaxed; when they let their guard down (either alone or with friends), they will be more likely to fiddle with an earlobe, twirl a strand of hair, or clean their fingernails.

The amount and type of gesturing a person does can be a measure of power and status (Andersen, 1999). For example, people who gesture more are rated by observers as being in positions of control and power, whereas those who gesture less are judged by observers as being subordinate. And pointing is judged by observers as one indicator of power, since it implies at least some ability to order other people around.

Gestures can produce a wide range of reactions in receivers (Druckmann et al., 1982). In many situations, the right kinds of gestures can increase persuasiveness. Making more hand and arm movements, leaning forward, fidgeting less, and keeping one's limbs open all make a speaker more effective at influencing others (Leathers, 1992). Even more interesting is the fact that persuasiveness increases when one person mirrors another's movements. When the persuader and the audience are reasonably similar, reciprocating the other person's gestures has a positive effect, whereas acting in a contrary manner is likely to have the opposite result.

People who gesture appropriately often create impressions that differ from those of less-expressive people. They are rated as being warmer, more casual, agreeable, and energetic. They also are viewed as more enthusiastic, considerate, approachable, and likeable.

© iStockPhoto/Jason Lugo.

People who gesture appropriately often create impressions that differ from those of less-expressive people. They are rated as being warmer and more casual, agreeable, and energetic. They also are viewed as more enthusiastic, considerate, approachable, and likeable. How expressive do you think you are?

On the other hand, less expressive people are viewed as more logical, cold, and analytical. Not only are they less persuasive, but they are also viewed as less likeable in general.

As with almost any non-verbal behaviour, the context in which gestures occur makes all the difference in the results they produce. Animated movements that are well received in a co-operative social setting may seem like signals of aggression or attempts at domination in a more competitive setting. Fidgeting that might suggest deviousness in a bargaining session could be appropriate when you offer a nervous apology in a personal situation. In any case, trying to manufacture insincere, artificial gestures (or any other non-verbal behaviour)

TAKE TWO

- **Kinesics:** the study of how people communicate through body movements.
- **Manipulators:** movements in which one part of the body grooms, massages, rubs, holds, pinches, picks, or otherwise manipulates another part.

will probably backfire. A more useful goal is to recognize the behaviour you find yourself spontaneously delivering and to consider how it expresses the attitudes you already feel.

Touch

Social scientists use the term **haptics** to describe communication involving touch. Interpersonal touch is a powerful way to communicate our feelings and it plays an important role in our emotional well-being (Gallace and Spence, 2010). Contemporary research confirms the value of touch for infants (Feldman et al., 2010; Whitman et al., 1999; Underdown et al., 2010). Infant massage has been shown to help premature babies grow faster and gain more weight, and help healthy infants in their sleep patterns, responses to stress, and formation of positive relationships with their parents (Adler, 1993; Feldman et al., 2010; Underdown et al., 2010). Massage helps newborn babies thrive, and it also helps depressed mothers of newborns feel better and facilitate the delivery process (Mwakalyelye and DeAngelis, 1995). Massage can also boost the immune function of cancer and HIV patients. In addition to *being* touched, studies have found that touching soft things (i.e., soft grip pen, teddy bear) can reassure people in times of uncertainty or social exclusion (Tai et al., 2011; Van Horen and Mussweiler, 2014).

Touch also plays a large part in how we respond to others. For instance, in a laboratory task, subjects evaluated partners more positively when they were touched (appropriately, of course) by them (Burgoon et al., 1992). Besides increasing likeability, touch also boosts compliance. In a study by Chris Kleinke (1977), subjects were approached by an undercover researcher who asked them to return a coin she had left in the phone booth they had just used. When the request was accompanied by a light touch on the subject's arm, the subject was significantly more likely to return the coin. In a similar experiment (Willis and Hamm, 1980), subjects were asked by researchers either to sign a petition or complete a rating scale. Again, subjects were more likely to co-operate when they were touched lightly on the arm. In the rating-scale variation of the study, the results were especially dramatic: 70 per cent of those who were touched complied, whereas only 40 per cent of the untouched subjects were willing to co-operate.

Arguing that these small solicitations hardly get at the power of touch, Gueguen and Fischer-Lokou (2002) conducted an experiment in which researchers asked sidewalk passersby to look after a large and very excited dog for 10 minutes so the owner could go into a pharmacy where animals were prohibited. In half of the cases, the passersby were touched during the request. When touched, 55 per cent agreed with the request, whereas only 35 per cent of those who were not touched agreed. The results confirmed that touch has a large effect on compliance.

Touch seems to have a powerful effect on decision making in the world of business and finance too. For instance, when business students received a pat on the back or shoulder from a female experimenter they were more likely than their peers who were not touched to make a riskier financial investment (Levav and Argo, 2010). The same pat on the back or shoulder by a male experimenter did not lead to riskier investments.

An additional power of touch is its on-the-job utility. One study showed that fleeting touches on the hand and shoulder resulted in larger tips for restaurant waiters (Crusco and Wetzel, 1984). In addition, both women and men in pubs and taverns, whether in same-sex or opposite-sex dyads, drink more alcohol if they are touched by the server (Kaufman and Mahoney, 1999).

In contemporary society, unwanted touching is cause for concern, and even legal action. In North America, touching is generally more appropriate for women than for men (Derlega et al., 1989; Jones, 1986). Males touch their male friends less than they touch their female friends, and also less than females touch their female friends. Although women

Touch is a powerful form of communication. Next time you touch or are touched by someone, think about how the touch is part of the communication.

are generally more comfortable about touching than men, sex is not the only factor that shapes contact. In general, the degree of touch comfort goes along with openness to expressing intimate feelings, an active interpersonal style, and satisfactory relationships (Fromme et al., 1989). Culture also plays a role in same-sex and opposite-sex touching. For example, Saudi businessmen often hold hands as a sign of trust—a kind of touching that might easily be misinterpreted by North Americans. In contrast, Saudi women are never to be touched in public (Remland et al., 1995).

There is considerable variation around the world in the amount of touch viewed as appropriate. Canada is regarded as a moderate touch culture. Most Asian cultures are considered non-contact cultures, whereas many South and Central American cultures, and southern European cultures, are viewed as contact cultures (Hall, 1963).

Voice

Social scientists use the term **paralanguage** to describe the way a message is spoken. Vocal rate, pitch, tone, volume, and so on can give the same word or phrase many meanings. For example, note how many meanings come from a single sentence just by shifting the emphasis from one word to another:

This is a fantastic communication book.
(Not just any book, but *this* one in particular.)

This is a *fantastic* communication book.
(This book is superior, exciting.)

This is a fantastic *communication* book.
(The book is good as far as the study of communication goes, but it may not be as great as a work of literature.)

This is a fantastic communication *book*.
(It's not a play or a movie; it's a book.)

Along with tone, speed, pitch, and volume, paralanguage includes length of pauses and **disfluencies** (such as stammering and the use of *uh*, *um*, and *er*). All these factors can do a great deal to reinforce or contradict the messages that words convey.

The effect of paralinguistic cues is strong. In fact, listeners pay more attention to paralanguage than to the content of the words when asked to determine a speaker's attitudes (Burns and Beier, 1973). Furthermore, when vocal factors contradict a verbal message (as when a speaker shouts, "I am *not* angry!"), listeners tend to judge the speaker's intention from the paralanguage, not the words themselves (Mehrabian and Weiner, 1967). Vocal changes that contradict spoken words are not easy to conceal. If the speaker is trying to hide fear or anger, the voice will probably sound higher and louder, and the rate of talk may be faster than normal. Sadness produces the opposite vocal pattern: quieter, lower-pitched speech delivered at a slower rate (Ekman, 1985).

Paralanguage can affect behaviour in many ways, some of which are rather surprising. Studies by David Buller and Kelly Aune (1988, 1992) reveal that communicators are most likely to comply with requests delivered by speakers whose rate is similar to their own. However, speaking rate is not constant. For example, it changes when a speaker's first message does not seem to get the desired results. Charles Berger and Patrick diBattista (1993) discovered that when communicators gave directions that weren't followed, the wording of their second attempts didn't change significantly. Instead, they simply slowed down and spoke more loudly.

Sarcasm is one approach in which we use both emphasis and tone of voice to change the meaning of a statement to the opposite of its verbal message. Experience this reversal yourself with the following three statements. First say them literally, and then say them sarcastically.

"You look terrific!"

"I really had a wonderful time on my blind date."

"There's nothing I like better than calves' brains on toast."

As with other non-verbal messages, people often ignore or misinterpret the vocal nuances of sarcasm. Members of certain groups—children, people with weak intellectual skills, poor listeners, and people with certain forms of brain damage—are more likely to misunderstand sarcastic messages than are others (Andersen, 1991; Dennis et al., 2001; Shamay et al., 2002). Experiments by J. Bruce Morton and Sandra Trehub (2001) reveal that children interpret mixed messages in ways very different from adults. When youngsters aged four to eight were presented with positive statements (such as "Dad gave me a new bike for my

birthday") delivered in a sad tone of voice, they gauged the speaker as happy because they paid attention to the words rather than the vocal cues. When a negative statement was read in an upbeat tone, children interpreted the message as negative—again, relying more on the content than the paralanguage. There was a direct relationship between age and sensitivity to non-verbal cues, with the youngest children relying most heavily on the words spoken. This study helps us appreciate the often taken-for-granted importance of non-verbal cues. It also serves as a reminder that communication with children may require different approaches than those that work with adults.

Communication through paralanguage is not always intentional. Our voices often give us away when we're trying to create an impression different from our actual feelings. You have probably had the experience of trying to sound calm and serene when you were really shaking with inner nervousness. Maybe your deception succeeded for a while—just the right smile, no telltale fidgeting of the hands, posture appearing relaxed—and then, without being able to do a thing about it, right in the middle of your relaxed comments, your voice squeaked! The charade was over.

In addition to reinforcing or contradicting messages, some vocal factors influence the way a speaker is perceived by others (Castelan-Cargile and Bradac, 2001). For example, people who speak more slowly are judged as having greater conversational control than fast talkers (Tusing and Dillard, 2000), and people who judge a speaker's speech rate as similar to their own perceive the speaker as more competent and socially attractive than when the rate is different (Feldstein et al., 2001). Communicators with more attractive voices are rated higher than those whose speech sounds less attractive (Francis and Wales, 1994; Zuckerman and Driver, 1989). Just what makes a voice attractive can vary. As Figure 7.1 shows, culture can make a difference. Surveys have found that there are similarities *and* differences between what Mexicans and Americans

IDEAL MEXICAN SPEAKER'S VOICE

Medium in pitch
Medium in rate
Loud in volume

Clear enunciation
Well-modulated
Without regional accent
Cheerful

Firm
Low in pitch
Somewhat slow, with pauses

IDEAL AMERICAN SPEAKER'S VOICE

Figure 7.1 ● A Comparison of the Ideal Speaker's Voice Types in Mexico and the United States

SOURCE: Reproduced from C.A. Valentine and B. Saint Damian (1988), *Communicative power: Gender and culture as determinants of the ideal voice* (p. 54) in C.A. Valentine and N. Hoar (eds), *Women and communicative power: Theory, research, and practice.* Washington, DC: National Communication Association. Reprinted with permission from the National Communication Association. All rights reserved.

view as the "ideal" voice. Howard Giles, Anthony Mulac, and their associates (1992) found that age combines with accent to form preferences by listeners. Older-sounding communicators whose language was accent-free were rated as being most competent, while older-sounding people who did not speak in a culturally standard way were judged as being least competent.

Distance

Proxemics is the study of how people use the space around them. Each of us carries around a sort of invisible bubble of **personal space** wherever we go. We think of the area inside this bubble as our own—almost as much a part of us as our own bodies. Our personal bubbles vary in size according to the culture in which we were raised, the person we're with,

Paralanguage: the way a message is spoken. The speaker's mode of delivery is governed by vocal rate, pitch, tone, volume, pauses, and disfluencies (e.g., stammering, use of *um, er*, etc.).

as well as the situation. The varying size of our personal space—the distance we put between ourselves and others—gives a non-verbal clue to our feelings (Sommer, 2002).

D. Russell Crane (1987) and other researchers tested more than 100 married couples, asking partners to walk toward one another and stop when they reached a "comfortable conversational distance." Then, they gave each partner a battery of tests to measure their marital intimacy, desire for change, and potential for divorce. The researchers discovered that there was a strong relationship between distance and marital happiness. The average space between distressed couples was about 25 per cent greater than that between satisfied partners. On average, the happy couples stood 28.5 centimetres apart, while

© iStockPhoto/Geber86.

Our personal space differs depending on our relationship with the other person as well as cultural norms. Think about this the next time you're comfortable being close to another person, or uncomfortable being close to another. How far apart are you in those interactions?

the distance between unhappy spouses averaged 37 centimetres.

Preferred spaces are largely a matter of cultural norms. In hyper-dense Hong Kong, people manage to live in crowded residential quarters that most North Americans would find intolerable (Chan, 1999). The distance between communicators during a conversation is very much influenced by culture. Looking at the distances that North American communicators use in everyday interaction, Edward T. Hall (1969) developed a "theory of proxemics." This theory identifies four specific distances—beginning with skin contact and ranging out to about 45 centimetres—each reflecting a different way we feel toward others at a given time. By "reading" which distance people select, we can get some insight into their feelings.

Intimate Distance

The first of Hall's four zones, **intimate distance**, begins with skin contact. We usually use this intimate distance with people who are emotionally close to us, and then mostly in private situations—making love, caressing, comforting, protecting. By allowing people to move into our intimate distance, we let them enter our personal space. When we let them in voluntarily, it is usually a sign of trust: we have willingly lowered our defences. On the other hand, when someone invades this most personal area without our consent, we usually feel threatened.

Personal Distance

The second spatial zone, **personal distance**, ranges from 45 centimetres at its closest point to 1.2 metres at its farthest. Its closer end of the range is the distance at which most couples stand in public. If at a party, a third person stands that close, the other person is likely to become alert. This "moving in" often is taken to mean that something more than casual conversation is taking place. The far end of the personal distance range (from roughly 0.75 m to 1.2 m) is the area just beyond the other person's reach. As Hall puts it, at this distance,

we can keep someone "at arm's length." His choice of words suggests the type of communication that goes on at this range: the contacts are still reasonably close, but they're much less personal than the ones that occur 30 centimetres or so closer.

Social Distance

The third zone is **social distance**. It ranges from 1.2 metres to about 3 metres at the outside. Within this zone, the distance between communicators can have a powerful effect on how we regard and respond to others. For example, students are more satisfied with teachers who reduce (at appropriate levels, of course) the distance between themselves and their classes. They also are more satisfied with the course itself and are more likely to follow the teacher's instructions (Hackman and Walker, 1990). Likewise, medical patients are more satisfied with doctors who use close physical proximity to convey warmth and concern (Conlee et al., 1993; Grant et al., 2000).

Public Distance

Public distance is Hall's term for the farthest zone, running outward from 3 metres. The closer range of public distance is the one that most teachers use in the classroom. In the farther reaches of public space—7.5 metres and beyond—two-way communication is almost impossible. Sometimes, speakers must use public distance to reach a large audience, but we can assume that anyone who chooses to use it when more closeness is possible is not interested in a dialogue.

When our spatial bubble is invaded, we usually experience stress and respond with **barrier behaviours**: strategies designed to create a barrier (or fix a broken one) between ourselves and other people (Kanaga and Flynn, 1981). Invade someone's personal space, and notice the reaction. At first, the person is most likely to simply back away, probably without realizing what is happening. Next, your partner might attempt to put an object between you, such as a desk, a chair, or some books clutched to the chest, all in an effort to get some separation. Then, the other person will probably decrease eye contact (the "elevator syndrome," in which we can crowd in and even touch one another so long as we avoid eye contact). Furthermore, your reluctant partner might sneeze, cough, scratch, and exhibit various gestures to discourage your anti-social behaviour. In the end, if none of these actions achieves the desired goal of getting some space between the two of you, the other person might leave or "counterattack," gently at first ("Will you move back, please?"), then more forcefully (probably with a shove).

Territoriality

While personal space is the invisible bubble we carry around, the area that serves as an extension of our physical being, **territory** remains stationary (Hidalgo and Hernandez, 2001). To lay claim a piece of territory requires that you mark it with your ownership, such as an OCCUPIED sign on an airplane seat, a coat over the back of a chair in a restaurant, or books on a desk in the library. Sometimes, people formally mark their territory with a name or some representative symbol, such as a sign in a personal parking space. Similarly, a fence may separate your property from your neighbour's, and a closed door clearly separates your room from the rest of the residence.

Robert Sommer (1969) watched students in a college library and found that there is a definite pattern for people who want to study alone. When the library was not crowded, students almost always chose corner seats at one of the empty rectangular tables. After each table was occupied by one reader, new readers would choose a seat on the opposite side and at the far end, thus keeping the maximum distance between themselves and the other readers. One of Sommer's associates tried breaking these "rules" by sitting next to and across from other female readers even though distant seats were available. She found that the women reacted defensively, signalling their discomfort through shifts in posture, by gesturing, or by moving away.

How you respond to such a manoeuvre depends on *who* enters and uses your territory (a friend is less threatening than a stranger); *why* she or he enters or uses it (for instance, a "mistake" is less important than a "planned attack"); *what* territory is entered or used (you may care more about a territory over which you have exclusive rights, such as your bedroom, than about a territory in a public area, such as your seat in class); and *how* it is entered or used (an invasion is more threatening than a violation). Generally, we grant people with higher status more personal territory and greater privacy. We knock before entering our supervisor's office, whereas the supervisor can usually walk into our work area without hesitating.

Time

Social scientists use the term **chronemics** to describe the study of how humans use and structure time. The way we handle time can

- **Personal space:** the invisible bubble of space we consider as our own; it varies in size according to the person we're with, the culture in which we were raised, and the situation at hand.
- **Intimate distance:** the first of Hall's spatial distances, skin contact to about 45 cm.
- **Personal distance:** the second of Hall's spatial distances, 45 cm to 1.2 m.
- **Social distance:** the third of Hall's spatial distances, 1.2 m to 3 m.
- **Public distance:** the fourth of Hall's spatial distances, 7.5 m and beyond.
- **Barrier behaviours:** strategies to create or fix a barrier between ourselves and other people (e.g., avoiding eye contact).

express both intentional and unintentional messages. Social psychologist Robert Levine (1988) describes several ways that time can communicate. For instance, in cultures like those of Canada, the United States, and northern Europe, which highly value time, waiting can be an indicator of status. "Important" people (whose time is supposedly more valuable than others) may be seen by appointment only, while it is acceptable to intrude without notice on lesser beings. To see how this rule operates, consider how natural it is for a boss to drop into a subordinate's office unannounced, while the employee would never intrude into the boss's office without an appointment. A related rule is that low-status people must never make more important people wait. It would be a serious mistake to be late for a job interview, although the interviewer may keep you cooling your heels in the lobby.

The use of time depends greatly on culture. In some cultures, punctuality is critically important, but in others it is barely considered (Arman and Adir, 2012; Levine and Norenzayan, 1999). Punctual Canadians often report welcoming the easygoing approach to time that is characteristic of many Caribbean countries. One psychologist discovered the difference between North and South American attitudes when he was teaching at a university in Brazil (Levine, 1988). He found that some students arrived halfway through a two-hour class and that most of them stayed and kept asking questions when the class was scheduled to end. Half an hour after the official end of the period, the professor finally closed off discussion, since there was no indication that the students intended to leave. This flexibility of time is quite different from what is common in most North American colleges and universities.

Even within a culture, rules of time vary. Consider your own experience. In school, some instructors begin and end class punctually, while others are more casual. With some people, you feel comfortable talking for hours in person or on the phone, while with others, time seems precious and not to be "wasted."

Physical Attractiveness

The importance of beauty has been emphasized in the arts for centuries. More recently, social scientists have begun to measure the degree to which physical attractiveness affects interaction between people. Findings, summarized by Knapp and Hall (2013), indicate that women who are perceived as attractive have more dates, receive higher grades in college (or university), persuade males with greater ease, and receive lighter court sentences. Both men and women whom others view as attractive are rated as being more sensitive, kind, strong, sociable, and interesting than their less-fortunate brothers and sisters.

The influence of attractiveness begins early in life (Dion et al., 1972). In one study, preschoolers were shown photographs of children their own age and asked to choose potential friends and enemies. The researchers found that children as young as three agreed as to who was attractive ("cute") and unattractive ("homely"). Furthermore, they valued their attractive counterparts—both of the same and the opposite sex—more highly. Also, preschool children rated by their peers as attractive were most liked, and those identified as least attractive were least liked. Children who were interviewed rated good-looking children as having positive social characteristics ("He's friendly to other children") and unattractive children negatively ("He hits other children without reason").

Teachers also are affected by students' attractiveness. Vicki Ritts and her colleagues (1992) found that physically attractive students are usually judged to be more intelligent, friendly, and popular. Even the parents of attractive students benefit from their children's good looks: they are judged by strangers as caring more about education than are parents of less attractive youngsters.

Fortunately, attractiveness is something we can control without having to call the plastic surgeon. We view others as beautiful or ugly, not just on the basis of the "original equipment" they come with, but also on *how they*

Focus on RESEARCH

COMMUNICATION ENHANCES PHYSICAL ATTRACTIVENESS

How can you make yourself more physically attractive to a romantic partner? Most of us think of ways to change our appearance such as a new hairstyle or wardrobe and trips to the gym. Kelly F. Albada, a communication professor, and her associates have explored a different approach, which they have labelled Interaction Appearance Theory (IAT). IAT predicts that rewarding interactions with a partner will make him or her see you as more physically attractive (Albada, Knapp, and Theune, 2002).

Albada and her colleagues collected data to test IAT in three different ways:

1. a series of interviews with people in romantic relationships;
2. a survey of college students in newly formed dating relationships; and
3. an analysis of diaries kept by romantic partners.

Time and again, the researchers found support for the notion that partners find one another more physically attractive as they communicate with one another in positive ways, such as offering compliments, expressing affection, and buying gifts. Here is how one man in the study recounts the shift in his appraisal of the woman he eventually married:

Initially, I saw her as pretty average in physical attractiveness . . . But after we dated and I fully appreciated how well we related to each other, I saw her as much more physically attractive. I actually saw her differently. Now, I can't see her as any less physically attractive.

Interaction appearance theory suggests that physical attractiveness is not a static property of an individual; instead, it is a perception that can be enhanced through good communication skills.

Critical thinking: *Do you have anecdotal evidence from your own life to support or refute Interaction Appearance Theory? Have people you initially perceived as physically attractive lost some of their appeal due to their poor communication skills?*

use that equipment. Posture, gestures, facial expressions, and other behaviours can increase the attractiveness of a seemingly unremarkable person. Exercise can improve the way each of us looks. In addition, attractiveness is at least partly in the mind of the beholder. Some evidence suggests that, as we get to know more about people and begin to like them, we start to regard them as better looking (Bazil, 1999; Swami et al, 2010). (See the accompanying "Focus on Research" box for further evidence of this phenomenon.) Finally, our style of dress can make a significant difference in the way others perceive us.

Clothing

Besides protecting us from the elements, clothing is a tool of non-verbal communication. One writer has suggested that clothing conveys at least 10 types of messages to others (Thourlby, 1978) including:

1. economic level,
2. educational level,
3. trustworthiness,
4. social position,
5. level of sophistication,
6. economic background,
7. social background,
8. educational background,
9. level of success, and
10. moral character.

We do make assumptions about people on the basis of their style of clothing. For example, the way people are dressed affects judgments of their credibility. In one experiment, college students judged victims of sexual harassment

Focus on RESEARCH

DESIGNER KNOCKOFFS AND THE COUNTERFEIT SELF

Have you ever wondered whether wearing counterfeit products has any effect on people's behaviour and their self-perceptions? Most of us probably haven't thought too much about these things, but researchers Francesca Gino, Michael Norton, and Dan Ariely have. Gino and her colleagues (2010) randomly assigned female students to one of two groups to perform a series of very difficult puzzles while wearing sunglasses. The first group believed they were wearing authentic designer sunglasses, while the second group believed the sunglasses they wore were designer knockoffs. Actually, all participants wore authentic designer sunglasses while completing the puzzles. The participants were told they would be rewarded for the number of puzzles they solved and that the investigators were using an honour system—participants would tally up their own scores and submit them. In fact, the experimenters tracked the number of puzzles each participant solved and the number each claimed to have solved. As predicted, participants lied about their performance, reporting more solved puzzles than they actually completed. The surprising finding was that significantly more participants in the "fake sunglasses" group cheated (71 per cent) compared to the participants in the "authentic sunglasses" group (30 per cent). In a second study these investigators found that female participants wearing what they believed to be fake sunglasses were also more cynical in their ratings of people they knew than were participants knowingly wearing authentic sunglasses. The "fake sunglasses" participants rated people they knew as more dishonest. Finally, after they had completed the puzzles, participants in these two groups, and a third group not wearing sunglasses, were asked to complete a survey that measured the extent to which they felt alienated from their authentic selves (e.g., "Right now I feel out of touch with the real me"). These investigators found that the women who thought they were wearing fake designer sunglasses felt significantly less authentic compared to both women not wearing sunglasses at all and those knowingly wearing authentic designer sunglasses. Francesca Gino and her colleagues conclude that there are negative consequences of wearing designer knock-offs, including a greater likelihood of behaving dishonestly, seeing others more cynically, and feeling less true to ourselves.

Critical thinking: *These researchers used only female participants in their study, because previous research had suggested that women care more than men about brand-name fashion products, and that women have more interest in fashion. What implications might these assumptions have for their research?*

© Zoe Waelchli.

Clothing, personal space, and body language communicate a lot about us. Look at what you're wearing and how you're sitting right now. What does it communicate about yourself?

differently depending on their attire. Victims dressed in black were rated as less honest and more aggressive than those dressed in light colours (Vrij and Akehurst, 1999). Not surprisingly, the perception of a woman's sexual intent increased when she wore more revealing clothes, although this effect was greater for men in the study (Koukounas and Letch, 2001). In another study, a man and a woman were stationed in a hallway so that anyone who wished to go by had to avoid them or pass between them. In one condition, the conversationalists wore "formal daytime dress"; in the other, they wore "casual attire." Passersby behaved differently toward the couple, depending on the style of clothing.

Self-Assessment

Below is a series of statements regarding inter-cultural communication. There are no right or wrong answers. Imagine yourself interacting with people from a wide variety of cultural groups, not just one or two. Record your first impression of the following statement by indicating the degree to which you agree or disagree, using the following scale.

5 = strongly agree
4 = agree
3 = uncertain
2 = disagree
1 = strongly disagree

_____ 1. I enjoy interacting with people from different cultures.

_____ 2. I think people from other cultures are narrow-minded.

_____ 3. I am pretty sure of myself in interacting with people from different cultures.

_____ 4. I find it very hard to talk in front of people from different cultures.

_____ 5. I always know what to say when interacting with people from different cultures.

_____ 6. I can be as sociable as I want to be when interacting with people from different cultures.

_____ 7. I don't like to be with people from different cultures.

_____ 8. I respect the values of people from different cultures.

_____ 9. I get upset easily when interacting with people from different cultures.

_____ 10. I feel confident when interacting with people from different cultures.

_____ 11. I tend to wait before forming an impression of culturally distinct counterparts.

_____ 12. I often get discouraged when I am with people from different cultures.

_____ 13. I am open-minded to people from different cultures.

_____ 14. I am very observant when interacting with people from different cultures.

_____ 15. I often feel useless when interacting with people from different cultures.

_____ 16. I respect the ways people from different cultures behave.

_____ 17. I try to obtain as much information as I can when interacting with people from different cultures.

_____ 18. I would not accept the opinions of people from different cultures.

_____ 19. I am sensitive to my culturally distinct counterpart's subtle meanings during our interaction.

_____ 20. I think my culture is better than other cultures.

_____ 21. I often give positive responses to my culturally different counterpart during our interaction.

_____ 22. I avoid those situations where I will have to deal with culturally distinct persons.

_____ 23. I often show my culturally distinct counterpart my understanding through verbal or non-verbal cues.

_____ 24. I have a feeling of enjoyment toward differences between my culturally distinct counterpart and me.

To determine your score, begin by reverse-scoring (i.e., 5 = 1, 4 = 2, 3 = 3, 2 = 4, and 1 = 5) items 2, 4, 7, 9, 12, 15, 18, 20, and 22.

Sum items 1, 11, 13, 21, 22, 23, and 24 = _____ Interaction Engagement (range is 7–35)

Sum items 2, 7, 8, 16, 18, and 20 = _____ Respect for Cultural Differences (6–30)

Sum items 3, 4, 5, 6, and 10 = _____ Interaction Confidence (5–25)

Sum items 9, 12, and 15 = _____ Interaction Enjoyment (3–15)

Sum items 14, 17, and 19 = _____ Interaction Attentiveness (3–15)

Sum of all the items = _____ (24–120, with a midpoint of 48)

Higher scores on the total instrument and each of the five sub-scales indicate a greater probability of intercultural communication competence.

SOURCE: G.M. Chen and W.J. Starosta (2000). "The development and validation of the Intercultural Sensitivity Scale," *Human Communication*, 3, 1–14. Permission to use courtesy of *Guo-Ming Chen Human Communication: A Journal of the Pacific and Asian Communication Association*.

They responded positively to the well-dressed couple and showed more annoyance when the same people were casually dressed (Fortenberry et al., 1978).

Attire makes a difference in the classroom, too. College students' perceptions of expertise decreases if their graduate teaching assistant's attire becomes more casual. On the other hand, teaching assistants who dress casually are seen as more interesting, extroverted, and sociable than those who dress more formally (Morris et al., 1996; Roach, 1997). Finally, there is fascinating research regarding the effects of wearing designer knock-off clothing and accessories. Students who believed they were wearing counterfeit sunglasses were more likely to behave unethically than their peers who were given authentic designer apparel (Gino et al., 2010). See the "Focus on Research" box for details about how our clothing decisions affect our sense of self and our behaviour.

Like all our perceptions based on appearances, judgments of others based on their clothing choices need to be made carefully and put into the larger context of what we know about the subjectivity and biases inherent in human perception.

Physical Environment

We conclude our discussion of non-verbal communication by examining how physical settings, architecture, and interior design affect communication. Begin by remembering the different homes you have visited lately. Were some of them more comfortable to be in than others? Certainly, a lot of your feelings were shaped by the people you were with, but there are some houses in which it seems impossible to relax, no matter how friendly the hosts. We've spent what seemed like endless evenings in what Knapp and Hall (2013) call "unliving rooms," where the spotless floors, furniture coverings, and plastic lamp covers send non-verbal messages telling us not to touch anything, not to put our feet up, and not to be comfortable. People who live in such houses probably wonder why nobody ever seems

REFLECTION

HEAD SCARVES

I consider myself to be an independent, liberated, Western woman with a fundamental belief in my equality with men. Attending university, I met several Muslim women who wore head scarves. I had always seen the head scarf as a sign of the male subjugation of women. I had this stereotype of demure, soft-spoken, obliging women, sort of like the "ideal" 1950s housewife, but from a different culture. As I got to know these Muslim women, my perception (or bias) seemed really wrong! I observed these women to be outspoken, articulate, independent-minded individuals. They spoke up in class, challenged their peers' ideas (both male and female), and clearly had a strong sense of their worth. They told me that rather than being a symbol of subservience to men, the head scarf served as a guard against the eyes of men and freed them from being "sexual objects." For me, this was a whole new way of interpreting the meaning of the head scarf. It gave me a new perspective, and now I'm wondering about the meaning of those low-cut tops and low-rise jeans . . .

© carlosphotos/iStockphoto.

Building WORK SKILLS

CULTURAL VALUES AT WORK

The Public Service Commission of Canada has published a variety of resources to help their managers promote equity in the workplace. Many of their recommendations involve strategies to deal with cultural differences in non-verbal communication (physical appearance, patterns of eye contact, speaking cadence, gestures, and so on). An important beginning strategy is being aware of your workplace values and behaviour that are influenced by your culture.

Take a moment to assess your workplace or your school environment in terms of some of the types of non-verbal communication discussed in this chapter. Pay particular attention to touch, proxemics and territoriality, time, clothing, and physical environment. Describe your workplace in terms of these elements,

and then identify the values communicated. Here are some questions to get your started:

- Who initiates touch? Who touches whom?
- Who gets the most territory? Who gets the least? Who gets the window?
- Do some people prefer greater or less social distance? Who? How do you know?
- How important is punctuality? Can some people keep others waiting with impunity?
- What do people wear? Are there differences?
- Is the physical environment clean? Are some places cleaner than others? Is the space well designed for the work to be done? Are some places better than others?

---

to relax and enjoy themselves at their parties. They don't seem to understand that the environment they have created can communicate discomfort to their guests.

The impressions that home designs communicate can be remarkably accurate. Edward Sadalla (1987) showed 99 students slides of the insides or outsides of twelve upper-middle-class homes and then asked them to infer the personality of the owners from their impressions. The students' inferences were especially accurate after glancing at interior photos. The decorating schemes conveyed clear information about the homeowners' intellectualism, politeness, maturity, optimism, and tenseness, their willingness to have adventures, family orientation, and reserve. The home exteriors also gave viewers accurate perceptions of the owners' artistic interests, graciousness, privacy, and quietness. Similarly, our personalities are revealed to others through our tastes in art, books, and music (Gelitz, 2011).

Besides communicating information about the designer, an environment can also shape the kind of interaction that takes place in it. In one experiment, subjects working in a

"beautiful" room were more positive and energetic than those working in "average" or "ugly" spaces (Maslow and Mintz, 1956). Inner-city adults and children who have access to landscaped public spaces interact in ways that are much more pro-social than those who have to interact in more barren environments (Taylor et al., 1998). Kuo and Sullivan (2001) found that residents of inner-city public housing who lived in relatively barren buildings reported more mental fatigue, aggression, and violence than their counterparts in buildings with nearby grass and trees. Similarly, researchers (Keizer et al., 2008) have found that in environments that contain graffiti, are strewn with litter, and have an abundance of unreturned shopping carts, people are more likely to similarly violate norms or social rules governing public spaces (e.g., they too litter, vandalize, or fail to return their shopping carts). In contrast, exposure to natural environments has been found to be associated with increased generosity and caring for others (Weinstein et al., 2009)

Students see professors who have well-decorated offices as more credible than those

REFLECTION

SIDE-BY-SIDE VERSUS HEAD-TO-HEAD

After three years at university, I've met with plenty of professors during their office hours to discuss papers and exams. I have noticed that some of them sit behind their desks, so that we discuss my work across a barrier. Other professors set up their offices or move their chairs so that we sit next to each other while we're looking at the work.

The two layouts seem to make a difference. Having that barrier between us leaves me feeling that the conferences are more adversarial than collaborative, and I definitely feel there's a greater power difference in this setup. I don't know whether the furniture layout causes my feelings or if professors who want to exert more power choose to set up their offices in a way that reflects their attitudes. In either case, I've come to think that the significance of office design goes beyond aesthetics.

 **CHECK** IT!

List the ten types of non-verbal communication and provide an example of each.

with less attractive work areas (Teven and Comadena, 1996). Some doctors have shaped environments to improve the quality of interaction with their patients. According to environmental psychologist Robert Sommer (1969), simply the absence of a doctor's desk made patients feel almost five times more at ease during office visits. Sommer also found that redesigning the convalescent ward of a hospital greatly increased the interaction between patients. In the old design, seats were placed shoulder to shoulder around the edges of the ward. By grouping the chairs around small tables so that patients faced each other at a comfortable distance, the number of conversations doubled.

SUMMARY

Non-verbal communication consists of messages expressed by non-linguistic means. It is pervasive; in fact, non-verbal messages are always available as a source of information about others. Most non-verbal behaviour conveys messages about relational attitudes and feelings, in contrast to verbal statements, which are better suited to expressing ideas. Messages that are communicated non-verbally are usually more ambiguous than verbal communication.

Non-verbal communication serves many functions. It can repeat, substitute for, complement, accent, regulate, and contradict verbal messages, and it can also be used as a tool for enhancing the success of deceptive verbal messages. When people are presented with conflicting verbal and non-verbal messages, they are more likely to rely on the non-verbal ones.

Non-verbal messages can be communicated in a variety of ways—through the face and eyes, body movement, touch, voice, distance, time, physical appearance, clothing, and environment. Culture plays a significant role in determining the rules and meanings for each of these factors.

MULTIPLE-CHOICE QUESTIONS

1. The best definition of non-verbal communication is
   a. communication without words.
   b. a message expressed by non-linguistic means.
   c. a message expressed vocally.
   d. all of the above.
2. Which of the following statements is true about non-verbal communication?
   a. Not all behaviour has communicative value.
   b. Non-verbal communication is best suited to communicate ideas.
   c. Unlike language, non-verbal communication is rarely influenced by culture.
   d. Non-verbal communication is ambiguous.
3. Esther points her finger at her son when she tells him he is not to have any more candy. Esther's pointing is an example of
   a. a regulator.
   b. an emblem.
   c. a contradiction.
   d. an illustrator.
4. Illustrators are usually unconscious.
   a. true
   b. false
5. People are effective at uncovering deceptive messages about _____ of the time.
   a. 20%
   b. 40%
   c. 50%
   d. 70%
6. Research has shown that women who think they are wearing fake designer sunglasses are no more likely to cheat than women not wearing designer knock-off sunglasses.
   a. true
   b. false
7. Paralanguage refers to
   a. communication through body movements.
   b. communication with facial expressions.
   c. the way a message is spoken.
   d. the way people use personal space.
8. The influence of physical attractiveness begins early in life.
   a. true
   b. false
9. On a crowded elevator people often avoid eye contact. This is referred to as a
   a. barrier behaviour.
   b. territory behaviour.
   c. social distance behaviour.
   d. public distance behaviour.
10. The way your personal space is decorated communicates information about you, but has little effect on the interactions that take place in the space.
    a. true
    b. false

Answers: 1. b; 2. d; 3. d; 4. a; 5. c; 6. b; 7. c; 8. a; 9. a; 10. b

ACTIVITIES

1. Invitation to Insight

Demonstrate for yourself that it is impossible to avoid communicating non-verbally by trying *not* to communicate with a friend or family member. (You be the judge of whether to tell the other person about this experiment beforehand.) See how long it takes for your partner to ask what you are doing and to report what he or she thinks you might be thinking and feeling.

2. Critical Thinking Probe

Interview someone from a culture different from your own, and learn at least three ways in which non-verbal codes differ from those of the place where you were raised. Together, develop a list of ways you could break unstated, but important, rules about non-verbal behaviour in your partner's culture in three of the following areas:

eye contact
posture
gesture
facial expression
distance
voice
touch
time
clothing
environmental design
territory

Describe how a failure to recognize different cultural codes could lead to misunderstandings, frustrations, and dissatisfaction. Discuss how an awareness of cultural rules can be developed in an increasingly multicultural world.

3. Invitation to Insight

Using the video of a television program or film, find examples of the non-verbal functions listed below. If time allows, show the video examples to your classmates.

repeating
substituting
complementing
accenting
regulating
contradicting
deceiving

4. Skill Builder

Sharpen your ability to distinguish between *observing* and *interpreting* non-verbal behaviour by following these directions:

a. Sit or stand opposite a partner at a comfortable distance. For a one-minute period, report your observations of the other person's behaviour by repeatedly completing the statement, "Now I see _____ (*non-verbal behaviour*)." For example, you might report, "Now I see you blinking your eyes. Now I see you looking down at the floor. Now I see you fidgeting with your hands." Notice that no matter what your partner does, you have an unending number of non-verbal behaviours to observe.

b. For a second one-minute period, complete the sentence "Now I see _____ (*non-verbal behaviour*), and I think _____," filling in the blank with your interpretation of the other person's non-verbal behaviour. For instance, you might say, "Now I see you look away, and I think you are nervous about looking me in the eye. Now I see you smiling and I think you are imagining that you agree with my interpretation." Notice that by clearly labelling your interpretation, you give the other person a chance to correct any mistaken hunches.

c. Repeat the first two steps, changing roles with your partner.

5. Invitation to Insight

How satisfied are you with the way your body looks? If you are extremely satisfied, mark 7; if you are satisfied, mark 6; if you are slightly satisfied, mark 5; if you are neither satisfied nor unsatisfied, mark 4; if you are slightly unsatisfied, mark 3; if you are unsatisfied, mark 2; and if you are extremely unsatisfied, mark 1.

_____	hair	_____	eyes
_____	nose	_____	mouth
_____	back	_____	chest or breasts
_____	stomach	_____	hips
_____	sex organs	_____	teeth
_____	chin	_____	cheeks
_____	arms	_____	elbows
_____	forearms	_____	wrists
_____	hands	_____	fingers
_____	thighs	_____	knees
_____	calves	_____	buttocks

_____ height   _____ weight
_____ overall facial attractiveness
_____ overall body appearance

How does the way you feel about a particular body part affect how you behave? How is your self-esteem affected by your physical appearance?

6. Invitation to Insight

Learn more about the non-verbal messages you send by interviewing someone who knows you well, such as a friend, family member, or co-worker. Ask your interview subject to describe how he or she knows when you are feeling each of the following emotions, even though you may not announce your feelings verbally:

anger or irritation
boredom or indifference
happiness
sadness
worry or anxiety

Which of these non-verbal behaviours do you display intentionally, and which are not conscious? Which functions does your non-verbal behaviour perform in the situations your partner described: repeating, substituting, complementing, accenting, regulating, contradicting, and/or deceiving feelings?

7. Invitation to Insight

Explore your territoriality by listing the spaces you feel you "own," such as your parking space, parts of the place you live in, or a seat in a particular classroom. Describe how you feel when your territory is invaded and identify things you do to "mark" it.

8. Invitation to Insight

This activity requires you to observe how people use space in a particular setting and to note reactions to violations of spatial expectations. Choose a supermarket, department store, university bookstore, or some other common setting in which people shop for things and then pay for them in a checkout line. Observe the interaction distances that seem usual between clerks and customers, between customers as they shop, and between customers in the checkout line.

a. What are the average distances between the people you observed?
b. How do people respond when one person comes too close to another or when one person touches another? How do people react to these violations of their space? How could they avoid violating each other's personal space?
c. Think back to a foreign film or a film that contains interaction between North Americans and people of another culture, as well as between people from the same culture—or try to observe people from a culture other than your own. Describe how they use spatial distance during conversations.

9. Role Play

This role play allows you to become more aware of your non-verbal behaviour and then gives you an opportunity to pay attention to all the facets of non-verbal communication by observing and copying someone else.

a. Think of an important message you need to deliver to someone significant (e.g., declining an invitation, asking for something the person may be unwilling to give). If you can't think of anything currently, think of a message you had to deliver in the past.
b. Deliver the message to your partner and ask her or him to copy all your non-verbal actions (except paralanguage) while you are giving the message—like you are looking into a mirror. When you are finished, discuss what you and your partner noticed about your non-verbal message.
c. Next, reverse roles. Have your partner deliver the message and you copy his or her behaviour. Be sure to pay attention to as many facets as possible (e.g., face and eyes, posture and body movement, touch, gestures). Again, discuss your observations.

DISCUSSION QUESTIONS

1. Describe similarities and differences between verbal and non-verbal communication.
2. Why do you think non-verbal communication has so much influence on human perception? Why do we value it more than verbal communication when we are evaluating the relational content of messages? What are the limitations of non-verbal communication in this regard?
3. Describe nine types of non-verbal behaviour and rate the significance of each in your communication with others.
4. The eyes have been described as the windows to the soul. Do you agree? What channels or types of non-verbal communication are most powerful for you? Why?
5. The research evidence regarding the power of physical attractiveness over human perception is disconcerting (unless you happen to be gorgeous). What can we do to overcome our biases (both positive and negative) in this area?

JOURNAL IDEAS

1. Pay attention to the types of non-verbal communication that you notice most in others. What kinds of things do you tend to notice? Why do you think that is? Are these observations helpful? Are there other types of non-verbal communication that you overlook? Would it be helpful to pay more attention to these areas? Why or why not?
2. Pay attention to the flow of various conversations you have with others or that you observe others having. What regulators do people use to establish turn taking? Where did you learn the strategies you use? Do they change significantly depending on who you are talking to? What larger forces have influenced your choice of non-verbal behaviours?

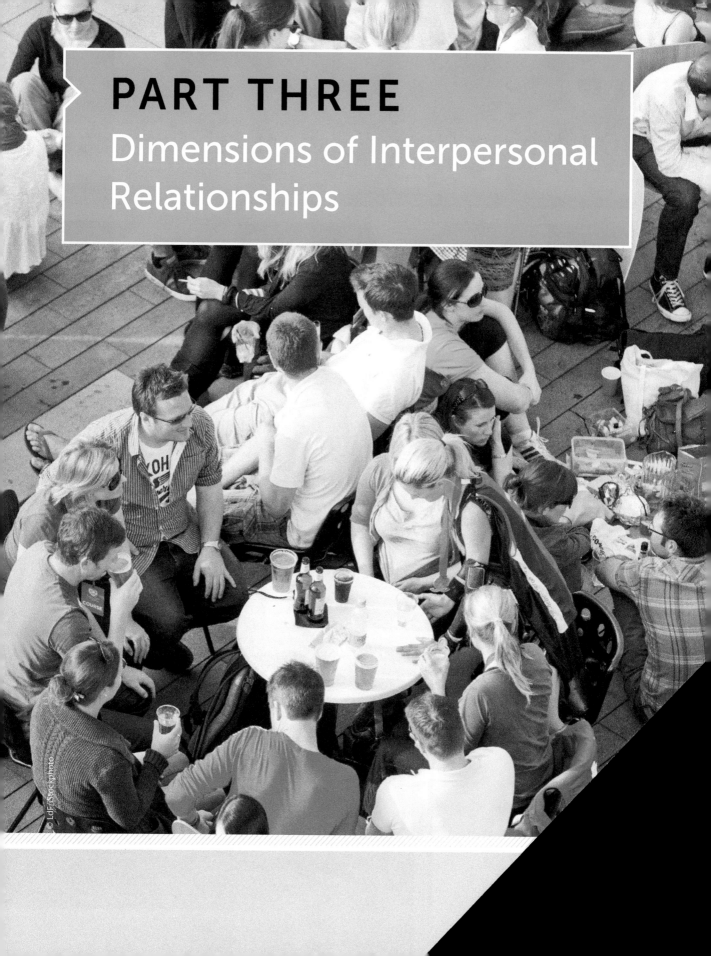

PART THREE
Dimensions of Interpersonal Relationships

8

Dynamics of Interpersonal Relationships

Key Terms

avoiding
bonding
circumscribing
comparison level (CL)
comparison level of
    alternatives (CL^{alt})
connection–autonomy
    dialect
dialectical tensions
differentiating
experimenting
expression–privacy dialectic
initiating

integrating
integration–separation
    dialectic
intensifying
intimacy
metacommunication
openness–closedness
    dialectic
relational maintenance
social exchange theory
stability–change dialectic
stagnating
terminating

Learning Objectives

YOU SHOULD UNDERSTAND:

- the reasons people choose others as potential relational partners;
- the dimensions of intimacy and distance in interpersonal relationships;
- the stages of relational development and the characteristics of movement between these stages;
- the dialectical tensions that can arise as communicators attempt to satisfy conflicting needs; and
- the ways content and relational messages are communicated in interpersonal relationships.

YOU SHOULD BE ABLE TO:

- identify the bases of interpersonal attraction in one of your relationships;
- identify the optimal blend of intimacy and distance in your personal relationships;
- describe the current stage of an important personal relationship and predict whether and how that relationship might move to a more satisfying stage; and
- identify the dialectical tensions that influence your communication goals, the strategies you use to manage these tensions, and alternative strategies you might consider using.

We are like islands in the sea, separate on the surface but connected in the deep.

—William James

There is no question that personal relationships matter. The development and maintenance of stable and satisfying interpersonal relationships is fundamental to human motivation (Baumeister and Leary, 1995). Our interconnectedness to others affects our biology, our physical health and survival, and our emotional health and well-being (Gable and Gosnell, 2013). It's no surprise that respondents to one survey identified interpersonal relationships as more important than anything else in making their lives meaningful (Campbell et al., 1976). While interpersonal relationships can be highly gratifying they can also cause much distress. In this chapter, we introduce some of

© Claudiad/iStockphoto.

Relationships are processes. Think about some of your closest relationships. How have they changed over time? Do you have relationships that haven't changed?

the dynamics that characterize interpersonal relationships and the communication that occurs within them. After reading the chapter, you will see that relationships are not fixed or unchanging. Rather, they can, and often do, change over time. In other words, a relationship is more a *process* than a *thing*.

Why We Form Relationships

As we discussed in Chapter 1, interpersonal relationships can be distinguished from less personal ones in many ways. Specifically, interpersonal relationships are unique, intrinsically rewarding, and irreplaceable; and the individuals involved are interdependent and disclose personal information to each other. While our closest relationships may not embody *all* these qualities, they do help us distinguish where relationships fall on the impersonal–interpersonal continuum. So, why do we form interpersonal relationships with some people and not with others? Sometimes, we have no choice. Children can't choose their parents, and most workers aren't able to choose their colleagues. In many other cases, however, we seek out some people and actively avoid others. Social scientists have collected an impressive body of research on interpersonal attraction (Eastwick et al., 2013; Krause et al., 2014). Following are some of the factors that they have identified as influences on our choice of relational partners.

Appearance

Most people claim that we should judge others on the basis of how they act, not how they look. However, the reality is quite the opposite, at least in terms of first impressions. Appearance is especially important in the early stages of a relationship (Lemay et al., 2010). In one study, a group of more than 700 men and women were matched as blind dates, allegedly for a "computer dance." After the party was over, they were asked whether or not they would like to date their partners again. The result? The more physically attractive the person (as judged in advance by independent raters), the more likely he or she was seen as desirable. Other factors—social skills and intelligence, for example—did not seem to affect the decision (Walster et al., 1966). Similarly, in one study, it was found that physical attractiveness can predict dating among adolescents (Cawley et al., 2006); in another study, it was found that online daters tend to strategically provide slightly deceptive information about themselves in order to enhance their appearance and attract more potential dates (Toma and Hancock, 2012).

Although we might assume that attractive people are radically different from those who are less attractive, the truth is that we view the familiar as beautiful. Langlois and Roggman (1990) presented raters with two types of photos. Some were of people from northern European, Asian, and Latino backgrounds, while others were computer-generated images that combined the characteristics of several individuals. Surprisingly, the judges consistently preferred the composite photos of both men and women. When the features of eight or more individuals were combined into one image, viewers rated the picture as more attractive than the features of a single person or of a smaller combination of people. Even if your appearance is not beautiful by societal standards, consider the following encouraging facts. After initial impressions have passed, ordinary-looking people with pleasing personalities are likely to be judged as attractive (Berscheid and Walster, 1978; Lewandowski et al., 2007). Our interactions with others change our perceptions of their physical appearance. Recall from Chapter 7 that positive communication increases perceptions of physical

attractiveness (Albada et al., 2002). Physical factors become less important as a relationship progresses. As Don Hamachek (1982, p. 59) puts it, "Attractive features may open doors, but apparently, it takes more than physical beauty to keep them open."

Similarity

It's comforting to know someone who likes the same things you like, has similar values, and may even be of the same race, economic class, or educational standing. The basis for this sort of relationship, commonly known as the *similarity thesis*, is the most frequently discussed of the several bases of relationship formation (Buss, 1985; Reis et al., 2011). As early as three years of age, North American children have been observed to show a preference for puppets who look similar to themselves (e.g., have the same hair colour) and were said to like the same foods and toys (Fawcett and Markson, 2010). By the time children reach middle and high school, they report being similar to each other in many ways, including having mutual friends, enjoying the same sports, liking the same social activities, and using (or not using) alcohol and cigarettes to the same degree (Aboud and Mendelson, 1998; Urberg

As North Americans, we tend to seek friendships with others who are like us. In what ways are your friends like you? What are the advantages and disadvantages of having friends who are similar to you?

© iStockPhoto/Andrew Rich.

et al., 1998). For adults, similarity is more important to relational happiness than even communication ability. Friends who have low levels of communication skills are just as satisfied with their relationships as are friends having high levels of skills (Burleson and Samter, 1996). Even online, people are attracted to others they consider similar to themselves on the basis of their blogs and web pages (Li and Chignell, 2010), and online dating services match partners based on the similarity of their personalities, preferences, and interests.

The similarity thesis has a great deal of support in cultures such as Canada and the United States; however among other cultures, the attraction to people similar to oneself may not be quite as strong. Steven Heine and his colleagues (2009) found that in comparison to Canadians, Japanese people were less attracted to those who had similar personalities, attitudes, and demographics. These investigators suggest that it may be the degree to which you are pleased with yourself and the extent to which your culture promotes a positive view of the self that determines the extent to which you are attracted to people similar to yourself. This idea makes sense when we consider the reasons why similarity is a strong foundation for interpersonal attraction in many Western cultures. First, the other person serves as an external indication—a social validation—that you are not alone in your thinking, that you're not too peculiar. Someone else *did* like the same controversial book you liked; therefore, this other person offers good support for you, reinforcing your own sense of what is right. Second, when someone is similar to you, you can make fairly accurate predictions—such as whether the person will want to eat at a Thai restaurant or attend the concert you're so excited about. This ability to make confident predictions reduces uncertainty and anxiety (Duck and Barnes, 1992). Third, it may be that when we learn that other people are similar to us, we assume they will probably like us, so we in turn like them. The self-fulfilling prophecy creeps into the picture again.

Similarity turns from attraction to dislike when we encounter people who are like us in many ways, but who behave in a strange or socially offensive manner (Cooper and Jones, 1969; Taylor and Mette, 1971). For instance, you have probably disliked people who others have said were "just like you," but who talked too much, were complainers, or had some other unappealing characteristic. In fact, there is a tendency to have stronger dislike for similar, but offensive people than for those who are offensive, but different. One likely reason is that such people threaten our self-esteem, causing us to fear that we may be as unappealing as they are. In such circumstances, the reaction is often to put as much distance as possible between ourselves and this threat to our ideal self-image.

Complementarity

The old saying "opposites attract" seems to contradict the principle of similarity we just described. In truth, though, both are valid. Differences strengthen a relationship when they are *complementary*—when each partner's characteristics satisfy the other's needs. Relationships also work well when the partners agree that one will exercise control in certain areas ("You make the final decisions about money") and the other will take the lead in different ones ("I'll decide how we ought to decorate the place"). Strains occur when control issues are disputed.

Studies that have examined successful and unsuccessful couples over a twenty-year period show the interaction between similarities and differences. When partners are radically different, the dissimilar qualities that at first appear intriguing later become cause for relational breakups (Felmlee, 1998). Partners in successful marriages were similar enough to satisfy each other physically and mentally, but were different enough to meet each other's needs and keep the relationship interesting. The successful couples found ways to keep a balance between their similarities and differences while adjusting to the changes that occurred over the years.

Opposites can attract at work too. There is evidence that teams made up of people with different personality traits function better and are more productive. Employees are more attracted to their team members when the team is made up of people with differing personality traits, particularly when the team has a balance of people with differing levels of extroversion. People who are extroverted tend to be more sociable, assertive, and dominant, and to like excitement. A study of teams employed at manufacturing firms, as well as teams of MBA students, found that people got along better and liked their team members more when their own level of extroversion was different from the average level of their team (Kristof-Brown et al., 2005). However, when team members differ in their goals and values, productivity and harmony at work is compromised (Kristof-Brown and Stevens, 2001).

Rewards

Some relationships are based on an economic model called **social exchange theory** (Hand and Furman, 2009; Thibaut and Kelley, 1959). This approach suggests that we often seek out people who can give us rewards that are greater than or equal to the costs we encounter in dealing with them. Social exchange theorists define rewards as being any outcomes we desire. They may be tangible (a nice place to live, a high-paying job) or intangible (prestige, emotional support, companionship). Costs are defined as undesirable outcomes, such as unpleasant work, emotional pain, and so on.

A simple formula captures the social exchange explanation for why we form and maintain relationships:

$$\text{Rewards} - \text{Costs} = \text{Outcome}$$

According to social exchange theorists, we use this formula (often unconsciously) to calculate whether a relationship is a "good deal" or "not worth the effort"—that is, whether the outcome is positive or negative.

At its most blatant level, an exchange approach seems cold and calculating, but it seems quite appropriate in some types of relationships. A healthy business relationship is based on how well the parties help one another, and some friendships are based on an informal kind of barter: "I don't mind listening to the ups and downs of your love life because you rescue me when my house needs repairs." Even close relationships have an element of exchange. Friends and lovers often tolerate each other's quirks because the comfort and enjoyment they experience makes the less-than-pleasant times worth accepting.

Costs and rewards do not exist in isolation. We define them by comparing a certain situation with alternatives. For example, consider a hypothetical woman, Maryam, who is struggling to decide whether to remain in a relationship with Ahmed, her long-time boyfriend. Ahmed does love Maryam, but he has a hair-trigger temper and he has become verbally abusive from time to time. Also, Maryam knows that Ahmed was unfaithful to her at least once. In deciding whether or not to stay with Ahmed, Maryam will use two standards.

The first is her **comparison level (CL)**—her minimum standard of acceptable behaviour. If Maryam believes that relational partners have an obligation to be faithful and treat one another respectfully at all times, then Ahmed's behaviour will fall below her comparison level. On the other hand, if Maryam adopts a "nobody's perfect" standard, she is more likely to view Ahmed's behaviour as meeting or exceeding her comparison level.

Maryam will also rate Ahmed according to her **comparison level of alternatives (CL^{alt})**. This standard refers to a comparison between the rewards she is receiving in her present situation and those she could expect to receive in others. If, for example, Maryam doesn't want to be alone, her CL^{alt} would be lower than her present situation; but if she is confident that she could find a kinder partner, her CL^{alt} would be higher than the status quo.

Social exchange theorists suggest that communicators unconsciously use this calculation to decide whether to form and stay in relationships. At first, this information seems to offer little comfort to communicators who are in unsatisfying relationships, such as those where CL > CL^{alt}. But there are alternatives to being stuck in situations where the costs outweigh the rewards. First, you might make sure that you are judging your present relationship against a realistic comparison level. Expecting a situation to be perfect can be a recipe for unhappiness. (Recall the discussion of the "fallacy of *should*" in Chapter 4.) If you decide that your present situation truly falls below your comparison level, you might look for alternatives you have not considered. And finally, the skills introduced throughout this book may help you negotiate a better relationship with the other person.

Competence

We like to be around talented people, probably because we hope their skills and abilities will rub off on us. On the other hand, we are uncomfortable around those who are too competent—probably because we look bad by comparison. Elliot Aronson and his associates (1966) demonstrated how competence and imperfection combine to affect attraction by having subjects evaluate tape recordings of candidates for a quiz program. One was a "perfect" candidate who answered almost all the questions correctly and modestly admitted that he was an honours student, athlete, and college yearbook editor. The "average" candidate answered fewer questions correctly, had average grades, was a less successful athlete, and was a low-level member of the yearbook staff. In half the tapes, the candidates committed a blunder near the end, spilling coffee all over themselves. The remaining half of the tapes contained no such blunder. These, then, were the four experimental conditions: (1) a person with superior ability who blundered; (2) a person with superior ability who did not blunder; (3) an average person who blundered; and (4) an average person who did not blunder. The students who rated the attractiveness of these four types of people revealed an interesting and important principle of interpersonal attraction. The most attractive person was the superior candidate who blundered. Next was the superior person who did not blunder. Third was the average person who did not blunder. The least attractive person was the average person who committed the blunder. Aronson's

TAKE TWO

- **Social exchange theory:** the practice of seeking out people who can give us rewards greater than the costs of dealing with them.
- **Comparison level (CL):** a minimum standard of acceptable behaviour.
- **Comparison level of alternatives (CL^{alt}):** a comparison between rewards in the present situation and those one could expect to receive from others.

conclusion was that we tend to like people who are somewhat flawed because they remind us of ourselves.

Proximity

As common sense suggests, we are likely to develop relationships with people whom we often interact with. In many cases, proximity leads to liking. For instance, we're more likely to develop friendships with close neighbours than with distant ones, and the chances are good that we will choose a mate with whom we often cross paths. Facts like these are understandable when we consider that proximity allows us to

You are likely to develop strong personal feelings toward others you encounter frequently, like classmates, co-workers, and club mates. Who are the five people you come in contact with most in your life? Do you have strong positive or negative feelings about them?

get more information about other people and benefit from a relationship with them. Also, people in close proximity may be more similar to us than those who aren't—for example, if we live in the same neighbourhood, the odds are we have the same socio-economic status.

Familiarity, on the other hand, can breed contempt. Evidence to support this fact comes from police blotters as well as university laboratories. Thieves frequently prey on nearby victims, even though the risk of being recognized is greater. Most aggravated assaults occur within the family or among close neighbours. Similarly, you are likely to develop strong personal feelings, either positive or negative, toward others you encounter frequently.

Disclosure

Telling others important information about yourself can help build liking in person (Derlega et al., 1993; Dindia, 2002) and online (Ledbetter et al., 2011). Sometimes, the basis of this attraction comes from learning about ways we are similar, either in experiences ("I broke off an engagement as well") or in attitudes ("I feel nervous with strangers, too").

Self-disclosure also increases liking because it is a sign of regard. Sharing private information is a form of respect and trust—a kind of liking that we have already seen increases attractiveness.

Not all disclosure, however, leads to liking. Research shows that the key to satisfying self-disclosure is *reciprocity*—that is, getting back an amount and kind of information equivalent to that which you reveal (Dindia, 2000a). A second important ingredient in successful self-disclosure is *timing*. It's probably unwise to talk about your sexual insecurities with a new acquaintance or express your pet peeves to a friend at your birthday party.

Figuring out what is appropriate to disclose when, where, and to whom can be difficult. In addition to factoring in reciprocity and timing, we need to consider the stage of the relationship and the setting, and the influences of culture and gender on disclosure and intimacy. Later in this chapter, we will examine how gender and culture both influence disclosure and intimacy, as well as examine relationship stages and the tensions inherent in relationships that influence self-disclosure. In terms

CHECK IT!

Why do we communicate? Describe the four types of needs communication helps us to meet.

of the setting, it is important to understand that social norms, or rules about appropriate self-disclosure online and in face-to-face interactions, appear to be different. People reveal a great deal of personal information about themselves to others online (Joinson and Paine, 2007; Mesch and Beker, 2010). Theorists originally thought that people in face-to-face interactions would disclose more than those who interact online because face-to-face interactions include the non-verbal elements that more easily help communicate feelings and establish trust. However, it appears that that the anonymity and the lack of non-verbal cues allow people to disclose more personal information more easily online, and that it is through disclosure that trust is established (Mesch and Beker, 2010). As we explained in Chapter 2, while online disclosure can certainly increase likeability, it needs to be understood that there still is risk involved.

Intimacy and Distance in Relationships

The 1970s musical group Three Dog Night said it well: one *can* be the loneliest number. For most of us, the desire to connect with others is a powerful force. As we explained in Chapter 1, strong attachments with others not only make us happier, they can also make us healthier and help us live longer.

In their book *Intimacy: Strategies for Successful Relationships*, C. Edward Crowther and Gayle Stone (1986) offer a reminder of just how important close relationships can be. As part of a study of people who were dying in hospices and hospitals in the United States and England, Crowther and Stone asked each person what mattered most in his or her life. Fully 90 per cent of these terminally ill patients put intimate relationships at the top of the list. As a 50-year-old mother of three children who was dying of cancer put it, "You need not wait until you are in my condition to know nothing in life is as important as loving relationships" (p. 13).

Dimensions of Intimacy and Distance

What does it mean to be intimate? Does intimacy mean spending time together? Sharing feelings? Having sex? Going through thick and thin? Are intimacy and love identical?

Relationship **intimacy** is often described as a motivation to share one's private self with another person (Aron et al., 2004). This closeness and commitment can occur in a variety of relationships (Berscheid et al., 1989). When researchers asked several hundred college students to identify their "closest, deepest, most involved, and most intimate relationship," the answers were varied. Roughly half (47 per cent) identified a romantic partner. About a third (36 per cent) chose a friendship. Most of the rest (14 per cent) cited a family member.

Intimacy comes in many forms (Lippert and Prager, 2001). One type is *emotional*: sharing important information and feelings.

REFLECTION

INTIMACY THROUGH GRIEF

I have grown closer to many people through shared activities. My soccer teammates and I definitely bonded over the past season, and my best friend and I moved to a new level after backpacking through South America. But the "shared activity" that stands out for me as an intimacy builder is death. Last year, I experienced the tragedy of losing a friend who died in a car accident. Grieving with our surviving group was the saddest thing I've ever experienced, and I wouldn't wish the experience on anyone. But I must say that our shared loss has created a special bond among the four of us.

Sharing distressing emotions with others can help to reduce stress and provide support and comfort (Taylor, 2007). Sharing positive emotions also supports relationship development, because when others respond enthusiastically to our happy news it helps to build trust (Reis et al., 2010). In addition, as we described in Chapter 4, sharing positive emotions helps to make the good feelings last, and that makes us happier.

Dimensions of Intimacy

Another form of intimacy is *physical*. Even before birth, the developing fetus experiences a kind of physical closeness with its mother that will never happen again, "floating in a warm fluid, curling inside a total embrace, swaying to the undulations of the moving body and hearing the beat of the pulsing heart" (Morris, 1973, p. 7). As they grow up, fortunate children are continually nourished by physical intimacy by being rocked, fed, hugged, and held. As we grow older, the opportunities for physical intimacy are less regular, but still possible and important. Some physical intimacy is sexual, but this category also can include affectionate hugs, kisses, and even struggles. Companions who have endured physical challenges together—for example, in sports or during emergencies—form a bond that can last a lifetime.

In other cases, intimacy comes from *intellectual* sharing. Not every exchange of ideas counts as intimacy, of course. Talking about next week's mid-term with your professor or classmates isn't likely to forge strong relational bonds. But when you engage another person in an exchange of important ideas, a kind of closeness develops that can be powerful and exciting.

Shared activities can provide a fourth way to emotional closeness (Girme et al., 2014; Wood and Inman, 1993). Not all shared activities lead to intimacy. You might work with a colleague for years without feeling any sort of emotional connection. But some shared experiences—struggling together against obstacles or living together as housemates are good examples—can create strong bonds. Play is one valuable form of shared activity. Leslie Baxter (1992) found that both same-sex friendships and opposite-sex romantic relationships were characterized by several forms of play. Partners invented private codes, fooled around by acting like other people, teased one another, and played games—everything from having punning contests to arm wrestling.

The amount and type of intimacy can vary from one relationship to another (Speicher, 1999). Some intimate relationships exhibit all four qualities of emotional disclosure, physical intimacy, intellectual exchanges, and shared activities. Other intimate relationships exhibit only one or two. Of course, some relationships aren't close ones in any way. Acquaintances,

© iStockPhoto/dchadwick.

Companions who have endured physical challenges together form a bond that can last a lifetime. Do you have friends with whom you've played sports, climbed mountains, or survived other physical adversity together? How has that affected your relationship?

roommates, and co-workers may never become intimate. In some cases, even family members develop smooth, but relatively impersonal relationships.

Not even the closest relationships always operate at the highest level of intimacy. At some times, you may share all of your thoughts or feelings with a friend, family member, or lover; at other times, you may withdraw. You may freely share your feelings about one topic and stay more distant regarding another one. The same principle holds for physical intimacy, which waxes and wanes in most relationships.

Despite the fact that no relationship is *always* intimate, it is hardly desirable to live without *any* sort of intimacy. For example, one study revealed that subjects who fear intimacy while dating expect less satisfaction in a long-term relationship and report feeling more distant from even long-time dating partners (Sherman and Thelen, 1996; Thelen et al., 2000).

Dimensions of Distance

Intimacy in a relationship is important, but so is distance. Sometimes, we create physical and emotional space between ourselves and others whose behaviour we find bothersome, such as intrusive relatives or annoying co-workers. There are also times when we feel the need to distance ourselves, at least temporarily, from people we genuinely care for (Hess, 2000).

Just as there are a variety of ways to be intimate, there are different ways to gain distance in a relationship. The most common strategy for creating distance, at least among students, is *avoidance* (Hess, 2000). We can avoid unwanted contact physically, or by other means. For example, you can screen your incoming messages and ignore those that are unwanted.

Other common avoidance tactics include being *reserved*—saying little when you're with the other person; by *shortening interaction*, perhaps by not asking questions or engaging in non-verbal behaviour that encourages the other person to talk; by *restricting topics*, especially those that might be personal or intimate; and by using *restraint*—for instance, avoiding joking or other attention-getting behaviours that often encourage unwanted contact. *Deception* is a sixth way to distance yourself. We discussed lying in Chapter 2 as an alternative to self-disclosure, and we will have more to say about managing the tension between intimacy (integration) and distance (separation) when we examine the dialectic tensions inherent in our relationships a little later in this chapter.

Intimacy and distance are both important. It is impossible to have a close relationship with everyone we encounter, because there simply isn't enough time and energy. Even if we could become intimate with everyone, few

Dimensions of Intimacy

- **Emotional:** the exchange of important information and feelings.
- **Physical:** physical closeness, both sexual and non-sexual.
- **Intellectual:** the exchange of important and profound ideas.
- **Shared activities:** mutual experiences such as struggling together or playing.

Forms of Distance

- **Avoidance:** evading contact with others.
- **Being reserved:** holding back expression of thoughts and feelings.
- **Shortening interactions:** not asking questions or providing non-verbal cues to encourage conversation.
- **Restricting topics:** limiting what is discussed.
- **Restraint:** not joking or encouraging contact.
- **Deception:** lying.

of us would want that much closeness. Consider the range of everyday contacts that do not require any sort of intimacy. Some are based on economic exchange (with the people at work or the shopkeeper you visit several times a week); some are based on group membership (in a place of worship or school); some are based on physical proximity (to neighbours or through carpooling); and some grow out of third-party connections (mutual friends, child care). Simply engaging in conversational give-and-take with both strangers and acquaintances can be enjoyable.

These examples suggest that intimacy isn't essential in every relationship. Even with people we encounter often it's possible to have very satisfying relationships without a high degree of closeness (Weiss, 1998), but living without any sort of intimacy in relationships is hardly desirable. Some people fear intimacy in relationships and this can cause major problems in establishing and maintaining satisfying and meaningful relationships (Montesi et al., 2013). Normally, our desire for intimacy waxes and wanes in our relationships. As we will discuss a bit later in this chapter, individuals need both closeness and distance even in their most intimate relationships. Lovers and married couples often go through periods of much sharing, alternating with times of relative withdrawal. Likewise, they experience periods of passion and then times of little physical contact (Ben-Ari, 2012; Van Lear, 1991). Friends, too, have times of high disclosure, when they share almost every feeling and idea, and then disengage for days, months, or even longer. Given the equally important needs for intimacy and distance, the challenge is to communicate in a manner that provides the best possible mix of intimate and non-intimate relationships (Petronio, 1991).

Influences on Intimacy and Distance

What is the ideal amount of intimacy? The answer varies according to who is giving the answer. You know from personal experience that different people seek different levels of intimacy. What factors lead to these differences? Two of the most powerful influences are gender and culture.

Gender and Intimacy

Until recently, most social scientists believed that women were better than men at developing and maintaining intimate relationships. This view grew from the assumption that the disclosure of personal information is the most important ingredient of intimacy. Most research *does* show that women (taken as a group, of course) are somewhat more willing than men to share their most personal thoughts and feelings (Dindia and Allen, 1992), although the differences aren't as dramatic as most people believe (Dindia, 2000b, 2002).

© iStockPhoto/shaunl.

Whereas women place a somewhat higher value on talking about personal matters as a measure of closeness, men are more likely to create and express closeness by doing things together. How do you see this in the relationships of the men and women around you? How do you develop close relationships?

But more recent scholarship has begun to show that emotional expression is not the *only* way to develop close relationships (Floyd, 1996; Inman, 1996; Johnson, 1996). Whereas women place a somewhat higher value on talking about personal matters as a measure of closeness, men are more likely to create and express closeness by doing things together. In one study, more than 75 per cent of the men surveyed said that their most meaningful experiences with friends came from shared activities (Swain, 1989). They reported that through shared activities they "grew on one another," developed feelings of interdependence, showed appreciation for one another, and demonstrated mutual liking. Likewise, men regarded practical help as a measure of caring. Findings like these show that, for many men, closeness grows from activities that do not always depend heavily on disclosure. A friend is a person who does things *for* you and *with* you. Of course, it's important not to assume that all men who value shared activities are reluctant to share feelings, or that doing things together isn't important to women. There is evidence that, in many respects, the meaning of intimacy is more similar than different for men and women (Goldsmith and Fulfs, 1999).

Whatever differences do exist between male and female styles of intimacy help explain some of the stresses and misunderstandings that can arise between the sexes. For example, a woman who looks for emotional disclosure as a measure of affection may overlook an "inexpressive" man's efforts to show he cares by doing favours or spending time with her. Fixing a leaky tap or taking a hike may look like ways to avoid getting close, but to the man who proposes them, they may be measures of affection and bids for intimacy. Likewise, differing ideas about the timing and meaning of sex can lead to misunderstandings. Whereas many women think of sex as a way to *express* an intimacy that has already developed, men are more likely to see it as a way to *create* that intimacy (Reissman, 1990). In this sense, the man who encourages sex early in a

relationship or after a fight may not just be a testosterone-crazed lecher. Rather, he may view the shared activity as a way to build closeness. By contrast, the woman who views personal talk as the pathway to intimacy may resist the idea of physical closeness before the emotional side of the relationship has been discussed.

As with all research that examines women's and men's communication, it is important to realize that no generalization applies to every person. Furthermore, stereotypes are changing. For example, an analysis of prime-time television sitcoms showed that male characters who reveal personal information generally receive favourable responses from other characters (Good et al., 2002). In addition, researchers Mark Morman and Kory Floyd (2002) note that a cultural shift is taking place in North America, in that fathers are becoming more affectionate with their sons than they were in previous generations—although some of that affection is still expressed through shared activities.

Culture and Intimacy

Historically, the notions of public and private behaviour have changed dramatically (Adamopoulos, 1991; Gadlin, 1977). What would be considered intimate behaviour today was quite public at times in the past. For example, in 16th-century Germany, newlyweds were often expected to consummate their union in a bed carried by witnesses who would validate the marriage! Conversely, in England as well as in colonial North America, the customary level of communication between spouses was once quite formal—not much different from the way acquaintances or neighbours spoke to one another.

Today, the notion of intimacy varies from one culture to another. In one study, researchers asked residents of Britain, Japan, Hong Kong, and Italy which of the 33 rules that regulated interaction in social relationships they followed (Argyle and Henderson, 1985). The rules governed a wide range of communication behaviour: everything from the use of humour, to shaking hands and the management of money. The results showed that the greatest differences between Asian and European cultures involved the rules for dealing with intimacy, including showing emotions, expressing affection in public, sexual activity, and respecting privacy. Canadians often have multiple cultures that influence their behaviour in relationships. Tara Marshall (2010) was interested in how these multiple cultures influenced intimacy and commitment in the romantic rela-

© iStockPhoto/101dalmations.

Do you think you are easy to meet, but difficult to know, or difficult to meet, but easy to know? Or some other combination?

tionships of Chinese-Canadians. She found that when Chinese-Canadian men identified more with mainstream Canadian culture, they reported greater intimacy in their relationships and so did their romantic partners. When Chinese-Canadian women identified more strongly with their Chinese heritage, they reported greater commitment to their partners. Marshall argues that both culture and gender roles interact to explain these findings. She suggests that the more traditional gender roles that are highly valued in Chinese culture may account for women's greater commitment to relationships, and the more egalitarian norms for men's behaviour in mainstream Canadian culture may allow for greater self-disclosure thereby promoting greater intimacy.

In addition to differences in notions of intimacy, the amount that individuals desire also varies from one culture to another. In a comparison of members of collectivistic and individualistic cultures (Turkish and mainstream Canadian), researchers from Toronto's York University studied the participants' ratings of ideal closeness in a variety of relationships (i.e., with friends, family, and acquaintances) (Uskul et al., 2004). Both the Turkish and the Canadian participants ideally

wanted to be closest to their romantic partner; however, the Turkish participants wanted to have greater intimacy than the Canadians in all types of relationships. The Turks also said they did feel closer to friends, family, and acquaintances than the Canadians did.

Disclosure is especially high in mainstream North American society. In fact, United States citizens do more disclosing than members of any other culture studied (Gudykunst, 1986). They are likely to reveal more about themselves to acquaintances and even to strangers. By contrast, Germans and Japanese tend to reveal little about themselves, except in personal relationships with a select few (Schug et al., 2010; Seki et al., 2002). In some collectivistic cultures, such as those of Taiwan and Japan, there is a significant difference in the way people communicate with members of their in-groups (such as family and close friends) and with those they view as outsiders (Seki et al., 2002; Triandis, 1994). They generally do not reach out to strangers, often waiting until they are properly introduced before entering into a conversation. Once introduced, they address outsiders with formality and go to extremes to hide unfavourable information about in-group members from them. By

Focus on TECHNOLOGY

SOCIAL MEDIA AND INTIMACY

Computer-mediated communication provides opportunities to meet and interact with people whose interests and experiences are similar to our own. Chat rooms, blogs, social networking sites, and online dating services allow us access to people we may otherwise never have a chance to meet. This is one of the main advantages of online dating sites—they provide access to a much larger pool of potential romantic partners than our personal social networks could ever provide (Finkel et al., 2012). Online social gaming provides us with opportunities to interact with both old and new friends, some of whom we interact with in person and some of whom we engage with exclusively online (Domahidi et al., 2014). Social media platforms allow us to connect with others socially and professionally, while text messaging allows us constant contact with our loved ones. There is no doubt that CMC is often personal and helps us establish and maintain our intimate relationships. However, it is somewhat ironic that CMC *feels* so intimate. When we are online we are often alone, in the privacy of our homes sending messages intended for a chosen few. But there is no guarantee that our chosen recipients are our only audience. Recall from Chapter 2 that privacy settings can be breached (never mind what you agreed to when you checked that box in the "terms and conditions") and there are a variety of organizations that have a vested interest in knowing more about us (Madrigal, 2012).

In addition, there are times when members of our own social networks can hurt us, either intentionally or accidently, by sharing information we wanted to keep private. In a clever experiment, researchers at the University of Haifa found that contrary to popular thought it is not the anonymity or invisibility afforded by the Internet that predicts how unkind people are to each other, but the lack of eye contact (Lapidot-Lefler and Barak, 2012). In their experiment 71 pairs of college students were instructed to debate an issue, and agree on a solution, while using instant messaging. Each partner was seated in a different room, using a computer to communicate. Partners debated in one of three conditions. One group of partners was asked to share personal, identifying details before debating. A second group could see the profiles of their partners, and a third group was instructed to maintain eye contact via close up cameras attached to their monitors. Participants in the first two conditions (in which eye contact was unavailable) were twice as likely to send hostile messages to their partners as compared to the pairs who were required to maintain eye contact. The researchers speculated that lack of eye contact reduces empathy and allows greater aggressiveness. All of the factors that contribute to peoples' lack of inhibition on the Internet have yet to be identified, but there is increasing evidence that people online behave in ways that they are less likely to behave in person. Recall from Chapter 2 that people often disclose more personal information about themselves online compared to when they are face-to-face with others (Christofides et al., 2012) and that sharing information about ourselves triggers reward pathways in our brains (Tamir and Mitchell, 2012). Being aware of the inhibition that is associated with CMC, combined with the knowledge that the privacy we experience online is not the reality of the Internet, helps us monitor our communication to ensure that the messages we send via CMC are those we would be comfortable sending in face-to-face interactions.

contrast, members of more individualistic cultures—such as those of Canada, the United States, and Australia—make less distinction between personal and casual relationships. They are more familiar with strangers and reveal more personal information, making them excellent "cocktail party conversationalists." Social psychologist Kurt Lewin (1936) captured the difference nicely when he noted that Americans were easy to meet, but difficult to get to know, while Germans were difficult to meet, but easy to know well.

Differences like these mean that the level of self-disclosure that is appropriate in one culture may seem completely inappropriate in another one. If you were raised in Canada or the United States, you may view people from other cultures as reserved and perhaps standoffish. The converse is also true. To members of other cultures, North Americans probably appear like exhibitionists who spew out personal information to anyone within earshot.

When communicating with people from different cultures, it is important to consider their norms for appropriate intimacy. Do not mistakenly judge them according to your own standards. Likewise, be sensitive about honouring their standards when talking about yourself. In this sense, choosing the proper level of intimacy is not too different from choosing the appropriate way of dressing or eating when encountering members of a different culture: what seems familiar and correct at home may not be suitable with strangers.

Communication and Relational Dynamics

Even the most stable relationships vary from day to day and over longer periods of time. Communication scholars have tried to describe and explain how communication creates and reflects the changing dynamics of relational interaction. In the following sections, we describe two very different characterizations of relational development and interaction.

A Developmental Model of Interpersonal Relationships

One of the best-known models of relational stages was developed by Mark Knapp (Knapp and Vangelisti, 2009; Avtgis et al., 1998; Welch and Rubin, 2002), who broke the waxing and waning of relationships into 10 steps. Other researchers have suggested that in addition to explaining how people come together and come apart, any model of relational communication ought to contain a third area, **relational**

maintenance—communication aimed at keeping relationships operating smoothly and satisfactorily. Relational maintenance includes behaving in a positive way, being open, and assuring your partner that you are committed to the relationship (Dainton, 2000). Figure 8.1 shows how Knapp's 10 stages fit into this three-part view of relational communication. This model seems most useful for describing communication between romantic partners, but in many respects, it works well for other types of close relationships. As you read the following section, consider how the stages could describe a long-term friendship, a couple in love, or even business partners.

Initiating

The goals in the **initiating** stage are to show that you are interested in making contact and to demonstrate that you are a person worth talking to. Communication during this stage is usually brief, and it generally follows conventional formulas, such as handshakes, comments about innocuous subjects such as the weather, and friendly remarks. Such behaviour may seem superficial and meaningless, but it is a way of

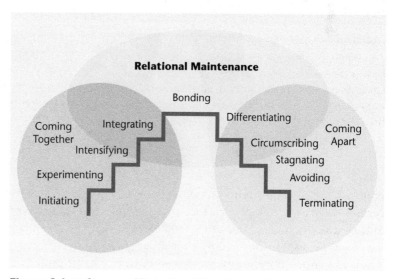

Figure 8.1 ● Stages of Relational Development

signalling that you are interested in building some kind of relationship with the other person. It allows us to indicate, "I'm a friendly person, and I'd like to get to know you."

Beginning a relationship requires a fair measure of skill. One study revealed several strategies that are both efficient and socially acceptable ways to learn about others (Douglas, 1987). The first is *networking*—getting information about the other person from a third party who helps the first moments of contact go well. Another strategy is *offering*—putting yourself in a favourable position to be approached by the desired partner. Offering strategies might include picking a seat in class near the person you would like to meet. A third technique is *approaching*—signalling your desire for contact, either verbally or non-verbally. Typical approaches include smiles and self-introductions. (Incredibly, there are people who never even try such seemingly obvious strategies, instead waiting for interesting people to approach them.) A final initiating strategy is *sustaining*—behaving in ways to keep the conversation going. Asking questions is a typical sustaining technique.

Beginning a relationship—especially a romantic one—can be particularly difficult for people who are shy. As we noted in Chapter 4, computer-mediated communication can make it easier for people to strike up a relationship. Those who become anxious in social situations, often prefer using text messages to attempt intimate contact with others rather than talking to them on the phone (Reid and Reid, 2007, 2010). CMC has the advantage of allowing the sender to carefully compose the message and present him or herself in a particular way (identity management)—as a result, many people are often more candid in their text messages (Reid and Reid, 2005, 2010). Social networking profiles provide an inconspicuous way to find out more about people we might be interested in knowing better. Among college and university students, relationship development typically begins with communication through social networking sites, and progresses to text messaging and later face-to-face and phone conversations (Yang et. al., 2014). Online dating sites also provide opportunities to initiate contact with many more potential romantic partners than people might otherwise have access to. The primary benefit of online dating is that it provides opportunities for short-term CMC before actually meeting a potential romantic partner face-to-face.

There is evidence to suggest that spending too much time communicating through computer-mediated channels (e.g., six weeks rather than three weeks) can actually hurt people's romantic prospects. People tend to optimistically over-interpret social cues in CMC, which in turn increases the chances for disappointment when they actually meet face-to-face (Finkel at al., 2012).

© iStockPhoto/TriggerPhoto.

Beginning a relationship requires a fair measure of skill. Think about your current or last romantic relationship. How did it begin? Who made the first move? Was it difficult to start?

Experimenting

After meeting someone new, we generally begin the search for common ground.

Self-Assessment

WHAT IS YOUR FLIRTING STYLE?

Research on initiating relationships has identified five styles of communicating romantic interest. The scale below has been abbreviated, but will give you a flavour for your flirting tendencies. Use the numbers 1 to 7 to indicate how strongly you agree or disagree with each of the following statements, according to the following scale:

strongly disagree   1 2 3 4 5 6 7   strongly agree

_____   1. Men should pursue women, not the other way around.

_____   2. I am good at using my body language to flirt.

_____   3. Flirting is just for fun; people don't need to be serious.

_____   4. Making a real connection with others can be exciting.

_____   5. In today's society, people have to be careful about flirting.

_____   6. Despite how quickly our society is changing, it is still up to a man to take control in initiating relationships.

_____   7. I am good at picking up on the sexual interest of others.

_____   8. I flirt with people I have absolutely no interest in.

_____   9. I really enjoy learning about another person's interests.

_____   10. When dating, people should always be polite and use proper manners.

_____   11. Men should make the first move.

_____   12. I have no problem letting others know I am interested in them.

_____   13. Flirting can be harmless fun.

_____   14. I really look for an emotional connection with someone I'm interested in.

_____   15. People should be cautious when letting someone know they are interested.

Add up your scores for each flirting style.

Traditional: add items 1, 6, and 11 =___ /21
Physical: add items 2, 7, and 12 = ___/21
Playful: add items 3, 8, and 13 = ___/21
Sincere: add items 4, 9, and 14 = ___/21
Polite: add items 5, 10, and 15 = ___/21

Higher agreement ratings indicate a tendency toward that flirting style. The physical, playful, and sincere styles have been correlated with more dating success.

SOURCE: Adapted from J.A. Hall, S. Carter, M.J. Cody, and J.M. Albright (2010), "Individual differences in the communication of romantic interest: Development of the Flirting Styles Inventory," *Communication Quarterly*, 58(4) (pp. 365–393).

This search usually begins with the basics: "Where are you from? What program are you in?" From there, we look for other similarities: "You're a runner, too? How many kilometres do you run a week?"

It usually doesn't take long for communicators who are interested in one another to move from initiating to **experimenting**. The shift seems to occur even more rapidly in cyberspace than in person (Ho and McLeod, 2008; Pratt et al., 1999; Tidwell and Walther, 2002). People who develop relationships online begin asking questions about attitudes, opinions, and preferences more quickly than those in face-to-face contact. It probably helps that when online, people can't see each other's non-verbal reactions—they don't have to worry about blushing, stammering, or looking away if they realize that they asked for too much information too quickly.

The hallmark of experimenting is small talk. We tolerate the ordeal of small talk because it serves several functions. First, it is a useful way to find out what interests we share with the other person. It is also a way to "audition" the other person—to help us decide whether a relationship is worth pursuing. In addition, small talk is a safe way to ease into a relationship. You have not risked much as you decide whether to proceed further. Finally, small talk does provide some kind of link to others. It's often better than being alone.

The kind of information we look for during the experimentation stage depends on the nature of the relationship we are seeking (Miller, 1998; Stewart et al., 2000). For example, both men and women who are seeking short-term relationships look for someone with an exciting personality and a good sense of humour. Being trustworthy and romantic becomes more important to people who are seeking long-term relationships.

Intensifying

During the **intensifying** stage, the kind of qualitatively personal relationship that we defined in Chapter 1 begins to develop. Friendships deepen when friends spend more time together and engage in shared activities such as shopping, eating together, hanging out, playing games, studying, watching movies and sharing their lives with each other (Lee, 2008). Dating couples use a wide range of communication strategies to express their feelings of attraction (Tolhuizen, 1989). About a quarter of the time, they express their feelings directly to discuss the state of the relationship. More often, they use less-direct methods of communication—spending an increasing amount of time together, asking for support from one another, doing favours for the partner, giving tokens of affection, hinting and flirting, expressing feelings non-verbally, getting to know the partner's friends and family, and trying to look more physically attractive (Richmond et al., 1987).

Although commitment grows as a relationship intensifies, communication between partners shows that doubts can still remain. Romantic partners use a variety of strategies to test each other's commitment (Baxter and Wilmot, 1985; Bell and Buerkel-Rothfuss, 1990) including: asking direct questions, testing the partner by presenting challenges that require proof of commitment, hinting in order to gain expressions of commitment, and asking third parties for information. While that kind of behaviour is frequent in the early stages of a relationship, it usually declines as the partners spend more time together.

The intensifying stage is usually a time of relational excitement and even euphoria. For friends it's a time of increased eagerness, positivity and patience (Lee, 2008). For romantic partners, it is often filled with star-struck gazes, goosebumps, and daydreaming. As a result, it's a stage that is regularly depicted in movies and romance novels—after all, we love to watch lovers in love. The problem, of course, is that this stage doesn't last forever. Sometimes, romantic partners who stop feeling goosebumps begin to question whether they are still in love. While it is possible that they are not, it also could be that they've simply moved on to a different stage in their relationship—such as integrating.

Integrating

As the relationship strengthens, the individuals enter an **integrating** stage. They begin to take on an identity as a social unit. Invitations begin to come addressed to a couple. Social circles merge. The partners share each other's commitments: "Sure, we'll spend Thanksgiving with your family." Common property may begin to be designated—our apartment, our car, our song (Baxter, 1987). Partners develop their own personal idioms (Dunleavy and Booth-Butterfield, 2009) and forms of play (Baxter, 1992). They develop routines and rituals that reinforce their identity as a couple—jogging together, eating at a favourite restaurant, expressing affection with a goodnight kiss, and worshipping together (Afifi and Johnson, 1999). As these examples illustrate, the stage of integrating is a time when we give up some characteristics of our former selves and become different people.

As we become more integrated with another person, our sense of obligation to him or her grows (Roloff et al., 1988). We feel required to provide a variety of resources, such as class notes and money, whether or not the other person asks for them. When intimates do make requests of one another, they are relatively straightforward. Gone are the elaborate explanations, inducements, and apologies. In short, partners in an integrated relationship

As integration increases and we become more intimate, uncertainty about our relationship decreases. We become clearer about relationship norms and what behaviour is appropriate and inappropriate. How is getting to this stage of a relationship difficult?

their relationship exists. These gestures can take the form of a contract between business partners or a licence to be married. Bonding signifies a committed relationship that can include cohabitation and common-law relationships, as well as more formal, legally recognized relationships like marriage. Bonding usually generates social support for the relationship. This may be particularly true for lesbian, gay, bisexual, transgendered, and queer (LGBTQ) people. For instance, in one study, gay and lesbian Canadians who were legally married reported feeling better understood by their friends and family. One participant summarized it nicely: "The language of marriage helped us feel more a part of this world. Everyone knows what it means. It helps others start to realize that a relationship is a relationship and we are dealing with the same issues that everyone else deals with." (MacIntosh, Reissing, and Andruff, 2010, p. 84). In addition to social support, customs and laws impose certain rights and responsibilities on partners who have officially bonded.

Bonding usually marks an important turning point in a relationship. Up to now, the relationship may have developed at a steady pace. Experimenting gradually moved into intensifying and then into integrating. Now, however, there is a spurt of commitment. The public display and declaration of exclusivity make this a critical period in the relationship.

Differentiating

Now that the two people have formed this commonality, they need to re-establish individual identities. "How are we different?" "How am I unique?" Former identifications as "we" now emphasize "I." **Differentiating** often takes place when a relationship begins to experience the first, inevitable feelings of stress. Whereas happy employees might refer to "our company," the description might change to "this company" when a raise or some other request isn't forthcoming. We see this kind of differentiation when parents argue over the misbehaviour of a child: "Did you see what *your* daughter just did?"

expect more from each other than they do in less intimate associations.

As integration increases and we become more intimate, uncertainty about our relationship decreases: we become clearer about relationship norms and what behaviour is appropriate and inappropriate. In addition, our ability to influence each other's daily activities increases, such as the amount of time spent with friends and studying (Solomon and Knobloch, 2001). Reducing uncertainty about our partner and the relationship enhances attraction and feelings of closeness (Knobloch and Solomon, 2002).

Bonding

During the **bonding** stage, the partners make symbolic public gestures to show the world that

Differentiation can also be positive—people need to be individuals as well as part of a relationship. The key to successful differentiation is to maintain commitment to a relationship while creating the space for being individuals as well (we will describe this later in the chapter as the connection–autonomy dialectic).

Circumscribing

So far, we have been looking at the growth of relationships. Although some reach a plateau of development, continuing successfully for as long as a lifetime, others pass through several stages of decline and dissolution. In the **circumscribing** stage, communication between members decreases in quantity and quality (Duck, 1987). Subtle hints of dissatisfaction grow more evident. When one or both partners start working later at the office, seeking less and less romance, and arguing more and more, there begins to form a pattern that is hard to ignore (Kellermann et al., 1991). Ironically, both partners in a circumscribed relationship still co-operate in one way, namely by suppressing the true state of the relationship. They hide its decline from others and even from themselves (Vaughn, 1987). Restrictions and restraints characterize this stage, and dynamic communication becomes static. Rather than discussing a disagreement (which requires some degree of energy on both parts), members opt for withdrawal, either mental (through silence or daydreaming and fantasizing) or physical (by spending less time together). Circumscribing doesn't involve total avoidance, which comes later. Rather, it entails a shrinking of interest and commitment.

Stagnating

If circumscribing continues, the relationship begins **stagnating**. Members behave toward each other in old, familiar ways without much feeling. No growth occurs. The stagnating relationship is a hollow shell of its former self. We see stagnation in many workers who have lost enthusiasm for their job yet continue to go through the motions for years. The same sad event occurs for some couples who unenthusiastically have the same conversations, see the same people, and follow the same routines without any sense of joy or novelty.

Avoiding

When stagnation becomes too unpleasant, people in a relationship begin to create distance between each other by **avoiding**. Sometimes, they do it under the guise of excuses ("I've been sick lately and can't see you"); at other times, directly ("Please don't call me; I don't want to see you now"). In either case, by this point, the writing is on the wall about the future of the relationship.

Research by Jon Hess (2000) reveals that there are several ways we gain distance. One way is *expressing detachment*, such as avoiding

© Thinkstock/Pixland.

There are a lot of reasons why relationships don't last and some breakups are more positive than others. What is the "best" breakup you or one of your friends ever had? What was the worst?

the other person altogether, or "tuning them out." A second way is *avoiding involvement*, such as leaving the room, ignoring the person's questions, steering clear of touching, and being superficially polite. *Showing antagonism* is a third technique, which includes behaving in a hostile way and treating the other person as a lesser person. A fourth strategy is to *dissociate mentally* from the other person, such as by thinking about the other person as less capable or as unimportant. A vicious circle is started when one person avoids the other: the more one person avoids the other, the greater the odds the other will reciprocate. And the more topics for discussion that are avoided, the less satisfactory the relationship will be (Sargent, 2002).

Terminating

Not all relationships end, many last a lifetime, but some do end. **Terminating** a relationship has its own distinguishable pattern (Battaglia et al., 1998). Characteristics of this stage often include summary dialogues of where the relationship has gone and the desire to dissociate. The relationship may end with a cordial dinner, a note left on the kitchen table, a phone call, a text message, a social network posting, or a legal document stating the dissolution, or a combination of several methods. Depending on each person's feelings, the terminating stage can be quite short or it may be drawn out over time, with bitter jabs made at each other. In either case, termination doesn't have to be completely negative. Understanding each other's investments in the relationship and needs for personal growth may dilute the hard feelings.

Baxter (1982) and Cody (1982) found that the strategy partners use to disengage depends on the degree of intimacy their relationship had reached. In the least intimate relationships, one partner simply withdraws (physically or emotionally) from the other. In slightly more intimate relationships, one partner is likely to request they see less of each other. When intimacy has been greater, the disengaging partner

REFLECTION

CULTURE AND RELATIONAL STAGES

I think Knapp's model does a good job of describing relational stages in Western culture, but it doesn't work everywhere in the world. My parents were born in India, and their families arranged their marriage when my mother and dad were children. They hardly knew one another when they were married, so most of the experimenting, integrating, and intensifying actually came after their official bonding (i.e., marriage), not before. I'm happy to say that they do love one another, but it happened in a very different way than it usually does in this part of the world

makes an effort to explain the reason for leaving in a way that takes the other's feelings into account. In the most intimate relationships, the initiator expresses grief over the disengagement. In fact, Cody found that the more intimate the relationship, the greater the feeling of obligation to justify terminating it.

Ilana Gershon (2010) interviewed college students about their romantic relationship breakups and found the "channel" or medium (face-to-face, phone, text, or social network) by which the breakup information was communicated mattered a great deal. When students described their breakup stories to her, they always included descriptions of *how* they or their romantic exes chose to communicate during the breakup—although many of the participants were nostalgic for the days when there were far fewer choices about how to communicate the end of a relationship, they found pros and cons for each media choice.

How do the individuals deal with each other after a romantic relationship has ended? The best predictor of whether the individuals will become friends is whether they were friends before their romantic involvement (Metts et al., 1989). The way the couple splits up also makes a difference. It is no surprise to find that friendships are most possible when communication during the breakup was positive, such as expressions that there were no regrets for time spent together and other attempts to minimize hard feelings. When communication during the breakup is negative (manipulative, complaining to third parties), friendships are less likely.

Survivors of broken relationships offer a number of reasons why their relationships do not last (Cupach and Metts, 1986). These reasons are summarized in Table 8.1. The tendency is to blame the breakup on the other person more than on oneself. While women are more likely to blame themselves during a divorce, men are more likely to pin the responsibility on their ex-wives or on outside forces.

Dialectical Tensions in Relationships

Stage-related views, like the one described in the preceding pages, characterize communication as differing in important ways at various points in the life of a relationship. According to the stage approach, what happens during initiating, experimenting, or intensifying is different from the kind of communication that occurs during differentiating, circumscribing, or avoiding.

Not all theorists agree that relational stages are the best way to explain interaction in relationships. Some suggest that communicators grapple with the same kinds of challenges whether a relationship is brand new or has lasted decades. Their focus, then, is on the ongoing maintenance of relationships (Lee, 1998). They argue that communicators seek important, but apparently incompatible, goals. The struggle to achieve these goals creates **dialectical tensions**, conflicts that arise when two opposing or incompatible forces exist simultaneously.

Communication scholars such as Leslie Baxter (Baxter and Braithwaite, 2006; Baxter and Montgomery, 1996), William Rawlins (1992), and Brian Spitzberg (1994) have identified several dialectical forces that make successful communication challenging. They

Stages of Relational Development

Coming Together

- **Initiating:** making contact; demonstrating that you are worth talking to.
- **Experimenting:** searching for common ground; engaging in small talk.
- **Intensifying:** beginning to develop a personal relationship; spending more time together and experiencing excitement.

Relational Maintenance

- **Integrating:** taking on an identity as a social unit; routines, rituals, and obligations grow.
- **Bonding:** making a symbolic gesture to announce the relationship publicly (e.g., marriage, business partnership).
- **Differentiating:** re-establishing individual identities; can be stressful, positive, or both.
- **Circumscribing:** decreasing the quantity and quality of communication; avoiding conversations about problems in the relationship.

Coming Apart

- **Stagnating:** going through hollow routines; no growth in the relationship; little joy or novelty.
- **Avoiding:** creating distance; expressing detachment, avoiding involvement, showing antagonism, dissociating mentally.
- **Terminating:** ending the relationship; can be negative, positive, or both.

Table 8.1 ● Reasons Offered for Termination of Relationship

1. Characteristics of the individuals themselves:
   "I began to feel lonely."
   "She said she felt trapped."
   "He was too conservative."

2. Lack of fulfilment of relational roles:
   "He found no joy in being a father."
   "There were no sexual relations."
   "He tried to tell me what I had to do to be his wife."
   "She went back to school."

3. Unsatisfactory relational cohesiveness and intimacy:
   "We no longer wanted the same things in life."
   "We did nothing together as a couple."
   "We had different needs."

4. Poor regulation of interaction:
   "He wouldn't listen."
   "All our discussions ended in arguments."
   "He threatened me."

5. Third-party involvements:
   "I had an affair with an exciting older man."
   "When I found out she'd been seeing other guys, I was very hurt."
   "The unexpected pregnancy was more than we could handle."
   "I lost my job."

SOURCE: Adapted from W.R. Cupach and S. Metts (1986), "Accounts of relational dissolution: A comparison of marital and non-marital relationships," *Communication Monographs*, 53 (pp. 311–354).

suggest that the struggle to manage these tensions creates the most powerful dynamics in relational communication. In the following pages, we will discuss three influential dialectical tensions, which are summarized in Table 8.2. As the table shows, we experience dialectical challenges both *internally*, vis-à-vis our partners, and *externally* as we and our relational partners encounter other people whose desires clash with our own.

Integration versus Separation

No one is an island. Recognizing this fact, we seek out involvement with others. But, at the same time, we are unwilling to sacrifice our entire identity to even the most satisfying relationship. The conflicting desires for connection and independence are embodied in the **integration–separation dialectic**. This set of apparently contradictory needs creates communication challenges that can show up both within a relationship and between the partners and the world.

We want to be close and connected to others, but at the same time, we seek autonomy and independence. Sociolinguist Deborah Tannen (1986, p. 17) captures the insoluble integration–separation dialectic nicely by evoking the image of two porcupines trying to get through a cold winter:

> They huddle together for warmth, but their sharp quills prick each other, so they pull away. But then they get cold. They have to keep adjusting their closeness and distance to keep from freezing and from getting pricked by their fellow porcupines—the source of both comfort and pain.

Table 8.2 ● Dialectical Tensions

	Dialectic of Integration–Separation	Dialectic of Stability–Change	Dialectic of Expression–Privacy
Our seemingly incompatible goals	connection–autonomy	predictability–novelty	openness–closedness
External manifestations	inclusion–seclusion	conventionality–uniqueness	revelation–concealment

SOURCE: Adapted from D.J. Canary and L. Stafford (eds) (1994). "A dialogic approach to relationship maintenance," *Communication and relational maintenance* (p. 240). Elsevier: Maryland Heights, MO.

We need to get close to each other to have a sense of community, to feel we're not alone in the world. But we need to keep our distance from each other to preserve our independence, so others do not impose on or engulf us. This duality reflects the human condition. We are both individual *and* social creatures. We need other people to survive, but we want to survive as individuals.

Baxter (1994) describes the consequences for relational partners who cannot manage the conflicting needs for connection and autonomy. Some of the most common reasons that relationships break up involve the failure of partners to satisfy one another's needs for connection: "We barely spent any time together"; "My partner wasn't committed to the relationship"; "We had different needs." But other complaints involve excessive demands for connection: "I was feeling trapped"; "I needed freedom."

In accounts of relational turning points, both men and women in heterosexual romantic pairs cited the **connection–autonomy dialectic** as one of the most significant factors affecting their relationship (Baxter and Erbert, 1999). This dialectical tension was crucial when they were negotiating turning points related to commitment, conflict, disengagement, and reconciliation. Research also shows that managing the dialectical tension between connection and autonomy is as important during divorce as it is at the beginning of a marriage, as partners seek ways to salvage and reconcile the unbreakable bonds of their personal history (including

Focus on TECHNOLOGY

CELLPHONES AS A SOURCE OF INTEGRATION–SEPARATION CONFLICT

Cellphones allow us to be in constant contact with our colleagues, friends, family, and romantic partners. While they allow us to be more integrated into each other's lives, they also have the potential to reduce opportunities for separation and independence. They create the expectation that we are always available. This constant connection can create tension in relationships. For instance, teenagers may perceive parents' monitoring via cellphones as a violation of their need for independence (Weisskirch, 2009; 2011). Similarly, smart phones have been described as "tethers" that enable employers and employees to be constantly connected infringing on each other's autonomy and work–life balance (Sullivan, 2014). Round the clock contact has been found to take its toll on the romantic relationships of young adults too (Duran et al., 2011; Luo, 2014). In one study, young couples with lower levels of relationship satisfaction were more likely to report that they experienced conflict about cellphone use and availability expectations. Participants who had higher availability expectations (e.g., "We expect each other to have our cellphones on." "We are expected to call or text when we change locations."), and who disagreed with their partner about cellphone use, were more likely to report being less satisfied with their romantic relationships. Some participants' dissatisfaction stemmed from the feeling that their independence was being restricted. They felt their freedom to see their friends and engage in activities was constrained—they wanted more separation from their partner. Conversely, some participants reported feeling less satisfied about the time they spent with their partner and wanted more control over their partner—they wanted more integration with their partner (Duran et al., 2011). The integration–separation tensions inherent in their relationships were revealed in their conflicts about cellphone use. Finally, cellphones have been associated with both increased relationship satisfaction among friends (because they allow for increased relationship maintenance), as well as decreases in relationship satisfaction (when they are associated with overdependence) (Hall and Baym, 2012). The increased access to our friends, romantic partners, family, and colleagues provided by cellphones and the interpersonal conflict that constant availability can create helps to highlight the integration–separation tension that is part of all our interpersonal relationships.

finances, children, and friends) with their new independence (Pam and Pearson, 1998). Even at the end of life, the connection–autonomy dialectic comes into play. When a loved one is in an extended period of declining health, the partner often feels torn between the desire to stay close and the need to let go. This tension is especially poignant when one partner suffers from Alzheimer's disease and becomes mentally absent while physically present (Baxter et al., 2002).

Parents and children must deal constantly with the conflicting tugs of connection and autonomy, as we describe in Chapter 9 in some detail. These struggles do not end when children grow up and leave home. Parents experience the mixed feelings of relief at their new freedom and a longing to stay connected to their adult children. Likewise, grown children feel excitement at being on their own, and yet miss the bonds they had likely taken for granted since the beginning of their lives (Blacker, 1999; Fulmer, 1999).

Stability versus Change

Stability is an important need in relationships, but too much of it can lead to feelings of staleness. The **stability–change dialectic** captures the tensions between the need for predictability and the need for novelty in our relationships. Although nobody wants a completely unpredictable relational partner ("You are not the person I married!"), humorist Dave Barry (1990, p. 47) exaggerates only slightly when he talks about the boredom that can come from spouses knowing each other too well:

> After a decade or so of marriage, you know *everything* about your spouse, every habit and opinion and twitch and tic and minor skin growth. You could write a seventeen-pound book solely about

the way your spouse eats. This kind of intimate knowledge can be very handy in certain situations—such as when you are on a TV quiz show where the object is to identify your spouse from the sound of his or her chewing—but it tends to lower the passion level of a relationship.

REFLECTION

ONE PLUS ONE MAKES THREE

I've been to a lot of weddings in the last few years, and several couples have included a ceremony that got me thinking about dialectical challenges in a marriage. There are usually three candles in a holder—two that are lit on the outsides and a centre one that is not. The bride and groom each take an outside candle and light the centre one, symbolizing that they've created a new union together.

The part that comes next is most interesting to me. Some couples blow out their own individual candles, leaving only the centre one burning. Others leave their own individual candles burning.

I like the symbolism of leaving all three candles burning. It reminds me of the connection–autonomy dialectic that we talked about in class. If only the centre one is burning, there's connection without autonomy. If only the outside ones are burning, it is autonomy without connection. Leaving all three lit says to me that being a couple is important, but so is being an individual.

© lulu27/iStockphoto

Expression versus Privacy

Disclosure is one characteristic of interpersonal relationships. Yet, along with the drive for intimacy, we have an equally important need to maintain some space between ourselves and others. These sometimes-conflicting drives create the **expression–privacy dialectic.**

The internal struggle between expression and privacy shows up in our need to be open with our relationship partners (and have them be forthcoming with us) and our simultaneous need to keep some things to ourselves (and their need to do the same). What do you do in an intimate relationship when a person you care about asks an important question that you don't want to answer? (e.g., "Do you think I'm attractive?" "Are you having a good time?") Because of your commitment to the relationship, you may wish to be honest, but your concern for the other person's feelings and a desire for privacy may lead you to be less than completely honest. Partners use a variety of strategies to gain privacy from each other (Burgoon et al., 1989; Petronio, 2000). For example, they may confront the other person directly and explain that they do not want to continue a discussion, or they may be less direct and offer non-verbal cues, change the topic, or leave the room.

Although all of the dialectical tensions play an important role in relationships, some are more frequent than others depending on the type of relationship. For instance, young married couples have reported that autonomy–connection was the most frequent tension in their relationships (Pawlowski, 1998), while adolescents whose parents had divorced have reported that the **openness–closedness dialectic** is the biggest tension in their relationships with the parent they no longer live with (Braithwaite and Baxter, 2006). Women in abusive relationships wrestle with the dialectic of staying private or disclosing the abuse (Dieckmann, 2000). Telling other people that she is being abused by her partner can be the first step in a woman's disengaging from a violent relationship, but it can also threaten her self-esteem, her security, and her very life.

Of all the dialectical tensions, the most important ones to manage, in most relationships, seem to be autonomy–connection and openness–closedness (Baxter and Erbert 1999; Erbert, 2000).

Strategies for Managing Dialectical Tensions

Managing the dialectical tensions outlined in these pages presents communication challenges. There are at least eight ways these challenges can be managed (Baxter and Braithwaite, 2006; Griffin, 2009):

1. *Denial.* In the strategy of denial, communicators respond to one end of the dialectical spectrum and ignore the other. For example, a couple caught between the conflicting desires for stability and novelty might find their struggle for change too difficult to manage. So they choose to follow predictable, if unexciting, patterns of relating to one another.
2. *Disorientation.* In this mode, communicators feel so overwhelmed and helpless,

TAKE TWO

- **Dialectical tensions:** conflicts that arise when two opposing forces exist simultaneously; they exist within personal relationships and also between individuals/couples and the external world.
- **Integration–separation:** conflicting desires for connection and independence within a relationship.
- **Stability–change:** conflicting needs for constancy and variation within a relationship.
- **Expression–privacy:** conflicting needs to share information, but also to keep things confidential within a relationship.

they are unable to confront their problems. They might fight, freeze, or even leave the relationship. Partners who discover soon after the honeymoon that living a "happily-ever-after," conflict-free life is impossible might become so terrified that they decide their marriage is a mistake.

3. *Alternation.* Communicators who use this strategy choose one end of the dialectical spectrum at some times, and the other end on different occasions. Friends, for example, might manage the integration–separation dialectic by alternating between times when they spend a large amount of time together and other periods when they live independent lives.

4. *Segmentation.* Partners who use this tactic compartmentalize different areas of their relationship. For example, a couple might manage the expression–privacy dialectic by sharing almost all their feelings about mutual friends with one another, but keeping certain parts of their romantic histories private.

5. *Balance.* Communicators who try to balance dialectical tensions recognize that both forces are legitimate and try to manage them through compromise. As we point out in Chapter 10, compromise is inherently a situation in which everybody loses at least a little of what he or she wants. A couple caught between the conflicting desires for stability and change might seek balance by compromising with a lifestyle that is neither as predictable as one wants nor as surprise-filled as the other seeks—not an ideal outcome.

6. *Integration.* With this approach, communicators simultaneously accept opposing forces without trying to diminish them. Barbara Montgomery (1993) describes a couple who accept the need both for stability and for change by devising a "predictably novel" approach. Once a week, they would do something together that they had never done before. Similarly, Dawn Braithwaite and her colleagues (1998) found that step-families often manage the tension between the "old family" and the

"new family" by adapting and blending their family rituals.

7. *Recalibration.* Communicators can respond to dialectical challenges by reframing them so that the apparent contradiction disappears. Consider how a couple who felt hurt by each other's unwillingness to share parts of their past might redefine the secrets as creating an attractive aura of mystery instead of being a problem to be solved. The desire for privacy would still remain, but it would no longer compete with a need for openness about every aspect of the past.

8. *Reaffirmation.* This approach acknowledges that dialectical tensions will never disappear. Instead of trying to make them go away, reaffirming communicators accept—or even embrace—the challenges they present. The metaphorical view of relational life as a kind of roller coaster reflects this orientation, and communicators who use reaffirmation view dialectical tensions as part of the ride.

Characteristics of Relational Development

Whether you analyze a relationship in terms of stages or dialectical dynamics, two characteristics are true of every interpersonal relationship.

Relationships Are Constantly Changing

Relationships are rarely stable for long periods of time. In fairy tales, a couple may live happily ever after, but in real life this sort of equilibrium is less common. Consider a husband and wife who have been married for some time. Although they have formally bonded, their relationship will probably shift forward and backward along the spectrum of stages, and different dialectical tensions will become more or less important at different times.

Richard Conville (1991) captures this constant change by describing relational cycles in which the partners continually move through a series of stages before returning to ones they previously encountered, although at a new level. He pictures this movement as a kind of

Focus on RESEARCH

HUMOUR AND ROMANTIC RELATIONSHIPS

There is a good deal of research that suggests that people value a sense of humour in their friends and romantic partners (Kuiper, 2010; Treger et al., 2013). People rate those with a good sense of humour as more attractive than their less funny peers. Bethany Butzer and Nicholas Kuiper (2008), researchers at the University of Western Ontario, wanted to find out what types of humour romantic partners use in two types of situations—a typical conflict and a typical pleasant event. These investigators presented two vignettes to 155 undergraduate students who were currently involved in romantic relationships. The conflict vignette was designed to invoke feelings of jealousy and described a situation in which the partner had lunch with an opposite-sex friend. The participant was asked to imagine a discussion with their partner about this event and indicate how frequently they would use positive, negative, or avoiding humour in this discussion. In the pleasant vignette, participants were asked to imagine having lunch with their partner and describing to each other the events of the previous day, during which they had not been in touch. Again, participants rated the frequency with which they would use positive, negative, and avoiding humour

during this discussion. Finally, participants rated their satisfaction with their romantic relationships. Individuals in this study reported that they would use positive humour most often with their partners—humour that made them feel closer as a couple and eased the tension. They used negative humour—put-downs highlighting their partners' weaknesses—the least, and they used avoiding humour—changing the subject, avoiding saying what was on their mind—with medium frequency. In addition, individuals who reported high levels of positive humour and low levels of negative and avoiding humour also reported being more satisfied in their romantic relationships. In the conflict situation, participants were less likely to use negative and avoiding humour, but were not more likely to use positive humour than in the positive event scenario. These researchers conclude that positive humour contributes to romantic satisfaction and that satisfied partners are careful not to escalate conflicts through the use of negative and avoiding humour.

Critical thinking: *Do you think that the stage of the relationship might affect couple uses of humour? Why or why not?*

---

helix, as shown in Figure 8.2. According to Conville, we move from security (*integration* in Knapp's terminology) to disintegration (*differentiating*) to alienation (*circumscribing*) to resynthesis (*intensifying, integrating*) to a new level of security. This cycle repeats itself again and again. This back-and-forth movement reflects the dialectical tensions identified by Baxter and others.

Movement Is Always to a New Place

Even though a relationship may move back to a stage it has experienced before, it will never be the same as before. For example, most healthy long-term relationships will go through several phases of experimenting, as the partners try out new ways of behaving with each other. Although each phase has the same general features, the specifics will feel different each time.

Similarly, how partners manage the openness–closedness dialectic at one time will affect how they experience and manage it at another time with the same or different relational issues. As you learned in Chapter 1, communication is irreversible. Partners can never go back to "the way things were." Sometimes, this fact may lead to regrets, but it can also make relationships exciting since it lessens the chance for boredom and can lead to novelty and growth (Montgomery, 1993).

Communicating about Relationships

By now, it is clear that relationships are complex, dynamic, and important. How do communicators address relational issues with one another?

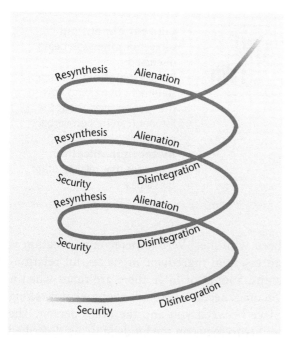

Figure 8.2 ● A Helical Model of Relational Cycles

Content and Relational Messages

In Chapter 1, we saw that every message has a content dimension and a relational dimension. The most obvious component of most messages is their content—the subject being discussed. The content of statements like "It's your turn to do the dishes" or "I'm busy Saturday night" is obvious.

But content messages are not the only information being exchanged when two people communicate. In addition, every message—both verbal and non-verbal—has a second, relational dimension, which makes statements about how the communicators feel toward one another (Dillard et al., 1999; Watzlawick et al., 1967). These relational messages deal with one or more of the social needs: intimacy, affinity, respect, and control. Consider the two examples we just mentioned:

- Imagine two ways of saying, "It's your turn to do the dishes"—one that is demanding and another that is matter-of-fact. Notice how the different non-verbal messages

make statements about how the sender views control in this part of the relationship. The demanding tone says, in effect, "I have a right to tell you what to do around the house," whereas the matter-of-fact one suggests, "I'm just reminding you of something you might have overlooked."

- You can easily imagine two ways to deliver the statement, "I'm busy Saturday night"—one with some affection and the other without.

Like these messages, every statement we make goes beyond discussing the subject at hand and says something about the way the speaker feels about the recipient. You can prove this fact by listening for the relational messages implicit in your own statements to others and theirs to you.

Most of the time, we are unaware of the relational messages that bombard us every day. Sometimes, these messages don't capture our awareness because they match our belief about the amount of control, liking, or intimacy that is appropriate in a relationship. For example, you would probably not be offended if your boss told you to drop everything and tackle a certain job, because you agree that supervisors

REFLECTION

SENDING THE WRONG RELATIONAL MESSAGE

I work 30 hours a week and have a full course load at school, so I am very busy. Sometimes, when my little brother wants to hang out and talk, I give him the brush-off. While he's telling me about his day, I keep typing on the computer or reading a book. After a while, I sigh and start replying automatically, "Yeah, yeah." Last night, he asked, "Why don't you like me anymore?" I realized that, in my obsession with staying on top of my work, I've been giving him the wrong impression. Next time, I'll either give him my attention or let him know explicitly that I can't.

have the right to direct employees. However, if your boss delivered the order in a condescending, sarcastic, or abusive tone of voice, you would probably be offended. Your complaint wouldn't be with the order itself, but with the way it was delivered. "I may work for this company," you might think, "but I'm not a slave or an idiot. I deserve to be treated like a human being."

Expression of Relational Messages

Exactly how are relational messages communicated? As the boss–employee example suggests, they are usually expressed non-verbally. To test this fact for yourself, imagine how you could act while saying, "Can you help me for a minute?" in a way that communicates each of the following messages:

- superiority
- helplessness
- friendliness
- aloofness
- sexual desire
- irritation

Although non-verbal behaviour is a good source of relational messages, remember that it is ambiguous. The sharp tone you take as a personal insult might be due to fatigue, and the interruption you take as an attempt to ignore your ideas might be a sign of pressure that has nothing to do with you. Before you jump to conclusions about relational clues, it is a good idea to verify the accuracy of your interpretation with the other person: "When you cut me off, I got the idea you are angry at me. Is that right?"

Not all relational messages are non-verbal. Social scientists use the term **metacommunication** to describe messages that refer to other messages (Ruesch and Bateson, 1951). In other words, metacommunication is communication about communication. Whenever we discuss a relationship with others, we are metacommunicating: "I wish we could stop arguing so much," or "I appreciate how honest you've

- **Content dimension:** the subject of a message being discussed.
- **Relational dimension:** a statement describing how the speaker feels about the listener (can be non-verbal or verbal).
- **Metacommunication:** messages that refer to other messages.

been with me." Verbal metacommunication is an essential ingredient in successful relationships. Sooner or later, there are times when it becomes necessary to talk about what is taking place between you and the other person. The ability to focus on the kinds of issues described in this chapter can be the tool for keeping your relationship on track.

Despite its importance, overt metacommunication is not a common feature of most relationships (Fogel and Branco, 1997; Wilmot, 1987). In fact, there seems to be an aversion to it, even among many intimates. When 90 people were asked to identify the taboo subjects in their personal relationships, the most frequent topics involved metacommunication (Baxter and Wilmot, 1985). For example, people were reluctant to discuss the state of their current relationships and the norms ("rules") that governed their lives together. Nevertheless metacommunication can play an important role in relational maintenance and repair (Becker et al., 2008).

Communication that Keeps Relationships Going

We have all heard the advice that we must "work" at relationships if we want them to be positive and fulfilling, but rarely do we hear about exactly what that "work" involves. Daniel Canary and his colleagues (1993) have identified a number of communication strategies that are used by friends, relatives, romantic partners, and co-workers to maintain positive relationships. The four strategies most commonly used by university students were:

- *Openness:* disclosing information, being empathetic, talking about the relationship, and listening to each other.
- *Assurances:* letting each other know that the relationship is important, comforting each other, and being supportive.
- *Joint activities:* spending time with each other.
- *Positivity:* trying to make interactions pleasant and cheerful, showing affection, and doing favours for each other.

Of the strategies listed above, positivity and assurances are the best predictors of marital satisfaction (Dainton et al., 1994). In addition to the strategies described above, communication researchers have found that routinely communicating affection is a strategy married couples employ in maintaining their relationships. Giving and receiving both verbal (e.g., "I love you") and non-verbal (e.g., hugs, kisses, holding hands) affection is another strong predictor of marital satisfaction and commitment (Dainton et al., 1994; Horan and Booth-Butterfield, 2010). In addition to communicating affection, being open, giving assurances, doing things together, and being positive, how we give and receive advice and criticism, and how we resolve conflicts also contribute a great deal to the satisfaction we experience in our relationships (Afifi et al., 2009; Busby and Holman, 2009; Laursen and Hafen, 2010; Renshaw et al., 2010; Stafford et al., 2000). We have discussed giving advice in Chapter 7, and in the next two chapters we will examine ways to give others feedback and methods of resolving conflicts that can go a long way in developing and maintaining fulfilling interpersonal relationships. Finally, it is important to remember that making relationships work is a transactional endeavour. The communication strategies of both partners contribute to the quality and ebb and flow of the relationship they share.

SUMMARY

There are several explanations for why we form relationships with some people and not with others. These explanations include appearance (physical attractiveness), similarity, complementarity, rewards, competence, proximity, and disclosure. Intimacy and distance are important parts of our relationships with others and there are several ways to establish both. Gender and culture exert a strong influence on both the amount of intimacy in a relationship and how that intimacy is communicated. A female intimacy style is usually characterized by self-disclosure and a male intimacy style by shared activities. These differences exist within larger cultural differences. Each culture has rules that govern intimate communication, from touching in public to the disclosure of personal information. Also, each culture defines the extent to which any relationship should be formal and distant or close and intimate.

Some theorists argue that interpersonal relationships may go through as many as ten stages of growth and deterioration. They suggest that communication may reflect more than one stage at a given time, although one stage will be dominant. Another way to analyze the dynamics of interpersonal communication is in terms of dialectical tensions, that is, mutually opposing, incompatible desires that are part of our relationships and that can never be completely resolved. These tensions include integration–separation, stability–change, and expression–privacy. Both views characterize relationships as constantly changing, so that communication is more of a process than a static thing.

Relationships are developed and maintained through communication. Messages have both content and relational dimensions. Relational messages are sometimes expressed overtly by verbal metacommunication; however, they are conveyed non-verbally more frequently. There are many communication strategies that partners use to maintain satisfying relationships. They include communicating affection, being open, giving assurances, doing things together, and being positive. In addition, the ways we give and receive advice and criticism, as well as our approaches to resolving conflicts, contribute to the quality of our relationships. We will deal with these last two elements in the next two chapters.

MULTIPLE-CHOICE QUESTIONS

1. We seek to have relationships with people who give us rewards that are equal to or greater than the costs we encounter in dealing with them. This statement is the basis of
   a. social exchange theory.
   b. comparison level theory.
   c. the theory of complementarity.
   d. proximity theory.

2. In their study of how competence and imperfection combine, Elliot Aronson and his colleagues found that people found which of the following quiz show contestants most attractive?
   a. The person with superior ability who did not spill the coffee.
   b. The person with average ability who did not spill the coffee.
   c. The person with superior ability who spilled the coffee.
   d. The person with average ability who spilled the coffee.

3. Networking, offering, approaching, and sustaining are all strategies that people use during which stage of relationship development?
   a. initiating
   b. experimenting
   c. intensifying
   d. integrating

4. People who become anxious in social situations often prefer to use text-based communication to initiate relationships with others.
   a. true
   b. false

5. What is the name for the conflicts that arise when two incompatible forces exist simultaneously in a relationship?
   a. integration–separation dialectic
   b. stability–change dialectic
   c. expression–privacy dialectic
   d. dialectic tension

6. People tend to blame themselves for their relationship breakups.
   a. true
   b. false

7. Grace and Zoe enjoy sharing their beliefs about spirituality, politics, and the meaning of life with each other. They find these discussions interesting and they feel secure in knowing they can safely share their deeply held beliefs with each other. Their relationship involves which type of intimacy?
   a. emotional
   b. physical
   c. intellectual
   d. shared activities

8. Physical and verbal affection is an important component of satisfying marriages.
   a. true
   b. false

9. Laura is very reserved with George. She talks very little and doesn't laugh at his jokes or ask any questions. Laura is trying to
   a. establish distance.
   b. resolve the stability–change dialectic.

c. provide assurances.

d. accomplish all of the above.

10. The part of the message that expresses how the communicators feel about

each other is referred to as the content dimension.

a. true

b. false

Answers: 1. a; 2. c; 3. a; 4. a; 5. d; 6. b; 7. c; 8. c; 9. a; 10. b

ACTIVITIES

1. Invitation to Insight

What kinds of intimacy characterize your relationships? Answer the questions below as you think about your relationship with an important person in your life.

a. What is the level of physical intimacy in your relationship?

b. What intellectual intimacy do you share?

c. How emotionally intimate are you? Is your emotional intimacy deeper in some ways than in others?

d. What shared activities are important in this relationship?

e. Has your intimacy level changed? If so, in what ways?

After answering these questions, ask yourself how satisfied you are with the amount of intimacy in this relationship. Identify any changes you would like to occur, and describe the steps you could take to make them happen.

2. Critical Thinking Probe

Some critics claim that Knapp's model of relational stages is better at describing romantic relationships than other types. Use a variety of romantic and non-romantic interpersonal relationships from your experience to evaluate the breadth of his model. If the model does not describe the developmental path of all types of interpersonal relationships, can you suggest alternative models?

3. Invitation to Insight

How do you manage the dialectical tensions in your important relationships? Is there a pattern to what you and the other person do, or does it depend on the type of relationship you

have? Identify at least two dialectical tensions in two different relationships—one relationship, perhaps, with a person with whom you work closely, and the other with a romantic partner. How is each tension managed? Which approach do you and your partner tend to use (denial, disorientation, alternation, segmentation, balance, integration, recalibration, or reaffirmation)? What seem to be the conditions that determine which method you and your partner use?

4. Ethical Challenge

Consider the notion that we often face conflicting goals when we communicate in an attempt to meet our own needs and those of others. Use the information found on pages 274–279 to identify a situation in which your personal goals conflict with those of another person. What obligation do you have to communicate in a way that helps the other person reach his or her goals? Is it possible to honour this obligation and still try to satisfy your own needs?

5. Skill Builder

Describe three unexpressed relational messages in one or more of your interpersonal relationships.

a. Explain how you could have used metacommunication to express each one. Consider skills you learned in other chapters, such as perception checking, "I" language, and paraphrasing.

b. Discuss the possible benefits and drawbacks of this kind of metacommunication in each of the situations you identified. On the basis of your discussion here, what principles do you believe should guide your decisions about whether and when to focus explicitly on relational issues?

6. Role Play

Choose a partner. Pretend you don't know each other and you want to initiate contact with this person in class. What strategies might you use? (Review the strategies listed on pages 267–268.) Role-play your attempts to initiate contact. Which strategies worked well? Are there any you would not try in this context? Now reverse roles and think of another context or situation in which your partner might want to initiate contact with you (e.g., at work, at a party) Role-play initiating contact in this new situation. Afterward, again analyze the strategies that worked, those that didn't, and the ones that felt appropriate or inappropriate in this situation, and discuss why.

DISCUSSION QUESTIONS

1. Why do we form relationships with other people?
2. Describe the four different types of intimacy presented in the chapter and give an example of each from your own relationships. Do you think an ideal intimate relationship would include all four? Why or why not?
3. Describe the different ways men and women develop and maintain intimacy in relationships. Is one style better than the other? Why or why not?
4. The level of intimacy viewed as appropriate in certain relationships varies between cultures. Describe some of the differences. What is your experience?
5. Do you think Knapp's model of the stages of relational development can be adapted to more collectivistic cultures? Why or why not?
6. Describe the dialectical tensions that exist in one of your relationships (e.g., with your parents, a friend, or a romantic partner). How do you manage these tensions in that relationship?
7. Despite its importance, metacommunication is not a common feature of most relationships. Why do you think this is?
8. Review the strategies for relationship maintenance described on pages 270–272. Which do you use in your most satisfying relationships? Which do you use in your least satisfying relationships? Is there a relationship between the number of maintenance strategies you use and your satisfaction with your relationships? Why or why not?

JOURNAL IDEAS

1. You can get a sense of how your desires for both intimacy and distance operate by reflecting on a relationship with an important person you see regularly. For this journal exercise you might choose a friend, family member, or romantic partner. For at least a week, chart how your communication with this relational partner reflects your desire for either intimacy or distance. Use a 7-point scale, in which behaviour seeking high intimacy receives a 7 and behaviour designed to avoid physical, intellectual, and/or emotional contact receives a 1. Use ratings from 2 to 6 to represent intermediate stages. Record at least one rating per day, making more detailed entries if your desire for intimacy or distance changes during that period. What tactics did you use to establish or maintain distance? After charting your communication, reflect on what the results tell you about your personal desire for intimacy and distance. Consider the following questions:

   - Was there a pattern of alternating phases of intimacy and distance during the time you observed?
   - Was this pattern typical of your communication in this relationship over a longer period of time?
   - Does your communication in other relationships contain a similar mixture of intimacy and distance?
   - Most importantly, are you satisfied with the results you discovered in this exercise?
   - If you are not satisfied, how would you like to change your communication behaviour?

2. Choose one of the dialectal tensions described in this chapter and describe how it operates in one of your close relationship. Review this journal entry in a couple of weeks and see if the tension has changed during the interval. If so, how has it changed? Why do you think it has changed? If no change has occurred, why do you think it has remained so stable? Are there environmental factors that influence how these competing needs affect this relationship? If so, what are they?

9

Communication Climate

Chapter Outline

Key Terms

aggressiveness	face-threatening acts
ambiguous response	impersonal response
argumentativeness	impervious response
certainty	incongruous response
communication climate	interrupting response
complaining	irrelevant response
confirming communication	neutrality
controlling communication	problem orientation
defensiveness	provisionalism
description	spiral
disagreeing message	spontaneity
disconfirming communication	strategy
equality	superiority
evaluation	tangential response

Learning Objectives

YOU SHOULD UNDERSTAND:

- the definition of communication climate;
- the importance of being valued and confirmed;
- the characteristics of confirming, disagreeing, and disconfirming messages;
- the nature of positive and negative communication spirals;
- the relationship between the presenting self (face) and defensiveness;
- the types of messages that are likely to create positive communication climates; and
- the various ways to transform negative communication climates.

YOU SHOULD BE ABLE TO:

- identify confirming, disagreeing, and disconfirming messages and patterns in your own relationships;
- identify the parts of your presenting self (face) that you defend, and the consequences of doing so;
- create messages that are likely to build supportive rather than defensive communication climates; and
- create appropriate non-defensive responses to real or hypothetical criticisms.

How would you describe your most important relationships? Fair or stormy? Hot or cold? Just as physical locations have characteristic weather patterns, interpersonal relationships have unique climates, too. You can't measure the interpersonal climate by looking at a thermometer or glancing at the sky, but it's there nonetheless. Every relationship has a feeling, a pervasive mood that colours the actions of the participants.

What Is Communication Climate?

The term **communication climate** refers to the social tone of a relationship. A climate doesn't involve specific activities as much as the way people feel about each other as they carry out those activities. Consider two interpersonal communication classes. Both meet for the same length of time and follow the same syllabus. It's easy to imagine how one of these classes might be a friendly, comfortable place to learn, whereas the other could be cold and tense—even hostile. It is not the course content that differs—it is the way the people in the classroom feel about and treat each other.

Just as every classroom has a unique climate, so does every relationship. Romances, friendships, and families—just like neighbourhoods, cities, and countries—can be defined by their social tone. Another obvious place for observing the effect of a climate impact is the workplace, which may explain why the topic is so widely studied (Scarpero, 2000; Sopow, 2007). Have you ever held a job where backbiting, criticism, and suspicion were the norm? Or have you been lucky enough to work where the atmosphere was positive, encouraging, and supportive? If you have experienced both, you know what a difference climate makes. Other studies reinforce the fact that employees are more creative and willing to solve problems when they feel supported at work (Kholer et al., 2010). People are more committed to jobs in which they experience a positive communication climate (e.g., Bakar et al., 2010; Guzley,

1992; Madlock and Kennedy-Lightsey, 2010). Like their meteorological counterparts, communication climates are shared by everyone involved. It's rare to find one person describing a relationship as open and positive while another characterizes it as cold and hostile. And, just like the weather, communication climates can change over time. A relationship can be overcast at one time and sunny at another. Carrying the analogy to its conclusion, we should say that communication climate forecasting is not a perfect science. Unlike the weather, however, people can change their communication climates—and that's why it is important to understand them. We'll look at several climate issues in this chapter: how communication climates develop, how and why we respond defensively in certain climates, and what can be done to create positive climates and transform negative ones.

How Communication Climates Develop

Why does some communication create a positive climate while other communication has the opposite effect? A short, but accurate answer is that communication climates are determined by the degree to which people see themselves as *valued*. Communicators who perceive others as liking, appreciating, and respecting them react positively, whereas those who feel unimportant or abused react negatively. Social scientists use the term **confirming communication** to describe messages that convey valuing. In one form or another, confirming messages say, "you exist," "you matter," "you're important." By contrast, **disconfirming communication** signals a lack of regard. In one form or another, disconfirming messages say, "I don't care about you," "I don't like you," "you're not important to me."

As we have stressed throughout this book, every message has a relational dimension along with its content. This means that we send and receive confirming and disconfirming messages virtually whenever we communicate. Serious conversations about our relationships may not be common (Goldsmith and Baxter, 1996), but we convey our attitudes about one another even when we talk about everyday matters. In other words, it isn't *what* we communicate about that shapes a relational climate as much as *how* we speak and act toward one another.

It is hard to overstate the importance of confirming messages and the impact of disconfirming ones. Victims of hateful speech can experience the same long-term consequences that follow other traumas: feeling dazed, shocked, ill, and angry (Leets, 2002). Children who lack confirmation suffer more intense feelings of anxiety, depression, grief, jealousy, and loneliness; higher incidences of mental and physical illness; and a broad range of behavioural problems, such as criminality and suicide (Osterman, 2001). In school, a sense of belonging is associated with a positive attitude toward school, class work, and teachers, and greater participation, school engagement, and achievement. Both teachers' and parents' supportive interactions help to moderate the daily challenges and frustrations children face at school and help them to be more successful (Strom and Boster, 2007). Even in post-secondary settings when instructors behave in ways that are confirming to students (e.g., respond to student questions, employ and interactional teaching style, demonstrate interest in students' learning) their students experience an abundance of emotional benefits (Goldman and Goodboy, 2014; Titsworth et al., 2013). A confirming climate is also important in marriage, where it is the best predictor of marital satisfaction (Clarke, 1973; Veroff et al., 1998). Satisfied couples have a 5:1 ratio of positive to negative statements, while the ratio for dissatisfied partners is 1:1 (Gottman, 2003).

Like beauty, the decision about whether a message is confirming or disconfirming is in the eyes of the beholder. Consider, for example, times when you took a comment that might have sounded unsupportive to an outsider ("You turkey!") as a sign of affection within the context of your personal relationship. Likewise, a comment that the sender might have meant to be helpful ("I'm telling you this for your own good . . .") could easily be regarded as a disconfirming attack.

Levels of Message Confirmation

Figure 9.1 shows that the range of confirming and disconfirming communication includes several categories of messages, which we describe in the following pages.

Confirming Messages

There is no guarantee that others will regard even your best attempts at confirming messages the way you intend them, but research shows that three increasingly positive types of messages have the best chance of being perceived as confirming (Cissna and Sieberg, 2006)

Recognition The most fundamental act of confirmation is to recognize the other person. Recognition seems easy and obvious, yet there are many times when we do not respond to others on this basic level. Failure to call or visit a friend is a common example. So is failure

Confirming	Disagreeing	Disconfirming
Endorsement	Argumentativeness	Impervious
Acknowledgment	Complaining	Interrupting
Recognition	Aggressiveness	Irrelevant
		Tangential
		Impersonal
		Ambiguous
		Incongruous
VALUING		**NON-VALUING**

Figure 9.1 ● Confirmation–Disconfirmation Continuum

to return an email or text message. Likewise, avoiding eye contact and not approaching someone you know can send a negative message. Of course, this lack of recognition may simply be an oversight. You may not notice your friend, or the pressures of work and school may prevent you from staying in touch. Nonetheless, if the other person *thinks* you avoided contact, the message has the effect of being disconfirming.

Acknowledgment   Acknowledging the ideas and feelings of others is a stronger form of confirmation than simple recognition. Listening is probably the most common form of acknowledgment. Silently and attentively paying attention to another person's words is one measure of your interest. Not surprisingly, employees give high marks to managers who solicit their opinions—even when the managers don't accept every suggestion (Allen, 1995). As we saw in Chapter 5, reflecting the speaker's thoughts and feelings can be a powerful way to offer support when others have problems.

Endorsement   Whereas acknowledgment says you are interested in another person, endorsement means that you agree with her or him or otherwise find that person important. It's easy to see why endorsement is the strongest type of confirming message, since it communicates the highest form of valuing. The most obvious form of endorsement is agreeing, but it isn't necessary to agree completely with other people in order to endorse their message. You can probably find something in the message that you endorse. "I can see why you were so angry," you might reply to a friend, even if you don't approve of his or her outburst. Of course, outright praise is a strong form of endorsement, one you can use surprisingly often once you look for opportunities to do so. Non-verbal endorsement also can enhance the quality of a relational climate. For example, simple acts like maintaining eye contact and nodding while someone speaks can confirm the value of a speaker's idea. On a more intimate level, hugs can sometimes communicate endorsement in ways that words cannot.

Disagreeing Messages

Between confirming and disconfirming lies a type of message that isn't always easy to categorize. A **disagreeing message** essentially says, "You're wrong." In its most constructive form, disagreement includes two confirming components: recognition and acknowledgment. At its worst, a brutal disagreeing message can so devastate another person

© MarcusPhoto1 /iStockphoto.

There is no guarantee that others will regard even your best attempts at confirming communication the way you intend it, but research shows that recognition, acknowledgment, and endorsement have the best chance at being perceived as confirming. When have you used confirming communication and found the other person felt valued? When have you felt valued when others use confirming communication? Have you ever used confirming communication, only to find the other person did not feel valued? Has this happened to you in return?

that the benefits of recognition and acknowledgment are lost. Because there are better and worse ways to disagree with others, disagreeing messages need to be put on a positive-to-negative scale. We will do just that in this section as we discuss three types of disagreement: *argumentativeness*, *complaining*, and *aggressiveness*.

Argumentativeness Normally when we call a person argumentative, we're making an unfavourable evaluation because they argue too much. However, the ability to create and deliver a sound argument is something we admire in lawyers, talk-show participants, writers of "letters to the editor," and politicians. Taking a positive approach to the term, communication researchers define **argumentativeness** as presenting and defending positions on issues while attacking positions taken by others (Infante and Rancer, 1982). The key to maintaining a positive climate while arguing a point is the *way* you present your ideas. It is crucial to attack issues, not people. In addition, a sound argument is received better when it's delivered in a supportive, affirming manner (Infante and Gorden, 1989). The supportive kinds of messages outlined on pages 291–292 show how it is possible to argue in a respectful, constructive way. It is important to keep in mind that not all cultures value a clear and assertively made argument. Cultures that value collectivism, high power distance, and high-context communication patterns may be less appreciative of this kind of assertive communication than people in more individualistic, low power distance, and low-context cultures such as Canada and the United States (e.g., Koc, 2010; Ma and Jaeger, 2010).

Complaining When communicators aren't prepared to argue, but still want to register dissatisfaction, they often complain. As for all disagreeing messages, some ways of **complaining** are better than others. Jess Alberts (1988, 1990) found that satisfied couples tend to offer behavioural complaints ("You always throw your socks on the floor"), while dissatisfied couples make more complaints aimed at personal characteristics ("You're a slob"). Personal complaints are more likely to result in an escalated conflict episode (Alberts and Driscoll, 1992). The reason should be obvious—complaints about personal characteristics attack a more fundamental part of the presenting self. Talking about socks deals with a habit that can be changed; calling someone a slob is a character assault that is unlikely to be forgotten when the conflict is over. Marriage researcher John Gottman (2000) has found that complaining is not a sign of a troubled relationship—in fact, it's usually healthy for spouses to get their concerns out in the open. However, when a couple's communication is filled with personal and disrespectful criticism, it is often a symptom of a marriage headed for divorce.

Aggressiveness The most destructive way to disagree with another person is through **aggressiveness**. Dominic Infante and his associates (1992, p. 116) define verbal aggressiveness as the tendency to "attack the self-concepts of other people in order to inflict psychological pain." Unlike argumentativeness, aggressiveness demeans the worth of others. Name calling, put-downs, sarcasm, taunting, yelling, badgering—all are methods of "winning" disagreements at someone else's expense.

It should come as no surprise that aggressiveness has been found to have a variety of serious consequences. Aggressive behaviour is especially hurtful when it comes from people who are close to us (Martin et al., 1996). Research shows it is associated with physical violence in marriages (Infante et al., 1989), juvenile delinquency (Atkin et al., 2002; Straus et al., 1989), depression (Dutton and Karakanta, 2013), and a negative climate in both the workplace (Infante and Gorden, 1989; Hershcovis et al, 2007) and the classroom (Myers, 2001; Myers and Rocca, 2001). Myers and Rocca compared argumentativeness and verbal aggressiveness and found that "when instructors are perceived to engage in

Self-Assessment

ARGUMENTATIVENESS AND VERBAL AGGRESSION

The following items are from two research instruments, one developed by Infante and Rancer (1982) and the other by Infante and Wigley (1986). Use the following scale to indicate how true each statement is for you.

1 = almost never true
2 = rarely true
3 = occasionally true
4 = often true
5 = almost always true

Part 1

_____ 1. While in an argument, I worry that the person I am arguing with will form a negative impression of me.

_____ 2. Arguing over controversial issues improves my intelligence.

_____ 3. Once I finish an argument, I promise myself that I will not get into another.

_____ 4. Arguing with a person creates more problems than it solves.

_____ 5. I have a pleasant, good feeling when I win a point in an argument.

_____ 6. When I finish arguing with someone I feel nervous and upset.

_____ 7. I enjoy a good argument over a controversial issue.

_____ 8. I have the ability to do well in an argument.

_____ 9. I try to avoid getting into arguments.

_____ 10. I enjoy defending my point of view on an issue.

Part 2

_____ 1. I am extremely careful to avoid attacking a person's intelligence when I attack their ideas.

_____ 2. When someone is very stubborn, I use insults to soften the stubbornness.

_____ 3. I try to make people feel good about themselves, even when their ideas are stupid.

_____ 4. When people refuse to do a task I know is important, without good reason, I tell them they are unreasonable.

_____ 5. When people criticize my shortcomings, I take it in good humour and do not try to get back at them.

_____ 6. When people simply will not budge on a matter of importance, I lose my temper and say rather strong things to them.

_____ 7. I refuse to participate in arguments when they involve personal attacks.

_____ 8. I like poking fun at people who do things that are very stupid in order to stimulate their intelligence.

_____ 9. When an argument shifts to personal attacks, I try very hard to change the subject.

_____ 10. When I am not able to refute others' positions, I try to make them feel defensive in order to weaken their positions.

For Part 1, add your scores on items 2, 5, 7, 8, and 10. This is your tendency to approach argumentative situations. Now, add your scores on 1, 3, 4, 6, and 9. This is your tendency to avoid argumentative situations. To compute your argumentativeness score, subtract the second sum from the first. The higher your score, the greater your predisposition to be argumentative (the possible range is from 0 to 20).

For Part 2, sum the scores on the 10 items after reverse-scoring for items 1, 3, 5, 7, and 9 (i.e., 5 = 1, 4 = 2, 3 = 3, 2 = 4, and 1 = 5). This is your verbal aggressiveness score—the higher the score, the greater your tendency to be verbally aggressive (the possible range is 10 to 50, with a midpoint of 30).

argumentativeness, they promote student . . . motivation; when instructors are perceived to engage in verbal aggressiveness, they contribute negatively to student perceptions of classroom climate and diminish student . . . motivation" (p. 131). In Chapter 10, we describe how "win–win" approaches to conflict are healthier and more productive than the "win–lose" tactics of aggressiveness.

Disconfirming Messages

Disconfirming messages are subtler than confirming ones, but potentially more damaging. Disconfirming communication implicitly says, "You don't exist; you are not valued."

Disconfirming messages, unfortunately, are part of everyday life. Though an occasional disconfirming message may not injure a relationship, a pattern of them usually indicates a negative communication climate. Sieberg and Larson (1971) found it was easiest to recognize disconfirming communication by observing responses to the messages of others. They noted seven types of disconfirming responses.

Impervious Response An **impervious response** fails to acknowledge the other person's communicative attempt, either verbally or non-verbally. Failing to return a phone call or answer a letter or email is an impervious response. Impervious responses also happen in face-to-face settings. They are especially common when adults and children communicate. Parents often become enraged when they are ignored by their children; likewise, children feel diminished when adults pay no attention to their questions, comments, or requests. Most experts agree that being ignored by significant others is psychologically damaging (Holte and Wichstrom, 1990; Laing, 1961). This explains why the "silent treatment" can be so disturbing, and why the cruelest punishment children can bestow on others is to ignore them.

Interrupting Response As its name implies, an **interrupting response** is made when one person begins to speak before the other is through making a point.

> Customer (C): I'm looking for an outfit I can wear on a trip I'm . . .
> Salesperson (S): I've got just the thing. It is part wool and part polyester, so it won't wrinkle at all.
> C: Actually, wrinkling isn't that important. I want something that will work as a business outfit and . . .
> S: We have a terrific blazer that you can dress up or down, depending on the accessories you choose.
> C: That's not what I was going to say. I want something that I can wear as a business outfit, but it ought to be on the informal side. I'm going to . . .
> S: Say no more. I know just what you want.
> C: Never mind. I think I'll look in some other stores.

Irrelevant Response It is disconfirming to give an **irrelevant response**, making comments totally unrelated to what the other person was just saying.

> A: What a day! I thought it would never end. First, the car overheated and I had to call a tow truck, and then the server crashed at work.
> B: Listen, we have to talk about a present for Ann's birthday. The party is on Saturday, and I have only tomorrow to shop for it.
> A: I'm really beat. You won't believe what the boss did. Like I said, the server was down, and in the middle of that mess, he decided he absolutely had to have the sales figures for the last six months.
> B: I just can't figure what would suit Ann. She's been so generous to us, and I can't think of anything she needs.
> A: Why don't you listen to me? I beat my brains out all day and you don't give a damn!
> B: And you don't care about me!

REFLECTION

DRIVING MY FATHER CRAZY

My brother had a very bad habit. Whenever our father would call him, Leo would simply not answer—I mean, he would just sit there and act as if he hadn't heard my dad. Most of the time, our father just figured Leo wasn't at home, but those times he knew he was home and was *purposefully* ignoring him, he'd get a bit crazy.

Now that I have children of my own, I can understand how my father was feeling. There's nothing quite as disconfirming as being ignored—being told "You don't exist!"—by your own child.

Tangential Response   Unlike the three kinds of behaviour just discussed, a **tangential response** does acknowledge the other person's communication. However, the acknowledgment is used to steer the conversation in a new direction. Tangents can come in two forms: One is the "tangential shift," which is an abrupt change in conversation. For example, a little boy runs into the house excited, showing his mother the rock he found. She says, "Wash your hands; that rock is dirty." In a "tangential drift," the speaker makes a token connection with what the other person is saying and then moves the conversation in another direction entirely. In the same scenario, the mother might look at the rock, say, "Hmmm, nice rock," and then immediately add, "Go and wash your hands before dinner."

Impersonal Response   In an **impersonal response**, the speaker conducts a monologue filled with impersonal, intellectualized, and generalized statements. The speaker never really interacts with the other on a personal level.

> Employee: I've been having some personal problems lately, and I'd like to take off early a couple of afternoons to clear them up.
> Boss: Ah, yes. We all have personal problems. It seems to be a sign of the times.

Ambiguous Response   An **ambiguous response** contains a message with more than one meaning. The words are highly abstract or have private meanings for the speaker alone.

> A: I'd like to get together with you soon. How about Tuesday?
> B: Uh, maybe so. Anyhow, see you later.
> A: How can I be sure you mean it?
> B: Who knows what anybody means?

Incongruous Response   An **incongruous response** contains two messages that seem to deny or contradict each other, one at the verbal level and the other at the non-verbal level.

> He: Darling, I love you!
> She: I love you, too. [*giggles*]

> Teacher: Did you enjoy the class?
> Student: Yes. [*yawns*]

It is important to note again that disconfirming messages, like virtually every other type of communication, are a matter of

TAKE TWO

- **Communication climate:** the social tone of a relationship.
- **Confirming communication:** messages that convey valuing (levels: recognition, acknowledgment, endorsement).
- **Disagreeing messages:** messages that say, "You're wrong," but which can include confirming components (types: argumentativeness, complaining, aggressiveness).
- **Disconfirming communication:** messages that signal a lack of regard (types: impervious, interrupting, irrelevant, tangential, impersonal, ambiguous, incongruous).

perception. A message that might not be intended to devalue the other person can be interpreted as disconfirming. For example, your failure to return a phone call or respond to the email of an out-of-town friend might simply be the result of a busy schedule, but if the other person views the lack of contact as a sign that you don't value the relationship, the effect will be just as strong as if you had deliberately intended to convey a slight.

Defensiveness

It is no surprise that disconfirming and disagreeing messages can pollute a communication climate. Perhaps the most predictable reaction to a hostile or indifferent message is defensiveness.

The word *defensiveness* suggests protecting yourself from attack, but what kind of attack? Seldom when you become defensive is a physical threat involved. If you are not threatened by bodily injury, what *are* you guarding against? To answer this question, we need to talk more about notions of *presenting self* and *face*, both of which were introduced in Chapter 2. Recall that the presenting self consists of the physical traits, personality characteristics, attitudes, aptitudes, and all the other parts of the image you want to present to the world. Actually, it is a mistake to talk about a single face, as we try to project different selves to different people. You might try to impress a potential employer with your seriousness, but also want your friends to see you as a joker. Of course, not all parts of your presenting self are equally significant. Letting others know that you are left-handed or a Gemini is probably less important to you than convincing them you are good-looking or loyal.

The word *defensiveness* suggests protecting yourself from attack, but what kind of attack? Seldom when you become defensive is a physical threat involved. If you are not threatened by bodily injury, what *are* you guarding against? Think back to the last time you felt defensive or threatened. Did you feel it physically? What were you guarding against? How did you deal with the situation?

When others are willing to accept and acknowledge important parts of our presenting image, there is no need to feel defensive. On the other hand, when others confront us with **face-threatening acts**—messages that seem to challenge the image we want to project—we are likely to resist what they say. **Defensiveness**, then, is the process of protecting our presenting self, our face.

You can understand how defensiveness operates by imagining what might happen if an important part of your presenting self were attacked. Suppose an instructor criticized you for making a stupid mistake. Or consider how you would feel if a friend called you self-centred or your boss labelled you as lazy. You would probably feel threatened if these attacks were untrue. But your own experience will probably show that you sometimes respond defensively even when you know that the criticism is justified. For instance, you have probably responded defensively at times when you *did* make a mistake, act selfishly, or cut corners in your work. In fact, we often feel most defensive when criticism is right on target (Becker at al., 2008; Stamp et al., 1992).

Some people are more prone to defensiveness than others. Individualistic people are more likely to interpret other people's messages as neutral or critical and more inclined to deflect criticism, whereas people with a communal orientation are more likely to interpret ambiguous messages as supportive and be more accepting of criticism (Edwards, 1998; Suzuki et al., 2008).

The topics that trigger defensiveness also vary. Sometimes, sensitive topics are personal. You may feel a strong need to protect your image of athletic skill or intelligence, while another person may be more concerned with appearing fashionable or funny. Some research suggests that defence-provoking topics can vary by sex. In one study, men interpreted messages about mental or physical errors (such as misfiling a document or tripping on a carpet) more defensively than women did. Males and females were equally defensive about messages regarding their clothes and hair, but women were more defensive about messages that focused on weight (Futch and Edwards, 1999).

Who offers the potentially defence-arousing remark or criticism also matters. Matthew Hornsey and his colleagues (2002) conducted three experiments examining group members' responses to criticism from in-group (other Australians) and out-group (people from another country) members. They found that in-group criticisms were tolerated surprisingly well, whereas out-group criticisms were met with defensiveness—probably because in-group criticisms are seen as more legitimate and constructive.

Snapp and Leary (2001) found parallel results. When participants in their study were ignored by a person they hardly knew, they were significantly more hurt than when ignored by someone who knew them better. The researchers offer several reasons for this result, one of which is that familiar relationships provide a buffer against hurt feelings. Defensive responses to being ignored by a stranger may include "He's such a social idiot" and "What's wrong with *me*?" But if the other

person is a friend, you are more likely to make an excuse: "She didn't see me" or "He must be preoccupied."

So far, we have talked about defensiveness as if it is only the responsibility of the person who feels threatened. If this were the case, the prescription would be simply to grow a thicker skin, admit your flaws, and stop trying to manage impressions. This approach isn't just unrealistic—it also ignores the role played by those who send face-threatening messages. In fact, competent communicators protect the face needs of others as well as their own. For example, the people whom college students judge as close friends are those who provide "positive face support" by endorsing the presenting image of others (Cupach and Messman, 1999). Findings like this make it clear that defensiveness is *interactive*: all communicators contribute to the climate of a relationship.

At this point, you might be wondering how you can send a face-honouring message when you have a genuine complaint against someone. The answer lies in the two-dimensional nature of communication. On a content level, you can express dissatisfaction with the other person, but on a relational level you can be saying—explicitly or non-verbally—that you value him or her. In the second half of this chapter, we make specific suggestions for creating messages that are both honest and supportive.

Climate Patterns

Once a communication climate is formed, it can take on a life of its own. The pattern can be either positive or negative. In one study of married couples, each spouse's response in conflict situations was found to be similar to the other's statement (Burggraf and Sillars, 1987). Conciliatory statements (for example, support, accepting responsibility, agreeing) were likely to be followed by conciliatory responses. Confrontational acts (i.e., criticism, hostile questions, fault finding) were likely to trigger an aggressive response. The same pattern held for other kinds of messages. Avoidance

Focus on RESEARCH

ORGANIZATIONAL CLIMATE: BULLYING IN THE WORKPLACE

In April 1999, a former employee of OC Transpo in Ottawa went on a shooting rampage at his former workplace, killing four employees. He then took his own life. The investigation that followed revealed that the killer had been the victim of workplace harassment. In November 2005, Lori Dupont, a nurse at Hotel-Dieu hospital in Windsor, was stabbed to death at work by Dr Marc Daniel, with whom she had had a failed romantic relationship. Earlier that year she had reported to hospital administration that she feared for her safety and was being harassed by Daniel, but the hospital concluded there was insufficient evidence to take action. More recently, in March 2014, an employee of a Canadian grocery chain shot and killed two of his co-workers and injured four others at the grocery's distribution centre, in Alberta.

Though most provinces in Canada require employers to have policies on workplace violence and/or harassment, there is no current national legislation specific to bullying in the workplace (Canadian Centre for Occupational Health and Safety, 2014). Legislation that requires employers to prevent psychological harassment and violence in the workplace sends a powerful message about the importance of creating a safe and respectful workplace environment.

According to the International Labour Organization (2006), workplace bullying, mobbing, and harassment, and threats by unstable co-workers are all on the rise throughout the world. Data from a variety of Canadian sources—the Canadian Human Rights Commission, Statistics Canada, the Canadian Union of Public Employees, and the Association of Workers' Compensation Boards of Canada—all suggest that violence and hostility at work in Canada are serious problems with multiple costs to both the victims and organizations (Hughes and Rutten, 2010; Trepaniér et al., 2013).

Who bullies others at work? The overwhelming majority of bullies are bosses, some are co-workers, and a minority are people who bully employees in more senior positions. A bully is equally likely to be a woman or a man. Who gets bullied? Contrary to the popular stereotype of the victim being an oddball or loner, the majority of victims of workplace bullying are competent and capable employees who are generally well-liked by their co-workers. Workplace bullies are most likely to pick on someone who is co-operative and non-confrontational (Canada Safety Council, 2004; Workplace Bullying Institute, 2010).

Violence in the workplace has enormous costs for the individuals involved and also for the organizational climate as a whole. Victims of workplace bullying have increased anxiety, confusion, sadness, anger, physical and mental health problems, and domestic difficulties (because of the stress at work); they experience declining productivity and are more likely to be absent from work, eventually leaving the organization (Brotheridge and Lee, 2010; Hershcovis et al., 2007; MacIntosh, Wuest et al., 2010; Trepaniér et al., 2013). Given that they are capable and competent employees, this is a loss to the organizations they work for. Bullying lowers morale for all employees and contributes to an atmosphere of fear, anger, and depression. The employer pays for bullying with lost productivity, absenteeism, high staff turnover, severance packages, and lawsuits (Canada Safety Council, 2004; Hynes 2001; MacIntosh, Wuest et al., 2010).

Among Canadian corporations, the most frequent response to bullying seems to be to ignore it. Most corporate boards have not put any structures in place to deal with the prevention and management of workplace violence and harassment (Hughes and Rutten, 2010). Developing a policy or corporate strategy on workplace violence that focuses on prevention is the first step. Creating a communication climate that includes clear expectations for civility and consequences for violations is an essential first step. At an individual level, it is important for victims of workplace bullying to assert their right to a healthy, respectful workplace environment.

Critical thinking: *In what ways does disconfirming communication contribute to a communication climate that might encourage workplace harassment and bullying to develop?*

- **Presenting self:** the person you believe yourself to be in moments of honest self-examination; physical traits, personality characteristics, attitudes, aptitudes, and all other parts of the image you want to present to the world.
- **Faces:** different selves we present to different people; your socially-approved identity.
- **Face-threatening acts:** messages that seem to challenge the image we want to project.
- **Defensiveness:** process of protecting our presenting self (face).

led to avoidance, analysis evoked analysis, and so on. This was also found in a study on disagreements of married couples (Newton and Burgoon, 1990). Videotaped interactions revealed that accusations from one partner triggered accusations in response, and that communication satisfaction was highest when both partners used supportive rather than accusatory tactics.

This reciprocal pattern can be represented as a **spiral** (Wilmot, 1987). Some spirals are negative. In poorly adjusted and abusive couples, for example, one spouse's complaint is likely to produce a counter-complaint or denial by the other (Sabourin and Stamp, 1995; Sutter and Martin, 1999). The cartoon below provides an amusing, but sad image of how tit-for-tat spirals can take on lives of their own.

Fortunately, spirals can also work in a positive direction. One confirming behaviour leads to a similar response from the other person, which in turn leads to further confirmation by the first person (Le Poire and Yoshimura, 1999).

Spirals—whether positive or negative—rarely go on indefinitely. When a negative spiral gets out of hand, the partners may agree to back off from their disconfirming behaviour. "Hold on," one may say, "this is getting us nowhere." At this point, there may be a cooling-off period, or the partners may work together more constructively to solve their problem (Becker et al., 2008). This ability to end and recover from negative communication spirals is characteristic of successful relationships (Gottman and Levenson, 1999). But, if the partners continually pass "the point of no return," the relationship may end. As we saw in Chapter 1, it is impossible to take back a message once it has been sent, and some exchanges are so lethal that the relationship can't survive them. Positive spirals also have their limit. Even the best relationships

"To be fair, Martha, you started it."

© Matthew Diffee, *The New Yorker* Collection/The Cartoon Bank.

go through rocky periods in which the climate suffers. However, the accumulated goodwill and communication ability of the partners can make these times less frequent and intense.

Creating Positive Climates

Even the "best" message is not guaranteed to create a positive climate. A complimentary comment can be interpreted as sarcasm; an innocent smile can be perceived as a sneer; an offer to help can be seen as condescension. Because human communication is so complex, there are no foolproof words, phrases, or formulas for creating positive climates.

However, there is a helpful study that has stood the test of time: Jack Gibb's (1961) categorization of supportive and defensive behaviour (see Table 9.1). After observing groups for several years, Gibb was able to isolate six types of defence-arousing communication and six contrasting kinds of behaviour that seem to reduce the level of threat and defensiveness. His findings have common-sense appeal and multiple applications. As a result, they've played an important part in communication textbooks, training seminars, journals, and research studies (Becker et al., 2008; Stewart, 2012). We will use them here to discuss how positive climates can be created by sending supportive rather than defence-provoking messages.

Evaluation versus Description

The first type of defence-arousing message Gibb identified is **evaluation**. An evaluative message judges the other person, usually in a negative way. Consider this message: "You don't care about me!" Evaluative messages like this have several characteristics that make them so face-threatening. They judge what the other person is feeling rather than describing the speaker's thoughts, feelings, and wants. They don't explain how the speaker arrived at his or her conclusion, and they lack specifics. Furthermore, they are often phrased in the kind of defence-arousing "you" language that we described in Chapter 5. It's easy to

 **CHECK IT!**

Describe the characteristics of communication spirals.

understand why evaluative statements often trigger a defensive spiral.

Do the climate-threatening properties of evaluative messages mean that it's impossible to tell others how some of the things that they do bother you? No. It simply means that you must be alert to more constructive ways to do so. **Description** is a way to offer your thoughts, feelings, and wants without judging the listener. Descriptive messages make documented observations that are specific and concrete. As we mentioned earlier when discussing complaining, description focuses on behaviour that can be changed rather than on personal characteristics that cannot be changed. In addition, descriptive messages often use "I" language, which tends to provoke less defensiveness than "you" language (Proctor and Wilcox, 1993). Contrast the evaluative "You don't care about me" with this more descriptive message: "I'm sorry that we don't spend as much time together as we did during the summer. When we don't talk during the week, I sometimes feel unimportant. Maybe we could set up a phone call time on Wednesdays—that would mean a lot to me."

Note several things about this descriptive message. First, the focus is on the speaker's

Table 9.1 ● The Gibb Categories of Defensive and Supportive Behaviour

Defensive Behaviour	Supportive Behaviour
1. Evaluation	1. Description
2. Control	2. Problem orientation
3. Strategy	3. Spontaneity
4. Neutrality	4. Empathy
5. Superiority	5. Equality
6. Certainty	6. Provisionalism

Focus on TECHNOLOGY

DOES THE CHANNEL AFFECT THE CLIMATE?

Does the channel you choose to send your message influence the receiver's interpretation? Are text messages and emails perceived differently from voice messages? It appears that the channel you choose influences some relational aspects of the message for both the receiver and the sender.

Joseph Walther (1996, 2007, 2011; Walther et al., 2010) argues that computer-mediated communication (CMC) technologies, particularly text-based CMC, such as email that are asynchronous and devoid of many non-verbal cues, can facilitate socially desirable communication. The act of sending an email message, instead of a voice mail or face-to-face one, eliminates the need to monitor and control non-verbal behaviours and allows the sender more time to carefully compose a message. Kirk Duthler (2006) explored Walther's proposition in his examination of the relative politeness of voice mail requests versus email requests. He found that email requests were typically more polite than their voice mail counterparts.

In her study of evaluative feedback, Stephanie Watts (2007) compared feedback delivered by voice mail to feedback delivered by email. Students attending a large university in the American Midwest were required to compose and deliver positive and negative feedback messages about a group project to a receiver who had participated in the project. The participants were randomly assigned to the voice mail or the email condition, and both senders and receivers completed a questionnaire about the experience of delivering or receiving the feedback. Watts found that there were no differences in the effectiveness of the email and the voice mail messages. She did find differences in the perceptions of the messages between the senders and the receivers.

Senders of negative email feedback perceived it as more negative than did its recipients, but this was not true for voice mail messages. Also, senders of negative voice mail feedback felt more uncomfortable delivering their messages than recipients felt receiving the negative comments.

Most of us feel uncomfortable when we have to give negative comments in person or over the phone, but sending an email to convey bad news at work can be perceived as rude. In their study of cyber incivility, Vivien Lim and Thompson Teo (2009) found that employees considered their supervisors to be rude when they sent emails about problems that really required face-to-face dialogue. Clearly, in these instances the supervisors' choice of communication channel, in addition to the content of the message, contributed to the email being perceived as rude.

In addition to the channel and the main message content, little things seem to count, too. In her case study of email correspondence in employment settings, Joan Waldvogel (2005, 2007) found that people used cordial greetings and closings significantly more in the workplace that valued harmony and interpersonal relationships, and where co-operation and solidarity were highly valued. In contrast, in the organization Waldvogel studied that had low morale and high mistrust of management, emails were indirect and socially distant. Senders were much less likely to use a greeting such as the recipient's name or a word (e.g., "Hello," "Good morning all") or a farewell statement (e.g., "Cheers," "Have a good day").

Relational aspects of messages between individuals and within larger organizations involve a complex mix of factors, not the least of which is the channel selected to send a message.

honest thoughts, feelings, and wants, with little or no judgment. Second, the message addresses something specifically (a desire to talk more often) and refrains from making sweeping character generalizations ("You don't care!"). The message also provides information about how the speaker arrived at this conclusion.

Although it may seem ideal, even this sort of message may not get a non-defensive response. Its effectiveness will be determined by when, where, and how it is communicated (you can imagine how it would be received if it were said in front of a roomful of relatives or in a whining tone of voice). The point is, by contrasting evaluative and descriptive messages, you can see how and why some messages are more likely to create positive climates than others.

Let's look at more examples:

Evaluation	Description
You're not making any sense.	I don't understand the point you're trying to make.
You're inconsiderate.	I would appreciate it if you'd let me know when you're running late—I was worried.
That's an ugly tablecloth.	I'm not crazy about big blue stripes; I like something subtler.

Control versus Problem Orientation

A second defence-provoking message involves some attempt to control another. **Controlling communication** occurs when a sender seems to be imposing a solution on the receiver with little regard for the receiver's needs or interests. The object of control can involve almost anything: where to eat dinner, what television program to watch, whether to remain in a relationship, or how to spend a large sum of money. Whatever the situation, people who act in controlling ways create a defensive climate. None of us likes to feel that our ideas are worthless and that nothing we say will change other people's determination to have their way. Yet, this is precisely the attitude a controller communicates. Whether with words, gestures, tone of voice, or through some other channel, whether control is accomplished through status, insistence on obscure or irrelevant rules, or physical power, the controller generates hostility wherever he or she goes. The unspoken message is "I know what's best for you, and if you do as I say, we will get along."

In **problem orientation**, however, communicators focus on finding a solution that satisfies both their own needs and those of the others involved. The goal here is not to "win" at the expense of your partner, but to work out some arrangement in which everybody feels like a winner. (See Chapter 10 for a thorough discussion on "win–win" problem solving as a way to find problem-oriented solutions.) Problem orientation is often typified by "we" language (see Chapter 5), which suggests the speaker is making decisions *with* rather than *for* other people.

Here are some examples of how some controlling and problem-orientation messages might sound:

Controlling	Problem Orientation
Get off the phone—now!	I need to interrupt your call in order to make an important call. It will only take a couple of minutes and you can use the phone for as long as you'd like once I am done.
There's only one way to handle this problem . . .	Looks like we have a problem. Let's work out a solution that we can both live with.
Either you start working harder, or you're fired!	The production in your department hasn't been as high as I'd hoped. Any ideas on what we could do?

Strategy versus Spontaneity

Gibb uses the word **strategy** for defence-arousing messages in which speakers hide their ulterior motives. The terms *dishonesty* and *manipulation* reflect the nature of strategy. Even if the intentions that motivate strategic communication are honourable, the victim of deception who discovers the attempt to deceive is likely to feel offended at having been tricked.

As we discussed in Chapter 5, counterfeit questions are a form of strategic communication because they try to trap others into desired responses. Indirect and double messages also can be strategic ploys that lead to defensive reactions. In addition, many sales techniques are strategic, as they give customers limited information and then make it difficult to say no. This is not to say that all sales techniques are wrong or unethical, but most strategic ones are not well-suited to interpersonal relationships. If you have ever become defensive when you thought a friend was doing a "sales job" on you, you understand the concept.

Spontaneity is the behaviour that contrasts with strategy. Spontaneity simply means being honest with others instead of trying to manipulate them. What

Can you think of a situation in which communication which at first sounds "spontaneous" should actually be classified as "strategy?" Or messages that blur the lines between evaluation and description and control and problem solving? Can you think of examples from your own life? How did you address these issues?

it does not mean is blurting out what you're thinking as soon as an idea comes to you. As we discussed in Chapter 2, there are appropriate (and inappropriate) times for self-disclosure. You would undoubtedly threaten other people's presenting selves if you were "spontaneous" about every opinion that crossed your mind. That's not what Gibb intended in using the term *spontaneity*, but rather to set aside hidden agendas that others will sense and resist. You can probably remember times when someone asked you a question and you answered suspiciously with "Hmmm . . . why do you want to know?" Your defensive antennae were up because you detected an underlying strategy. If the person had told you honestly why he or she was asking the question, then your defences probably would have been lowered. That's what we mean by spontaneity.

Here are some examples:

Strategy	Spontaneity
What are you doing Friday after work?	I have a piano I need to move Friday after work. Can you give me a hand?
Have you ever considered another line of work?	I'm concerned about your job performance over the last year; let's set up a time to talk about it.
Trevor and Alicia go out to dinner every week.	I'd like to go out for dinner more often.

This is a good place to pause and talk about larger issues regarding the Gibb model. First, Gibb's emphasis on being direct is better suited for low-context cultures like Canada and the United States, which value a straightforward approach, than for high-context cultures. Second, there are ways in which each of the communication approaches Gibb labels as "supportive" can be used to exploit others and, therefore, violate the spirit of positive climate building. For instance, consider spontaneity. Although it sounds paradoxical at first, spontaneity can be a strategy, too. Sometimes, you'll see people using honesty in a calculating way, being just frank enough to win someone's trust or sympathy. This "levelling" is probably the most defence-arousing strategy

© iStockPhoto/davidf.

of all because once we've learned someone is using frankness as a manipulation, there is almost no chance we will ever trust that person again.

Neutrality versus Empathy

Gibb uses the term **neutrality** to describe a fourth behaviour that arouses defensiveness. Probably a better word would be *indifference*. For example, 911 emergency telephone dispatchers are taught to be neutral in order to calm down the caller, but they should not communicate indifference (Shuler and Sypher, 2000). In Gibb's terminology, a neutral attitude is disconfirming because it communicates a lack of concern for the welfare of another and implies that the other person is not very important to you. This apparent indifference is likely to promote defensiveness, because people do not like to think of themselves as worthless, and they will protect a self-concept that sees them as worthwhile.

The poor effects of neutrality become apparent when you consider the hostility that most people have for the large, impersonal organizations they have to interact with: "They think of me as a number instead of a person"; "I felt as if I were being handled by computers and not human beings." These common statements reflect reactions to being handled in an indifferent, neutral way.

The behaviour that contrasts with neutrality is empathy. Gibb found that empathy helps rid communication of the quality of indifference. When people show that they care for the feelings of another, there's little chance that the person's self-concept will be threatened. Empathy means accepting another's feelings, putting yourself in another's place. This does not mean you need to agree with that person. By simply letting someone know you care and have respect for them, you will be acting in a supportive way. Gibb noted the importance of non-verbal messages in communicating empathy. He found that facial and bodily expressions of concern are often more important to the recipient than the words used.

We have addressed the concept of empathy in Chapter 3 and the skill of empathizing in Chapter 7; now let's see what empathic messages look like when contrasted with neutral ones:

Neutrality	Empathy
This is what happens when you don't plan properly.	Ouch—looks like this didn't turn out the way you expected.
Sometimes, things just don't work out. That's the way it goes.	I know you put a lot of time and effort into this project.
Don't get too excited—everybody gets promoted sooner or later.	I'll bet you're pretty excited about the promotion.

Superiority versus Equality

A fifth behaviour creating a defensive climate involves **superiority**. Jake Harwood, Howard Giles, and their associates (Draper, 2005; Harwood et al., 1997) summarize a body of research that describes how patronizing messages irritate recipients ranging from young students to senior citizens. Any message that suggests "I'm better than you" is likely to arouse feelings of defensiveness in the recipients.

Many times in our lives, we communicate with people who possess less talent or knowledge than we do, but it is not necessary to convey an attitude of superiority in these situations. Gibb found ample evidence that many who have superior skills and talents are capable of projecting feelings of **equality** rather than superiority. Such people communicate that, although they may have greater talent in certain areas, they see other human beings as having just as much worth as themselves.

Charles Beck and Elizabeth Beck (1996) observed that equality is put to the test when a person *does not* have superior skills, yet is in a position of authority. Supervisors sometimes have less expertise in certain areas than their subordinates, but believe it would be beneath them to admit it. You have probably been in

Focus on RESEARCH

COMMUNICATION CLIMATE AND INTERPROFESSIONAL COLLABORATION

Contributing to positive communicate climates in the workplace often requires regulating emotions. Managing and sometimes suppressing emotions is referred to as "emotion labour" and has been studied in a variety of workplace settings, particularly those of first responders (e.g., 911 operators, paramedics, fire-fighters, and police officers), corrections officers, and health-care professionals (Giardini and Frese, 2006; Scott and Myers, 2005; Tracy et al., 2006). People in human services occupations are often required to manage difficult emotions—their own and those of the people they serve. In addition, in many of these occupations people work in interprofessional teams which can serve to increase the amount of emotion work required (Miller et al., 2008).

Karen-Lee Miller and her colleagues (2008) inves-tigated interprofessional collaboration (or the lack of it) within three Canadian hospitals (all were large, urban, and publicly funded facilities). They found that a major obstacle to nurses' participation in inter-professional collaboration was the amount of emotion work involved. Nurses reported that the importance of nursing's core caring values was not recognized in formal interprofessional meetings—or professional development activities—by their multi-disciplinary colleagues (e.g., social workers, dieticians, phys-icians, etc.). In addition, they experienced conflict with physicians in "hallway consultations." The extra emotion work, that these slights and conflicts cre-ated, came on top of the nurses' primary obligation to care for their patients in a warm, competent, and genial manner. Miller and her colleagues found that the long-standing, antagonistic interpersonal dynam-ics between medicine and nursing undermined the reciprocity, knowledge sharing, and equity required for successful interprofessional collaboration. These investigators suggested that other medical profes-sionals need help in understanding the core values and emotion work that are central to nursing in order to better support collaborative practice.

Given the improved quality of care and improved patient satisfaction associated with successful collab-oration (Kenaszchuk et al. 2010; Shen et al. 2011), as well as the increased job satisfaction and retention associated with successful nurse–physician collabor-ation (Hughes and Fitzpatrick 2010; Ritter 2011), it is vital that health-care professionals develop skills to transform potentially negative communication cli-mates and support interprofessional collaboration.

Critical thinking: *How can we best prepare human service professionals (and possibly change work set-tings) to ensure human service providers are equipped and able to contribute positively to supportive com-munication climates that facilitate interprofessional collaboration?*

situations where you knew more about the subject than the person in charge—be it a boss, a teacher, a parent, or a salesperson—yet this person acted as if he or she knew more. Did you feel defensive? No doubt. Did that person feel defensive? Absolutely. Both of you were challenging each other's presenting self, so the climate probably became hostile. A truly secure person can treat others with equality even when there are obvious differences in knowledge, talent, and status. Doing so creates a positive climate in which ideas are evaluated not on the basis of who contributed them, but rather on the merit of the ideas themselves.

What does equality sound like? Here are some examples:

Superiority	Equality
When you get to be in my position someday, then you'll understand.	I'd like to hear how the issue looks to you. Then I can tell you how it looks to me.
You don't know what you're talking about.	I'm not sure I agree.
No, that's not the right way to do it!	I'd be happy to help if you'd like—just let me know.

REFLECTION

Certainty versus Provisionalism

Have you ever run into people who are positive they are right? Who know that theirs is the only, or proper, way of doing something? Who insist that they have all the facts and need no additional information? If you have, you have met individuals who project the defence-arousing behaviour that Gibb calls **certainty**.

How do you react when you are the target of such certainty? Do you suddenly find your energy directed to proving the dogmatic individual wrong? If you do, you're reacting normally—if not very constructively.

Communicators who regard their own opinions with certainty, while disregarding the ideas of others, demonstrate a lack of respect for others. It's likely the recipient will take the certainty as a personal affront and react defensively.

In contrast to dogmatic certainty is **provisionalism**, in which people may have strong opinions, but are willing to acknowledge that they don't have a monopoly on the truth, and will change their stand if another position seems more reasonable. Provisionalism often surfaces in a person's choice of words. While certainty regularly uses the terms *can't*, *never*, *always*, *must*, and *have to*, provisionalism uses *perhaps*, *maybe*, *possibly*, *might*, and *may*. It's not that provisional people are spineless—they simply recognize that discussion is aided by open-minded messages. Winer and Majors (1981) found that provisional word choice does indeed enhance communication climate.

Let's look at some examples:

Certainty	Provisionalism
That will *never* work!	My guess is that you'll run into problems with that approach.
You'll hate that class! Stay away from it!	I didn't like that class very much; I'm not sure you would, either.
You won't get anywhere without a university education. Mark my words.	I think it's important to get that degree. I found it was hard to land an interview until I had one.

You have probably noticed a great deal of overlap between the various Gibb components. For instance, look at the final example under "provisionalism." The statement is likely to create a positive climate, not only because it is provisional rather than certain, but also because it is descriptive rather than evaluative; problem-oriented rather than controlling; and equal rather than superior. You may also have noticed a tone underlying all of the supportive examples: *respect*. By valuing and confirming others—even if you disagree with them—you create a respectful climate that helps enhance a positive communication climate, both now and in future interactions. Communication scholars Sonja Foss and Cindy Griffin (1995) use the term *invitational rhetoric* to describe this sort of respectful approach that strives to understand others and invite them to see your point of view, rather than dominating them in defence-provoking ways.

There are no guarantees that you will achieve positive responses or outcomes, but if you send supportive messages, your odds for interpersonal success should improve.

Building WORK SKILLS

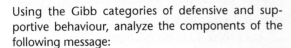

CRITICISM THAT AROUSES LESS DEFENSIVENESS

Using the Gibb categories of defensive and supportive behaviour, analyze the components of the following message:

> This project coordinator job seems to be too challenging for you! You're constantly wasting my time. *You* need to take minutes of the team meetings and send them to me if I am unable to attend. *You're* the coordinator, after all. These things happen when you don't plan properly. When you have been here as long as I have, you'll know better.

What defensive-arousing elements does it include? Now, rewrite the criticism using more supportive statements.

Transforming Negative Climates

The world would be a happier place if everyone communicated supportively. But how can you respond non-defensively when others use evaluation, control, superiority, and all the other attacking behaviours Gibb identified? Despite your best intentions, it is difficult to be reasonable when you are faced with a torrent of criticism. Being attacked is hard enough when the critic is clearly being unfair, but it's often even more threatening when the

How can you respond non-defensively when others use evaluation, control, superiority, and all the other attacking behaviours Gibb identified? Can you think of situations in which you've sought more information or agreed with the critic? Did that change the climate of the communication?

judgments are accurate. Despite the accuracy of your critic, the tendency is either to counter-attack aggressively with a barrage of verbal aggression or to withdraw non-assertively.

Since neither of these responses is likely to resolve a dispute, we need other ways of behaving. There are two such methods. Despite their apparent simplicity, they have proved to be among the most valuable skills communicators can learn.

Seek More Information

The response of seeking more information makes good sense, when you realize that it's foolish to respond to a critical attack, until you understand what the other person has said. Even comments that at first appear to be totally unjustified or foolish often prove to contain at least a grain of truth and, sometimes, much more.

Many readers object to the idea of asking for details when they are criticized. Their resistance grows from confusing the act of *listening open-mindedly* to a speaker's comments with *accepting* them. Once you realize that you can listen to, understand,

© iStockPhoto/Terry J. Alcorn.

Focus on RESEARCH

EMOTIONAL REGULATION: THE KEY TO REDUCING DEFENSIVENESS

In the research conducted for the completion of a master's degree in psychology at the University of British Columbia, Edward Peck (1998) described how effective group counsellors reduce defensive communication and create group climates that foster trust. In these climates people are more productive, content, and resourceful.

Using Gibb's categories, Peck documented actual techniques that effective counsellors used to reduce defensiveness in their group therapy sessions. Peck then analyzed this interview data in relationship to the literature on effective group leadership, using Gibb's theory as a theoretical framework. The leaders described challenging incidents, their internal and external responses, and the outcomes of these incidents.

The most critical feature identified by the counsellors was how they used their own emotional reactions to recognize when incidents were arousing defensiveness within the group. They needed to start with themselves and regulate their own internal emotions before they could apply any of the strategies to reduce defensiveness in the group.

Peck's research has implications for all of us. Before we can use Gibb's categories to create a more positive communication climate, we must find resources to regulate our own emotions. The therapists in Peck's study used self-talk to help them gain control of their feelings in defence-arousing situations. Once again that little voice in our heads can help us to create more constructive communications.

Critical thinking: *In your experience, in what situations or circumstances does a leader's ability to regulate his or her own emotions have a powerful effect on the communication climate? Less powerful effect?*

and even acknowledge the most hostile comments without necessarily accepting them, it becomes much easier to hear another person out. If you disagree with a speaker's objections, you will be in a much better position to explain yourself once you understand the criticism. On the other hand, after carefully listening to the other person's remarks, you may just see that they are valid, in which case you have learned some valuable information about yourself. In either case, you have everything to gain and nothing to lose by paying attention to the critic.

Of course, after one has spent years of instinctively resisting criticism, learning to listen to the other person will take some practice. To make matters clearer, here are several ways in which you can seek additional information from your critics.

Ask for Specifics

Often, the vague attack of a critic is virtually useless even if you sincerely want to change. Abstract accusations such as "You're being unfair" or "You never help out" can be difficult to understand. In such cases, it is a good idea to request more specific information from the sender. "What do I *do* that's unfair?" is an important question to ask before you can judge whether the accusation is correct. "When haven't I helped out?" you might ask before agreeing with or disputing the accusation.

If you already solicit specifics by using questions and are still accused of reacting defensively, the problem may be in the *way* you ask. Your tone of voice and facial expression, posture, or other non-verbal clues can give the same words radically different connotations. For example, think of how you could use the question, "Exactly what are you talking about?" to communicate either a genuine desire

✔ CHECK IT!

Describe the Gibb categories of defensive and supportive behaviours and how they can contribute to creating a more defence-arousing or a less defence-arousing response.

to know or your belief that the speaker is crazy. It is important to ask for specific information only when you genuinely want to learn more from the speaker, as asking under any other circumstances will merely make matters worse.

Guess about Specifics

Sometimes, even your sincere and well-phrased requests for specific details won't meet with success. There may be instances when your critics won't be able to define precisely the behaviour they find offensive. If such is the case, you will hear comments like "I can't tell you exactly what's wrong with your sense of humour—all I can say is that I don't like it." In other cases, your critics may know exactly what they don't like, but for some reason they seem to get a perverse satisfaction out of making you struggle to figure them out. In instances like these, you can often learn more clearly what is bothering your critic by *guessing* at the specifics of a complaint. In a sense, you become both detective and suspect, the goal being to figure out exactly what "crime" you have committed. Like the technique of asking for specifics, guessing must be done with goodwill if it is to produce satisfying results. You need to convey to the critic that for both of your sakes, you are truly interested in finding out what is the matter. Once you have communicated this intention, the emotional climate generally becomes more comfortable because, in effect, both you and the critic are seeking the same goal.

Here are some typical questions you might hear from someone guessing about the details of another person's criticism:

"So, you object to the language I used in writing the paper. Was my language too informal?"

"Okay, I understand that you think the outfit looks funny. What is it that's so bad? Is it the colour? Does it have something to do with the fit? The fabric?"

"When you say that I'm not doing my share around the house, do you mean that I haven't been helping enough with the cleaning?"

Paraphrase the Speaker's Ideas

Another strategy is to draw out confused or reluctant speakers by paraphrasing their thoughts and feelings, using the reflective listening skills that we described in Chapter 5. Paraphrasing is especially good in helping others solve their problems—and since people generally criticize you because your behaviour creates some problem for them, the method is especially suitable at such times.

One advantage of paraphrasing is that you don't have to guess about the specifics of your behaviour that might be offensive. By clarifying or amplifying what you understand critics are saying, you will learn more about their objections. A brief dialogue between a disgruntled customer and a store manager who is an exceptional listener might sound like this:

Customer (C): The way you people run this store is disgusting! I just want to tell you that I'll never shop here again.

Manager (M) [*reflecting the customer's feeling*]: It seems that you're quite upset. Can you tell me your problem?

C: It isn't *my* problem; it is the problem your salespeople have. They seem to think it's a great inconvenience to help a customer find anything around here.

M: So, you didn't get enough help finding the items you were looking for, is that it?

C: Help? I spent twenty minutes looking around in here before I even talked to a staffer. All I can say is that it's a hell of a way to run a store.

M: So, what you're saying is that the salespeople seemed to be ignoring the customers?

C: No. They were all busy with other people. It just seems to me that you ought to have enough help around to handle the crowds that come in at this hour.

M: I understand now. You were most frustrated because we didn't have enough staff to serve you promptly.

C: That's right. I have no complaint with the service I get once I'm waited on, and I've always thought you had a good selection here. It's just that I'm too busy to wait so long for help.

M: Well, I'm glad you brought this to my attention. We certainly don't want loyal customers going away mad. I'll try to see that it doesn't happen again.

This conversation illustrates two advantages of paraphrasing. First, the critic often reduces the intensity of the attack once he or she realizes that the complaint is being heard. Criticism often grows from the frustration of unmet needs—which, in this case, was partly a lack of attention. As soon as the manager genuinely demonstrated interest in the customer's plight, the customer began to feel better and was able to leave the store relatively calmly. Of course, paraphrasing won't always mollify your critic, but even when it does not, there is still another benefit that makes the technique worthwhile. In the sample conversation, the manager learned some valuable information by taking time to understand the customer. As you read earlier, even apparently outlandish criticism often contains at least a grain of truth, and, thus, a person who is genuinely interested in improving would be wise to hear it out.

Ask What the Critic Wants

Sometimes, your critic's demand will be obvious:

"Turn down that music!"

"I wish you'd remember to tell me about phone messages."

"Would you clean up your dirty dishes now!?"

In other cases, however, you will need to do some investigating to find out what the critic wants from you:

A: I can't believe you invited all those people over without asking me first!
B: Are you saying you want me to cancel the party?

A: No, I just wish you'd ask me before you make plans.

C: You are so critical! It sounds as if you don't like *anything* about this paper.
D: But you asked for my opinion. What do you expect me to do when you ask?
C: I want to know what's wrong, but I don't just want to hear criticisms. If you think there's anything good about my work, I wish you'd tell me that, too.

This last example illustrates the importance of accompanying your questions with the right non-verbal behaviour. It's easy to imagine two ways D could have said, "What do you expect me to do when you ask?" One would show a genuine desire to clarify what C wanted, whereas the other would have been clearly hostile and defensive. As with all of the styles in this section, your responses to criticism have to be sincere in order to work.

Ask about the Consequences of Your Behaviour

As a rule, people complain about your actions only when some need of theirs is not being met. One way to respond to this kind of criticism is to find out exactly what troublesome consequences your behaviour has for them. You will often find that actions which seem perfectly legitimate to you cause some difficulty for your critic. Once you have understood this, comments that previously sounded foolish take on a new meaning:

Neighbour A: You say that I ought to have my cat neutered. Why is that important to you?
Neighbour B: Because at night, he picks fights with my cat, and I'm tired of paying the vet's bills.

Worker A: Why do you care whether I'm late for work?
Worker B: Because when the boss asks, I feel obliged to make up some story so you won't get into trouble, and I don't like to lie.

Husband: Why does it bother you when I lose money at poker? You know I never gamble more than I can afford.

Wife: It's not the cash itself. It's that when you lose, you're in a grumpy mood for two or three days, and that's no fun for me.

Ask What Else Is Wrong

It might seem crazy to invite more criticism, but sometimes asking about other complaints can uncover the real problem:

A: Are you mad at me?

B: No, why are you asking?

A: Because the whole time we were at the picnic you hardly spent any time talking to me. In fact, it seemed as if whenever I came over to where you were, you went off somewhere else.

B: Is anything else wrong?

A: Well, to be honest, I've been wondering lately if you are tired of me.

This example shows that asking if anything else bothers your critic is not just an exercise in masochism. If you can keep your defensiveness in check, probing further can lead the conversation to issues that are the source of the critic's real dissatisfaction.

But sometimes, it is not enough to solicit more information from a critic. For instance, what do you do when you fully understand the other person's objections and still feel a defensive response on the tip of your tongue? You know that if you try to protect yourself, you'll wind up in an argument; on the other hand, you simply cannot accept what the other person is saying about you. The solution to such a dilemma is outrageously simple and is discussed in the following section.

Agree with the Critic

But, you protest, how can I honestly agree with comments that I don't believe are true? In the following pages, we will answer this question by showing that there is virtually no situation in which you can't honestly accept the other person's point of view and still maintain your position. To see how this can be so, you need to realize that there are several different types of agreement, one of which you can use in almost any situation.

Agree with the Truth

Agreeing with the truth is easy to understand, though not always easy to practise. You agree with the truth when another person's criticism is factually correct:

"You're right; I am angry."

"I suppose I was just being defensive."

"Now that you mention it, I did get pretty sarcastic."

Agreeing with the facts seems quite sensible when you realize that certain matters are indisputable. If you agree to be somewhere at

"That's just great. I discover the cure for the common cold and all you can do is criticize."

Christopher Weyant/*The New Yorker* Collection/The Cartoon Bank

✅ CHECK IT!

Describe the ways you can seek more information from your critic and how these strategies can contribute to a more positive communication climate.

4:00 and don't show up until 5:00, you are late, no matter how good your excuse is. If you have broken something you borrowed, run out of gas, or failed to finish a job you started, there's no point in denying the fact. In the same way, if you are honest you will have to agree with many interpretations of your behaviour, even when they are not flattering. You do get angry, act foolishly, fail to listen, and behave inconsiderately. Once you rid yourself of the myth of perfection, it's much easier to acknowledge these truths.

If it is so obvious that the descriptions others give of your behaviour are often accurate, why is it so difficult to accept them without being defensive? The answer lies in a confusion between agreeing with the *facts* and accepting

REFLECTION

AGREEING WITH A CRITIC CAN BE LIBERATING

I've always been a very thrifty person. Sometimes, I wish I were more of a free-and-easy spender, but I'm just not. When my housemates and I shop for food, I'm always looking for bargains.

Just after we covered the part of our textbook that talked about agreeing with a critic, we were in the market and I was doing my usual "we can't afford that" routine. One of my housemates said, "You are really a tightwad!" Instead of arguing, I agreed with the truth of his accusation and said, "You're right, I am!" This surprised us both, and we both started to laugh. It felt great to acknowledge the reality of his claim without getting defensive.

the *judgment* that so often accompanies them. Most critics don't merely describe the action that offends them; they also evaluate it, and it is the evaluation that we resist:

> "It's silly to be angry."

> "You have no reason for being defensive."

> "You were wrong to be so sarcastic."

It is such judgments that we resent. By realizing that you can agree with—even learn from—the descriptive part of many criticisms and still not accept the accompanying evaluations, you will often have a response that is both honest and non-defensive. A conversation between a teacher and a student illustrates this point:

Teacher (T): Look at this paper! It's only two pages long and it contains 12 misspelled words. I'm afraid you have a real problem with your writing.

Student (S): You're right. I know I don't spell well at all.

T: I don't know what's happening in the lower grades. They just don't seem to be turning out people who can write a simple, declarative sentence.

S: You're not the first person I've heard say that.

T: I should think you'd be upset by the fact that after so much time in English composition classes, you haven't mastered the basics of spelling.

S: You're right. It does bother me.

Notice that in agreeing with the teacher's comments, the student did not in any way demean herself. Even though there may have been extenuating circumstances to account for her lack of skill, the student didn't find it necessary to justify her errors—because she wasn't saddled with the burden of pretending to be perfect. By simply agreeing with the facts, she was able to maintain her dignity and avoid an unproductive argument.

Of course, in order to reduce defensiveness it is important that your agreement with the facts be honest and admitted without malice. It's humiliating to accept inaccurate descriptions, and maliciously pretending to agree with these only leads to trouble. You can imagine how unproductive the above conversation would have been if the student had spoken the same words in a sarcastic tone. Agree with the facts only when you can do so sincerely. Although it will not always be possible, you'll be surprised at how often you can use this simple response.

Agreeing with criticism is fine, but by itself, it isn't an adequate response to your critic. For instance, once you have admitted to someone that you are defensive, habitually late, or sarcastic, you can expect that person to ask what you intend to do about this behaviour. Such questions are fair. In most cases, it would be a mistake simply to understand another's criticism, to agree with the accusations, and then to go on behaving as before. Such behaviour makes it clear that you have no concern for the speaker. The message that comes through can sound like this: "Sure, I now understand what I've done to bother you. You're right, I have been doing it and I'll probably keep on doing it. If you don't like the way I've been behaving, that's tough!" Such a response might be appropriate for dealing with people you genuinely don't care about—someone who is manipulative or abusive, for example—but it is clearly not suitable for people who matter to you.

Before reading on, then, understand that responding non-defensively to criticism is just the *first* step in resolving the conflicts that usually prompt an attack. In order to resolve your conflicts fully, you will need to learn the skills that we describe in Chapter 10.

Agree with the Odds

Sometimes, a critic will point out possible unpleasant consequences of your behaviour:

> "If you don't talk to more people, they'll think you're a snob."

> "If you don't exercise more, you'll wind up having a heart attack one of these days."

> "If you run around with that crowd, you'll probably be sorry."

Often, such comments are genuinely helpful suggestions that others make for your own good. In other cases, however, they are really devices for manipulating you into behaving the way your critic wants you to. For instance, "If we go to the football game, you might catch cold" could mean "I don't want to go to the football game." "You'll probably be exhausted tomorrow if you stay up late" could be translated as "I want you to go to bed early." In Chapter 10, we will have more to say about such methods of indirect aggression, but for now, it is sufficient to state that such warnings

REFLECTION

COPING WITH CRITICISM AS A MARTIAL ART

I've been taking self-defense lessons for a year, and I think there are a lot of similarities between judo and agreeing with your critic. In both techniques, you don't resist your attacker. Instead you use the other person's energy to your advantage. You let your opponent defeat himself.

Last week, I used "verbal judo" on a very judgmental friend who called me a hypocrite because I'm a vegetarian, but still wear leather shoes. I knew that nothing I could say would change his mind, so I just agreed with his perception by saying, "I can see why you think I'm not consistent." (I really *could* see how my lifestyle looks hypocritical to him, although I don't agree.) No matter what he said, I replied (in different ways), "I understand why it looks that way to you." And each time, I *meant* it. I won't always agree with my critics this way, any more than I'll always use judo. But it certainly is a useful approach to have at my disposal.

often generate defensiveness. A mother–son argument shows this outcome:

Mother (M): I don't see why you want to ride that motorcycle. You could wind up in an accident so easily. [*states the odds of having an accident*]

Son (S): Oh, don't be silly. I'm a careful driver, and besides you know that I never take my bike on the highway. [*denies the odds*]

M: Yes, but every time I pick up the paper I read about someone being hurt or killed. There's always a danger that some crazy driver will miss seeing you and run you off the road. [*states the odds of incurring an injury*]

S: Oh, you worry too much. I always look out for the other driver. And besides, you have a lot better manoeuvrability on a motorcycle than in a car. [*denies the odds of incurring an injury*]

M: I know you're careful, but all it takes is one mistake and you could be killed. [*states the odds of being killed*]

S: Somebody is killed shaving or taking a shower every day, but you don't want me to stop doing those things, do you? You're just exaggerating the whole thing. [*denies the odds of being killed*]

From this example, you can see that it is usually self-defeating to deny another person's predictions. You don't convince the critic, and your opinions stay unchanged as well. Notice the difference when you agree with the odds (though not the demands) of the critic:

M: I don't see why you want to drive that motorcycle. You could wind up in an accident so easily. [*states the odds of having an accident*]

S: I suppose there is a chance of that. [*agrees with the odds*]

M: You're darned right. Every time I pick up the newspaper, I read about someone being hurt or killed. There's always a danger that some crazy driver will miss seeing you and run you off the road. [*states the odds of incurring an injury*]

S: You're right; that could happen [*agrees with the odds*], but I don't think the risk is great enough to keep me off the bike.

M: That's easy for you to say now. Someday, you could be sorry you didn't listen to me. [*states the odds of having regrets*]

S: That's true. I really might regret driving the bike someday—but I'm willing to take that chance. [*agrees with the odds*]

Notice how the son simply considers his mother's predictions and realistically acknowledges the chance that they might come true. While such responses may at first seem indifferent and callous, they can help the son avoid the pitfall of indirect manipulation. Suppose the conversation were a straightforward one, in which the mother was simply pointing out

In addition to bringing hidden agendas into the open for resolution, agreeing with the odds also helps you become aware of some possible previously unconsidered consequences of your actions. Think about a situation in which you agreed with the critic. How did it change the communication climate? How did it change your perspective?

to her son the dangers of motorcycle riding. He acknowledges that he understands her concern and even agrees with the possibility that her prediction could come true. If, however, her prediction were really an indirect way of saying, "I don't want you to ride anymore," then the son's response would force her to clarify her demand so that he could deal with it openly. At this point, they might be able to figure out a solution that would let the son satisfy his need for transportation and excitement and, at the same time, allow his mother to alleviate her concern.

In addition to bringing hidden agendas into the open for resolution, agreeing with the odds also helps you become aware of some possible previously unconsidered consequences of your actions. Instead of blindly denying the chance that your behaviour is undesirable, agreeing with the odds will help you look objectively at whether your course of action is in fact the best one. You may agree with your critic that you really should change your behaviour.

Agree in Principle

Criticism often comes in the form of abstract ideals against which you are unfavourably compared:

> "I wish you wouldn't spend so much time on your work. Relaxation is important, too, you know."

> "You shouldn't expect so much from your kids. Nobody's perfect."

> "What do you mean, you're not voting? The government is going to get better only when people like you take more of an interest in it."

> "You mean you're still upset by that remark? You ought to learn how to take a joke better."

In cases like these, you can accept the principle that the criticism is based on and still behave as before. After all, some rules do allow occasional exceptions, and people are often inconsistent. Consider how you might sincerely agree with the criticisms above without necessarily changing your behaviour:

> "You're right. I am working hard right now. It probably is unhealthy, but finishing the job is worth the extra strain to me."

> "I guess my expectations for the kids are awfully high, and I don't want to drive them crazy. I hope I'm not making a mistake."

> "You're right: if everybody stopped voting, the system would fall apart."

> "Maybe I *would* be happier if I could take a joke in stride. I'm not ready to do that, though, at least not for jokes like that one."

Agree with the Critic's Perception

What about times when there seems to be no basis whatsoever for agreeing with your critics? You've listened carefully and asked questions to make sure you understand the objections, but the more you listen, the more positive you are that they are totally wrong. There is no truth to the criticisms, you can't agree with the odds, and you can't even accept the principle the critics are putting forward. Even here, there's a way of agreeing—this time, not with the critics' conclusions, but with their right to perceive things their way:

A: I don't believe you have been to all the places you were just describing. You're probably just making all this up so that we will think you are hot stuff.

B: Well, I can see how you might think that. I've known people who lie to get approval.

C: I want to let you know right from the start that I was against hiring you for the job. I think the reason you got it was because you're a woman.

D: I can understand why you'd believe that with all the anti-discrimination laws on the books. I hope that after I've been here for a while, you'll change your mind.

E: I don't think you're being totally honest about your reasons for wanting to stay home. You say it's because you have a headache, but I think you're avoiding Li Ping and Owen.

F: I can see why that would make sense to you since Li Ping and I got into an argument the last time we were together. All I can say is that I do have a headache.

Such responses tell your critics that you are acknowledging the reasonableness of their perceptions, even though you don't agree or wish to change your behaviour. This coping style is valuable, as it lets you avoid debates over who is right and who is wrong, which can turn an exchange of ideas into an argument. Notice the difference in the following scenes.

Dispute the Perception

A: I don't see how you can stand to be around Josh. The guy is so crude—he gives me the creeps.

B: What do you mean, crude? He's a really nice guy. I think you're just touchy.

A: Touchy! If it's touchy to be offended by disgusting behaviour, then I'm guilty.

B: You're not guilty about anything. It's just that you are too sensitive when people kid around.

A: Too sensitive, huh? I don't know what's happened to you. You used to have such good judgment about people . . . .

Agree with the Perception

A: I don't see how you can stand to be around Josh. The guy is so crude—he gives me the creeps.

B: Well, I enjoy being around him, but I guess I can see how his jokes would be offensive to some people.

A: You're darned right. I don't see how you can put up with him.

B: Yeah. I guess if you didn't appreciate his humour, you wouldn't want to have much to do with him.

Notice how in the second exchange, person B was able to maintain his own position without attacking A's in the least. Such acceptance is the key ingredient for successfully agreeing with your critic's perceptions. Using acceptance, you clarify that you are in no way disputing his or her views. Because you have no intention of attacking your critic's views, your critic is less likely to be defensive.

 CHECK **IT!**

Explain the ways you can agree with your critic and how this approach contributes to a more positive communication climate.

Building WORK SKILLS

RESPONDING NON-DEFENSIVELY TO CRITICISM

As a student (in a co-op work placement, field practicum, or work-placement setting) or as a new employee, you often get a lot of evaluative feedback or "constructive criticism." Think of a time when your job-related skills were criticized and you reacted defensively. If you are having trouble getting started, imagine yourself receiving one of the following comments:

"You are not taking enough initiative."

"You are not very receptive to feedback."

"You are not acting like a team player."

Now, use the strategies described in the "Transforming Negative Climates" section (page 308) to seek more information from your critic and/or agree with that person. What might you say? Role-play your response with a classmate. Make sure your non-verbal communication agrees with your sincere intent to gather more information. Does your partner think you are genuine?

All these responses to criticism may appear to buy peace at the cost of denying your feelings. However, as you can see by now, counterattacking usually makes matters worse. The non-defensive responses you have just learned will not solve problems or settle disputes by themselves. Nevertheless, they *will* make a constructive dialogue possible, setting the stage for a productive solution. How to achieve productive solutions is the topic of Chapter 10.

SUMMARY

Communication climate refers to the social tone of a relationship. The most influential factor in shaping a communication climate is the degree to which the people involved see themselves as being valued and confirmed. Messages have differing levels of confirmation. We can categorize them as confirming, disagreeing, or disconfirming.

Confirming messages, which communicate that "you exist and are valued," involve recognition, acknowledgment, or endorsement of the other party. Disagreeing messages, which communicate "you are wrong," use argumentativeness, complaining, or aggressiveness. Disconfirming messages, which communicate "you do not exist and are not valued," include responses that are impervious, interrupting, irrelevant, tangential, impersonal, ambiguous, or incongruous. Over time, these messages form climate patterns that often take the shape of positive or negative spirals.

Defensiveness is at the core of most negative spirals. Defensiveness occurs when individuals perceive that their presenting self is being attacked by face-threatening acts. We become particularly defensive about flaws that we don't want to admit and those that touch on sensitive areas. Both the attacker and the person attacked are responsible for creating defensiveness, since competent communicators protect other people's face needs as well as their own.

Jack Gibb suggested a variety of ways to create a positive and non-defensive communication climate. These include being descriptive rather than evaluative, problem-oriented rather than controlling, spontaneous rather than strategic, empathic rather than neutral, equal rather than superior, and provisional rather than certain.

When you are faced with criticism by others, there are two ways to respond less defensively: seek additional information from the critic and agree with some aspect of the criticism. When performed sincerely, these approaches can transform an actual or potentially negative climate into a more positive one.

MULTIPLE-CHOICE QUESTIONS

1. Messages that communicate a lack of regard for another person are
   a. argumentative.
   b. confirming.
   c. incongruous.
   d. disconfirming.

2. The most fundamental act of confirmation is
   a. acknowledgment.
   b. endorsement.
   c. recognition.
   d. listening.

3. When another person fails to acknowledge what you have just said—or they
   just ignore you—their response would be
   best described as
   a. impervious.
   b. argumentative.
   c. impersonal.
   d. irrelevant.
4. According to John Gottman's research,
   complaining is *not* a sign of a troubled
   marriage.
   a. true
   b. false
5. A reciprocal pattern of interaction which
   escalates either positive or negative emotions is called
   a. an escalation.
   b. a de-escalation.
   c. an interactive twist.
   d. a spiral.
6. Defensive responses are designed to protect your presenting self from attack.
   a. true
   b. false
7. Hamid's boss says "When you get to
   be in my position someday, then you'll
   understand," rather than listening to
   Hamid's ideas to solve a problem at
   work. This boss's approach could be
   described as
   a. using neutrality rather than empathy.
   b. using certainty rather than
      provisionalism.
   c. using superiority rather than equality.
   d. using strategy rather than spontaneity.
8. When receiving criticism, it is a good idea
   to seek more information.
   a. true
   b. false
9. Sam says that Julie was angry and over-
   reacted to his suggestion. Julie agrees with
   Sam and admits that she really was angry
   when he suggested they skip the movie
   they had planned to see. Julie was agreeing with
   a. the truth.
   b. the odds.
   c. the principle.
   d. Sam's perception.
10. Non-defensive responses solve disputes.
    a. true
    b. false

Answers: 1. d; 2. c; 3. a; 4. a; 5. d; 6. a; 7. c; 8. a; 9. a; 10. b

ACTIVITIES

1. Invitation to Insight
Identify three personal relationships that matter to you. For each relationship:
a. Come up with a weather phrase that
   describes the current climate of the
   relationship.
b. Come up with a weather phrase that fore-
   casts the climate of the relationship over
   the next year.
c. Consider why you chose the phrases
   you did. In particular, describe how
   feeling valued and confirmed played a
   part in the climates you perceived and
   predicted.

2. Critical Thinking Probe
Mental-health experts generally believe it is
better to have others disagree with you than
ignore you. Express your opinion on this
matter, using specific examples from personal
experiences to support your position. Next,
discuss whether (and how) it is possible to disagree without being disconfirming.

3. Skill Builder
Develop your ability to communicate supportively instead of triggering defensive reactions
in others. Restate each of the following "you"
statements as an "I" message. Use details from

your own personal relationships to create messages that are specific and personally relevant.

a. "You're thinking only of yourself."

b. "Don't be so touchy."

c. "Quit fooling around!"

d. "Stop beating around the bush and tell me the truth."

e. "You're a slob!"

4. Ethical Challenge

Gibb argues that spontaneous rather than strategic communication reduces defensiveness. However, in some situations a strategic approach may hold the promise of a climate better than that created by a completely honest message. Consider situations such as these:

a. You don't find your partner very attractive. He or she asks, "What's the matter?"

b. You intend to quit your job because you hate your boss, but you don't want to offend him or her. How do you explain the reasons for your departure?

c. You are tutoring a high school student in reading or math. The student is sincere and a hard worker, but is perhaps the most dull-witted person you have ever met. What do you say when the teenager asks, "How am I doing?"

Describe at least one situation from your experience where complete honesty increased another person's defensiveness. Discuss whether candour, or another strategy, might have been the best approach in this situation. How can you reconcile your approach with Gibb's arguments in favour of spontaneity?

5. Invitation to Insight

Review the Gibb behaviours discussed on pages 301–308, and then answer the following questions:

a. Which defence-provoking behaviour do you find most annoying?

b. Who in your life uses that behaviour most often?

c. What part of your presenting self is threatened by that behaviour?

d. How do you normally respond to that behaviour?

e. What behaviour do you wish that person would do instead?

6. Role Play

Practise responding non-defensively to critical attacks by following these steps:

a. Describe five criticisms you are likely to encounter from others in your day-to-day communication. If you have trouble thinking of criticisms, invite people who know you well to supply some real, sincere grievances.

b. For each criticism, write one or more non-defensive responses using the categories on pages 308–318. Be sure your responses are sincere and that you can offer them without counterattacking your critic.

c. Practise your responses, either by inviting a friend or classmate to play the role of your critics or by approaching your critics directly and inviting them to share their complaints with you.

DISCUSSION QUESTIONS

1. Describe the three levels of confirming messages and give examples of each. Can you endorse another person without recognizing and acknowledging him or her? Why or why not?

2. The authors argue that argumentativeness is a more positive approach to disagreeing than complaining or aggressiveness. Do you agree? Why or why not?

3. What elements do all types of disconfirming messages have in common? Explain.

4. Explain how defensiveness is the process of protecting your presenting self. Give an example to illustrate.

5. It has been said that we often feel most defensive when the criticism we receive is accurate. Would you agree or disagree? Why?

6. How can Jack Gibb's categories of supportive behaviour help you to reduce defensiveness in others?

7. What are the advantages and disadvantages of seeking more information when you are criticized?

JOURNAL IDEAS

1. Think of a criticism or complaint you have about someone important to you. Write down your complaint, review the Gibb categories, and rewrite your complaint using:
   a. a description (rather than an evaluation);
   b. a problem orientation (rather than a control orientation);
   c. spontaneity (rather than strategy);
   d. empathy (rather than neutrality);
   e. equality (rather than superiority); and
   f. provisionalism (rather than certainty).

   Have you lost any of your meaning and intention? If so, what and how can it be incorporated? Look at your two complaints and pretend someone was making them about you. Which would you rather hear and why?

2. Describe a time recently when you responded defensively to a comment or criticism made by someone important to you. Review the strategies for seeking more information and agreeing with the critic described in this chapter. How could you have used these strategies in the situation you just described, and what might the challenges and benefits be?

10
Managing Conflict

Chapter Outline

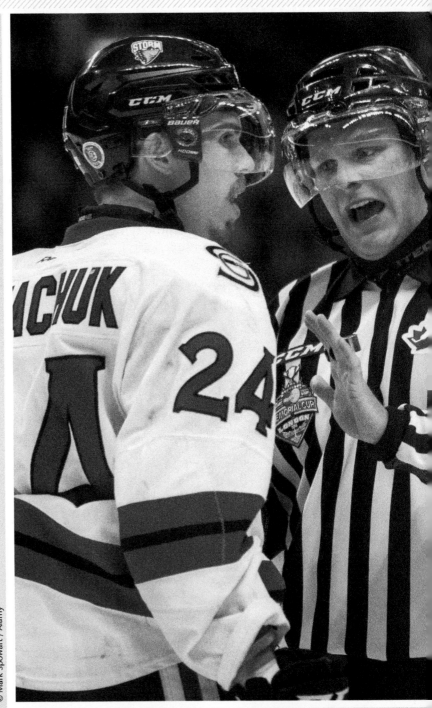

© Mark Spowart / Alamy

Key Terms

assertion
collaborative problem
  solving
complementary conflict style
compromise
conflict
conflict rituals
de-escalatory spiral
direct aggression
dysfunctional conflict
escalatory spiral

functional conflict
indirect communication
lose–lose problem solving
non-assertion
parallel conflict style
passive aggression
relational conflict style
symmetrical conflict style
win–lose problem solving
win–win problem solving

Learning Objectives

YOU SHOULD UNDERSTAND:

- the five elements of conflict;
- that conflict is natural and inevitable;
- the characteristics of functional and dysfunctional conflicts;
- the differences among non-assertiveness, indirect communication, passive aggression, direct aggression, and assertiveness;
- the influence of gender and culture on interpersonal conflict; and
- the characteristics of win–lose, lose–lose, and win–win problem solving.

YOU SHOULD BE ABLE TO:

- recognize and accept the inevitability of conflicts in your life;
- identify the behaviours that characterize your dysfunctional conflicts and suggest more functional alternatives;
- identify the conflict styles you use most commonly and evaluate their appropriateness;
- use the assertive message format;
- describe the relational conflict system in one of your important relationships; and
- use the win–win problem-solving approach to resolve an interpersonal conflict.

Once upon a time, there was a world without conflicts. The leaders of each nation recognized the need for co-operation and met regularly to solve any potential problems before they could grow. They never disagreed on matters needing attention or on ways to handle these matters, and so there were never any international tensions, and of course there was no war.

Within each nation, things ran just as smoothly. The citizens always agreed on who their leaders should be, so elections were always unanimous. There was no social friction among various groups. Age, race, and educational differences did exist, but each group respected the others, and all got along harmoniously.

Human relationships were always perfect. Strangers were always kind and friendly to each other. Neighbours were considerate of each other's needs. Friendships were always mutual, and no disagreements ever spoiled people's enjoyment of one other. Once people fell in love—and everyone did—they stayed happy. Partners liked everything about each other and were able to fully satisfy each other's needs. Children and parents agreed on every aspect of family life and were never critical or hostile toward each other. Each day was better than the one before.

Of course, everybody lived happily ever after.

This story is obviously a fairy tale. Regardless of what we may wish for or dream about, a conflict-free world just doesn't exist. Even the best communicators, the luckiest people, are bound to wind up in situations when their needs don't match the needs of others. Money, time, power, sex, humour, aesthetic taste, and a thousand other issues arise and keep us from living in a state of perpetual agreement.

For many people, the inevitability of conflict is a depressing fact. They think that the existence of ongoing conflict means that there is little chance for happy relationships with others. Effective communicators know differently. They realize that although it's impossible to *eliminate* conflict, there are ways to *manage* it effectively. The skilful management of conflict can open the door to healthier, stronger, and more satisfying relationships.

What Is Conflict?

Stop reading for a moment and make a list of as many different conflicts as you can think of. Include conflicts you have experienced personally and those that involved other people only. The list will probably show you that conflict takes many forms. Sometimes, there is angry shouting, as when parents yell at their children. In other cases, conflicts involve restrained discussion, as in labour–management negotiations or court trials. Sometimes, conflicts are carried on through hostile silence, as in the unspoken feuds of angry couples. Finally, conflicts may wind up with physical fighting between friends, enemies, or even total strangers.

Whatever forms they may take, all interpersonal conflicts share certain similarities. William Wilmot and Joyce Hocker (2010)

© iStockPhoto/ LPETTET.

Conflict can appear in many forms in many different relationships. Think about the most recent conflicts you've had—with a co-worker, friend, parent, or partner. How did the conflict change your relationship?

provide a thorough definition of conflict. They state that **conflict** is an expressed struggle that inevitably occurs between at least two interdependent parties who perceive incompatible goals, scarce rewards, and interference from the other party in achieving their goals. The various parts of this definition can help you gain a better understanding of how conflict operates in everyday life.

Expressed Struggle

In order for conflict to exist, all the people involved must know that there is some disagreement. You may be upset for months because a neighbour's loud music keeps you awake at night, but no conflict exists until the neighbour learns about your problem. An expressed struggle does not have to be verbal. You can show your displeasure with someone without saying a word. A dirty look, the silent treatment, and avoiding the other person are all ways of expressing yourself. One way or another, both people must know that a problem exists before it fits our definition of conflict.

Perceived Incompatible Goals

All conflicts look as if one person's gain would be another's loss. For instance, consider the neighbour whose music keeps you awake at night. It appears that someone has to lose. If the neighbour turns down the noise, then she loses the enjoyment of hearing the music at full volume, but if she keeps the volume up, then you're still awake and unhappy.

The goals in this situation really aren't completely incompatible—solutions do exist that allow both people to get what they want. For instance, you could achieve peace and quiet by closing your windows or getting the neighbour to close hers. You might use earplugs, or perhaps the neighbour could get a set of earphones, which would allow the music to play at full volume without bothering anyone. If any of these solutions prove workable, the conflict disappears.

Unfortunately, people often fail to see mutually satisfying answers to their problems.

As long as they *perceive* their goals to be mutually exclusive, the conflict is real, albeit unnecessary.

Perceived Scarce Rewards

Conflicts also exist when people believe there is not enough of something to go around: affection, money, space, and so on. Time is often a scarce commodity. As authors, teachers, and people who value their families, the writers of this textbook are constantly in the middle of struggles about how to use the limited time we have at home. Should we work on this book? Spend time with our families? Enjoy the luxury of being alone? With only 24 hours in a day, we're bound to wind up in conflicts with our families, editors, students, colleagues, and friends—all of whom want more of our time than we have available to give.

Interdependence

However antagonistic they may feel, the people in a conflict are dependent upon each other. The welfare and satisfaction of one depends on the actions of another. If this were not true, there would be no need for conflict, even in the face of scarce resources and incompatible goals. In fact, many conflicts remain unresolved because the people fail to understand their interdependence. One of the first steps toward resolving a conflict is to take the attitude that "we're all in this together."

Inevitability

Conflicts are bound to happen, even in the best relationships. College students who have kept diaries of their relationships report that they take part in about seven arguments a week (Benoit and Benoit, 1987). In addition, most people report having repeated arguments about the same issues in their relationships (Malis and Roloff, 2006; Radanielina-Hita, 2010). In another survey (Samter and Cupach, 1998), 81 per cent of the respondents acknowledged that they had conflicts with friends. Even the 19 per cent who claimed their friendships were conflict-free used terms like "push and pull" or "little disagreements" to describe the tensions that inevitably occurred. Among families, conflict can be even more frequent. Researchers who recorded dinner conversations of 52 families found an average of 3.3 "conflict episodes" per meal (Vuchinich, 1987). The frequency of conflicts does vary over the life of a relationship. For example, partners married 40 years or more report having fewer conflicts than earlier in their relationship, since many contested issues (such as those involving children, in-laws, and money) are no longer present (Dickson et al., 2002). But for most of us, most of the time, conflict is an inescapable fact of life.

Since it is impossible to *avoid* conflicts, the challenge is to handle them effectively when they do arise. More than 20 years of research shows that both happy and unhappy relationships have conflicts, but that they perceive them and manage them in very different ways (Bertoni and Bodenmann, 2010; Wilmot and Hocker, 2010). Unhappy couples argue in ways categorized in this book as destructive. The partners are more concerned with defending themselves than solving problems; they fail to listen carefully to each another, have little or no empathy for their partners, use evaluative "you" language, and ignore each other's relational messages.

Many satisfied couples handle their conflicts more effectively. They recognize that disagreements are healthy and know that conflicts need to be faced (Burleson and Denton, 2014; Crohan, 1992; Ridley et al., 2001). While they may argue vigorously they value supportive communication skills such as helping each other feel better when upset and communicating in ways that make their partners feel good about their qualities and accomplishments (Burleson and Denton, 2014). These partners use skills such as perception checking to find out what the other person is thinking, and they let the other person know that they understand the other side of the dispute (Canary et al., 1991). Satisfied couples believe they have empathy for each other's position (Cramer and Jowett, 2010). These people are willing to

admit their mistakes, a habit that contributes to a harmonious relationship and also helps solve the problem at hand.

Functional and Dysfunctional Conflicts

Some bacteria are "good," aiding digestion and cleaning up waste, whereas others are "bad," causing infection. There are helpful forest fires, which clean out dangerous accumulations of underbrush, and harmful ones, which threaten lives and property. In the same way, some conflicts can be beneficial. They provide a way for relationships to grow by solving the problem at hand and often improving other areas of interaction. Other conflicts can be harmful, causing pain and weakening a relationship. Communication scholars usually describe harmful conflicts as *dysfunctional* and beneficial ones as *functional* (Canary and Messman, 2000). In a **dysfunctional conflict**, the outcomes fall short of what is possible and have a damaging effect on the relationship. By contrast, participants in a **functional conflict** achieve the best possible outcome, even strengthening the relationship.

- **Conflict:** an expressed struggle between at least two interdependent parties who perceive incompatible goals, scarce rewards, and interference from the other party in achieving goals; conflict is inevitable.
- **Functional conflict:** a struggle between two participants that is resolved so as to achieve the best possible outcome, even strengthening the relationship.
- **Dysfunctional conflict:** a struggle between two participants in which the outcomes fall short of what is possible and have a damaging effect on the relationship.

What makes some conflicts functional and others dysfunctional? Usually, the difference does not rest in the subject of the conflict, as it is possible to have good or poor results on almost any issue. The factors that distinguish functional conflicts from their more destructive counterparts are complex and include the quality of the relationship itself and the partners' conflict styles (Laursen and Hafen, 2010). In addition, certain individual styles of communication can be more productive than others, and the success or failure of a conflict may well depend on the method of resolution the communicators choose (Alberts and Driscoll, 1992). We will talk more about types of conflict resolution later in this chapter. Now, though, we will describe some characteristics that distinguish functional from dysfunctional conflicts.

In a dysfunctional conflict, the outcomes fall short of what is possible and have a damaging effect on the relationship, while in a functional conflict the participants achieve the best possible outcome, even strengthening the relationship. Think of one example of a functional conflict and a dysfunctional conflict in your life. What were the characteristics that distinguished one from the other?

Integration versus Polarization

In a dysfunctional conflict partners take oppositional positions. They see themselves as "good" and the other person as "bad," their actions as "protective" and the other's as "aggressive," their behaviour as "open and trustworthy" and the other's as "sneaky and deceitful." Alan Sillars and his colleagues (2000) found that in severe conflicts and dissatisfied relationships, married people saw their spouses as more blameworthy than themselves. Researchers Robert Blake and Jane Mouton (1964) found that people engaged in this kind of polarization underestimate the commonalities shared with the other person and miss areas of agreement and goodwill.

By contrast, participants who take a more integrating approach to conflict realize that the other person's needs may be legitimate, too. They display a high concern for both themselves and the other person. They take a problem-oriented approach and see the other person as a partner in resolving the issue rather than an opponent who should be controlled or defeated. Functional conflict is marked by mutual respect and an appreciation of people's differences (Connolly and Sicola, 2005; Foss and Griffin, 1995).

Co-operation versus Opposition

Participants in a dysfunctional conflict see each other as opponents and view the other's gain as their loss: "If you win, I lose" is the attitude. This belief keeps partners from looking for ways to agree or finding solutions that can satisfy them both. People rarely try to redefine the situation in more constructive ways, and they seldom give in, even on non-critical issues.

A more functional approach recognizes that co-operation may bring about an answer that leaves everyone happy. Even nations basically hostile to each other often recognize the functional benefits of co-operating. For example, although many member countries of the United Nations have clear-cut differences in certain areas, they work together to alleviate world hunger and to encourage peaceful solutions to world conflict. Such co-operation is also possible in interpersonal conflicts. Co-operative problem solving is discussed in greater detail later in this chapter.

Confirmation versus Disconfirmation

When people involved in disagreements attack and belittle each other they create dysfunctional conflicts. Marital researcher John Gottman and his colleagues have identified four disconfirming behaviours that accurately predict (90 per cent of the time) that newly married couples will wind up getting divorced (Gottman and Notarius 2000, 2002). Gottman calls them the "Four Horsemen of the Apocalypse" and they are: criticism, defensiveness, contempt, and stonewalling (also known as the silent treatment). As we learned in Chapter 9 about negative communication, criticism (which involves negative evaluation), contempt (which involves taking a position of superiority) and stonewalling (which denies the most fundamental act of confirmation–recognition) all contribute to creating defensiveness and counterattacks, which poison the communication climate. These destructive types of communication are as predictive of relationship dissatisfaction and dissolution among gay and lesbian couples as they are among heterosexual couples (Gottman et al., 2003) and similar types of disconfirming behaviour have been linked to less than satisfying friendships (Koh et al., 2003) and workplace conflict (Madlock and Kennedy-Lightsey, 2010). In contrast, during functional conflicts the people involved may disagree, but they are not disagreeable. By using the kinds of supportive behaviour described on pages 301–308 in Chapter 9 (description instead of evaluation, equality instead of superiority, problem orientation rather than control, etc.), it is possible to tackle disagreements without attacking the person. When partners treat one another with empathy and affection, and without behaving dominantly or dismissively, relational satisfaction increases—even in the face of conflict (Askari et al., 2012; Gottman et al., 2003; Hubbard, 2001).

Agreement versus Coercion

In destructive conflicts, the participants rely heavily on power to get what they want. "Do it my way, or else" is a threat commonly stated or implied in dysfunctional conflicts. Money, favours, friendliness, sex, and sometimes even physical coercion become tools for forcing the other person to give in. Needless to say, victories won with such power plays do not do much for a relationship.

More enlightened communicators realize that power plays are usually a bad idea, not only on ethical grounds, but also because they can often backfire. Rarely is a person in a relationship totally powerless; it is often possible to win a battle only to lose the war. One classic case of the dysfunctional consequences of using power to resolve conflicts occurs in families where authoritarian parents turn their children's requests into "unreasonable demands." It's easy enough to send five-year-olds out of the room for some real or imagined misbehaviour, but when they grow into teenagers they acquire many ways of striking back.

De-escalation versus Escalation

In destructive conflicts, the problems seem to grow larger instead of smaller. As we saw in Chapter 9, defensiveness is reciprocal: the person you attack is likely to strike back even harder. We all have seen a small incident get out of hand and cause damage out of proportion to its importance.

One clear sign of functional conflict is that in the long run, the behaviour of the participants solves more problems than it creates. We say "long run" because facing up to an issue instead of avoiding it will usually make life more difficult for a while. In this respect, handling conflicts functionally is rather like going to the dentist: you may find it painful for a short time, but you are only making matters worse if you don't face the problem.

Focusing versus Drifting

In dysfunctional conflicts, the partners often bring in issues having little or nothing to do with the original problem. Take, for example, a wife and husband having trouble deciding whether to spend the holidays at his or her parents' home. As they begin to grow frustrated at their inability to solve the disagreement, their interaction sounds like this:

A: Your mother is always trying to latch onto us!

B: If you want to talk about latching on, what about your folks? Ever since they loaned us that money, they've been asking about every dime we spend.

A: Well, if you could ever finish with school and hold down a decent job, we wouldn't have to worry about money so much. You're always talking about wanting to be an equal partner, but I'm the one paying all the bills around here.

You can imagine how the conversation would go from here. Notice how the original issue became lost as the conflict expanded. Such open-ended hostility is unlikely to solve any of the problems it brings up, not to mention its potential for creating problems that didn't even exist before.

One characteristic of communicators who handle conflict well is their ability to keep focused on one subject at a time. Unlike those dysfunctional battlers that George Bach and Peter Wyden (1968) call "kitchen sink fighters," skilful communicators might say, "I'm willing to talk about how my parents have been acting since they made us that loan, but first let's settle the business of where to spend the holidays." In other words, for functional problem solving, the rule is "one problem at a time."

 **CHECK IT!**

Describe the characteristics that distinguish functional conflict from dysfunctional conflict.

Foresight versus Short-Sightedness

Short-sightedness can produce dysfunctional conflicts even when partners do not lose sight of the original issue. One common type of short-sightedness occurs when disputants try to win a battle and wind up losing the war. Friends may argue about who started a fight, but if you succeed in proving that you were "right" at the cost of the friendship, then the victory is a hollow one. In another type of short-sightedness, partners are so interested in defending their own solution to a problem that they overlook a different solution that would satisfy both their goals. A final type of short-sightedness occurs when one or both partners jump into a conflict without thinking about how they can approach the issue most constructively. More details about preventing these last two types of short-sightedness are discussed later in this chapter. Foresight, in contrast helps individuals pick their battles wisely. They look ahead and anticipate the consequences of the conflict on the relationship and weigh the benefits and possible costs of various approaches to resolving the problem.

REFLECTION

EMAIL DE-ESCALATES CONFLICT SPIRAL

My mother is a family lawyer who specializes in divorce cases. She says that email has been a good way to get angry couples to communicate. Some husbands and wives can't be in the same room without getting into a shouting match, but email slows things down and gives them a chance to think before they answer each other. My mother asks each person in a divorcing couple to wait overnight before answering to the other's message, which cuts down on the angry and hurtful replies.

She often says that email doesn't save failing marriages, but it certainly makes the breakup more civilized and less painful.

Positive versus Negative Results

So far, we have looked at the differences between the *processes* of functional and dysfunctional conflicts. Now, we will compare the *results* of these different styles.

Dysfunctional conflict usually has two consequences. First, no one is likely to get what they originally wanted. In the short run, it may *look* as if one person is winning a dispute while the other person loses, but today's victor is likely to suffer tomorrow at the hands of the original loser. Second, dysfunctional conflicts can threaten the future of a relationship. Family members, lovers, friends, neighbours, or fellow workers are usually bound together by webs of commitments and obligations that are not easy to break. If they cannot find satisfactory ways of resolving their differences, their connections will become strained and uncomfortable. Even when it is possible, dissolving a relationship in the face of a conflict is hardly a satisfying practice.

In contrast to these dismal outcomes, functional conflicts have positive results. One benefit of handling issues skilfully is the reward of successfully facing a challenge. Finding a solution that works for you and the other person can leave partners feeling better about themselves and each other. Partners learn more about each other's needs and how they can be satisfied. Feelings are clarified. Backgrounds are shared. The relationship grows deeper and stronger. Of course, growth can take place in non-conflict situations, too, but the point here is that dealing with problems can be an opportunity for getting to know each other better and appreciating each other more. Constructive conflict also provides a safe outlet for the feelings of frustration and aggression that are bound to occur. Without this kind of release, partners can build up a list of grudges that interfere with their everyday functioning and their goodwill toward each other.

Individual Conflict Styles

People have their individual styles of handling conflict—characteristic approaches they take when their needs appear incompatible with what others want. As you will read, the most effective style often changes from one situation to another. Despite this fact, many people have one or two "default" styles that can be effective at some times and ineffective at others. What styles do you tend to use to deal with conflict? Find out by thinking about how two hypothetical characters—Chris and Pat—manage a problem that you might find familiar.

Chris and Pat have been friends for several years, ever since they moved into the same apartment building. They had always exchanged favours in a neighbourly way, but Pat has recently been depending more and more on Chris. Pat asks Chris to take care of her cat and houseplants almost every other weekend when she is travelling; borrows food and money without returning them; and drops in to talk about her unhappy love life at least once a week. Until lately, Chris hasn't minded much, but now she is getting tired of Pat's behaviour.

Read the five groups of responses below and rank them in the order you would be most likely to use them if you were Chris. Mark your most likely response as number 1, your next most likely as number 2, and so on.

1. Steer clear of Pat as much as possible. Pretend not to be home when Pat drops by. Make excuses for why you can't help with the endless list of demands and problems *or* do the favours for Pat, hoping the imposing will stop soon. After all, nobody's perfect, and it isn't worth making an issue.

   Ranking = _____

2. Hint to Pat that you are not happy with all her demands. When she asks you to take care of her cat, hesitate and talk about your busy schedule. When Pat doesn't pay back the loans, mention that you're short of money and may need to borrow some from your friends and family. When Pat starts to talk about her romantic problems, mention

that you need to study for an exam.

Ranking = _____

3. Do the favours for Pat, but send out signals that you aren't happy. Sigh when Pat asks another favour. Make an occasional sarcastic remark about how much you enjoy being Pat's housekeeper and psychotherapist. When Pat asks if you are upset, deny that anything is wrong. If Pat doesn't notice your dissatisfaction, express your resentment by saying you'll do the favours, then don't do them.

Ranking = _____

4. Pat can't take a hint, so be direct and say that you are fed up with all her demands. Say you don't mind helping once in a while, but that you feel that she is taking advantage of your friendship. Warn Pat that continued impositions will threaten your friendship.

Ranking = _____

5. Tell Pat that you're beginning to feel uneasy about the barrage of requests. Let her know that you value the friendship and want to keep feeling good about it. Explain that's why you are telling her this. Ask Pat to work with you to find a way to solve the problems that's less of a strain for you.

Ranking = _____

Make sure you have ranked your responses before going on. Each of the choices above represents a different style of behaviour used

© iStockPhoto/PhotoEuphoria.

Conflict with a person with whom you are close or see frequently can be difficult to deal with. What is your style of conflict management? Do you have different styles for different people? What style seems to dominate?

in conflicts (Tangney et al., 1996). These five styles are explained below and summarized in Table 10.1. As you read on, see which ones best describe the way you manage your own conflicts.

Non-assertion

The inability or unwillingness to express thoughts or feelings in a conflict is called **non-assertion**. Non-assertion can often come from a lack of confidence, but in many cases, people lack the awareness or skill to use a more direct means of expression. Sometimes, people know how to communicate in a straightforward way, but choose to behave non-assertively.

Non-assertion can take a variety of forms. One is *avoidance*—either physical (steering clear of a friend after having an argument) or conversational (changing the topic, joking, or denying that a problem exists). People who avoid conflicts usually believe it is easier to put up with the status quo than to face the problem head-on and try to solve it. *Accommodation* is another type of non-assertive response. Accommodators deal with conflict by giving in, putting the other's needs ahead of their own.

While non-assertion may be the easiest response in the short term, research suggests that it can lead to less satisfaction and security over the life of a relationship (Ruvolo et al., 2001). Our example of Chris and Pat illustrates the perils of non-assertion. Every time Chris hides from Pat or changes the subject so Pat won't ask for a favour, Chris becomes uncomfortable and probably leaves Pat feeling the same way. After this avoidance goes on for a while, it's likely that whatever enjoyment Chris and Pat had found together will be eclipsed by their new way of relating and that the friendship will degenerate into an awkward, polite charade.

Non-assertive behaviour is not always a bad idea. You may choose to keep quiet or give in if the risk of speaking up is too great, such as getting fired from a job you can't afford to lose, being humiliated in public, or even risking physical harm. You may also avoid a conflict if the relationship it involves isn't worth the effort. Even in close relationships, though, non-assertion has its logic. If the issue is temporary or minor, you may let it pass. It might even make sense to keep your thoughts to yourself and give in if the issue is more important to the other person than it is to you. These reasons help explain why the communication of many happily married couples is characterized by "selectively ignoring" the other person's minor flaws (Cahn, 1992). This doesn't mean that a key to successful relationships is to avoid *all* conflicts. Instead, it suggests that it is smart to save energy for the truly important ones.

Indirect Communication

Sometimes, we choose to convey messages indirectly instead of expressing ourselves outright. **Indirect communication** is often conveyed through a third party ("Kiera is driving

Table 10.1 ● Individual Styles of Conflict

	Non-assertive	Directly Aggressive	Passive Aggressive	Indirect	Assertive
Approach to others	I'm not OK; you're OK.	I'm OK; you're not OK.	I'm OK; you're not OK. (But I'll let you think you are.)	I'm OK; you're not OK.	I'm OK; you're OK.
Decision making	Lets others choose.	Chooses for others. They know it.	Chooses for others. They don't know it.	Chooses for others. They don't know it.	Chooses for self.
Self-sufficiency	Low.	High or low.	Looks high, but usually low.	High or low.	Usually high.
Behaviour in problem situations	Flees; gives in.	Outright attack.	Concealed attack.	Strategic, oblique.	Direct confrontation.
Response of others	Disrespect, guilt, anger, frustration.	Hurt, defensiveness, humiliation.	Confusion, frustration, feelings of manipulation.	Unknowing compliance or resistance.	Mutual respect.
Success pattern	Succeeds by luck or charity of others.	Beats out others.	Wins by manipulation.	Gains unwitting compliance of others.	Attempts win–win solutions.

SOURCE: Adapted from Stanlee Phelps and Nancy Austin (2002), *The assertive woman*, 4th edn. American Orthopsychiatric Association, 1975. Impact Publishers, Inc.

me crazy!"); in other cases, the message is delivered to the person involved, but in an obscure way ("You must have been really hungry. You ate all the leftover pie and finished off that carton of milk.").

Consider again the case of Chris and Pat. Rather than risk triggering a defensive reaction, Chris decides to try to change Pat's bad habits with an indirect approach. If Pat has the kind of sensitivity that characterizes most competent communicators, Pat may get Chris's message without forcing a confrontation with Chris. In her analysis of radio and television interviewers, Marcia Macaulay (2001) found that female interviewers employed indirect requests for "tough" or delicate information so as not to jeopardize a line of questioning.

An indirect approach can save face for the other person. If your guests are staying too long at a party, it's probably kinder to yawn and hint about your big day tomorrow than to bluntly ask them to leave. Likewise, if you are not interested in going out with someone who has asked you for a date, it may be more compassionate to claim that you are busy than to say, "I'm not interested in seeing you."

Sometimes, indirect communication can be a form of self-protection. You may test the waters by hinting instead of directly asking the boss for a raise, or by letting your partner know you could use some affection instead of asking outright. At times like these, an oblique approach may get the message across while minimizing the risk of a negative response.

The advantages of saving face for others and protecting oneself help explain why indirect communication is the most common way people make requests (Jordan and Roloff, 1990). The risk of an indirect message, of course, is that the other person will misunderstand you or fail to get the hint. There are also times when the importance of an idea is great enough that hinting lacks the necessary punch. When clarity and directness are your goals, the assertive approach, which we describe later in this section, can be more effective.

Passive Aggression

Passive aggression occurs when a communicator expresses dissatisfaction in a disguised manner. Passive aggression can take the form of "crazy making" (Bach and Wyden, 1968)—tactics designed to punish another person without direct confrontation. "Crazy making" takes its name from the effect such behaviour usually has on its target. There are a number of crazy-making ways to deal with conflict. One is through guilt: "Never mind. I'll do all the work myself. Go ahead and have a good time. Don't worry about me." Another crazy-maker involves someone agreeing with you face-to-face, but then showing a different agenda behind your back—such as the teenager who says he'll clean his room, then doesn't do so as a means of getting back at the parent who grounded him. Some passive aggression is non-verbal: a loud sigh, a pained expression, or a disdainful laugh can get a message across. If the target of these messages asks about

Nina Paley/Creative Commons Attribution Share-Alike

them, the passive aggressor can always deny the conflict exists. Even humour—especially sarcasm—can be used as passive aggression.

There are a number of risks to passive-aggressive approaches like these. First, they may not work. The other person may miss your message and continue with the undesirable behaviour. Second, the target of your passive aggression may understand your message clearly, but refuse to comply, possibly out of irritation at your underhanded style of communicating. Even when passive aggression proves successful in the short run, it can have unpleasant consequences over a longer period of time. You may get immediate compliance ("All right, I'll help you with the damn thing!"), but create a resentful climate that will harm the relationship in the future.

Direct Aggression

Whereas a non-asserter under-reacts, a directly aggressive communicator does just the opposite, lashing out to attack the source of displeasure. Dominic Infante (1987) identifies nine types of **direct aggression**: *character attacks, competence attacks, physical appearance attacks, maledictions* (wishing the other bad fortune), *teasing, ridicule, threats, swearing,* and *non-verbal emblems* (shaking a fist, waving arms, etc.). Like all types of relational communication, direct aggression has both verbal and non-verbal dimensions.

The results of direct aggression can have a severe impact on the target. There is a significant connection between verbal aggression and physical aggression (Cui et al., 2010; Infante et al., 1989; Kwong et al., 2003). Even if the attacks never lead to blows, the psychological effects can be harmful or even devastating. Recipients can feel embarrassed, inadequate, humiliated, hopeless, desperate, or depressed. These results can lead to decreased effectiveness in personal relationships (Perlman, 2007), on the job (Madlock and Kennedy-Lightsey, 2010), in classrooms (Martin et al., 2010; Myers et al., 2013) and in families (Cui et al., 2010). Verbal aggression can affect the

relationship as well as the target. One aggressive remark can lead to an equally combative reaction, starting a destructive spiral that can expand beyond the original dispute and damage the entire relationship (Infante, 1988; Olson and Braithwaite, 2004).

Assertion

People who take an assertive approach face conflict directly. It is an important element of a problem-solving approach to conflict in which people try to find solutions that meet both their own needs and the needs of their partner. In **assertion**, a speaker's statement expresses thoughts and feelings clearly. Unlike an aggressive message, it does not attack the other person (Infante and Wigley, 1986). One format for an assertive message consists of five elements (Miller, Nunnally et al., 1975):

1. *A description of the observable behaviour that prompted your message.* The key here is to describe the behaviour objectively, without blaming or name calling. Notice how each of the following statements just describes the facts: "When you didn't call me after you said you would . . ." and "Last week, you asked me to buy the tickets, and now you tell me you don't want them."
2. *Your interpretation of the behaviour.* Be sure to label the interpretation as subjective, not as a matter of fact. For example, "I get the idea you're mad at me" is a better statement than "Why are you mad at me?"
3. *The feelings that arise from your interpretation.* Notice the difference between saying, "I get the idea you are mad at me" and the more complete description "I get the idea you are mad at me *and I feel hurt* (or *defensive, confused,* or *sorry*)." Review Chapters 4 and 5 for suggestions on how to express emotions clearly.
4. *The consequences of the information you have shared so far.* Consequences can describe what happens to *you,* the speaker ("When you tease me, I avoid you"), what happens to the *target of the message*

("When you drink too much, you start to drive dangerously"), or what happens to *others* ("When you play the radio so loudly, it wakes up the baby").

5. *An intention statement.* Some intention statements are requests ("I hope you'll come again"). Others describe how you plan to act ("Unless we can work out some sort of studying arrangement, I may have to find a new place to live").

Chris could have used this format to speak assertively, without blaming Pat:

> I've been bothered by some things lately, and I'd like to talk them over with you. When you ask me to take care of your apartment two or three times a month and borrow food and money without returning them [*behaviour*], I don't think you realize the inconveniences I face [*interpretation*]. I didn't mind until recently—that's why I haven't said anything before—but I'm starting to feel resentful [*feeling*], and I'm afraid it might spoil our friendship [*consequence*]. I don't want that to happen [*intention*], so I'd like to figure out some way I can help you when you really need it, but without it being quite so much of a burden on me [*another intention*].

This sort of assertive message gets results, especially in our most important interpersonal relationships. While less direct forms may work in non-intimate situations, directness is more effective at getting compliance in intimate relationships (Jordan and Roloff, 1990). Furthermore, a straightforward approach is likely to result in greater relational satisfaction (Honeycutt and Wiemann, 1999; Ridley et al., 2001). When the issue is important and the commitment between partners is high, speaking from the heart instead of beating around the bush seems to be the best approach.

Besides boosting your chances of getting what you want, an assertive approach maintains the self-respect of both people. As a result, people who manage their conflicts assertively usually feel better about themselves

and each other afterward, which is not always the case with other styles.

Which Style to Use?

Although communicating assertively might seem like the most attractive alternative to the other styles described in this chapter, it is an oversimplification to imagine that there is one "right" way to respond to conflicts (Canary and Cupach, 1988; Canary and Spitzberg, 1987). Generally speaking, assertive tactics, such as asking for information and considering alternatives, are preferable to such aggressive tactics as shouting or blaming. But we have already seen that there are times when aggression or even non-assertion is desirable. Occasionally, you may have to shout to get the other person's attention, and at other times, the smartest approach may be to quietly abide someone else's abuse instead of responding.

A personal conflict style is not necessarily a personality "trait" that carries across all situations. Wilmot and Hocker (2010) suggest that

Individual Conflict Styles

- **Non-assertion:** avoiding (physical or conversational) and accommodating (putting other people's needs ahead of your own).
- **Indirect communication:** delivering information through another person or in an obscure way.
- **Passive aggression:** expressing dissatisfaction in a disguised manner.
- **Direct aggression:** attacking another person, verbally, non-verbally, or both.
- **Assertion:** delivering a message which includes a description of observable behaviour that prompted the message, your interpretation, your feelings, the consequences, and your intentions.

Focus on RESEARCH

HOW IMPORTANT IS AN APOLOGY TO YOU?

We have all wanted an apology when someone has harmed us in some way, but how much difference will it actually make? David De Cremer and his colleagues (2011) were interested in the value of an apology. Participants in their study were presented with 10 euros each and told that they could choose to keep the money or transfer it to a partner, who was in a separate area in the same lab and was an associate of the experimenters. They were told that if they decided to transfer their money, it would be tripled to 30 euros and then the partner, who received the tripled sum, would decide how much to give back to the first participant. Only 90 per cent of the participants decided to transfer their money; they were told that the person who had received the money chose to give them back only 5 euros. Half of these participants received a message (via computer) from their partner who apologized and took full responsibility for the unfair offer of 5 euros. The other half, instead of actually receiving an apologetic message, were told to imagine an apology. The researchers found that the people who imagined the apology valued it more than the people who actually received one. These investigators suggest that while an apology is an important first step in reconciliation and repairing

relationships, because it allows us to understand the transgressors' good or bad intentions, an apology alone will probably not repair the relationship.

Perhaps what was missing in the actual apologies, and what was included in the participants' imagined apologies, was some explanation (beyond greed) for the unfair division of the money. In addition, it is quite possible that the receivers of the apology did not feel that their experience of being cheated was adequately understood by the apologizers, particularly in this experimental situation. Finally, researchers have identified that in addition to feeling understood, the sincerity and timing of the apology matters too (Ebesu Hubbard et al., 2013). Apologies acknowledge that social rules have been broken, but in order to facilitate forgiveness they must be sincere, provided earlier rather than later in the conflict and include empathy for the recipient (Ebesu Hubbard et al., 2013).

Critical thinking: *Do you think a sincere, prompt apology and explanation are usually sufficient? Is something else required to repair relationships? Why? Under what circumstances might an apology be sufficient? Why?*

roughly 50 per cent of the population change their style from one situation to another. As we saw in Chapter 1, this sort of behavioural flexibility is a characteristic of competent communicators. Several factors govern which style to use.

The Situation

When someone clearly has more power than you, non-assertion may be the best approach. If the boss tells you to fill that order *now*, you probably ought to do it without comment. A more assertive response ("When you use that tone of voice, I feel defensive") might be clearer, but it could also cost you your job.

The Other Person

Although assertiveness has the best chance of success with many people, some recipients

respond better to other approaches. You probably know some communicators who are so sensitive or defensive that an assertive approach would be too much for them to handle. Others are so competitive and insensitive that an assertive approach might not be powerful enough to get their attention.

Your Goals

When you want to solve a problem, assertiveness is probably the best approach. But there are other reasons for communicating in a conflict. Sometimes, your overriding goal is to calm down an enraged or upset person. For example, tolerating an outburst from your crotchety and sick neighbour is probably better than standing up for yourself and triggering a stroke. Likewise, you might choose to

Building WORK SKILLS

ASSERTIVE MESSAGES

With the help of a classmate, construct an assertive message that you could deliver to someone in your work or school life (boss, co-worker, or professor).

Once you have rehearsed the message, discuss the risks and benefits of delivering it. Decide whether the assertive approach is justified in this case.

sit quietly through the harangue of a family member rather than ruin Thanksgiving dinner. In other cases, your moral principles might demand an aggressive statement even though it might not get you what you originally sought: "I've had enough of your racist jokes. I've tried to explain why they're so offensive, but you obviously haven't listened. I'm leaving!" Or your goal may be to be seen in a favourable way, in which case, you may want to avoid being aggressive.

Conflict in Relational Systems

So far, we have been describing individual conflict styles. Even though the style you choose in a conflict is important, your approach is not the only factor that will determine how a conflict unfolds. In reality, it is a **relational conflict style**. That is, its character is usually determined by the way the people involved interact (Wilmot and Hocker, 2010; Knapp et al., 1988). For example, you might be determined to handle a conflict with your neighbours assertively, only to be driven to aggression by their uncooperative nature, or even to non-assertion by their physical threats. Likewise, you might plan to hint to a professor that you are bothered by his apparent indifference, but wind up discussing the matter in an open,

 CHECK IT!

What factors should be considered before deciding which individual conflict to use?

assertive way in reaction to his constructive suggestion. Examples like these indicate that conflict is not just a matter of individual choice. Rather, it depends on how the partners interact.

Complementary, Symmetrical, and Parallel Styles

Partners in interpersonal relationships—and impersonal ones, too—can use one of three styles to manage their conflicts. In relationships with a **complementary conflict style**, the partners use different, but mutually reinforcing behaviour. In a **symmetrical conflict style**, both people use the same tactics. Some relationships are characterized by a **parallel conflict style**, which shifts between complementary and symmetrical patterns from one issue to another. Table 10.2 illustrates how the same conflict can unfold in very different ways, depending on whether the partners' communication is symmetrical or complementary. A parallel style would alternate between these two forms, depending on the situation.

Research shows that a complementary "fight-or-flight" style is common in many unhappy marriages. One partner (most commonly the wife) addresses the conflict directly, while the other (usually the husband) withdraws (Burleson and Denton, 2014). As we discussed in Chapter 3, it is easy to see how this pattern can lead to a cycle of increasing hostility and isolation, since each partner punctuates the conflict differently, blaming the other for making matters worse. "I withdraw because she's so critical," a husband might say. However, the wife wouldn't organize the

Table 10.2 ● Complementary and Symmetrical Styles

Situation	Complementary Styles	Symmetrical Styles
Wife is upset because husband is spending little time at home.	Wife complains; husband withdraws, spending even less time at home (*destructive complementarity*).	Wife complains; husband responds angrily and defensively (*destructive symmetry*).
Female employee is offended when male boss jokingly calls her "sweetie."	Employee objects to boss, explaining her reasons for being offended; boss apologizes for his unintentional insult (*constructive complementarity*).	Employee tries to make boss understand how she feels by calling him "cutie"; boss gets the hint and stops using the term (*constructive symmetry*).
Parents are uncomfortable about teenager's new friends.	Parents express concerns; teenager dismisses them, saying, "There's nothing to worry about" (*destructive complementarity*).	Teenager expresses concern that parents are being too protective; parents and teenager negotiate a mutually agreeable solution (*constructive symmetry*).

sequence in the same way. "I criticize because he withdraws," would be her perception. Couples who engage in this demand–withdraw pattern report being less satisfied with their relationships when the initiators' communication is perceived as unsupportive. If the initiator engages in highly supportive communication (rather than criticism and nagging) then mutual problem solving is much more likely (Burleson and Denton, 2014). It is the initiators' supportive communication that has the potential to break the "fight-or-flight" pattern. Complementary styles are not the only ones that can lead to problems. Some distressed relationships suffer from destructively symmetrical communication. If both partners treat one another with matching hostility, one threat or insult leads to another in an **escalatory spiral**. If the partners both withdraw from one another instead of facing their problems, a complementary **de-escalatory spiral** results, in which the satisfaction and vitality ebb from the relationship, leaving it a shell of its former self.

As Table 10.2 shows, both complementary and symmetrical behaviour can produce good results as well as bad ones. If the complementary behaviours are positive, then a positive spiral results, and the conflict stands a good chance of being resolved. This is the case in the second example in Table 10.2, in which the boss is open to hearing the employee's concerns and listens willingly as the employee talks. Here, a complementary talk–listen pattern works well.

Symmetrical styles can also be beneficial, as another look at the boss–employee example

TAKE TWO

- **Complementary conflict style:** partners use different, but mutually reinforcing behaviour; can lead to cycle of increasing hostility and isolation; can lead to positive outcomes as well.
- **Symmetrical conflict style:** partners use the same behaviours; can lead to escalatory and de-escalatory conflict spirals; can lead to positive outcomes, too.
- **Parallel conflict style:** partners shift between complementary and symmetrical styles, depending on the situation.

shows. Many women have found that giving insensitive men a taste of their own sexist medicine is an effective way to end harassment without provoking an argument. The clearest example of a constructive symmetry occurs when both people communicate assertively, listen to one another's concerns, and work together to resolve them. Couples using symmetrical styles appraise their marriages more positively than any other type of couple (Ridley et al., 2001). The potential for this sort of solution occurs in the parent–teenager conflict in Table 10.2. With enough mutual respect and careful listening, both the parents and their teenager can understand one another's concerns and possibly find a way to give all three people what they want.

When people have been in a relationship for some time, their communication often develops into conflict rituals—unacknowledged, but very real repeating patterns of interlocking behaviour. What relationships in your life have conflict rituals? Are these rituals problematic?

Conflict Rituals

When people have been in a relationship for some time, their communication often develops into **conflict rituals**—unacknowledged, but very real repeating patterns of interlocking behaviour (Wilmot and Hocker, 2010). Consider a few common rituals:

A young child interrupts his parents, demanding to be included in their conversation. At first, the parents tell the child to wait, but he whines and cries until the parents find it easier to listen than to ignore the fussing.

A couple fights. One partner leaves. The other accepts blame for the problem and begs forgiveness. The first partner returns, and a happy reunion takes place. Soon, they fight again.

One friend is unhappy with the other. He or she withdraws until the other asks what's wrong. "Nothing," the first replies. The questioning persists until the problem is finally out in the open. The friends then solve the issue and continue happily until the next problem arises, when the pattern repeats itself.

There's nothing inherently wrong with the interaction in many rituals (Olson, 2002). Consider the examples above. In the first, the child's whining may be the only way he can get his parents' attention. In the second, both partners might use the fighting as a way to blow off steam, and both might find that the joy of a reunion is worth the grief of the separation. The third ritual might work well when one friend is more assertive than the other.

Rituals can cause problems, though, when they become the *only* way relational partners handle their conflicts. As you learned in Chapter 1, competent communicators have a large repertoire of behaviours, and they are able to choose the most effective response for a given situation. Relying on one pattern to handle all conflicts is no more effective than using a screwdriver to handle every home repair, or putting the same seasoning in every dish you cook. What works in one situation is not likely to succeed in many others. Conflict rituals may

Focus on TECHNOLOGY

Does conflict escalate more rapidly through email? Email and text messages certainly have a greater potential for miscommunication and misunderstanding than face-to-face interactions or telephone conversations. Recall from Chapter 6 that Kristen Byron (2008) found that people are more likely to perceive positive emails as more neutral than intended and neutral emails as more negative than intended, particularly when the communicators didn't know each other well.

Email appears to have both advantages and disadvantages related to managing workplace conflict. On the positive side, as we discussed in Chapter 9, it allows the sender to carefully consider and compose his or her message and has the potential to be perceived as more polite and non-threatening than some face-to-face encounters (Duthler, 2006; Walther, 1996). In addition, it has the potential to reduce the incidence of heated exchanges between people engaged in ongoing conflicts such as divorce (see the "Reflection" box about email and divorce cases on page 329). On the more negative side, the absence of non-verbal cues that help us decipher the relational tone of the message, combined with the lack of inhibition we might feel because the receiver is not physically present, can contribute to a situation in which we are more likely to quickly fire off a curt or less-than-polite email response in the heat of the moment. Often, these emails are intended only to justify our position or defend our presenting self from the perceived attack. We have no intention of soliciting or listening to the other person's point of view or engaging in resolving the issue at hand. It's easy to see how a back-and-forth exchange of email messages like this can quickly escalate a conflict.

Here are some guidelines to consider before you respond to a situation or email that has aroused strong emotions:

- Wait—take time to regulate your emotions before you respond.
- Consider trying to talk to the person on the phone—or, better yet, meeting them face to face.
- Think before you hit SEND—you really can't take your words back. Email and text messages provide exact transcripts of your words.

Raymond Friedman and Steven Currall (2003) also point out that we pay more attention, perhaps too much attention, to statements made in email, and this is another factor that leads to greater conflict escalation than that in face-to-face and phone communication. They suggest that we exercise caution when using email to try to resolve disputes.

be familiar and comfortable, but they aren't the best way to solve the variety of conflicts that are part of any relationship.

Variables in Conflict Styles

By now, you can see that every relational system is unique. The communication patterns in one family, business, or classroom are likely to be very different from those in any other. But along with the differences that arise in individual relationships, there are two powerful variables that affect the way people manage conflict: gender and culture. We will now take a brief look at each of these factors and see how they affect the ways that conflict is managed.

Gender

Some research suggests that men and women often approach conflicts differently (Ansara and Hinden, 2010; Archer, 2002). Even in childhood, there is evidence that boys are (on average, of course) more likely to be aggressive, demanding, and competitive, while girls are more co-operative and accommodating. Studies of children from preschool age to early adolescence have shown that boys try to get their way by ordering one another around: "Lie down"; "Get off my steps"; "Gimme your arm." By contrast, girls are more likely to make proposals for action that begin with the word *let's*: "Let's go and find some"; "Let's ask her if she has any bottles"; "Let's move *these* out *first*" (Tannen, 1990). Whereas boys tell each other what role to take in pretend play ("Come on, be a doctor"), girls more commonly ask each other what role they want ("Will you be the patient for a few minutes?") or make a joint proposal ("We can both be doctors"). Furthermore, boys often make demands without offering an explanation ("I want the stethoscope right now"). In contrast, girls often give reasons for their suggestions ("We have to clean them because they've got germs").

Differences like these often persist into adulthood. Esin Tezer and Ayhan Demir (2001) studied the conflict behaviour that late adolescents use with same-sex and opposite-sex peers. They found that compared to females, males use more competing behaviours with same-sex peers and more avoiding behaviours with opposite-sex peers. In addition, in the workplace, women are more likely to endorse compromising to resolve conflicts and men are more likely to report that they would force a solution to a problem (Holt and DeVore, 2005).

Another body of research suggests that the differences in how the two sexes handle conflict are rather small, and not at all representative of the stereotypical picture of aggressive men and passive women (Afifi et al., 2012; Gayle et al., 1998). Gender differences in communication during conflict appear to be less important and less predictive of relationship satisfaction than factors such as the value

individuals place on supportive communication (Burleson and Denton, 2014) or their standards for openness in relationships (Afifi et al., 2012). People may *think* that there are greater differences in male and female ways of handling conflicts than actually exist (Allen, 1998). People who assume that men are aggressive and women accommodating may notice behaviour that fits these stereotypes ("See how much he bosses her around? A typical man!"). On the other hand, behaviour that does not fit these preconceived ideas (accommodating men, pushy women) goes unnoticed.

What, then, can we conclude about the influence of gender on conflict? Research has demonstrated that there are, indeed, some small, but measurable differences between the two sexes. But, while men and women may have characteristically different conflict styles, the individual style of each communicator is more important than his or her gender in shaping the way he or she handles conflict.

Culture

People from most cultures prefer mutually beneficial resolutions to disagreements whenever possible (Cai and Fink, 2002). Nonetheless, the ways in which people communicate during conflicts do vary from one culture to another (Holt and DeVore, 2005; Radanielina-Hita, 2010).

The kind of direct approach that characterizes many North Americans is not the norm in other parts of the world. Members of collectivist cultures are more inclined to use avoidance, compromise, and problem solving to resolve conflicts when compared to individualistic cultures (Holt and De Vore, 2005). The assertiveness that might seem perfectly reasonable to a Canadian would be rude and insensitive in many Asian countries (Gudykunst and Ting-Toomey, 1988; Samovar et al., 2012).

Many Asian cultures value self-restraint, avoid confrontation, and place a premium on preserving and honouring the "face" of the other person. For this reason, what seems like "beating around the bush" to a Canadian would be

TAKE TWO

Conflict rituals: unacknowledged but real repeating patterns of interlocking behaviour; they become problematic when they reduce flexibility and limit the repertoire of behaviour choices.

polite to an Asian. In Japan, for example, even a simple request like "Close the door" would be too straightforward (Okabe, 1987). A more indirect statement, such as "It is somewhat cold today," would be more appropriate. To take a more important example, Japanese are reluctant to say no to a request. A more likely answer would be "Let me think about it for a while," which anyone familiar with Japanese culture would recognize as a refusal.

The Japanese notion of self-restraint is reflected in the important concept of *wa*, or harmony. Interpersonal harmony in Japanese culture includes a tendency for individuals to be self-critical, rather than to find fault in others. A cross-cultural study compared Canadian and Japanese university students' *willingness* to accept information that they were better at completing a task than other students at their university and their *reluctance* to accept information that they had performed worse than their peers (Heine et al., 2000). The results of their investigation supported the idea that Canadians, on average, find it difficult to believe that they were outperformed by their average classmate, but easily accept that their own performance was superior. Japanese students, in contrast, were reluctant to believe

that they had outperformed the average student from their university. While North Americans, on average, are motivated to find out what is good about themselves and reluctant to find fault with themselves, Japanese tend to search for their weaknesses in order to correct them. This Japanese tendency to avoid self-enhancement that is typical of more individualistic cultures and to engage in significantly more self-criticism, serves to enhance the collectivistic value of interpersonal harmony (*wa*) with others. There are at least two motives in collectivistic cultures related to harmony. The first is to enhance harmony and actively promote group cohesiveness, and in these instances taking a more assertive problem-solving approach to interpersonal conflict is preferred. When the motive is to avoid the disintegration of group harmony, avoidance or non-assertion are the preferred approaches to conflict resolution (Lim, 2009).

Similar attitudes toward conflict prevail in China, where one proverb states, "The first person to raise his voice loses the argument." Among Chinese college students (in both the People's Republic and Taiwan), the three most common methods of persuasion used are *hinting, setting an example by one's own actions,* and *strategically agreeing to whatever pleases others* (Ma and Chuang, 2001). It appears that with globalization, some of these preferences may be changing. Yan Bing Zhang and her colleagues (2005) found that while older Chinese adults still preferred an accommodating style of conflict resolution, the younger adults in their study viewed a problem-solving style just as positively as an accommodating style.

It isn't necessary to look at Asia to encounter cultural differences in conflict.

© iStockPhoto/liannelin.

Do you often have to navigate cultural differences when dealing with conflicts in your life? How do you manage?

Many First Nations people in North America approach conflict very differently than do individualistic Westerners. When disciplining their children, Aboriginal people often avoid direct criticism or reprimands. Instead, storytelling is the primary means of teaching proper behaviour (Keeshig-Tobias, 1990). In addition to storytelling, parents model the behaviours expected of their children. The importance of developing and maintaining good relationships is a fundamental value of First Nations culture, and there is a belief that personal criticism is damaging and should be avoided (LaLonde, 1992).

Despite these differences, it is important to realize that culture is not the only factor that influences the way people think about conflict or how they act when they disagree. Some research (e.g., Beatty and McCroskey, 1997) suggests that our approach to conflict may be part of our biological makeup. Furthermore, scholarship suggests a person's self-concept is more powerful than his or her culture in determining conflict style (Oetzel et al., 2001; Ting-Toomey et al., 2001). For example, people who view themselves as mostly independent of others are likely to use a direct, solution-oriented conflict style, regardless of their cultural heritage. Those who see themselves as mostly interdependent are likely to use a style that avoids direct confrontation. And those who see themselves as both independent and interdependent are likely to have the widest variety of conflict behaviours on which to draw.

Beyond individual temperament and self-concept, the environment in which we are raised can shape the way we approach conflict. Parental conflict style plays a role. Parents who use spanking and other forms of corporal punishment with their children are more likely to have children who approve of using aggressive approaches to problem solving—such as hitting—with their siblings and peers (Simons and Wurtele, 2010). The influence of parental modelling and style of conflict resolution can be seen in adults as well. Research has revealed a significant relationship between the way a mother handles conflict and the style used by her adult children (Martin et al., 1997). Finally, the status of the people involved in a dispute has a powerful effect on conflict styles, at least in individualistic cultures (Kim et al., 2007). When given two conflict scenarios, one involving a classmate and the other involving a professor, students with a more individualistic orientation indicated that they would use a more argumentative approach with their classmate and feel more apprehension about the conflict with the professor. In contrast, students with a more collectivistic orientation were not more likely to be more argumentative with a peer and more avoidant with a professor, but like their more individualistic peers, they too reported feeling more apprehension about having a conflict with a professor (Kim et al., 2007).

Along with family influences, the "culture" of each relationship can shape how we behave (Messman and Canary, 1998). You might handle disagreements calmly in a job where rationality and civility are the norm, but shriek like a banshee at home if that's the way you and a relational partner handle disputes.

Methods of Conflict Resolution

Whatever the style, every conflict is a struggle to have one's goals met. Sometimes, that struggle succeeds, and in other cases, it fails. In the remainder of this chapter, we look at various approaches to resolving conflicts and see which ones are most promising.

Win–Lose

In **win–lose problem solving**, one person gets satisfaction while the other comes up short. People resort to this method of resolving

CHECK IT!

What is the evidence regarding gender and cultural differences in conflict style and what conclusions can be reached?

disputes when they perceive a situation as being an "either–or" one: either I get my way, or you get yours. The most clear-cut examples of win–lose situations are certain games, such as hockey or poker, in which the rules require that there be a winner and a loser. Some interpersonal issues seem to fit into this win–lose framework: two co-workers seeking a promotion to the same job, or a couple arguing over how to spend their limited money. In the "Self-Assessment" box on page 345, the win–lose problem-solving method in which *you* win is *dominance*, and the win–lose methods in which you let the *other person* win are *accommodation* and *avoidance*. How do your three scores compare with each other, and how do they compare with the other two methods?

Power is the distinguishing characteristic in win–lose problem solving, as it's necessary to defeat an opponent to get what you want. The most obvious kind of power is physical. Some parents threaten their children with warnings such as "Stop misbehaving or I'll send you to your room." Real or implied force is not the

only kind of power used in conflicts. People who rely on authority of many types engage in win–lose methods without ever threatening physical coercion. In most jobs, supervisors can use their authority in the assignment of working hours, job promotions, desirable or undesirable tasks, and, of course, in firing an unsatisfactory employee. Teachers can use the power of grades to coerce their students into acting in desired ways. Even the usually admired, democratic principle of majority rule is a win–lose method of resolving conflicts. However fair it may be, the system results in one group getting its way and another being unsatisfied.

The win–lose method may sometimes be necessary when there are truly scarce resources, or when only one person can achieve satisfaction. If two suitors want to marry the same person, only one can succeed. To return to an earlier example, it is often true that only one applicant can be hired for a job. Still, don't be too willing to assume that your conflicts are necessarily win–lose. Many situations that seem to require a loser can be resolved to everyone's satisfaction.

There is a second kind of situation in which win–lose is the best method of conflict. Even when co-operation is possible, if the other person insists on defeating you, then the most logical response might be to defend yourself by fighting back. "It takes two to tango," the saying goes, and it takes two to co-operate. Some people are so resistant to constructive problem solving that it may be fruitless to try that approach. In one study, employees identified by their managers as "difficult" consistently refused to co-operate in constructive

"It's not enough that we succeed. Cats must also fail."

Leo Cullum/*The New Yorker Collection*/The Cartoon Bank.

Self-Assessment

YOUR METHOD OF CONFLICT RESOLUTION

Think of a relationship with someone with whom you interact regularly and with whom you engage in conflict (for example, a parent, sibling, roommate, close friend, spouse, partner, or lover). How do you usually respond to your conflict with this person? In each pair below, circle the A or B statement that is most *characteristic* of your behaviour. In some cases, neither answer may be very typical of your behaviour. If this happens, select the response that you would be *more likely* to use.

1. A. There are times when I let the other person take responsibility for solving the problem.
    B. Rather than negotiating the things on which we disagree, I try to stress those things upon which we both agree.
2. A. I try to find a compromise solution.
    B. I attempt to deal with all of the other person's *and* my concerns.
3. A. I am usually firm in pursuing my goals.
    B. I might try to soothe the other's feelings and preserve our relationship.
4. A. I try to find a compromise solution.
    B. I sometimes sacrifice my own wishes for the wishes of the other person.
5. A. I consistently seek the other's help in working out a solution.
    B. I don't worry about my own concerns if satisfying them means damaging the relationship.
6. A. I try to avoid creating unpleasantness for myself.
    B. I try to win my position.
7. A. I try to postpone the issue until I have had some time to think it over.
    B. I give up some points in exchange for others.
8. A. I am usually firm in pursuing my goals.
    B. I attempt to get all concerns and issues immediately out in the open.
9. A. I feel that differences are not always worth worrying about.
    B. I try to integrate my concerns with the other person's concerns.
10. A. I am firm in pursuing my goals.
    B. I try to find a compromise solution.
11. A. I attempt to get all concerns and issues immediately out in the open.

B. I might try to soothe the other's feelings and preserve our relationship.

12. A. I sometimes avoid taking positions that would create controversy.
    B. I will let the other person have some of what she or he wants if she or he lets me have some of what I want.
13. A. I propose a middle ground.
    B. I press to get my points made.
14. A. I tell the other person my ideas and ask for his or hers.
    B. I try to show the other person the logic and benefits of my position.
15. A. I might try to soothe the other's feelings and preserve our relationship.
    B. I try to do what is necessary to avoid tensions.

Scoring: For each question, circle the A or B below according to your answer.

	D	I	C	A	AC
1.				A	B
2.		B	A		
3.	A				B
4.			A		B
5.		A			B
6.	B			A	
7.			B	A	
8.	A	B			
9.		B		A	
10.	A		B		
11.		A			B
12.			B	A	
13.	B		A		
14.	B	A			
15.				B	A

Total the number of circled responses in each column:

D (**D**ominance) _____
I (**I**ntegration) _____
C (**C**ompromise) _____
A (**A**voidance) _____
AC (**AC**commodation) _____

How do your five scores compare? Which is your highest, or your most likely, method of conflict resolution? Which is your lowest, or your least likely, method of conflict resolution?

problem solving (Monroe et al., 1989). Instead, they responded with passive-aggressive strategies—refusing to accept managers' feedback, offering excuses, and using avoidance. When faced with this sort of absolute refusal to co-operate, it may be self-defeating for you to hang on to a collaborative approach.

A final and much less frequent justification for trying to defeat another person occurs when the other person is clearly behaving wrongly and when defeating that person is the only way to stop the wrong behaviour. Few people would deny the importance of restraining a person who is deliberately harming others, even if the belligerent person's freedom is sacrificed in the process. However, only in the most extreme circumstances is it productive in the long run to coerce others into behaving as we think they should.

From the discussion so far, you might assume that a win–lose orientation is always destructive. The truth is not so simple. Susan Messman and Rebecca Mikesell (2000) found that some men and women in satisfying dating relationships used competition to enrich their relationships. Some found satisfaction by competing in play (who's the better racquetball player?), in achievement (who gets the better job offer?), and in altruism (who's more romantic?). These satisfied couples developed a shared narrative (see Chapter 3) that defined competition as a measure of regard, quite different from conflict, which signalled a lack of appreciation and respect.

Lose–Lose

In **lose–lose problem solving**, neither side is satisfied with the outcome. Although the name of this approach is so discouraging that it's hard to imagine how anyone could willingly use it,

lose–lose is a fairly common way to handle conflicts. Often, the partners will both strive to be winners, but as a result of the struggle, both wind up losers. On the international scene, many wars illustrate this sad point. A nation that gains military victory at the cost of thousands of lives, large amounts of resources, and a damaged national consciousness hasn't truly won much. On an interpersonal level, the same principle holds true. Most of us have seen battles of pride in which both people strike out and both suffer.

Compromise

A **compromise** gives both people at least some of what they want, although both sacrifice part of their goals. People usually settle for a compromise when it seems that partial satisfaction is the best they can hope for. What was your score for Compromise in the "Self-Assessment" exercise, and how does it compare with the other scores?

Although a compromise may be better than losing everything, this approach hardly seems to deserve the positive image it has with some people. In his valuable book on conflict resolution, Albert Filley (1975, p. 23) makes

Compromise can produce either win–win or lose–lose outcomes, depending upon the perceptions of the people involved and the effectiveness of the solution they devise. What kind of compromises have you experienced lately? How were the outcomes reached?

© iStockPhoto/kevinruss.

an interesting observation about our attitudes toward this method. Why is it, he asks, that if someone says, "I will compromise my values," we view the action unfavourably, yet we talk admiringly about people in a conflict who compromise to reach a solution? Although compromises may be the best result obtainable in some conflicts, it is important to realize that both people in a dispute can often work together to find much better solutions. In such cases, *compromise* is a negative word.

Most of us are surrounded by the results of bad compromises. Consider a common example: the conflict between one person's desire to smoke and another's need for clean air. The win–lose outcomes on this issue are obvious: Either the smoker abstains or the non-smoker gets polluted lungs—neither option is a very satisfying one. But a compromise in which the smoker gets to enjoy only a rare cigarette or must retreat outdoors, and in which the non-smoker must still inhale some fumes or feel like an ogre, is hardly better. Both sides have lost a considerable amount of both comfort and goodwill. Of course, the costs involved in other compromises are even greater. If a divorced couple compromises on child care by haggling over custody and then finally grudgingly agrees to split the time with their children, it is hard to say that anybody has won.

Some compromises do satisfy everyone. You and the seller might settle on a price for a used car that is between what the seller was asking and what you wanted to pay. While neither of you got everything you wanted, the outcome would still leave both of you satisfied. Likewise, you and your companion might agree to see a film that is the second choice for both of you in order to spend an evening together. As long as everyone is satisfied with an outcome, compromise can be an effective way to resolve conflicts. Catherine Sanderson and Kim Karetsky (2002) found that college students with a strong focus on intimacy goals were likely to engage in open discussion and compromise, show concern for their partner, and seek social support—and, particularly

important, they were likely to resolve the conflict successfully. Table 10.3 presents a summary of the differences between win–lose and win–win problem-solving scenarios.

By now, you can see that compromise can produce either win–win or lose–lose outcomes, depending upon the perceptions of the people involved and the effectiveness of the solution they devise. When you consider compromising, ask yourself whether it leaves you and the other party better or worse off. If it's the latter, you may want to consider other approaches.

Win–Win

Win–win problem solving is different in approach and outcome from both win–lose and lose–lose styles. This **collaborative problem-solving** approach requires concern for both oneself and others. In win–win problem solving, the goal is to find a solution that satisfies the needs of everyone involved. Not only do the partners avoid trying to win at each other's expense, but there is also a belief that working together can provide a solution in which all reach their goals without needing to compromise. In the "Self-Assessment" exercise, the win–win problem-solving method is called Integration. How does your score on Integration compare to the other approaches?

One way to understand how win–win problem solving works is to look at a few examples:

- A boss and her employees get into a disagreement over scheduling. The employees often want to shift the hours they're

Table 10.3 ● Differences between Win–Lose and Win–Win Problem Solving

Win–Lose	Win–Win
Conflicting interests.	Shared interests.
Negotiations based on power.	Negotiations based on trust.
Low self-disclosure.	High self-disclosure.
Concern only for self.	Concern for self and for other.

scheduled to work so that they can accommodate personal needs; the boss needs to be sure that the operation is fully staffed at all times. After some discussion, they arrive at a solution that satisfies everyone. The boss works up a monthly master schedule showing the hours during which each employee is responsible for being on the job. Employees are free to trade hours among themselves, as long as the operation is fully staffed at all times.

- A dispute about testing arises in a college class. Because of sickness and for other reasons, a certain number of students need to take makeup exams. The instructor doesn't want to give these students any advantage over their peers and also doesn't want to have to create a brand-new test for just a few people. After working on the problem together, the instructor and students arrive at a win–win solution: the instructor will hand out a list of 20 possible exam questions in advance of the test day. At examination time, 5 of these questions are randomly drawn for the class to answer. Students who take makeup exams will draw from the same pool of questions at the time of their test. In this way, makeup students are taking a fresh test without the instructor having to create a new exam.

- A newly married husband and wife find themselves arguing frequently over their budget. The husband enjoys buying impractical and enjoyable items for himself and for the house, whereas the wife fears that such purchases will ruin their carefully constructed budget. Their solution is to set aside a small amount of money each month for "fun" purchases. The amount is small enough to be affordable, but it gives the husband a chance to escape from their "Spartan" lifestyle. The wife is satisfied with the arrangement because the luxury money is now a budget category by itself, which gets rid of the "out-of-control" feeling that comes when her husband makes

unexpected purchases. The plan works so well that the couple continues to use it even after their income rises—they increase the amount devoted to luxuries.

Although such solutions might seem obvious when you read them here, a moment's reflection will show you that such co-operative problem solving is all too rare. People faced with these types of conflicts often resort to such dysfunctional styles of communicating as withdrawing, avoiding, or competing, and they wind up handling the issues in a manner that results in either a win–lose or lose–lose outcome. As we pointed out earlier, it is a shame to see one or both partners in a conflict come away unsatisfied when they could both get what they're seeking by communicating in a win–win manner.

Steps for the Win–Win Approach

Win–win problem solving works best when it follows a eight-step approach that is based on a plan developed by Deborah Weider-Hatfield (1981):

1. Define Your Needs

Begin by deciding what you want or need. Sometimes, the answer is obvious, as in our earlier example of the neighbour whose loud music kept others awake. There are times, however, when the apparent problem masks a more fundamental one. Consider an example: after dating for a few months, Sophia started to call Mehmet after they parted for the evening—a "goodnight call." Although the calling was fine with Mehmet at the beginning, he began to find it irritating after several weeks.

At first, Mehmet thought he was annoyed by the nuisance of talking late at night when he was ready for sleep. More self-examination showed that his irritation centred on the relational message he thought Sophia's calls implied: that she was either snooping on him or was so insecure she needed constant assurances of his love. Once Mehmet recognized the true sources of his irritation, his needs became

Focus on TECHNOLOGY

CHANNEL SELECTION AND CONFLICT IN ROMANTIC RELATIONSHIPS

Do people with different individual conflict styles prefer different channels (e.g., face-to-face, telephone, text, chat, social networking, email) when they are engaged in conflict with their significant other? Brandi Frisby and David Westerman (2010) wanted to find out what factors predicted romantic partners' channel choice during their disputes. They asked 129 undergraduate students who were currently in romantic relationships (15 casually dating, 82 seriously dating, 2 engaged, 29 married, and 1 "other") to complete a conflict style questionnaire and a relationship satisfaction questionnaire, and to provide demographic information and responses to six open-ended questions about their conflicts and use of face-to-face and computer-mediated communication (CMC; e.g., text, phone, chat, social networking) with their romantic partners. They found that participants whose conflict style was integrating—a win–win collaborative problem-solving style—were less likely to choose CMC when experiencing a conflict with their romantic partners. They preferred face-to-face communication, because

they wanted the non-verbal cues that they felt were necessary in conflicts, they believed it was better at communicating emotions, and it was more personal. The participants who preferred CMC for their conflicts described technological advances that benefited them (e.g., "It is easier to say what I want without being interrupted") and not advances that benefited their partner (e.g., "It can keep the fight from being too mean"). Participants with a dominating conflict style—a win–lose aggressive style—were more likely to prefer CMC for their conflicts with their romantic partners. Finally, relationship characteristics such as the length of the relationship or relationship satisfaction did not predict channel choices. However, conflict styles with a high concern for one's partner (win–win methods and accommodating styles) did predict higher levels of relationship satisfaction. The authors concluded that people are aware of their own preferences and consider the impact of the channel they choose when engaged in conflict. They are able to find ways to use technology to accomplish their relationship goals.

---

clear: (1) to have Sophia's trust and (2) to be free of her insecurities.

Because your needs will not always be clear, it is often necessary to think about a problem alone, before approaching the other person involved. Talking to a third person can sometimes help you sort out your thoughts. In either case, you should explore both the apparent content of your dissatisfaction and the relational issues that may lurk behind it.

2. Choose the Best Time and Place

Before you initiate a discussion with your partner you need to think about the best time and place to share your concerns. If your partner is tired or busy, your concerns may not be well received. Likewise, be sure you are at your best. Don't bring an issue up when your anger may cause you to say things you'll later regret, when your discouragement blows the problem

out of proportion, or when you are distracted by other business. Making a date to discuss the problem—after dinner, over a cup of coffee, or even a day in advance—can often boost the odds of a successful outcome.

3. Share Your Needs with the Other Person

Once you have defined your needs, and chosen the best time and place to discuss them with your partner it is important to think about *how* you will communicate. If it is an ongoing issue or a conflict that your partner has already expressed then it might be best to listen to your partner's point of view first (see Step 4). On the other hand, if it is a problem you are bringing up then you will need to describe your perceptions first.

Using the descriptive "I" language that we outlined in Chapter 5 and the assertive message

REFLECTION

WIN–WIN SOLUTION REDUCES FRICTION

After four months of living together, my two neat roommates were fed up with cleaning up after me and the other messy member of our little household, and the two of us were tired of hearing the neat freaks complain about our habits.

Last week, we had a meeting (again) about the dishes and glasses. But this time, we didn't argue about who was right or wrong. Instead, we looked for a win–win solution. And once we started looking, we found it. Each of us gets his own dishes, glasses, and silverware—two of each item per person. We are responsible for cleaning only our own things. Now, if you look in our kitchen cabinets, you find only eight glasses, eight plates, and so on. There isn't enough stuff to make a mess, and each of us has to wash his own things if he wants to eat. Everybody is happy. Some people might think our solution is silly, but it has certainly worked well for us—and that's all that matters.

format on pages 334–335 of this chapter will increase the odds of your partner listening to your concerns. Rather than implying blame, messages worded in this way describe how your partner's behaviour affects you. Notice how Mehmet's use of the assertive message format conveys a descriptive, non-judgmental attitude in his discussion with Sophia:

> When you call me after every date [*sense data*], I begin to wonder whether you are checking up on me [*interpretation of Sophia's behaviour*]. I've also started to think that you're feeling insecure about whether I care about you and that you need lots of reassurance [*more interpretation*]. I'm starting to feel closed in by the calls [*feeling*], and I feel myself pulling back from you [*consequence*]. I don't like the way we're headed, and I don't think it is necessary. I'd like to know whether you are feeling insecure and to find a way that we can feel sure

about each other's feelings without needing so much reassurance [*intentions*].

4. Listen to the Other Person's Needs

It is essential to find out what the other person wants and needs. (Now, the listening skills described in Chapter 7 and the supportive behaviour described in Chapter 9 become most important.) When Mehmet began to talk to Sophia about her calling, he learned some interesting things. In his haste to hang up the phone the first few times she called, he had given her the impression that he didn't care about her once the date was over. Feeling insecure about his love, she called as a way of getting attention and expressions of love from him.

Once Mehmet realized this fact, it became clear that he needed to find a solution that would make Sophia feel secure and at the same time relieve him of feeling pressured.

Arriving at a shared definition of the problem requires skills associated with creating a supportive and confirming climate. The ability to be non-judgmental, descriptive, and empathic is an important, support-producing skill. Both Mehmet and Sophia needed to engage in paraphrasing to discover all the details of the conflict.

When they are really communicating effectively, partners can help each other clarify what they're seeking. Truly believing that their happiness depends on each other's satisfaction, they actively try to analyze what obstacles need to be overcome.

5. Generate Possible Solutions

In the next step, the partners try to think of as many ways to satisfy both of their needs as possible. They can best do so by *brainstorming*—inventing as many potential solutions as they can. The key to success in brainstorming is to seek quantity without worrying about quality. The rule is to prohibit criticism of all ideas, no matter how outlandish they may sound. An idea that seems far-fetched can sometimes lead to a more workable one. Another rule of brainstorming is that ideas are not personal property. If one person makes a suggestion, the other should feel free to suggest another solution that builds upon or modifies the original one. The original suggestion and its offshoots are all potential solutions that will be considered later. Once partners get over their possessiveness about ideas, the level of defensiveness drops, and both people can work together to find the best solution without worrying about whose idea it is.

Much of the time, however, good intentions and creative thinking can lead to outcomes that satisfy everyone. In what way can a third party help with the conflict resolution process?

All of the supportive and confirming behaviours that we discussed in Chapter 9 are important during this step. However, two of them stand out as crucial: the ability to communicate provisionalism rather than certainty, and the ability to refrain from premature evaluations of any solution. The aim of this step is to generate *all* the possible solutions—whether they are immediately reasonable or not. If the partners behave provisionally and avoid any evaluation until all the solutions are generated, creative and spontaneous behaviour is encouraged. The result is a long list of solutions that most likely contains the best solution, one that might not have been expressed if the communication climate were defensive.

Mehmet and Sophia used brainstorming to generate solutions to their telephone problem. Their list consisted of continuing the calling, but limiting the time spent on the phone; limiting the calls to once in a while; Sophia's keeping a journal that could serve as a substitute for calling; Mehmet's calling Sophia once in a while; cutting out all calling; moving in together to eliminate the necessity for calling; getting married; and breaking up. Although some of these solutions were clearly unacceptable to both partners, they listed all the ideas they could think of, preparing themselves for the next step in no-lose problem solving.

6. Evaluate the Possible Solutions and Choose the Best One

The time to evaluate the solutions is after they all have been generated, after the partners feel they have exhausted all the possibilities. In this step, the possible solutions generated during the previous step are evaluated for their ability to satisfy the mutually shared goal. How does each solution stand up against the individual and mutual goals? Which solution satisfies the most goals? Partners need to work co-operatively in examining each solution and in finally selecting the best one.

It is important during this step to react spontaneously rather than strategically. Choosing a particular solution because the other person finds it satisfactory (an accommodation strategy), while seemingly a "nice" thing to do, is as manipulative a strategy as getting the other person to accept a solution satisfactory only to you (a win–lose strategy). Respond honestly as solutions are evaluated, and encourage your partner to do the same. Any solution agreed upon as "best" has little chance of satisfying both partners' needs if it was strategically manipulated to the top of the list.

The solution Sophia and Mehmet chose as satisfying her need to feel secure, his need to be undisturbed before turning in, and their mutual goal of maintaining their relationship at a highly intimate level was to limit both the frequency and length of the calls. Also, Mehmet agreed to share in the calling.

7. Implement the Solution

Now, the time comes to try out the idea selected to see if it does, indeed, satisfy everyone's needs. The key questions to answer are *who* does *what* to *whom*, and *when*?

Before Mehmet and Sophia tried out their solution, they went over the agreement to make sure it was clear. This step proved to be important, for a potential misunderstanding existed. When will the solution be implemented? Should Sophia wait a few weeks before calling? Should Mehmet begin the calling? They agreed that Mehmet would call after their next date.

Another problem concerned their different definitions of length. How long is too long? They decided that more than a few minutes would be too long.

The solution was implemented after they discussed it in detail and came to a mutual agreement about its particulars. This process may seem awkward and time-consuming, but both Sophia and Mehmet decided that without a clear understanding of the solution, they were opening the door to future conflicts.

Interestingly, the discussion concerning their mutual needs and how the solution satisfied them was an important part of their relationship's development. Mehmet learned that Sophia did, sometimes, feel insecure about his love. Sophia learned that Mehmet needed time to himself and that this need did not reflect on his love for her. Soon after implementing the solution, they found that the problem ceased to exist. Mehmet no longer felt the calls were invading his privacy, and Sophia, after talks with Mehmet, felt more secure about his love.

8. Follow Up on the Solution

To stop after selecting and implementing a particular solution assumes any solution is forever,

Methods of Conflict Resolution

- **Win–lose:** one person gets what he or she wants and the other does not.
- **Lose–lose:** neither person gets what he or she wants.
- **Compromise:** both people get some of what they want and sacrifice part of what they want.
- **Win–win:** everyone involved has needs satisfied.

that time does not change things, that people remain constant, and that events never alter circumstances. Of course, this assumption is incorrect. As people and circumstances change, a particular solution may lose or increase its effectiveness. Regardless, a follow-up evaluation needs to take place.

After you have tested your solution for a short time, it's a good idea to plan a meeting to talk about how things are going. You may find that you need to make some changes or even rethink the whole problem.

Reviewing the effects of your solution does not mean that something is wrong and must be corrected. Indeed, everything may point to the conclusion that the solution is still working to satisfy your needs and the mutually shared goal, and that this goal is still important to both of you.

It is important at this stage in the win–win problem-solving process to be honest with yourself as well as with the other person. It may be difficult for you to say, "We need to talk about this again," yet it could be essential if the problem is to remain resolved. Planning

CHECK IT!

Explain the eight steps involved in win–win problem solving and the times when it is the desired approach.

Table 10.4 ● Choosing the Best Method of Conflict Resolution

Win–Lose (*You Lose*)	Win–Lose (*You Win*)	Compromise	Win–Win
When you discover you are wrong.	When there is not enough time to seek a win–win outcome.	When the issue is important and the other person will take advantage of your non-competitive approach.	When the issue is too important for a compromise.
When the issue is more important to the other person than it is to you.	When the issue is not important enough to negotiate at length.	When sustaining or maintaining a relationship with the other person is unimportant to you.	When a long-term relationship between you and the other person is important.
To let others learn by making their own mistakes.	When the other person is not willing to seek a win–win outcome.		When the other person is willing to use a win–win strategy.
When the long-term cost of winning may not be worth the short-term gains.			

a follow-up talk when the solution is first implemented is important.

Sophia and Mehmet decided to wait one month before discussing the effects of their solution. Their talk was short, because both felt the problem no longer existed. Also, their discussions helped their relationship grow: they learned more about each other, felt closer, and developed a way to handle their conflicts constructively.

Although a win–win approach sounds ideal, it is not always possible, or even desirable (Budescu et al., 1999). Table 10.4 lists some factors to consider when deciding which approach to take when facing a conflict. There will certainly be times when compromising is the most sensible approach. You will even encounter instances when pushing for your own solution is reasonable. Even more surprisingly, you will probably discover that there are times when it makes sense to willingly accept the loser's role. Much of the time, however, good intentions and creative thinking can lead to outcomes that satisfy everyone.

SUMMARY

Despite wishes and cultural myths to the contrary, conflict is a natural and unavoidable part of any relationship. Since conflict cannot be escaped, the challenge is how to deal with it so that it strengthens a relationship rather than weakens it.

All conflicts have the same characteristics: expressed struggle, perceived incompatible goals, perceived scarce rewards, interdependence, and inevitability. Functional conflicts cope with these characteristics in very different ways from dysfunctional ones. Partners strive to co-operate instead of competing; to focus on rather than avoid the issues in dispute; and to seek positive, long-term solutions that meet each other's needs.

Individuals can respond to conflicts in a variety of ways: non-assertively, indirectly, with direct or passive aggression, and assertively. Each of these approaches can be justified in certain circumstances. The way a conflict is handled is not always the choice of a single person, since the people involved influence one another as they develop a relational conflict style. This style is influenced by the partners' genders and the influences of their cultural backgrounds.

There are four possible outcomes to a particular conflict: lose–lose, win–lose, compromise, and win–win. In most circumstances, a win–win outcome is best, and it can be achieved by following the guidelines outlined on pages 348–353.

MULTIPLE-CHOICE QUESTIONS

1. Sandra is furious with her brother: he has asked to use their parents' only car this weekend, when he knows she has a gymnastics competition out of town and that her having the car would make her life so much easier. She hasn't said anything about it yet, however, because she fears he will just start yelling. Sandra is experiencing
   a. an expressed struggle with her brother.
   b. a perception that she and her brother have incompatible goals
   c. an interpersonal conflict with her brother.
   d. all of the above.
2. A conflict in which outcomes fall short of what is possible and have a damaging effect on the relationship is called
   a. functional.
   b. dysfunctional.
   c. de-escalating.
   d. aggressive.
3. Josh dislikes conflict. His style involves giving in to the other person: going along with what the other person wants and putting their needs ahead of his own. His conflict style would be best described as
   a. avoidant.
   b. indirect.
   c. impersonal.
   d. accommodating.

4. Sarcasm can be used as a passive-aggressive approach to conflict.
   a. true
   b. false
5. Both Tommy and Daisy get very angry during their conflicts, use aggressive tactics, and then frequently storm off and give each other the silent treatment (not talking to each other for several days). The pattern is always the same. Their relational conflict style would be best described as
   a. complementary.
   b. symmetrical.
   c. parallel.
   d. direct aggression.
6. Conflict rituals become a problem when they are the only way relational partners handle their conflicts.
   a. true
   b. false
7. In collectivistic cultures people are more likely to take which of the following approaches to conflict?
   a. assertiveness
   b. passive aggression
   c. confrontation avoidance
   d. direct aggression
8. Compromise is what people involved in a conflict should aim for in their conflict resolution.
   a. true
   b. false

9. Which of the following influence the ways in which people manage conflict?
   a. gender
   b. culture
   c. temperament
   d. all of the above

10. Win–win problem solving is always the most desirable method of conflict resolution.
    a. true
    b. false

ACTIVITIES

1. Invitation to Insight

Even the best relationships have conflicts. Using the characteristics on pages 324–326, describe at least five conflicts in one of your important relationships. Then answer the following questions:

a. Which conflicts involve primarily content issues? Which involve primarily relational issues?

b. Which conflicts were one-time affairs, and which recur?

2. Invitation to Insight

From your recent experiences, recall two conflict incidents—one functional and one dysfunctional. Then answer the following questions:

a. What distinguished these two conflicts?

b. What were the consequences of each?

c. How might the dysfunctional conflict have turned out differently if it had been handled in a more functional manner?

d. How could you have communicated differently to make the dysfunctional conflict more functional?

3. Invitation to Insight

Interview someone who knows you well. Ask your interviewee which personal-conflict styles (non-assertive, indirect, etc.) you use most often and what effect each of these styles has on your relationship with this person. Using your findings, discuss whether different behaviour might produce more productive results.

4. Invitation to Insight

This activity will be most productive if, in answering the following questions about yourself, you consult several people with whom you share an interpersonal relationship:

a. Is your relational style of handling conflict complementary, symmetrical, or parallel? What are the consequences of this style?

b. What combination of intimacy and aggressiveness characterizes your approach to conflict? Are you satisfied with this approach?

c. What conflict rituals do you follow in this relationship? Are these rituals functional or dysfunctional? What might be better alternatives?

5. Skill Builder

To explore how the win–win approach might work in your life, try one of the following alternatives:

a. Use the steps on pages 348–353 to describe how you could manage a conflict by following the win–win approach. How could you try this approach in your personal life? What difference might such an approach make?

b. Try the win–win approach with a relational partner. What parts prove most helpful? Which are most difficult? How can you improve your relationship by using some or all of the win–win approach in future conflicts?

6. Role Play

Think of an interpersonal conflict you recently engaged in that you believe was not resolved well. Review the individual approaches to conflict described on pages 330–337 and decide on the approach you would take if you had the opportunity to do it over. To a partner, briefly describe the conflict and the person you had it with, and role-play your new approach to the conflict. Discuss the strengths and challenges of the approach you chose. Now, reverse roles.

DISCUSSION QUESTIONS

1. Wilmot and Hocker (2010) provide a definition of conflict that includes five parts. Must all five elements be present in order for conflict to exist? Why or why not?

2. Explain the concept of functional conflict and contrast it with dysfunctional conflict.

3. Which conflict style do you think poses the most risks to interpersonal relationships? Why?

4. Explain why assertion is often more effective than the other four conflict styles described in this chapter.

5. We have suggested that the supposed differences in how men and women handle conflict may have more to do with people's preconceived notions (stereotypes) about how men and women handle conflict. What do you think? Why?

6. Recent research suggests a person's self-concept is more powerful than his or her culture in determining conflict style. Given the role of culture in the development of self-concept (see Chapter 2), how could this be true?

7. Contrast win–win problem solving with compromise. What are the advantages and disadvantages of each approach? Why is compromise celebrated in our culture and win–win problem solving often ignored?

JOURNAL IDEAS

1. Describe at least two relatively recent conflicts that you had with two different people and how you resolved them. Compare the two. Things to compare might include the emotions you experienced throughout and afterward, the methods you employed, the content of the disagreements, the length of the disputes, the outcomes, and anything else that you believe is significant. Look for both similarities and differences. What factors account for the similarities and differences? If you had these situations to do over, what might you change (focus here on your own behaviour and approach, rather than the other person's)? Do you have any insight into your conflict style tendencies?

2. For some people, reviewing conflict situations can cause them to ruminate on negative events and create debilitating emotions that do not contribute to immediate conflict resolution or more satisfying conflict resolution in the future. There is a Swedish proverb that states "Worry gives a small thing a big shadow." If you find yourself worrying or having debilitating emotions frequently when you reflect on conflict situations, go back to Chapter 4 and review the information regarding self-talk—particularly the "Self-Assessment" on page 136 and the information regarding irrational thoughts. Use your journal to dispute those thoughts and record what is good about you and your life (savour your happiness).

PART FOUR
Contexts of Interpersonal Communication

11
Communicating with Family

Chapter Outline

© Geber86/iStockphoto

Key Terms

attachment
boundaries
chaotic family
communication rules
conformity orientation
conversation orientation
disengaged family

enmeshed family
family
family of origin
rigid family
roles
system

Learning Objectives

YOU SHOULD UNDERSTAND:

- the defining characteristics of a family and family communication;
- issues related to communication between spouses or partners, children, and siblings;
- the significance of family systems, roles, narratives, models, and rules; and
- the nature of cohesion, adaptability, and conflict in functional and dysfunctional families.

YOU SHOULD BE ABLE TO:

- describe the defining characteristics of the families to which you belong;
- differentiate between three couple types and their unique characteristics and communication patterns;
- explain the influence of parent–child relationships on human development;
- identify the roles, narratives, models, and rules of your family system;
- analyze your families' boundaries, adaptability, and conflict-management styles.

What is a family? A few decades ago, this was an easy question for most people to answer. Common notions of a family in the Western world stressed shared residence, reproduction or adoption of children by different-sexed adults, and a "socially approved sexual relationship" (Murdock, 1965, p. 1). In recent years, social scientists, lawyers, judges, and theologians have grappled with much broader definitions as they considered matters such as deciding who can marry, who the parents are when there is an egg or sperm donor, determining the rights of adoptive parents and adopted children, and negotiating grandparents' access to their grandchildren.

Each of us understands what "family" means in our own personal way, but understanding what it means to be a family in Canada requires that we take a much broader perspective. While the majority of Canadians live in private households with people who are related to them, families have changed throughout history and continue to change (The Vanier Institute of the Family, 2010). Canadians increasingly choose to cohabit or remain single rather than marrying or remarrying, they have fewer children than in previous decades, and they wait longer before marrying or having children. While the divorce rate continues to increase in Canada, the majority of divorced people do not remarry, but they do "re-partner," choosing to cohabit instead. As a result, children experience transitions in their living arrangements, often living in more than one household with both biological parents and step-parents. Almost half of these step-families are blended families—they include children from two or more different previous marriages or children from previous marriages and the current relationship. Finally, Canada was the third country in the world to legalize same-sex marriage, and the reported number of same-sex couples has continued to grow (The Vanier Institute of the Family, 2010). Thus, in Canada today, people are freer than ever before to create the kinds of family arrangements that are best for them (Brym, 2011).

After reviewing various definitions over the last century, Kathleen Galvin and her colleagues (2008) define **family** broadly enough to include many types of relationships: a family is a system with two or more interdependent people who have a common history and a present reality, and who expect to influence each other in the future. This definition includes the following different family arrangements:

- two parents (of opposite or same sex) and their children (biological or adopted)
- a couple (married or not, heterosexual or not) who live together for a period of time and have a committed, binding relationship
- a single parent (married, never married, widowed, or divorced) who lives with his or her biological or adopted children
- two adults and their children, all, some, or none of whom may be the offspring of their union
- groups of relatives who have blood or legal ties and who live with or near each other

All these arrangements share important characteristics that make communication among members different from that in other sorts of relationships.

Types of Family Communication

Within families, each type of communication between different family members has its own characteristics.

Communication between Spouses or Partners

Research on communication in committed, romantic relationships has identified communication patterns characteristic of couple types as well as research about general, everyday patterns of interactions between partners that have been linked to more and less satisfying relationships.

Focus on RESEARCH

IT TAKES A VILLAGE: FIRST NATIONS CONCEPTUALIZATIONS OF FAMILY

In First Nations communities many people may help to raise young children. The clan system extends the network of caring and nurturing future generations beyond parents to grandparents, aunts, uncles, cousins, and community elders (Castellano, 2002). Even when aboriginal people move to different locations the idea of a caring, extended family and community is a powerful principle that informs their concept of family. Children have a special place in many aboriginal cultures because they are believed to be gifts from the spirit world that help to renew the strength of the family, clan, and community.

According to tradition, children are gifts from the spirit world and have to be treated very gently lest they become disillusioned with this world and return to a more congenial place. They must be protected from harm because there are spirits that would wish to entice them back to that other realm. They bring a purity of vision to the world that can teach their elders. They carry within them the gifts that manifest themselves as they become teachers, mothers, hunters, councillors, artisans and visionaries. They renew the strength of the family, clan and village and make the elders young again with their joyful presence. (Report of the Royal Commission on Aboriginal Peoples, 1996).

The Aboriginal Children's Survey revealed that over 90 per cent of Métis, Inuit, and off-reserve First Nations children under six years of age in Canada were being raised by a variety of different people within their communities (Statistics Canada, 2006a). Children played with, talked to, and were supported by siblings, grandparents, aunts, uncles, cousins, and elders daily or weekly. In trying to repair the intergenerational damage inflicted by residential schools in Canada, many First Nations researchers and community leaders are calling on governments, organizations, communities, and service providers to be sensitive to cultural traditions and beliefs, and use those to inform their policies and practices in relation to First Nations families (Blackstock, 2010; Brown et al., 2012; Castellano, 2002; Fuller-Thompson, 2005; Trocmé et al., 2004). While we all have our ideas about what constitutes a family it is essential to remember our perceptions are not the only meaningful interpretations of families.

Critical thinking: *Taking into account all you have learned about communication so far (e.g., self-concept, perception, culture, language, communication climate, conflict resolution), what would you suggest are the fundamental skills required for delivery of culturally sensitive social, health, and education services in Canada?*

The way spouses or partners communicate with each other reflects both their personal style and their thinking about what their relationship should be like. In Chapter 3 we explained that our perceptions of gender-related communication can be categorized as masculine, feminine, androgynous, and undifferentiated. Recall that stereotypical masculine communication is described as goal-oriented or instrumental. Stereotypical female communication is described as expressive and androgynous communication is a combination of the two. Undifferentiated communicators are low in both instrumental and expressive communication. These communication styles have been related to marital satisfaction (Helms et al., 2006). Couples with more stereotypical male (instrumental)/female (expressive) communication patterns report lower marital satisfaction when compared to couples whose communication patterns are more androgynous or undifferentiated (Helms et al., 2006). Similarly, higher levels of marital satisfaction have been associated with more egalitarian division of household labour among heterosexual, gay, and lesbian relationships (Farr and Patterson, 2013).

More than 35 years of research on marriage and divorce, by John Gottman and his colleagues, has revealed several important communication habits of successful couples (Gottman, 2007; Gottman and Notarius, 2000, 2002). Gottman's research involved interviewing couples and taping both their positive interactions and their interactions during conflicts. After just three hours with a couple, Gottman and his colleagues at the "Love Lab" can predict with 90 per cent accuracy whether or not the couple will still be together in three to five years. Gottman suggests that lasting romantic relationships include an accentuation of the positive.

While a beautiful wedding is nice, it is through the daily drip of ordinary, often mundane interactions that intimacy, trust, and connection are developed. What are some small, everyday things that you believe make a happy marriage?

Partners say "yes" more often than "no," saying things such as, "Yes, I like that idea," "Yes, I hadn't thought of that before," or "Yes, let's do that if you think it is important." Gottman gives the analogy of a salt shaker filled with all the ways you can say "yes." He suggests it should be sprinkled liberally throughout your interactions with your partner. In addition, he has found that successful couples don't necessarily have clear communication, but they do communicate attachment and intimacy. Finally, he has found that embracing conflict and working though it constructively strengthens, rather than diminishes, relationships. These findings hold true for same-sex couples as well as heterosexual couples (Gottman et al., 2003; Kurdek, 2008). It is through the daily drip of ordinary, often mundane interactions that intimacy, trust, and connection are developed. Happy couples and families find their happiness in seemingly trivial, everyday occurrences and events such as shared routines and chores, solving problems together, being silly, and being physically close and affectionate with each other.

In addition to being affectionate and receptive to your partner (e.g., using the "yes" salt shaker), in constructively solving conflicts and creating intimacy and trust in everyday interactions, it is important to use the strategies described in Chapter 9 to avoid reacting defensively and being critical of your partner. Jack Gibb (see Chapter 9) described ways to give feedback that reduce the level of threat and arouse less defensiveness (recall they included description, problem orientation, spontaneity, empathy, equality, and provisionalism). They are particularly helpful in creating a positive climate between romantic partners. In particular it is important that both partners take a position of equality rather than superiority when discussing problems in romantic relationships. When a partner takes a position of superiority, the emotional message conveyed is one of contempt. John Gottman and his colleagues have found that contempt is a very good predictor of relational dissatisfaction and relationship dissolution in both same-sex couples and heterosexual couples (Gottman, 2007; Gottman et al, 2003).

Communication between Parents and Children

The Transition to Parenthood

With the arrival of the first child, communication within the family becomes more complicated. Along with being a threesome, the members can form three very different dyads: wife–husband, father–child, and mother–child. In gay and lesbian families the same dyads are formed, the labels are just different. These combinations lead to at least seven influence patterns:

1. The father influences the mother's interaction with the child (e.g., the father says, "Please don't coddle the baby").
2. The mother influences the father's interaction with the child (e.g., the wife says, "Give her a kiss good night").
3. The father–child relationship influences mother–child interaction (e.g., the father yells at the child, and the child runs to her mother for comfort).
4. The mother–child relationship influences the father–child interaction (e.g., the wife teaches the child that his father is a hard worker).
5. The father–child relationship influences husband–wife interaction (e.g., the husband spends time playing tennis with the child instead of spending time with his wife).
6. The mother–child relationship influences husband–wife interaction (e.g., the wife discloses personal information to her adult child and not to her husband).
7. The husband–wife relationship influences the interaction among all the family members (e.g., a conflict between the husband and wife spills over to a conflict with the child).

The birth or adoption of a child also influences other aspects of family communication (Huston and Vangelisti, 1995). For example, role patterns may change, and the change may

© iStockPhoto/Ceneri.

Everything changes when a baby is born. What are some of the things new parents can do to make this transition go smoothly? What are some things the community can do?

be reflected in the division of labour in housework. Also, changes in the extent to which the couple enjoys leisure activities and engages in interaction with friends and relatives are likely after the birth of their child. The transition to parenthood is both extremely stressful and pleasurable. Most couples, regardless of sexual orientation, report a decline in marital satisfaction, an increase in conflict and, at the same time, an increase in joy and pleasure with their child (Bergman et al., 2010; Goldberg and Sayer, 2006; Gottman and Notarius, 2002; Halford et al., 2010; Kluwer and Johnson, 2007).

Jay Belsky and his colleagues (Belsky, 2008; Belsky and Kelly, 1994; Belsky et al., 1985; Belsky et al., 1983) have done considerable research on the transition to parenthood and the effects this transition has on individual parents as well as on their romantic relationship. Couples who have well-developed constructive problem-solving strategies are able to manage the transition more effectively. Common areas of disagreement for new parents include the division of household chores, money, and work outside the home, as well as their relationship and social lives. Partners who can resolve these issues in mutually satisfying ways improve their satisfaction with their relationship, but partners who are unable to resolve them become increasingly unhappy and dissatisfied. The strategies described in Chapter 8 are fundamental to creating a relationship climate that allows couples to deal with the changes that are inevitable during this transition. In addition, Chapter 9 describes effective methods for resolving conflicts in ways that demonstrate high concern for both oneself and one's partner.

The First Relationship

For most of us our parents are our first teachers. We learn about ourselves and the world through our interactions with our parents. A great deal of research has examined children's first relationships with significant adults in their lives. John Bowlby (1969, 1976, 1982) believed that infants form an **attachment** or lasting social–emotional relationships with adults, usually their mothers, but it could be with fathers, grandparents, childcare providers, or any consistent caregiver. This first relationship begins gradually during the first few months of life and is built on the caregivers' responses to the infants' needs. If caregivers are consistently warm and responsive to the infants' needs, children are more likely to develop a positive self-concept and a positive view of others. They learn that they can effectively influence the world around them and trust others to take care of them. These individuals would be described as having developed a secure attachment. Conversely, if infants receive inconsistent or insensitive care from their parents, they may develop what Bowlby described as an insecure attachment. Over the years attachment theory has been further developed and tested, and researchers have found that patterns of attachment can persist into adulthood and influence adult relationships (Fraley and Shaver, 2000; Mikulincer and Shaver, 2012; Moller et al., 2006; Rholes et al, 2014; Winterheld et al., 2013). People with secure attachments have the least

difficulty establishing and maintaining interpersonal relationships. For instance, female university students who were classified as securely attached to their parents reported greater ease forming friendships and greater satisfaction with their friendships during their first year of university (Parade et al., 2010). Developmental psychologists (e.g., Cortina and Liotti, 2010) argue that attachment relationships inform our ideas about safety and protection, and that individuals with a history of secure attachment find it easier to trust others. As a result, attachment style helps to explain individual differences in our orientations toward forming close committed relationships with others. Richard Bello and his colleagues (2008) found that spouses' attachment classification influenced how positively they viewed their partners' attempts to repair the marital relationship. Securely attached individuals perceived their spouses' conciliatory messages, following a disagreement, as more positive than did insecurely attached individuals. The way we respond when others make attempts at reconciliation is a strong predictor of the quality of our relationships. Spouses who accept their partners' attempts to repair transgressions in the relationship are more likely to experience better-quality and longer-lasting marriages Similarly, Rachel Domingue and Debra Mollen (2009) examined how the combination of both partners' attachment styles affected their communication during conflicts. They included both opposite- and same-sex couples in their study and found that when both partners were classified as securely attached, they engaged in more constructive communication during conflicts compared to couples who were both insecurely attached and to couples in which one partner was securely attached and the other was insecurely attached. They concluded that their findings support the idea that different attachment classifications lead to different communication styles. Securely attached individuals are more likely to engage in direct and assertive communication during conflict, whereas insecurely

REFLECTION

LEARNING TO TRUST

My mom really didn't want another baby, but she had me anyway, and then was very depressed after I was born. She went back to work fairly soon, and I had a great child-care provider whom I loved very much. But when I was about three years old my mom stopped working, and I never saw my nanny again. As a young adult I had many failed romantic relationships. I just didn't want to get too close. Now that I think about it, I was probably scared they would leave me, so I made sure I left first. I am a very independent person, and I don't like to rely on others, but then I met Chris. Chris just wouldn't let me go, and no matter how badly I behaved he just stuck around. When I got seriously ill he really showed me that he was in it for the long haul. I really had to rely on him when I was sick. I had no choice. Discovering he wouldn't leave was a really big deal for me. It sounds so corny, but it changed the way I understood relationships. We have been together for 14 years now and I can honestly say he changed my life so much for the better.

TAKE TWO

- **Stereotypically feminine communication** is characterized as emotionally expressive.
- **Stereotypically masculine communication** is characterized as instrumental or task-focused.
- **Androgynous communication** is high in both emotional expression and instrumental or task-related messages.
- **Undifferentiated communication** is low in both instrumentality and expressiveness.

attached individuals are more likely to use avoidant or demanding communication during conflicts. Although our first relationships can have a profound influence on our subsequent relationships, it is important to keep in mind that our attachment classifications do not necessarily *determine* our future relationships. As we gain insight into our early relationships and develop greater self-awareness and more effective communication skills, we can challenge ourselves to develop healthier and more fulfilling relationships.

Continuity and Change in Parent–Child Communication

Parents play a central role in their children's development, and while some elements of their communication and their relationship remain constant, many aspects change over the course of their children's development. The same dialectic tensions that exist in romantic relationships (discussed in Chapter 8) exist in parent–child relationships. These include the tensions between stability and change, expression and privacy, and integration and separation. Toddlers and adolescents often want greater autonomy than parents are willing to allow. Similarly, they may want a degree of privacy that parents are not comfortable with. During different developmental periods these tensions reveal themselves in various issues and conflicts. Families who are most successful in managing these tensions tend to be those with high flexibility who can change their approach as the situation requires. This is true for parents who need to allow more time for their toddlers to do things themselves, for adolescents who want to explore some alternative identities without criticism from their parents and siblings.

In the past, entrance into adulthood was marked by biological changes (e.g., reproductive capacity) and clear social transitions (e.g., entry into the workforce, moving out of the parental home), but in recent years that transition has emerged more slowly for young Canadian adults and their parents (Daly, 2013). In Canada, adult children frequently stay in the family home longer than they did in the past and this can create more tension and conflict in families as well as more relationship satisfaction. Not surprisingly, one source of conflict is lack of clarity about roles (as both a parent and a child) and ambiguity about household responsibilities and conflicts about everyday living (e.g., cleanliness, scheduling activities, shared space, etc.). When young adults show more maturity and independence and parents shift from treating them as children to recognizing them as adults their relationships tend to be more positive (Daly, 2013). Parents of young adults are most successful in managing the tensions between connection and autonomy when they relinquish some control while still being responsive and maintaining the relationship.

Finally, communication between elderly parents and their adult children has its own set of challenges. In many families the caring relationship comes full circle with adult children caring for now frail and elderly parents. Caring for elderly parents usually creates stress for individual children and between siblings, but it can also provide families with opportunities to work together and increase closeness (Van Volkom, 2006).

Communication between Siblings

Sibling relationships are usually the longest-lasting ones in our lives. Think about your interaction with your siblings over the years, and you can probably identify many roles you played in each other's lives: playmate, confidant, friend, counsellor, role model, and perhaps even adversary. Research shows that sibling relationships can offer vital support throughout our lives (Goetting, 1986; Myers and Bryant, 2008), and, thus, it is important to maintain them by sharing tasks, expressing positivity, offering assurances, and so on (Myers, 2003). Another way adult siblings can nurture their relationships is by talking about their family—reminiscing about their childhood, crazy family events, and wild relatives. Sharing these stories can hold the siblings together, help them clarify family events, and validate their feelings and life choices (McGoldrick et al., 1999).

Siblings' experiences in the family often vary greatly, given their differences in age and birth order. Children close in age usually spend more time together than those further apart and likely share many similar experiences (McGoldrick et al., 1999). However, siblings close in age also tend to compete for their parents' attention more than siblings separated by more than approximately five years. Parents' different treatment of each child is important to the children and is scrutinized very carefully, especially regarding who is closer to the mother, who has a greater say in family decisions, and who has the most-favoured relationship with the father (Noller and Fitzpatrick, 1993; Suitor et al., 2008). The effects of parental favouritism persist into adulthood and affect the quality of siblings' relationships throughout their lives. Jill Suitor and her colleagues (2009) found that adult

siblings who recalled their mother favouring one child when they were growing up had more distant and more conflictual adult relationships with each other, as compared to siblings who perceived that their mother treated them more equitably during childhood. Even a mother's favouritism of one of her adult children is related to a reduced closeness among them.

Biological sex matters, too. Sister pairs tend to be closer than brother–sister or brother–brother pairs, and both brothers and sisters feel closer to sisters (Riggio, 2006; Spitze and Trent, 2006). Like romantic partners and friends, siblings use relational strategies to sustain their relationships, particularly when they are adults. These strategies include many of the same behaviours we described in Chapter 8—providing assurances, being open and positive, giving and asking for advice, communicating through social networks, and resolving conflicts constructively. The extent to which people use these strategies with their siblings varies depending on the type of relationship they share (Myers and Goodboy, 2010). Siblings, particularly sisters, who enjoy an intimate relationship (best friends) or whose relationship could be described as congenial (good friends) use these relational maintenance strategies more frequently and also use a greater variety of communication channels (face-to-face, phone, email, text, chat, social networking) to keep in touch with their siblings. Siblings who are loyal (but not really friends) and those who have apathetic or hostile relationships are less inclined to work at maintaining their relationships. The degree of adults' psychological closeness with their siblings predicts the extent to which they work to maintain their relationships with their brothers

Sibling relationships are usually the longest-lasting ones in our lives. What was your relationship like with your siblings growing up? How do you relate to them now?

© iStockPhoto/VikramRaghuvanshi.

and sisters (Myers et al., 2008). Adult sibling relationships offer social, emotional, and instrumental support over their lifetimes, but are often harder to maintain than friendships.

Elements of Family Communication

Whatever form families take, the communication that occurs within them shares some important characteristics, which we will examine now.

Families as Communication Systems

Every family has its own unique ways of communicating. Despite these differences, a family is a **system** whose members interact with one another to form a whole. Families, like all systems, have a number of characteristics that shape the way members communicate (Lerner et al., 2002; Whitchurch and Constantine, 1993).

Family Members Are Interdependent

If you touch one piece of a mobile, all the other parts will move in response. In the same way, one family member's feelings and behaviour affect all the other members. If, for example, a family member leaves home to

> Define what a family is and describe the three general types of communication that occur within families.

marry, a parent loses a job, two brothers get angry with each other and decide to stop talking, or a member wins the lottery, the system is no longer the same. Each event is a reaction to the family's history, and each event shapes future interaction.

A Family Is More than the Sum of Its Parts

Even if you knew each member of a family separately, you still would not know the family in its entirety. As the accompanying "Reflection" box illustrates, family members can take on new ways of behaving when they are operating in the context of their family system. This means that to understand a family you must see it as a whole.

Families Have Systems within the Larger System

Like boxes within boxes, families have subsystems (systems within the family). For example, a traditional family of four can have six two-person communication subsystems: mother–father, mother–son, mother–daughter, father–son, father–daughter, and daughter–son. If you add three-person subsystems to these six (e.g., mother–father–daughter), the number of combinations is even greater. The nuclear family itself is a subsystem of larger supra-systems that include aunts, uncles, cousins, grandparents, in-laws, and so on.

Family Systems Are Affected by Their Environment

As "open systems," families are influenced by the world in which they are situated. Some environmental influences are personal. If, for example, one member has a bad (or good) day at work or school, her experiences will

REFLECTION

WHEN A MARRIAGE CATCHES COLD, EVERYBODY SNEEZES

When I was about eight years old, my parents went through a crisis that almost led to the breakup of their marriage. My siblings and I weren't aware of the details, but the strain changed everything. My older brother, who was a star student, started getting Cs and Ds instead of As and Bs. I used to pretend to be sick so my mom and dad would co-operate to take care of me. And my five-year-old brother started having temper tantrums and wetting his bed. I learned several years later that our family business had almost gone bankrupt. After learning about family communication, I understand how problems in one part of a system affect every other part.

probably shape the way she acts at home. Other environmental influences involve social forces. For example, a family that wants to maintain traditional values will be challenged by media images that present very different depictions of how to behave.

Roles

Although they are rarely discussed, the **roles** family members play shape the way they communicate. Some roles are obvious: income earner, child-care provider, and so on. Others are less obvious, but just as important: harmonizer, problem solver, tension reliever, helpless victim, and so on. A bit of reflection may reveal some of the roles in your family. Perhaps one child is the athletic one, while another is the academic star. One parent may be the emotional person, while the other is the voice of reason. One sibling may be responsible, another irresponsible.

Some important roles centre on how the family handles conflict and stress. From her many years of experiences as a family therapist, Virginia Satir (1972; Bermudez, 2008) noticed four roles that arise during family

Focus on TECHNOLOGY

FEELING CLOSER AND DRIFTING APART?

Cellphones serve a number of functions in the communication habits of families. Studies have shown that cellphones have changed the way families organize their everyday activities. Studies have documented how mobile communication technologies allow friends and family members to organize and re-organize activities continuously. Rich Ling and Brigitte Yttri (2002) have called this practice "micro-coordination" or "hyper-coordination" and they suggest that cellphones operate like quasi umbilical cords between adolescents and their parents—a source of both security and resentment (Ling and Yttri, 2006). Parents use cellphones to engage in remote parenting. Parents can communicate caring and affection to their children when they are apart, and they can monitor and control their children's activities remotely as well. Parents routinely make sure that children have arrived or returned from school and children use their cellphones to get parental approval for their activities. Toke Christensen (2009) was interested in exploring how these calls and text messages contributed to the general sense of closeness between family members. He interviewed nine Danish families about their cellphone use. He found that cellphone conversations between family members covered a wide range of issues that included asking for permission, expressing affection, sharing news of the day, sharing personal problems, planning of activities, greetings (saying good night if parents were not home at night), and calling for no real reason other than to "check in" or find out how things were going. He speculated that families' numerous conversations throughout the day created the experience of closeness and allowed them to transcend their physical separation. Christensen suggests that even the shortest, most instrumental, text messages and cellphone calls "contribute to the continuous flow of interaction that keeps intimate relations between family members alive, and the concept of connected presence helps to draw attention to the experience of interpersonal closeness" (Christensen, 2009, p. 446). While this ability to create presence-at-a-distance creates closeness in families, Christensen wonders if it also assists in allowing family members to actually spend less and less time in each other's physical presence—the very aspect of modern life to which it is a response.

conflicts. The first role is the *blamer*, who judges others and holds them responsible for anything that goes wrong: "You never do anything right. What is the matter with you?" (p. 66). According to Satir, blamers may look powerful from the outside, but inside they often feel lonely and unsuccessful.

A second conflict role is the *placater*—the person who agrees with whatever is said so the other person will not get angry: "Whatever you want is okay. I am just here to make you happy" (p. 63). According to Satir, the person who placates feels helpless and worthless without the other family member.

A third role is the *computer*, the family member who uses reasonableness and dispassion to defuse the conflict—and also to boost his or her self-esteem. According to Satir, "the *computer* is very correct, very reasonable with no semblance of showing any emotion" (p. 68). In an effort to sound intelligent, the computer uses long words (whether or not he or she knows what they mean). The computer's image is one of someone cool and calm, but on the inside Satir suggests that this person feels very vulnerable.

The fourth role is the *distracter*, the person who says something irrelevant so the threat will be forgotten. Satir suggests that the unrelated and pointless behaviours that distracters use mask their belief that nobody cares about them and that there is no place for them in the family.

Take a moment to consider who plays which of these four roles in your family. You may decide that your family members sometimes switch roles, depending upon the issue or situation. In any case, these categories offer assurance that these roles are a normal part of most family systems.

Family Narratives

In Chapter 3, we described how shared *narratives* provide a storyline that keeps relationships operating harmoniously. These themes are especially important in families, where they reinforce shared goals, values, and concerns (Androutsopoulou, 2001). Narratives may reflect a family's view of how members relate to one another: "We help each other a lot" or "We are proud of our heritage." Others reflect values about how to operate in the world: "It's impossible to be successful without a good education" or "It's our responsibility to help others less fortunate than ourselves." Even dysfunctional families can be united by a shared narrative: "What a hopeless bunch! We can never get along." With a bit of thought, you can probably come up with several phrases that capture your family's narratives.

Models for Other Relationships

In addition to providing us with our very first relationships, our experiences in our **family of origin**, the family in which we grow up, shape the way we communicate throughout life. They teach us important lessons—sometimes positive, sometimes negative—about future relationships. Perhaps most important, families of origin are the primary model for how we will create our own families. Should family members share personal information or keep it to themselves? How is power distributed among the members? How much time should family members spend together and apart? How do we handle conflicts? We form our answers to these questions in large measure by observing our family of origin (Huang, 1999; Koerner and Fitzpatrick, 2002; Van Lear, 1992).

Unfortunately, some types of family dysfunction are passed from one generation to another. Adolescents in homes where there is spousal abuse, for example, are particularly liable to be physically abused themselves (Tajima, 2002), and a son's exposure to parental physical or verbal aggression is a good predictor of his perpetrating violence on a female partner (Shook et al., 2000; Schumacher et al., 2001).

Along with our personal experiences, each culture's model for family interaction shapes our notion of how to communicate (Hines et al., 1999; Koerner and Fitzpatrick, 2002). In the dominant culture of North America, for example, children often have an image of their family in which emotional support and loyalty comes from a small number of people; in general, the family is isolated from other families (Moghaddam, 1993). In these types of families, children quickly learn to be independent and self-reliant. In many other cultures, the image of the family is very different. In the extended families typical of First Nations Canadians, Mexico, Latin America, Africa, parts of Europe, the Middle East, and Asia, support and loyalty extend beyond the immediate family of parents and siblings to include grandparents, cousins, aunts, uncles, great-aunts and great-uncles, and even godparents.

Communication Rules

Despite their similar properties, not all families communicate in the same way. As unique cultures, families have their own sets of rules about a variety of communication practices. Some **communication rules** are explicit: "If you're going to be more than half an hour late, call or text." Other rules are not ever discussed, but they are just as important: "If Mom slams the door after coming home from work, wait until she's had time to relax before speaking to her."

Ascan Koerner and Mary Ann Fitzpatrick (2002) have defined two categories of rules about communication in the family: conversation and conformity. **Conversation orientation** involves the degree to which families have an open climate of discussing a wide array of topics. Families with a high conversation orientation interact freely, frequently, and spontaneously, without many limitations on topic or time spent interacting. They believe that this interaction is important in order to have an enjoyable and rewarding family life. On the other hand, members of families with a low conversation orientation interact less and there is less exchange of private thoughts. It's no surprise that families with a strong conversation orientation regard communication as rewarding, pleasurable, and relaxing (Avtgis, 1999; Barbato et al., 2003). Young adult children growing up in high-conversation-oriented families report feeling more confident and capable in their interpersonal skills when compared to young adult children growing up in high-conformity-oriented families (Schrodt et al., 2009).

Conformity orientation refers to the degree to which family communication stresses uniformity of attitudes, values, and beliefs. High-conformity families seek harmony, conflict avoidance, interdependence, and obedience. They are often hierarchical, with a clear sense that some members have more authority than others. Parents communicate with their children for the purposes of seeking control and escape (Barbato et al., 2003). By contrast, communication in families with a low conformity orientation is characterized by individuality, independence, and equality. The belief in such families is that individual growth should be encouraged and that family interests should be subordinated to individual interests. Figure 11.1 displays the four types of families that result from different combinations of conversation orientation and conformity orientation.

Families high in both conversation orientation and conformity orientation are *consensual*. Communication in these families reflects the tension between the pressure to agree and preserve the hierarchy, and an interest in open communication and exploration.

Families high in conversation orientation and low in conformity orientation are *pluralistic*. Communication in these families is open and unrestrained, with all family members' contributions evaluated on their own merits.

Families low in conversation orientation and high in conformity orientation are *protective*. In these families, communication emphasizes obedience to authority and a reluctance to share thoughts and feelings.

Elements of Family Communication

- **Systems:** members are interdependent; family is more than sum of its parts; families have subsystems; family systems are affected by their environment.
- **Roles:** can include the *blamer*, *placater*, *computer*, and *distracter*.
- **Narratives:** stories that keep relationships operating harmoniously.
- **Family of origin:** the family we grew up in—it provides a model for how we will create our own families.
- **Communication rules:** combinations of *conversation orientation* (high or low) and *conformity orientation* (high or low)—create four family types (consensual, pluralistic, protective, laissez-faire).

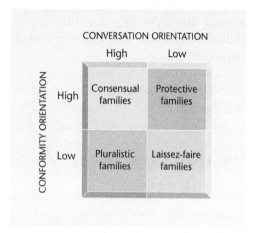

Figure 11.1 ● Conversation and Conformity Orientations in Families

Focus on RESEARCH

TOPIC AVOIDANCE IN STEPFAMILIES

Communication between teenagers and parents is often a delicate proposition. Teens tend to value their privacy and autonomy, whereas their parents want them to stay open and connected. These dialectical tensions can be even more dramatic in stepfamilies, where parent–child relationships face a unique set of challenges.

Tamara Afifi (nee Golish 2000; Afifi and Afifi, 2009) interviewed adolescents and young adults in divorced (stepfamilies) and non-divorced families to learn about topics they tend to avoid with their parents and step-parents. Not surprisingly, sex was the most frequently avoided topic across all relationship types. However, stepchildren say they avoid more topics with their step-parents than with their parents. In particular, stepchildren often avoid "deep conversations" or talking about money and family issues with their step-parents. In addition, children in divorced families avoid talking to their parents about their parents' relationship more than children in non-divorced families. Since relationships between ex-spouses are often difficult and children in stepfamilies often feel caught between their parents, their reluctance to discuss their parents seems warranted.

One factor affecting the comfort level in stepfamily communication is the type of parenting style used by the step-parents. Stepchildren feel more dissatisfied and avoid more topics with step-parents who are highly authoritarian (i.e., demanding and rigid). Interestingly, stepchildren also say they are dissatisfied with highly permissive step-parents. Afifi (nee Golish, 2000) concludes that step-parents need to strike a balance:

> Stepchildren may not be ready for too much closeness and need to progress at their own pace. At the same time, children need to know that their step-parent is interested in their well-being and will provide some sense of guidance.

Ultimately, stepchildren and step-parents face the same dialectical tensions that are true of all relationships. It would appear, however, that stepfamily tensions sometimes run stronger and deeper.

Critical thinking: *Given the increasing diversity of Canadian families, can you think of other topics that might be particularly sensitive for adolescents and young adults in other family configurations? Why do you think so?*

Families low in both conversation orientation and conformity orientation are laissez-faire. In these families, the communication reflects the members' lack of involvement with each other, the fact that they are emotionally divorced, and that decision making is individual.

Which of these styles best represents your family? Which style would you *like* to be true of your family?

Effective Communication in Families

It is impossible to cover every aspect of effective family communication in just a few pages. Still, the following points can offer guidelines

to make any family's interaction more satisfying and rewarding.

Strive for Closeness while Respecting Boundaries

In Chapter 8, we described the conflicting needs we all have for both integration and separation in our relationships, as well as for both expression and privacy. Nowhere are these opposing drives stronger than in families. We all know the importance of keeping close ties with our relatives, although too much cohesion can be a problem. When cohesion is too high, families may be **enmeshed**; that is they may suffer from too much consensus, too little independence, and a very high demand for loyalty—all of which may feel stifling. At the other extreme, of course, members of families with too little cohesion may be **disengaged**—disconnected, with limited attachment or commitment to one another (Olson, 2000).

Families cope with these dialectical tensions by creating **boundaries**, which are limits a family sets on its members' actions. Communication researchers have devoted a good deal of attention to the importance of boundary management in interpersonal and family relationships (Petronio, 2000). The most obvious boundaries are physical (e.g., do not enter a bedroom without knocking if the door is closed; stay out of the den when Mom is preparing her tax return). Other boundaries involve conversational topics. In some families, discussion of finances is off limits. In others, expression of certain emotions is restricted. As the "Focus on Research" box on page 372 notes, sex is one of the most-avoided topics with parents and step-parents (Golish and Caughlin, 2002).

In addition to governing what may be talked about, boundaries can also dictate how topics are handled. In some families, it is fine to persist if the first overture to discussion is rebuffed ("Come on, what's on your mind?"). In other families, privacy rules discourage this kind of persistence. While the particulars may differ, every family has communication boundaries—and newcomers would be wise to learn and heed those boundaries (consider the many TV shows and movies that poke fun at in-laws for violating each other's family rules).

The challenge that families face is to define boundaries that include important kinds of relational communication while allowing members to have the privacy and freedom that everyone desires. Sometimes, these boundaries need to be openly negotiated. At other times, they are established through trial and error. In either case, healthy boundaries allow us to balance the opposing and equally important needs for connection and autonomy, for openness and closedness. When cohesion is moderate, family members are able to be independent from each other while still remaining dependent on, loyal to, and connected to the family (Olson, 2000).

Strive for a Moderate Level of Adaptability

A family experiences stress both from within (e.g., children get older and their needs change) and from outside (e.g., the mother loses her job); therefore, it needs to make adaptations to how it operates in order to maintain itself. To see how adaptability can help a family to function, consider the stress a family experiences when a child reaches adolescence. To adapt to this change, parents can begin to share control with their teenager as they negotiate issues like schedules, responsibilities, and rules. Families with higher levels of adaptability and cohesion report being more supportive of their LGBTQ family members. These families have more knowledge of and more favourable attitudes toward LGBTQ issues, more contact with LGBTQ family members and friends when compared to families low in adaptability and cohesion (Reeves et al., 2010).

When adaptability is too high, the result may be a **chaotic family**, one that has erratic leadership or no leadership at all, dramatic shifts in roles, unclear roles, and impulsive decision making. When adaptability is too low, the result may be a **rigid family** with authoritarian leadership (usually in the hands of one person, the mother or father), strict discipline, roles that are inflexible, and unchanging rules. The extent to which a family is able to avoid these extremes in adaptability determines, to a large extent, how functional it is (Olson, 2000). Inasmuch as change is an inevitable fact of family life, it is important for healthy families to adapt, to a reasonable extent, to the changes that come their way.

Looking at possible combinations of cohesion and adaptability, Olson (1986, 2000) defines three types of families: *balanced*, *mid-range*, and *extreme*. Balanced families have moderate levels of both cohesion and adaptability. Mid-range families are moderate on one dimension and high or low on the other—for example, they have moderate cohesion and chaotic or rigid adaptability. Extreme families are high in both cohesion and adaptability (enmeshed and chaotic), low on both (disengaged and rigid), or high in one and low in the other (enmeshed and rigid, or disengaged and chaotic). Balanced and mid-range families generally function better than extreme families (Olson and Lavee, 1989). For example, members of extreme families are less satisfied with their families than are members of balanced and mid-range families. In addition, members of balanced families have more positive communication skills than do members of extreme families: they exhibit more supportive communication, give one another clearer and more explicit information, and display more positive emotions. Communication in a balanced family is likely to create a supportive and caring environment in which communication is open and accepting—in other words, a functional family.

Encourage Confirming Messages

In Chapter 9, we introduced the importance of confirming messages—ones that show in one way or another that we value the other person. Confirming messages from parents help satisfy a great many of their children's needs, such as the need to be nurtured and respected. Kathleen Ellis (2002) looked at the different ways mothers and fathers communicate valuing and support to their children. She found that two highly confirming behaviours parents offer are (1) telling their children that they are unique and valuable as human beings, and (2) genuinely listening to their children when they tell them something important. Two highly disconfirming behaviours are (1) belittling their children, and (2) making statements which mean that their ideas do not count: "Nobody asked for your opinion" or "What do you know about this anyway?" Confirming messages are as important for adolescents and young adults as they are for younger children. For adolescents, confirming messages from parents and

Self-Assessment

HOW COHESIVE AND ADAPTABLE IS YOUR FAMILY?

With either your current family or family of origin in mind, respond to each item, adapted from Olson's Family Adaptability and Cohesion Evaluation Scale (FACES III). How true of your family is each item?

Use the numbers 1 to 5 according to the following scale:

never true　　1　2　3　4　5　　always true

_____ 1. Family members feel closer to people inside the family than outside the family.
_____ 2. Family members are not afraid to say what is on their minds.
_____ 3. Our family does things together.
_____ 4. Each family member has input into major family decisions.
_____ 5. Family members know each other's close friends.
_____ 6. In our family, everyone shares responsibilities.
_____ 7. Family members feel very close to each other.
_____ 8. Our family tries new ways of dealing with problems.
_____ 9. Family members share interests and hobbies with each other.
_____ 10. We shift household responsibilities from person to person.

_____ Total your scores for item 1, 3, 5, 7, and 9. This is your cohesion score.
_____ Total your scores for item 2, 4, 6, 8, and 10. This is your adaptability score.

Scores of 20 and higher on the cohesion scale are high, scores of 10 and lower are low, and scores between 10 and 20 indicate moderate levels of cohesion. Scores of 17 and higher on the adaptability scale are high, scores of 10 and lower are low, and scores between 10 and 17 indicate moderate levels of adaptability. Give some thought to whether you're satisfied with your family's levels of cohesion and adaptability—and if you're not, consider ways that you might help bring about change.

SOURCE: D.H. Olson (1986). "Circumplex model VII: Validation studies and FACES III," *Family Processes, 25* (pp. 337–351).

siblings are related to higher levels of self-esteem, self-concept strength, and autonomy (Dailey, 2006, 2010). For young adults, confirming communication from mothers is related to increased communication initiation with their mothers and less communication avoidance (Kennedy-Lightsey and Dillow, 2011).

Confirming communication is also important to successful marriages. Marital researcher John Gottman (2003) acknowledges that most couples are not confirming in all of their communication—that would be unrealistic. The key, says Gottman, is to have the right ratio of positive-to-negative messages. His studies show that satisfied couples consistently have a 5-to-1 ratio of positive-to-negative communication, with positive messages including things such as humour, empathizing, and expressions of affection. It seems reasonable that this ratio would serve as an ideal for all family communication, not just between spouses.

Deal Constructively with Family Conflict

As we saw in Chapter 10, conflict is natural and inevitable. In families, as in other relationships, the question is not how to avoid conflict—that's impossible—but how to resolve conflicts in a way that makes relationships stronger rather than weaker.

Many family conflicts centre on recurring issues (Napier and Whitaker, 1989). One is *power struggles*—that is, how family rules are created and who enforces them. Family conflicts also occur over *differences in intimacy needs*: the amount of affection members are willing to give and receive, how much time members spend together, and how much praise should be expressed. Finally, families may have conflict related to *interactional difficulties*—including how to handle conflicts.

Sometimes, families handle their conflicts in destructive ways. For instance, displays of physical and verbal aggression are unsuitable responses to conflict; however, the other extreme—ignoring a conflict—may be just as destructive to the family. Families can improve their communication by recognizing that family conflict should be dealt with. Placing conflict on the back burner, attempting to ignore it, smoothing it over, or denying that it exists creates tensions. The key to resolution lies in how the conflict is dealt with. There are several general principles of conflict management in the family.

Don't Sweat the Small Stuff

There will always be differences of opinion and style in families. Many need attention, but others are simply not worth bothering about. (Of course, what is worth bothering about is often a matter of opinion.)

Focus on Manageable Issues

Many big issues can be broken down into smaller, more manageable parts. For example, instead of arguing about a family member's "controlling personality," consider addressing specific problems, such as differing opinions about household neatness, the need to be informed about family plans, interference with your personal decisions, and so on.

Express Appreciation as Well as Complaints

Along with addressing differences, let family members know that you appreciate them. As we saw in Chapter 9, hearing an abundance of confirming messages makes it easier for us to hear negative information without feeling defensive and unappreciated.

Seek Win–Win Solutions

Strong feelings that are not resolved in one conflict will probably resurface later in another. The guidelines for win–win problem solving that we provided in Chapter 10 can work especially well with family conflicts,

 CHECK IT!

Describe four aspects of effective communication in families.

particularly when family members realize that when one person is unhappy, all the others are likely to suffer. On the other hand, when all members contribute to and are satisfied with a solution to a family problem, it builds cohesion, trust, and goodwill.

From his own research and a review of the literature on "excellent family communication," John Caughlin (2003) offers a list of college students' standards for what constitutes effective family communication. Several of these standards highlight the points discussed above and are good predictors of family satisfaction. Family members who communicate well provide each other with emotional support, express affection verbally and non-verbally, are polite to one another, and base discipline on clear rules.

SUMMARY

Contemporary families have a variety of traditional and non-traditional arrangements. Family relationships often include those between spouses or partners, parents and children, and siblings—each with unique characteristics. Research on committed, romantic relationships has identified three couple types and corresponding communication patterns for each. In addition, there is evidence that lasting romantic relationships require partners who accentuate the positive, convey attachment and intimacy with each other, and deal with conflict constructively. Children influence patterns of communication within families in a variety of ways, and families of origin often serve as models for other relationships in our lives.

Over time, families develop into systems, as the members interact with one another to form a whole. Family members also adopt particular roles, share and live out narratives, and create rules for interaction. Effective communication in families requires that the members establish and maintain a moderate level of cohesion, and they do this by establishing appropriate boundaries. In addition, functional families are adaptable, managing change without too much rigidity or acquiescence. Members of healthy families encourage one another with confirming messages and strive for win–win solutions to their conflicts.

MULTIPLE-CHOICE QUESTIONS

1. Which of the following is an example of a family, according to Kathleen Galvin's definition?
   a. a heterosexual couple without children
   b. a same-sex couple with children
   c. two cousins and their children sharing a single-family dwelling
   d. all of the above

2. The degree to which families have an open climate of discussing a wide array of topics is referred to as:
   a. open orientation.
   b. conversation orientation.
   c. conformity orientation.
   d. laissez-faire orientation.

3. The transition to parenthood includes
   a. increased stress.

b. increased conflict.

c. increased joy.

d. all of the above.

4. Canadians are freer than ever before to create the family arrangements that best suit their needs.

a. true

b. false

5. Adult siblings who recall their mother favouring one of them during childhood are more likely to experience

a. increased closeness and harmony as they get older.

b. increased distance and conflict throughout their relationship.

c. increased closeness and conflict as they get older.

d. increased instrumental support as they grow older.

6. Children who experienced secure attachments to their caregivers early in life tend to have more successful and satisfying relationships as adults.

a. true

b. false

7. Linda always changes the topic or adds irrelevant comments during family

arguments. Linda's behaviour best fits which of the following roles?

a. blamer

b. placater

c. distracter

d. computer

8. When a family's adaptability is too high the family is best described as rigid.

a. true

b. false

9. According to John Gottman, satisfied couples have a ratio of positive-to-negative communication of approximately

a. 1:1

b. 1:5

c. 5:4

d. 5:1

10. When family cohesion is too high and family members are expected to always agree, be loyal, and have little independence the family can be described as

a. enmeshed.

b. disengaged.

c. chaotic.

d. rigid.

Answers: 1. d; 2. b; 3. d; 4. a; 5. b; 6. a; 7. c; 8. b; 9. d; 10. a

▶ ACTIVITIES

1. Invitation to Insight

Understand your own family system better by giving examples of each of the following characteristics (see descriptions on pages 367–372).

a. interdependence of members

b. how the family is more than the sum of its parts

c. family subsystems and suprasystems

d. how environmental influences affect the family

2. Invitation to Insight

What are some unstated yet important rules governing communication that you have experienced or observed in a family (yours or another's)? Discuss rules governing conversation orientation and conformity orientation, as well as other areas of communication.

3. Role Play

In a group of no more than four pretend to have a family discussion about any mildly controversial topic. Each member of the group will act out a different role (as described by Virginia Satir—see page 367–370). Afterward explain how playing that role affected your interactions with the other members of the group. Discuss the effects the different roles had on each other and your contributions to the discussion.

DISCUSSION QUESTIONS

1. Describe the four characteristics of family communication systems discussed in this chapter.
2. Is it useful to think of communication within a family as a communication system? Why or why not?
3. Do you think that the roles people adopt in their families influence their behaviour in other groups? Why or why not?
4. What are the family narratives of your family? What values do they communicate?
5. Describe the types of families that result from mixing conversation orientation and conformity orientation. Is there a best style? Why or why not?
6. Describe the guidelines given in this chapter for dealing with family conflict. Do you think they are realistic? Complete? Why or why not?

JOURNAL IDEAS

1. Families, like individuals, are unique; different topics covered in this chapter are more and less salient for different individuals. Review the chapter and pick a couple of topics that you can easily apply to your family. For instance: perhaps you and your siblings perceive parental favouritism, which has had an effect on your relationships; maybe you can easily think of an example of how your family members are interdependent and part of a larger family system; or perhaps your family narratives or communication rules came to mind when you read those sections. Once you have chosen a topic or two, describe how each topic applies to your family and evaluate its contribution—positive, negative, or both—to your family's communication patterns and relationships. Are there things you would like to ensure you keep? Change? What are they, and why do you feel that way?

2. According to the Vanier Institute of the Family, the majority of young Canadians would like to have children. The small percentage (7 to 8 per cent) who *don't* want to have children, still would like to create family arrangements of their own. After reviewing the material in this chapter, describe the elements of family communication (in your family of origin) that you would like to take forward—or are already taking forward—into your own family. What elements of communication and interaction would you prefer to leave behind or change. How will you accomplish this?

12

Work, Group, and Team Communication

Chapter Outline

Ammentorp Photography/Shutterstock

Key Terms

coercive power
designated leader
distributed leadership
downward communication
emergent leader
expert power
formal communication
groupthink
horizontal communication
informal communication
legitimate power

networking
power
referent power
reward power
social loafing
synergy
teams
upward communication
virtual teams
work groups

Learning Objectives

YOU SHOULD UNDERSTAND:

- the ways information can flow in work-related organizations and relationships;
- the importance of relational communication and organizational cultures in working groups;
- the advantages and drawbacks of work groups and teams;
- types of leadership in work groups and teams;
- the types of power individual group members can possess;
- the characteristics of effective networking and interviews.

YOU SHOULD BE ABLE TO:

- identify your formal and informal relationships on the job, and suggest how you can expand the number of relationships to operate most effectively in your career;
- identify situations in which groups and teams are most effective and appropriate;
- identify the relational roles you need to fulfill to help a working group operate effectively;
- diagnose the culture of an organization and determine how well it fits with your personal communication style;
- choose the type of interaction (face-to-face or mediated) that can maximize your on-the-job effectiveness;
- identify the types of power you possess in a given group, and describe how you can use them to help the group operate effectively; and
- apply the guidelines to plan, participate in, and follow up on an employment interview in a way that creates a positive relationship with a potential employer.

Interpersonal effectiveness is essential on the job. Employers consider communication to be the *most important* skill a job candidate can possess—greater than job-specific skills such as computer or technical abilities (Canadian Council of Chief Executives, 2014). Employment and Social Development Canada (2014) cites effective communication and the ability to work well with others as essential employability skills. Take a look at almost any job ad and you will find that employers want individuals with excellent communication skills. Interpersonal communication skills are increasingly important in workplaces where computers are performing the parts of the job that don't require the complexities of human interaction—leaving the building of and maintenance of relations with customers, clients, patients, and other professionals to people.

In the following pages, we cover some of the most common and important dimensions of interpersonal communication on the job. This information is no substitute for a full course in organizational or business and professional communication, but it will give you an appreciation of how competent communication on the job can lead to greater effectiveness and satisfaction.

Communicating in Organizations

Within the workplace, relationships differ in a number of ways. Each of these relationships brings its own set of communication characteristics and challenges. In this section we will take a look at both the officially established channels of communication that exist in organizations, as well as the ways that information is shared through unofficial personal relationships and associations that are inevitable in workplaces. Both formal and informal relationships influence the flow of information in organizations and the organizational climate, and affect job performance and satisfaction (Boudrias et al., 2010; Mills, 2010; Propp et al., 2010).

Formal Communication

In most work settings, people are identified by titles and roles, such as accounting supervisor, management trainee, service representative, and so on. These roles combine to create **formal communication**—interaction that follows officially established channels. There are three types of formal communication within all, but the very smallest organizations (Adler and Elmhorst, 2010; Sanchez, 1999).

Upward Communication

In **upward communication,** subordinates communicate with their bosses—sometimes in a way that distorts negative information and puts it in a positive light (Dansereau and Markham, 1987). Upward communication can cover a variety of topics:

- *What subordinates are doing*:

  "We'll certainly have that job finished by closing time today."

- *Unsolved work problems*:

  "We're still having trouble with our online connection."

- *Suggestions for improvement*:

  "I think we've figured out a way to give everybody the vacation schedules they requested."

- *How subordinates are feeling*:

  "I've been promised a promotion for six months, and it still hasn't happened."

Downward Communication

In **downward communication,** managers address messages to subordinates. Downward messages often include:

- *Job instructions*:

  "Here's the way to do it . . ."

- *Job rationale*:

  "We back up the files every night in case the hard drive crashes."

- *Feedback*:

    "Great job! Just one suggestion . . ."

Horizontal Communication

Horizontal communication occurs between people who do not have direct supervisor–subordinate relationships. These types of messages may include:

- *Task coordination*:

    "If you can get me the job tomorrow, I'll have it finished by Thursday."

- *Sharing information*:

    Sales rep to engineer: "The customers are asking for longer battery life. Is that possible?"

- *Conflict resolution*:

    "I was really unhappy when you criticized me in front of the boss. Can we talk about it?"

These examples suggest the importance of keeping formal channels open and operating; imagine the likely consequences if any one of these messages weren't delivered. In addition to providing task-related and emotional support, solving problems, and getting the job done, the quality of co-worker relationships is linked to satisfaction with and commitment to the job (Bryant and Sias, 2011; Sias, 2009). Communication with peers is the most common type of communication on the job and contributes significantly to whether people enjoy their work or feel stressed out and miserable. Ask anyone who has had a job they really disliked, and they will probably tell you the problems involved the people they worked with and not really the job requirements themselves. Both formal and informal communication with peers contributes to job satisfaction, and we will take a look at informal communication in the next section.

Informal Communication

Formal relationships are important, but they are not the only kinds that operate at work. People develop their own personal networks of relationships within the workplace. Communication in these networks is informal. **Informal communication** doesn't follow officially sanctioned routes (e.g., the administrator informs the frontline staff, who then let clients know); instead, it is based on friendships, shared personal or career interests, and proximity. Co-workers may have children in the same school, support the same sports team, belong to the same place of worship, or have mutual friends. They may carpool to share commuting expenses or work out together at the gym during lunch hour. They may develop a close friendship through self-disclosure and more frequent interaction, both on and away from the job (Mao and Hsieh, 2012; Morrison and Wright, 2009; Sias and Cahill, 1998).

Functions of Informal Communication

Informal messages can supplement more formal ones in a variety of ways. Sometimes, they

No matter what the workplace, there are titles and roles and various forms of communication. In what ways do you take part in formal and informal communication in your workplace?

© iStockPhoto/sturti.

function to *confirm* formal messages: "This time, they're really serious about our not using email for personal messages." At other times, they can *contradict* formal ones: "They say the deadline is Friday, but first thing Monday morning is okay." Some informal messages can *expand* on official information: "Khakis are fine. When they say 'no casual attire,' they mean no jeans or T-shirts." Informal communication can help you *circumvent* formal channels: "If you call Sharon in accounting, she can get you reimbursed quickly without all that paperwork."

Informal relationships are often more efficient and accurate than formal networks (Hellweg, 1987). An observation in the *Harvard Business Review* captured the relationship between formal and informal networks: "If the formal organization is the skeleton of a company, the informal is the central nervous system" (Krackhardt and Hanson, 1993, p. 104). The information exchanged in informal relationships often helps people to make sense of more formal types of workplace communication (Mills, 2010). Informal communication networks and friendships within workplaces can have a positive impact on the organization. They have been found to increase employee motivation and participation and they can contribute to more supportive and innovative climates and increase productivity (Berman et al., 2002; Fortado, 2011; Morrison 2004).

It is important to note that communication in the workplace doesn't always fall into neat and simple categories (Mills, 2010; Reamer, 2002). Often, we must move between formal and informal communication within a particular relationship. For instance, your boss might drop by your cubicle to share some office gossip with you—and a few minutes later take you to task about an assignment you neglected. Romantic partners who work together may have difficulty deciding where their personal relationship ends and their professional relationship begins. And many employees feel awkward when a co-worker is promoted to supervisor, because it changes the rules of their

- **Formal communication:** interaction that follows officially established channels.
- **Upward communication:** subordinates' communication with their bosses.
- **Downward communication:** managers' communication with subordinates.
- **Horizontal communication:** communication between people who do not have supervisor–subordinate relationships.
- **Informal communication:** communication in the workplace based on friendships, shared personal or career interests, and proximity; it can confirm, contradict, expand, or circumvent formal messages.

REFLECTION

ONLINE NEIGHBOURS— COMMUNITY TEAM

Recently, a developer presented the city council with a proposal to build a large, ostentatious house next door to me. I had lived on the street for 12 years, and I knew many of the neighbours well enough to wave and say hello to them, but our relations would be best described as superficial. This proposed threat to our neighbourhood called for united community action, and our united team came about on the Internet. With everyone's conflicting work and family schedules, we decided it would be easier to try to organize ourselves by email. This worked beautifully. Our united activism resulted in the building of a much smaller house that suited the neighbourhood better, and our email correspondence allowed us to deepen our friendships.

communication. These challenges are very apparent for people involved in family business. Family business employees are constantly negotiating their family and business roles and associated types of communication. It is interesting to note that family-business employees whose families are high in conversation orientation (see Chapter 11) report higher levels of both family and business satisfaction (Carmon and Pearson, 2013). Recall that families high in conversation orientation have a positive and open communication climate and discuss a wide array of topics. This allows family-business employees to better understand each other's point of view and increases the likelihood that they will be able to come to mutually satisfying resolutions to both family and business issues they face. As these examples suggest, the characteristics of competent communication that we discussed in Chapter 1 —such as adaptability, self-monitoring, and cultivating a large repertoire of skills—are as important in the workplace as they are in families and friendships.

Relationships in Work Groups and Teams

Working in groups is an essential part of almost every job (Hoch, 2013). Organizations use groups because they offer a number of advantages over people working on their own. **Work groups** can be defined as three or more people who have ongoing interactions with each other and who depend upon and support each other in order to accomplish a goal. **Teams** are specialized types of work groups. Teams often have members with distinct and complementary skills and resources. These individuals work together to accomplish a very specific task and usually have a strong sense of collective identity. Anyone with group experience knows that good personal relationships are essential in a well-functioning team. Communication researchers Carl Larson and Frank LaFasto (1989) studied over 75 top-notch work teams from a diverse range of settings that included 2 championship football teams, the scientists who developed the IBM personal computer, a Mount Everest expedition, and a heart surgery team. Among the qualities that distinguish winning teams is a collaborative climate in which the members trust and support one another. In the following pages, we will introduce some communication skills that can help build this sort of collaborative, confirming climate.

Characteristics of Groups and Teams

Groups and teams have a number of advantages in the workplace. First, it is important to consider the nature of the work before deciding whether a group is better suited to doing it than an individual. Generally, relatively simple tasks that require limited knowledge are better suited to an individual. This is particularly true if the time available for the job is limited. When time is available for deliberation, and a number of individuals have a stake in the outcome, a group approach might be best. This is often the case when a complicated task requires a broad range of knowledge.

Second, groups can often produce results that are greater than the strengths of the individuals involved. Groups and teams can create a special kind of energy that expands the contributions of the individual members through their interactions with each other. The energy that is created through these positive exchanges is sometimes referred to as **synergy** (Lumsden et al., 2009). Synergy allows groups to produce more creative results that integrate several individuals' thinking rather than just one person's ideas. Third, groups also tend to be more *accurate* in their work because individual members act as checks and balances for each other. Finally, they produce greater *commitment* to the outcomes because they consider multiple points of view and they encourage greater participation in decision making. It is easier for people to support efforts they had a hand in creating.

© iStockPhoto/Yuri_Arcurs.

Working in groups is an essential part of almost every job. What are some advantages and disadvantages of working in groups in your field?

Despite the advantages groups afford, they also have some drawbacks. First, groups require *time* to discuss ideas. All members of the group need to have an opportunity to contribute their ideas, and as a result working in groups takes longer than working alone. Second, individual members may feel pressure for acceptance in the group, and thus may be less likely to express disagreement. When people feel pressure to conform, they are more likely to go along with the thinking of the majority or the more powerful group members' decisions rather than speaking up. Sociologist Irving Janis (1983) identified a number of factors that increase the chances that group members will suspend their critical thinking to achieve agreement. He called this process **groupthink**, and suggested groups are most vulnerable when they are very cohesive, isolated, and under a lot of pressure to reach an agreement. In these situations group members fail to really consider the alternatives and the risks involved in their choices. Finally, as most students know too well, groups can include people who fail to do their fair share of the work. The tendency for people to work less hard in a group is called **social loafing**. Social loafing is more prevalent among those who are not committed to the goal of the group, who believe their individual performance is not being monitored, and who believe the task itself does not warrant a group effort—that it would be more efficient for one person to complete the task (Karau and Williams, 1993, 2001).

In order for groups to be effective and produce the benefits of combined expertise, increased creativity, accuracy, and commitment while avoiding the pitfalls of conformity, poor decision making, and unfair distribution of work, the individual participants need to communicate with each other effectively. The insights and skills you have read about in the preceding chapters will all contribute to effective communication in groups and teams. In the next section we will describe some skills that relate directly to working in groups and provide an orientation to typical patterns of group dynamics.

Personal Skills in Work Groups and Teams

Effective team members must, of course, have the task-related skills to tackle the job at hand. But relational skills are just as important. More than 60 years ago, Kenneth Benne and Paul Sheats (1948) identified a list of relational roles that need to be filled at one time or another in every group's life. These roles include:

- encouraging participation,
- harmonizing,
- relieving tension,
- evaluating the group's emotional climate,
- giving praise, and
- listening thoughtfully to the concerns of others.

If a group is not operating efficiently, one place to look for remedies is the communication climate among members. Ask yourself if any of these relational functions needs filling.

Don't get the idea that an effective group will be free of conflicts. Even the best team will experience struggles on the path to consensus. In fact, most groups go through a predictable series of stages as they work together (Brilhart et al., 2001). Figure 12.1 illustrates this pattern. Politeness and harmony are the norm during the *orientation* stage when a team first tackles a job. But as time goes on and differences emerge, the group enters a period of *conflict*. Disagreement does not necessarily involve hostility, but even civil and reasoned differences can require you to use the listening skills that we described in Chapter 5, the climate-building approaches

discussed in Chapter 9, and the conflict-management guidelines covered in Chapter 10. Once a group has worked through the conflict stage, it usually enters an *emergence* stage, where members accept—sometimes enthusiastically and sometimes reluctantly—the team's decision. The members recognize that this is a time to seek harmony. A fourth stage in group decision making is *reinforcement*. This is when the members not only accept the decision, but also endorse it.

This process repeats itself in a cyclical fashion—and different stages are likely to overlap somewhat—as a group faces each new challenge. Just like dyadic relationships, groups have their ups and downs. Knowing that each step—especially conflict—is a natural part of working together can be reassuring.

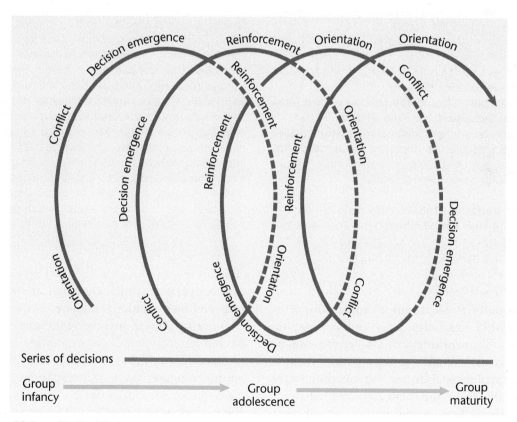

Figure 12.1 ● Cyclical Stages in an Ongoing Group

SOURCE: From J.K. Brilhart, G.J. Galanes, and K. Adams (2001), *Effective group discussion*, 10th edn (p. 289). New York: McGraw-Hill Ryerson. Reproduced with permission of the McGraw-Hill Companies.

Focus on TECHNOLOGY

Considerable research has been conducted on the influence of culture on the process and outcome of face-to-face negotiations between members of different cultures. However, considerably less is known about how culture influences negotiations when participants have no face-to-face or telephone contact. Three researchers—one Canadian and two Austrians—collaborated to investigate the influences of culture on anonymous negotiations (Kersten et al., 2002). They used a Web-based negotiation system and recruited subjects from Austria, Ecuador, Finland, and Switzerland. They contrasted the participants' cultures in terms of the five following attributes discussed earlier in this text:

- individualism (Austria, Finland, and Switzerland) versus collectivism (Ecuador);
- power distance (Austria = low, Finland and Switzerland = moderate, Ecuador = high);
- achievement (Austria, Switzerland, and Ecuador) versus nurturing (Finland);
- high context (Ecuador) versus low context (Austria, Switzerland, and Finland); and
- time orientation: monochronic—punctuality and schedules are important (Switzerland, Finland, and Austria); polychronic—more relaxed attitude toward time (Ecuador).

The participants—166 university students—were all given the same bargaining problem. They were not told whether they were negotiating with someone from their own country or a different country; however, they could choose to reveal their identity during the Web-based negotiations. Interestingly, even without visual or auditory sensory information, culture influenced participants' negotiations and their satisfaction with the negotiation process and outcomes. The researchers found several effects of culture on the participants' expectations before the negotiations as well as on the negotiators' behaviour during negotiations. For instance, negotiators from Ecuador, a collectivistic, polychronic, high-context and high-distance culture, had more positive expectations about the negotiation process and the friendliness of the negotiations before use of the Web-based negotiation system. Negotiators from Ecuador took more time between sending offers to their partners. Negotiators from low-context cultures (Austria, Finland, and Switzerland) included fewer text messages with their offers than the participants from high-context cultures (Ecuador). Although one could argue that anonymous, computer-mediated negotiations should be less influenced by the cultural background of the negotiators than face-to-face negotiations, this did not seem to be the case. The investigators hypothesized that, without the non-verbal communication information available in face-to-face negotiations, these Web-based, anonymous negotiators may have felt a high level of social uncertainty, which tied their behaviour closer to their own cultural norms.

Group Cultures

We usually think about cultures rooted in nationality, ethnicity, age, and geographic region, but working groups—entire organizations and smaller groups within them—have their own cultures, too (Ashkanasy et al., 2000; Deal and Kennedy, 1983; Rollinson, 2008). You can prove this for yourself by thinking about different classes you have attended as a student. Even though the basic process of learning is the same from one discipline and school to another, you probably can recognize that each class had its own culture—its own relational climate. The cultures of working groups involve many dimensions of communication such as *sociability* (friendly or aloof), *distribution of power* (controlled by authority figures or shared among members), *tolerance of new ideas* (welcome or resisted), *ways of managing conflict* (direct or indirect), and *emotional support* (more or less plentiful).

Perhaps the most important insight about cultures in working groups is that they can make the difference between satisfaction and misery (Mohr et al, 2012). If you are lucky enough to belong to a group that has a healthy culture—for example, one that is friendly, has shared power, welcomes new ideas, manages conflict directly, and provides emotional support—working on even the toughest jobs can be rewarding. On the other hand, if you are stuck in a group with an unsatisfying culture, great pay and plush working conditions will not prevent you from feeling miserable.

You may not be able to exert much influence on the culture of a large organization, whether it is a university you are attending or a corporation you work for. What you *can* do, though, is think about the culture of the organization before you decide to join it. Once you are on the job, you can help shape the culture of smaller groups to which you belong. The way you and your fellow workers treat one another, as well as your attitudes toward work, can make a tremendous difference in the quality of the many hours you spend on the job.

Face-to-Face and Mediated Relationships

As in personal settings, people in working relationships can communicate either face-to-face or through a variety of electronic media. Telephone and email are still the most common types of mediated communication channels, although not the only ones. Other ways to keep in touch include text messaging, video and teleconferencing, online discussion and information sharing forums, social media sites and instant messaging.

Face-to-face interaction is still the most common type of communication at work, but mediated relationships are becoming increasingly more common and essential. The most common methods for scheduling meetings are email or face-to-face communication and most people prefer to conduct meetings in person. However, among teams with members who work remotely, conference calls are favoured. In addition, most people prefer using face-to-face conversations, phone calls, and email to ask a work-related question and share work

related information with a fellow employee (Kiddie, 2014). Increasingly, many businesses communicate almost exclusively with their customers by phone and CMC, and employees within organizations are able to create effective working and personal relationships without spending much, if any, time together in person.

Virtual teams whose memberships transcend the boundaries of location and time can be a very effective and satisfying way to conduct business (Greer and Payne, 2014; Hambly et al., 2007; Martin and MacDonnell, 2012). Groups that operate electronically can communicate in ways that would otherwise not be possible. They can use the phone and Internet to tackle jobs much more quickly than a similar group that would have to assemble physically. They can use different working schedules to their advantage. For example, a person in the Maritimes—or even in Europe—can hand off work at the end of the day to a colleague in British Columbia, who can process and return it in time for the next morning.

As Table 1.1 on page 11 (Chapter 1) shows, each communication medium has its own advantages and drawbacks. And there are occasions where even the best technology is no substitute for "face time." Still, both face-to-face and mediated working relationships can clearly be interpersonal in every sense of the word.

Leadership, Power, and Influence in Working Groups

In order for groups and organizations to be effective, they require leadership. Leadership involves motivating and influencing people to accomplish a goal or objective. Leaders can be appointed or can emerge from the group. Throughout most of history people believed that leaders were people who were born with a set of traits that made them different from followers and contributed to their effectiveness. Research has identified factors that are related to people's ability to persuade and influence others; none of them appear to be entirely innate, and all can be learned. They include empathy, confidence, humour, and several factors related to the context of the situation (Dutton, 2010).

Types of Leadership

When most people think about influence in groups, they focus on the **designated leader**—the person (or people) with an official title that indicates authority, such as manager, chairperson, and so on. There is no doubt that designated leaders play an important role in making things happen. But you do not have to be a designated leader to influence the effectiveness of a group. An **emergent leader** is chosen by the group either formally or informally. For instance a sports team may elect a captain, or a group of unhappy employees may agree that one member of the group would be best suited to approach the boss to talk about their concerns. There can be a single leader in the group or leadership can be distributed among several group members. **Distributed leadership** relies on the collective efforts of several people to influence others and achieve goals rather than on the influence of a single person. In many workplaces such as schools and universities a model of distributed leadership is effective in achieving educational objectives and outcomes (Spillane, 2005). In addition, shared leadership has been associated with increased innovation in teams working on product development and training and development (Hoch, 2013). Regardless of whether leadership comes from an appointed individual or several emergent leaders, its effectiveness depends on the ways in which leaders use their power to influence and motivate others and achieve goals and objectives in their unique workplaces over both the short and long term.

Types of Power

Every member of a working team has at least one resource of power that can affect what happens in a group (Andrews and Baird, 2005; French and Raven, 1968). **Power** is the

REFLECTION

SHARING ROLES AND RESPONSIBILITIES

It never occurred to me that in some groups leadership is distributed throughout the group, but that's exactly what it was like when some fellow students and I decided to do some fundraising to help people who were victims of a recent disaster overseas. Once we had brainstormed our fundraising ideas, Jenn took the lead on making posters and signs to post throughout our campus, and Mohamed contacted some faculty to see if he could make announcements in classes. Keesha handled getting our message out on social media and I set up a bank account and contacted the Red Cross to see how the donations would work. We all just took on jobs that we were well-suited to—no one took "the lead"—we all just pitched in and it turned out great. We raised a lot of money, raised awareness, and had a lot of fun in the process.

potential to influence an individual or group. John French and Bertram Raven (1959, 1968) identified five bases of social power: *legitimate*, *expert*, *reward*, *coercive*, and *referent power*. Below we will discuss each type and current research and thinking about its effectiveness.

Legitimate Power

Legitimate power derives from the belief that a person in a particular position (e.g., a manager, supervisor, public relations advisor) has the right to tell others what to do. For instance, employees comply with their supervisor's requests (e.g., "Please have that report completed in time for Friday's meeting") because they understand that her position in the organization gives her the authority to make such demands. Raven and French (1958)

 **CHECK IT!**

Describe and distinguish between the three types of leadership described here.

found that when employees believed that the person in authority had a right to occupy that position, they were much more likely to comply with that person's demands. For instance, in their study, elected supervisors had more legitimate power, acceptance, and influence than appointed supervisors. Similarly, when employees perceive their boss as well qualified for the job they are more likely to consider him or her to have legitimate authority and to be influenced by it (Yoon and Thye, 2011).

Legitimate power and authority are conceived differently in different cultures. Recall the concept of power distance from Chapter 3. In cultures with high power distance, employees are more likely to feel comfortable with inequalities in power and to accept power based on one's position within the organization (Hofstede, 1980, 2001). In contrast, in cultures that expect more equitable distribution of power (e.g., low power distance) employees place a higher value on personal choice and prefer less hierarchical organizational structures (Lee and Antonakis, 2014). In low power distance cultures, such as Canada, staff are more inclined to expect authority figures to earn the respect and endorsement of their employees.

Expert Power

Expert power comes from the groups' belief that an individual has a high level of knowledge or a highly specialized skill. The designated leaders are often not the best or only experts; individual members often have a special kind of knowledge or talent, such as the ability to use a type of software or experience in the topic at hand. Wise leaders recognize the expert power of individual group members, and they also share their own expertise with the group.

Reward Power

Reward power, as its name implies, rests on the ability to give incentives and compensation. Rewards obviously include the designated leaders' hiring, paying, and promoting of employees, but they can also include less tangible benefits such as opportunities for creative and intellectual stimulation and a positive interpersonal climate in the workplace. For instance, providing people with opportunities to pursue the work they are most interested in creates a workplace culture that is inherently rewarding. Roger Martin (2014), former dean of the Rotman School of Management at the University of Toronto, for example, chose to allow his faculty to teach to their research passions. He figured that by doing so, he wouldn't have to choose between investing in faculty who were good at research or those who were good at teaching. Instead, he rewarded professors who were good at teaching in their own research areas. He eliminated courses that didn't correspond to any professor's area of research expertise and thus helped to create a business school that is highly regarded for both its research and teaching. Designated leaders are not the only

Building WORK SKILLS

Improve your ability to choose the most effective way of communicating in organizations by following these steps:

1. Think of an environment in which you work (you may use school for the following analysis).
2. Identify all the communication media used to convey messages in a one-week period:

face-to-face, print, telephone, email, Internet, instant messaging, fax, and so on.

3. Analyze each situation to determine whether the medium chosen was most effective. If not, suggest a better alternative.
4. Based on your observations, identify situations in which it is best to use each type of communication available to you.

---

ones who can influence others through the use of rewards. Group members can bestow their own rewards. Helping one another is a kind of reward that can help the group solve the job at hand. It also builds goodwill that serves both the giver and the team well.

Coercive Power

Along with rewarding one another, group members can use **coercive power** to get what they want by using unpleasant consequences, or the threat of them, to punish one another. You do not have to be a designated leader to punish. Complaining, withholding help, and blocking progress are examples of ways members can punish one another and their boss. Coercive power typically leads to short-term compliance, but is generally ineffective over the long term. It reduces employees' satisfaction with their jobs, erodes commitment, and diminishes creativity and productivity (Kiazad et al., 2010; Tepper, 2007). In contrast to reward power, which can create a workplace climate that is stimulating and engaging, coercive power creates a climate of fear and insecurity.

Referent Power

The clearest type of interpersonal influence is **referent power**—the influence that comes from the members' liking and respect for one another. Members with good interpersonal skills and integrity are likely to have high referent power, which enables them to shape the

way the group operates. People with referent power lead by example and have gained the trust of the group members. Referent power is the area in which the greatest difference between designated leaders and influential group members can exist. An unpopular manager might have to use the rewards and

Types of Power

- **Legitimate power:** lies in the perception that people who have rightfully achieved positions of power have a right to tell others what to do.
- **Expert power:** is based on an individual having specialized knowledge or skills and as a result has authority with the group.
- **Reward power:** is based on the provision of incentives and benefits in order to influence group members.
- **Coercive power:** is based on the use of force, threats, and punishments to influence group members.
- **Referent power:** the ability to influence others based on a person's strong interpersonal relationships with others that include being respected, admired, and seen as trustworthy.

punishments that come with the job title to gain members' compliance. But a popular manager or group member with no formal title can persuade others to co-operate because of the influence that comes with the high regard of other members (Leroy et al., 2012; Simons, 2008).

It appears that referent power is particularly dependent on employees' perceptions of the trustworthiness of the individual. Katie Dunleavy and her colleagues (2010) presented employees with a scenario in which an employee observes a co-worker putting office supplies in his car and claiming he will replace the supplies after payday. The manager later questions the pilfering employee about disappearing supplies, and the worker who observed the theft responds in one of three ways. He shares his observation of the employee putting supplies in his car (*truthful response*), agrees that things are missing, but doesn't share his observation (*withholding response*), or claims he hasn't noticed anything missing at all (*distorted response*). They found that employees reading the scenario perceived the individual who distorted the information as having significantly less credibility and referent power than the individuals who either told the truth or said nothing. The foundation of referent power, at least in Western cultures, appears to be strong interpersonal skills and trustworthiness.

By now, you can see that good relationships in working groups require some special skills. We will now look at another set of special skills that will help you gain entrance into an organization.

Advancing Your Career

The first steps in establishing a successful career require you to identify the types of

The majority of job seekers find employment through personal contacts and the majority of employers find good employees the same way. Does the field you're interested in have professional associations? Have you gone to any meetings?

work you find enjoyable and rewarding and obtain the required credentials. Next you need to gain access to the organizations and people who can help you get a job. The interpersonal communication skills you have been reading about in the previous chapters can help you to do just that.

Networking

For our purposes **networking** refers to the process of deliberately meeting people and maintaining contacts to get career information, advice, and leads. Most people are aware of the social network concept through popular online networking sites such as Facebook that focus primarily on linking friends for social purposes. In addition, there are also generic and career focused professional networking sites whose primary purpose is the facilitate connections and collaborations in the world of work. But people have been engaged in networking long before the Internet. The old saying, "It's not what you know, it's who you know," is a testament to both the power and endurance of social networking. The majority of job seekers find employment through personal contacts and the majority of employers find good employees the same way (Baker, 2000; Bolles, 2008; Yakubovich, 2005).The advantage of networking now is that the Internet can help job seekers gain access to a much wider variety of people who might be able to help advance their careers compared to in the past.

Identifying and Cultivating Your Networks

We are all members of informal social networks that include our friends, family, and neighbours. We interact with some of our contacts mostly face-to-face, some primarily via CMC and still others in person and through mediated communication. Our close personal contacts can be helpful in helping us gain access to potential employment and volunteer experiences, but sometimes our more distant contacts—old school friends, teachers, former colleagues, professionals whose services we have used, relatives, and acquaintances of family and friends—can provide even better connections. There are numerous online professional networking sites that can be helpful to connect with people who might provide job leads. In addition, these sites provide you with a platform to establish a professional online presence. It is important to look for every opportunity to connect with others that can help you advance in your career. At the same time it is also important to be sensitive to other peoples' needs and boundaries and to treat your contacts with respect and gratitude. Finally, it is important to reciprocate. Use your personal networks to help others who are either seeking employment or looking for an employee.

Keeping Your Online Profile Professional

Like it or not employers type job candidate's names into search engines and see what they can find. It is important to monitor your online profile and work to ensure that it works to your advantage rather than against you. The areas that are most likely to cause concern among potential employers include: drinking and drug use, inappropriate photos, bad mouthing previous employers or fellow employees, poor communication skills, discriminatory remarks, unprofessional screen names, criminal activity, and lying about credentials. In contrast, information that can help your chances of getting a position include: demonstration of good communication skills, creativity, information about awards and accolades, good references, and having a wide range of interests (Career Builder, 2006). It is important to keep in mind that the content you post on social media sites (i.e., Facebook, Twitter, Instagram, Vine, Snapchat, etc.) has the potential to be "out there" permanently. As we have mentioned throughout this book, privacy settings have limitations and the best way to manage your professional profile online is to treat the Internet as a public place.

Interviewing

While employment interviews are a type of conversation they are unlike the kinds of social exchanges we have in other situations. Employment interviews have qualities that distinguish them from other types of conversations (Stewart and Cash, 2011). The first is *purpose*. Most everyday conversations have no serious preconceived purpose. Two people chat between floors in an elevator; friends swap jokes at a party; a boss and employees take a break around the coffee machine. An employment interview, on the other hand, always has goals involving both the interviewer and the prospective employee. A second characteristic that distinguishes interviews is *structure*. In a typical conversation, neither person knows or cares when the exchange will end or exactly what topics will be covered. By contrast, any good interview has a distinct opening, body, and conclusion. A third feature of interviews is *control*. Whereas conversations do not require any guidance from one of the parties,

CHECK IT!

When people work in groups, what communication skills contribute to building a collaborative, confirming communication climate?

Focus on RESEARCH

LEADERSHIP—DO CULTURE AND GENDER MATTER?

Leadership is a popular topic for both researchers and popular media alike. Most research done on styles of leadership and their effectiveness has examined the leadership of white men in Western cultures. Increasingly investigators have wanted to find out whether men and women differ in their styles of leadership and whether effective leadership styles differ from culture to culture. It is important to understand diversity in leadership styles when we live in a diverse culture and organizations are increasingly global (Ayman and Korabik, 2010). Hetty van Emmerik and her colleagues (2008) examined subordinates' ratings of their managers' leadership in terms of two factors: the extent to which they showed consideration and to which they initiated structure. Consideration behaviours include a friendly interpersonal approach to supervision, while initiating behaviours involve assigning tasks, describing procedures, clarifying expectations, and scheduling work. Their study included 64,038 subordinates representing 42 different countries. These employees provided leadership evaluations for 13,595 different managers, 73 per cent of whom were men. Each response was placed in 1 of 10 cultural groups according to the participant's country. These cultural clusters were based on previous research into similarities in cultural values and beliefs across different countries as follows:

- *Anglo:* Canada, England, Australia, South Africa, New Zealand, Ireland, United States;
- *Arab:* Qatar, Morocco, Turkey, Egypt, Kuwait;
- *Eastern European:* Hungary, Russia, Kazakhstan, Albania, Poland, Greece, Slovenia, Georgia;
- *Germanic-European:* Austria, parts of Switzerland, the Netherlands, Germany;
- *Latin American:* Costa Rica, Venezuela, Ecuador, Mexico, El Salvador, Columbia, Guatemala, Bolivia, Brazil, Argentina;
- *Latin European:* Israel, Italy, Portugal, Spain, France, parts of Switzerland;
- *Nordic-European:* Finland, Sweden, Denmark;
- *South Asian:* India, Indonesia, Philippines, Malaysia, Thailand, Iran; and
- *Sub-Saharan:* Namibia, Zambia, Zimbabwe, Nigeria.

These investigators found that managers from Anglo, Latin American, and Arab cultures scored higher on consideration than managers from Germanic-European cultures. Managers from Latin American, South Asian, and Arab cultures scored higher on initiating structure than managers from Anglo, Latin European, Germanic-European, Eastern European, and sub-Saharan cultures.

In terms of gender, they found that, as gender stereotypes would predict, female managers scored higher on consideration than male managers, but this was true only when they included responses from all 42 countries or examined specific cultural groups. When they drilled down and looked at specific cultural clusters, this gender difference was observed only in managers from Anglo, Nordic-European, Germanic, and Eastern European cultural clusters. Female managers from other cultural backgrounds did not differ from male managers in the amount of consideration shown. Contrary to gender stereotypes, female managers also scored higher on initiating structure than their male counterparts; however, cultural differences were greater than gender differences here too. These investigators suggest that the effects of culture are more powerful in explaining managerial differences than are the effects of gender. They did not find support for the stereotype that women leaders are more concerned with relationships and are less task-oriented; instead, they found that female leaders scored higher than males in both areas, and that females in Western cultures show significantly more consideration for employees than female managers from non-Western cultures. They conclude that gender differences in management styles appear limited to Western culture, and that culture is more powerful worldwide in predicting differences in leadership style than is gender.

Critical thinking: *Do you think the small percentage of females currently in management positions worldwide (in Canada it is currently about 28 per cent) would have an effect on the popularity of certain styles of leadership? Why or why not?*

an interviewer's job is to keep the exchange moving toward the preset purpose. Finally, interviews usually have a unique *balance of participation*. Though most conversations involve roughly the same amount of speaking by each person, in an interview, the person being interviewed should do about 70 per cent of the talking.

To make an interview successful, both the interviewer and interviewee have responsibilities before, during, and after they meet. As an interviewee, you can make the experience pay off by following the guidelines that we present in the rest of this chapter.

Before the Interview

A good interview begins before the people sit down to talk. You can make your interviews more successful through careful planning (Government of Canada, 2014; Service Canada, 2011).

1. Clarify the Interviewer's Goals   Imagine you are preparing for an employment interview. You know that the company is looking for the best applicant, but just what qualities are they seeking? Are education and training most important? Experience? Initiative? Knowing these criteria in advance will improve your chances of doing well in the interview. Examine the job description provided in the job advertisement carefully and use any relevant contacts in your social network to find out more about what skills, abilities, and past experiences might be most relevant. Besides arriving with a basic understanding of what skills and abilities they are looking for, you can impress the interviewer, and serve yourself well, by doing advance research on the organization. What products or services does it sell? What is its position in the marketplace and the community? What challenges and trends does the organization face? What makes this organization unique among its competitors? If you show your awareness of this information, you will distinguish yourself as a serious candidate.

2. Be Prepared to Make a Good First Impression   First impressions can make or break an interview. Usually, the first impression you make will be based on your cover letter and resumé, which is why it's important for them to be well-constructed and error-free. There are many books and online resources that offer tips on developing these important documents (e.g., Brown, 2007; Ontario Public Service, 2011). In addition, your punctuality (or lack thereof) will make a statement about how you manage your time. Plan to arrive 10 to 15 minutes early in order to leave room for any unexpected delays. If you're unsure of the company's location, make a test run ahead of time.

A good interviewee does not go to an interview empty-handed. You will want to take materials with you that will help the employer learn more about why you are ready, willing, and able to do the job. For instance, take extra copies of your resumé, because more than one person may interview you that day. Go prepared to take notes; you will need something to write on, as well as a pen or pencil. If it is relevant, take copies of your past work, such as reports you have helped prepare, performance reviews by former employers, drawings or designs you have created in work or school, letters of recommendation, and so on. Besides demonstrating your qualifications, items like these show that you know how to sell yourself. Take along the names, addresses, and phone numbers of any references you haven't listed in your resumé.

Finally, research shows that many interviewers form their opinions about candidates based on the non-verbal cues that candidates display during the interaction (De Groot and Gooty, 2009). Physical attractiveness is a major influence on how applicants are rated, so it makes sense to do everything possible to look your best (Shannon and Stark, 2003). The proper style of clothing can vary from one type of job or organization to another. When in doubt, it is best to dress formally and conservatively. It's unlikely an employer will think less of you for being overdressed, but looking too casual can be taken as a sign that you don't take the job or the interview seriously.

During the Interview

Once you are in the interview itself, there are several important points to keep in mind. These guidelines both show your competence and help you build a good relationship with your interviewer.

1. Get Off to a Good Start   The usual format for an opening begins with some sort of greeting, which includes any introductions that are necessary. A period of informal conversation often follows, in which the interviewer and applicant talk about subjects of mutual interest not necessarily related to the interview topic. This period gives both people a chance to get settled and acquainted before getting down to business. The idea is to establish some common ground between interviewer and applicant. One way to do so is to look around the interviewer's office for information about that person's interests and hobbies. A prominent plaque, a sports pennant, a wall photo, or a piece of art can all be topics for conversation.

2. Give Clear, Detailed Answers   Put yourself in the interviewer's shoes and be as specific and helpful as you hope others would be for you. A good answer provides a general theme and then offers specifics. For example, suppose a potential employer asks, "What did you learn in your interpersonal communication course that will help you in this job?" You could follow this theme-specific format with an answer like, "I learned how to build and maintain positive relationships, and that can help me with people in the company and with customers. For example, we learned how to listen well, negotiate win–win solutions, raise difficult issues skilfully, and handle criticism without getting defensive." Be prepared, because a good interviewer will probably ask a follow-up question such as, "Give me an example of a time when you've used those skills." It's a good idea to come to an interview with several brief stories, illustrations, and examples that provide evidence of your abilities and skills.

3. Keep Your Answers Focused   It is easy to rattle on in an interview, either out of enthusiasm, a desire to show off your knowledge, or nervousness; but in most cases, long answers are not a good idea. The interviewer probably has lots of ground to cover, and long-winded answers will not help this task. As a general rule, your answers should not run much over a minute or two without inviting the interviewer either to follow up or to move on to the next question. Of course, you'll want to give clear, detailed answers with examples, as described above. Keep in mind, though, that an interview is a conversation—and as is true of any conversation, a dialogue in which people take turns is better than a long monologue.

© iStockPhoto/Neustockimages.

Job interviews can be difficult. Think back to your last job interview. What did you do well for the interview? What could you do better next time?

REFLECTION

SELF-CRITICISM AND SELF-PRAISE

Perhaps the thing I have found most difficult as a student from Japan studying in Canada is the performance evaluations that have been part of my work placements. These evaluations involve a self-assessment of strengths and areas for improvement. Then, together with my supervisor we develop goals for my professional development. I enjoy discovering areas for improvement and developing goals for myself, but when it comes to describing my strengths I feel very uncomfortable. My supervisors have been sympathetic, and I believe they know how much I want to improve my skills, but they always say I am too hard on myself. In my culture, to say I am good at something or to describe myself as superior in some area of the job would be considered rude and boastful. I find it hard to even think in such terms. I don't find it distressing to be self-critical, but as hard as I try, I can't bring myself to "sing my own praises." I realize "selling yourself" is a skill you need in the North American job market, but I'm appreciative of my colleagues' patience because I feel I'm a slow learner in this regard.

4. Follow the Interviewer's Lead   Let the interviewer set the emotional tone of the session. If he or she is informal, you can loosen up a bit; but if the approach is formal and dignified, you should act the same way. Since a great deal depends on the personal interaction between the interviewer and the candidate, you should try to match the interviewer's style without becoming insincere. If the tone of the interview does not fit well with you, this may be a signal that you will not feel comfortable with this organization. It may be wise to see whether the interviewer's approach represents the whole company, either by asking for a tour or by speaking to other employees on your own. This desire to learn about the company shows that you are a thinking person who takes the job seriously, so your curiosity is not likely to offend the interviewer.

5. Arrive Prepared to Answer the Interviewer's Questions   Whatever specific questions you might be asked, the employer is always asking, "How can you help us?" If you remember this, you can respond in ways that show how you can meet the employer's needs. If you have spent time learning about your potential employer, you will be in a good position to talk about that company's needs and how you can satisfy them. Knowing that you can indeed help the company, should raise your self-confidence and lead you to feel more comfortable when facing a potential employer (Linden et al., 1993). Table 12.1 provides suggestions for answering common questions employers ask.

6. Arrive Prepared to Ask the Interviewer Questions   Near the end of an employment interview, it is typical for an interviewer to ask the applicant, "Do you have any questions?" An ineffective response would be "No, I can't think of any," which suggests a lack of initiative and inquisitiveness. Instead, go prepared with a list of questions about the company and the position you are applying for (Fry, 2003). Don't forget that you are trying to determine if this job is a good match for you, so you are interviewing the company as much as they are interviewing you. Good questions will allow you to demonstrate that you have done your homework on the organization. It is wise to save questions about salary and benefits to later stages of the negotiation process. In this interview your goal is to show the organization what you can offer them.

Good questions will allow you to demonstrate the homework you've done on the organization. For example, you could say, "I saw on your website that the company is developing new training programs. How might these programs help me in my position?" Questions to avoid include those about salary or benefits—at least in an initial interview. Such questions focus on what the company will do for you, whereas your goal is to show what you can do for the company.

Table 12.1 ● Common Employment Interview Questions

1. Tell me something about yourself. This broad, opening question gives you a chance to describe what qualities you possess that can help the employer. Remember that your response should be job-related—this is not the time to talk about where you grew up or your hobbies.

2. What makes you think you're qualified to work for this company? This question may sound like an attack, but it really is another way of asking, "How can you help us?" It gives you another chance to show how your skills and interests fit with the company's goals.

3. What accomplishments have given you the most satisfaction? The accomplishments you choose need not be directly related to former employment; however, they should demonstrate qualities that would help you be successful in the job for which you are being interviewed. Your accomplishments might demonstrate creativity, perseverance in the face of obstacles, self-control, or dependability.

4. Why do you want to work for us? Employers are impressed by candidates who have done their homework about the organization. This question offers the chance to demonstrate your knowledge of the employer's organization and to show how your talents fit with its goals.

5. What university subjects did you like best and least? Whatever your answer, show how your preferences about your courses are related to the job you are applying for. When necessary, show how apparently unrelated subjects do illustrate your readiness for a job. For example, you might say, "I really enjoyed cultural anthropology courses because they showed me the importance of understanding different cultures. I think those courses would help me a lot in relating to our overseas customers and suppliers."

6. Where do you see yourself in five years? This familiar question is really asking, "How ambitious are you?" "How compatible are your plans with this company's goals?" "How realistic are you?" If you have studied the industry and the company, your answer will show an understanding of the workplace realities and a sense of personal planning that should impress an employer.

7. What major problems have you faced, and how have you dealt with them? The specific problem isn't as important as the way you responded to it. What (admirable) qualities did you demonstrate as you grappled with the problem you have chosen to describe? Perseverance? Calmness? Creativity? You may even choose to describe a problem you didn't handle well, and show what you learned from it that can help you in the future.

8. What are your greatest strengths? The "strength" question offers another chance to sell yourself. Emphasize qualities that apply to employment. "I'm a pretty good athlete" isn't a persuasive answer unless you can show how your skill is job-related. For instance, you might talk about being a team player, your competitive drive, or your ability to work hard and not quit in the face of adversity.

9. What are your greatest weaknesses? Whatever answer you give to the "weakness" question, try to show how your awareness of your flaws makes you a desirable person to hire. There are four ways to respond to this question.
   - You can discuss a weakness that also can be viewed as a strength: "When I'm involved in a big project I tend to work too hard, and I can wear myself out."
   - You can discuss a weakness that is not related to the job at hand, but then end your answer with a strength that is related to the job. For a job in sales: "I'm not very interested in accounting. I'd much rather work with people selling a product I believe in."
   - You can discuss a weakness the interviewer already knows about from your resumé application, or the interview. "I don't have a lot of experience in multimedia design at this early stage of my career. But my experience in other kinds of computer programming and my internship in graphic arts have convinced me that I can learn quickly."
   - You can discuss a weakness you have been working to remedy. "I know being bilingual is important for this job. That's why I've enrolled in a French course."

SOURCES: Adapted from R.B. Adler and G. Rodman (2008), *Understanding human communication*, 10th edn (pp. A16–A19). New York: Oxford University Press; and K.O. Locker, (2000). *Business and Administrative Communication*, 5th edn (pp. 574–5). Homewood, IL: Irwin.

After the Interview

Follow up your meeting with a note of thanks to the interviewer. (A typed letter is usually more appropriate than either a handwritten note or an email.) Since most candidates don't take this step, your letter will be especially impressive. Express your appreciation for the chance to get acquainted with the company, and let the interviewer know that the session left you excited about the chance of becoming associated with it. It's also a good idea to mention specific information you learned about the company during the interview: "I enjoyed hearing about the new software program your company is using to facilitate performance reviews." Whenever possible, show how the things you learned make you a good match for the job: "My familiarity with a variety of computer programs should help me learn your new system quickly, and my training in communication will assist me in conducting performance reviews." Finally, your note can confirm the next steps in the interviewing process: "You explained that I should be hearing from the company within the next week. I'll be looking forward to speaking with you."

✓ CHECK IT!

Describe what an interviewee can do (before, during, and after) a job interview in order to make the interview successful.

SUMMARY

Effective interpersonal skills are essential for effectiveness in the workplace, so much so that they are considered essential employability skills by the Conference Board of Canada. Relationships in the workplace include both formal and informal networks, and using upward, downward, and horizontal communication. On-the-job communication often takes place in work groups and teams, which are work groups with some unique characteristics. Groups and teams offer some advantages in the workplace, but also have some drawbacks. In addition, work groups go through predictable stages, create their own cultures, and provide opportunities for leadership, power, and influence.

Leaders can be designated or emerge from a group of co-workers. In addition, leadership can also be centralized or distributed throughout a work group. Leaders influence group members through their use of different kinds of power. French and Raven (1968) described the five types of social power: legitimate, expert, reward, coercive, and referent. Well-developed and flexible interpersonal communication skills are essential to both effective leadership and effective group membership.

Interviews are used for a variety of purposes. Before an employment interview, an applicant should clarify the interviewer's goals and come prepared. During an interview, it is important to make a good first impression and opening, and to give answers that are clear, detailed, and focused. A good interviewee will follow the interviewer's lead, be prepared to answer questions that the interviewer is likely to ask, and ask questions about the company and the position. When the interview is over, the applicant should send a thank-you note and confirm the next steps in the interview process.

> ## MULTIPLE-CHOICE QUESTIONS

1. When subordinates communicate with their boss according to officially established channels, the communication is referred to as
   a. informal communication.
   b. downward communication.
   c. horizontal communication.
   d. upward communication.

2. The transit authority has issued an official statement warning employees not to use their cellphones when they are working. The statement says employees may use their phones on their breaks. Sam, an employee of the transit authority, has told his co-workers that he heard that the company has recently fired two employees for using their cellphones during their breaks. Sam's communication with his co-workers serves which function?
   a. confirms the formal message
   b. contradicts the formal message
   c. expands the formal message
   d. circumvents the formal message

3. The fourth stage in group decision making, in which the group members not only accept the decision, but also endorse it, is called
   a. reinforcement.
   b. emergence.
   c. conflict.
   d. orientation.

4. Work groups are best suited to uncomplicated tasks for which there is a very limited amount of time.
   a. true
   b. false

5. The culture of work groups can involve which of the following dimensions?

   a. sociability
   b. distribution of power
   c. tolerance of new ideas
   d. all of the above

6. Teams whose memberships transcend the boundaries of location and time are called virtual teams.
   a. true
   b. false

7. Salome has been appointed to lead the occupational health and safety committee in her workplace. Her leadership would best be described as
   a. emergent.
   b. coercive.
   c. designated.
   d. distributed.

8. Unlike informal conversations between people in a workplace, an interview always has a goal.
   a. true
   b. false

9. Ricardo is very aloof with the group he manages, and he often hints that if people complain about the schedule or working conditions, he will have to increase the number of evening shifts and get rid of the break room. These strategies best reflect Ricardo's use of
   a. referent power.
   b. reward power.
   c. expert power.
   d. coercive power.

10. Following up a job interview by sending a note of thanks is generally not acceptable practice.
    a. true
    b. false

Answers: 1. d; 2. b; 3. a; 4. b; 5. d; 6. a; 7. c; 8. a; 9. d; 10. b

ACTIVITIES

1. Invitation to Insight

Think about group projects you have done throughout your school or work career. Choose a successful project and describe the factors that made the group work effectively. Now contrast that group experience with one that was less satisfying. What are the differences between the two experiences? Use the characteristics of work groups and teams, the personal skills in groups and teams, and the information about group cultures as the basis for your comparisons.

2. Invitation to Insight

Analyze the types of power used by various members of your class. Which types of power have you observed? What types of power does your professor use? What kinds of power do you have in your class? Who has the most influence? Why do you think so?

3. Ethical Challenge

Imagine yourself interviewing for a job you really want. Consider how you will represent yourself in a way that maximizes the chances of your receiving an offer of employment. To what degree is the narrative that you would create in presenting yourself, accurate; to what degree is it less than totally honest? Could you justify the approach you would take as being ethical?

4. Role Play

Describe to a partner a job that you would like to apply for. Have your partner take the role of the interviewer and you take the role of the interviewee. Use Table 12.1, "Common Employment Interview Questions," to help guide the interview. Role-play the job interview and ask your partner to give you feedback. Refer to the "During the Interview" section on pages 397–400 of this chapter for criteria to evaluate your communication during the interview. Now, reverse roles.

DISCUSSION QUESTIONS

1. What functions can informal communication serve in a workplace? Are they important? Why or why not?

2. Describe some of the communication skills that can help to build a positive communication climate in a working group. How much influence can one group member have? Why do you think so?

3. Discuss the advantages and disadvantages of working in virtual teams. What steps can be taken to mitigate some of the drawbacks of relying so heavily on computer-mediated communication to get work done?

4. Are there situations where the use of coercive power is appropriate? When and why, or why not?

5. In your experience, what kinds of skills and personal qualities do people who

   have referent power possess? Do you think these skills and qualities can be developed? Why or why not?

6. In order to be competitive and attract the best employees, many companies (e.g., Google, Apple, and the Rotman School of Management as described in this chapter) work hard to create an organizational climate (a big part of which is communication climate) that is attractive to smart, creative people. They provide rewards that are both tangible (e.g., a cafeteria with healthy, good-tasting food; a fitness centre) and intangible (e.g., the opportunity for employees to focus on work that interests them most). What are you looking for in a workplace?

JOURNAL IDEAS

1. Think about a group or team you were involved in, the roles you took, and the types of power you had. Were you satisfied with your contributions? What might you do differently if you were involved in a similar situation in the future?

2. Think about teachers or supervisors you have enjoyed working with. What types of power did they use? What did the class or group members contribute to this experience? Why do you think you liked learning with or working for these people?

GLOSSARY

abstraction ladder A range of more-to-less abstract terms describing an event or object.

achievement culture Term used to describe a culture that places a high value on the achievement of material success and a focus on the task at hand.

advising response A listening response in which the receiver offers suggestions about how the speaker should deal with a problem.

aggressiveness A verbal attack that demeans another person's self-concept and inflicts psychological pain.

ambiguous language Language that consists of words and phrases that have more than one commonly accepted definition.

ambiguous response A response with more than one meaning, leaving the other person unsure of the responder's position.

ambushing A style in which the receiver listens carefully in order to gather information to use in an attack on the speaker.

analyzing response A listening response in which the listener offers an interpretation of a speaker's message.

androgynous Possessing both masculine and feminine traits.

argumentativeness Presenting and defending positions on issues while attacking positions taken by others.

assertion A direct expression of a sender's needs, thoughts, or feelings, delivered in a way that does not attack a receiver's dignity. See also *passive aggression* and *indirect communication*.

asynchronous A time gap between when the message was sent and when it is received.

attachment Lasting social–emotional relationships, such as with an infant and its mother or father.

attending A phase of the listening process in which the communicator focuses on a message, excluding other messages.

attribution The process of attaching meaning to another person's behaviour.

avoiding A relational stage immediately before terminating, in which the partners minimize contact with one another.

barrier behaviours Strategies designed to create a barrier (or fix a broken one) between ourselves and other people.

benevolent lie A lie that is not considered malicious by the person who tells it.

bonding A stage of relational development in which the partners make symbolic public gestures to show that their relationship exists.

boundaries Limits that a family sets on its members' actions, such as what topics are permissible to discuss, how to discuss certain topics, or whom family members may interact with outside the family.

breadth In the *social penetration model*, it is the first dimension of self-disclosure; it comprises the range of subjects being discussed.

"but" statement A statement in which the second half cancels the meaning of the first, for example, "I'd like to help you, *but* I have to go or I'll miss my bus."

certainty Absolute belief that one's position is correct and the ideas of others are not worth considering. Likely to arouse defensiveness, according to Gibb.

channel The medium through which a message passes from sender to receiver.

chaotic family A family that has erratic leadership or no leadership at all, dramatic shifts in roles, unclear roles, and impulsive decision making.

chronemics The study of how people use and structure time.

circumscribing A relational stage in which partners begin to reduce the scope of their contact and commitment to one another.

closed questions Questions that limit the range of possible responses, such as questions that seek a yes or no answer.

co-culture A group within an encompassing culture with a perceived identity.

coercive power Influence achieved by using unpleasant consequences or threats to punish others.

cognitive complexity The ability to construct a variety of frameworks for viewing an issue.

cognitive conservatism The tendency to seek out information that conforms to an existing self-concept and to ignore information that contradicts it.

cognitive reappraisal Rethinking or reinterpreting the meaning of a situation in ways that change the emotional impact.

collaborative problem solving An approach to resolving conflict that requires participants to show concern for both themselves and others.

collectivistic culture A culture whose members feel loyalties and obligations to an in-group, such as one's extended family, community, or even the organization one works for.

communication climate The emotional tone of a relationship between two or more individuals.

communication competence The ability to achieve one's goals in a manner that is personally acceptable and, ideally, acceptable to others.

communication rules Sets of (usually) unwritten principles that families, as unique cultures, have about a variety of communication practices. Despite their similar properties, not all families communicate in the same way.

comparison level (CL) The minimum standard of what behaviour is acceptable from a relationship partner.

comparison level of alternatives (CL^alt) A comparison between the rewards one is receiving in a present situation and those one could expect to receive in others.

complaining A disagreeing message that directly or indirectly communicates dissatisfaction with another person.

complementary conflict style The use by partners in a conflict of different, but mutually reinforcing behaviour.

compromise An approach to conflict resolution in which both people attain at least part of what they want through self-sacrifice.

computer-mediated communication (CMC) Communication that occurs through computerized channels (e.g., email, instant messaging, computer conferencing).

confirmation bias A tendency to seek out, remember, and organize information that supports our impressions and beliefs.

confirming communication A message that expresses caring or respect for another person.

conflict An expressed struggle between at least two interdependent people who perceive incompatible goals, scarce rewards, and interference from the other person in achieving their goals.

conflict rituals Repeating patterns of interlocking conflict behaviour.

conformity orientation The degree to which family communication stresses uniformity of attitudes, values, and beliefs.

connection–autonomy dialectic The tension between the need for integration and the need for independence in a relationship.

content message A message that communicates information about the subject being discussed. See also *relational message*.

controlling communication According to Gibb, messages that attempt to impose some sort of outcome on another person, resulting in a defensive response.

convergence The process of adapting one's speech style to match that of others with whom one wants to identify. See also *divergence*.

conversation orientation The degree to which families favour an open climate of discussion of a wide array of topics.

counterfeit questions Questions that are disguised attempts to send a message rather than elicit information.

culture According to Samovar and Porter, "the language, values, beliefs, traditions, and customs people share and learn."

debilitative emotions Emotions that prevent a person from functioning effectively.

de-escalatory spiral A reciprocal communication pattern in which one person's non-threatening behaviour leads to reduced hostility by the other, with the level of hostility steadily decreasing. See also *spiral* and *escalatory spiral*.

defensive listening A response style in which the receiver perceives a speaker's comments as an attack.

defensiveness The attempt to protect a presenting image that a person believes is being attacked.

depth In the *social penetration model*, it is the second dimension of self-disclosure; here, the people interacting shift from relatively unrevealing messages to more personal ones.

description Messages that describe a speaker's position without evaluating others.

designated leader The person (or people) with official titles that indicate authority, for example, "manager."

dialectical tensions Relational tensions that arise when two opposing or incompatible forces exist simultaneously.

differentiating A relational stage in which the partners re-establish their individual identities after having bonded together.

direct aggression An expression of the sender's thoughts and/or feelings that attacks the position and dignity of the receiver.

disagreeing message A message that essentially tells to another person, "You are wrong"; includes argumentativeness, complaining, and aggressiveness.

disconfirming communication A message that expresses a lack of caring or respect for another person.

disengaged family Families with too little cohesion in which members have limited attachment or commitment to one another.

disfluencies Non-linguistic verbalizations, for example, *um, er, ah*.

distorted feedback Information that can skew a person's self-concept; such feedback might be excessively favourable because of others' less-than-honest behaviour (e.g., a boss may claim to be an excellent manager because his assistants pour on false praise in order to keep their jobs).

distributed leadership Several people working collectively to influence others and achieve goals rather than relying on one person.

divergence A way of speaking that emphasizes difference from others. See also *convergence*.

downward communication Communication from managers to subordinates.

dyad Two communicators who interact with each other.

dysfunctional conflict Harmful conflicts characterized by communication that is coercive, uncooperative, and unfocused, which often results in a win–lose outcome and the damaging of a relationship.

emblems Culturally understood substitutes (nonverbal behaviour) for verbal expressions.

emergent leader Leader chosen by the group either formally or informally.

emotions Feeling states that includes physiological changes, a cognitive interpretations, and an outward expression.

emotional contagion The process by which emotions are transferred from one person to another.

emotional intelligence The ability to recognize emotions in ourselves and others, to manage our emotions, and to use emotions to enhance our self-motivation, our empathy, and our relationships with others.

emotionally counterfeit Communications where the sender thinks she or he is expressing a feeling when, in fact, her or his statement is devoid of emotional content.

emotive language Language that expresses the sender's attitude rather than simply offering an objective description.

empathizing response A listening response that conveys identification with a speaker's perceptions and emotions.

empathy The ability to project oneself into another person's point of view in an attempt to experience his or her thoughts and feelings.

enmeshed family Families with too much consensus, too little independence, and a very high demand for loyalty.

environment Both the physical setting in which communication occurs and the personal perspectives of the people involved.

equality A type of supportive communication described by Gibb which suggests that the sender regards the receiver with respect.

equivocal language Ambiguous language that has two or more equally plausible meanings.

escalatory spiral A reciprocal communication pattern in which one person's attack leads to a counterattack by the other, with the level of hostility steadily increasing. See also *spiral* and *de-escalatory spiral*.

ethnocentrism An attitude that one's own culture is superior to that of others.

euphemism A pleasant term substituted for a blunt one in order to soften the impact of unpleasant information.

evaluating response A listening response that appraises a sender's thoughts or behaviour and implies that the person evaluating is qualified to pass judgment on the other.

evaluation A message in which a sender judges a receiver in some way, usually resulting in a defensive response.

experimenting An early stage in relational development, consisting of a search for common ground. If the experimentation is successful, the relationship progresses to intensifying. If not, it may go no further.

expert power Influence that arises from the group's belief that an individual has a high level of knowledge or specialized skill.

expression–privacy dialectic The tension between the desire to share information, and the need keep things confidential within a relationship.

face The image an individual wants to project to the world. See also *presenting self*.

face-threatening acts Behaviour by another that is perceived as attacking an individual's presenting image or face.

facework Actions people take to preserve their own and others' presenting images.

facilitative emotions Emotions that contribute to effective functioning.

factual statement A statement that can be verified as true or false. See also *inferential statement, opinion statement*.

fallacy of approval The irrational belief that it is vital to win the approval of virtually every person with whom a communicator interacts.

fallacy of catastrophic expectations The irrational belief that the worst possible outcome will probably occur.

fallacy of causation The irrational belief that emotions are caused by others and not by the person who has them.

fallacy of helplessness The irrational belief that satisfaction in life is determined by forces beyond one's control.

fallacy of overgeneralization Irrational beliefs in which conclusions (usually negative) are based on limited evidence, or communicators exaggerate their shortcomings.

fallacy of perfection The irrational belief that a worthwhile communicator should be able to handle every situation with complete confidence and skill.

fallacy of *should* The irrational belief that people *should* behave in the most desirable way.

family A system with two or more interdependent people who have a common past history and a present reality, and who expect to influence each other in the future.

family of origin The family in which a person grows up.

filling in the gaps A listening habit that involves adding details never mentioned by a speaker to complete a message.

formal communication An interaction that follows officially established channels.

functional conflict Beneficial conflicts characterized by communication that is respectful, co-operative, and focused, which results in the resolution of a problem and the strengthening of a relationship.

fundamental attribution error A mistaken human tendency that has two main parts: on the one hand, when others suffer, we often blame the problem on their personal qualities and we underestimate the impact of the situation; on the other hand, when we experience failure, we find explanations outside ourselves, but we are quick to take credit when we succeed.

gender Psychological sex type.

groupthink The phenomenon of group members suspending their critical thinking in order to achieve agreement.

halo effect The power of a first impression to influence subsequent perceptions.

haptics Communication involving touch.

hearing The first stage in the listening process, in which sound waves are received by a communicator.

high-context culture A culture that relies heavily on verbal and non-verbal cues to maintain social harmony.

horizontal communication Communication between people who do not have direct supervisor–subordinate relationships.

"I" language A statement that describes the speaker's reaction to another person's behaviour without making judgments about its worth. See also *"we" language* and *"you" language*.

identity management The communication strategies people use to influence how others view them.

illustrators Non-verbal behaviours that accompany and support verbal messages.

impersonal response A disconfirming response that is superficial or trite.

impervious response A disconfirming response that ignores another person's attempt to communicate.

incongruous response A disconfirming response in which two messages, one of which is usually non-verbal, contradict one another.

indirect communication Hinting at a message instead of expressing thoughts and feelings directly. See also *passive aggression* and *assertion*.

individualistic culture A culture in which people view their primary responsibility as being to themselves.

inferential statement A statement based on an interpretation of evidence. See also *factual statement*, *opinion statement*.

informal communication Communication based on friendships, shared personal or career interests, and proximity.

in-groups Groups with which an individual identifies her or himself.

initiating The first stage in relational development, in which those who are interacting express interest in one another; making contact; demonstrating that you are worth talking to.

insulated listening A style in which the receiver ignores undesirable information.

integrating A relational stage in which those who are interacting begin to take on a single identity; taking on an identity as a social unit; routines, rituals, and obligations grow.

integration–separation dialectic The tension between the desire for connection with others and the desire for independence.

intensifying A relational stage following experimenting, in which those who are interacting move toward integration by increasing their amount of contact, as well as the breadth and depth of their self-disclosure.

intercultural communication Communication that occurs when members of two or more cultures or other groups exchange messages in a manner that is influenced by their different cultural perceptions and symbol systems.

interpretation The process of attaching meaning to sense data.

interrupting response A disconfirming response in which one communicator interrupts another.

intimacy A state achieved by intellectual, emotional, and/or physical closeness, as well as shared activities.

intimate distance One of Hall's four distance zones, ranging from skin contact to eighteen inches away.

irrelevant response A disconfirming response in which one communicator's comments bear no relationship to the previous speaker's ideas.

"it" statement A statement in which *it* replaces the personal pronoun *I*, making the statement less direct and more evasive.

Johari Window A model that describes the relationship between self-disclosure and self-awareness.

kinesics The study of body movements.

legitimate power Influence that arises when the group believes that the person in charge is qualified to have authority.

lie A deliberate act of deception.

linguistic relativism The notion that the language individuals use exerts a strong influence on their perceptions.

listening The process of hearing, attending, understanding, remembering, and responding to messages.

lose–lose problem solving An approach to conflict resolution in which neither party achieves its goals.

low-context culture A culture that uses language primarily to express thoughts, feelings, and ideas as clearly and logically as possible.

manipulators Movements in which one part of the body grooms, massages, rubs, holds, fidgets with, pinches, picks, or otherwise manipulates another part.

media richness A concept used to describe the amount and type of information that can be conveyed through a communication channel.

metacommunication Messages (usually relational) that refer to other messages: communication about communication.

myth of perfection Along with *obsolete information* and *distorted feedback*, another cause for low self-esteem or skewed self-concept that is common in our society. From the time most of us learn to understand language, we are exposed to models who appear to be perfect at whatever they do. As we grow up, though, we learn that this "perfection" is a facade.

narratives The stories we use to describe our personal worlds.

negative mood A state of being where people view themselves more harshly than the facts warrant (e.g., we have all experienced a temporary case of the "uglies," convinced we look much worse than others say that we do). Research confirms what common sense suggests: people are more critical of themselves when they are experiencing negative moods than when they are feeling more positive.

negotiation A process in which two or more people discuss specific proposals in order to find a mutually acceptable agreement.

networking The process of deliberately meeting people and maintaining contacts to get career information, advice, and leads.

neutrality A defence-arousing behaviour described by Gibb in which a sender expresses indifference toward a receiver.

noise External, physiological, and psychological distractions that interfere with the accurate transmission and reception of a message.

non-assertion The inability to express one's thoughts or feelings when necessary. Non-assertion may be due to a lack of confidence, communication skill, or both.

non-verbal communication Messages expressed by other than linguistic means.

nurturing culture A culture that regards the support of relationships as an especially important goal.

obsolete information Information that can skew a person's self-concept; such information is usually out-dated and unhelpful to the person in question (e.g., perhaps your jokes used to be well-received, or your grades were high, or your work was superior, but now the facts have changed).

openness–closedness dialectic The tension between the desire to be honest and open, and the desire for privacy.

open questions Questions that allow for a variety of extended responses.

opinion statement A statement based on a speaker's beliefs. See also *factual statement*, *inferential statement*.

organization The stage in the perception process that involves arranging data in a meaningful way.

out-groups Groups that an individual sees as different from him or herself.

paralanguage Non-linguistic means of vocal expression (e.g., rate, pitch, and tone).

parallel conflict style The practice by partners in a conflict of shifting from complementary to symmetrical patterns from one conflict issue to another.

paraphrasing Restating a speaker's thoughts and feelings in the listener's own words.

passive aggression An indirect expression of aggression delivered in a way that allows the sender to maintain a facade of kindness. See also *indirect communication* and *assertion*.

perceived self The person we believe ourselves to be in moments of candour. It may be identical with or different from the presenting and desired selves.

perception checking A three-part method for verifying the accuracy of interpretations, including a description of the sense data, two possible interpretations, and a request for confirmation of the interpretations.

permanence How long a message endures.

personal distance One of Hall's four distance zones, ranging from 18 inches to 4 feet away.

personal space The distance we put between ourselves and others.

phonological rules Rules governing the way in which sounds are pronounced in a language.

power A source of influence, such as expert power.

power distance The degree to which members of a society accept the unequal distribution of power among members.

powerless speech mannerisms Forms of speech that express to others a lack of power in the speaker (i.e., hedges, hesitations, intensifiers, and so on).

pragmatic rules Rules that govern the interpretation of language in terms of its social context. See also *semantic rules* and *syntactic rules*.

prejudice An unfairly biased and intolerant attitude toward members of an out-group.

presenting self The image a person presents to others. It may be identical with or different from the perceived and desired selves. See also *face*.

problem orientation A supportive style of communication described by Gibb in which the communicators focus on working together to solve their problems instead of trying to impose their own solutions on one another.

provisionalism A supportive style of communication described by Gibb in which a sender expresses open-mindedness to the ideas and opinions of others.

proxemics The study of how people and animals use space.

pseudo-listening An imitation of true listening in which the receiver's mind is elsewhere.

psychological sex type A person, regardless of his or her biological sex, can act in a masculine manner, a feminine manner, or exhibit both types of characteristics (androgynous), or exhibit neither strongly (undifferentiated); the word *gender* is a short-hand term for psychological sex-type.

public distance One of Hall's four distance zones, extending outward from 12 feet away.

punctuation The process of determining the causal order of events.

qualitative interpersonal communication Interpersonal communication that occurs when people treat one another as unique individuals, regardless of the context in which the interaction occurs or the number of people involved.

quantitative interpersonal communication Any interaction or communication between, or among, a small number of people, usually two.

questioning response A listening response in which the receiver seeks additional information from the sender.

rational–emotive approach A method for getting rid of debilitative feelings while remaining sensitive to the more facilitative emotions; the method is based on the idea that the key to changing feelings is to change unproductive thinking.

reference groups Groups against which we compare ourselves, which thereby influence our self-concept and self-esteem.

referent power Influence that comes from group members' liking and respect for one another.

reflected appraisal The theory that a person's self-concept matches the way the person believes others regard him or her.

regulators Non-verbal behaviours that control verbal interaction. The best example of such regulation is the wide array of turn-taking signals that people utilize in everyday conversation.

relational conflict style A pattern of managing disagreements that repeats itself over time.

relational messages Messages that expresses the social relationship between two or more individuals. See also *content message.*

relational maintenance Communication aimed at keeping relationships operating smoothly and satisfactorily (e.g., behaving in a positive way, being open, and assuring your partner that you're committed to the relationship).

relative language Words that gain their meaning by comparison.

remembering A phase of the listening process in which a message is recalled.

responding A phase of the listening process in which feedback occurs, offering evidence that the message has been received.

reward power Influence achieved by giving incentives and compensation.

rigid family Families with authoritarian leadership, strict discipline, roles that are inflexible, and unchanging rules.

roles The long-term "parts" members play within the family unit. Roles shape the way family members communicate—some are obvious: income earner, child-care provider, and so on; others are less obvious, but just as important: harmonizer, problem solver, tension reliever, helpless victim, and so on.

rumination Recurrent negative thoughts not demanded by the immediate environment. Sometimes called "brooding."

selection A phase of the perception process in which a communicator attends to a stimulus from the environment. Also, a way communicators manage dialectical tensions by responding to one end of the dialectical spectrum and ignoring the other.

selective listening A listening style in which the receiver responds only to messages that interest her or him.

self-concept The relatively stable set of perceptions each individual holds of him or herself. See also *self-esteem.*

self-control The ability to change (one's thoughts, behaviours, emotions, etc.) in order to conform to an expectation.

self-disclosure The process of deliberately revealing information about oneself that is important and that would not normally be known by others.

self-esteem The part of the self-concept that involves evaluations of self-worth. See also *self-concept.*

self-fulfilling prophecy A person's expectations of an event and his or her subsequent behaviour based on those expectations that make the outcome more likely to occur than would otherwise have been true.

self-monitoring The process of observing one's behaviour and using these observations to shape the way one behaves.

self-serving bias The tendency to judge one's self in the most generous terms possible, while being more critical of others.

self-talk The non-vocal, internal monologue that is our process of thinking.

semantic rules Rules that govern the meaning of language, as opposed to its structure. See also *pragmatic rule* and *syntactic rules.*

significant other A person whose opinion is important enough to affect one's self-concept strongly.

silent listening Staying attentive and non-verbally responsive without offering verbal feedback.

sincere questions Genuine attempts to elicit information from others.

social comparison An evaluation of oneself by way of comparison to others.

social distance One of Hall's distance zones, ranging from four to twelve feet away.

social exchange theory The supposition that we use an economic model on which to base some of our relationships. This approach suggests that we often seek out people who can give us rewards that are greater than or equal to the costs we encounter in dealing with them.

social expectations A societal convention that leads most of us to talk freely about our shortcomings while downplaying our accomplishments. For example, it's okay to proclaim that you are miserable if you have failed to do well on a project, but it's boastful to express your pride at a job well done. It's fine to remark that you feel unattractive, but it's egocentric to say that you think you look good.

social loafing The tendency for people to work less hard in a group.

social penetration model A model that describes relationships in terms of their *breadth* and *depth*.

spiral A reciprocal communication pattern in which messages reinforce one another. See also *escalatory spiral* and *de-escalatory spiral*.

spontaneity A supportive communication behaviour described by Gibb in which the sender expresses a message without any attempt to manipulate the receiver.

stability–change dialectic The tension between the desire to keep a relationship predictable and stable, and the desire for novelty and change.

stage hogging A listening style in which the receiver is more concerned with making his or her own point than in understanding the speaker.

stagnating Term used to describe a relational stage characterized by declining enthusiasm and standardized forms of behaviour.

standpoint theory A body of scholarship that explores how one's position in a society shapes one's view of society in general, and of specific individuals.

static evaluation Treating people or objects as if they were unchanging.

stereotyping Exaggerated beliefs associated with a categorizing system.

strategy A defence-arousing style of communication described by Gibb in which a sender tries to manipulate or deceive a receiver.

superiority A defence-arousing style of communication described by Gibb in which the sender states or implies that the receiver is not worthy of respect.

supporting response A listening response in which the receiver reveals her or his solidarity with the speaker's situation.

symmetrical conflict style The use of the same tactics by both partners in a conflict.

synchronous Refers to communication that occurs in real time so that messages are sent and received simultaneously.

synergy The creativity that results from the integration of several individuals' thinking.

syntactic rules Rules that govern the ways symbols can be arranged, as opposed to the meanings of those symbols. See also *semantic rules* and *pragmatic rules*.

system A group, such as a family, whose members interact with one another to form a whole.

tangential response A disconfirming response that uses the speaker's remark as a starting point for a shift to a new topic.

teams Specialized types of work groups often comprising members with distinct and complementary skills and resources.

terminating The conclusion of a relationship, characterized by the acknowledgment of one or both partners that the relationship is over.

territory A stationary area claimed by a person or animal.

transactional communication A dynamic process created by the participants through their interaction with one another.

uncertainty avoidance The extent to which a culture's members feel threatened by ambiguous situations and try to avoid them.

understanding A stage in the listening process in which the receiver attaches meaning to a message.

upward communication Communication from subordinates to their superiors.

virtual teams Teams whose membership transcends the boundaries of location and time.

"we" language The use of first-person-plural pronouns to include others, either appropriately or inappropriately. Language that implies the issue being discussed is the concern and responsibility of both the speaker and receiver of a message. See also *"I" language* and *"you" language*.

win–lose problem solving An approach to conflict resolution in which one person reaches her or his goal at the expense of the other.

win–win problem solving An approach to conflict resolution in which people work together to satisfy all their goals.

work groups Three or more people who have ongoing interactions with each other and depend on each other to accomplish a goal.

"you" language A statement that expresses or implies a judgment of the other person. See also *evaluation*, *"I" language*, and *"we" language*.

REFERENCES

Aamodt, M.G., and Custer, H. (2006). "Who can best catch a liar? A meta-analysis of individual differences in detecting deception," *The Forensic Examiner*, *15*(1), 6–11.

Aboud, F.E., and Mendelson, M.J. (1998). "Determinants of friendship selection and quality: Developmental perspectives," in W.M. Bukowski and A.F. Newcomb (eds), *The company they keep: Friendship in childhood and adolescence*, 87–112. New York: Cambridge University Press.

Adamopoulos, J. (1991). "The emergence of interpersonal behavior: Diachronic and cross-cultural processes in the evolution of intimacy," in S. Ting-Toomey and F. Korzenny (eds), *Cross-cultural interpersonal communication*, 155–170. Newbury Park, CA: Sage.

——, and Bontempo, R.N. (1986). "Diachronic universals in interpersonal structures," *Journal of Cross-Cultural Psychology*, *17*, 169–189.

Adams, M. (2003). *Fire and ice: The United States, Canada and the myth of converging values*. Toronto: Penguin.

—— (2005). "Sex and fire. Religion, homosexuality and authority in Canada and the United Sates," *Environics Research Group News*, 7 April.

—— (2007a). "Surprise, Canadian pluralism is working," *Environics Research Group News*, 20 November.

—— (2007b). *Unlikely utopia: The surprising triumph of Canadian pluralism*. Toronto: Viking.

—— (2010). "Michael Adams on how we see ourselves," *2010 in Review. Canada's Values*, 23 December.

Adeniran, R., Healy, D., Sharp, H., and Williams, J.M.G. (1996). "Interpersonal sensitivity predicts depressive symptom response to the circadian rhythm disruption of night work," *Psychological Medicine*, *26*, 1211–1221.

Adler, R.B., and Elmhorst, J.M. (2008). *Communicating at work: Principles and practices for business and the professions*, 8th edn. New York: McGraw-Hill.

—— (2010). *Communicating at work: Principles and practices for business and the professions*, 10th edn. New York: McGraw-Hill.

——, and Rodman, G. (2008). *Understanding human communication*, 10th edn. New York: Oxford University Press.

Adler, T. (1993). "Congressional staffers witness miracle of touch," *APA Monitor*, February, 12–13.

Afifi, T., Coughlin, J., and Afifi, W. (2007). "The dark side (and light side) of avoidance and secrets," in B. Spitzberg and W. Cupach (eds), *The dark side of interpersonal communication*. New Jersey: Lawrence Erlbaum.

——, Joesph, A., and Aldeis, D. (2012). "The standards for openness hypothesis: Why women find (conflict) avoidance more dissatisfying than men," *Journal of Social and Personal Relationships*, *29*(1), 102–125.

——, McManus, T., Steuber, K., and Coho, A. (2009). "Verbal avoidance and dissatisfaction in intimate conflict situations," *Human Communication Research*, *35*, 357–383.

Afifi, W.A., and Afifi, T.D. (2009). "Avoidance among adolescents in conversations about their parents' relationship: Applying the theory of motivated information management," *Journal of Social and Personal Relationships*, *26*(4), 488–511.

——, and Johnson, M.L. (1999). "The use and interpretation of tie signs in a public setting: Relationship and sex differences," *Journal of Social and Personal Relationships*, *16*, 9–38.

Agne, R., Thompson, T.L., and Cusella, L.P. (2000). "Stigma in the line of face: Self-disclosure of patients' HIV status to health care providers," *Journal of Applied Communication Research*, *28*, 235–261.

Ala-Kortesmaa, S., and Isotalus, P. (2014). "Relational tensions and optimal listening in the communication relationships of American and Finnish legal professionals," *Journal of Intercultural Communication Research*, May, 1–21.

Albada, K.F., Knapp, M.L., and Theune, K.E. (2002). "Interaction appearance theory: Changing perceptions of physical attractiveness through social interaction," *Communication Theory*, *12*, 8–40.

Alberts, J.K. (1988). "An analysis of couples' conversational complaints," *Communication Monographs*, *55*, 184–197.

—— (1990). "Perceived effectiveness of couples' conversational complaints," *Communication Studies*, *40*, 280–291.

——, and Driscoll, G. (1992). "Containment versus escalation: The trajectory of couples' conversational complaints," *Western Journal of Communication*, *56*, 394–412.

——, Kellar-Guenther, U., and Corman, S.R. (1996). "That's not funny: Understanding recipients' responses to teasing," *Western Journal of Communication*, *60*, 337–357.

——, Yoshimura, C.G., Rabby, M., and Loschiavo, R. (2005). "Mapping the topography of couples' daily conversation," *Journal of Social and Personal Relationships*, *22*(3), 299–322.

Albrecht, T.L., and Adelman, M.B. (1987). "Communicating social support: A theoretical perspective," in T.L. Albrecht and M.B. Adelman (eds), *Communicating social support*, 18–39. Newbury Park, CA: Sage.

Allen, B. (1995). "Diversity and organizational communication," *Journal of Applied Communication Research*, *23*, 143–155.

Allen, A.J.H., Forrest, J.I., . . . Hogg, R.S. (2014). "Factors associated with disclosure of HIV status among a cohort of individuals on antiretroviral therapy in British Columbia, Canada," *AIDS and Behavior*, *18*, 1014–1026.

Allen, K. (2010). "Vantage theory and linguistic relativity," *Language Sciences*, *32*, 158–169.

Allen, M. (1998). "Methodological considerations when examining a gendered world," in D.J. Canary and K. Dindia (eds), *Handbook of sex differences and similarities in communication*, 427–444. Mahwah, NJ: Lawrence Erlbaum.

Allen, M.W. (1995). "Communication concepts related to perceived organizational support," *Western Journal of Communication, 59*, 326–346.

Almaney A., and Alwan, A. (1982). *Communicating with the Arabs.* Prospect Heights, IL: Waveland.

Altman, I. (1973). "Reciprocity of interpersonal exchange," *Journal for the Theory of Social Behavior, 3*, 249–261.

———, and Taylor, D.A. (1973). *Social penetration: The development of interpersonal relationships.* New York: Holt, Rinehart and Winston.

Ambady, N., and Gray, H. (2002). "On being sad and mistaken: Mood effects on the accuracy of thin-slice judgments," *Journal of Personality and Social Psychology, 83*(4), 947–961.

———, Koo, J., Lee, F., and Rosenthal, R. (1996). "More than words: Linguistic and nonlinguistic politeness in two cultures," *Journal of Personality and Social Psychology, 70*, 996–1011.

Amieva, H., Stoykova, R., Matharan, F., Helmer, C., Antonucci, T., and Dartigues, J.F. (2010). "What aspects of social networks are protective for dementia? Not the quantity but the quality of social interactions is protective up to 15 years later," *Psychosomatic Medicine, 72*(9), 905–911.

Andersen, P.A. (1991). "Nonverbal communication in the small group," in L. A. Samovar and R.S. Cathcart (eds), *Small group communication: A reader*, 6th edn, 272–286. Dubuque, IA: Wm.C. Brown.

——— (1999). *Nonverbal communication: Forms and functions.* Mountain View, CA: Mayfield.

Anderson, C., Brion S., Moore D.A., and Kennedy J.A. (2012) "A status-enhancement account of overconfidence," *Journal of Personality and Social Psychology, 103*(4), 718–735.

Anderson, R., and Fetner, T. (2008). "Cohort differences in tolerance of homosexuality: Attitudinal change in Canada and the United States 1982–2000," *Public Opinion Quarterly, 72*(2), 311–330.

Andrews, P.H., and Baird, J.E. (2005). *Communication for business and the professions*, 8th edn. New York: McGraw-Hill Ryerson.

Androutsopoulou, A. (2001). "The self-characterization as a narrative tool: Applications in therapy with individuals and families," *Family Process, 40*, 79–94.

Ansara, D.L., and Hindin, M.J. (2010). "Exploring gender differences in patterns of intimate partner violence in Canada: A latent class approach," *Journal of Epidemiology and Community Health, 64*, 849–854.

Antioch College. (2006). *The Antioch College sexual offense prevention policy.* http://antiochcollege.org/campus-life/residence-life/health-safety/sexual-offense-prevention-policy

Applegate, J. (1990). "Constructs and communication: A pragmatic integration," in G.J. Neimeyer and R.A. Neimeyer (eds), *Advances in personal construct psychology*, 203–230. Stamford, CT: JAI Press.

Archer, J. (2002). "Sex differences in physically aggressive acts between heterosexual partners: A meta-analytic review," *Aggression and Violent Behavior, 7*, 313–351.

Argyle, M., Alkema, F., and Gilmour, R. (1971). "The communication of friendly and hostile attitudes by verbal and nonverbal signals," *European Journal of Social Psychology, 1*, 385–402.

———, and Henderson, M. (1985). "The rules of relationships," in S. Duck and D. Perlman (eds), *Understanding personal relationships: An interdisciplinary approach*, 63–84. Beverly Hills, CA: Sage.

Arman, G., and Adair, C.K. (2012). "Cross-cultrual differences in perception of time: Implications for multinational teams," *European Journal of Work and Organizational Psychology, 21*(5), 657–680.

Armarego, J. (2007). "Learning from reflection: Practitioners as adult learners," *Proceedings of the 20th Conference on Software Engineering, Education and Training*, 3–5 July 2007, 55–63. www2.computer.org/portal/web/csdl/doi/10.1109/CSEET.2007.33

Armstrong, G.B., Boiarsky, G.A., and Mares, M.L. (1991). "Background television and reading performance," *Communication Monographs, 58*, 235–253.

Aron, A., Aron, E.N., Tudor, M., and Nelson, G. (2004). "Close relationships as including other in the self," in H.T. Reis, and C.E. Rusbult (eds), *Close relationships: Key readings*, 365– 379. Philadelphia, PA: Taylor and Francis.

Aronson, E., Willerman, B., and Floyd, J. (1966). "The effect of a pratfall on increasing interpersonal attractiveness," *Psychonomic Science, 4*, 227–228.

Asante, M.K. (2002). "Language and agency in the transformation of American identity," in W.F. Eadie and P.E. Nelson (eds), *The changing conversation in America: Lectures from the Smithsonian*, 77–89. Thousand Oaks, CA: Sage.

Ashkanasy, N.M., Wilderom, C., and Peterson, M.F. (eds). (2000). *Handbook of organizational culture and climate.* Thousand Oaks, CA: Sage.

Askari, M., Noah, S.B., Hassan, S.A., and Baba, M.B. (2012). "Comparison effects of communication and conflict resolution skills training on marital satisfaction," *International Journal of Psychological Studies, 4*(1), 182–195.

Atkin, C.K., Smith, S.W., Roberto, A.J., Fediuk, T., and Wagner, T. (2002). "Correlates of verbally aggressive communication in adolescents," *Journal of Applied Communication Research, 30*, 251–268.

Au, K., Hui, M.K., and Leung, K. (2001). "Who should be responsible? Effects of voice and compensation on responsibility attribution, perceived justice, and post-complaint behaviors across cultures," *International Journal of Conflict Management, 12*, 350–364.

Aune, R.K., and Kikuchi, T. (1993). "Effects of language intensity similarity on perceptions of credibility, relational attributions, and persuasion," *Journal of Language and Social Psychology, 12*, 224–238.

Aura, S., and Hess, G. (2004). "What's in a name?" CESifo GmbH, CESifo Working Paper Series: CESifo Working Paper no. 1190, 2004.

Avery, R.D., and Campion, J.E. (1982). "The employment interview: A summary and review of recent research," *Personnel Psychology, 35*, 284–308.

Avtgis, T.A. (1999). "The relationship between unwillingness to communicate and family communication patterns," *Communication Research Reports, 16*, 333–338.

———, West, D.V., and Anderson, T.L. (1998). "Relationship stages: An inductive analysis identifying cognitive, affective, and behavioral dimensions of Knapp's relational stages model," *Communication Research Reports, 15*, 280–287.

Ayman, R., and Korabik, K. (2010). "Leadership: Why culture and gender matter," *American Psychologist, 65*(3), 157–170.

Ayres, J., and Crosby, S. (1995). "Two studies concerning the predictive validity of the personal report of communication apprehension in employment interviews," *Communication Research Reports, 12*, 145–151.

———, and Hopf, T. (1993). *Coping with speech anxiety*. Norwood, NJ: Ablex.

Babson, K.A., Trainor, C.D., Feldner, M.T., and Blumenthal, H. (2010). "A test of the effects of acute sleep deprivation on general and specific self-reported anxiety and depressive symptoms: An experiment extension," *Journal of Behavior Therapy and Experimental Psychiatry, 41*, 297–303.

Bach, G.R., and Wyden, P. (1968). *The intimate enemy*. New York: Avon.

Bakar, H.A., Dilbeck, K.E., and McCroskey, J.C. (2010). "Mediating role of supervisory communication practices on relations between leader–member exchange and perceived employee commitment to workgroup," *Communication Monographs, 77* (4), 637–656.

Baker, C. (2001). *Service provision by representative institutions and identity*. Paper commissioned by the Department of Canadian Heritage for the Ethno-cultural, Racial, Religious, and Linguistic Diversity and Identity Seminar, Halifax, NS, 1–2 November.

——— (2002) "What September 11th teaches us about Canada," *Environics Research Group News*. 12 September.

Baker, W. (2000). *Achieving success through social capital*. San Francisco, CA: Jossey-Bass.

Baker, L.R., and Oswald, D.L. (2010). "Shyness and online social networking services," *Journal of Social and Personal Relationships, 27*(7), 873–889.

Balcetis, E. (2009). "Claiming a moral minority, saccades help create a biased majority: Tracking eye movements to base rates in social predictions," *Journal of Experimental Social Psychology, 45*, 970–973.

Baldwin, M.W., and Keelan, J.P.R. (1999). "Interpersonal expectations as a function of self-esteem and sex," *Journal of Social and Personal Relationships, 16*, 822–833.

Balswick, J.O. (1988). *The inexpressive male: A tragedy of American society*. Lexington, MA: Lexington Books.

Bane, C., Cornish, M., Erspamer, N., and Kampman, L. (2010).

"Self-disclosure through weblogs and perceptions of online and real life friendships among female bloggers," *Cyberpsychology, Behavior and Social Networking, 13*(2), 131–139.

Barak, A., Boniel-Nissim, M., and Suler, J. (2008). "Fostering empowerment in online support groups," *Computers in Human Behavior, 24*, 1867–1883.

Barbato, C.A., Graham, E.E., and Perse, E.M. (2003). "Communicating in the family: An examination of the relationship of family communication climate and interpersonal communication motives," *Journal of Family Communication, 3*(3), 123–148.

Barbee, P.P., Gulley, M.R., and Cunningham, M.R. (1990). "Support seeking in personal relationships," *Journal of Social and Personal Relationships, 7*, 531–540.

Bargh, J.A. (1988). "Automatic information processing: Implications for communication and affect," in L. Donohew and H.E. Sypher (eds), *Communication, social cognition, and affect*, 9–32). Hillsdale, NJ: Lawrence Erlbaum.

Barker, L.L. (1971). *Listening behavior*. Englewood Cliffs, NJ: Prentice-Hall.

Barnes, S.B. (2003). *Computer-mediated communication: Human-to-human communication across the Internet*. Boston: Allyn and Bacon.

Baron, R., Cutrona, C., Hicklin, D., Russell, D., and Lubaroff, D. (1990). "Social support and immune responses among spouses of cancer patients," *Journal of Personality and Social Psychology, 59*, 344–352.

Barr, L.K., Kahn, J.H., and Schneider, W.J. (2008). "Individual differences in emotional expression: Hierarchal structure and relation with psychological distress," *Journal of Social and Clinical Psychology, 27*(10), 1045–1077.

Barry, D. (1990). *Dave Barry Turns 40*. New York: Fawcett Columbine.

Bartholomew, K. (1990). "Avoidance of intimacy: An attachment perspective," *Journal of Social and Personal Relationships, 7*, 147–178.

Bartoshuk, L. (1980). "Separate worlds of taste," *Psychology Today, 14*, September, 48–63.

——— (2000). "Psychophysical advances aid the study of genetic variation in taste," *Appetite, 34*(1): 105.

Basso, K. (1970). "To give up on words: Silence in Western Apache culture," *Southern Journal of Anthropology, 26*, 213–230.

Bateson, G., and Jackson, D.D. (1964). "Some varieties of pathogenic organization," *Disorders of Communication* [Research Publications: Association for Research in Nervous and Mental Disease], *42*, 270–283.

Battaglia, D.M., Richard, F.D., Datteri, D.L., and Lord, C.G. (1998). "Breaking up is (relatively) easy to do: A script for the dissolution of close relationships," *Journal of Social and Personal Relationships, 15*, 829–845.

Baumeister, R.F., and Alquist, J.L. (2009). "Is there a downside to good self-control?" *Self and Identity, 8*, 115–130.

———, Bratslavsky, E., Finkenauer, C., and Vohs, K.D. (2001). "Bad is stronger than good," *Review of General Psychology, 5*, 323–370.

———, Gailliot, M., DeWall, C.N., and Oaten, M. (2006). "Self-regulation and personality: How interventions increase regulatory success, and how depletion moderates the effects of traits on behavior," *Journal of Personality, 74*, 1773–1801.

———, and Leary, M.R. (1995). "The need to belong: Desire for interpersonal attachments as a fundamental human motivation," *Psychological Bulletin, 117*, 497–529.

Bavelas, J.B., Black, A., Chovil, N., and Mullett, J. (1990). *Equivocal communication*. Newbury Park, CA: Sage.

Baxter, L.A. (1982). "Strategies for ending relationships: Two studies," *Western Journal of Speech Communication, 46*, 223–241.

——— (1987). "Symbols of relationship identity in relationship culture," *Journal of Social and Personal Relationships, 4*, 261–280.

——— (1992). "Forms and functions of intimate play in personal relationships," *Human Communication Research, 18*, 336–363.

——— (1994). "A dialogic approach to relationship maintenance," in D.J. Canary and L. Stafford (eds), *Communication and relational maintenance*, 233–254. San Diego: Academic Press.

———, and Braithwaite, D.O. (2006). "Social dialectics: The contradictions of relating," in B. Whaley and W. Samter (eds), *Explaining communication: Contemporary communication theories and exemplars*, 305–324. Mahwah, NJ: Erlbaum.

———, ———, Golish, T.D., and Olson, L.N. (2002). "Contradictions of interaction for wives of elderly husbands with adult dementia," *Journal of Applied Communication Research, 30*, 1–20.

———, and Erbert, L.A. (1999). "Perceptions of dialectical contradictions in turning points of development in heterosexual romantic relationships," *Journal of Social and Personal Relationships, 16*, 547–569.

———, and Montgomery, B.M. (1996). *Relating: Dialogues and dialectics.* New York: Guilford Press.

Baxter, L.A., and Pittman, G. (2001). "Communicatively remembering turning points of relational development in heterosexual romantic relationships," *Communication Reports, 14*, 1–17.

———, and Wilmot, W.W. (1985). "Taboo topics in close relationships," *Journal of Social and Personal Relationships, 2*, 253–269.

Bazil, L.G.D. (1999). "The effects of social behavior on fourth- and fifth-grade girls' perceptions of physically attractive and unattractive peers," (Doctoral dissertation, California School of Professional Psychology, San Diego, 1999). *Dissertation Abstracts International, 59*, 4533B.

Bearman, P., and Moody, J. (2004). "Suicide and friendships among American adolescents," *American Journal of Public Health, 94*(1), 89–95.

Beatty, M.J. (1998). "Interpersonal communication as temperamental expression: A communibiological paradigm," in J.C. McCroskey, J.A. Daly, M.M. Martin, and M.J. Beatty, (eds), *Communication and personality: Trait perspectives*, 41–67. Cresskill, NJ: Hampton Press.

———, Burant, P.A., Dobos, J.A., and Rudd, J.E. (1996). "Trait verbal aggressiveness and the appropriateness and effectiveness of fathers' interaction plans," *Communication Quarterly, 44*, 1–15.

———, Marshall, L.A., and Rudd, J.E. (2001). "A twins study of communicative adaptability: Heritability of individual differences," *Quarterly Journal of Speech, 87*, 366–377.

———, and McCroskey, J.C. (1997). "It's in our nature: Verbal aggressiveness as temperamental expression," *Communication Quarterly, 45*, 446–460.

Beaupré, P., Turcotte, P., and Milan, M. (2006). "Junior Comes Back Home: Trends and Predictors of Returning to the Parental Home," *Canadian Social Trends*, Ottawa: Statistics Canada, Catalogue no. 11–008 (Winter), 28–34.

Bechara, A. (2004). "The role of emotion in decision-making: Evidence from neurological patients with orbitofrontal damage," *Brain and Cognition, 55*, 30–40.

Beck, C.E., and Beck. E.A. (1996). "The manager's open door and the communication climate," in K.M. Galvin and P. Cooper (eds), *Making connections: Readings in relational communication*, 286–290. Los Angeles: Roxbury.

Becker, J.A.H., Ellevold, B., and Stamp, G.H. (2008). "The creation of defensiveness in social interaction II: A model of defensive communication among romantic couples," *Communication Monographs, 75*, 1, 86–110.

Bell, B.S., and Kozlowski, S.W.J. (2002). "A typology of virtual teams: Implications for effective leadership," *Group and Organization Management, 27*(1), 14–49.

Bell, R.A., and Buerkel-Rothfuss, N.L. (1990). "(S)he loves me, s(he) loves me not: Predictors of relational information-seeking in courtship and beyond," *Communication Quarterly, 38*, 64–82.

———, ———, and Gore, K.E. (1987). "Did you bring the yarmulke for the cabbage patch kid?: The idiomatic communication of young lovers," *Human Communication Research, 14*, 47–67.

———, and Healey, J.G. (1992). "Idiomatic communication and interpersonal solidarity in friends' relational cultures," *Human Communication Research, 18*, 307–335.

Bellah, R.N., Madsen, R., Sullivan, W.M., Swidler, A., and Tipton, S.M. (1985). *Habits of the heart: Individualism and commitment in American life.* Berkeley: University of California Press.

Bello, R.S., Brandau-Brown, F.E., and Ragsdale, J.D. (2008). "Attachment style, marital satisfaction, commitment and communal strength effects on relational repair message interpretation among remarrieds," *Communication Quarterly, 56*(1) 1–16.

Belsky, J. (2008). "The transition to parenthood," in H.T. Reis and S.K. Sprecher (eds), *Encyclopedia of Human Relationships*. Thousand Oaks, CA: Sage.

———, and Kelly, J. (1994). *The transition to parenthood.* New York: Delacorte.

———, Lang, M.E., and Rovine, M. (1985). "Stability and change in marriage across the transition to parenthood: A second study," *Journal of Marriage and the Family, 47*, 855–865.

———, Spanier, G.B., and Rovine, M. (1983). "Stability and change in marriage across the transition to parenthood," *Journal of Marriage and the Family, 45*, 567–577.

Bem, S.L. (1974). "The measurement of psychological androgyny," *Journal of Consulting and Clinical Psychology, 42*, 155–162.

Ben-Ari, A. (2012). "Rethinking closeness and distance in intimate relationships: Are they really two opposites," *Journal of Family Issues, 33*(3), 391–412.

Benenson, J.F., Gordon, A.J., and Roy, R. (2000). "Children's evaluative appraisals of competition in tetrads versus dyads," *Small Group Research, 31*, 635–652.

Benne, K.D., and Sheats, P. (1948). "Functional roles of group members," *Journal of Social Issues, 4*, 41–49.

Benoit, W.L., and Benoit, P.J. (1987). "Everyday argument practices of naive social actors," in J. Wenzel (ed.), *Argument and critical practice.* Annandale, VA: Speech Communication Association.

Berger, C.R. (1979). "Beyond initial interactions: Uncertainty, understanding, and the development of interpersonal relationships," in H. Giles and R. St. Clair (eds), *Language and social psychology*, 122–144. Oxford, UK: Blackwell.

——— (1988). "Uncertainty and information exchange in developing relationships," in S. Duck and D.F. Hay (eds), *Handbook of personal relationships: Theory, research and interventions*, 239–255. Chichester, UK, and New York: John Wiley & Sons.

——— (1993). "Revisiting the relationship construct," *Personal Relationship Issues, 1*, July, 25–27.

———, and diBattista, P. (1993). "Communication failure and plan adaptation: If at first you don't succeed, say it louder and slower," *Communication Monographs, 60*, 220–238.

Bergman, K., Rubio R.J., Green, R.J., and Padrón, E. (2010). "Gay men who become fathers via surrogacy: The transition to parenthood," *Journal of GLBT Family Studies, 6*, 111–141.

Bergner, R.M., and Holmes, J.R. (2000). "Self-concepts and self-concept change: A status dynamic approach," *Psychotherapy: Theory, Research, Practice, Training, 37*, 36–44.

Berman, E.M., West, J.P., and Richter, N.M. (2002). "Workplace relations: Friendship patterns and consequences (according to managers)," *Public Administration Review, 62*, (2), 217–230.

Bermudez, D. (2008). "Adapting Virginia Satir techniques to Hispanic families," *The Family Journal: Counselling and Therapy for Couples and Families, 16*(1), 51–57.

Berscheid, E., Schneider, M., and Omoto, A.M. (1989). "Issues in studying close relationships: Conceptualizing and measuring closeness," in C. Hendrick (ed.), *Close relationships*, 63–91. Newbury Park, CA: Sage.

———, and Walster, E.H. (1978). *Interpersonal attraction*, 2nd edn. Reading, MA: Addison-Wesley.

Bertoni, A., and Bodenmann, G. (2010). "Satisfied and dissatisfied couples: Positive and negative dimensions, conflict styles, and relationship with family of origin," *European Psychologist, 15*(3), 175–184.

Bertrand, M., and Mullainathan, S. (2004). "Are Emily and Greg more employable than Lakisha and Jamal? A field experiment on labor market discrimination," *American Economic Review, 94*(4), September, 991–1013.

Bharti, A. (1985). "The self in Hindu thought and action," in A.J. Marsella, G. DeVos, and F.L. K. Hsu (eds), *Culture and self: Asian and Western perspectives*. New York: Tavistock.

Bibby, R.W. (2001). *Canada's teens: Today, yesterday and tomorrow*. Toronto: Stoddart.

Bippus, A.M. (2001). "Recipients' criteria for evaluating the skillfulness of comforting communication and the outcomes of comforting interactions," *Communication Monographs, 68*, 301–313.

Birdwhistell, R.L. (1970). *Kinesics and context*. Philadelphia: University of Pennsylvania Press.

Birnie, S., and Horvath, P. (2002). "Psychological predictors of internet social communication," *Journal of Computer-Mediated Communication, 7*(4). http://jcmc.indiana.edu/vol7/issue4/horvath.html

Bischoping, K. (1993). "Gender differences in conversation topic, 1922–1990," *Sex Roles, 28*, 1–18.

Bjorklund, D.F., Cassel, W.S., Bjorklund, B.R., Brown, R.D., Park, C.L., and Ernst, K. (2000). "Social demand characteristics in children's and adults' eyewitness memory and suggestibility: The effect of different interviewers on free recall and recognition," *Applied Cognitive Psychology, 14*, 421–433.

Blacker, L. (1999). "The launching phase of the life cycle," in B. Carter and M. McGoldrick (eds), *The expanded family life cycle: Individual, family, and social perspectives*, 3rd edn, 287–306. Boston: Allyn and Bacon.

Blackstock, C. (2010). "Supporting First Nations adoption," First Nations Child and Family Caring Society of Canada. Submission to: Standing Committee on Human Resources, Skills and Development and Status of Persons with Disabilities. www.fncaringsociety.com

Blake, R.R., and Mouton, J.S. (1964). *The managerial grid*. Houston: Gulf Publishing.

Blank, P.D. (ed.). (1993). *Interpersonal expectations: Theory, research, and applications*. Cambridge, UK: Cambridge University Press.

Boase, J., Horrigan, J., Wellman, B., and Rainie, L. (2006). "The strength of internet ties: The internet and e-mail aid users in maintaining their social networks provide pathways to help when people face big decisions," Pew Internet and American Life Project, Washington, DC, January. www.pewinternet.org/files/old-media/Files/Reports/2006/PIP_Internet_ties.pdf.pdf

Boatswain, S., and Lalonde, R. (2000). "Social identity and preferred ethnic/racial labels for blacks in Canada," *Journal of Black Psychology, 26*, 216–234.

Bok, S. (1978). *Lying: Moral choice in public and private life*. New York: Pantheon.

Bolles, R.N. (2008). *What colour is your parachute? A practical manual for job hunters and careers changers*. Berkeley, CA: Ten Speed Press.

Bolton, G. (2005). *Reflective practice: Writing and professional development*, 2nd edn. Thousand Oaks, CA: Sage.

Bond, C.F., Jr., and DePaulo, B.M. (2006). "Accuracy of deception judgments," *Personality and Social Psychology Review, 10*(3), 214–234.

———, and ——— (2008). "Individual differences in judging deception:

Accuracy and bias," *Psychological Bulletin, 134*(4), 477–492.

Booth-Butterfield, M., and Booth-Butterfield, S. (1998). "Emotionality and affective orientation," in J.C. McCroskey, J.A. Daly, M.M. Martin, and M.J. Beatty (eds), *Communication and personality: Trait Perspectives*, 171–190. Cresskill, NJ: Hampton.

———, and Jordan, F. (1989). "Communication adaptation among racially homogeneous and heterogeneous groups," *Southern Communication Journal, 54*, 253–272.

Boroditsky, L. (2009). "How does language shape the way we think?" in M. Brockman (ed.) *What's Next? Dispatches on the future of science*. Toronto: Random House.

———, and Gaby, A. (2010). "Remembrance of times east: Absolute spatial representations of time in an Australian Aborginal community," *Psychology Science, 21*(11), 1635–1639.

Bostrom R.N. (1996). "Aspects of listening behavior," in O. Hargie (ed.), *Handbook of communication skills*, 2nd edn, 236–259. London: Routledge.

———, and Waldhart, E.S. (1980). "Components in listening behavior: The role of short-term memory," *Human Communication Research, 6*, 221–227.

Boucher, C. (2004). "Canada–US Values. Distinct, inevitably carbon copy or narcissism of small differences," *Horizons: Policy Research Initiative, 7*, 42–49.

Bourdrias, J.S., Brunet, L., Morin, A.J., Savoie, A., Plunier, P., and Cacciatore, G. (2010). "Empowering employees: The moderating role of perceived organizational climate and justice," *Canadian Journal of Behavioural Science, 42*(4), 201–211.

Bourgeois, P., and Hess, U. (2007). "The impact of social context on mimicry," *Biological Psychology, 77*, 343–352.

Bourhis, J., and Allen, M. (1992). "Meta-analysis of the relationship between communication apprehension and cognitive performance," *Communication Education, 41*, 68–76.

Bower, B. (1998). "Social disconnections online," *Science News*, 12 September, 168.

Bowers, A.L., Crawford, S.C., Saltuklaroglu, T., and Kalinowski, J. (2010). "Gaze aversion to stuttered speech:

A pilot study investigating differential visual attention to stuttered and fluent speech," *International Journal of Language and Communication Disorders, 45*(2), 133–144.

Bowlby, J. (1969). *Attachment and loss* (vols 1). New York: Basic Books.

——— (1976). *Attachment and loss* (vol. 2). New York: Basic Books.

——— (1982). *Attachment and loss* (vol. 3). New York: Basic Books.

Brackett, M.A., Warner, R.M., and Bosco, J. (2005). "Emotional intelligence and relationship quality among couples," *Personal Relationships, 12,* 197–212.

Bradbury, T.N., and Fincham, F.D. (1990). "Attributions in marriage: Review and critique," *Psychological Bulletin, 107,* 3–33.

Braithwaite, C. (1990). "Communicative silence: A cross cultural study of Basso's hypothesis," in D. Carbaugh (ed.), *Cultural communication and intercultural contact,* 321–328. Hillsdale, NJ: Erlbaum.

Braithwaite, D.O., and Baxter, L.A. (2006). "You're my parent but you're not: Dialectical tensions in stepchildren's perceptions about communicating with the nonresidential parent," *Journal of Applied Communication Research, 34*(1), 30–48.

———, ———, and Harper, A.M. (1998). "The role of rituals in the management of the dialectical tension of 'old' and 'new' in blended families," *Communication Studies, 49,* 101–120.

Brajer, V., and Gill, A. (2010). "Yakity-yak: Who talks back? An e-mail experiment," *Social Science Quarterly, 91*(4), 1007–1024.

Brashers, D.E., and Jackson, S. (1999). "Changing conceptions of 'message effect': A 24–year overview," *Human Communication Research, 25,* 457–477.

Brescoll, V.L., and Uhlmann, E.L. (2008). "Can an angry woman get ahead? Status conferral, gender, and expression of emotion in the workplace," *Psychological Science, 19*(3), 268–275.

Brightman, V., Segal, A., Werther, P., and Steiner, J. (1975). "Ethological study of facial expression in response to taste stimuli," *Journal of Dental Research, 54,* 141.

Brilhart, J.K., Galanes, G.J., and Adams, K. (2001). *Effective group discussion,* 10th edn. New York: McGraw-Hill Ryerson.

Broome, B.J. (1991). "Building shared meaning: Implications of a relational approach to empathy for teaching intercultural communication," *Communication Education, 40,* 235–249.

Brotheridge, C., and Lee, R.T. (2010). "Restless and confused: Emotional responses to workplace bullying in men and women," *Career Development International, 15*(7), 687–707.

Brown, D. (1991). *Human universals.* New York: McGraw-Hill Ryerson.

Brown, J.D., Gerritts, J., Ivanova, V., Mehta, N., and Skrodzki, D. (2012). "Motives of aboriginal foster parents," *Children and Youth Services Review, 34,* 1298–1304.

———, and Mankowski, T.A. (1993). "Self-esteem, mood, and self-evaluation: Changes in mood and the way you see you," *Journal of Personality and Social Psychology, 64,* 421–430.

Brown, J.E. (2009). "Reflective practice: A tool for measuring the development of generic skills in the training of professional musicians," *International Journal of Music Education, 27*(4), 372–382.

Brown, L. (2007). *Resume writing made easy,* 8th edn. Upper Saddle River, NJ: Prentice Hall PTR.

Brown, T.L., and Alderson, K.G. (2010). "Sexual identity and heterosexual male students' usage of homosexual insults: An exploratory study," *The Canadian Journal of Human Sexuality, 19*(1–2), 27–42.

Brownell, J. (1990). "Perceptions of effective listeners: A management study," *Journal of Business Communication, 27,* 401–415.

Browning, S., and Waite, R. (2010). "The gift of listening: JUST listening," *Nursing Forum, 45,* (3), 150–158.

Brunet, P.M., and Schmidt, L.A. (2010). "Sex differences in the expression and use of computer-mediated affective language: Does context matter? "*Social Science Computer Review, 28*(2), 194–205.

Bryant, E.M., and Sias, P.M. (2011). "Sensemaking and relational consequences of peer co-worker deception," *Communication Monographs, 78*(1), 115–137.

Bryant, G.A., and Barrett, H.C. (2008). "Vocal emotion recognition across disparate cultures," *Journal of Cognition and Culture, 8,* 135–148.

Brym, R.J. (ed.) (2011). *Society in Question,* 6th custom edn. Toronto: Nelson.

———, and Lenton, R. (2003). "Love at first byte: Internet dating in Canada," *Online Articles.* Nelson Thompson.

Buck, R., and Van Lear, C.A. (2002). "Verbal and nonverbal communication: Distinguishing symbolic, spontaneous and pseudo-spontaneous nonverbal behavior," *Journal of Communication, 52,* 522–541.

Buckman, R., and Baile. W. (2005). "Truth telling: Yes but how?" *Community Oncology,* March–April, 138–142.

———, Tulsky, J.A., and Rodin, G. (2011). "Empathic responses in clinical practice: Intuition or tuition?" *Canadian Medical Association Journal Online,* 24 January. www.ecmaj.ca/cgi/content/citation/cmaj.090113v1

Budescu, D.V., Erev, I., and Zwick, R. (eds). (1999). *Games and human behavior: Essays in honor of Amnon Rapoport.* Mahwah, NJ: Lawrence Erlbaum.

Buller, D.B., and Aune, K. (1988). "The effects of vocalics and nonverbal sensitivity on compliance: A speech accommodation theory explanation," *Human Communication Research, 14,* 301–332.

———, and ——— (1992). "The effects of speech rate similarity on compliance application of communication accommodation theory," *Western Journal of Communication, 56,* 37–53.

———, and Burgoon, J.K. (1994). "Deception: Strategic and nonstrategic communication," in J.A. Daly and J.M. Wiemann (eds), *Strategic interpersonal communication,* 191–223. Hillsdale, NJ: Lawrence Erlbaum.

Buote, V.M., Wood, E., and Pratt, M. (2009). "Exploring similarities and differences between online and offline friendships: The role of attachment style," *Computers in Human Behavior, 25,* 560–567.

Burggraf, C.S., and Sillars, A.L. (1987). "A critical examination of sex differences in marital communication," *Communication Monographs, 54,* 276–294.

Burgoon, J.K., and Buller, D.B. (2008). "Interpersonal deception theory," in L.A. Baxter and D.O. Braithwaite (eds), *Engaging theories in interpersonal communication: Multiple perspectives,* 227–239. Thousand Oaks, CA: Sage Publications.

———, ———, and Guerrero, L.K. (1995). "Interpersonal deception: IX. Effects of social skill and nonverbal communication on deception success and detection accuracy," *Journal of*

Language and Social Psychology, 14, 289–311.

——, ——, ——, and Feldman, C.M. (1994). "Interpersonal deception: VI. Effects of pre-interactional and interactional factors on deceiver and observer perceptions of deception success," *Communication Studies, 45*, 263–280.

——, and Le Poire, B.A. (1999). "Nonverbal cues and interpersonal judgments: Participant and observer perceptions of intimacy, dominance, and composure," *Communication Monographs, 66*, 105–124.

——, Parrott, R., LePoire, B.A., Kelley, D.L., Walther, J.B., and Perry, D. (1989). "Maintaining and restoring privacy through different types of relationships," *Journal of Social and Personal Relationships, 6*, 131–158.

——, Walther, J., and Baesler, E. (1992). "Interpretations, evaluations, and consequences of interpersonal touch," *Human Communication Research, 19*, 237–263.

Burke, M., Marlow, C., and Leto, T. (2010). "Social network activity and social well-being," *Proceedings of the 2010 ACM Conference on Human Factors in Computing Systems*, 1909–1912.

Burleson, B.R. (1982). "The development of comforting communication skills in childhood and adolescence," *Child Development, 53*, 1578–1588.

—— (1984). "Comforting communication," in H. Sypher and J. Applegate (eds), *Communication by children and adults: Social cognitive and strategic processes*, 63–104. Beverly Hills, CA: Sage.

—— (1994). "Comforting messages: Features, functions and outcomes," in J.A. Daly and J.M. Wiemann (eds), *Strategic interpersonal communication*, 135–161. Hillsdale, NJ: Lawrence Erlbaum.

—— (2007). "Constructivism: A general theory of communication skill," in B.B. Whaley and W. Samter (eds) *Explaining communication: Contemporary theories and exemplars*, 105–128. Mahwah, N.J.: Erlbaum.

—— (2008). "What counts as effective emotional support?" in M.T. Motley (ed.) *Studies in applied interpersonal communication*, 207–227. Thousand Oaks, CA: Sage.

——, and Caplan, S.E. (1998). "Cognitive complexity," in J.C. McCroskey, J.A. Daly, M.M. Martin, and M.J. Beatty (eds), *Communication and personality: Trait*

perspectives, 233–286. Cresskill, NJ: Hampton Press.

——, and Denton, W.H. (2014). "The association between spousal initiator tendency and partner marital satisfaction: Some moderating effects of supportive communication values," *The American Journal of Family Therapy, 42*, 141–152.

——, Kunkel, A.W., Samter, W., and Werking, K.J. (1996). "Men's and women's evaluations of communication skills in personal relationships: When sex differences make a difference—and when they don't," *Journal of Social and Personal Relationships, 13*, 201–224.

——, and Samter, W. (1985). "Individual differences in the perception of comforting messages: An exploratory investigation," *Central States Speech Journal, 36*, 39–50.

——, and —— (1994). "A social skills approach to relationship maintenance," in D.J. Canary and L. Stafford (eds), *Communication and relationship maintenance: How individual differences in communication skills affect the achievement of relationship functions*, 61–90. San Diego: Academic Press.

——, —— (1996). "Similarity in the communication skills of young adults: Foundations of attraction, friendship, and relationship satisfaction," *Communication Reports, 9*, 127–139.

Burn, S.M., Kadlec, K., and Rexter, R. (2005). "Effects of subtle heterosexism on gays, lesbians and bisexuals," *Journal of Homosexuality, 49*(2), 23–38.

Burns, K.L., and Beier, E.G. (1973). "Significance of vocal and visual channels for the decoding of emotional meaning," *Journal of Communication, 23*, 118–130.

Burton, C.M., and King, L.A. (2008). "Effects of very brief writing on health: The two minute miracle," *British Journal of Health Psychology, 13*, 9–14.

Busby, D.M., and Holman, T.B. (2009). "Perceived match or mismatch on the Gottman conflict styles: Associations with relationship outcome variables," *Family Process, 48*(4), 531–545.

Bushman, B.J. (2002). "Does venting anger feed or extinguish the flame? Catharsis, rumination, distraction, anger and aggressive responding," *Personality and Social Psychology Bulletin, 28*, 724–731.

——, Baumeister, R.F., and Stack, A.D. (1999). "Catharsis, aggression,

and persuasive influence: Self-fulfilling or self-defeating prophecies?" *Journal of Personality and Social Psychology, 76*, 367–376.

——, Bonacci, A.M., Pedersen, W.C., Vasquez, E.A., and Miller, N. (2005). "Chewing on it can chew you up: Effects of rumination on triggered displaced aggression," *Journal of Personality and Social Psychology, 88*, 969–983.

——, DeWall, C.N., Pond, R.S., and Hanus, M.D. (2014). "Low glucose relates to greater aggression in married couples," *Proceedings of the National Academy of Sciences*, published ahead of print, 14 April, doi:10.1073/pnas.1400619111

Buss, D.M. (1985). "Human mate selection," *American Scientist*, January–February. *73*, 47–51.

Buttny, R. (1997). "Reported speech in talking race on campus," *Human Communication Research, 23*, 477–506.

Butzer, B., and Kuiper, N.A. (2008). "Humour use in romantic relationships: The effects of relationship satisfaction in pleasant versus conflict situations," *Journal of Psychology, 142*(3), 245–260.

Byrne, D. (1997). "An overview (and underview) of research and theory within the attraction paradigm," *Journal of Social and Personal Relationships, 14*, 417–431.

Byron, K. (2008). "Carrying too heavy a load? The communication and miscommunication of emotion by email," *Academy of Management Review, 33*(2), 309–327.

Cahn, D.D. (1992). *Conflict in intimate relationships*. New York: Guilford Press.

Cai, D.A., and Fink, E.L. (2002). "Conflict style differences between individualists and collectivists," *Communication Monographs, 69*, 67–87.

Camden, C., Motley, M.T., and Wilson, A. (1984). "White lies in interpersonal communication: A taxonomy and preliminary investigation of social motivations," *Western Journal of Speech Communication, 48*, 315.

Cameron, D. (2008). "Talk from the top down," *Language and Communication, 28*, 143–155.

Campbell, A., Converse, P.E., and Rogers, W.L. (1976). *The quality of married life*. New York: Russell Sage Foundation.

Campbell, S., Cumming, S., and Hughes, I. (2006). "Internet use by the socially fearful: Addiction or therapy?" *CyberPsychology and Behavior*, *9*(1) 69–81.

———, and Russo, T. (2003). "The social construction of mobile telephony: An application of the social influence model to perception and uses of mobile phones within personal communication networks," *Communication Monographs*, *70*, 317–334.

Canada Safety Council (2004). "Bullying in the workplace." https://canadasafetycouncil.org/workplace-safety/bullying-workplace

Canadian Centre for Occupational Health and Safety (2014). *VOSH Answers fact sheets: Violence in the workplace*. www.ccohs.ca/osh answers/psychosocial/violence.html

Canadian Council of Chief Executives (2014). "Preliminary survey report: The skill needs of major Canadian employers. Taking action for Canada: Jobs and skills for the 21st century." www.ceocouncil.ca/wp-content/uploads/2014/01/Preliminary-report-on-skills-survey-Jan-20-2014-2.pdf

Canadian Council on Social Development (2000). "Unequal access: A report card on racism," *Perception*, *24* (3).

Canadian Internet Registration Authority (2013). "Factbook 2013." www.cira.ca/factbook/2013/index.html

Canadian Press (2010). "16 million Canadians on Facebook," *Globe and Mail*, 2 June. www.theglobeandmail.com/news/technology/personal-ech/16-million-canadians-on-facebook-report/article1589749/

Canadian Wireless Telecommunications Industry (2010). *Canada's Wireless Industry.*

Canary, D.J., and Cupach, W.R. (1988). "Relational and episodic characteristics associated with conflict tactics," *Journal of Social and Personal Relationships*, *5*, 305–325.

———, ———, and Messman, S.J. (1995). *Relationship conflict*. Newbury Park, CA: Sage.

———, and Emmers-Sommer, T.M. (1997). *Sex and gender differences in personal relationships*. New York: Guilford Press.

———, and Hause, K. (1993). "Is there any reason to research sex differences in communication?" *Communication Quarterly*, *41*, 482–517.

———, and Messman, S.J. (2000). "Relationship conflict," in C. Hendrick and S.S. Hendrick (eds), *Close relationships: A sourcebook*, 261–270. Thousand Oaks, CA: Sage.

———, and Spitzberg, B.H. (1987). "Appropriateness and effectiveness perceptions of conflict strategies," *Human Communication Research*, *15*, 93–118.

———, Stafford, L., Hause, K.S., and Wallace, L.A. (1993). "An inductive analysis of relational maintenance strategies: Comparisons among lovers, relatives, friends and others," *Communication Research Reports*, *10*(1), 3–14.

———, Weger, H. Jr., and Stafford, L. (1991). "Couples' argument sequences and their associations with relational characteristics," *Western Journal of Speech Communication*, *55*, 159–179.

Canli, T., Desmond, J.E., Zhao, Z., and Gabrieli, J.D.E. (2002). "Sex differences in the neural basis of emotional memories," *Proceedings of the National Academy of Sciences*, *10*, 10789–10794.

———, Zhao, Z., Desmond, J.E., Kang, E., Gross, J., and Gabrieli, J.D.E. (2001). "An fMRI study of personality influences on brain reactivity to emotional stimuli," *Behavioral Neuroscience*, *115*, 33–42.

Cantazaro, A., and Wei, M. (2010). "Adult attachment, dependence, self-criticism and depressive symptoms: A test of a meditational model," *Journal of Personality*, *78*(4), 1135–1162.

Career Builder (2006). "One-in-four hiring managers have used internet search engines to screen job candidates; one-in-ten have used social networking sites, careerbuilder.com survey finds." www.careerbuilder.com/share/aboutus/pressreleases detail.aspx?id=pr331&ed=12%2F31%2F2006&sd=10%2F26%2F2006

Carlson E.N., Vazire S, Oltmanns T.F. (2011). "You probably think this paper's about you: Narcissists' perceptions of their personality and reputation," *Journal of Personality and Social Psycholology*, *10*1(1), 185–201.

Carmon, A.F., and Pearson, J.C. (2013). "Family business employees' family communication and workplace experiences," *Journal of Family Business Management*, *3*(2), 88–107.

Carney, D. (2010). "Powerful people are better liars," *Harvard Business Review*, *88*(5), 32–33.

Carrell, L.J. (1997). "Diversity in the communication curriculum: Impact on student empathy," *Communication Education*, *46*, 234–244.

———, and Willmington, S.C. (1996). "A comparison of self-report and performance data in assessing speaking and listening competence," *Communication Reports*, *9*, 185–191.

Carroll, J.M., and Russell, J.A. (1996). "Do facial expressions signal specific emotions? Judging emotion from the face in context," *Journal of Personality and Social Psychology*, *70*, 205–218.

Carter, A., Davis, K.A., Evans, L.V., and Cone, D.C. (2009). "Information loss in handover of trauma patients," *Prehospital Emergency Care*, *13*, 280–285.

Carton, J., Kessler, E., and Pape, C. (1999). "Nonverbal decoding skills and relationship wellbeing in adults," *Nonverbal Behaviour*, *23*(1), 91–100.

Casmir, F.L. (1991). "Culture, communication, and education," *Communication Education*, *40*, 229–234.

Castelan-Cargile, A., and Bradac, J.J. (2001). "Attitudes towards language: A review of speaker-evaluation research and a general process model," in W.B. Gudykunst (ed.), *Communication Yearbook 25*, 347–382. Thousand Oaks, CA: Sage.

Castellano, M.B. (2002). "Aborginal family trends: Extended families, nuclear families, families of the heart," *Contemporary Family Trends*, The Vanier Institute of the Family. www.vanierinstitute.ca/include/get.php?nodeid=1142

Castells, M. (2001). *The internet galaxy: Reflections on the internet, business and society*. New York: Oxford University Press.

Caughlin, J.P. (2003). "Family communication standards: What counts as excellent family communication and how are such standards associated with family satisfaction?" *Human Communication Research*, *29*, 5–40.

Cavaliere, F. (1995). "Society appears more open to gay parenting," *American Psychological Association Monitor*, July, 51.

Cawley, J., Joyner, K., and Sobal, J. (2006). "Size matters. The influence of adolescents' weight and height on dating and sex," *Rationality and Society*, *18*(1), 67–94.

CBC News (2010). "Saving First Nations languages from extinction," 3 September. www.cbc.ca/news/

canada/new-brunswick/saving-first-nations-languages-from-extinction-1.885932

Cegala, D.J., Savage, G.T., Brunner, C.C., and Conrad, A.B. (1982). "An elaboration of the meaning of interaction involvement: Toward the development of a theoretical concept," *Communication Monographs*, 49, 229–248.

Cerasaro, A. (2008). "Employers defy privacy by using Facebook," *Tennessee Journalist*, 8, April.

Chan, Y.K. (1999). "Density, crowding, and factors intervening in their relationship: Evidence from a hyper-dense metropolis," *Social Indicators Research*, 48, 103–124.

Chandler, D. (1998). *Personal home pages and the construction of identities on the web*. http://visual-memory.co.uk/daniel/Documents/short/webident.html

Chen, G.M., and Starosta, W.J. (1996). "Intercultural communication competence: A synthesis," in B.R. Burleson and A.W. Kunkel, (eds), *Communication Yearbook 19*, 353–383. Thousand Oaks, CA: Sage.

———, and ——— (2000). "The development and validation of the intercultural sensitivity scale," *Human Communication*, 3, 1–14.

Chen, L. (1997). "Verbal adaptive strategies in US American dyadic interactions with US American or East-Asian partners," *Communication Monographs*, 64, 302–323.

Choi, M., and Toma, C.L. (2014). "Social sharing through interpersonal media: Patterns and effects on emotional well-being," *Computers in Human Behaviour*, 36, 530–541.

Chou, H. G., and Edge, N. (2012). "'They are happier and having better lives than I am': The impact of using Facebook on perceptions of others' lives," *Cyberpsychology, Behavior and SocialNetworking*, 15(2), 117–121.

Chovil, N. (1991). "Social determinants of facial displays," *Journal of Nonverbal Behavior*, 15, 141–154.

Christenfeld, N., and Larsen, B. (2008). "The name game," *Psychologist*, 21, 210–213.

Christensen, T.H. (2009). "Connected presence in distributed family life," *New Media and Society*, 11(3), 433–451.

Christofides, E., Muise, A., and Desmarais, S. (2012). "Risky disclosures on Facebook: The effect of having a bad experience on online behavior,"

Journal of Adolescent Research, 27(6), 714–731.

Chuang, L., Wu, C., Lin, K., and Hsieh, C. (2014). "Relative and absolute reliability of a vertical numerical pain rating scale supplements with a faces pain scale," *Physical Therapy*, 94(1), 129–138.

Cissna, K.N., and Sieberg, E. (1999). "Patterns of interactional confirmation and disconfirmation," in J. Stewart (ed.), *Bridges not walls*, 7th edn, 336–346. New York: McGraw-Hill Ryerson.

Cissna, K.N., and Sieberg, E. (2006). "Patterns of interactional confirmation and disconfirmation," in J. Stewart (ed.), *Bridges not walls*, 9th edn, pp. 429–439. New York: McGraw-Hill Ryerson.

Clark, A. (2000). *A theory of sentience*. New York: Oxford University Press.

Clark, R.A. (1998). "A comparison of topics and objectives in a cross section of young men's and women's everyday conversations," in D.J. Canary and K. Dindia (eds), *Sex differences and similarities in communication: Critical essays and empirical investigations of sex and gender in interaction*, 303–319. Mahwah, NJ: Lawrence Erlbaum.

———, Pierce, A.J., Finn, K., Hsu, K., Toosley, A., and Williams, L. (1998). "The impact of alternative approaches to comforting, closeness of relationship, and gender on multiple measures of effectiveness," *Communication Studies*, 49, 224–239.

Clarke, F.P. (1973). *Interpersonal communication variables as predictors of marital satisfaction-dissatisfaction*. Unpublished doctoral dissertation, University of Denver.

Clevenger, T. (1991). "Can one not communicate? A conflict of models," *Communication Studies*, 42, 340–353.

Cline, R.J., and McKenzie, N.J. (2000). "Interpersonal roulette and HIV/AIDS as disability: Stigma and social support in tension," in D.O. Braithwaite and T.L. Thompson (eds), *Handbook of communication and people with disabilities: Research and application*, 467–483. Mahwah, NJ: Lawrence Erlbaum.

Clinton, B.L., and Hancock, G.R. (1991). "The development of an understanding of comforting messages," *Communication Reports*, 4(2), 54–63.

Cloven, D.H., and Roloff, M.E. (1991). "Sense-making activities and

interpersonal conflict: Communicative cures for the mulling blues," *Western Journal of Speech Communication*, 55, 134–158.

Coates, J. (1986). *Women, men and language*. London: Longman.

Cody, M.J. (1982). "A typology of disengagement strategies and examination of the role of intimacy, reactions to inequity, and relational problems in strategy selection," *Communication Monographs*, 49, 148–170.

Cohen, E.L., Bowman, N.D., and Borchert, K. (2014). "Private flits, public friends: Understanding romantic jealousy responses to an ambiguous social network site message as a function of message exclusivity," *Computers in Human Behavior*, 35, 535–541.

Cohen, S., Doyle, W.J., Skoner, D.P., Rabin, B.S, and Gwaltney, J.M. (1997). "Social ties and susceptibility to the common cold," *Journal of the American Medical Association*, 277, 1940–1944.

Cole, P.M., Bruschi, C.J., and Tamang, B.L. (2002). "Cultural differences in children's emotional reactions to difficult situations," *Child Development*, 73, 983–996.

Cole, T. (2001). "Lying to the one you love: The use of deception in romantic relationships," *Journal of Social and Personal Relationships*, 18, 107–129.

Coleman, L.M., and DePaulo, B.M. (1991). "Uncovering the human spirit: Moving beyond disability and 'missed' communications," in N. Coupland, H. Giles, and J.M. Wiemann (eds), *"Miscommunication" and problematic talk*, 61–84. Newbury Park, CA: Sage.

Colleges Ontario (2015). "Sexual assault and sexual violence policy and protocol template," March. www.collegesontario.org/policy-positions/health/CO_Sexual%20Violence%20PP%20template_March%202015.pdf

Collier, M.J. (1996). "Communication competence problematics in ethnic relationships," *Communication Monographs*, 63, 314–336.

Conference Board of Canada (2000). *Employability Skills 2000*. www.conferenceboard.ca/topics/education/learning-tools/employability-skills.aspx

Conlee, C., Olvera, J., and Vagim, N. (1993). "The relationships among physician nonverbal immediacy and measures of patient satisfaction with physician care," *Communication Reports*, 6, 25–33.

Connolly, C.M., and Sicola, M.K. (2005). "Listening to lesbian couples: Communication competence in long-term relationships," *Journal of GLBT Family Studies*, 1(2), 143–167.

Conville, R.L. (1991). *Relational transitions: The evolution of personal relationships*. New York: Praeger.

Coon, D. (2001). *Psychology: Gateways to mind and behavior*, 9th edn. Belmont, CA: Wadsworth.

Cooper, J., and Jones, E.E. (1969). "Opinion divergence as a strategy to avoid being miscast," *Journal of Personality and Social Psychology*, 13, 23–30.

Cooper, L.O., Seibold, D.R., and Suchner, R. (1997). "Listening in organizations: An analysis of error structures in models of listening competency," *Communication Research Reports*, 14, 312–320.

Copeland, L., and Griggs, L. (1985). *Going international*. New York: Random House.

Corballis, M.C. (2002). *From hand to mouth: The origins of language*. Princeton, NJ: Princeton University Press.

Cordova, J.V., Gee, C.B., and Warren, L.Z. (2005). "Emotional skillfulness in marriage: Intimacy as a mediator of the relationship between emotional skillfulness and marital satisfaction," *Journal of Social and Clinical Psychology*, 24, 218–235.

Cormier, N.S., and Woodworth, M.T. (2008). "So you see what I see? The influence of gender stereotypes on student and Royal Canadian Mounted Police (RCMP) perceptions of violent same-sex and opposite-sex relationships," *Journal of Aggression, Maltreatment and Trauma*, 17(4), 478–505.

Cortina, M., and Liotti, G. (2010). "Attachment is about safety and protection, intersubjectivity is about sharing and social understanding," *Psychoanalytic Psychology*, 27(4), 410–441.

Cory, C.T. (1980). "Bafflegab pays," *Psychology Today*, 13, May, 12.

Costa, P.T., and McCrae, R.R. (1980). "Influence of extraversion and neuroticism on subjective well-being: Happy and unhappy people," *Journal of Personality and Social Psychology*, 38, 668–678.

Cox, S.J., Mezulis, A.H., and Hyde, J.S. (2010). "The influence of child

gender role and maternal feedback on the emergence of gender difference in depressive rumination in adolescence," *Developmental Psychology*, 46(4), 842–852.

Cozby, P.C. (1973). "Self-disclosure: A literature review," *Psychological Bulletin*, 79, 73–91.

Cramer, D., and Jowett, S. (2010). "Perceived empathy, accurate empathy and relationship satisfaction in heterosexual couples," *Journal of Social and Personal Relationships*, 27(3), 327–249.

Crane, D.R. (1987). "Diagnosing relationships with spatial distance: An empirical test of a clinical principle," *Journal of Marital and Family Therapy*, 13, 307–310.

Crohan, S.E. (1992). "Marital happiness and spousal consensus on beliefs about marital conflict: A longitudinal investigation," *Journal of Social and Personal Relationships*, 9, 89–102.

Cronen, V., Chen, V., and Pearce, W.B. (1988). "Coordinated management of meaning: A critical theory," in Y.Y. Kim and W.B. Gudykunst (eds), *Theories in intercultural communication*, 66–98. Newbury Park, CA: Sage.

———, and Chetro-Szivos, J. (2001). "Pragmatism as a way of inquiring with special reference to a theory of communication and the general form of pragmatic social theory," in D.K. Perry (ed.), *American pragmatism and communication research*, 27–65. Mahwah, NJ: Lawrence Erlbaum.

Cronkhite, G. (1976). *Communication and awareness*. Menlo Park, CA: Cummings.

Crowley, J.P. (2014). "Expressive writing to cope with hate speech: Assessing psychobiological stress recovery and forgiveness promotion for lesbian, gay, bisexual, or queer victims of hate speech," *Human Communication Research*, 40, 238–261.

———, and Knowles, J.H. (2014). "Gender differences in happiness and well-being of individuals who engage in contemptuous communication," *Communication Reports*, 27,(1), 27–38.

Crowther, C.E., and Stone, G. (1986). *Intimacy: Strategies for successful relationships*. Santa Barbara, CA: Capra Press.

Crusco, A.H., and Wetzel, G.G. (1984). "The Midas Touch: Effects of interpersonal touch on restaurant tipping," *Personality and Social Psychology Bulletin*, 10, 512–517.

Cuddy, A.J., Fiske, S.T. . . ., and Ziegler, R. (2009). "Stereotype content model across cultures: Towards universal similarities and some differences," *British Journal of Social Psychology*, 48, 1–33.

Cui, M., Durtschi, J.A. . . ., and Conger, R.D. (2010). "Intergenerational transmission of relationship aggression: A prospective longitudinal study," *Journal of Family Psychology*, 24(6), 688–697.

Cunningham, M.R., and Barbee, A.P. (2000). "Social support," in C. Hendrick and S.S. Hendrick (eds), *Close relationships: A sourcebook*, 273–285. Thousand Oaks, CA: Sage.

Cupach, W.R., and Messman, S.J. (1999). "Face predilections and friendship solidarity," *Communication Reports*, 12, 117–124.

———, and Metts, S. (1986). "Accounts of relational dissolution: A comparison of marital and non-marital relationships," *Communication Monographs*, 53, 311–334.

Daft, R.L., and Lengel, R.H. (1984). "Information richness: A new approach to managerial behavior and organizational design," in L.L. Cummings, and B.M. Staw, B.M. (eds), *Research in Organizational Behavior*, 6, (191–233). Homewood, IL: JAI Press.

Dailey, M.N., Joyce, C., Lyons, M.J., Kamachi, M., Ishi, H., Gyoba, J., and Cottrell, G.W. (2010). "Evidence and a computational explanation of cultural differences in facial expression recognition," *Emotion*, 10(6), 874–893.

Dailey, R.M. (2006). "Confirmation in parent-adolescent relationships and adolescent openness: Toward extending Confirmation Theory," *Communication Monographs*, 73, 434–458.

Dainton, M. (2000). "Maintenance behaviors, expectations for maintenance, and satisfaction: Linking comparison levels to relational maintenance strategies," *Journal of Social and Personal Relationships*, 17, 827–842.

———, and Aylor, B. (2002). "Patterns of communication channel use in the maintenance of long-distance relationships," *Communication Research Reports*, 19, 118–129.

———, Stafford, L., and Canary, D.J. (1994). "Relational maintenance strategies and physical affection as predictors of love, liking and satisfaction in marriage," *Communication Reports*, 7(2), 88–98.

Dallimore, K.S., Sparks, B.A., and Butcher, K. (2007). "The influence of angry customer outbursts on service providers' facial displays and affective states," *Journal of Service Research, 10*(1), 78–92.

Daly, K. (2013). "Prolonged parenting. Extending the limits of active parenting," *Transition, 43*(2), The Vanier Institute of the Family.

Danner, D.D., Snowdon, D.A., and Friesen, W.V. (2001). "Positive emotions in early life and longevity: Findings from the nun study," *Journal of Personality and Social Psychology, 80*, 804–813.

Dansereau, F., and Markham, S.E. (1987). "Superior-subordinate communication: Multiple levels of analysis," in F.M. Jablin, L.L. Putnam, K.H. Roberts, and L.W. Porter (eds), *Handbook of organizational communication*, 343–388. Newbury Park, CA: Sage.

Danzinger, S., Levav, J., Avnaim-Presso, L., and Kahneman, D. (2013). "Extraneous factors in judicial decisions," *Proceedings of the National Academy of Sciences, 108*(17), 6889–6892.

Daubs, K. (2008). "Don't LOL, but linguists like teens' text talk: Instant messaging creates language renaissance," 20 May. *Ottawa Citizen*.

Davidowitz, M., and Myrick, R. (1984). "Responding to the bereaved: An analysis of 'helping' styles," *Death Education, 8*, 1–10.

Davis, S.F., and Kieffer, J.C. (1998). "Restaurant servers influence tipping behavior," *Psychological Reports, 83*, 223–226.

Deal, T.E., and Kennedy, A.A. (1983). "Culture and school performance," *Educational Leadership, 40*(5), 14–15.

DeAngelis, T. (1992). "Illness linked with repressive style of coping," *APA Monitor*, 14–15.

Deaux, K. (1972). "To err is humanizing: But sex makes a difference," *Representative Research in Social Psychology, 3*, 20–28.

De Cremer, D., Pillutla, M.M., and Folmer, C.R. (2011). "How important is an apology to you? Forecasting errors in evaluating the value of apologies," *Psychological Science, 22*(1), 45–48.

De Groot, T., and Gooty, J. (2009). "Can nonverbal cues be used to make meaningful personality attributions in employment interviews," *Journal of Business Psychology, 24*, 179–192.

De Mol, J., and Buysse, A. (2008). "Understanding children's influence in parent–child relationships: A Q-methodological study. *Journal of Social and Personal Relationships, 25*(2), 359–379.

de Monteflores, C., and Schultz, S.J. (1978). "Coming out: Similarities and differences for lesbians and gay men," *Journal of Social Issues, 34*(3), 59–72.

Dennis, A.R., Kinney, S.T., and Hung, Y.T. (1999). "Gender differences in the effects of media richness," *Small Group Research, 30*, 405–437.

Dennis, M., Purvis, K., Barnes, M., Wilkinson, M., and Winner, E. (2001). "Understanding of literal truth, ironic criticism, and deceptive praise following childhood head injury," *Brain and Language, 78*(1), 1–16.

Deny, B.T., and Ochsner, K.N. (2014). "Behavioral effects of longitudinal training in cognitive reappraisal," *Emotion, 14*(2), 425–433.

DePaulo, B.M. (1992). "Nonverbal behavior and self-presentation," *Psychological Bulletin, 3*, 203–243.

———, Kashy, D.A., Kirkendol, S.E., and Wyer, M.M. (1996). "Lying in everyday life," *Journal of Personality and Social Psychology, 70*, 779–795.

———, Lindsay, J.J., Malone, B.E., Muhlenbruk, L., Charlton, K., and Cooper, H. (2003). "Cues to deception," *Psychological Bulletin, 129*(1), 74–118.

Derks, D., Bos, A., and Von Grumbkow, J. (2008). "Emoticons in computer-mediated communication: Social motives and social context," *Cyber-Psychology and Behavior, 11*(1), 99–101.

Derlega, V.J., Barbee, A.P., and Winstead, B.A. (1994). "Friendship, gender, and social support: Laboratory studies of supportive interactions," in B.R. Burleson, T.L. Albrecht, and I.G. Sarson (eds), *Communication of social support: Message, interactions, relationships, and community*, 36–151. Newbury Park, CA: Sage.

———, and Grzelak, J. (1979). "Appropriateness of self-disclosure," in G.J. Chelune (ed.), *Self-disclosure: Origins, patterns and implications of openness in interpersonal relationships*, 151–176. San Francisco: Jossey-Bass.

———, Lewis, R.J., Harrison, S., Winstead, B.A., and Costanza, R. (1989). "Gender differences in the initiation and attribution of tactile intimacy,"

Journal of Nonverbal Behavior, 13, 83–96.

———, Metts, S., Petronio, S., and Margulis, S.T. (1993). *Self-disclosure*. Newbury Park, CA: Sage.

———, Wilson, M., and Chaikin, A.L. (1976). "Friendship and disclosure reciprocity," *Journal of Personality and Social Psychology, 34*, 578–582.

———, Winstead, B.A., and Folk-Barron, L. (2000). "Reasons for and against disclosing HIV-seropositive test results to an intimate partner: A functional perspective," in S. Petronio (ed.), *Balancing the secrets of private disclosures*, 71–82. Mahwah, NJ: Lawrence Erlbaum.

Derwing, T. (2003). "What do ESL students say about their accents?" *Canadian Modern Language Review, 59*, 545–564.

———, and Munro, M. (2009a). "Comprehensibility as a factor in listener interaction preferences: Implications for the workplace," *The Canadian Modern Language Review, 66*(2), 181–202.

———, and ——— (2009b). "Putting accent in its place: Rethinking obstacles to communication," *Language Teaching, 42*, 476–490.

deTurck, M.A., and Miller, G.R. (1990). "Training observers to detect deception: Effects of self-monitoring and rehearsal," *Human Communication Research, 16*, 603–620.

Devine, D.J., Clayton, L.D., Phillips, J.L., Dunford, B.B., and Melner, S.B. (1999). "Teams in organizations: Prevalence, characteristics, and effectiveness," *Small Group Research, 30*, 678–711.

DeWall, C.N., Pond, R.S. Jr., and Deckman, T. (2011). "Aceta-minophen dulls psychological pain," in G. MacDonald and L. Jensen-Campbell (eds), *Social pain: Neuropsychological and health implications of loss and exclusion*, 123–140. Washington, DC: APA.

Dickson, F.C., Hughes, P.C., Manning, L.D., Walker, K.L., Bollis-Pecci, T., and Gratson, S. (2002). "Conflict in later-life, long-term marriages," *Southern Communication Journal, 67*, 110–121.

Dieckmann, L.E. (2000). "Private secrets and public disclosures: The case of battered women," in S. Petronio (ed.), *Balancing the secrets of private disclosures*, 275–286. Mahwah, NJ: Lawrence Erlbaum.

Dillard, J.P. (1990). *Seeking compliance: The production of interpersonal influence messages.* Scottsdale, AZ: Gorsuch Scarisbrick.

——, Solomon, D.H., and Palmer, M.T. (1999). "Structuring the concept of relational communication," *Communication Monographs, 66,* 49–65.

Dindia, K. (2000a). "Self-disclosure research: Advances through meta-analysis," in M.A. Allen, R.W. Preiss, B.M. Gayle, and N. Burrell (eds), *Interpersonal communication: Advances through meta-analysis.* Mahwah, NJ: Lawrence Erlbaum.

—— (2000b). "Sex differences in self-disclosure, reciprocity of self-disclosure, and self-disclosure and liking: Three meta-analyses reviewed," in S. Petronio (ed.), *Balancing the secrets of private disclosures,* 21–35. Mahwah, NJ: Lawrence Erlbaum.

—— (2002). "Self-disclosure research: Knowledge through meta-analysis," in M. Allen and R.W. Preiss (eds), *Interpersonal communication research: Advances through meta-analysis,* 169–185. Mahwah, NJ: Lawrence Erlbaum.

——, and Allen, M. (1992). "Sex differences in self-disclosure: A meta-analysis," *Psychological Bulletin, 112,* 106–124.

——, Fitzpatrick, M.A., and Kenny, D.A. (1997). "Self-disclosure in spouse and stranger dyads: A social relations analysis," *Human Communication Research, 23,* 388–412.

Dion, K., Berscheid, E., and Walster, E. (1972). "What is beautiful is good," *Journal of Personality and Social Psychology, 24,* 285–290.

Doherty, R.W. (1997). "The emotional contagion scale: A measure of individual differences," *Journal of Nonverbal Behavior, 21,* 131–154.

Domahidi, E., Festl, R., and Quandt, T. (2014). "To dwell among gamers: Investigating the relationship between social online game use and gaming-related friendships," *Computers in Human Behavior, 35,* 107–115.

Domingue, R., and Mollen, D. (2009). "Attachment and conflict in adult romantic relationships," *Journal of Social and Personal Relationships, 26*(5), 678–696.

Dougherty, D.S. (2001). "Sexual harassment as [dys]functional process: A feminist standpoint analysis," *Journal of Applied Communication Research, 29,* 372–402.

Dougherty, T., Turban, D., and Collander, J. (1994). "Conforming first impressions in the employment interview," *Journal of Applied Psychology, 79, 659–665.*

Douglas, W. (1987). "Affinity testing in initial interactions," *Journal of Social and Personal Relationships, 4,* 3–16.

Doura, D. (2014). Michael Sam's spectacular ESPY speech is a real tear jerker. *Globe and Mail,* 17 July. www.theglobeand mail.com/life/celebrity-news/ the-a-list/michael-sams-spectacular-espy-speech-is-a-real-tear-jerker/ article19655272/

Downey, G., and Feldman, S.I. (1996). "Implications of rejection sensitivity for intimate relationships," *Journal of Personality and Social Psychology, 70,* 1327–1343.

Downs, V.G. (1988). "Grandparents and grandchildren: The relationship between self-disclosure and solidarity in an intergenerational relationship," *Communication Research Reports, 5,* 173–179.

Draper, P. (2005). "Patronizing speech to older patients: A literature review," *Review of Clinical Gerontology, 15,* 273–279.

Drews, F.A., Pasupathi, M., and Strayer, D.L. (2008). "Passenger and cell phone conversations in simulated driving," *Journal of Experimental Psychology, 14*(4), 392–400.

Drigotas, S.M. (2002). "The Michelangelo phenomenon and personal well-being," *Journal of Personality, 70,* 59–79.

——, Rusbult, C.E., Weiselquist, J., and Whitton, S. (1999). "Close partner as sculptor of the ideal self: Behavioral confirmation and the Michelangelo phenomenon," *Journal of Personality and Social Psychology, 77,* 293–323.

Driscoll, M.S., Newman, D.L., and Seal, J.M. (1988). "The effect of touch on the perception of counselors," *Counselor Education and Supervision, 27,* 344–354.

Druckmann, D., Rozelle, R.M., and Baxter, J.C. (1982). *Nonverbal communication: Survey, theory, and research.* Beverly Hills, CA: Sage.

Drullman, R., and Smoorenburg, G.F. (1997). "Audio–visual perception of compressed speech by profoundly hearing-impaired subjects," *Audiology, 36*(3), 165–177.

Drummond, K., and Hopper, R. (1993). "Acknowledgment tokens in series," *Communication Reports, 6,* 47–53.

Duck, S. (1987). "How to lose friends without influencing people," in M.E.

Roloff and G.R. Miller (eds), *Interpersonal processes: New directions in communication research,* 278–298. Beverly Hills, CA: Sage.

—— (1992). "Social emotions: Showing our feelings about other people," in *Human Relationships,* 1–34. Newbury Park, CA: Sage.

—— (1994). "Maintenance as a shared meaning system," in D.J. Canary and L. Stafford (eds), *Communication and relationship maintenance: How individual differences in communication skills affect the achievement of relationship functions,* 45–60. San Diego: Academic Press.

—— (1998). *Human relationships,* 3rd edn. London: Sage.

——, and Barnes, M.K. (1992). "Disagreeing about agreement: Reconciling differences about similarity," *Communication Monographs, 59,* 199–208.

——, and Miell, D.E. (1986). "Charting the development of personal relationships," in R. Gilmour and S. Duck (eds), *The emerging field of personal relationships.* Hillsdale, NJ: Lawrence Erlbaum.

——, and Pittman, G. (1994). "Social and personal relationships," in M.L. Knapp and G.R. Miller (eds), *Handbook of interpersonal communication,* 2nd edn. Newbury Park, CA: Sage.

Dunleavy, K.N and Booth-Butterfield, M. (2009). "Idiomatic communication in stages of coming together and falling apart," *Communication Quarterly, 57*(4), 416–432.

——, Chory, R.M., and Goodboy, A.K. (2010). "Responses to deception in the workplace: Perceptions of credibility, power and trustworthiness," *Communication Studies, 61*(2), 239–255.

Duran, R.L., Kelly, L., and Rotaru, T. (2011). "Mobile phones in romantic relationships and the dialectic of autonomy versus connection," *Communication Quarterly, 59*(1), 19–36.

Duthler, K.W. (2006). "The politeness of requests made via email and voicemail: Support for the hyperpersonal model," *Journal of Computer-Mediated Communication, 11*(2), article 6. http://jcmc.indiana.edu/vol11/issue2/ duthler.html

Dutton, D.G., and Karakanta, C. (2013). "Depression as a risk marker for aggression: A critical review," *Aggression and Violent Behavior, 18,* 310–319

Dutton, K. (2010). *Split-second persuasion. The ancient art and new science of changing minds*. Scarborough, ON: Doubleday Canada.

Dweck, C.S. (2006). *Mindset*. New York: Random House.

——— (2010). "Even geniuses work hard," *Educational Leadership*, *68*(1), 16–20.

Eastwick, P.W., Luchies, L.B., Finkel, E.J., and Hunt, L.L. (2013). "The predicative validity of ideal partner preferences: A review and meta-analysis," *Psychological Bulletin*, *140* (3), 623–665.

Ebesu Hubbard, A.S., Hendrickson, B., Fehrenbach, K.S., and Sur, J. (2013). "Effects of timing and sincerity of an apology on satisfaction and changes in negative feelings during conflicts," *Western Journal of Communication*, *77*(3), 305–322.

Edgar, C., McRoroe, M., and Sneddon, I. (2012). "Emotional intelligence, personality and the decoding of non-verbal expressions of emotion," *Personality and Individual Differences*, *52*, 295–300.

Edwards, R. (1998). "The effects of gender, gender role, and values on the interpretation of messages," *Journal of Language and Social Psychology*, *17*, 52–71.

———, and Bello, R. (2001). "Interpretations of messages: The influence of equivocation, face concerns, and ego involvement," *Human Communication Research*, *27*, 597–691.

———, and Caballero, C. (2008). "What's in a name? An exploration of the significance of personal naming of 'mixed' children for parents from different racial, ethnic and faith backgrounds," *Sociological Review*, *56*(1) 39–60.

Eibl-Eibesfeldt, I. (1972). "Similarities and differences between cultures in expressive movements," in R.A. Hinde (ed.), *Nonverbal communication*. Oxford, UK: Cambridge University Press.

Eisenberg, E.M. (1984). "Ambiguity as strategy in organizational communication," *Communication Monographs*, *51*, 227–242.

——— (1990). "Jamming: Transcendence through organizing," *Communication Research*, *17*, 139–164.

———, and Goodall Jr., H. (2001). *Organizational communication*, 3rd edn. New York: Bedford/St. Martin's.

———, and Witten, M.G. (1987). "Reconsidering openness in organizational communication," *Academy of Management Review*, *12*, 418–426.

Ekenrode, J. (1984). "Impact of chronic and acute stressors on daily reports of mood," *Journal of Personality and Social Psychology*, *46*, 907–918.

Ekman, P. (1981). "Mistakes when deceiving," in T.A. Sebeok and R. Rosenthal (eds), *The Clever Hans phenomenon: Communication with horses, whales, apes, and people*, 269–278. New York: New York Academy of Sciences.

——— (1985). *Telling lies: Clues to deceit in the marketplace, politics, and marriage*. New York: Norton.

——— (2009), *Telling lies: Clues to deceit in the marketplace, politics and marriage*, 4th edn. New York: W.W. Norton.

———, and Friesen, W.V. (1974a). "Detecting deception from the body or face," *Journal of Personality and Social Psychology*, *29*, 288–298.

———, and ——— (1974b). "Nonverbal behavior and psychopathology," in R.J. Friedman and M.N. Katz (eds), *The psychology of depression: Contemporary theory and research*. Washington, DC: J. Winston.

———, and ——— (1975). *Unmasking the face: A guide to recognizing emotions from facial clues*. Englewood Cliffs, NJ: Prentice Hall.

———, ———, and Baer, J. (1984)." The international language of gestures," *Psychology Today*, *18*, May, 64–69.

———, Levenson, R.W., and Friesen, W.V. (1983). "Autonomic nervous system activity distinguishes among emotions," *Science*, *221*, September, 1208–1210.

Elfenbein, H.A., and Ambady, N. (2002a). "Is there an in-group advantage in emotion recognition?" *Psychological Bulletin*, *128*, 243–249.

———, and Ambady, N. (2002b). "On the universality and cultural specificity of emotion recognition: A meta-analysis," *Psychological Bulletin*, *128*, 203–235.

———, Beaupre, M., Levesque, M., and Hess, U. (2007). "Toward a dialect theory: Cultural differences in the expression and recognition of posed facial expressions," *Emotion*, *7*(1), 131–146.

Elias, F.G., Johnson, M.E., and Fortman, J.B. (1989). "Task-focused self-disclosure: Effects on group cohesiveness, commitment to task, and productivity," *Small Group Behavior*, *20*, 87–96.

Ellis, A. (2001). *Overcoming destructive beliefs, feeling and behaving: New directions for rational emotive behavior therapy*. Amherst, NY: Prometheus Books.

———, and Dryden, W. (1997). *The practice of rational emotive behavior therapy*, 2nd edn. New York: Springer.

———, and Ellis, D.J. (2011). "Rational emotive therapy," in J. Carlson and M. Englar-Carson (Series eds.) *Theories of psychotherapy series*. Washington, DC: American Psychological Association.

Ellis, D.G., and McCallister, L. (1980). "Relational control sequences in sex-typed and androgynous groups," *Western Journal of Speech Communication*, *44*, 35–49.

Ellis, K. (2002). "Perceived parental confirmation: Development and validation of an instrument," *Southern Communication Journal*, *67*, 319–334.

Ellison, N., Steinfield, C., and Lampe, C. (2007). "The benefits of Facebook 'friends': Social capital and students' use of online social network sites," *Journal of Computer-Mediated Communication*, *12*(4), 1143–1168.

Emanuel, R., Adams, J., Baker, K., Daufin, E., Coke, E., Fitts, E., Himsel, J., Holladay, L., and Okeowo, D. (2008). "How college students spend their time communicating," *International Journal of Listening*, *22*, 13–28.

Employment and Social Development Canada (2014). "Reader's guide to essential skill profiles." www.esdc.gc.ca/eng/jobs/les/profiles/readersguide.shtml

Ennis, E., Vriji, A., and Chance, C. (2008). "Indivdual differences and lying in everyday life," *Journal of Social and Personal Relationships*, *25*, 105–118.

Environics Institute (2012). *Focus Canada 2012*. Toronto: The Environics Institute. www.environicsinstitute.org/uploads/institute-projects/environics%20institute%20-%20focus%20canada%202012%20final%20report.pdf

Erbert, L.A. (2000). "Conflict and dialectics: Perceptions of dialectical contradictions in marital conflict," *Journal of Social and Personal Relationships*, *17*, 638–659.

Eslinger, P.J., and Tranel, D. (2005). "Integrative study of cognitive, social and emotional processes in clinical neuroscience," *Cognitive and Behavioral Neurology*, *18*(1), 1–4.

Etter, G.W., Sr. (1998). "Common characteristics of gangs: Examining the cultures of the new urban tribes," *Journal of Gang Research, 5,* 19–33.

Fabri, M., and Moore, D. (2005). "Is empathy the key? Effective communication via instant messaging," in Proceedings of the 11th International Conference on Networking Entities, October, St. Polten, Austria.

Farah, A., and Atoum, A. (2002). "Personality traits as self-evaluated and as judged by others," *Social Behavior and Personality, 30,* 149–156.

Farh, J., Hackett, R.D., and Liang, J. (2007). "Individual-level cultural values as moderators of perceived organizational support–employee outcome relationships in China: Comparing the effects of power distance and traditionality," *Academy of Management Journal, 50,* 715–729.

Farley, S.D., Ashcraft, A.M., Stasson, M.F., and Nusbaum, R.L. (2010). "Nonverbal reactions to conversational interruption: A test of complementarity theory and the status/gender parallel," *Journal of Nonverbal Behavior, 34,* 193–206.

Farr, R.H., and Patterson, C.J. (2013). "Coparenting among lesbian, gay and heterosexual couples: Associations with adopted children's outcomes," *Child Development, 84*(4), 1226–1240.

Fast, L.A., Reimer, H.M., and Funder, D.C. (2008). "The social behavior and reputation of the attributionally complex," *Journal of Research in Personality, 42*(1), 208–222.

Fawcett, C.A., and Markson, L. (2010). "Similarity predicts liking in 3-year-old children," *Journal of Experimental Child Psychology, 105*(4), 345–358.

Fay, N., Page, A., and Serfaty, C. (2010). "Listeners influence speakers' perceived communication effectiveness," *Journal of Experimental Social Psychology, 46,* 689–692.

———, ———, ———, Tai, V., and Winkler, C. (2008). "Speaker overestimation of communication effectiveness and fear of negative evaluation: Being realistic is unrealistic," *Psychonomic Bulletin and Review, 15*(6), 1160–1165.

Fehr, B. (1996). *Friendship processes.* Thousand Oaks, CA: Sage.

Feldman, R., Gordon, I., Schneiderman, I., Weisman, O., and Zagoory-Sharon, O. (2010). "Natural variations in maternal and paternal care are associated with systematic changes in oxytocin following parent–infant contact,"

Psychoneuroendocrinology, 35, 1133–1141.

———, Tomasian, J.C., and Coats, E.J. (1999). "Non-verbal deception abilities and adolescents' social competence: Adolescents with higher social skills are better liars," *Non-Verbal Behavior, 23*(3), 237–249.

Feldstein, S., Dohm, F.A., and Crown, C.L. (2001). "Gender and speech rate in the perception of competence and social attractiveness," *Journal of Social Psychology, 141,* 785–806.

Felmlee, D.H. (1998). "'Be careful what you wish for . . .': A quantitative and qualitative investigation of 'fatal attractions.'" *Personal Relationships, 5,* 235–253.

Felson, R.B. (1985). "Reflected appraisal and the development of self," *Social Psychology Quarterly, 48,* 71–78.

Fernald, A. (2001). "Hearing, listening, and understanding: Auditory development in infancy," in G. Bremner and A. Fogel (eds), *Blackwell handbook of infant development,* 35–70. Malden, MA: Blackwell Publishers.

Festinger, L. (1954). "A theory of social comparison processes," Human Relations, 7(2), 117–140.

Filley, A.C. (1975). *Interpersonal conflict resolution.* Glenview, IL: Scott Foresman.

Findley, M.B., Carvallo, M., and Bartak, C.P. (2014). "The effect if self-control on willingness to sacrifice in close relationships," *Self and Identity, 13*(3), 334–344.

Finkel, E.J., and Campbell, W.K. (2001). "Self-control and accommodation in close relationships: An interdependence analysis," *Journal of Personality and Social Psychology, 81,* 263–277.

———, Eastwick, P.W., Karney, B.R., Reis, H.T., and Sprecher, S. (2012). "Online dating: A critical analysis from the perspective of psychological science," *Psychology Science in the Public Interest, 13,* 3–66.

First People's Cultural Foundation. Language services. www.fpcf.ca/language-index.html

Fisher, B.A. (1983). "Differential effects of sexual composition and interactional content on interaction patterns in dyads," *Human Communication Research, 9,* 225–238.

———, and Adams, K. (1994). *Interpersonal communication: Pragmatics of human relationships,* 2nd edn. New York: Random House.

Fisher, D.V. (1986). "Decision-making and self-disclosure," *Journal of Social and Personal Relationships, 3,* 323–336.

Fitts, W.H. (1971). *The self-concept and self-actualization.* Nashville, TN: Counselor Recordings and Tests.

Fitzpatrick, J., and Sollie, D.L. (1999). "Influence of individual and interpersonal factors on satisfaction and stability in romantic relationships," *Personal Relationships, 6,* 337–350.

Fitzpatrick, M.A. (1977). "A typological approach to communication in relationships," in B. Rubin (ed.), *Communication Yearbook 1,* 263–275. New Brunswick, NJ: Transaction Books.

——— (1988). *Between husbands and wives: Communication in marriage.* Newbury Park, CA: Sage.

———, Fallis, S., and Vance, L. (1982). "Multifunctional coding of conflict resolution strategies in marital dyads," *Family Relations, 21,* 61–71.

Fletcher, G.J.O., Fincham, F.D., Cramer, L., and Heron, N. (1987). "The role of attributions in the development of dating relationships," *Journal of Personality and Social Psychology, 53,* 481–489.

Flora, J., and Segrin, C. (2000). "Relationship development in dating couples: Implications for relational satisfaction and loneliness," *Journal of Social and Personal Relationships, 17,* 811–825.

Floyd, J.J. (1985). *Listening: A practical approach.* Glenview, IL: Scott Foresman.

Floyd, K. (1996). "Communicating closeness among siblings: An application of the gendered closeness perspective," *Communication Research Reports, 13,* 27–34.

Floyd, K., Hess, J.A., Miczo, L.A., Halone, K.K., Mikkelson, A.C., and Tusing, K. (2005). "Human affection exchange: VIII. Further evidence of the benefits of expressed affection," *Communication Quarterly, 53,* 285–303.

Flynn, F.J., Reagans, R.E., and Amanatullah, E.T. (2006). "Helping one's way to the top: Self-monitors achieve status by helping others and knowing who helps whom," *Journal of Personality and Social Psychology, 91,* 1123–1137.

Fogel, A., and Branco, A.U. (1997). "Metacommunication as a source of indeterminism in relationship development," in A. Fogel and M.C.D.P. Lyra (eds), *Dynamics and indeterminism in developmental and social processes*, 65–92. Hillsdale, NJ: Lawrence Erlbaum.

———, de Koeyer, I., Bellagamba, F., and Bell, H. (2002). "The dialogical self in the first two years of life: Embarking on a journey of discovery," *Theory and Psychology*, 12, 191–205.

Forest, A.L., and Wood, J.V. (2012). "When social networking is not working: Individuals with low self-esteem recognize but do not reap the benefits of self-disclosure on Facebook," *Psychological Science*, 23(3), 295–302.

Forgays, D.K., Hyman, I., and Schreiber, J. (2014). "Texting everywhere for everything: Gender and age differences in cell phone etiquette and use," *Computers in Human Behavior*, 31, 314–321.

Fortado, B. (2011). "A field exploration of informal workplace communication," *Sociology Mind*, 1 (4), 212–220.

Fortenberry, J.H., Maclean, J., Morris, P., and O'Connell, M. (1978). "Mode of dress as a perceptual cue to deference," *Journal of Social Psychology*, 104, 131–139.

Fortney, S.D., Johnson, D.I., and Long, K.M. (2001). "The impact of compulsive communicators on the self-perceived competence of classroom peers: An investigation and test of instructional strategies," *Communication Education*, 50, 357–373.

Foss, S.K., and Griffin, C.L. (1995). "Beyond persuasion: A proposal for an invitational rhetoric," *Communication Monographs*, 62, 2–18.

Fraley, R.C., and Shaver, P.R. (2000). "Adult romantic attachment: Theoretical developments, emerging controversies and unanswered questions," *Review of General Psychology*, 4, 132–154.

Francis, J., and Wales, R. (1994). "Speech a la mode: Prosodic cues, message interpretation, and impression formation," *Journal of Language and Social Psychology*, 13, 34–44.

Freeman, J.B., and Ambady, N. (2011). "A dynamic interactive theory of person construal," *Psychological Review*, 118(2), 247–279.

French, J.R., and Raven, B. (1959). "The bases of social power," in D. Cartwright (ed.), *Studies in social power*. Ann Arbor, MI: Institute for Social Research.

———, and ——— (1968). "The bases of social power," in D. Cartwright

and A. Zander (eds), *Group dynamics: Research and theory*, 259–269. New York: Harper and Row.

Friedman, R., and Currall, S. (2003). "Conflict escalation: Dispute exacerbation elements of e-mail communication," *Human Relations*, 56(11), 1325–1347.

Frisby, B.N., and Westerman, D. (2010). "Relational actors: Channel selection and rational choices in romantic episodes," *Journal of Social and Personal Relationships*, 27(7), 970–981.

Fromme, D.K., Jaynes, W.E., Taylor, D.K., Hanold, E.G., Daniell, J., Rountree, J.R., and Fromme, M. (1989). "Nonverbal behavior and attitudes toward touch," *Journal of Nonverbal Behavior*, 13, 3–14.

Fry, R.W. (2003). *101 smart questions to ask on your interview*. Franklin Lakes, NJ: Career Press.

Fu, G., Brunet, M.K., Lv, Y., Ding, X., Heyman, G.D., Cameron, A., and Lee, K. (2010). "Chinese children's moral evaluation of lies and truths— Roles of context and parental individualism-collectivism tendencies," *Infant and Child Development*, 19(5), 498–515.

———, Lee, K., Cameron, C.A., and Xu, F. (2001). "Chinese and Canadian adults' categorization and evaluation of lie and truth-telling about prosocial and antisocial behaviors," *Journal of Cross-Cultural Research*, 32, 740–747.

Fuller-Thompson, E. (2005). "Canadian First Nations grandparents raising grandchildren: A portrait in resilience," *International Journal of Aging and Human Development*, 60(4), 331–342.

Fulmer, R. (1999). "Becoming an adult: Leaving home and staying connected," in B. Carter and M. McGoldrick (eds), *The expanded family life cycle: Individual, family, and social perspectives*, 3rd edn, 215–230. Boston: Allyn and Bacon.

Fussell, S.R. (ed.). (2002). *The verbal communication of emotions: Interdisciplinary perspectives*. Mahwah, NJ: Lawrence Erlbaum.

Futch, A., and Edwards, R. (1999). "The effects of sense of humor, defensiveness, and gender on the interpretation of ambiguous messages," *Communication Quarterly*, 47, 80–97.

Gable, S.L., and Gosnell, C.L. (2013). "Approach and avoidance behavior in interpersonal relationships," *Emotion Review*, 5(3), 269–274.

Gabric, D., and McFadden, K.L. (2001). "Student and employer perceptions of desirable entry-level operations management skills," *Mid-American Journal of Business*, 16, 51–59.

Gadlin, H. (1977). "Private lives and public order: A critical view of the history of intimate relations in the United States," in G. Levinger and H.L. Raush (eds), *Close relationships: Perspectives on the meaning of intimacy*, 33–72. Amherst, MA: University of Massachusetts Press.

Gallace, A., and Spence, C. (2010). "The science of interpersonal touch: An overview," *Neuroscience and Biobehavioral Reviews*, 34, 246–259.

Gallois, C. (1993). "The language and communication of emotion: Universal, interpersonal, or intergroup?" *American Behavioral Scientist*, 36, 309–338.

Galloway, G., and Moore, O. (2005). "Senate approves same-sex marriage," *Globe and Mail*, 20 July.

Galvin, K.M., Bylund, C.L., and Brommel, B.J. (2008). *Family communication: Cohesion and change*, 7th edn. New York: Longman.

Gara, M.A., Woolfolk, R.L., Cohen, B.D., Gioldston, R.B., and Allen, L.A. (1993). "Perception of self and other in major depression," *Journal of Abnormal Psychology*, 102, 93–100.

Garcia, S.M., and Tor, A. (2007). "Rankings, standards, and competition: Task vs. scale comparisons," *Organizational Behavior and Human Decision Processes*, 102(1), 95–108.

Garfield, R. (2010). "Male emotional intimacy: How therapeutic men's groups can enhance couples therapy," *Family Process*, 49, 109–122.

Gayle, B.M., and Preiss, R.W. (1999). "Language intensity plus: A methodological approach to validate emotions in conflicts," *Communication Reports*, 12, 43–50.

———, ———, and Allen, M.A. (1998). "Embedded gender expectations: A covariate analysis of conflict situations and issues," *Communication Research Reports*, 15, 379–387.

Geangu, E., Benga, O., Stahl, D., and Striano, T. (2010). "Contagious crying beyond the first days of life," *Infant Behavior and Development*, 33(3), 279–288.

Geddes, D. (1992). "Sex-roles in management: The impact of varying power of speech style on union members' perception of satisfaction and effectiveness," *Journal of Psychology*, 126, 589–607.

Gelitz, C. (2011). "You are what you like," *Scientific American Mind*, March–April, 38–43.

Gentile, B., Grabe, S., Dolan-Pascoe, B., Twenge, J., Wells, B.E., and Maitino, A. (2009). "Gender difference in domain specific self-esteem: A meta-analysis," *Review of General Psychology*, 13(1), 34–45.

——, Anderson, C.A., Yukawa, S., . . ., and Sakamoto, A. (2009). "The effects of prosocial video games on prosocial behaviors: International evidence from correlational, longitudinal, and experimental studies," *Personality and Social Psychology Bulletin*, 35(6), 752–763.

George, J.F., Marett, K., and Tilley, P.A. (2008). "The effects of warnings, computer based media and probing on successful lie detection," *Professional Communication*, 51(1), 1–17.

Gergen, K.J. (1971). *The concept of self.* New York: Holt, Rinehart and Winston.

—— (1991). *The saturated self: Dilemmas of identity in contemporary life.* New York: Basic Books.

Gershon, I. (2010). "Breaking up is hard to do: Media switching and media ideologies," *The Journal of Linguistic Anthropology*, 20(2), 389–405.

Giardini, A., and Frese, M. (2006). "Reducing the negative effects of emotion work in service occupations: Emotional competence as a psychological resource," *Journal of Occupational Health Psychology*, 11, 63–75.

Gibb, J.R. (1961). "Defensive communication," *Journal of Communication*, 11, 141–148.

Gibson, D.E., and Callister, R.R. (2010), "Anger in organizations: Review and integration," *Journal of Management*, 36(1), 66–93.

Giles, H. (1971). "Evaluation of personality content from accented speech as a function of listeners' social attitudes," *Perceptual and Motor Skills*, 34, 168–170.

——, Coupland, N., and Wiemann, J.M. (1992). "'Talk is cheap . . .' but 'my word is my bond': Beliefs about talk," in K. Bolton and H. Kwok (eds), *Sociolinguistics today: International perspectives*, 218–243. London, UK: Routledge and Kegan Paul.

——, and Franklyn-Stokes, A. (1989). "Communicator characteristics," in M.K. Asante and W.B. Gudykunst (eds), *Handbook of international and intercultural communication*, 117–144. Newbury Park, CA: Sage.

——, Henwood, K., Coupland, N., Harriman, J., and Coupland, J. (1992). "Language attitudes and cognitive mediation," *Human Communication Research*, 18, 500–527.

——, Mulac, A., Bradac, J.J., and Smith, P.J. (1992). "Speech accommodation," in W.B. Gudykunst and Y.Y. Kim (eds), *Readings on communicating with strangers.* New York: McGraw-Hill Ryerson.

Gino, F., Norton, M., and Ariely, D. (2010). "The counterfeit self: The deceptive costs of faking it," *Psychological Science*, 21(5), 712–720.

Giordano, G., Stoner, S., Brouer, R., and George, J. (2007). "The influences of deception and computer mediation on dyadic negotiations," *Journal of Computer-Mediated Communication*, 12(2), article 2. http://jcmc.indiana.edu/vol12/issue/2/giordana.html

Girme, Y.U., Overall, N.C., and Faingataa, S. (2014). "'Date nights' take two: The maintenance of shared relationship activities," *Personal Relationships*, 21, 125–149.

Gleason, J.B., and Greif, E.B. (1983). "Men's speech to young children," in B. Thorne, C. Kramarae, and N. Henley (eds), *Language, gender, and society*, 140–150. Rowley, MA: Newbury House.

Gluszek, A., and Dovidlo, J.F. (2010). "The way they speak: A social psychological perspective on the stigma of nonnative accents in communication," *Personality and Social Psychology Review*, 14, (2), 214–237.

Goetting, A. (1986). "The developmental tasks of siblingship over the life cycle," *Journal of Marriage and the Family*, 48, 703–714.

Goffman, E. (1959). *The presentation of self in everyday life.* Garden City, NY: Doubleday.

—— (1971). *Relations in public.* New York: Basic Books.

Goldberg, A.E., and Sayer, A. (2006). "Lesbian couples' relationship quality across the transition to parenthood," *Journal of Marriage and Family*, 68, 87–100.

Goldman, Z.W., and Goodboy, A.K. (2014). "Making students feel better: Examining the relations between teacher confirmation and college students' emotional outcomes," *Communication Education*, 63(3), 259–277.

Goldschmidt, W. (1990). *The human career.* Cambridge, MA: Basil Blackman.

Goldsmith, D.J. (2000). "Soliciting advice: The role of sequential placement in mitigating face threat," *Communication Monographs*, 67, 1–19.

——, and Baxter, L.A. (1996). "Constituting relationships in talk: A taxonomy of speech events in social and personal relationships," *Human Communication Research*, 23, 87–114.

——, and Fitch, K. (1997). "The normative context of advice as social support," *Human Communication Research*, 23, 454–476.

——, and Fulfs, P.A. (1999). "'You just don't have the evidence': An analysis of claims and evidence in Deborah Tannen's *You just don't understand*," in M.E. Roloff (ed.), *Communication Yearbook 22*, 1–49. Thousand Oaks, CA: Sage.

——, and MacGeorge, E.L. (2000). "The impact of politeness and relationship on perceived quality of advice about a problem," *Human Communication Research*, 26, 234–263.

Goleman, D. (1995). *Emotional intelligence: Why it can matter more than IQ.* New York: Bantam.

Golen, S. (1990). "A factor analysis of barriers to effective listening," *Journal of Business Communication*, 27, 25–36.

Golish, T.D. (2000). "Is openness always better? Exploring the role of topic avoidance, satisfaction, and parenting styles of stepparents," *Communication Quarterly*, 48, 137–158.

——, and Caughlin, J.P. (2002). "'I'd rather not talk about it': Adolescents' and young adults' use of topic avoidance in stepfamilies," *Journal of Applied Communication Research*, 30, 78–106.

Gonsalkorale, K., and Williams, K.D. (2007). "The KKK won't let me play: Ostracism even by a despised out-group hurts," *European Journal of Social Psychology*, 37, 1176–1186.

Good, G.E., Porter, M.J., and Dillon, M.G. (2002). "When men divulge: Men's self-disclosure on prime time situation comedies," *Sex Roles*, 46, 419–427.

Goodman, G., and Esterly, G. (1990). "Questions—The most popular piece of language," in J. Stewart (ed.), *Bridges not walls*, 5th edn, 69–77. New York: McGraw-Hill Ryerson.

Goodvin, S.H., Meyer, S., Thompson, R.A., and Hayes, R. (2008). "Self-understanding in early childhood: Associations with child attachment security and maternal negative affect," *Attachment and Human Development, 10*, 433–450.

Gordon, T. (1970). *P.E.T.: Parent effectiveness training.* New York: Wyden.

Gore, J.S. (2009). "The interaction of sex, verbal and nonverbal cues in same-sex first encounters," *Journal of Nonverbal Behavior, 33*, 279–299.

Gorham, J. (1988). "The relationship between verbal teacher immediacy behaviors and student learning," *Communication Education, 37*, 40–53.

Gosine, K. (2008). "Living between stigma and status: A qualitative study of the social identities of highly educated Black Canadian adults," *Identity, 8*(4), 307–333.

Gottman, J. (2000). "Welcome to the love lab," *Psychology Today Online*, September. www.psychology today.com/articles/200009/welcome-the-love-lab

——— (2003). "Why marriages fail," in K.M. Galvin and P.J. Cooper (eds), *Making connections: Readings in relational communication*, 258–266. Los Angeles: Roxbury.

——— (2007). "Making relationships work," *Harvard Business Review, 85*(12), 45–50.

———, Katz, L.F., and Hooven, C. (1997). *Meta-emotion: How families communicate emotionally.* Mahwah, NJ: Lawrence Erlbaum.

———, and Levenson, R.W. (1999). "Rebound from marital conflict and divorce prediction," *Family Process, 38*(3), 287–292.

———, ———, Gross, J., Fredrickson, B., McCoy, K., Rosenthal, L., Ruel, A., and Yoshimoto, D. (2003). "Correlates of gay and lesbian couples' relationship satisfaction and relationship dissolution," *Journal of Homosexuality, 45*(1), 23–43.

———, and Notarius, C.I., (2000). "Decade review: Observing marital interaction," *Journal of Marriage and the Family, 62*(4), 927–947.

———, and ———, (2002). "Marital research in the 20th century and a research agenda for the 21st century," *Family Process, 41*(2), 159–197.

Government of Canada (2014). "Preparing for a job interview," *Services for Youth*. www.youth.gc.ca/eng/topics/jobs/interview.shtml

Government of Ontario, Ministry of Education (2009). "Leadership and integrative thinking. An interview with Roger Martin," *In Conversation, 1*(3). www.rotman.utoronto.ca/rogermartin/Ministryof Education.pdf

Grabb, E., and Curtis, J. (2010). *Regions apart: The four societies of Canada and the United Sates.* Toronto: Oxford University Press.

Grace, A., Kemp, N., Martin, F., and Parrila, R. (2014). "Undergarduates' text messaging language and literacy skills," *Reading and Writing, 17*, 855–873.

Granic, I., Lobel, A., and Engels, R.C.M.E., (2014). "The benefits of playing video games," *American Psychologist, 69*(1), 66–78.

Grant, C.H., III, Cissna, K.N., and Rosenfeld, L.B. (2000). "Patients' perceptions of physicians' communication and outcomes of the accrual to trial process," *Health Communication, 12*(1), 23–39.

Gray, J. (1992). *Men are from Mars; women are from Venus: A practical guide for improving communication and getting what you want in your relationship.* New York: HarperCollins.

Greene, K., Derlega, V.J., and Mathews, A. (2006). "Self-disclosure in personal relationships," in A. Vangelisti and D. Perlman (eds), *The Cambridge handbook of personal relationships* (409–428). New York: Cambridge University Press.

Greenwald, A.G. (1995). "Getting (my) self into social psychology," in G.G. Brannigan and M.R. Merrens (eds), *The social psychologists: Research adventures*, 3–16. New York: McGraw-Hill Ryerson.

Greer, T.W., and Payne, S.C. (2014). "Overcoming telework challenges: Outcomes of successful telework strategies," *The Psychologist-Management Journal, 17*(2), 87–111.

Greimel, E., Schulte-Ruther, M., Kircher, T., Kamp-Becker, I., Remschmidt, H., and Konrad, K. (2010). "Neural mechanisms of empathy in adolescents with autism spectrum disorder and their fathers," *NeuroImage, 49*, 1055–1065.

Greitemeyer, T., and Osswald, S. (2010). "Effects of prosocial video games on prosocial behavior," *Journal of Personality and Social Psychology, 98*(2), 211–221.

Griffin, E.A. (2009). *A first look at communication theory*, 7th edn. New York: McGraw-Hill.

Grob, L.M., Meyers, R.A., and Schuh, R. (1997). "Powerful/powerless language use in group interactions: Sex differences or similarities?" *Communication Quarterly, 45*, 282–303.

Grodin, D., and Lindlof, T.R. (1995). *Constructing the self in a mediated world.* Newbury Park, CA: Sage.

Gross, E. (2004). "Adolescent internet use: What we expect, what teens report," *Journal of Applied Developmental Psychology, 25*(6), 633–649.

Gross, J.J., Sutton, S.K., and Ketelaar, T.V. (1998). "Relations between affect and personality: Support for the affect-level and affective-reactivity views," *Personality and Social Psychology Bulletin, 24*, 279–288.

Gudykunst, W.B. (1986). "The influence of cultural variability on perceptions of communication behavior associated with relationship terms," *Human Communication Research, 13*, 147–166.

——— (1993). *Communication in Japan and the United States.* Albany, NY: State University of New York Press.

——— (2005). *Theorizing about interpersonal communication.* Thousand Oaks, CA: Sage.

———, and Kim, Y.Y. (2003). *Communicating with strangers: An approach to intercultural communication.* New York: McGraw-Hill Ryerson.

———, and Ting-Toomey, S. (1988). *Culture and interpersonal communication.* Newbury Park, CA: Sage.

Gueguen, N., and Fischer-Lokou, J. (2002). "An evaluation of touch on a large request: A field setting," *Psychological Reports, 90*, 267–269.

Guzley, R. (1992). "Organizational climate and communication climate: Predictors of commitment to the organization," *Management Communication Quarterly, 5*, 379–402.

Hackman, M., and Walker, K. (1990). "Instructional communication in the televised classroom: The effects of system design and teacher immediacy," *Communication Education, 39*, 196–206.

Haddon, L. (2000). "The social consequences of mobile telephony: Framing questions," in R. Ling and K. Thrane (eds) *The social consequences of mobile telephony.* Norway: Telenor R&D.

——— (2006). "Communication problems," *Knowledge, Technology and Policy, 19*(1), 19–27.

Hale, J.L., Tighe, M.R., and Mongeau, P.A. (1997). "Effects of event type and sex on comforting messages,"

Communication Research Reports, *14,* 214–220.

Halford, W.K., Petch, J., and Creedy, D.K. (2010). "Promoting positive transition to parenthood: A randomized clinical trial of couple relationship education," *Prevention Science,* *11,* 89–100.

Hall, E.T. (1959). *Beyond culture.* New York: Doubleday.

—— (1963) "A system for the notion of proxemic behaviour," *American Psychologist,* *65,* 1003–1026.

—— (1969). *The hidden dimension.* Garden City, NY: Anchor.

Hall, J.A. (2006). "Women and men's nonverbal communication: Similarities, differences, stereotypes, and origins," in V. Manusov and M.L. Patterson (eds), *The Sage handbook of nonverbal communication,* 201–218. Thousand Oaks, CA: Sage.

——, and Baym, N.K. (2012). "Calling and texting (too much): Mobile maintenance expectations, (over) dependence, entrapment, and friendship satisfaction," *New Media and Society,* *14,* 316–331.

——, ——, Miltner, K.M. (2014). "Put down that phone and talk to me: Understanding the roles of mobile phone norm adherence and similarity in relationships," *Mobile Media and Communication,* *2*(2), 134–153.

——, Carter, S., Cody, M.J., and Albright, J.M. (2010). "Individual differences in the communication of romantic interest: Development of the flirting styles inventory," *Communication Quarterly,* *58*(4), 265–393.

——, and Pennington, N. (2013). "Self-monitoring, honesty and cue use on Facebook: The relationship with user extraversion and conscientiousness," *Computers in Human Behavior,* *29,* 1556–1564.

Hall, M., and Havens, B. (2002). "Social isolation and loneliness," *NCA Writings in Gerontology on Mental Health and Aging,* Spring/Summer.

Halone, K.K., and Pecchioni, L.L. (2001). "Relational listening: A grounded theoretical model," *Communication Reports,* *14,* 59–65.

Hamachek, D.E. (1982). *Encounters with others: Interpersonal relationships and you.* New York: Holt, Rinehart, and Winston.

—— (1992). *Encounters with the self,* 3rd edn. Fort Worth, TX: Harcourt Brace.

Hambly, L.A., O'Neill, T.A., and Kline, T.J.B. (2007). "Virtual team leadership: Perspectives from the field," *International Journal of e-Collaboration,* *3*(1), 40–64.

Hammick, J.K., and Lee, M.J. (2014). "Do shy people feel less communication apprehension online? The effects of virtual reality on the relationship between personality characteristics and communication outcomes," *Computers in Human Behavior,* *33,* 302–310.

Hample, D. (1980). "Purposes and effects of lying," *Southern Speech Communication Journal,* *46,* 33–47.

——, and Dallinger, J.M. (2000). "The effects of situation on the use or suppression of possible compliance gaining appeals," in M.A. Allen, R.W. Preiss, B.M. Gayle, and N. Burrell (eds). *Interpersonal communication: Advances through meta-analysis,* 187–209. Mahwah, NJ: Lawrence Erlbaum.

Hampton, K.N., Sessions, L.F., and Her, E.J. (2011). "Core networks, social isolation and new media. How the internet and mobile phone use is related to network size and diversity," *Information, Communication and Society,* *14*(1), 130–155.

Han, S. (2001). "Gay identity disclosure to parents by Asian American gay men," *Dissertation Abstracts International,* *62,* 329.

Hancock, J. (2007). "Digital Deception: When, where, and how people lie online," in K. McKenna, T. Postmes, U. Reips, and A. Joinson (eds), *Oxford handbook of internet psychology,* 287–301. Oxford: Oxford University Press.

——, Birnholtz, J., Bazarova, N., Guillory, J., Perlin, J., and Amos, B. (2009). "Butler lies: Awareness, deception and design," Proc. ACM CHI, 517–526.

——, Curry, L., Goorha, S., and Woodworth, M. (2004). "Lies in conversation: An examination of deception using automated linguistic analysis," in *Proceedings of the 26th Annual Conference of the Cognitive Science Society.*

——, Thom-Santelli, J., and Ritchie, T. (2004). "Deception and design: Effects of communication technology on lying behavior," in *Proceedings of CHI 2004,* 129–134. New York: ACM Press.

Hand, L.S., and Furman, W. (2009). "Rewards and costs in adolescent other-sex friendships: Comparisons to same-sex friendships and romantic relationships," *Social Development,* *18*(2), 270–287.

Haney, C., and Zimbardo, P. (2009). "Persistent dispositionalism in interactionist clothing: Fundamental attribution error in explaining prison abuse," *Personality and Social Psychology Bulletin,* *35*(6), 807–814.

Hansson, G. (1996). "Emotions in poetry: Where are they and how do we find them?" in R.J. Kreuz and M.S. MacNealy (eds), *Empirical approaches to literature and aesthetics. Advances in discourse processes* (52) 275–288. Norwood, NJ: Ablex.

Harding, S. (1991). *Whose science? Whose knowledge? Thinking from women's lives.* Ithaca, NY: Cornell University Press.

Harley, D., Winn, S., Pemberton, S., and Wilcox, P. (2007). "Using texting to support students' transition to university," *Innovations in Education and Teaching International,* *44*(3), 229–241.

Hart Research Associates (2013). "It takes more than a major: Employer priorities for college and student success." An online survey among employers conducted on behalf of the Association of American Colleges and Universities. www.aacu.org/liberaleducation/le-sp13/hartresearchassociates.cfm

Harter, S. (2006). "The self," in N. Eisenberg (ed.), *Handbook of child psychology Vol 3: Social, emotional and personality development,* 6th edn, 505–570. Hoboken, NJ: John Wiley & Sons.

Hartley, M. (2008). "YouTube told to hand over users' data," *Globe and Mail,* 3 July. www.theglobeandmail.com/technology/youtube-told-to-hand-over-users-data/article1057052/

Hartwig, M., Granhag, P., Stromwall, L., and Kronkvist, O. (2006). "Strategic use of evidence during police interviews: When training to detect deception works," *Law and Human Behavior,* *30*(5), 603–620.

Harwood, J., Bouchard, E., Giles, H., and Tyoski, S. (1997). "Evaluations of patronizing speech and three response styles in a non-service-providing context," *Journal of Applied Communication Research,* *25,* 170–195.

——, and Giles, H. (1996). "Reactions to older people being patronized: The roles of response strategies and attributed thoughts," *Journal of Language and Social Psychology,* *15,* 395–421.

Hatfield, E., and Sprecher, S. (1986). *Mirror, mirror: The importance of looks in everyday life*. Albany: State University of New York Press.

Hayes, A., Shanahan, J., and Glynn, C. (2001). "Willingness to express one's opinion in a realistic situation as a function of perceived support of that opinion," *International Journal of Public Opinion Research*, *13*(1), 45–58.

Hegelson, V.S., and Gottlieb, B.H. (2000). "Support groups," in S. Cohen, L.G. Underwood, and B.H. Gottlieb (eds), *Social support measurement and intervention*, 221–245. New York: Oxford University Press.

Hegstrom, T.G. (1979). "Message impact: What percentage is nonverbal?" *Western Journal of Speech Communication*, *43*, 134–142.

Heine, S.J., Foster, J.A.B., and Spina, R. (2009). "Do birds of a feather universally flock together? Cultural variation in the similarity-attraction effect," *Asian Journal of Social Psychology*, *12*(4), 247–258.

——, Takata, T., and Lehman, D. (2000). "Beyond self-presentation: Evidence for self-criticism among Japanese," *Personality and Social Psychology Bulletin*, *26*, 71–78.

Hellweg, S. (1987). "Organizational grapevines: A state of the art review," in B. Dervin and M. Boight (eds), *Progress in the Communication Sciences*, *8*. Norwood, NJ: Ablex.

Helms, H.M., Proulx, C.M., Klute, M.M., McHale, S.M., and Crouter, A.C. (2006). "Spouses' gender-typed attributes and their links with marital quality: A pattern analytic approach," *Journal of Social and Personal Relationships*, *23*(6), 843–864.

Helmreich, R., Aronson, E., and Lefan, J. (1970). "To err is humanizing—sometimes: Effects of self-esteem, competence, and a pratfall on interpersonal attraction," *Journal of Personality and Social Psychology*, *16*, 259–264.

Hendrick, C., Hendrick, S.S., and Dicke, A. (1998). "The love attitudes scale: Short form," *Journal of Social and Personal Relationships*, *15*, 147–159.

Henningsen, D.D., Cruz, M.G., and Morr, M.C. (2000). "Pattern violations and perception of deception," *Communication Reports*, *13*, 1–9.

Henry, F., and Tator, C. (2003). *Racial profiling in Toronto: Discourses of domination, mediation, and opposition*. Ottawa: Canadian Race Relations Foundation.

Hershcovis, M.S., Tuner, N., Barling, J., Arnold, K., Dupre, K., Inness, M., Leblanc, M.M., and Sivanathan, N. (2007). "Predicting workplace aggression: A meta-analysis," *Journal of Applied Psychology*, *92*(1), 228–238.

Hess, J.A. (2000). "Maintaining non-voluntary relationships with disliked partners: An investigation into the use of distancing behaviors," *Human Communication Research*, *26*, 458–488.

Hett, A.M. (1993). "Language of silence: An ethnographic case study of the expressive language skills of preschool Native American girls," *Dissertation Abstracts International*, *53*, 3062.

Hicks, C.B., and Tharpe, A.M. (2002). "Listening effort and fatigue in school-age children with and without hearing loss," *Journal of Speech, Language, and Hearing Research*, *45*, 573–584.

Hidalgo, M.C., and Hernandez, B. (2001). "Place attachment: Conceptual and empirical questions," *Journal of Environmental Psychology*, *21*, 273–281.

Hinde, R.A., Finkenauer, C., and Auhagen, A.E. (2001). "Relationships and the self-concept," *Personal Relationships*, *8*, 187–204.

Hines, P.M., Preto, N.G., McGoldrick, M., Almeida, R., and Weltman, S. (1999). "Culture and the family life cycle," in B. Carter and M. McGoldrick (eds), *The expanded family life cycle: Individual, family, and social perspectives*, 3rd edn, 69–87. Needham Heights, MA: Allyn and Bacon.

Ho, S.S., and McLeod, D.M. (2008). "Social-psychological influences on opinion expression in face-to-face and computer-mediated communication," *Communication Research*, *35*, 190–207.

Hoch, J.E. (2013). "Shared leadership and innovation: The role of vertical leadership and employee integrity," *Journal of Business Psychology*, *28*, 159–174.

Hochberg, J. (ed.). (1998). *Handbook of perception and cognition*, 2nd edn. San Diego, CA: Academic Press.

Hocker, J.L., and Wilmot, W.W. (1997). *Interpersonal conflict*, 5th edn. New York: McGraw-Hill Ryerson.

Hoffman, M.L. (1991). "Empathy, social cognition, and moral action," in W. Kurtines and J. Gerwirtz (eds), *Moral behavior and development:*

Theory, research, and applications (1) 275–301. Hillsdale, NJ: Lawrence Erlbaum.

Hoffnung, M. (2006). "What's in a name? Marital name choice re-visited." *Sex Roles*, *55*, 817–825.

Hofstede, G. (1980, 2001). *Culture's consequences: Comparing values, behavior, institutions and organizations across nations*. Thousand Oaks, CA: Sage.

Holt, J.L., and DeVore, C.J. (2005). "Culture, gender, organizational role and styles of conflict resolution: A meta-analysis," *International Journal of Intercultural Relations*, *29*, 165–196.

Holte, A., and Wichstrom, L. (1990). "Disconfirmatory feedback in families of schizophrenics," *Scandinavian Journal of Psychology*, *31*, 198–211.

Homans, G.C. (1961). *Social behavior: Its elementary form*. New York: Harcourt Brace.

Honeycutt, J.M. (1999). "Typological differences in predicting marital happiness from oral history behaviors and imagined interactions," *Communication Monographs*, *66*, 276–291.

——, and Wiemann, J.M. (1999). "Analysis of functions of talk and reports of imagined interactions (IIs) during engagement and marriage," *Human Communication Research*, *25*, 399–419.

Horan, S.M., and Booth-Butterfield, M. (2010). "Investing in affection: An investigation of affection exchange theory and relational qualities," *Communication Quarterly*, *58*(4), 394–413.

Hornsey, M.J., Oppes, T., and Svensson, A. (2002). "'It's ok if we say it, but you can't: Responses to intergroup and intragroup criticism." *European Journal of Social Psychology*, *32*, 293–307.

Horrey, W.J., and Wickens, C.D. (2006). "Examining the impact of cell phone conversations on driving using meta-analytic techniques," *Human Factors*, *48*, 196–205.

Hosman, L.A. (1989). "The evaluative consequences of hedges, hesitations, and intensifiers: Powerful and powerless speech styles," *Human Communication Research*, *15*, 383–406.

House, J.S., Landis, K.R., and Umberson, D. (1988). "Social relationships and health," *Science*, *241*, 540–545.

Howard, C.S., Munro, K.J., and Plack, C.J. (2010). "Listening effort at signal-to-noise ratios that are typical of the school classroom," *International Journal of Audiology, 49*(12), 928–932.

Huang, L. (1999). "Family communication patterns and personality characteristics," *Communication Quarterly, 47*, 230–243.

Hubbard, A.S.E. (2001). "Conflict between relationally uncertain romantic partners: The influence of relational responsiveness and empathy," *Communication Monographs, 68(4)*, 400–414.

Hughes B., and Fitzpatrick J. (2010). "Nurse–physician collaboration in an acute care community hospital," *Journal of Interprofessional Care, 24*(6), 625–632.

Hughes, L., and Rutten, B. (2010). *Managing the risks of workplace violence and harassment*. The Conference Board of Canada, October. www.conferenceboard.ca/documents.aspx?did=3822

Hulbert, J.E. (1989). "Barriers to effective listening," *Bulletin for the Association for Business Communication, 52*, 3–5.

Human, L.J., and Biesanz, J.C. (2011). "Through the looking glass clearly: Accuracy and assumed similarity in well-adjusted indivduals' first impressions," *Journal of Personality and Social Psychology, 100*, 349–364.

Hussain, Z., and Griffiths, M. (2008). "Gender swapping and socializing in cyberspace: An exploratory study," *CyberPsychology and Behavior, 11*(1), 47–53.

Huston, T.L., and Vangelisti, A.L. (1995). "How parenthood affects marriage," in M.A. Fitzpatrick and A.L. Vangelisti (eds), *Explaining family interactions*, 147–176. Thousand Oaks, CA: Sage.

Hyde, R.B. (1993). "Council: Using a talking stick to teach listening," *Speech Communication Teacher, 7*, Winter, 1–2.

Hyman, I.R., Boss, S.M., Wise, B.M., McKenzie, K.E., and Caggiano, J.M. (2010). "Did you see the unicycling clown? Inattentional blindness while walking and talking on a cell phone," *Applied Cognitive Psychology, 24*, 597–607.

Hynes, D. (2001). *Preventing workplace violence: Towards an aggression-free workplace*. Ottawa: Conference Board of Canada.

Iacoboni, M., Dapretto, M., (2006). "The mirror neuron system and the consequences of its dysfunction," *National Review, Neuroscience. 7*, 942–951.

Ifert, D.E., and Roloff, M.E. (1997). "Overcoming expressed obstacles to compliance: The role of sensitivity to the expressions of others and ability to modify self-presentation," *Communication Quarterly, 45*, 55–67.

Industry Canada (2012). "Archived—Key small business statistics—July 2012." www.ic.gc.ca/eic/site/061.nsf/eng/02724.html

Ilies, R., Wagner, D.T., and Morgeson, F.P. (2007). "Explaining affective linkages in teams: Individual differences in susceptibility to contagion and individualism-collectivism," *Journal of Applied Psychology, 92*(4), 1140–1148.

Infante, D.A. (1987). "Aggressiveness," in J.C. McCroskey and J.A. Daly (eds), *Personality and interpersonal communication*, 157–192. Newbury Park, CA: Sage.

—— (1988). *Arguing constructively*. Prospect Heights, IL: Waveland Press.

——, Chandler, T.A., and Rudd, J.E. (1989). "Test of an argumentative skill deficiency model of interspousal violence," *Communication Monographs, 56*, 163–177.

——, and Gorden, W.I. (1985). "Superiors' argumentativeness and verbal aggressiveness as predictors of subordinates' satisfaction," *Human Communication Research, 12*, 117–125.

——, and —— (1987). "Superior and subordinate communication profiles: Implications for independent mindedness and upward effectiveness," *Central States Speech Journal, 38*, 73–80.

——, and —— (1989). "Argumentativeness and affirming communicator style as predictors of satisfaction/dissatisfaction with subordinates," *Communication Quarterly, 37*, 81–90.

——, and Rancer, A.S. (1982). "A conceptualization and measure of argumentativeness," *Journal of Personality Assessment, 46*, 72–80.

——, Riddle, B.L., Horvath, C.L., and Tumlin, S.A. (1992). "Verbal aggressiveness: Messages and reasons," *Communication Quarterly, 40*, 116–126.

——, and Wigley, C.J., III. (1986). "Verbal aggressiveness: An interpersonal model and measure," *Communication Monographs, 53*, 61–69.

Inman, C. (1996). "Friendships among men: Closeness in the doing," in J.T. Wood (ed.), *Gendered relationships*, 95–110. Mountain View, CA: Mayfield Publishing.

International Labour Organization. (2006). *New forms of violence at work on the rise worldwide, says ILO*. Press Release, 14 June. Ref: ILO/06/33.

Ipsos Reid (2010). *The Ipsos Canadian inter@active Reid report 2010 fact guide*.

—— (2012). *The Ipsos Canadian inter@active Reid report 2012 fact guide: The definitive Resource on Canadians and the Internet*. www.ipsos.ca/common/dl/pdf/Ipsos_InteractiveReidReport_FactGuide_2012.pdf

Iverson, J.M. (1999). "How to get to the cafeteria: Gesture and speech in blind and sighted children's spatial descriptions," *Developmental Psychology, 35*, 1132–1142.

——, and Goldin-Meadow, S. (1997). "What's communication got to do with it? Gesture in children blind from birth," *Developmental Psychology, 33*, 453–467.

Izard, C.E. (2010). "The many meanings/aspects of emotion: Definitions, functions, activation and regulation," *Emotion Review, 2*(4), 363–370.

—— (2011). "Forms and functions of emotions: Matters of emotion-cognition interactions," *Emotion Review, 3*(4), 371–378.

Jackson, M. (2002). *Justice behind the walls: Human rights in Canadian prisons*. Toronto: Douglas and McIntyre.

Jackson, W.C. (1978). *Wisconsin State Journal*, 7 September. UPI.

Janas, M. (2001). "Getting a clear view," *Journal of Staff Development, 22*(2), 32–34.

Janis, I.L. (1983). *Groupthink: Psychological studies of policy decisions and fiascos*, 2nd edn. Boston: Houghton Mifflin.

Janoff-Bulman, R., and Leggatt, H.K. (2002). "Culture and social obligation: When 'shoulds' are perceived as 'wants.'" *Journal of Research in Personality, 36*, 260–270.

Janusik, L.A., and Wolvin, A.D. (2009). "24 hours in a day: A listening update to the time studies," *The International Journal of Listening, 23*, 104–120.

Jedwab, J. (2003). *Perceived threat to the French language and culture and support for bilingualism in Canada*.

Press release. Toronto: Environics Research.

——— (2004a). "Collective and individual perceptions of discrimination in Canada," Poll conducted for the Association for Canadian Studies, 29 April. www.acs-aec.ca/en/social-research/?start=250&csort=&order=

——— (2004b). "Canadian society: More American than European," Poll conducted for Association for Canadian Studies, 29 April. www.acs-aec.ca/en/social-research/?start=250&csort=&order=

Jett, C. (2005). "E-mail etiquette," *Freelance Star*, 30 July.

Job Outlook '99. (2010). "National Association of Colleges and Employers." www.jobwell.org/pubs/joboutlook/want.htm

Johnson, F. (1996). "Friendships among women: Closeness in dialogue," in J.T. Wood (ed.), *Gendered relationships*, 79–94. Mountain View, CA: Mayfield Publishing.

Johnson, H.M. (1998). *How do I love me?* 3rd edn. Salem, WI: Sheffield.

Johnson, P., Lindsey, A.E., and Zakahi, W.R. (2001). "Anglo-American, Hispanic American, Chilean, Mexican and Spanish perceptions of competent communication in initial interaction," *Communication Research Reports, 18*, 36–43.

Johnson, S. (1987). *Going out of our minds: The metaphysics of liberation*. Freedom, CA: Crossing.

———, and Bechler, C. (1998). "Examining the relationship between listening effectiveness and leadership emergence: Perceptions, behaviors, and recall," *Small Group Research, 29*, 452–471.

Joinson, A.N., and Paine, C.B. (2007). "Self-disclosure, privacy and the internet," in A. Joinson, K. McKenna, T. Postmes, and U. Reips (eds), *The Oxford handbook of internet psychology*, 237–252. Oxford University Press.

Jones, S.E. (1986). "Sex differences in touch behavior," *Western Journal of Speech Communication, 50*, 227–241.

Jordan, J., and Roloff, M.E. (1990). "Acquiring assistance from others: The effect of indirect requests and relational intimacy on verbal compliance," *Human Communication Research, 16*, 519–555.

Jorgenson, J. (1992). "Communication, rapport, and the interview: A social perspective," *Communication Theory, 2*, 148–157.

Jourard, S. (1966). "An exploratory study of body accessibility," *British Journal of Social and Clinical Psychology, 5*, 221–231.

Kalist, D., and Lee, D.Y. (2009). "First names and crime: Does unpopularity spell trouble?" *Social Science Quarterly, 90*, 39–49.

Kanaga, K.R., and Flynn, M. (1981). "The relationship between invasion of personal space and stress," *Human Relations, 34*, 239–248.

Karau, S.J., and Williams, K.D. (1993). "Social loafing: A meta-analytic review and theoretical integration," *Journal of Personality and Social Psychology, 65*, 681–706.

———, and ——— (2001). "Understanding individual motivation in groups: The collective effort model," in M.E. Turner (ed.), *Groups at work: Theory and Research. Applied social research*. Mahwah, NJ: Lawrence Erlbaum.

Karl, K., Peluchette, J., and Schlaegel, C. (2010). "Who's posting Facebook faux pas? Cross-cultural examination of personality differences," *International Journal of Selection and Assessment, 18*(2), 174–186.

Kashima, Y., Lyons, A., and Clark, A. (2013). "The maintenance of cultural stereotypes in the conversational retelling of narratives," *Asian Journal of Social Psychology, 16*, 60–70.

Katz, J.E., Rice, E.E., and Aspden, P. (2001). "The internet, 1995–2000: Access, civic involvement, and social interaction," *American Behavioral Scientist, 45*, 404–419.

Kaufman, D., and Mahoney, J.M. (1999). "The effect of waitresses' touch on alcohol consumption in dyads," *Journal of Social Psychology, 139*, 261–267.

Kaufmann, P.J. (1993). *Sensible listening: The key to responsive interaction*, 2nd edn. Dubuque, IA: Kendall/Hunt.

Keefe, W.F. (1971). *Listen, management!* New York: McGraw-Hill Ryerson.

Keeshig-Tobias, L. (1990). "Stop stealing our stories," *Globe and Mail*, 26 January.

Keizer, K., Lindenberg, S., and Steg, L. (2008). "The spreading of disorder," *Science, 322*, 12 December, 1681–1685.

Kellermann, K. (1989). "The negativity effect in interaction: It's all in your point of view," *Human Communication Research, 16*, 147–183.

———, Reynolds, R., and Chen, J.B. (1991). "Strategies of conversational retreat: When parting is not sweet sorrow," *Communication Monographs, 58*, 362–383.

Kelley, D.L. (1999). "Relational expectancy fulfillment as an explanatory variable for distinguishing couple types," *Human Communication Research, 25*, 420–442.

Kelly, A.E. (1999). "Revealing personal secrets," *Current Directions in Psychological Science, 8*(4), 105–108.

———, Klusas, J.A., von-Weiss, R.T., and Kenny, C. (2001). "What is it about revealing secrets that is beneficial?" *Personality and Social Psychology Bulletin, 27*, 651–665.

Kelly, L., and Brown, J.B. (2002). "Listening to Native patients: Changes in physicians' understanding and behaviour," *Canadian Family Physician, 48*, 1645–1652.

———, Duran, R.L., and Zolten, J.J. (2001). "The effect of reticence on college students' use of electronic mail to communicate with faculty," *Communication Education, 50*, 170–176.

———, and Watson, A.K. (1986). *Speaking with confidence and skill*. Lanham, MD: University Press of America.

Keltner, D., and Haidt, J. (2001). "Social function of emotions," in T.J. Mayne and G.A. Bonanno (eds), *Emotions: Current issues and future directions*. New York: Guilford Press.

Kenaszchuk C., Wilkins K., Reeves S., Zwarenstein M., and Russell A. (2010). "Nurse–physician relations and quality of nursing care: Findings from a national survey of nurses," *Canadian Journal of Nursing Research 42*, 120–136.

Kendon, A. (1994). "Do gestures communicate? A review," *Research on Language and Social Interaction, 27*, 175–200.

Kennedy-Lightsey, C.D., and Dillow, M.R. (2011). "Initiating and avoiding communication with mothers: Young adult children's perceptions of hurtfulness and affirming styles," *Southern Communication Journal, 76*(5), 482–501.

Kennedy-Moore, E., and Watson, J.C. (1999). *Expressing emotion: Myths, realities, and therapeutic strategies*. New York: Guilford Press.

Kerem, E., Fishman, N., and Josselson, R. (2001). "The experience of empathy in everyday relationships: Cognitive and affective elements," *Journal of Social and Personal Relationships, 18*, 709–729.

Kersten, G., Koszegi, S., and Vetschera, R. (2002). *Cultural influences in anonymous business negotiations.* Paper presented at the 35th Hawaii International Conference on System Sciences.

Khanna, N. (2004). "The role of reflected appraisals in racial identity: The case of multiracial Asians," *Social Psychology Quarterly, 67*(2), 115–131.

——— (2010). "If you are half black, you're just black: Reflected appraisals and the persistence of the one-drop rule," *Sociological Quarterly, 51*(1), 96–121.

Kholer, T., Jansen, C., Plath, S., Reese, J., Lay, J., . . . and Pfaff, H. (2010). "Communication, social capital, and workplace health management as determinants of the innovative climate in German banks," *International Journal of Public Health, 55*(6), 561–570.

Kiazad, K., Restubog, S.L., Zagenczyk, T.J., Kicwitz, C., and Tang, R.L. (2010). "In pursuit of power: The role of authoritarian leadership in the relationship between supervisors' Machiavellianism and subordinates' perceptions of abusive behavior," *Journal of Research in Personality, 44*, 512–519.

Kiddie, T.J. (2014). "Text(ing) in context: The future of workplace communication in the United States," *Business and Professional Communication Quarterly, 77*(1), 65–88.

Kihlstrom, J.F., and Klein, S.B. (1994). "The self as a knowledge structure," in R.S. Wyer and T.K. Srull (eds), *Handbook of social cognition, volume 1: Basic processes,* 2nd edn, 153–208. Hillsdale, NJ: Lawrence Erlbaum.

Kilbride, K.M., and Ali, M.A. (2010). "Striving for voice: Language acquisition and Canadian immigrant women," *Current Issues in Language Planning, 11*(2), 173–189.

Killgore, W.D.S. (2010). "Effects of sleep deprivation on cognition," in G.A. Kerkhof and H.P.A. Van Dongen (eds). *Progress in Brain Research, 185*, 105–129.

Kim, E.J., and Buschmann, M.T. (1999). "The effect of expressive physical touch on patients with dementia," *International Journal of Nursing Studies, 36*, 235–243.

Kim, M.S., Hunter, J.E., Miyahara, A., Horvath, A.M., Bresnahan, M., and Yoon, H. (1996). "Individual vs. culture-level dimensions of individualism and collectivism: Effects on preferred conversational styles," *Communication Monographs, 63*, 28–49.

———, Shin, H.C., and Cai, D. (1998). "Cultural influences on the preferred forms of requesting and re-requesting," *Communication Monographs, 65*, 47–66.

———, Tasaki, K., Kim, I.D., and Lee, H. (2007). "The influence of social status on communication predispositions. Focusing on independent and interdependent self-construals," *Journal of Asian Pacific Communication, 17*(2), 303–329.

Kinney, T., and Segrin, C. (1998). "Cognitive moderators of negative reactions to verbal aggression," *Communication Studies, 49*, 49–72.

Kinzler, K.D., Shutts, K., Dejesus, J., and Spelke, E. (2009). "Accent trumps race in guiding children's social preferences," *Social Cognition, 27*(4), 623–634.

Kirchler, E. (1988). "Marital happiness and interaction in everyday surroundings: A time-sample diary approach for couples," *Journal of Social and Personal Relationships, 5*, 375–382.

Kirkland, S.L., Greenberg, J., and Pyszczynski, T. (1987). "Further evidence of the deleterious effects of overheard derogatory ethnic labels: Derogation beyond the target," *Personality and Social Psychology Bulletin, 12*, 216–227.

Kirkpatrick, D. (1992). "Here comes the payoff from PCs," *Fortune,* 23 March, 93–102.

Kito, M. (2005). "Self-disclosure in romantic relationships and friendships among American and Japanese college students," *Journal of Social Psychology, 145*, 127–140.

Kleinke, C.L., Peterson, T.R., and Rutledge, T.R. (1998). "Effects of self-generated facial expressions on mood," *Journal of Personality and Social Psychology, 74*, 272–279.

Kleinke, C.R. (1977). "Compliance to requests made by gazing and touching experimenters in field settings," *Journal of Experimental Social Psychology, 13*, 218–223.

Kline, S.L., and Chatani, K. (2001). "Social perception and message awareness as correlates of person-centered regulative messages," *Communication Research Reports, 18*, 274–284.

Klopf, D. (1984). "Cross-cultural apprehension research: A summary of Pacific Basin studies," in J. Daly and J. McCroskey (eds), *Avoiding communication: Shyness, reticence, and communication apprehension,* 157–169. Beverly Hills, CA: Sage.

Kluwer, E.S., and Johnson, M.D. (2007). "Conflict frequency and relationship quality across the transition to parenthood," *Journal of Marriage and Family, 69*(5), 1089–1106.

Knafo, A., Zahn-Waxler, C., Van Hulle, C., Robinson, J.L., and Rhee, S.H. (2008). "The developmental origins of a disposition toward empathy: Genetic and environmental contributions," *Emotion, 8*(6), 737–752.

Knapp, M.L., and Hall, J.A. (2006). *Nonverbal communication in human interaction,* 5th edn. Belmont, CA: Wadsworth.

———, and ——— (2013). *Nonverbal communication in human interaction,* 8th edn. Belmont, CA: Wadsworth.

———, Putnam, L.L., and Davis, L.J. (1988). "Measuring interpersonal conflict in organizations: Where do we go from here?" *Management Communication Quarterly, 1*, 414–429.

———, and Vangelisti, A. (2000). *Interpersonal communication and human relationships,* 4th edn. Boston: Allyn and Bacon.

———, and ———. (2009). *Interpersonal communication and human relationships,* 6th edn. Boston: Allyn and Bacon.

Knobloch, L.K., and Solomon, D.H. (2002). "Information seeking beyond initial interaction: Negotiating relational uncertainty within close relationships," *Human Communication Research, 28*, 243–257.

Knowles, E.D., Wearing, J.R., and Campos, B. (2011). *Social, Psychological and Personality Science, 2*(4), 408–415.

Koc, E. (2010). "Services and conflict management: Cultural and European integration perspectives," *International Journal of Intercultural Relations, 34*, 88–96.

Kock, N. (2005). "Media richness or media naturalness? The evolution of our biological communication apparatus and its influence on our behaviour toward e-communication tools," *IEEE Transactions on Professional Communication, 48*, 117–130.

Koerner, A.F., and Fitzpatrick, M.A. (2002). "Toward a theory of family communication," *Communication Theory, 12*, 70–91.

Koh, Y., Mendelson, M., and Rhee, U. (2003). "Friendship satisfaction in Korean and Canadian university students," *Canadian Journal of Behavioural Science*, *35*(2), 239–253.

Kolb, J.A. (1998). "The relationship between self-monitoring and leadership in student project groups," *Journal of Business Communication*, *35*, 264–282.

Kolligan, J., Jr. (1990). "Perceived fraudulence as a dimension of perceived incompetence," in R.J. Sternberg and J. Kolligan, Jr. (eds), *Competence considered*, 261–285. New Haven, CT: Yale University Press.

Kollock, P., Blumstein, P., and Schwartz, P. (1985). "Sex and power in interaction: Conversation privileges and duties," *American Sociological Review*, *50*, 34–46.

Kopp, J. (1988). "Self-monitoring: A literature review of research and practice," *Social Work Research and Abstracts*, *24*(4), 8–20.

Korabik, K., and McCreary, D.R. (2000). "Testing a model of socially desirable and undesirable gender-role attributes," *Sex Roles*, *43*, 665–685.

Korzybski, A. (1933). *Science and sanity*. Lancaster, PA: Science Press.

Koukounas, E., and Letch, N.M. (2001). "Psychological correlates of perception of sexual intent in women," *Journal of Social Psychology*, *141*, 443–456.

Krackhardt, D., and Hanson, J.R. (1993). "Informal networks: The company behind the chart," *Harvard Business Review*, *71*, 104–111.

Krause, S., Back, M.D., Egloff, B., and Schmukle, S.C. (2014). "Implicit interpersonal attraction in small groups: Automatically activated evaluations predict actual behaviour toward social partners," *Social Psychological and Personality Science*, *5*(6), 671–679.

Krauss, C. (2003). "Canada's view on social issues is opening rifts with the US," *New York Times*, 2 December.

Krauss, R.M., Morrel-Samuels, P., and Colasante, C. (1991). "Do conversational hand gestures communicate?" *Journal of Personality and Social Psychology*, *61*, 743–754.

Kraut, R., Patterson, M., Lundmark, V., Kiesler, S., Mukopadhyay, T., and Scherlis, W. (1998). "Internet paradox: A social technology that reduces social involvement and psychological well-being?" *American Psychologist*, *53*(9), 1017–1031.

Kristof-Brown, A.L., Barrick, M.R., and Stevens, C.K. (2005). "Opposites attract: A multi-sample demonstration of complementary person–team fit on extraversion," *Journal of Personality*, *73*(4), 935–958.

———, and Stevens, C.K. (2001). "Goal congruence in project teams: Does the fit between members' personal mastery and performance goals matter?" *Journal of Applied Psychology*, *86*, 1083–1095.

Kroeber, A.L., and Kluckholn, C. (1952). *Culture: A critical review of concepts and definitions*. Harvard University, Peabody Museum of American Archeology and Ethnology Papers 47.

Krokoff, L.J. (1990). "Hidden agendas in marriage: Affective and longitudinal dimensions." *Communication Research*, *17*, 483–499.

Kross, E., Verduyn, P., Demiralp, E., Park, J., Lee, D.S., et al. (2013). "Facebook use predicts declines in subjective well-being in young adults," *PLoS ONE 8*(8): e69841.

Krpan, K.M., Kross, E., Berman, M.G., Deldin, P.J., Askren, M.K., and Jonides, J. (2013). "An everyday activity treatment for depression: The benefits of expressive writing for people diagnosed with major depressive disorder," *Journal of Affective Disorders*, *150*, 1148–1151.

Kruger, J., Epley, N., Parker, J., and Ng, Z. (2005). "Egocentrism over e-mail: Can we communicate as well as we think?" *Journal of Personality and Social Psychology*, *89*, 925–936.

Kubany, E.S., Richard, D.C., Bauer, G.B., and Muraoka, M.Y. (1992). "Impact of assertive and accusatory communication of distress and anger: A verbal component analysis," *Aggressive Behavior*, *18*, 337–347.

Kuiper, N.A. (2010). "Introductory comments: Special issue of EJOP on humor research in personality and social psychology," *Europe's Journal of Psychology*, *6*(3), 1–8.

Kunkel, A.W., and Burleson, B.R. (1999). "Assessing explanations for sex differences in emotional support: A test of the different cultures and skill specialization accounts," *Human Communication Research*, *25*, 307–340.

Kuo, F.E., and Sullivan, W.C. (2001). "Aggression and violence in the inner city: Effects of environment via mental fatigue," *Environment and Behavior*, *33*, 543–571.

Kurdek, L.A. (2008). "Change in relationship quality for partners from lesbian, gay male and heterosexual couples," *Journal of Family Psychology*, *22*(5), 701–711.

Kwan V.S.Y., John O.P., Kenny D.A, Bond M.H., Robins R.W. (2004). "Reconceptualizing individual differences in self-enhancement bias: An interpersonal approach," *Psychological Review*, *111*(1), 94–110.

Kwong, M.J., Bartholomew, K., Henderson, A.J.Z., and Trinke, S.J. (2003). "The intergenerational transmission of relationship violence," *Journal of Family Psychology*, *17*, 288–301.

Laing, R.D. (1961). *The self and others: Further studies in sanity and madness*. London: Tavistock.

LaLonde, M. (1992). "Parents as role models," *Ha-Shilth-Sa*, *19*, 2–3.

Lane, K., Balleweg, B.J., Suler, J.R., Fernald, P.S., and Goldstein, G.S. (2000). "Acquiring skills—Undergraduate students," in M.E. Ware and D.E. Johnson (eds), *Handbook of demonstrations and activities in the teaching of psychology, Vol. III: Personality, abnormal, clinical-counseling, and social*, 2nd edn, 109–124. Mahwah, NJ: Lawrence Erlbaum.

Lang, E.V., Hatsiopoulou, O., Koch, T. . . ., and Kaptchuk, T.J. (2005). "Can words hurt? Patient–provider interactions during invasive procedures," *Pain*, *114*, 303–9

Lange, P. (2007). "Publicly private and privately public: Social networking on YouTube," *Journal of Computer-Mediated Communication*, *13*(1).

Langlois, J.H., and Roggman, L.A. (1990). "Attractive faces are only average," *Psychological Science*, *1*, 115–121.

Lapakko, D. (1997). "Three cheers for language: A closer examination of a widely cited study of nonverbal communication," *Communication Education*, *46*, 63–67.

Lapidot-Lefler, N., and Barak, A. (2012). "Effects of anonymity, invisibility, and lack of eye-contact on toxic online disinhibition," *Computers in Human Behavior*, *28*, 434–443.

LaRochelle-Côté, S. (2010). "Self-employment in the downturn," *Perspectives*, March. Statistics Canada Catalogue no. 75-001-X.

Larose, H., and Standing, L. (1998). "Does the halo effect occur in the elderly?" *Social Behavior and Personality*, *26*, 147–150.

Larsen, K.R.T., and McInerney, C.R., (2002). "Preparing to work in the virtual organization," *Information and Management*, *39*(6), 445–456.

Larson, C.E., and LaFasto, F.M. (1989). *Team Work: What must go right/What can go wrong*. Newbury Park, CA: Sage.

Larson, J.H., Crane, D.R., and Smith, C.W. (1991). "Morning and night couples: The effect of wake and sleep patterns on marital adjustment," *Journal of Marital and Family Therapy, 17,* 53–65.

Lassonde, K.A., and O'Brien, E.J. (2013). "Occupational stereotypes: Activation of male bias in a gender-neutral world," *Journal of Applied Social Psychology, 43,* 387–396.

Laursen, B., and Hafen, C.A. (2010). "Future directions in the study of close relationships: Conflict is bad (except when it's not)," *Social Development, 19*(4), 858–872.

Leaper, C., and Ayres, M.M. (2007). "A meta-analytic review of gender variations in adults' language use: Talkativeness, affiliative speech and assertive speech," *Personality and Social Psychology Review, 11*(4), 328–363.

Learning Partnership (2004). *Take our kids to work*. www.takeourkidstowork.ca

Leary, M.R., and Kowalski, R.M. (1990). "Impression management: A literature review and two-component model," *Psychological Bulletin, 107,* 34–47.

Leathers, D.G. (1992). *Successful nonverbal communication: Principles and applications*, 2nd edn. New York: Macmillan.

Lebula, C., and Lucas, C. (1945). "The effects of attitudes on descriptions of pictures," *Journal of Experimental Psychology, 35,* 517–524.

Ledbetter, A.M., Mazer, J.P., DeGroot, J.M., Meyer, K.R., Mao, Y., and Swafford, B. (2011). "Attitudes toward online social connection and self-disclosure as predictors of Facebook communication and relational closeness," *Communication Research, 38*(1), 27–53.

Lee, J. (1998). "Effective maintenance communication in superior–subordinate relationships," *Western Journal of Communication, 62,* 181–208.

Lee, J.A. (1973). *The colors of love: Exploration of the ways of loving*. Don Mills, ON: New Press.

Lee, K., Cameron, C.A., Xu, F., Fu, G., and Board, J. (1997). "Chinese and Canadian children's evaluations of lying and truth telling," *Child Development, 64,* 924–934.

Lee, P. (2008). "Stages and transitions if relational identity formation in intercultural friendship: Implications for identity management theory," *Journal of International and Intercultural Communication, 1*(1), 51–69.

Lee, T.M.C., Sun, D., Leung, M.K., Chu, L.W., and Keysers, C. (2013). "Neural activities during affective processing in people with Alzheimer's disease," *Neurobiology of Aging, 34,* 706–715.

Lee, Y., and Antonakis, J. (2014). "When preference is not satisfied but the individual is: How power distance moderates person–job fit," *Journal of Management, 40*(3), 641–675.

Leets, L. (2002). "Experiencing hate speech: Perceptions and responses to anti-semitism and antigay speech," *Journal of Social Issues, 58,* 341–361.

Lehdonvirta, V., and Rasanen, P. (2010). "How do young people identify with online and offline peer groups? A comparison between UK, Spain, and Japan," *Journal of Youth Studies, 14*(1), 91–108.

Lemay, E.P., Clark, M.S., and Greenberg, A. (2010). "What is beautiful is good because what is beautiful is desired: Physical attractiveness stereotyping as projection of interpersonal goals," *Personality and Social Psychology Bulletin, 36*(3), 339–353.

———, and Dudley, K.L. (2009). "Implications of reflected appraisals of interpersonal insecurity for suspicion and power," *Personality and Social Psychology Bulletin, 35*(12), 1672–1686.

Lenhart, A., Madden, M., Cacgill, A.R., and Smith, A. (2007). *Teens and social media*. Washington, DC: Pew Internet and American Life Project.

———, Rainie, L., and Lewis, O. (2001). *Teenage life online*. Pew Internet and American Life Project. www.pewinternet.org/2001/06/21/teenage-life-online/

Leone, C., and Hall, I. (2003). "Self-monitoring, marital dissatisfaction, and relationship dissolution: Individual differences in orientations to marriage and divorce," *Self and Identity, 2,* 189–202.

———, and Hawkins, L.B. (2006). "Self-monitoring and close relationships," *Journal of Personality, 74,* 739–788.

Le Poire, B.A., and Yoshimura, S.M. (1999). "The effects of expectancies and actual communication on nonverbal adaptation and communication outcomes: A test of interaction adaptation theory," *Communication Monographs, 66,* 1–30.

Lerner, R.M., Rothbaum, F., Boulos, S., and Castellino, D.R. (2002). "Developmental systems perspective on parenting," in M. Bornstein (ed), *Handbook of parenting, Vol. 2: Biology and ecology of parenting*, 2nd edn, 315–344. Mahwah, NJ: Lawrence Erlbaum.

Leroy, H., Palanski, M., and Simons, T. (2012). "Authentic leadership and behavioral integrity as drivers of follower commitment and performance," *Journal of Business Ethics, 107,* 255–264.

Leung, L., and Lee, P.S.N. (2005). "Multiple determinants of life quality: The roles of internet activities, use of new media, social support and leisure activities," *Telematics and Informatics, 22*(3), 161–180.

Levav, J., and Argo, J. (2010). "Physical contact and financial risk taking," *Psychological Science, 21*(6), 804–810.

Levine, R.V. (1988). "The pace of life across cultures," in J.E. McGrath (ed.), *The social psychology of time,* 39–60. Newbury Park, CA: Sage.

———, and Norenzayan, A. (1999). "The pace of life in 31 countries," *Journal of Cross-Cultural Psychology, 30,* 178–205.

Lewandowski, G.W. Jr., Aron, A., and Gee, J. (2007). "Personality goes a long way: The malleability of opposite-sex physical attractiveness," *Personal Relationships, 14,* 571–585.

Lewin, K. (1936). *Principles of topological psychology*. New York: McGraw-Hill.

Lewis, M.H., and Reinsch, N.L. Jr. (1988). "Listening in organizational environments," *Journal of Business Communication, 25,* 49–67.

Li, H.Z. (2002). "Culture, gender and self-close-other(s) connectedness in Canadian and Chinese samples," *European Journal of Social Psychology, 32,* 93–114.

Li, J., and Chignell, M. (2010). "How personality influences blog writing and reading," *International Journal of Human-Computer Studies, 68,* 589–602.

Lim, G.Y., and Roloff, M.E. (1999). "Attributing sexual consent," *Journal of Applied Communication Research, 27,* 1–23.

Lim, L.L. (2009). "The influences of harmony motives and implicit beliefs on conflict styles of the collectivist,"

International Journal of Psychology, *44*(6), 401–409.

Lim, V.K., and Teo, T.S.H. (2009). "Mind your e-manners: Impact of cyber incivility on employees' work attitude and behavior," *Information and Management, 46*, 419–425.

Linden, R.B., Martin, C.L., and Parsons, C.K. (1993). "Interviewer and applicant behaviors in employment interviews," *Academy of Management Journal, 36*, 372–386.

Lindsey, A.E., and Vigil, V. (1999). "The interpretation and evaluation of winking in stranger dyads," *Communication Research Reports, 16*, 256–265.

Ling, R. (2004). *The mobile connection: The cell phone's impact on society.* New York: Morgan Kaufmann Pub.

——, Bertel, F.B., and Sundsoy, P.R. (2011). "The socio-demographics of texting: An analysis of traffic data," *New Media and Society, 14*(2), 281–298.

——, and Yttri, B. (2002). "Hyper-co-ordination via mobile phones in Norway," in J.E. Katz and M. Aakhus (eds), *Perpetual contact: Mobile communication, private talk, public performance.* Cambridge: Cambridge University Press, 139–169.

——, and —— (2006). "Control, emancipation and status: The mobile telephone in teens' parental and peer relationships," in R. Kraut, M. Brynin, and S. Kiesler (eds), *Computers, phones and the internet: Domesticating information technology.* Oxford series in human–technology interaction. New York: Oxford University Press, 219–234.

Lippard, P.V. (1988). "Ask me no questions, I'll tell you no lies: Situational exigencies for interpersonal deception," *Western Journal of Speech Communication, 52*, 91–103.

Lippert, T., and Prager, K.J. (2001). "Daily experiences of intimacy: A study of couples," *Personal Relationships, 8*, 283–298.

Littlejohn, S.W., and Foss, K.A. (2008). *Theories of human communication,* 9th edn. Belmont, CA: Wadsworth.

Litzinger, S., and Gordon, K.C. (2005). "Exploring relationships among communication, sexual satisfaction and marital satisfaction," *Journal of Sex and Marital Therapy, 31,*(5), 409–424.

Locker, K.O. (2000). *Business and administrative communication,* 5th edn. Homewood, IL: Irwin.

Long, E.C.J., Angera, J.J., Carter, S.J., Nakamoto, M., and Kalso, M. (1999). "Understanding the one you love: A longitudinal assessment of an empathy training program for couples in romantic relationships," *Family Relations: Interdisciplinary Journal of Applied Family Studies, 48*, 235–242.

Lourenco, O., and Machado, A. (1996). "In defense of Piaget's theory: A reply to 10 common criticisms," *Psychological Review, 103*, 143–164.

Loyd, D.L., Phillips, K.W., Whitson, J., and Thomas-Hunt, M.C. (2010). "Expertise in your midst: How congruence between status and speech style affects reactions to unique knowledge," *Group Processes and Intergroup Relations, 13*(3), 379–395.

Luft, J. (1969). *Of human interaction.* Palo Alto, CA: National Press Books.

Lumsden, G., Lumsden, D., and Wiehoff, C. (2009). *Communicating in groups and teams: Sharing leadership.* Boston, MA: Wadsworth.

Luo, S. (2014). "Effects of texting on satisfaction in romantic relationships: The role of attachment," *Computer and Human Behavior, 33*, 145–152.

Lustig, M.W., and Koester, J. (1999). *Intercultural competence: Interpersonal communication across cultures,* 3rd edn. New York: Longman.

Lyons, A., and Kashima, Y. (2003). "How are stereotypes maintained through communication? The influence of stereotype sharedness," *Journal of Personality and Social Psychology, 85*, 989–1005.

——, and —— (2006). "Maintaining stereotypes in communication: Investigating memory biases and coherence-seeking in storytelling," *Asian Journal of Social Psychology, 9*, 59–71.

Lyubomirsky, S., Sousa, L., and Dickerhoof, R. (2006). "The costs and benefits of writing, talking and thinking about life's triumphs and defeats," *Journal of Personality and Social Psychology, 90*(4), 692–708.

Ma, R., and Chuang, R. (2001). "Persuasion strategies of Chinese college students in interpersonal contexts," *Southern Communication Journal, 66*, 267–278.

Ma, Z., and Jaeger, A.M. (2010). "A comparative study of the influence of assertiveness on negotiation outcomes in Canada and China," *Cross Cultural Management: An International Journal, 17*(4), 333–346.

Macagno, F., and Walton, D. (2010). "What we hide in words: Emotive words and persuasive defintions," *Journal of Pragmatics, 42*, 1997–2013.

Macaulay, M. (2001). "Tough talk: Indirectness and gender in requests for information," *Journal of Pragmatics, 33*, 293–316.

MacDonald, G., and Leary, M. (2005). "Why does social exclusion hurt? The relationship between social and physical pain," *Psychological Bulletin, 131*(2), 202–223.

MacGeorge, E.L., Lichtman, R.M., and Pressey, L.C. (2002). "The evaluation of advice in supportive interactions: Facework and contextual factors," *Human Communication Research, 28*, 451–463.

MacIntosh, H., Reissing, E.D., and Andruff, H. (2010). "Same-sex marriage in Canada: The impact of legal marriage on the first cohort of gay and lesbian Canadians wed," *The Canadian Journal of Human Sexuality, 19*(3), 79–90.

MacIntosh, J., Wuest, J., Gray, M.M., and Aldous, S. (2010). "Effects of workplace bullying on how women work," *Western Journal of Nursing Research, 32*(7), 910–931.

Macrae, C.N., and Bodenhausen, G.V. (2001). "Social cognition: Categorical person perception," *British Journal of Psychology, 92*, 239–256.

Maczewski, M. (2002). "Exploring identities through the internet: Youth experiences online," *Child and Youth Care Forum, 31*(2), April, 111–129.

—— (2007). "Understanding how information and communication technologies matter to youth," Ph.D. thesis. http://web.uvic.ca/~mecht/dissapril27final.pdf

Madden, M., and Smith, A. (2010). *Reputation management and social media.* Pew Internet and American Life Project. www.pewinternet.org/2010/05/26/reputation-management-and-social-media/

Madell, D., and Muncer, S. (2006). "Internet communication: An activity that appeals to shy and socially phobic people?" *CyberPsychology and Behavior, 9*(5), 618–622.

Madlock, P.E., and Kennedy-Lightsey, C. (2010). "The effects of supervisors' verbal aggressiveness and mentoring on their subordinates," *Journal of Business Communication, 47*(1), 42–62.

Madrigal, A.C. (2012). "I'm being followed: How Google and 104 other companies are tracking me on the web," *The Atlantic*, 29 February. www.theatlantic.com/technology/archive/2012/02/im-being-followed-how-google-151-and-104-other-companies-151-are-tracking-me-on-the-web/253758/

Malis, R.S., and Roloff, M.E. (2006). "Correlates of the perceived resolvability and relational consequences of serial arguing in dating relationships: Argumentative features and the use of coping strategies," *Journal of Social and Personal Relationships, 17,* 676–686.

Manusov, V. (1993). "It depends on your perspective: Effects of stance and beliefs about intent on person perception," *Western Journal of Communication, 57,* 27–41.

Manzi, C., Vignoles, V.L., and Regalia, C. (2010). "Identity changes and wellbeing across two life-transitions," *European Journal of Social Psychology, 40*(6), 970–984.

Mao, H., and Hsieh, A. (2012). "Organizational level and friendship expectation at work," *Asian Business and Management, 11*(4), 485–506.

Mar, R.A., and Oatley, K. (2008). "The function of fiction is the abstraction and simulation of social experience," *Perspectives on Psychological Science, 3,* 173–192.

——, ——, and Peterson, J.B., (2009). "Exploring the link between reading fiction and empathy: Ruling out individual differences and examining outcomes," *Communications, 34,* 407–428.

Marangoni, C., and Ickes, W. (1989). "Loneliness: A theoretical review with implications for measurement," *Journal of Social and Personal Relationships, 6,* 93–128.

Marchant, V. (1999). "Listen Up!" *Time, 153,* 28 June, 74.

Marcus, M.G. (1976). "The power of a name," *Psychology Today, 9,* October, 75–77, 106.

Marriott, M. (1998). "The blossoming of internet chat," *The New York Times* [online], 2 July. www.nytimes.com/1998/07/02/technology/the-blossoming-of-internet-chat.html?scp=1&sq=the%20blossoming%20of%20internet%20chat&st=cse

Marriott, T.C., and Buchanan, T. (2014). "The true self online: Personality correlates of preference for self-expression online, and observer ratings of personality online and offline," *Computers in Human Behavior, 32,* 171–177.

Marshall, T. (2010). "Love at the cultural crossroads: Intimacy and commitment in Chinese Canadian relationships," *Personal Relationships, 17,* 391–411.

Martin, B.H., and MacDonnell, R. (2012). "Is telework effective for organizations? A meta-analysis of empirical research on perceptions of telework and organizational outcomes," *Management Research Review, 35,* 602–616.

Martin, M.M., Anderson, C.M., Burant, P.A., and Weber, K. (1997). "Verbal aggression in sibling relationships," *Communication Quarterly, 45,* 304–317.

——, ——, and Hovarth, C.L. (1996). "Feelings about verbal aggression: Justifications for sending and hurt from receiving verbally aggressive messages," *Communication Research Reports, 13,* 19–26.

——, ——, and Mottet, T.P. (1999). "Perceived understanding and self-disclosure in the stepparent–stepchild relationship," *Journal of Psychology, 133,* 281–290.

——, Dunleavy, K.N., Kennedy-Lightsey, C. (2010). "Can verbally aggressive messages in the instructor–student relationship be constructive," *College Student Journal, 44*(3), 726–736.

Martin, R. (2014). "Leadership and integrative thinking," *In Conversation, 5*(1), 2–8.

Martz, J.M., Verette, J., Arriaga, X.B., Slovik, L.F., Cox, C.L., and Rusbult, C.E. (1998). "Positive illusion in close relationships," *Personal Relationships, 5,* 159–181.

Masip, J., Alonso, H., Garrido, E., and Herrero, C. (2009). "Training to detect what? The biasing effects of training on veracity judgments," *Applied Cognitive Psychology, 23,* 1282–1296.

Maslow, A.H. (1968). *Toward a psychology of being.* New York: Van Nostrand Reinhold.

——, and Mintz, N.L. (1956). "Effects of aesthetic surroundings: Initial effects of those aesthetic surroundings upon perceiving 'energy' and 'well-being' in faces," *Journal of Psychology, 41,* 247–254.

Maté, G. (2003). *When the body says no: Understanding the stress–disease connection.* Toronto: Alfred A. Knopf.

Matsuba, M.K. (2006). "Searching for self and relationships online," *CyberPsychology and Behavior, 9*(3), 275–284.

Matsumoto, D. (1991). "Cultural influences on facial expressions of emotion," *Southern Communication Journal, 56,* 128–137.

——, and Hwang, H.C. (2013). "Cultural similarities and differences in emblematic gestures," *Journal of Nonverbal Behavior, 37*(1), 1–27.

——, LeRoux, J., Wilson-Cohn, C., Raroque, J., Kooken, J., Ekman, P., et al. (2000). "A new test to measure emotion recognition ability: Matsumoto and Ekman's Japanese and Caucasian Brief Affect Recognition Test (JACBART)," *Journal of Nonverbal Behavior, 24,* 179–209.

——, Yoo, S.H., Fontaine, J., Anguas-Wong, A.M., Arriola, M., Ataca, B., et al. (2008). "Mapping expressive differences around the world: The relationship between emotional display rules and individualism versus collectivism," *Journal of Cross-Cultural Psychology, 39,* 55–74.

Mayer, J., Salovey, P., and Caruso, D. (2004). "Emotional intelligence: Theory, findings and implications," *Psychological Inquiry, 15*(3), 197–215.

——, Slaovey, P., and Caruso, D. (2008). "Emotional intelligence: New ability or eclectic traits?" *American Psychologist, 63*(6), 503–517.

Mayne, T.J. (1999). "Negative affect and health: The importance of being earnest," *Cognition and Emotion, 13,* 601–635.

Mazur, E., and Kozarian, L. (2010). "Self-presentation and interaction in blogs of adolescents and young emerging adults," *Journal of Adolescent Research, 25*(1), 124–144.

McCarty, M.K., Kelly, J.R., and Williams, K.D. (2014). "The cognitive costs of counter-stereotypic: Gender, emotion and social presence," *Journal of Social Psychology, 154,* 447–462.

McClelland, D.C., and Atkinson, J.W. (1948). "The projective expression of needs: The effect of different intensities of the hunger drive on perception," *Journal of Psychology, 25,* 205–222.

McCornack, S.A., and Levine, T.R. (1990). "When lies are uncovered: Emotional and relational outcomes of discovered deception," *Communication Monographs, 57,* 119–138.

McCrae, R.R., and Costa, P.T., Jr. (2008). "Empirical and theoretical status of the five-factor model of personality traits," in G. Boyce, G. Methews and D. Saklofske (eds), *The SAGE handbook of personality theory and assessment, volume 1: Personality theories and models*, 273–279. Thousand Oaks, CA: Sage.

McCroskey, J.C. (2009). "Communication apprehension: What we learned from the last four decades," *Human Communication, 12*, 157–171.

———, and Richmond, V.P. (1996). *Fundamentals of human communication: An interpersonal perspective*. Prospect Heights, IL: Waveland.

———, and Wheeless, L. (1976). *Introduction to human communication*. Boston: Allyn and Bacon.

McGee, D.S., and Cegala, D.J. (1998). "Patient communication skills training for improved competence in the primary care medical consultation," *Journal of Applied Communication Research, 26*, 412–430.

McGoldrick, M., Watson, M., and Benton, W. (1999). "Siblings through the life cycle," in B. Carter and M. McGoldrick (eds), *The expanded family life cycle: Individual, family, and social perspectives*, 3rd edn, 153–168. Needham Heights, MA: Allyn and Bacon.

McGregor, D. (1960). *The human side of enterprise*. New York: McGraw-Hill Ryerson.

McLean, K., and Fournier, M. (2008). "The content and processes of autobiographical reasoning in narrative identity," *The Journal of Research in Personality, 42*, 527–545.

McLuhan, M. (1964). *Understanding media: The extensions of man*. New York: McGraw-Hill Ryerson.

Meaux, J.B. (2002). "Time perception, behavioral inhibition, and ADHD," *Dissertation Abstracts International, 62*, 3556.

Mehl, M.R., Simine, V., Ramirez-Esparza, N.R., Slatcher, R.B., and Pennebaker, J.W. (2007). "Are women really more talkative than men?" *Science, 317*, 82.

Mehrabian, A. (1972). *Nonverbal communication*. Chicago: Aldine-Atherton.

Mehrabian, A., and Weiner, M. (1967). "Decoding of inconsistent communications," *Journal of Personality and Social Psychology, 6*, 109–114.

Mesch, G.S., and Beker, G. (2010). "Are norms of disclosure of online and offline personal information associated with the disclosure of personal information online?" *Human Communication Research, 36*, 570–592.

Merkin, R., Taras, V., and Steel, P. (2014). "State of the art themes in cross-cultural communication research: A systematic and meta analytic review," *International Journal of Intercultural Relations, 38*, 1–23.

Messman, S.J., and Canary, D.J. (1998). "Patterns of conflict in personal relationships," in B.H. Spitzberg and W.R. Cupach (eds), *The dark side of close relationships*, 121–152. Mahwah, NJ: Lawrence Erlbaum.

———, and Mikesell, R.L. (2000). "Competition and interpersonal conflict in dating relationships," *Communication Reports, 13*, 21–34.

Metts, S. (1989). "An exploratory investigation of deception in close relationships," *Journal of Social and Personal Relationships, 6*, 159–179.

———, and Cupach, W.R. (1990). "The influence of relationship beliefs and problem-solving relationships on satisfaction in romantic relationships," *Human Communication Research, 17*, 170–185.

———, ———, and Bejllovec, R.A. (1989). "'I love you too much to ever start liking you': Redefining romantic relationships," *Journal of Social and Personal Relationships, 6*, 259–274.

———, ———, and Imahori, T.T. (1992). "Perceptions of sexual compliance-resisting messages in three types of cross-sex relationships," *Western Journal of Communication, 56*, 1–17.

Microsoft. (2007). "Lack of emotion, inadequate time lead Canadians to question efficiency of e-mail," Study conducted by Strategic Counsel, press release, 16 October.

Middleton. C., Veenhof, B., and Leith, J. (2010). "Intensity of internet use in Canada: Understanding different types of Users," Ottawa: Statistics Canada, Catalogue no. 88F0006X, no. 2. www.statcan.gc.ca/pub/88f0006x/88f0006x2010002-eng.pdf

Midlarsky, E., Jones, S.F., and Corley, R.P. (2005). "Personality correlates of heroic rescue during the Holocaust," *Journal of Personality, 73*(4), 907–934.

Mikulincer, M and Shaver, P.R. (2012). "Adult attachment orientations and relationship processes," *Journal of Family Theory and Review, 4*, 259–274.

Miller, G.F. (1998). "How mate choice shaped human nature: A review of sexual selection and human evolution," in C.B. Crawford and D.L. Krebs, *Handbook of evolutionary psychology: Ideas, issues, and applications*, 87–129. Mahwah, NJ: Lawrence Erlbaum.

———, and Steinberg, M. (1975). *Between people: A new analysis of interpersonal communication*. Chicago: SRA.

Miller, K., Joseph, L., and Apker, J. (2000). "Strategic ambiguity in the role development process," *Journal of Applied Communication Research, 28*, 193–214.

———, Reeves, S., Zwarenstein, M., Beales, J., Kenazchuk, C., and Gotlib. C.L. (2008). "Nursing emotion work and interprofessional collaboration in general internal medicine wards: A qualitative study," *Journal of Advanced Nursing 64*, 332–343.

Miller, L.C., Cooke, L.L., Tsang, J., and Morgan, F. (1992). "Should I brag? Nature and impact of positive and boastful disclosures for women and men," *Human Communication Research, 18*, 364–399.

Miller, S., Nunnally, E.W., and Wackman, D.B. (1975). *Alive and aware: How to improve your relationships through better communication*. Minneapolis, MN: Interpersonal Communication Programs.

Millikan, R.G. (2001). "The language–thought partnership: A bird's eye view," *Language and Communication, 21*, 157–166.

Mills, C. (2010). "Experiencing gossip: The foundations for a theory of embedded organizational gossip," *Group and Organization Management, 35*(2), 213–240.

Mitchell, P.J. (2014). "The world family map. Canadian families in the global context," *eReview. Institute of Marriage and Family Canada, 14*(9). www.imfcanada.org/issues/canadian-families-global-context

Modayil, M., Thompson, A., Varnhagen, S., and Wilson, D. (2003). "Internet users' prior psychological and social difficulties," *CyberPsychology and Behavior, 6*(6), 585–594.

Moghaddam, F.M., Taylor, D.M., and Wright, S.C. (1993). *Social-psychology in cross-cultural perspective*. New York: W.H. Freeman.

Mohr, D.C., Young, G.J., and Burgess, J.F. (2012). "Employee turnover and operational performance: The moderating effect of group-oriented organizational culture," *Human Resource Management Journal, 4*(22), 216–233.

Mok, D., Wellman, B., and Carrasco, J. (2010). "Does distance matter in the age of the internet?" *Urban Studies, 47*(13), 2747–2783.

Moller, K., Hwang, C.P., and Wickberg, B. (2006). "Romantic attachment, parenthood and marital satisfaction," *Journal of Reproductive and Infant Psychology, 24*, 233–240.

Monk, A.F., Carroll, J., Parker, S., and Blythe, M. (2004a). "Why are mobile phones so annoying?" *Behaviour and Information Technology, 23*(5), 33–42.

——, Fellas, E., Ley, E. (2004b). "Hearing only one side of normal and mobile phone conversations," *Behaviour and Information Technology, 23*(5), 301–305.

Monroe, C., Borzi, M.G., and DiSalvo, V.S. (1989). "Conflict behaviors of difficult subordinates," *Southern Communication Journal, 34*, 311–329.

Montcrieff, R.W. (1966). *Odor preferences*. New York: John Wiley & Sons.

Montesi, J.L., Conner, B.T., Gordon, E.A., Fauber, R.L., Kim, K.H., and Heimberg, R.G. (2013). "On the relationship among social anxiety, intimacy, sexual communication, and sexual satisfaction in young couples," *Archives of Sexual Behavior, 42*, 81–91.

Montgomery, B.M. (1993). "Relationship maintenance versus relationship change: A dialectical dilemma," *Journal of Social and Personal Relationships, 10*, 205–223.

Monty, J.C. (1998). "Remarks from the 452 Convocation," *University of Chicago Record, 33*, 12–13.

Moody, E.J. (2001). "Internet use and its relationship to loneliness," *CyberPsychology and Behavior, 4*, 393–401.

Moore, J. (2010). "Survey says . . . . Time spent on various communication channels," 10 July. http://thesocialcustomer.com

Morgan, H.J., and Shaver, P.R. (1999). "Attachment processes and commitment to romantic relationships," in J.M. Adams and W.H. Jones (eds), *Handbook of interpersonal commitment and relationship stability*, 109–124. New York: Kluwer Academic/Plenum.

Morman, M.T., and Floyd, K. (2002). "A 'changing culture of fatherhood': Effects of affectionate communication, closeness, and satisfaction in men's relationships with their fathers and their sons," *Western Journal of Communication, 66*, 395–411.

Morreale, S.P., and Pearson, J.C. (2008). "Why communication education is important: The centrality of the discipline in the 21st century," *Communication Education, 57*(2), 224–240.

Morris, D. (1973). *Intimate behavior*. New York: Bantam.

Morris, M., Robinson, J., and Simpson, J. (1999). *The changing nature of home care and its impact on women's vulnerability to poverty*. Ottawa: Status of Women Canada.

Morris, T.L., Gorham, J., Cohen, S.H., and Huffman, D. (1996). "Fashion in the classroom: Effects of attire on student perceptions of instructors in college classes," *Communication Education, 45*, 135–148.

Morrison, M.A., Morrison, T.G., and Franklin, R. (2009). "Modern and old-fashioned homonegativity among samples of Canadian and American university students," *Journal of Cross Cultural Psychology, 40*(4), 523–542.

Morrison, R.L. (2004). "Informal relationships in the workplace: Associations with job satisfaction, organizational commitment and turnover decisions," *New Zealand Psychological Society, 33*(3), 114–128.

—— (2009) "Are women tending and befriending in the workplace? Gender differences in the relationship between workplace friendships and organizational outcomes," *Sex Roles 60*(1): 1–13.

——, and Wright, S.L. (2009). *Friends and enemies in organizations*. London: Palgrave Macmillan.

Morse, D.S., Edwardsen, E.A., and Gordon, H.S. (2008). "Missed opportunities for interval empathy in lung cancer communication," *Archives of Internal Medicine, 168*(17), 1853–1658.

Morton, J.B., and Trehub, S.E. (2001). "Children's understanding of emotion in speech," *Child Development, 72*, 834–843.

Moss, D. (1999). "The humanistic psychology of self-disclosure, relationship, and community," in D. Moss (ed.), *Humanistic and transpersonal psychology: A historical and biographical sourcebook*, 66–84. Westport, CT: Greenwood Press.

Most, S.B., Laurenceau, J.-P., Graber, E., Belcher, A., and Smith, C.V. (2010). "Blind jealousy? Romantic insecurity increases emotion-induced failures in visual perception," *Emotion, 10*(2), 250–256.

Motley, M.T. (1990). "On whether one can(not) communicate: An examination via traditional communication postulates," *Western Journal of Speech Communication, 54*, 1–20.

—— (1992). "Mindfulness in solving communicators' dilemmas," *Communication Monographs, 59*, 306–314.

—— (1993). "Facial affect and verbal context in conversation: Facial expression as interjection," *Human Communication Research, 20*, 3–40.

Mulac, A. (1998). "The gender-linked language effect: Do language differences really make a difference?" in D.J. Canary and K. Dindia (eds), *Sex differences and similarities in communication: Critical essays and empirical investigations of sex and gender in interaction*, 127–153. Mahwah, NJ: Lawrence Erlbaum.

Mulac, A., Bradac, J.J., and Gibbons, P. (2001). "Empirical support for the gender-as-culture hypothesis: An intercultural analysis of male–female language differences," *Human Communication Research, 27*, 121–152.

——, Wiemann, J.M., Widenmann, S.J., and Gibson, T.W. (1988). "Male/female language differences and effects in same-sex and mixed-sex dyads: The gender-linked language effect," *Communication Monographs, 55*, 315–335.

Mulford, M., Orbell, J., Shatto, C., and Stockard, J. (1998). "Physical attractiveness, opportunity, and success in everyday exchange," *American Journal of Sociology, 103*, 1565–1592.

Murdock, G.P. (1965). *Social structure*. New York: Free Press.

Munroe, D., and Watt, D. (2014). "Skills for business innovation success: It's people who innovate," Conference Board of Canada. www.conference board.ca/e-library/abstract.aspx?did=6069

Murray, S.L., Holmes, J.G., and Griffin, D.W. (1996). "The benefits of positive illusions: Idealization and the construction of satisfaction in close relationships," *Journal of Personality and Social Psychology, 70*, 79–98.

Mwakalyelye, N., and DeAngelis, T. (1995). "The power of touch helps vulnerable babies thrive," *APA Monitor, 25*, October.

Myers, D. (1980). "The inflated self," *Psychology Today, 14*, 16, May.

Myers, S.A. (1998). "Students' self-disclosure in the college classroom," *Psychological Reports, 83*(3, Pt 1), 1067–1070.

Myers, S. (2000). "Empathic listening: Reports on the experience of being heard," *Journal of Humanistic Psychology*, *40*, 148–173.

Myers, S.A., (2001). "Perceived instructor credibility and verbal aggressiveness in the college classroom," *Communication Research Reports*, *18*(4), 354–364.

———— (2003). "Sibling use of relational maintenance behaviors," in K.M. Galvin and P.J. Cooper (eds), *Making connections: Readings in relational communication*, 300–308. Los Angeles: Roxbury.

————, Brann, M., and Martin, M.M. (2013). "Instructor use of verbally aggressive messages," *Communication Research Reports*, *30*, 252–258.

————, ————, and Rittenour, C.E. (2008). "Interpersonal communication motives as a predictor of early and middle adulthood siblings' use of relational maintenance behaviors," *Communication Research Reports*, *25*, 155–167.

————, and Bryant, L.E. (2008). "The use of behavioral indicators of sibling commitment among emerging adults," *Journal of Family Communication*, *8*, 101–125.

————, and Goodboy, A.K. (2010). "Relational maintenance behaviors and communication channel use among adult siblings," *North American Journal of Psychology*, *12*(1), 103–116.

————, and Rocca, K.A. (2001). "Perceived instructor argumentativeness and verbal aggressiveness in the college classroom: Effects on student perceptions of climate, apprehension, and state motivation," *Western Journal of Communication*, *65*, 113–137.

Naftulin, D., Ware, J., and Donnelly, F. (1973). "The Doctor Fox lecture: A paradigm of educational seduction," *Journal of Medical Education*, *48*, 630–635.

Naito, T., Wangwan, J., and Tani, M. (2005). "Gratitude in university students in Japan and Thailand," *Journal of Cross Cultural Psychology*, *36*, 247–263.

Napier, A.Y., and Whitaker, C.A. (1989). *The family crucible: The intense experience of family therapy*. New York: Harper Trade.

National Communication Association. (1999). "How Americans communicate." www.natcom.org

Neidenthal, P.M., Brauer, M., Halberstadt, J.B., and Innes-Ker, A.H. (2001). "When did her smile drop? Facial mimicry and the influences of emotional state on the detection of change in emotional expression," *Cognition and Emotion*, *15*, 853–864.

Nelson, J. (2013). "The power of stereotyping and confirmation bias to overwhelm accurate assessment: The case of economics, gender, and risk aversion." Working Paper, Department of Economics, University of Massachusetts, Boston.

Nelton, S. (1996). "Emotions in the workplace," *Nation's Business*, 25–30, February.

Neuliep, J.W. (1996). "The influence of theory x and y management style on the perception of ethical behavior in organizations," *Journal of Social Behavior and Personality*, *11*, 301–311.

————, and Grohskopf, E.L. (2000). "Uncertainty reduction and communication satisfaction during initial interaction: An initial test and replication of a new axiom," *Communication Reports*, *13*, 67–77.

Newton, D.A., and Burgoon, J.K. (1990). "The use and consequences of verbal influence strategies during interpersonal disagreements," *Human Communication Research*, *16*, 477–518.

Ng, S.H., and Bradac, J.J. (1993). *Power in language: Verbal communication and social influence*. Newbury Park, CA: Sage, 1993.

Nichols, R.G. (1948). "Factors in listening comprehension," *Speech Monographs*, *1*, 154–163.

Nickerson, R.S. (1998). "Confirmation bias: A ubiquitous phenomenon in many guises." *Review of General Psychology 2* (2): 175–220.

Nie, N.H. (2001). "Sociability, interpersonal relations, and the internet," *American Behavioral Scientist*, *45*, 420–435.

————, and Erbring, L. (2000). *Internet and society: A preliminary report*. Stanford, CA: Stanford Institute for the Quantitative Study of Society (SIQSS), 17 February. www.stanford.edu

————, and Hillygus, D. (2002). "The impact of internet use on sociability: Time-diary findings," *IT and Society* *1*(1), 1–20.

Niederhoffer, K.G., and Pennebaker, J.W. (2002). "Sharing one's story: On the benefits of writing or talking about emotional experience," in C.R. Snyder and S.J. Lopez (eds), *Handbook of positive psychology*, 573–583. London: Oxford University Press.

Nielsenwire. (2010). "Global audience spends two hours more a month on social networks," 19 March. http://blog.nielsen.com/nielsenwire/global/global-audience-spends-two-hours-more-a-month-on-social-networks-than-last-year/

Noller, P., and Fitzpatrick, M.A. (1993). *Communication in family relationships*. Englewood Cliffs, NJ: Prentice Hall.

Noordewier, M.K., van Horen, F., Ruys, K., and Stapel, D. (2010). "What's in a name? 361.708 Euros: The effects of marital name change," *Basic and Applied Social Psychology*, *32*(1), 17–25.

North, R.J., and Swann, W.B., Jr. (2009). "Self-verification 360: Illuminating the light and dark sides," *Self and Identity*, *8*(2), 131–146.

Northeastern University (2013). "Innovation imperative: Enhancing higher education outcomes," Public opinion survey results. www.northeastern.edu/innovationsurvey/pdfs/Northeastern_University_Innovation_Imperative_Higher_Ed_Outcomes_Poll_Deck_FINAL_Delivered.pdf

Nosko, A., Wood, E., and Molema, S. (2010). "All about me: Disclosure in online social networking profiles: The case of Facebook," *Computers in Human Behavior*, *26*, 406–418.

Notarius, C.I., and Herrick, L.R. (1988). "Listener response strategies to a distressed other," *Journal of Social and Personal Relationships*, *5*, 97–108.

Nowicki, S., and Manheim, S. (1991). "Interpersonal complementarity and time of interaction in female relationships," *Journal of Research in Personality*, *25*, 322–333.

Nussbaum, E. (2007). "Say everything," *New York*, 12 February.

Oaten, M., and Cheng, K. (2006). "Improved self-control: The benefits of a regular program of academic study," *Basic and Applied Social Psychology*, *28*(1), 1–16.

O'Barr, W.M. (1982). *Linguistic evidence: Language, power, and strategy in the courtroom*. New York: Academic Press.

O'Brien, M., and Bahadur, M.A. (1998). "Marital aggression, mother's problem-solving behavior with children, and children's emotional and behavioral problems," *Journal of Social and Clinical Psychology*, *17*(3), 249–272.

O'Byrne (2012). "Criminal law and public health practice: Are the Canadian HIV disclosure laws an effective HIV prevention strategy," *Sexuality Research and Social Policy, 9*, 70–79.

Ochsner, K.N., and Gross, J.J. (2008). "Cognitive emotion regulation: Insights from social cognitive and affective neuroscience," *Current Directions in Psychological Science, 17*, 153–158.

Odden, C.M., and Sias, P.M. (1997). "Peer communication relationships and psychological climate," *Communication Quarterly, 45*, 153–166.

Oetzel, J., Ting-Toomey, S., Masumoto, T., Yokochi, Y., Pan, X., Takai, J., and Wilcox, R. (2001). "Face and facework in conflict: A cross-cultural comparison of China, Germany, Japan, and the United States," *Communication Monographs, 68*, 235–258.

Officer, S.A., and Rosenfeld, L.B. (1985). "Self-disclosure to male and female coaches by high school female athletes," *Journal of Sport Psychology, 7*, 360–370.

Ogden, C.K., and Richards, I.A. (1923). *The meaning of meaning*. New York: Harcourt Brace.

O'Hair, D., and Cody, M.J. (1993). "Interpersonal deception: The dark side of interpersonal communication?" in B.H. Spitzberg and W.R. Cupach (eds), *The dark side of interpersonal communication*, 181–214. Hillsdale, NJ: Lawrence Erlbaum.

Office of the Privacy Commissioner of Canada (2009). "Privacy and social networking in the workplace," *Fact Sheet*. www.priv.gc.ca/resource/fs-fi/02_05_d_41_sn_e.asp

Okabe, K. (1987). "Indirect speech acts of the Japanese," in D.L. Kincaid (ed.), *Communication theory: Eastern and Western perspectives*, 127–136. San Diego: Academic Press.

Okamoto, D.G., and Smith-Lovin, L., (2001). "Gender, status and the dynamics of topic change," *American Sociological Review, 66*(6), 852–873.

Oliveira, M. (2014). "10 million Canadians use Facebook on mobile daily," *Globe and Mail*, 19 February.

——— (2010). "Canadians spend more time online than any others," *Globe and Mail*, 28 December.

Olivola, C.Y., and Todorov, A. (2010). "Fooled by first impressions? Reexamining the diagnostic value of appearance-based inferences," *Journal of Experimental Social Psychology, 46*, 315–324.

Olson, D.H. (1986). "Circumplex model VII: Validation studies and FACES III," *Family Processes 25*, 337–351.

——— (2000). "Circumplex Model of marital and family systems," *Journal of Family Therapy, 22*(2), 144–167.

———, and Lavee, Y. (1989). "Family systems and family stress: A family life cycle perspective," in K. Kreppner and R.M. Lerner (eds), *Family systems and life-span development*, 165–195. Hillsdale, NJ: Lawrence Erlbaum.

Olson, L.N. (2002). "'As ugly and painful as it was, it was effective.' Individuals' unique assessment of communication competence during aggressive conflict episodes," *Communication Studies, 53*, 171–188.

———, and Braithwaite, D.O. (2004). "'If you hit me again, I'll hit you back': Conflict management strategies of individuals experiencing aggression during conflicts," *Communication Studies, 55*, 271–285.

O'Neill, O.A. (2009). "Workplace expression of emotions and escalation of commitment," *Journal of Applied Social Psychology, 39*, 2396–2424.

Ontario Public Service (2011). "Writing a cover letter and resume: Tips, tools and resources," Human Resource Service and Delivery Excellence Branch. www.gojobs.gov.on.ca/docs%5COPS%20Cover%20Letter%20and%20Resume%20Writing%20Guide.pdf

Orbe, M.P. (1998). "From the standpoint(s) of traditionally muted groups: Explicating a co-cultural communication theoretical model," *Communication Theory, 8*, 1–26.

Orth, U., Trzesniewski, K.H., and Robbins, R.W. (2010). "Self-esteem development from young adulthood to old age: A cohort-sequential longitudinal study," *Journal of Personality and Social Psychology, 98*(4), 645–658.

Orth-Gomér, K., and Leineweber, C. (2005). "Multiple stressors and coronary disease in women: The Stockholm female coronary risk study," *Biological Psychology, 69*, 57–66.

Osterman, K. (2001). "Students' need for belonging in the school community," *Review of Educational Research, 70*, 323–367.

O'Sullivan, P.B. (2000). "What you don't know won't hurt me: Impression management functions of communication channels in relationships," *Human Communication Research, 26*, 403–431.

Oyamot, C.M., Jr., Fuglestad, P.T., and Snyder, M. (2010). "Balance of power and influence in relationships: The role of self-monitoring," *Journal of Social and Personal Relationships, 27*(1), 23–46.

Palmer, M.T., and Simmons, K.B. (1995). "Communicating intentions through nonverbal behaviors: Conscious and nonconscious encoding of liking," *Human Communication Research, 22*, 128–160.

Pam, A., and Pearson, J. (1998). *Splitting up: Enmeshment and estrangement in the process of divorce*. New York: Guilford Press.

Panksepp, J. (2011). "The neurobiology of social loss in animals: Some keys to the puzzle of psychic pain in humans," in G. MacDonald and L. Jensen-Campbell (eds), *Social pain: Neuropsychological and health implications of loss and exclusion*, 11–51. Washington, DC: APA.

Papa, M.J., and Natalie, E.J. (1989). "Gender, strategy selection, and discussion satisfaction in interpersonal conflict," *Western Journal of Speech Communication, 52*, 260–272.

Papousek, I., Freudenthaler, H.H., and Schulter, G. (2008). "The interplay of perceiving and regulating emotions in becoming infected with positive and negative moods," *Personality and Individual Differences, 45*, 463–467.

Parade, S.H., Leerkes, E.M., and Blankson, A.N. (2010). "Attachment to parents, social anxiety and close relationships of female students over the transition to college," *Journal of Youth and Adolescence, 39*, 127–137.

Park, H.S., Levine, T.R., McCornack, S.A., Morrison, K., and Ferrara, M. (2002). "How people really detect lies," *Communication Monographs, 69*, 144–157.

Park, J., Barash, V., Fink, C., and Cha, M. (2013). "Emoticon Style: Interpreting differences in emoticons across cultures," *Proceedings of the Seventh International AAAI Conference on Weblogs and Social Media*. Association for the Advancement of Artificial Intelligence. www.academia.edu/3361408/Emoticon_Style_Interpreting_Differences_in_Emoticons_Across_Cultures

Park, J., Kitayama, S., Markus, . . . and Ryff, C.D. (2013). "Social status and anger expression: The cultural moderation hypothesis," *Emotion, 13*(6), 1122–1131.

Parker, Y. (2003). *Damn good resume guide: A crash course in resume writing*, 4th edn. Berkeley, CA: Ten Speed Press.

Parks, J.B., and Robertson, M.A. (2000). "Development and validation of an instrument to measure attitudes toward sexist/nonsexist language," *Sex Roles, 42*, 415–438.

Parks, M.R. (1982). "Ideology in interpersonal communication: Off the couch and into the world," in M. Burgoon (ed.), *Communication Yearbook 5*, 79–107. New Brunswick, NJ: Transaction.

Parlamis, J.D. (2012). "Venting as emotion regulation," *International Journal of Conflict Management, 23*(1), 77–96.

———, Allred, K.G., and Block, C. (2010), "Letting off steam or just steaming? The influence of venting target and offender status on venting," *International Journal of Conflict Management, 21*(3), 260–80.

Parton, S., Siltanen, S.A., Hosman, L.A., and Langenderfer, J. (2002). "Employment interviews outcomes and speech style effects," *Journal of Language and Social Psychology, 21*, 144–161.

Pasupathi, M., and Hoyt, T. (2010). "Silence and the shaping of memory: How distracted listeners affect speakers' subsequent recall of a computer game experience," *Memory, 18*(2), 159–169.

———, Stallworth, L.M., and Murdoch, K. (1998). "How what we tell becomes what we know: Listener effects on speakers' long-term memory for events," *Discourse Processes, 26*, 1–25.

Pawlowski, D.R. (1998). "Dialectical tensions in marital partners' accounts of their relationships," *Communication Quarterly, 46*, 396–416.

Payne, B. (2010). "Your art is gay and retarded: Eliminating discriminating speech against homosexual and intellectually disabled students in secondary arts education classroom," *Art Education, 63*(5), 52–54.

Pearce, W.B., and Cronen, V. (1980). *Communication, action, and meaning*. New York: Praeger.

———, and Sharp, S.M. (1973). "Self-disclosing communication," *Journal of Communication, 23*, 409–425.

Pearson, J.C. (2000). "Positive distortion: 'The most beautiful woman in the world,'" in K.M. Galvin and P.J. Cooper (eds), *Making connections: Readings in relational communication*, 2nd edn, 184–190. Los Angeles: Roxbury.

Peck, E.W. (1998). *Leadership and defensive communication: A grounded theory study of leadership reaction to defensive communication*. Unpublished manuscript, University of British Columbia, Vancouver.

Peer, E., and Babad (2014). "The Doctor Fox research (1973) revisited: 'Educational seduction' ruled out," *Journal of Educational Psychology, 106*(1), 36–45.

Peluchette, J., and Karl, K. (2008). "Social networking profiles: An examination of student attitudes regarding the use and appropriateness of content," *CyberPsychology and Behavior, 11*(1), 95–97.

Pennebaker, J.W. (1995). *Emotion, disclosure and health*. Washington, DC: American Psychological Association.

——— (1997). *Opening up: The healing power of expressing emotions*. New York: Guilford Press.

———, and Chung, C.K. (2007). "Expressive writing, emotional upheavals, and health," in H.S. Friedman and R.C. Silver (eds), *Foundations of health psychology*, 263–284. New York, NY: Oxford University Press.

Peper, M. (2000). "Awareness of emotions: A neuropsychological perspective," in R.D. Ellis and N. Newton (eds), *The caldron of consciousness: Motivation, affect and self-organization—An anthology*, 243–269. Philadelphia, PA: John Benjamins.

Peplau, L.A., and Fingerhut, A.W. (2007). "The close relationships of lesbians and gay men," *Annual Review of Psychology, 58*, 405–424.

Perlman, D. (2007). "The best of times, the worst of times. The place of close relationships in psychology and our daily lives," *Canadian Psychology, 48*(1), 7–18.

Person-Lynn, K. (1994). "Language keeps racism alive," *Los Angeles Times*, B3, 28 November.

Pescosolido, A.T. (2001). "Informal leaders and the development of group efficacy," *Small Group Research, 32*, 74–93.

Petronio, S. (1991). "Communication boundary management: A theoretical model of managing disclosure of private information between marital couples," *Communication Theory, 1*, 311–335.

——— (2000). "The boundaries of privacy: Praxis of everyday life," in S. Petronio (ed.), *Balancing the secrets of private disclosures*, 37–49. Mahwah, NJ: Lawrence Erlbaum.

Pew Research Center for the People and the Press (2003). *Global attitudes project*. Washington, DC: Pew Research Center.

Pfeifer, J.H., Iacoboni, M., Mazziotta, J.C., Dapretto, M., (2008). "Mirroring others' emotions relates to empathy and interpersonal competence in children," *NeuroImage 39*, 2076–2085.

Pfeifer, T.H. (2009). "Deconstruction Cartesian dualisms of western racialized systems," *Journal of Black Studies, 39*(4), 528–547.

Pfister, H.R., and Bohm, G. (2008). "The multiplicity of emotions: A framework of emotional functions in decision making," *Judgment and Decision Making Journal, 3*(1), 5–17.

Phelps S., and N. Austin (2002), *The assertive woman*, 4th edn. American Orthopsychiatric Association, 1975. Impact Publishers, Inc.

Piaget, J. (1952). *The origins of intelligence in children*. New York: International Universities Press.

Piech, R.M., Pastorino, M.T., and Zald, D.H. (2010). "All I saw was the cake: Hunger effects on attentional capture by visual food cues," *Appetite, 54*, 579–582.

Pinker, S. (2011). *The better angels of our nature. Why violence has declined*. New York: Penguin.

Planalp, S. (1999). *Communicating emotion: Social, moral, and cultural processes*. New York: Cambridge University Press.

Plant, S. (2001). "On the mobile: The effects of mobile telephones on social and individual life," October. http://classes.dma.ucla.edu/Winter03/104/docs/splant.pdf

——— (2003). "A world of difference," *New Statesman*, 15 September, 9–10.

Plax, T.G., and Rosenfeld, L.B. (1979). "Receiver differences and the comprehension of spoken messages," *Journal of Experimental Education, 48*, 23–28.

Poirier, N., and Gaucher, M. (2009). "Asperger's syndrome and non-verbal learning disorder. Characteristics and differential diagnosis," *Evolution Pyschiatrique, 74*(4), 606–620.

Poloz, S. (2005). "The new global trade game: Will Canada be a player or just a spectator?" *Export Development Canada*, 20 January.

Poole, M.S., Folger, J.P., and Hewes, D.E. (1987). "Analyzing interpersonal attraction," in M.E. Roloff and G.R. Miller (eds), *Interpersonal processes: New directions in communication research*, 220–256. Beverly Hills, CA: Sage.

Porter, S., and Brinke, L. (2010). "The truth about lies: What works in detecting high-stakes deception?" *Legal and Criminological Psychology*, 15, 57–75.

Postman, N., and Weingartner, C. (1969). *Teaching as a subversive activity.* New York: Delacorte.

Powell, J. (1969). *Why am I afraid to tell you who I am?* Niles, IL: Argus Communications.

Prager, K.J., and Buhrmester, D. (1998). "Intimacy and need fulfillment in couple relationships," *Journal of Social and Personal Relationships*, 15, 435–469.

Pratt, L., Wiseman, R.L., Cody, M.J., and Wendt, P.F. (1999). "Interrogative strategies and information exchange in computer-mediated communication," *Communication Quarterly*, 47, 46–66.

Preto, N.G. (1999). "Transformation of the family system during adolescence," in B. Carter and M. McGoldrick (eds), *The expanded family life cycle: Individual, family, and social perspectives*, 3rd. edn, 274–286. Boston: Allyn and Bacon.

Priest, P.J., and Dominick, J.R. (1994). "Pulp pulpits: Self-disclosure on 'Donahue.'" *Journal of Communication*, 44, 74–97.

Proctor, R.F. (1989). "Responsibility or egocentrism? The paradox of owned messages." *Speech Association of Minnesota Journal*, 26, 57–69.

———, and Wilcox, J.R. (1993). "An exploratory analysis of responses to owned messages in interpersonal communication," *ETC: A Review of General Semantics*, 50, 201–220.

Prodanovic, K. (2013). "The silent genocide: Aboriginal language loss FAQ." www.terry.ubc.ca/2013/10/16/the-silent-genocide-aboriginal-language-loss-faq/

Pronovost, G. (2002). "The internet and time displacement: A Canadian perspective," *IT and Society*, 1(1), 44–53

Propp, K.M., Apker, J., Zabava Ford, W.S., Wallace, N., Serbenski, M., and Hofmeister, N. (2010). "Meeting the complex needs of the health care team: Identification of nurse-team communication practices perceived to enhance patient outcomes," *Qualitative Health Research*, 20(1), 15–28.

Putnam, R.D. (2000). *Bowling alone.* New York: Touchstone.

Qiu, L., Lin, H., Leung, A.K., and Tov, W. (2012). "Putting their best foot forward: Emotional disclosure on Facebook," *Cyberpsychology, Behavior, and Social Networking*, 15, 569 –572.

Quam, J.K., Whitford, G.S., Dziengel, L.E., and Knochel, K.A. (2010). "Exploring the nature of same-sex relationships," *Journal of Gerontological Social Work*, 53, 702–722.

Quek, K., and Fitzpatrick, J. (2013). "Cultural values, self-disclosure, and conflict tactics as predictors of marital satisfaction among Singaporean husbands and wives," *The Family Journal: Counseling and Therpay for Couples and Families, 12* (2), 208–216.

Qui, L., Lin, H., Leung, A. K., and Tov, W. (2012). "Putting their best foot forward: Emotional disclosure on Facebook," *Cyberpsychology, Behavior and Social Networking, 15*(10), 569–572.

Quoidbach, J., Berry, E.V., Hansenne, M., and Mikolajczak, M. (2010). "Positive emotion regulation and well being: Comparing the impact of eight savoring and dampening strategies," *Personality and Individual Differences*, 49, 368–373.

Radanielina-Hita, M.L. (2010). "Let's make peace! A cross-cultural analysis of the effects of serial arguing behaviors in romantic relationships: The case of Malagasy romantic partners," *Journal of Intercultural Communication Research*, 39(2), 81–103.

Rakow, L.F. (1992). "Don't hate me because I'm beautiful," *Southern Communication Journal, 57*, 132–142.

Ramirez, A., and Broneck, K. (2009). "'IM me': Instant messaging as relational maintenance in everyday communication," *Journal of Social and Personal Relationships*, 26(2–3), 291–314.

Raskin, R., and Shaw, R. (1988). "Narcissism and the use of personal pronouns," *Journal of Personality*, 56, 393–404.

Rawlins, W.K. (1992). *Friendship matters: Communication, dialectics, and the life course.* New York: Aldine De Gruyter.

Raven, B., and French, J. (1958a). "Group support, legitimate power and social influence," *Journal of Personality, 26*, 400–409.

———, and ——— (1958b). "Legitimate power, coercive power, and observability in social influence," *Sociometry, 21*(2), 83–97.

Ray, E.B. (1993). "When the links become chains: Considering the dysfunctions of supportive communication in the workplace," *Communication Monographs*, 60, 106–111.

Ray, R.D., McRae, K., Ochsner, K.N., and Gross, J.J. (2010). "Cognitive reappraisal of negative affect: Converging evidence from EMG and self-report," *Emotion*, 10, 587–592.

———, Wilhelm, F.H., and Gross, J.J. (2008). "All in the mind's eye? Anger rumination and reappraisal," *Journal of Personality and Social Psychology*, 94(1), 133–145.

Reamer, F.G. (2002). "Boundary issues in social work: Managing dual relationships," *Social Work*, 48, 121–133.

Redmond, M.V. (1986). *An inclusive conceptualization of empathy.* Paper presented at the November meeting of the Speech Communication Association, Chicago.

——— (1989). "The functions of empathy (decentering) in human relations," *Human Relations*, 42, 593–605.

——— (1995). "Interpersonal communication: Definitions and conceptual approaches," in M.V. Redmond (ed.), *Interpersonal communication: Readings in theory and research*, 4–27. Fort Worth, TX: Harcourt Brace.

Reeves, T., Horne, S.G., Rostosky, S.S., Riggle, E.D.B., Baggett, L.R., and Aycock, R.A. (2010). "Family members support for GLBT issues: The role of gamily adaptability and cohesion," *Journal of GLBT Family Studies*, 6, 80–97.

Rehman, U.S., and Holtzworth-Munroe, A. (2007). "A cross-cultural examination of the relation of marital communication behavior to marital satisfaction," *Journal of Family Psychology*, 21, 759–763.

Reid, D., and Reid, F. (2005). "Textmates and text circles: Insights into the social ecology of SMS text-messaging," in L. Hamill and A. Kansen (eds), *Mobile world: Past, present and future.* London: Springer-Verlag, 105–118.

———, and ———. (2007). "Text or talk? Social anxiety, loneliness and divergent preferences for cell phone use," *Cyber Psychology and Behavior, 10*(3), 424–436.

————, and ————. (2010). "The expressive and conversational affordances of mobile messaging," *Behavior and Information Technology*, *29*(1), 3–22.

Reid, S.A., and Ng, S.H. (1999). "Language, power, and intergroup relations," *Journal of Social Issues*, *55*, 119–139.

Reid, T.R. (1999). *Confucius lives next door: What living in the East teaches us about living in the West*. New York: Random House.

Reis, H.T., Maniaci, M.R., Eastwick, P.W., Caprariello, P.A., and Finkel, E.J. (2011). "Familiarity does indeed promote attraction in live interaction," *Journal of Personality and Social Psychology*, *101*(3), 557–570.

————, Smith, S.M., Tsai, F., Carmichael, C., Capariello, P., Rodrigues, A., and Maniaci, M. (2010). "Are you happy for me? How sharing positive events with others provides personal and interpersonal benefits," *Journal of Personality and Social Psychology*, *99*(2), 311–329.

Reissman, C.K. (1990). *Divorce talk: Women and men make sense of personal relationships*. New Brunswick, NJ: Rutgers University Press.

Reitz, J.G. (2011). "Pro-immigration Canada. Social and economic roots of popular views," IRPP Study no. 20, October.

Reivich, K., and Shatte, A. (2002). *The resilience factor*. New York: Broadway.

Remland, M., Jones, T., and Brinkman, H. (1995). "Interpersonal distance, body orientation and touch: Effects of culture, gender and age," *Journal of Social Psychology*, *135*, 281–298.

Renshaw, K.D., Blais, R.K., and Caska, C.M. (2010). "Distinctions between hostile and nonhostile forms of perceived criticism from others," *Behavior Therapy*, *41*, 264–374.

Report of the Royal Commission on Aboriginal Peoples (1996). Ottawa: Canada Communication Group-Publishing. www.ainc-inac.gc.ca/ch/rcap/sg/sgmm_e.html

Reynolds, L., Smith, M.E., Birnholtz, J., and Hancock, J. (2013). "Bulter lies from both sides: Actions and perceptions of unavailability management in texting," *Computer-Mediated Communication*, February, 23–27.

Rheingold, H. (1988). *They have a word for it*. New York: Tarcher/Putnam.

Rholes, W.S., Kohn, J.L., and Simpson, J.A. (2014). "A longitudinal study of cpnflict in new parents: The role of

attachment," *Personal Relationships*, *21*, 1–21.

Richards, I.A. (1948). "Emotive meaning again," *Philosophical Review New York*, *57*, 145–157.

Richardson, R.M., and Smith, S.W. (2007). "The influence of high/low-context culture and power distance on choice of communication media: Students' media choice to communicate with professors in Japan and America," *International Journal of Intercultural Relations*, *31*, 479–501.

Richman, J.M., and Rosenfeld, L.B. (1987). "Stress reduction for hospice workers: A support group model," *Hospice Journal*, *3*, 205–221.

Richmond, V., Gorham, J.S., and Furio, B.J. (1987). "Affinity-seeking communication in collegiate female–male relationships," *Communication Quarterly*, *35*, 334–348.

Richmond, V.P. (1995). "Amount of communication in marital dyads as a function of dyad and individual marital satisfaction," *Communication Research Reports*, *12*, 152–159.

Ridley, C.A., Wilhelm, M.S., and Surra, C.A. (2001). "Married couples' conflict responses and marital quality," *Journal of Social and Personal Relationships*, *18*, 517–534.

Riggio, H.R. (2006). "Structural features of sibling dyads and attitides toward sibling relationships in young adulthood," *Journal of Family Issues*, *27*(9), 1233–1254.

Riggio, R.E., and Friedman, H.S. (1983). "Individual differences and cues to deception," *Journal of Personality and Social Psychology*, *45*, 899–915.

Riordan, M.A., and Kreuz, R.J. (2010). "Emotion encoding and interpretation in computer-mediated communication: Reasons for use," *Computers in Human Behavior*, *26*, 1667–1673.

Ritter, D. (2011). "The relationship between healthy work environments and retention of nurses in a hospital setting," *Journal of Nursing Management 19*, 27–32.

Ritts, V., Patterson, M.L., and Tubbs, M.E. (1992). "Expectations, impressions, and judgments of physically attractive students: A review," *Review of Educational Research*, *62*, 413–426.

Rizzolatti, G., Craighero, L., (2004). "The Mirror-Neuron System," *Annual Review Neuroscience*, *27*, 169–192.

Roach, K.D. (1997). "Effects of graduate teaching assistant attire on student learning, misbehaviors, and ratings of instruction," *Communication Quarterly*, *45*, 125–141.

Robbins, J.E., and Rosenfeld, L.B. (2001). "Athletes' perceptions of social support provided by their head coach, assistant coach, and athletic trainer, pre-injury and during rehabilitation," *Journal of Sport Behavior*, *24*, 277–297.

Robbins, S.P., and Judge, T. (2010). *Essentials of organizational behavior*, 14th edn. New Jersey: Upper Saddle River, NJ: Prentice Hall

Robinson, W.P., Shepherd, A., and Heywood, J. (1998). "Truth, equivocation/concealment, and lies in job applications and doctor–patient communication," *Journal of Language and Social Psychology*, *17*, 149–164.

Rocca, K.A. (2004). "College student attendance: Impact of instructor immediacy and verbal aggression," *Communication Education*, *53*(2), 185–195.

Rockmann, K.W., and Northcraft, G.B. (2008). "To be or not to be trusted: The influence of media richness on defection and deception," *Organizational Behavior and Human Decision Processes*, *107*, 106–122.

Rockwell, P., Buller, D.B., and Burgoon, J.K. (1997). "The voice of deceit: Refining and expanding vocal cues to deception," *Communication Research Reports*, *14*, 451–459.

Roe, D. (2001). "Differences in self-disclosure in psychotherapy between American and Israeli patients," *Psychological Reports*, *88*, 611–624.

Rollinson, D. (2008). *Organisational behaviour and analysis: An integrated approach*, 4th edn. Harlow: Prentice Hall.

Roloff, M.E, Janiszewski, C.A., McGrath, M.A., Burns, C.S., and Manrai, L.A. (1988). "Acquiring resources from intimates: When obligation substitutes for persuasion," *Human Communication Research*, *14*, 364–396.

Romaine, S. (1999). *Communicating gender*. Mawah, NJ: Lawrence Erlbaum.

Romero, C. (2008)."Writing wrongs: Promoting forgiveness through expressive writing," *Journal of Social and Personal Relationships*, *25*, 625–642.

Rosenblith, J.F. (1992). *In the beginning: Development from conception to age two*. Newbury Park, CA: Sage.

Rosenfeld, H.M. (1987). "Conversational control functions of nonverbal behavior," in A.W. Siegman and S. Feldstein (eds), *Nonverbal behavior and communication*, 2nd edn, 563–601. Hillsdale, NJ: Lawrence Erlbaum.

Rosenfeld, L.B. (1979). "Self-disclosure avoidance: Why I am afrid to tell you who I am," *Communication Monographs*, 46, 63–74.

—— (1994). "Sex differences in response to relationship crises: A case study of the Hill-Thomas hearing," in P. Siegel (ed.), *Outsiders looking in: A communication perspective on the Hill/Thomas hearings*, 283–301. New York: Hampton Press.

—— (2000). "Overview of the ways privacy, secrecy, and disclosure are balanced in today's society," in S. Petronio (ed.), *Balancing the secrets of private disclosures*, 3–17. Mahwah, NJ: Lawrence Erlbaum.

——, and Bowen, G.L. (1991). "Marital disclosure and marital satisfaction: Direct-effect versus interaction-effect models," *Western Journal of Speech Communication*, 55, 69–84.

——, and Gilbert, J.R. (1989). "The measurement of cohesion and its relationship to dimensions of self-disclosure in classroom settings," *Small Group Behavior*, 20, 291–301.

——, and Richman, J.M. (1999). "Supportive communication and school outcomes, part II: Academically at-risk low income high school students," *Communication Education*, 48, 294–307.

——, ——, and Bowen, G.L. (1998). "Supportive communication and school outcomes for academically 'at-risk' and other low income middle school students," *Communication Education*, 47, 309–325.

Rosenthal, R., and Jacobson, L. (1968). *Pygmalion in the classroom*. New York: Holt, Rinehart and Winston.

Ross, J.B., and McLaughlin, M.M. (eds). (1949). *A portable medieval reader*. New York: Viking.

Ross, L. (1977). "The intuitive psychologist and his shortcomings: Distortions in the attribution process," in L. Berkowitz (ed.), *Advances in experimental psychology*. (Vol. 10). New York: Academic Press.

—— (2001). "Getting down to fundamentals: Lay dispositionism and the attributes of psychologists," *Psychological Inquiry*, 12, 37–40.

——, and Nisbett, R. (1991). *The person and the situation: Perspectives of social psychology*. New York: McGraw-Hill Ryerson.

Rourke, B.P. (1998). *Nonverbal learning disabilities: The syndrome and the model*. New York: Guilford Press.

Ruben, B.D. (1989). "The study of cross-cultural competence: Traditions and contemporary issues," *International Journal of Intercultural Relationships*, 13, 229–240.

Rubenstein, A.J., Kalakanis, L., and Langlois, J.H. (1999). "Infant preferences for attractive faces: A cognitive explanation," *Developmental Psychology*, 35, 848–855.

Ruberman, R. (1992). "Psychosocial influences on mortality of patients with coronary heart disease," *Journal of the American Medical Association*, 267, 559–560.

Rubin, D.L., Greene, K., and Schneider, D. (1994). "Adopting gender-inclusive language reforms: Diachronic and synchronic variation," *Journal of Language and Social Psychology*, 13, 91–114.

Rubin, R.B., and Graham, E.E. (1988). "Communication correlates of college success: An exploratory investigation," *Communication Education*, 37, 14–27.

——, ——, and Mignerey, J.T. (1990). "A longitudinal study of college students' communication competence," *Communication Education*, 39, 1–14.

——, Perse, E.M., and Barbato, C.A. (1988). "Conceptualization and measurement of interpersonal communication motives," *Human Communication Research*, 14, 602–628.

Ruesch, J., and Bateson, G. (1951). *Communication: The social matrix of psychiatry*, New York: Norton.

Rumble, A.C., Van Lange, P.A., and Parks, C.D. (2009). "The benefits of empathy: When empathy may sustain cooperation in social dilemmas," *European Journal of Social Psychology*, 40, (5), 856–866.

Ruvolo, A.P., Fabin, L.A., and Ruvolo, C.M. (2001). "Relationship experiences and change in attachment characteristics of young adults: The role of relationship breakups and conflict avoidance," *Personal Relationships*, 8, 265–281.

Rymer, R. (1993). *Genie: An abused child's flight from silence*. New York: HarperCollins.

Sabourin, T.C., and Stamp, G.H. (1995). "Communication and the experience of dialectical tensions in family life: An examination of abusive and non-abusive families," *Communication Monographs*, 62, 213–242.

Sacks, O. (1989). *Seeing voices: A journey into the world of the deaf*. Berkeley, CA: University of California Press.

Sadalla, E. (1987). "Identity and symbolism in housing," *Environment and Behavior*, 19, 569–587.

Safdar, S., Friedlmeier, W., Matsumoto, D., Yoo, S.H., Kwantes, C.T., Kakai, H., and Shigemasu, E. (2009). "Variations of emotional display rules within and across cultures. A comparison between Canada, USA, and Japan," *Canadian Journal of Behavioural Science*, 41(1), 1–10.

Sagarian, E. (1976). "The high cost of wearing a label," *Psychology Today*, 10, March, 25–27.

Sagioglou, C., and Greitemeyer, T. (2014). "Facebook's emotional consequences: Why Facebook causes a decrease in mood and why people still use it," *Computers in Human Behavior*, 35, 359–363.

Samovar, L.A., Porter, R.E., McDaniel, E.R., and Roy, C.S. (2012). *Communication between cultures*, 7th edn. Boston, MA: Wadsworth Cengage.

Samter, W., Burleson, B.R., Kunkel, A.W., and Werking, K.J. (1994). "Gender and beliefs about communication in intimate relationships: Moderating effects of type of communication and type of relationship (or, when gender differences make a difference—and when they don't)." Paper presented at the Annual Meeting of the International Communication Association, Sydney, Australia, May.

——, and Cupach, W.R. (1998). "Friendly fire: Topical variations in conflict among same and cross-sex friends," *Communication Studies*, 49, 121–138.

Sanchez (1999). "How to craft successful employee communication in the information age," *Communication World*, 16(7), August–September, 9–15.

Sanchez-Burks, J., Lee, F., Nisbett, R., Choi, I., Zhao, S., and Koo, J. (2003). "Conversing across cultures: East–West communication styles at work and non-work contexts," *Journal of Personality and Social Psychology*, 85, 363–372.

Sanderson, C.A., and Karetsky, K.H. (2002). "Intimacy goals and strategies of conflict resolution in dating relationships: A mediational analysis," *Journal of Social and Personal Relationships*, 19, 317–337.

Sangster, J. (2002). "'She is hostile to our ways': First Nations girls sentenced to Ontario training school for girls, 1933–1960," *Law and History Review*, 20, 1–36.

Saohir, M.N., and Chaffee, S.H. (2002). "Adolescents' contributions to family communication patterns," *Human Communication Research*, 28, 86–108.

Sarason, I.G., Sarason, B.R., and Pierce, G.R. (1990). "Social support: The search for theory," *Journal of Social and Clinical Psychology*, 9, 133–147.

Sargent, J. (2002). "Topic avoidance: Is this the way to a more satisfying relationship?" *Communication Research Reports*, 19, 175–182.

Satir, V. (1972). *Peoplemaking*. Palo Alto, CA: Science and Behavior Books.

Sato, K. (1998). "Evaluative reactions towards 'foreign accented' English speech: The effects of listeners' experience on their judgments" Unpublished master's thesis, University of Alberta, Edmonton.

Savin-Williams, R.C. (2001). *"Mom, dad. I'm gay." How families negotiate coming out.* Washington, DC: American Psychological Association.

Sawada, R., Sato, W., Kochiyama, T., Uono, S., Kubota, Y., et al. (2014). "Sex Differences in the Rapid Detection of Emotional Facial Expressions," *PLoS ONE*, 9(4).

Scarpero, D.B. (2000). "The relationship of organizational communication climates and interpersonal conflict management," *Dissertation Abstracts International*, 60, 4946.

Schachter, S. (1959). *The psychology of affiliation*. Stanford, CA: Stanford University Press.

Scharlott, B.W., and Christ, W.G. (1995). "Overcoming relationship-initiation barriers: The impact of a computer-dating system on sex role, shyness, and appearance inhibitions," *Computers in Human Behavior*, 11, 191–204.

Schauer, M., and Elbert, T. (2010). "Dissociation following traumatic stress: Etiology and treatment," *Journal of Psychology*, 218(2), 109–127.

Scherer, K.R. (2000). "Psychological models of emotion," in J.C. Borod (ed.), *The neuropsychology of emotion*, 137–162. New York: Oxford University Press.

Schmidt, J.J. (2006). *Social and cultural foundations of counseling and human services: Multiple influences on self concept development*. Boston: Pearson/Allyn and Bacon.

Schrodt, P., Ledbetter, A.M., Jernberg, K.A., Larson, L. Brown, N., and Glonek, K. (2009). "Family communication patterns as mediators of communication competence in the parent–child relationship," *Journal of Social and Personal Relationships*, 26(6–7), 853–874.

Schug, J., Yuki, M., and Maddux, W. (2010). "Relational mobility explains between and within-culture differences in self-disclosure to close friends," *Psychological Science*, 21(10), 1471–1478.

Schumacher, J.A., Feldbau-Kohn, S., Slep, A.M.S., and Heyman, R.E. (2001). "Risk factors for male-to-female partner physical abuse," *Aggression and Violent Behavior*, 6, 281–352.

Schütz, A. (1999). "It was your fault! Self-serving biases in auto-biographical accounts of conflicts in married couples," *Journal of Social and Personal Relationships*, 16, 193–208.

Schwarzer, R. (1998). "Stress and coping from a social-cognitive perspective," *Annals of the New York Academy of Sciences*, 851, 531–537.

Scott, C., and Myers, K.K. (2005). "The socialization of emotion: Learning emotion management at the fire station," *Journal of Applied Communication Research*, 33, 67–92.

Scudder, J.N., and Andrews, P.H. (1995). "A comparison of two alternative models of powerful speech: The impact of power and gender upon the use of threats," *Communication Research Reports*, 12, 25–33.

Sedikides, C., and Skowronski, J.J. (1995). "On the sources of self-knowledge: The perceived primacy of self-reflection," *Journal of Social and Clinical Psychology*, 14, 244–270.

Segrin, C., and Fitzpatrick, M.A. (1992). "Depression and verbal aggressiveness in different marital couple types," *Communication Studies*, 43, 79–91.

———, and Flora, J. (2005). *Family Communication*. Mahwah, NJ: Lawrence Erlbaum.

Sehulster, J.R. (2006). "Things we talk about, how frequently and to whom: Frequency of topics in everyday conversation as a function of gender, age and marital status," *The American Journal of Psychology*, 119(3), 407–432.

Seidlitz, L., and Diener, E. (1998). "Sex differences in the recall of affective experiences," *Journal of Personality and Social Psychology*, 74, 262–271.

Seki, K., Matsumoto, D., and Imahori, T.T. (2002). "The conceptualization and expression of intimacy in Japan and the United States," *Journal of Cross Cultural Psychology*, 33, 303–319.

Selfhout, M.H.W., Branje, S.J.T., Delsing, M., Bogt, T.F.M., and Meeus, W.H.J. (2009). "Different types of internet use, depression and social anxiety: The role of perceived quality of friendship," *Journal of Adolescence*, 32, 819–833.

Seligman, M. (1991). *Learned optimism*. New York: Harper Perennial.

Servaes, J. (1989). "Cultural identity and modes of communication," in J.A. Anderson (ed.), *Communication Yearbook 12*, 383–416. Newbury Park, CA: Sage.

Service Canada (2011). "Ace the interview." www.jobsetc.gc.ca/pieces.jsp?category_id=300&crumb=1&crumb=34&crumb=106

Shamay, S.G., Tomer, R., and Aharon-Peretz, J. (2002). "Deficit in understanding sarcasm in patients with prefrontal lesion is related to impaired empathic ability," *Brain and Cognition*, 48, 558–563.

Shannon, M.L., and Stark, C.P. (2003). "The influence of physical appearance on personnel selection," *Social Behavior and Personality*, 31(6), 613–623.

Shattuck, R. (1980). *The forbidden experiment: The story of the wild boy of Aveyron*. New York: Farrar, Straus and Giroux.

Shaw, C.L.M. (1997). "Personal narrative: Revealing self and reflecting other," *Human Communication Research*, 24, 302–319.

Shen H., Chiu H., Lee P., Hu Y., and Chang W. (2011). "Hospital environment, nurse–physician's relationships and quality of care: Questionnaire survey," *Journal of Advanced Nursing*, 67, 349–358.

Sherman, M.A., and Haas, A. (1984). "Man to man, woman to woman," *Psychology Today*, 17, June, 72–73.

Sherman, M.D., and Thelen, M.H. (1996). "Fear of Intimacy Scale: Validation and extension with adolescents," *Journal of Social and Personal Relationships*, 13, 507–521.

Shimanoff, S.B. (1985). "Rules governing the verbal expression of emotions between married couples," *Western Journal of Speech Communication*, *49*, 149–165.

—— (1988). "Degree of emotional expressiveness as a function of face-needs, gender, and interpersonal relationship," *Communication Reports*, *1*, 43–53.

Shiu, E., and Lenhart, A. (2004). *How Americans use instant messaging*. Washington, DC: Pew Internet and American Life Project.

Shoda, Y., Mischel, W., and Peake, P.K. (1990). "Predicting adolescent cognitive and self-regulatory competencies from preschool delay of gratification: Identifying diagnostic conditions," *Developmental Psychology*, *26*, 978–986.

Shoemaker, M.E., and Johlke, M.C. (2002). "An examination of the antecedents of a crucial selling skill: Asking questions," *Journal of Managerial Issues*, *14*, 118–131.

Shook, N.J., Gerrity, D.A., Jurich, J., and Segrist, A.E. (2000). "Courtship violence among college students: A comparison of verbally and physically abusive couples," *Journal of Family Violence*, *15*(1), 1–22.

Shuler, S., and Sypher, B.D. (2000). "Seeking emotional labor. Managing the heart enhances the work experience," *Management Communication Quarterly*, *14*(1), 50–89.

Sias, P.M. (2009). *Organizing relationships: Traditional and emerging perspectives on workplace relationships*. Los Angeles, CA: Sage.

——, and Cahill, D.J. (1998). "From coworkers to friends: The development of peer friendships in the workplace," *Western Journal of Communication*, *62*, 273–299.

Sieberg, E., and Larson, C. (1971). *Dimensions of interpersonal response*. Paper presented at the meeting of the International Communication Association, Phoenix, AZ.

Siegman, A.W., and Snow, S.C. (1997). "The outward expression of anger, the inward experience of anger and CVR: The role of vocal expression," *Journal of Behavioral Medicine*, *1*, 29–45.

Sillars, A., Roberts, L.J., Leonard, K.E., and Dun, T. (2000). "Cognition during marital conflict: The relationship of thought and talk," *Journal of Social and Personal Relationships*, *17*, 479–502.

——, Folwell, A.L., Hill, K.L., Maki, B.K., Hurst, A.P., and Casano, R.A. (1992). *Levels of understanding in marital relationships*. Paper presented at the meeting of the Speech Communication Association, Chicago, November.

——, Pike, G.R., Jones, T.S., and Murphy, M.A. (1984). "Communication and understanding in marriage," *Human Communication Research*, *10*, 317–350.

——, Shebellen, W., McIntosh, A., and Pomegranate, M. (1997). "Relational characteristics of language: Elaboration and differences in marital conversations," *Western Journal of Communication*, *61*, 403–422.

——, Weisberg, J., Burggraf, C.S., and Wilson, E.A. (1987). "Content themes in marital conversations," *Human Communication Research*, *13*, 495–528.

Simine, V., and Carlson, E.N. (2010). "Self-knowledge of personality: Do people know themselves?" *Social and Personality Psychology Compass*, *4*(8), 605–620.

Simon, R.W., and Nath, L.E. (2004). "Gender and emotion in the United States: Do men and women differ in self-reports of feelings and expressive behavior?" *American Journal of Sociology*, *109*(5), 1137–1176.

Simons, D.A., and Wurtele, S.K. (2010). "Relationships between parents' use of corporal punishment and their children's endorsement of spanking and hitting other children," *Child Abuse and Neglect*, *34*, 639–646.

Simons, T. (2008). *The integrity dividend: Leading by the power of your word*. San Francisco, CA: Jossey-Bass.

Simpson, J.A. (1990). "Influence of attachment styles on romantic relationships," *Journal of Personality and Social Psychology*, *59*, 971–980.

Sinclair, C., and Woodward, H. (1997). "The impact of reflective journal writing on student teacher professional development," *Journal of the International Society for Teacher Education*, *1*(1), 50–58.

Singer, J.K., Miller, L.C., and Murphy, S. (1998). "Sexual harassment and memory: How repetition of behavior and personal experience relate to judgments of sexual harassment." Paper presented at the annual conference of the International Communication Association, Jerusalem.

Singer, M. (1998). *Perception and identity in intercultural communication*. Yarmouth, ME: Intercultural Press.

Skovholt, K. Gronning, A., and Kankaanranta, A. (2014). "The communicative functions of emoticons in workplace e-mails," *Journal of Computer-Mediated Communication*, *19*(4), 780–797.

Smeltzer, L.R., and Watson, K.W. (1984). "Listening: An empirical comparison of discussion length and level of incentive," *Central States Speech Journal*, *35*, 166–170.

Smith, S. (2012). "Study of self-generated sexually explicit photos and videos featuring young people online," Internet Watch Foundation. www.iwf.org.uk/assets/media/resources/IWF%20study%20-%20self%20generated%20content%20online_Sept%202012.pdf

Smith, T.W. (1992). "Changing labels: From 'Colored' to 'Negro' to 'Black' to 'African Americans,'" *Public Opinion Quarterly*, *56*(4), 496–514.

Snapp, C.M., and Leary, M.R. (2001). "Hurt feelings among new acquaintances: Moderating effects of interpersonal familiarity," *Journal of Social and Personal Relationships*, *18*, 315–326.

Snyder, M. (1979). "Self-monitoring processes," in L. Berkowitz (ed.), *Advances in experimental social psychology*, (12), 86–128. New York: Academic Press.

——. (1980). "The many me's of the self-monitor," *Psychology Today*, *14*, March, 33–40, 92.

Solomon, D.H., and Knobloch, L.K. (2001). "Relationship uncertainty, partner interference, and intimacy within dating relationships," *Journal of Social and Personal Relationships*, *8*, 804–820.

——, and Williams, M.L.M. (1997). "Perceptions of social-sexual communication at work: The effects of message, situation, and observer characteristics on judgments of sexual harassment," *Journal of Applied Communication Research*, *25*, 197–216.

Sommer, R. (1969). *Personal space: The behavioral basis of design*. Englewood Cliffs, NJ: Prentice Hall.

—— (2002). "Personal space in a digital age," in R.B. Bechtel and A. Churchman (eds), *Handbook of environmental psychology*, 647–660. New York: John Wiley & Sons.

Sopow, E. (2007). "The communication climate change at the RCMP," *Strategic Communication Management*, *12*(1), 20–23.

Soroka, S., and Roberton, S. (2010). *A literature review of public opinion research on Canadian attitudes towards multiculturalism and immigration, 2006–2009*. Ottawa: Citizenship and Immigration Canada Report.

Sousa, L.A. (2002). "The medium is the message: The costs and benefits of writing, talking aloud, and thinking about life's triumphs and defeats," *Dissertation Abstracts International, 62*, 3397.

Sparks, E.A., and Baumeister, R.F. (2008). "If bad is stronger than good, why focus on human strength?" in S. Lopez (ed.), *Positive psychology: Exploring the best in people. Vol.1: Discovering human strengths*, 55–79. Westport, CT: Praeger.

Spasojevic, J., and Alloy, L.B. (2002). "Who becomes a depressive ruminator? Developmental antecedents of ruminative response style," *Journal of Cognitive Psychotherapy: An International Quarterly, 16*, 405–419.

Speicher, H. (1999). "Development and validation of intimacy capability and intimacy motivation measures," *Dissertation Abstracts International, 59*, 5172.

Spillane, J.P. (2005). "Distributed leadership," *The Educational Forum, 69*(2), 143–150.

Spinks, N., and Wells, B. (1991). "Improving listening power: The payoff," *Bulletin of the Association for Business Communication, 54*, 75–77.

Spitze, G., and Trent, K. (2006). "Gender differences in adult sibling relations in two-child families," *Journal of Marriage and Family, 68*, 977–992.

Spitzberg, B.H. (1991). "An examination of trait measures of interpersonal competence," *Communication Reports, 4*, 22–29.

——— (1994). "The dark side of (in)competence," in W.R. Cupach and B.H. Spitzberg (eds), *The dark side of interpersonal communication*, 25–50. Hillsdale, NJ: Lawrence Erlbaum.

——— (2000). "What is good communication?" *Journal of the Association for Communication Administration, 29*, 103–119.

Sprecher, S. (1987). "The effects of self-disclosure given and received on affection for an intimate partner and stability of the relationship," *Journal of Social and Personal Relationships, 4*, 115–128.

Staffieri, J.R. (1967). "A study of social stereotype of body image in children," *Journal of Personality and Social Psychology, 7*, 101–104.

Stafford, L., and Dainton, M. (1994). "The dark side of 'normal' family interaction," in B.H. Spitzberg and W.R. Cupach (eds), *The dark side of interpersonal communication*, 259–280. Hillsdale, NJ: Lawrence Erlbaum.

———, ———, and Haas, S. (2000). "Measuring routine and strategic relational maintenance: Scale revision, sex versus gender roles, and the prediction of relational characteristics," *Communication Monographs, 67*(3), 306–323.

———, and Kline, S.L. (1996). "Married women's name choices and sense of self," *Communication Reports, 9*, 85–92.

Stamp, G.H. (1999). "A qualitatively constructed interpersonal communication model: A grounded theory analysis," *Human Communication Research, 25*, 531–547.

———, Vangelisti, A.L., and Daly, J.A. (1992). "The creation of defensiveness in social interaction," *Communication Quarterly, 40*, 177–190.

Stanley, J.P. (1977). "Paradigmatic woman: The prostitute," in D.L. Shores and C.P. Hines (eds), *Papers in language variation*, 303–321. Tuscaloosa, AL: University of Alabama Press.

Starkweather, W.C. (2002) "The epigenesis of stuttering," *Journal of Fluency Disorders, 27*, 269–288.

Statistics Canada. (2001b). "Aboriginal peoples of Canada," 2001 Census Data. www.12.statcan.ca/english/census01

——— (2002). "Survey of self-employment," *The Daily*, 29 January.

——— (2005). "Study: Social relationships in rural and urban Canada," *The Daily*, 21 June.

——— (2006a). "Aboriginal peoples in Canada in 2006: Inuit, Métis and First Nations, 2006 census: First Nations people," *Census Data*. www.12.statcan.ca/census-recensement/2006/rt-td/ap-pa-eng.cfm

——— (2006b). "Health reports: Predictors of health in seniors," *The Daily*, 9 February.

Statistics Canada (2006c). "General Social Survey: The Internet and the way we spend our time," *The Daily*, 2 August.

——— (2007). "2006 census: Immigration, citizenship, language, mobility and migration," *The Daily*, 4 December.

——— (2008) "Sociodemographic factors influencing the use of the Internet," Connectedness Series, 56F0004M. www.statcan.gc.ca/pub/56f0004m/2008016/findings-resultats/socio-eng.htm

——— (2010a). "Canadian internet use survey," *The Daily*, 10 May.

——— (2010b). "Working at home," *The Daily*, 7 December.

——— (2011a). "Aboriginal language in Canada," *Language, 2011 Census of Population*. Ottawa: Government of Canada.

——— (2011b). "Immigration and ethnocultural diversity in Canada," *National Household Survey*. Analytical document. Ottawa: Government of Canada.

——— (2011c). "Mixed unions in Canada," *National Household Survey*. Catalogue no. 99-010-X2011003

——— (2013). "Canadian internet survey 2012," *The Daily*, 26 November.

Stearns, C.A., and Stearns, P. (1986). *Anger: The struggle for emotional control in America's history*. Chicago: University of Chicago Press.

Steen, S., and Schwartz, P. (1995). "Communication, gender, and power: Homosexual couples as a case study," in M.A. Fitzpatrick and A.L. Vangelisti (eds), *Explaining family interactions*, 310–343. Thousand Oaks, CA: Sage.

Stefanone, M.A., and Jang, C.Y. (2007). "Writing for friends and family: The interpersonal nature of blogs," *Journal of Computer-Mediated Communication, 13*(1), article 7.

Steil, L.K. (1996). "Listening training: The key to success in today's organizations," in M. Purdy and D. Borisoff (eds), *Listening in everyday life: A personal and professional approach*, 2nd edn, 213–237. Lanham, MD: University Press of America.

Steinfatt, T. (1989). "Linguistic relativity: Toward a broader view," in S. Ting-Toomey and F. Korzenny (eds), *Language, communication, and culture: Current directions*, 35–75. Newbury Park, CA: Sage.

Stephens, C., and Long, N. (2000). "Communication with police supervisors and peers as a buffer of work-related traumatic stress," *Journal of Organizational Behavior, 21*, 407–424.

Stets, J.E., and Cast, A.D. (2007). "Resources and identity verification from an identity theory perspective," *Sociological Perspectives, 50*(4), 517–543.

Stevens, S., and Morris, T. (2007). "College dating and social anxiety: Using the internet as a means of connecting to others," *CyberPsychology and Behavior, 10*(5), 680–688.

Stewart, C.J., and Cash, W.B. (2011). *Interviewing: Principles and practices*, 13th edn. New York: McGraw-Hill Ryerson.

Stewart, J. (1983). "Interpretive listening: An alternative to empathy," *Communication Education, 32,* 379–391.

———— (ed.). (2012). *Bridges not walls: A book about interpersonal communication*, 11th edn. New York: McGraw-Hill.

———— (ed.). (2009). *Bridges not walls: A book about interpersonal communication*, 10th edn. New York: McGraw-Hill Ryerson.

————, and Logan, C. (1993). *Together: Communicating interpersonally*, 4th edn. New York: McGraw-Hill Ryerson.

————, and ———— (1998). *Together: Communicating interpersonally*, 5th edn. New York: McGraw-Hill Ryerson.

Stewart, S., Stinnett, H., and Rosenfeld, L.B. (2000). "Sex differences in desired characteristics of short-term and long-term relationship partners," *Journal of Personal and Social Relationships, 17,* 843–853.

Stiff, J.B., Dillard, J.P., Somera, L., Kim, H., and Sleight, C. (1988). "Empathy, communication, and prosocial behavior," *Communication Monographs, 55,* 198–213.

Stiles, W.B., Walz, N.C., Schroeder, M.A.B., Williams, L.L., and Ickes, W. (1996). "Attractiveness and disclosure in initial encounters of mixed-sex dyads," *Journal of Social and Personal Relationships, 13,* 303–312.

Stith, S.M., Liu, T., Davies, L.C., Boykin, E.L., Alder, M.C. et al., (2009). "Risk factors in child maltreatment: A meta-analytic review of the literature," *Aggression and Violent Behavior, 14,* 13–29.

Stone, G., Lightbody, M., and Whait, R. (2013). "Developing accounting students' listening skills: Barriers, opportunities and an integrated stakeholder approach," *Accounting Education: An International Journal, 22*(2), 168–192.

Straus, M., Sweet, S., and Vissing, Y.M. (1989). "Verbal aggression against spouses and children in a nationally representative sample of American families." Paper presented at the November meeting of the Speech Communication Association, San Francisco.

Strayer, J., and Roberts, W. (2004). "Children's anger: Emotional expressiveness and empathy: Relations with parents' empathy, emotional expressiveness and parenting practices," *Social Development, 13*(2), 229–254.

Stritzke, W.G., Nguyen, A., Durkin, K. (2004). "Shyness and computer-mediated communication: A self-presentational theory perspective," *Media Psychology, 6,* 1–22.

Strom, R.E., and Boster, F.J. (2007). "Dropping out of high school: A meta-analysis assessing the effect of messages in the home and school," *Communication Education, 56*(4), 433–452.

Sugimoto, N. (1991). "'Excuse me and 'I'm sorry': Apologetic behaviors of Americans and Japanese," Paper presented at the March Conference on Communication in Japan and the United States, California State University, Fullerton, CA.

Suitor, J.J., Sechrist, J., Plikuhn, M., Pardo, S.T., Gilligan, M., and Pillemer, K. (2009). "Perceived maternal favoritism in sibling relations midlife," *Journal of Marriage and Family, 71*(4), 1026–1038.

————, ————, ————, ————, and Pillemer, K. (2008). "Within-family differences in parent–child relations across the life course," *Current Directions in Psychological Science, 17,* 334–338.

Sullins, E.S. (1991). "Emotional contagion revisited: Effects of social comparison and expressive style on mood convergence," *Personality and Social Psychology Bulletin, 17,* 166–174.

Sullivan, C.F. (1996). "Recipients' perceptions of support attempts across various stressful life events," *Communication Research Reports, 13,* 183–190.

Sullivan, M.J.L., Lynch, M.E., and Clark, A.J. (2005). "Dimensions of catastrophic thinking associated with pain experience and disability patients with neuropathic pain conditions," *Pain, 113*(3), 310–315.

Sullivan, T.A. (2014). "Greedy institutions, overwork, and work–life balance," *Sociological Inquiry, 84*(1), 1–15.

Sutter, D.L., and Martin, M.M. (1999). "Verbal aggression during disengagement of dating relationships,"

Communication Research Reports, 15, 318–326.

Suzuki, L.K., Davis, H.M., and Greenfield, P.M. (2008). "Self-enhancement and self-effacement in reaction to praise and criticism: The case of multiethnic youth," *Ethos, 36*(1), 78–97.

Swain, S. (1989). "Covert intimacy in men's friendships: Closeness in men's friendships," in B.J. Risman and P. Schwartz (eds), *Gender in intimate relationships: A microstructural approach*, 71–86. Belmont, CA: Wadsworth.

Swami, V., Furnham, A., Chamorro-Premuzic, T., . . . and Tovee, M.J. (2010). "More than just skin deep? Personality information influences men's ratings of the attractiveness of women's body sizes," *Journal of Social Psychology, 150*(6), 628–647.

Swann, W.B. Jr., Wenzlaff, R.M., Krull, D.S., and Pelham, B.W. (1992). "Allure of negative feedback: Self-verification strivings among depressed persons," *Journal of Abnormal Psychology, 101,* 293–306.

Swenson, J., and Casmir, F.L. (1998). "The impact of culture-sameness, gender, foreign travel, and academic background on the ability to interpret facial expression of emotion in others," *Communication Quarterly, 46,* 214–230.

Sypher, B.D., and Sypher, H.E. (1983). "Perceptions of communication ability: Self-monitoring in an organizational setting," *Personality and Social Psychology Bulletin, 9,* 297–304.

Tagliamonte, S.A. (2014). "Situating media influence in sociolinguistic context," *Journal of Sociolinguistics, 18*(2), 223–232.

Tagliamonte, S., and Denis, D. (2008). "Linguistic ruin LOL! Instant messaging and teen language," *American Speech, 83*(1), 3–34.

Tai, K., Zheng, X., and Narayanan, J. (2011). "Touching a teddy bear mitigates negative effects of social exclusion to increase prosocial behavior," *Social Psychological and Personality Science, 2*(6), 618–626.

Tajfel, H., and Turner, J.C. (1992). "The social identity theory of intergroup behavior," in W.B. Gudykunst and Y.Y. Kim (eds), *Readings on communicating with strangers*. New York: McGraw-Hill Ryerson.

Tajima, E.A. (2002). "Risk factors for violence against children: Comparing homes with and without wife abuse,"

Journal of Interpersonal Violence, 17, 122–149.

Tam, K.P., Au, A., and Leung, A.K. (2008). "Attributionally more complex people show less punitiveness and racism," *Journal of Research in Personality, 42,* 1074–1081.

Tangney, J.P., Baumeister, R.F., and Boone, A.L. (2004). "High self-control predicts good adjustment, less pathology, better grades, and interpersonal success," *Journal of Personality, 72,* 271–324.

———, Hill-Barlow, D., Wagner, P.E., and Marschall, D.E. (1996). "Assessing individual differences in constructive versus destructive responses to anger across the lifespan," *Journal of Personality and Social Psychology, 70,* 780–796.

Tamir, D.I., and Mitchell, J.P. (2012). "Disclosing information about the self is intrinsically rewarding," *PNAS, 109*(21), 8038–8043.

Tannen, D. (1986). *That's not what I meant! How conversational style makes or breaks your relations with others.* New York: Ballantine Books.

——— (1990). *You just don't understand: Women and men in conversation.* New York: William Morrow.

——— (1994). *Talking from 9 to 5: Women and men in the workplace: Language, sex and power.* New York: Morrow.

——— (1996). "Gender gap in cyberspace," *Newsweek,* 16 May, 52–53.

Taylor, A.F., Wiley, A., Kuo, F.E., and Sullivan, W.C. (1998). "Growing up in the inner city: Green spaces as places to grow," *Environment and Behavior, 30,* 3–27.

Taylor, D.A., and Altman, I. (1987). "Communication in interpersonal relationships: Social penetration processes," in M.E. Roloff and G.R. Miller (eds), *Interpersonal processes: New directions in communication research,* 257–277. Newbury Park, CA: Sage.

Taylor, S., and Mette, D. (1971). "When similarity breeds contempt," *Journal of Personality and Social Psychology, 20,* 75–81.

Taylor, S.E. (2007). "Social support," in H.S. Friedman and R.C. Silver (eds), *Foundations of health psychology, 145–171.* New York: Oxford University Press.

Teelucksingh, C., and Galabuzi, G.E. (2005). *Working precariously: The impact of race and immigrants status on employment opportunities and outcomes in Canada.* Ottawa: Canadian Race Relations Foundation.

Tenney, E.R., Vazire, S., and Mehl, M.R. (2013). "This examined life: The upside of self-knowledge for interpersonal relationships," PLoS ONE, 8(7). www.plosone.org/article/info%3Adoi%2F10.1371%2Fjournal.pone.0069605

Tepper, B.J. (2007). "Abusive supervision in work organizations: Review, synthesis, and research agenda," *Journal of Management, 33,* 261–289.

Teven, J.J., and Comadena, M.E. (1996). "The effects of office aesthetic quality on students' perceptions of teacher credibility and communicator style," *Communication Research Reports, 13,* 101–108.

Tezer, E., and Demir, A. (2001). "Conflict behaviors toward same-sex and opposite-sex peers among male and female late adolescents," *Adolescence, 36*(143), 525–533.

The Canadian Hearing Society (2007). The Canadian Hearing Society paper on discrimination and audism. www.chs.ca/en/position-papers/position-paper-on-discrimination-and-audism.html

Thelen, M.H., Vander Wall, J.S., Thomas, A.M., and Harmon, R. (2000). "Fear of intimacy among dating couples," *Behavior Modification, 24,* 223–241.

The Vanier Institute of the Family (2010). *Families count. Profiling Canada's families IV.* Ottawa, CA: Vanier Institute of the Family.

Thibaut, J.W., and Kelley, H.H. (1959). *The social psychology of groups.* New York: John Wiley & Sons.

Thompsen, P.A., and Foulger, D.A. (1996). "Effects of pictographs and quoting on flaming in electronic mail," *Computers in Human Behavior, 12*(2) June, 225–243.

Thourlby, W. (1978). *You are what you wear.* New York: New American Library.

Tidwell, L.C. (1998). "A comparison of anticipated interaction, channel, and communication goal on impression formation, self-disclosure, and relational orientation: Getting to know one another a bit at a time," *Dissertation Abstracts International, 58,* 4128.

———, and Walther, J.B. (2002). "Computer-mediated communication effects on disclosure, impressions, and interpersonal evaluations: Getting to know one another a bit at a time," *Human Communication Research, 28,* 317–348.

Tiewtrakul, T., and Fletcher, S.R. (2010). "The challenge of regional accents for aviation English language proficiency standards: A study of difficulties in understanding in air traffic control-pilot communications," *Ergonomics, 53* (2), 229–239.

Tillema, T., Schwanen, T., and Dijst, M. (2009). "Communicating something confidential while travelling by train: The use of a telephone conversation versus silent modes," *Transportation, 36,* 541–564.

Ting-Toomey, S. (1991). "Intimacy expressions in three cultures: France, Japan, and the United States," *International Journal of Intercultural Relations, 15,* 29–46.

——— (1999). *Communicating across cultures.* New York: Guilford Press.

———, Oetzel, J., and Yee-Jung, K. (2001). "Self-construal types and conflict management styles," *Communication Reports, 14,* 87–104.

Titsworth, S., McKenna, T.P., Mazer, J.P., and Quinlan, M.M. (2013). "The bright side of emotion in the classroom: Do teachers' behaviors predict students' enjoyment, hope and pride?" *Communication Education, 62*(2), 191–209.

Tokunaga, R.S. (2014). "A unique problem or the manifestation of a preexisting disorder? The mediating role of problematic internet use in the relationships between psychosocial problems and functional impairment," *Communication Research, 41*(4), 531–560.

Tolhuizen, J.H. (1989). "Communication strategies for intensifying dating relationships: Identification, use and structure," *Journal of Social and Personal Relationships, 6,* 413–434.

Toma, C.L., and Hancock, J.T. (2012). "What lies beneath: The linguistic traces of deception in online dating profiles," *Journal of Communication, 62,* 78–97.

Touitou, Y. (1998). "Biological clocks: Mechanisms and application," *Proceedings of the International Congress on Chronobiology.* New York: Elsevier Science.

Tracy, S.J. (2004). "The construction of correctional officers: Layers of emotionality behind bars," *Qualitative Inquiry, 10,* 509–533.

Tracy, S.J., Myers, K.K., and Scott, C.W. (2006). "Cracking jokes and crafting selves: Sense making and identity management among human service workers," *Communication Monographs, 73*(3), 28–308.

Treger, S., Sprecher, S., and Erber, R. (2013). "Laughing and liking: Exploring the interpersonal effects of humor use in initial interactions," *European Journal of Social Psychology, 43*, 532–543.

Trenholm, S., and Rose, T. (1980). "The compliant communicator: Teacher perceptions of appropriate classroom behavior," *Western Journal of Speech Communication, 44*, 13–26.

Trepaniér, S.G., Fernet, C., and Austin, S. (2013). "Workplace bullying and psychological health at work: The mediating role of satisfaction needs for autonomy, competence and relatedness," *Work and Stress, 27*(2), 123–140.

Triandis, H.C., (1990), "Cross-cultural studies of individualism and collectivism," in J. Berman (ed.), *Nebraska symposium on motivation*, pp. 41–133.

——— (1994). *Culture and social behavior*. New York: McGraw-Hill Ryerson.

——— (1995). *Individualism and collectivism*. Boulder, CO: Westview.

Trobst, K.K., Collins, R.L., and Embree, J.M. (1994). "The role of emotion in social support provision: Gender, empathy, and expressions of distress," *Journal of Social and Personal Relationships, 11*, 45–62.

Trocmé, N., Knoke, D., and Blackstock, C. (2004). "Pathways to the overrepresentation of aboriginal children in Canada's child welfare system," *Social Service Review, 78*(4), 577–600.

Tsaousis, I. (2010). "Circadian preferences and personality traits: A meta-analysis," *European Journal of Personality, 24*, 356–373.

Turk, D.R., and Monahan, J.L. (1999). "'Here I go again': An examination of repetitive behaviors during interpersonal conflicts," *Southern Communication Journal, 64*, 232–244.

Turkle, S. (2011). "Alone together," in *Why we expect more from technology and less from each other*. New York: Basic Books.

Turner, H.H., Dindia, K., and Pearson, J.C. (1995). "An investigation of female/male verbal behavior in same-sex and mixed-sex conversations," *Communication Reports, 8*, 86–96.

Tusing, K.J., and Dillard, J.P. (2000). "The sounds of dominance: Vocal precursors of perceived dominance during interpersonal influence," *Human Communication Research, 26*, 148–171.

Ulrey, K.L. (2001). "Intercultural communication between patients and health care providers: An exploration of intercultural communication effectiveness, cultural sensitivity, stress, and anxiety," *Health Communication, 13*, 449–463.

Ulrich, P.A., and Abner, N. (2010). "Diabetes under control. Meter, meds, meals, move and more," *American Journal of Nursing, 110*(7), 62–65.

Underdown, A., Barlow, J., and Stewart-Brown, S. (2010). "Tactile stimulation in physically healthy infants: Results of a systematic review," *Journal of Reproductive and Infant Psychology, 28*(1), 11–29.

United States Census Bureau (2014). "US and World Population Clocks." www.census.gov/main/www/popclock.html

Urberg, K.A., Degirmencioglu, S.M., and Tolson, J.M. (1998). "Adolescent friendship selection and termination: The role of similarity," *Journal of Social and Personal Relationships, 15*, 703–710.

Uskul, A.K., Hynie, M., and Lalonde, R.N. (2004). "Inter-dependence as a mediator between culture and interpersonal closeness for Euro-Canadians and Turks," *Journal of Cross-Cultural Psychology, 35*, 174–191.

Usunier, J.C., and Roulin, N. (2010). "The influence of high- and low-context communication styles on the design, content and language of business-to-business web sites," *Journal of Business Communication, 47*(2), 189–227.

Vaillant, G. (2002). *Aging well*. New York: Little, Brown.

Valentine, C. and B. Saint Damian (1988), "Communicative power: Gender and culture as determinants of the ideal voice" in C.A. Valentine and N. Hoar (eds), *Women and communicative power: Theory, research, and practice*. Washington, DC: National Communication Association, 54.

Vaish, A., Carpenter, M., and Tomasello, M. (2009). "Empathy through affective perspective taking and its relation to prosocial behavior in toddlers," *Developmental Psychology, 45*(2), 534–543.

Valins, S. (1966). "Cognitive effects of false heart-rate feedback," *Journal of Personality and Social Psychology, 4*, 400–408.

Valkenburg, P.M., and Peter, J. (2007). "Preadolescents and adolescents' online communication and their closeness to friends," *Developmental Psychology, 43*(2), 267–277.

———, Schouten, A.P., and Peter, J. (2005). "Adolescents' identity experiments on the internet," *New Media and Society, 7*(3), 383–402.

Van Emmerik, I.J.H., Euwema, M.C., and Wendt, H. (2008). "Leadership behaviors around the world: The relative importance of gender versus cultural background," *International Journal of Cross-Cultural Management, 8*, 297–315.

Vangelisti, A.L. (1994). "Couples' communication problems: The counselor's perspective," *Journal of Applied Communication Research, 22*, 106–126.

———, Caughlin, J.P., and Timmerman, L. (2001). "Criteria for revealing family secrets," *Communication Monographs, 68*, 1–27.

———, and Crumley, L.P. (1998). "Reactions to messages that hurt: The influence of relational contexts," *Communication Monographs, 65*, 173–196.

———, Knapp, M.L., and Daly, J.A. (1990). "Conversational narcissism," *Communication Monographs, 57*, 251–274.

Van Horen, F., and Mussweiler, T. (2014). "Soft assurance: Coping with uncertainty through haptic sensations," *Journal of Experimental and Social Psychology 54*, 73–80.

Vanlaere, L., Couke, T., and Gastmas, C. (2010). "Experiential learning of empathy in a care-ethics lab," *Nursing Ethics, 17*(3), 325–336.

Van Lear, C.A. (1987). "The formation of social relationships: A longitudinal study of social penetration," *Human Communication Research, 13*, 299–322.

——— (1991). "Testing a cyclical model of communicative openness in relationship development: Two longitudinal studies," *Communication Monographs, 58*, 337–361.

——— (1992). "Marital communication across the generations: Learning and rebellion, continuity and change," *Journal of Social and Personal Relationships 9*, 103–123.

Van Volkom, M. (2006). "Sibling relationships in middle and older adulthood," *Marriage and Family Review, 40*(2), 151–170.

Vaughn, D. (1987). "The long goodbye," *Psychology Today, 21*, July, 37–42.

Vazire, S., and Carlson, E.N. (2010). "Self-knowledge of personality: Do people know themselves?" *Social and Personality Psychology Compass, 4*(8), 605–620.

Veenhof, B. (2006). "The internet: Is it changing the way Canadians spend their time?" Ottawa: Statistics Canada, cat. no. 56F004MIE, no. 13. www.statcan.gc.ca/pub/56f0004m/56f0004m2006013-eng.htm

———, Wellman, B., Quell, C., and Hogan, B. (2008). "How Canadians' use of the internet affects social life and civic participation," Ottawa: Statistics Canada, cat. no. 56F0004M, no. 16. www.statcan.gc.ca/pub/56f0004m/56f0004m2008016-eng.pdf

Velez, J.A., Mahood, C., Ewoldsen, D.R., and Moyer-Guse, E. (2014). "Ingroup versus outgroup conflict in the context of violent video game play: The effect of cooperation on increased helping and decreased aggression," *Communication Research, 4*(5), 607–626.

Venable, K.V., and Martin, M.M. (1997). "Argumentativeness and verbal aggressiveness in dating relationships," *Journal of Social Behavior and Personality, 12*, 955–964.

Veroff, J., Douvan, E., Orbuch, T.L., and Acitelli, L.K. (1998). "Happiness in stable marriages: The early years," in T.N. Bradbury (ed.), *The developmental course of marital dysfunction*, 152–179. New York: Cambridge University Press.

Versfeld, N.J., and Dreschler, W.A. (2002). "The relationship between the intelligibility of time-compressed speech and speech-in-noise in young and elderly listeners," *Journal of the Acoustical Society of America, 111*(1, Pt 1), 401–408.

Vieta, M. (2004). "Interactions through the screen: The interactional self as a theory for internet-mediated communication." Master's thesis, School of Communication, Simon Fraser University: Burnaby, BC.

Vignovic, J.A., and Thompson, L.F. (2010). "Computer-mediated cross-cultural collaboration: Attributing communication errors to the person versus the situation," *Journal of Applied Psychology, 95*(2), 265–276.

Vilensky, D., and MacDonald, R. *Prehospital Emergency Care, 15*(1), 2011: 39–43.

Vito, D. (1999). "Affective self-disclosure, conflict resolution and marital quality," *Dissertation Abstracts International, 60*, 1319.

Vittengl, J.R., and Holt, C.S. (2000). "Getting acquainted: The relationship of self-disclosure and social attraction to positive affect," *Journal of Social and Personal Relationships, 17*, 53–66.

Vocate, D.R. (1994). "Self-talk and inner speech: Understanding the uniquely human aspects of intrapersonal communication," in D.R. Vocate (ed.), *Intrapersonal communication: Different voices, different minds*, 3–31. Hillsdale, NJ: Lawrence Erlbaum.

Vohs, K.D., Baumeister, R.F., and Ciarocco, N.J. (2005). "Self-regulation and self-presentation: Regulatory resource depletion impairs impression management and effortful self-presentation depletes regulatory resources," *Journal of Personality and Social Psychology, 88*, 632–657.

Voss, K., Markiewicz, D., and Doyle, A.B. (1999). "Friendship, marriage and self-esteem," *Journal of Social and Personal Relationships, 16*, 103–122.

Vranceanu, A.M., Elbon, M., Adams, M., and Ring, D. (2012). "The emotive impact of medical language," *Hand, 7*, 293–296.

Vranceanu, A.M., Elbon, M., and Ring, D. (2011). "The emotive impact of orthopedic words," *Journal of Hand Therapy, 24*, 112–8.

Vrij, A. (2000). *Detecting lies and deceit: The psychology of lying and the implications for professional practice*. Chichester, UK: John Wiley & Sons.

———, and Akehurst, L. (1999). "The existence of a black clothing stereotype: The impact of a victim's black clothing on impression formation," *Psychology, Crime and Law, 3*(3), 227–237.

———, Granhag, A., and Porter, S. (2010). "Pitfalls and opportunities in nonverbal and verbal lie detection," *Psychological Science, 11*(3), 89–121.

———, Paterson, B., Nunkoosing, K., Soukara, S., and Oosterwegel, A. (2003). "Perceived advantages and disadvantages of secrets disclosure," *Personality and Individual Differences, 35*, 593–602.

Vuchinich, S. (1987). "Starting and stopping spontaneous family conflicts," *Journal of Marriage and the Family, 49*, 591–601.

Waldvogel, J. (2005). "The role, status and style of workplace email: A study of two New Zealand workplaces," Unpublished doctoral dissertation, School of Linguistics and Applied Language Studies, Victoria University of Wellington, New Zealand.

——— (2007). "Greetings and closings in workplace email," *Journal of Computer-Mediated Communication, 12*(2), article 6. http://jcmc.indiana.edu/vol12/issue2/waldvogel.html

Wallenfelsz, K.P., and Hample, D. (2010). "The role of taking conflict personally in imagined interactions about conflict," *Southern Communication Journal, 75*(5), 471–487.

Walster, E., Aronson, E., Abrahams, D., and Rottmann, L. (1966). "Importance of physical attractiveness in dating behavior," *Journal of Personality and Social Psychology, 4*, 508–516.

Walther, J.B. (1996). "Computer-mediated communication: Impersonal, interpersonal, and hyperpersonal interaction," *Communication Research, 23*, 3–43.

——— (2007). "Selective self-presentation in computer-mediated communication: Hyperpersonal dimensions of technology, language, and cognition," *Computers in Human Behavior, 23*, 2538–2557.

——— (2011). "Theories of computer-mediated communication and interpersonal relations," in M.L. Knapp and J.A. Daly (eds), *The handbook of interpersonal communication*, 4th edn, 443–479. Thousand Oaks, CA: Sage.

———, and D'Addario, K.P. (2001). "The impacts of emoticons on message interpretation in computer-mediated communication," *Social Science Computer Review, 19*, 324–347.

———, Deandrea, D., and Tong, S.T. (2010). "Computer-mediated communication versus vocal communication and the attenuation of pre-interaction impressions," *Media Psychology, 13*(4), 364–386.

Wang, H., and Wellman, B. (2010). "Social connectivity in America: Changes in adult friendship network size from 2002 to 2007," *American Behavioral Scientist, 53*(8), 1148–1169.

Ware, J., and Williams, R. (1980). "A reanalysis of the Doctor Fox experiments," *Instructional Evaluation, 4*, 15–18.

Waring, E.M. (1981). "Facilitating marital intimacy through self-disclosure," *American Journal of Family Therapy, 9*, 33–42.

———, and Chelune, G.J. (1983). "Marital intimacy and self-disclosure," *Journal of Clinical Psychology, 39*, 183–190.

Warnecke, A.M., Masters, R.D., and Kempter, G. (1992). "The roots of nationalism: Nonverbal behaviour and xenophobia," *Ethology and Sociobiology*, *13*(4), 267–282.

Washington, M.C., Okoro, E.A., and Cardon, P.W. (2014). "Perceptions of civility for mobile phone use in formal and informal meetings," *Business and Professional Communication Quarterly*, *77*(1), 52–64.

Washington Post (2001). "Attacks on US soil," *Washington Post*, 12 September.

Watts, S.A. (2007). "Evaluative feedback: Perspectives onmedia effects," *Journal of Computer-Mediated Communication*, *12*(2), article 3. http://jcmc.indiana.edu/vol12/issue2/watts.html

Watzlawick, P., Beavin, J., and Jackson, D. (1967). *Pragmatics of human communication: A study of interactional patterns, pathologies, and paradoxes*. New York: W.W. Norton.

Weaver, J.B., and Kirtley, M.D. (1995). "Listening styles and empathy," *Southern Communication Journal*, *60*, 131–140.

Weger, H., Jr., Castle, G.R., and Emmett, M.C. (2010). "Active listening in peer interviews: The influence of message paraphrasing on perceptions of listening skill," *International Journal of Listening*, *24*, 34–49.

Wei, Y., and Li, Y. (2001). "The experimental research on the influence of different empathy training methods on children's sharing behavior," *Psychological Science China*, *24*, 557–562.

Weider-Hatfield, D. (1981). "A unit in conflict management skills," *Communication Education*, *30*, 265–273.

Weinstein, N., Przybyiski, A.K., and Ryan, R.M. (2009). "Can nature make us more caring? Effects of immersion in nature on intrinsic aspirations and generosity," *Personality and Social Psychology Bulletin*, *35*, (10), 1315–1329.

Weiss, L., and Lowenthal, M.F. (1975). "Life-course perspectives on friendship," in M.F. Lowenthal, M. Thurnher, and D. Chiriboga (eds), *Four stages of life: A comparative study of women and men facing transitions*, 48–61. San Francisco: Jossey-Bass.

Weiss, R.S. (1998). "A taxonomy of relationships," *Journal of Social and Personal Relationships*, *15*, 671–683.

Weisskirch, R.S. (2009) Parenting by Cell Phone: Parental Monitoring of Adolescents and Family Relations. *Journal of Youth Adolescence*. Vol. 38, 1123-1139.

—— (2011). "No crossed wires: Cell phone communication in parent–adolescent relationships," *Cyberpsychology, Behavior and Social Networking*, *14*(7–8), 447–451.

Welch, S.A., and Rubin, R.B. (2002). "Development of relationship stage measures," *Communication Quarterly*, *50*, 24–40.

Wellman, B. (1999). *Networks and the global village: Life in contemporary communities*. Boulder, CO: Westview Press

——, Boase, J., and Chen, W. (2002). "The networked nature of community: Online and offline," *IT and Society*, *1*(1), 151–165.

——, and Rainie, L. (2012). *Networked: The new social operating system*. Cambridge, MA: MIT Press.

Werner, E., and Smith, R. (2001). *Journeys from childhood to mid-life: Risk, resilience and recovery*. Ithaca, NY: Cornell University Press.

Wesselmann, E.D., Bagg, D., and Williams, K.D. (2009). "'I feel your pain': The effects of observing ostracism on the ostracism detection system," *Journal of Experimental Social Psychology*, *45*, 1308–1311.

Wester, S.R., Vogel, D.L., Pressly, P.K., and Heesacker, M. (2002). "Sex differences in emotion: A critical review of the literature and implications for counseling psychology," *Counseling Psychologist*, *30*, 630–652.

Westmyer, S.A., and DiCioccio, R.L. (1998). "Appropriateness and effectiveness of communication channels in competent interpersonal communication," *Journal of Communication*, *48*, 27–48.

Whitchurch, G.G., and Constantine, L.L. (1993). "Systems theory," in P.G. Boss, W.J. Doherty, R. LaRosa, W.R. Schumm, and S.K. Steinmetz (eds), *Source book of family theories and methods: A conceptual approach*, 325–352. New York: Plenum Press.

Whitman, T.L., White, R.D., O'Mara, K.M., and Goeke-Morey, M.C. (1999). "Environmental aspects of infant health and illness," in T.L. Whitman and T.V. Merluzzi (eds), *Life-span perspectives on health and illness*, 105–124. Mahwah, NJ: Lawrence Erlbaum.

Whitten, K.L., and Weaver, S.R. (2010). "Adoptive family relationships and healthy adolescent development: A risk and resilience analysis," *Adoption Quarterly*, *13*, 209–226.

Wiemann, J.M., Takai, J., Ota, H., and Wiemann, M. (1997). "A relational

model of communication competence," in B. Kovacic (ed.), *Emerging theories of human communication*. Albany: State University of New York Press.

Wilbur, J.R., Wilbur, M., Garrett, M.T., and Yuhas, M. (2001). "Talking circles: Listen, or your tongue will make you deaf," *Journal for Specialists in Group Work*, *26*, 368–384.

Williams, A. (2013). "The strategies used to deal with emotion work in student paramedic practice," *Nurse Education in Practice*, *13*, 207–212.

Williams, K.D., and Dolnik, L. (2001). "Revealing the worst first: Stealing thunder as a social influence strategy," in J.P. Forgas and K.D. Williams (eds), *Social influence: Direct and indirect processes*, 213–231. Hove, UK: Psychology Press.

Willington, R. (2011). "ITU finds 2 billion internet users worldwide, 5 billion mobile subscriptions," *Hot Hardware*, 30 January. http://hothardware.com/News/ITU-Finds-2-Billion-Internet-Users-Worldwide-5-Billion-Mobile-Subscriptions/

Willis, F.N., and Hamm, H.K. (1980). "The use of interpersonal touch in securing compliance," *Journal of Nonverbal Behavior*, *5*, 49–55.

Wilmot, W.W. (1987). *Dyadic communication*, 3rd edn. New York: Random House.

—— (1995). *Relational communication*, 5th edn. New York: McGraw-Hill Ryerson.

——, and Hocker, J.L. (2010). *Interpersonal conflict*, 8th edn. New York: McGraw-Hill.

Wilson, R.E., Gosling, S.D., and Graham, L.T. (2012). "A review of Facebook research in social sciences," *Perspectives Psychological Science*, *7*(3), 203–220.

Wilson, T.D. (2009). "Know thyself," *Perspectives on Psychological Science*, *4*, 384–389.

Winch, R. (1958). *Mate-selection: A study of complementary needs*. New York: Harper and Row.

Winer, S., and Majors, R. (1981). "A research note on supportive and defensive communication: An empirical study of three verbal interpersonal communication variables," *Communication Quarterly*, *29*, 166–172.

Winsor, J.L., Curtis, D.B., and Stephens, R.D. (1997). "National preferences in business and communication education: An update," *Journal of the Association for Communication Administration*, *3*, 170–179.

Winterheld, H.A., Simpson, J.A., and Orina, M.M. (2013). "It's in the way that you use it: Attachment and the duadic nature of humor during conflict negotiation in romantic couples," *Personality and Social Psychology Bulletin, 39*(4), 496–508.

Witmer, D.F., and Katzman, S.L. (1997). "Online smiles: Does gender make a difference in the use of graphic accents?" *Journal of Computer-Mediated Communication, 2*(4), np.

Wolff, F.I., and Marsnik, N.C. (1993). *Perceptive listening,* 2nd edn. Fort Worth, TX: Harcourt.

Wolvin, A.D. (1984). "Meeting the communication needs of the adult learner," *Communication Education, 33,* 267–271.

——, and Coakley, C. (1991). "A survey of the status of listening training in some Fortune 500 companies," *Communication Education, 40,* 152–164.

——, ——, and Gwynn, C. (1999). *Listening,* 6th edn. Boston: McGraw-Hill Ryerson.

Won-Doornick, M.J. (1979). "On getting to know you: The association between the stage of relationship and reciprocity of self-disclosure," *Journal of Experimental Social Psychology, 15,* 229–241.

Wood, J.T. (1994). "Gender and relationship crises: Contrasting reasons, responses, and relational orientations," in J. Ringer (ed.), *Queer words, queer images: The (re)construction of homosexuality,* 238–264. New York: New York University Press.

—— (2009). *Gendered lives: Communication, gender, and culture,* 8th edn. Belmont, CA: Wadsworth.

——, and Inman, C.C. (1993). "In a different mode: Masculine styles of communicating closeness," *Journal of Applied Communication Research, 21,* 279–295.

Woods, E. (1996). "Associations of nonverbal decoding ability with indices of person-centered communicative ability," *Communication Reports, 9,* 13–22.

Workplace Bullying Institute, (2010). *Results of the 2010 Workplace Bullying Institute US workplace bullying survey.* www.workplacebullying.org/research/WBI-NatlSurvey2010.html

World Gazetteer (2005). Population data arranged by country. www.world-gazetteer.com

Xu, F., Luo, Y.C., Fu, G., and Lee, K. (2009). "Children's and adult's conceptualization and evaluation of lying and truth-telling," *Infant and Child Development, 18*(4), 307–322.

Yakubovich, V. (2005). "Weak ties, information, and influence: How workers find jobs in a local Russian labor market." *American Sociological Review, 70*(3), 408–421.

Yang, C., Brown, B.B., and Braun, M.T. (2014). "From Facebook to cell calls: Layers of electronic intimacy in college students' interpersonal relationships," *New media and Society, 16*(1), 5–23.

Yingling, J. (1994). "Constituting friendship in talk and meta-talk," *Journal of Social and Personal Relationships, 11,* 411–426.

Yook, E.L., and Albert, R.D. (1998). "Perceptions of the appropriateness of negotiation in educational settings: A cross-cultural comparison among Koreans and Americans," *Communication Education, 47,* 18–29.

Yoon, J., and Thye, S. (2011). "A theoretical model and new test of managerial legitimacy in work teams," *Social Forces, 90*(2), 639–659.

Young, S. (2004). "A comparison of offline and online friendship qualities at different stages of relationship development," *Journal of Social and Personal Relationships, 21*(3), 305–320.

—— (2009). "The function of parental communication patterns: Reflection-enhancing and reflection-discouraging approaches," *Communication Quarterly, 57*(4), 379–394.

Yuki, M., Maddux, W., and Masuda, T. (2007). "Are the windows to the soul the same in the East and West: Cultural differences in using eyes and mouth as cues to recognize emotions in Japan and the United States," *Journal of Experimental and Social Psychology, 43,* 303–311.

Zack, J., Mannheim, A., and Alfano, M. (2010). "'I didn't know what to say?': Four archetypical responses to homophobic rhetoric in the classroom." *The High School Journal, 93*(3), 98–110.

Zahn, C.J. (1989). "The bases for differing evaluations of male and female speech: Evidence from ratings of transcribed conversation." *Communication Monographs, 56,* 59–74.

Zenmore, S.E., Fiske, S.T., and Kim, H.J. (2000). "Gender stereotypes and the dynamics of social interaction," in T. Eckes and H.M. Trautner (eds), *The developmental social psychology of gender,* 207–241. Mahwah, NJ: Lawrence Erlbaum.

Zepeda, O., and Hill, J.H. (1991). "The conditions of Native American languages in the United States," in R.H. Robbins and E.M. Uhlenbeck Robins (eds), *Endangered Languages.* Oxford, UK: Berg.

Zhang, Y.B., Harwood, J., and Hummert, M.L. (2005). "Perceptions of conflict management styles in Chinese intergenerational dyads," *Communication Monographs, 72*(1), 71–91.

Zheng, W., and Hart, R. (2004). "The effects of marital and non-marital union transition on health," *Journal of Marriage and Family, 64*(2), 420–432.

Zhong, C.B., and Leonardelli, G.J. (2008) "Cold and lonely: Does social exclusion literally feel cold?" *Psychological Science, 19*(9), 838–842.

Zickuhr, K. (2010). *Generations 2010.* Washington, D.C.: Pew Research Centre. http://pewinternet.org/~/media//Files/Reports/2010/PIP_Generations_and_Tech10.pdf

Zimbardo, P.G. (1971). *The psychological power and pathology of imprisonment.* Statement prepared for the US House of Representatives Committee on the Judiciary, Subcommittee No. 3, Robert Kastemeyer, Chairman. Unpublished manuscript. Stanford University, 1971.

—— (1977). *Shyness: What it is, what to do about it.* Reading, MA: Addison-Wesley.

Zimmerman, B.J. (1995). "Self-efficacy and educational development," in A. Bandura (ed), *Self-efficacy in changing societies,* 202–231. New York: Cambridge University Press.

Zuckerman, M., and Driver, R.E. (1989). "What sounds beautiful is good: The vocal attractiveness stereotype," *Journal of Nonverbal Behavior, 13,* 67–82.

——, Miserandino, M., Bernieri, F., Manusov, V., Axtell, R.E., Wiemann, J.M., Knapp, M.L., O'Leary, M.J., and Gallois, C. (1999). "Creating impressions and managing interaction," in L.K. Guerrero, J.A. DeVito, and M.L. Hecht (eds), *The nonverbal communication reader: Classic and contemporary readings,* 2nd edn, 379–422. Prospect Heights, IL: Waveland Press.

NAME INDEX

SUBJECT INDEX